KNIGHTS' GOLD

The Largest Documented KGC Treasure Ever Discovered

Jack Myers

Knights' Gold

Jack O'Lantern Press

A Jack O'Lantern Press book

© 2016 by Jack Myers
ISBN: 9781539896562

First edition: 2016

This book is an original publication of Jack O'Lantern Press.

Jack O'Lantern Press
For inquiries: jackmyers@peoplepc.com

To
Cecelia Reihl,
for her patience over the years it took to research and
write this very unusual book,
and

to
Bill Mountain,
for his hours of poring over the manuscript to find the
typos and mistakes all writers make, no matter how
careful,
and

to
Len Augsburger,
for writing the first book on this case, without which this
second book would certainly not have been written . . .
and for lending me valuable pieces of his research
materials,
and

to
Dr. E. Lee Spence, for encouraging me to self-publish
what will certainly be a most controversial theory,
and most of all,

to
Pat and Jack Myers, my parents.

Contents

Contents

Preface

During the time of the Great Depression, two teenaged pals in the City of Baltimore discovered — by pure stroke of luck — a fantastic treasure of historical proportions. The literal "pot of gold" the boys stumbled across was not found at the end of a mythical rainbow, nor did these youngsters live happily ever after. Rather, the copper pot bursting with rare gold coins had been buried for decades under the hard-packed dirt floor of a basement in a rundown harbor-district tenement building. In 2008, Illinois coin expert Leonard Augsburger researched and wrote the excellent book <u>Treasure in the Cellar.</u> Augsburger's narrative is a fine legal and numismatic account of what happened to the legendary hoard of thousands of gold coins uncovered in that dark, enigmatic, and long since forgotten inner-city location. Anyone interested in the details of this amazing and truly incredible legal case should undoubtedly read <u>Treasure in the Cellar.</u>

So who buried such a magnificent cache? And, more importantly, why did they bury it??

The judge who presided over the disposition of the coins in 1935 had reason to believe that a wealthy, 19th-century candle maker had stashed the loot. But an insufficient, tenuous chain of evidence was all that connected the 19th-century chandler to the buried gold. Augsburger himself points to the candle company executive as the logical suspect in this near 160-year mystery. The candle maker most certainly had the wealth to amass such a secret fortune. Also, he died unexpectedly in that same house in 1873 at age 46 — providing a convenient explanation as to why someone never returned to the cellar to dig up the gold.

Still, there have been continued nagging doubts in this most unusual of cases — unexplained discrepancies and curious tidbits of evidence that point in an altogether different direction. You see, both the judge in 1935, and author Len Augsburger in 2008, were likely led astray by extenuating though highly understandable circumstances. The coins were buried years earlier than suspected — before the Civil War, not during or after. And they were buried with the knowledge of perhaps five or more men.

The first conspirator was a Baltimore ship's captain who had been associated with both the treasure house and the illegal African slave trade.

Preface

The second, a 33rd-degree Mason and Grand Master for the State of Maryland, with connections to some of the most powerful and dangerous people in The Confederate States of America. The third, a wealthy Baltimore businessman and ardent secessionist who, after the war, hung portraits of Stonewall Jackson and Robert E. Lee in his parlor.

The fourth, a young executive who lived in a hotel close by the house where the coins were buried . . . a hotel which served as a nexus for clandestine rebel activity, and under which yet *another* fortune in gold coins would later be unearthed.

And the fifth conspirator, quite likely the most dangerous and daring of all, was the former chief of police in Baltimore, a friend to John Wilkes Booth, and a possible participant in multiple plots to kidnap or kill President Lincoln. This man, hailed in my book as the Confederate 007, would later be imprisoned without trial for sedition on orders from Lincoln. After his release, Confederate 007 would head north to Canada where he would join the Confederate Secret Service and participate in guerilla-styled operations against the Union. Circumstantial evidence points to this man having participated in the burial of yet another fabled treasure — the gold and silver of the Confederate treasury that went missing at the end of the Civil War. Confederate 007 would be elected, during the era of post-war Reconstruction, as Mayor of Baltimore.

All five men were likely involved, at various levels, with a secret, underground, nationwide pro-Confederate organization known as the Knights of the Golden Circle. The "KGC" was formed for the purpose of protecting the right of Southerners to own slaves — and to add new slave-holding territories through armed annexation. The Republic of Texas was their model. Cuba, Mexico, the entire Caribbean, Honduras, and even Nicaragua were KGC targets for violent takeover. Baltimore resident and stage actor John Wilkes Booth was purportedly a member of the KGC — as was the outlaw Jessie James. The U.S. government once identified the KGC as the most dangerous, subversive, treasonous group in U.S. history. President Abraham Lincoln, likely murdered as a result of a plot hatched by KGC zealots, had called the Knights of the Golden Circle a "fifth column" which threatened the very existence of our young nation.

Only the Civil War interrupted the KGC's grand plan to forge a slaveholding empire, one that would stretch from Delaware to Brazil, and from the Caribbean to Texas. Much of the gold collected and buried in anticipation of hatching this stupendous plot was never used. In slavery's defeat, the members of the KGC would eventually grow old and die, forever waiting for the day the "South would rise again." Much of their buried treasure would be guarded for a time, then abandoned, and ultimately by the 20th century, lost to history.

Today, treasure hunters and adventurers still seek the buried fortunes of the disbanded Knights of the Golden Circle — especially the legendary hidden treasures of the outlaw Jesse James. Their focus lies mainly on the Deep South, and also across the vast, arid wilderness and empty badlands of the southwestern United States. But now, a piece of the KGC treasure puzzle may have been solved. Possibly the greatest KGC treasure discovery ever made apparently took place 80 years ago in, of all places, an historical neighborhood just blocks north of Baltimore's famed Inner Harbor. For the "treasure in the cellar" found in 1934 by two bored teens was not the work of a lone miser. This king's fortune in gold was the result of a conspiracy — a conspiracy that, if successful, would have changed the history of the United States along with a sizable portion of the world's Western Hemisphere. That conspiracy, ultimately doomed to failure, did succeed in touching off the bloodiest conflict in U.S. history . . . and would, ultimately, cost President Abraham Lincoln his life.

The gold in the cellar was _Knights' Gold_.

This is the story of an immense, tantalizing golden hoard — today worth many millions of dollars — and of the daring, ambitious, yet reckless and often ruthless people who buried those 5,000+ highly valued gold coins in the year 1856.

The fantastic, mysterious "Baltimore gold hoard" was not discovered until almost 80 years after its pre-Civil War burial. Now, some 80 years after the gleaming pot of gold was unearthed, it is time for the full, shocking truth about the coins to finally be revealed.

"Truth," to quote the English poet Lord Byron, "is stranger than fiction." In response, American author Mark Twain quipped, "Truth is stranger than fiction, but it is because fiction is obliged to stick to possibilities; truth isn't."

Preface

The coins, which were cleaned, counted, logged into evidence, photographed, catalogued, and sold at public auction, were quite real. So were the wealthy pro-slavery individuals, existing at the pinnacle of mid-nineteenth century Baltimore society, who buried the coins under the auspices of the Knights of the Golden Circle.

The story you are about to read, <u>Knights' Gold</u>, may seem strange, even incredible, and perhaps at times will border on the near impossible. But it is nevertheless, as told to the best of my ability, the truth as I can interpret the myriad of facts across almost 200 years of rich American history.

To borrow a phrase from movie actress Bette Davis in the 1950 screen classic *All About Eve*, "*Fasten your seat belts, it's going to be a bumpy night!*"

Jack Myers
July, 2016

Serendipity

A reenactment of a most improbable
treasure discovery.

The year was 1934. An expanding drought was destroying
millions of acres of formerly fertile farmland across America's
heartland. The nationwide crime spree of Bonnie Parker and
Clyde Barrow had come to a violent end at the hands of "G" men
with blazing submachine guns on a dusty Louisiana back road.
Suspect Bruno Hauptmann was being arrested for the kidnapping
and murder of famed aviator Charles Lindbergh's infant son.
Hard-throwing Dizzy Dean was busy pitching his "Gashouse
Gang" St. Louis Cardinals to a World Series championship. And
Adolph Hitler had just declared himself the fuhrer of Germany.

A loaf of bread cost eight cents — and a gallon of gasoline 10
cents.[1]

The average annual wage was $1,600 . . . for those lucky
enough to have steady work.[2] Times were definitely tough in
Depression-era America of the 1930s. Nearly 25% of the work
force found itself unemployed in a time well before state and
federal unemployment benefits.

"Brother, can you spare a dime?"

One after another, banks and businesses closed their doors,
often forever. Families lost their homes and farms. Long lines of

weary, downtrodden folks stood outside soup kitchens, bellies aching for a hot meal. Others hustled selling apples or pencils on street corners, trying desperately to make ends meet.

"We have nothing to fear but fear itself," President Franklin Delano Roosevelt implored a distressed nation. But fear was everywhere — including fear's companions: poverty, hunger, homelessness, and hopelessness.

In a poor, dilapidated, East Baltimore neighborhood not far from the city's once-bustling harbor, two young, bored pals tried to pass the time on August 31 by forming their own secret boys' club. Theodore Jones, 14, and Henry Grob, 15, called their newly

founded organization the "Rinky Dinky Doos."[3] After collecting petty dues from new members and squirreling them away in a cigar box, Theodore and Henry decided to bury the dues, club papers, and assorted games (thought to be playing cards and dice) for safekeeping. The spot they chose was the hard-packed dirt floor in the dark, cramped cellar underneath the tenement house on South Eden Street where the Joneses rented an $8 per month apartment.[4] Both the Jones and Grob families were fatherless, and scraped by with the help of meager government assistance (the Joneses) or by picking tomatoes (Mrs. Grob). Theodore's parents, originally from Pittsburgh, had long been divorced, his father's whereabouts unknown. Henry's father had passed away shortly after Henry's birth, an apparent victim of the 1919 Spanish influenza epidemic which killed thousands in East Coast cities such as Baltimore and Philadelphia.[5]

Armed with a flashlight, axe, and a corn knife, the two buddies began digging in a secluded section by a brick wall, an area already covered by a layer of discarded oyster shells.[6] A few minutes had gone by when suddenly the axe wielded by Theodore Jones struck something — something unexpectedly hard. Theodore stooped down and plucked a shiny disc of yellowish metal out of the ground.[7]

"Hey look, a medal!" Theodore exclaimed.

But Henry Grob's eyes nearly popped out of his head when he saw what his friend was *really* holding.

"You're crazy!" Henry laughed. "That's not a medal . . . that's a twenty-dollar gold piece!"

Sure enough, Henry was absolutely correct. In a heartbeat, the boys dropped down on hands and knees, furiously clawing and brushing away the dirt in the widening treasure hole. At the bottom of that shallow hole lay an ancient, badly corroded, greenish copper pot or can, wrapped in a man's boot. The boys lugged the weighty container across the cellar and dropped it onto a discarded mattress. Theodore had Henry move aside, then raised the hammer, and with one hefty swing, split open the dried-out boot to reveal its contents. Thousands of old gold coins came spilling out before their disbelieving eyes, forming a shiny, yellow mound on the dusty, thrown away bedding.[8]

Theodore and Henry began splitting the coins one by one, starting with the large $20 coins. But soon, with so many gold pieces to divvy up, these newly minted treasure kids began dividing their loot by the fistful! A pile for Theodore, a pile for Henry. Another pile for me, and another pile for you.

Once Theodore had filled his pockets with yellow plunder, he began dumping additional fistfuls into his handy cigar box.

Henry, his trouser pockets likewise bulging, would remove his shoes and begin filling those with more coinage . . . $20, $10, $5, $2.50, and even $1 face value gold coins. The $1 gold coins, now much valued collector's items, had ceased being minted in the late 1800s.

When the cache of old coins, numbering in the thousands, had been divided, the boys parted ways. It was already growing late, and the two were naturally bursting with excitement. Theodore hauled his serendipitous take upstairs to the rear second-floor apartment he shared with his mother, Bessie Jones.

Henry, carrying his shoes full of gold and pants pockets crammed with weighty precious metal, had to barefoot it east across City Springs Square to his home on nearby South Caroline Street.[9]

One can scarcely imagine the wild thoughts that must have raced through the minds of these two Depression-era, inner-city youths. They had woken up poor, same as usual, and now would be going to bed both rich and soon-to-be famous. Neither boy could have possibly been fully aware of the furor and commotion their colossal discovery would soon bring. For the elusive, alluring yellow metal is truly a double-edged sword. During more than five thousand years of recorded history, gold has represented concentrated wealth and power. But with that wealth and power invariably comes conflict and trouble. Gold always comes with a price.

And as both the boys and the City of Baltimore would soon learn, there is no fever quite like gold fever.

Much like Aladdin, Theodore and Henry had awakened the long-slumbering golden genie in its buried hiding place. And only one thing was for certain — the boys' young and previously uncomplicated lives would never, ever be the same.

Because the golden genie was now loose . . . and he would soon have his capricious way with the boys, their families, their neighbors, and many other unsuspecting Baltimoreans.

The Republic of Texas

Remember the Alamo!

In the pantheon of American heroes, the defenders of the Alamo in San Antonio are reserved a special, exalted, indeed legendary status. They were some 182 patriots, holding out against impossible odds, waiting for reinforcements that would never come. Now immortal names such as William Travis, famed Louisiana knife fighter James Bowie, and Davy Crockett — King of the Wild Frontier. The battle, and those 182 lives, would be lost on that cold, March day in 1836 . . . but the war for independence from Mexico would soon be won.

The actual history, however, offers a more complex and somewhat darker tale.

Texas, or Tejas, had once been a far-flung province of New Spain. Hot, dry, and remote, it was largely under-populated save for the troublesome, warlike Comanches and other Native American tribes who made passage through Texas a daunting endeavor.

The wide-open spaces of Texas, however, still attracted early American settlers and adventurers, vanguards of the tacit although growing United States policy of "manifest destiny" on the North American continent. It was simply assumed that, one day, the American nation would extend from the Atlantic to the Pacific . . . . from sea to shining sea.

When Mexico fought and won its 1810 war of independence from Spanish rule, many American settlers in Texas sided with and aided the Mexican cause. Many were rewarded with additional land grants and greater autonomy.[1]

Under the newly established Mexican Empire, even more Americans were granted the privilege to settle in Texas. Soon, Americans in Texas (who would become known as "Texians") began to greatly outnumber the sparse Mexican population there.[2]

Mexican authorities required but three things of their new American guests and neighbors: [3]

1. That the Americans swear allegiance to Mexico.
2. That the Americans convert to Roman Catholicism.
3. That the Americans refrain from their peculiar custom of slave ownership.

The Texians, comprised largely of Protestant Anglos steeped in the long-standing Southern plantation culture that viewed slave ownership as a birthright, basically ignored all of the rules laid down for them. The fledgling Mexican government, confronted with more pressing issues in those early days after independence, basically turned a blind eye at the Texian indiscretions.

However, once the Mexican Empire was replaced by a new republican form of government in 1823, the laissez-faire attitude towards the cantankerous Americans started to shift. The new president of Mexico, Antonio Lopez de Santa Anna, began to centralize federal control over the Mexican nation[4] — and this included the outlying, renegade province of Texas. Now used to decades of doing things their own way, the emboldened American upstarts naturally resisted. The "Texians" had already begun to regard Texas as their own.

The situation came to a head in 1835 when the Texians banded together and forced all Mexican troops to retreat from Mexican Texas. The Americans then posted about a hundred troops in the former Alamo mission complex, later bolstered by a re-enforcement detachment led by Travis and Bowie, men who would soon become co-commanders of the former Catholic mission turned fortress. Meanwhile, down south, President General Santa Anna was attempting to muster an army of thousands in Mexico, anxious to crush the budding American rebellion.

On March 1, 1836 the Americans officially declared independence from Mexico.

Knowing what was coming, Travis sent messengers ahead, desperately pleading for more men, arms, and supplies. While the walled Alamo mission had been built by the Spaniards to protect against raids by Native Americans, it was not sufficiently fortified to withstand an assault by a modern federal army — one equipped with cannons and other heavy artillery. One of Travis' letters, written in later February as The Alamo came under its initial siege, reads as follows. The letter was addressed to "*The People of Texas and All Americans in the World*" . . . .

Fellow citizens and compatriots;

I am besieged, by a thousand or more of the Mexicans under Santa Anna. I have sustained a continual Bombardment and cannonade for 24 hours and have not lost a man. The enemy has demanded a surrender at discretion, otherwise, the garrison are to be put to the sword, if the fort is taken. I have answered the demand with a cannon shot, and our flag still waves proudly from the walls. <u>I shall never surrender or retreat</u>. Then, I call on you in the name of Liberty, of patriotism & everything dear to the American character, to come to our aid, with all dispatch. The enemy is receiving reinforcements daily and will no doubt increase to three or four thousand in four or five days. If this call is neglected, I am determined to sustain myself as long as possible and die like a soldier who never forgets what is due to his own honor & that of his country. <u>Victory or Death.</u>

William Barret Travis
Lt. Col. Comdt.

P.S. The Lord is on our side. When the enemy appeared in sight we had not three bushels of corn. We have since found in deserted houses 80 or 90 bushels and got into the walls 20 or 30 head of Beeves.

Travis [5]

Travis, a former lawyer and newspaperman from Alabama, had brought his slave Joe to Texas. Two more family slaves would remain with his wife and family back in Alabama.[6]

Crockett, the famed Kentucky woodsman, is not believed to have been a slave owner. In fact, Crockett himself spent some of his early years as an indentured servant.[7]

Jim Bowie's connection to slavery, however, was even stronger than Travis'. Bowie was a known slave trader, once doing a complicated deal that transferred ownership of 82 slaves and a large parcel of land for an immense sum of cash.[8] He is also reported to have bought slaves from the infamous French pirate, Jean Laffite, at a slave trading post (read smuggling post) located on Galveston Island, Texas. Laffite would prey on Spanish slave ships off the coast of Africa packed with human cargo for the return voyage. Laffite and his associates would then commandeer the pirated vessels across the Atlantic Ocean and Gulf of Mexico to Galveston Island. Bowie and others would be there waiting to buy up the hijacked slaves at bargain prices,[9] turning a quick profit by selling them to willing masters across the border in adjacent Louisiana (in blatant opposition to the 19th-century ban on the importation of slaves to the United States). Apparently, Bowie's get-rich-quick business plan was to buy low, sell high, and carry a big knife.

Not satisfied with the substantial profits he had already achieved in the illicit slave-trading business, Bowie next stumbled upon yet a new trafficking scheme. U.S. law in the 1830s encouraged anyone with knowledge of the illegal *foreign* importation of slaves to notify the authorities (domestic slave trading still being a legal, thriving, big business in the slave states of the South). The reward for turning in a wrongdoer? The right of the informant to then purchase those same illegally imported slaves at _half the going rate_. So, Bowie's racket involved purchasing slaves from Laffite on the cheap, selling them to customhouses in Louisiana on the sly, contacting the authorities with information that the customhouses were dealing in slaves imported from Africa — and then buying back those same people at half the price![10]

Bowie used this extra source of cash to become one of the hottest real estate speculators in all of fast-growing Louisiana. No doubt Jim Bowie was as slippery as his famous knife was sharp.

In the end, the Spanish finally caught up with pirate Jean Laffite off the coast of Honduras. Injured in an exchange of gunfire between Spanish privateers and his 43-ton schooner, the *General Santander*, Lafitte ultimately perished and was buried at sea in the Gulf of Honduras.[11] Treasure hunters have been seeking his fabled buried treasures to this day.

Back at the doomed Alamo, the 13-day siege was nearing its tragic conclusion. Travis had been placed in charge of the regular forces, and Bowie the fort's remaining volunteer fighters. Sometime during the siege, Bowie fell violently ill, and was confined to his quarters in bed.

In the predawn hours of March 6th, Mexican forces under Santa Anna began the assault. While the invaders were initially repelled, the Americans quickly ran low on both men and ammunition. With cannon fire bombarding the mission, Santa Anna's men began scaling the mission walls, forcing the Americans inside the Alamo's inner structures. The bloody confrontation would be over in mere minutes. The handful of Americans who attempted surrender were executed immediately.

Travis would be one of the first defenders to die, shot while manning the mission's outer wall. Crockett was slain shortly thereafter in hand-to-hand combat by the lower wall surrounding the church. An eyewitness account given by a former American slave employed as a cook for the Mexican Army put the number of dead Mexicans surrounding Crockett's corpse at "at least sixteen." Bowie, too sick from pneumonia to fight, would be bayonetted in his bed while braced against a wall with a gun and famed Bowie knife in hand.

Contrary to common belief, there were American survivors at the Alamo — noncombatants who managed to dodge the crossfire. These included the women and children of the Alamo[12], and also William Travis' slave, Joe.

The women were each given two silver pesos and a blanket and then sent home[13], some escorted by Ben, the former American slave.

There was a cruel calculation behind Santa Anna's handling of the noncombatants. The survivors were encouraged to spread the word far and wide. To warn other Texians that the army of President General Antonio Lopez de Santa Anna was both unbeatable and merciless, and that resistance to Mexican rule was futile. Santa Anna also hoped that Joe and Ben might help to incite a slave revolt against the Americans — with the Texians now in disarray and on the run.

The final cost of the Battle of the Alamo was horrific. All 182 or more defenders slain, along with 400-600 Mexicans killed or wounded. The violence inflicted on the Americans was savage. Forbidden to surrender, they were ultimately shot, stabbed, bludgeoned, hacked, and mutilated — killed many times over. Their bodies stacked and burned without benefit of proper burial. Santa Anna was sending a message . . . but his brazen message would backfire.

Upon hearing of the atrocities committed in San Antonio, fellow Texians rallied to confront the advancing Mexican army. Cries of "Remember the Alamo!" began punctuating battlefield skirmishes in the days and weeks following the Mexican assault on The Alamo.

On April 21, 1836, a rejuvenated though still outnumbered Texian army led by Sam Houston took to the offensive against their Mexican foes. Perhaps complacent, Santa Anna and his soldiers were caught totally by surprise within their own camp. The Battle of San Jacinto was a complete rout for the victorious Texians, with fighting lasting but a few minutes. All 1,600 Mexicans were either killed or surrendered. The Texians lost but nine men. By day's end Santa Anna was forced to begin withdrawing all Mexican troops from Texas territory — and to plead with Houston for mercy.

"You should have thought about that at The Alamo," the American leader replied. Though Santa Anna would be spared, he would return to Mexico in disgrace. The Republic of Texas had won its independence.

For most of ten years, Texas would remain a separate political entity. Cross border raids between the Mexicans and the Texans would continue to occur for some time. And though San Antonio would briefly fall again into Mexican hands . . . the sovereignty of the new republic was never seriously threatened. Some Texans, such as eventual Texas president Mirabeau Lamar, would favor a plan that would maintain Texas as a separate country while forcing all Native Americans from Texas soil.[14] But many others, including two-time Texas president Sam Houston, pushed for the annexation of Texas by the United States — along a proposed reconciliation with native peoples.

Texas leaders were initially ambitious to the extreme, envisioning a truly colossal Texas stretching west across the continent to the Pacific Ocean.[15] During the time of Texan independence, 1836-1845, Texas maintained claims to territory on vast swaths of land (including what would today encompass parts of Colorado, Kansas, New Mexico, Oklahoma, and even Wyoming).

One of the stumbling blocks to the U.S. annexation of Texas was its demand to remain a slaveholding state[16] — and also for the right of Texan emigrants to bring their slaves. Adding a slaveholding state to the Union during the 1840s was a decidedly touchy political matter. Early nineteenth century compromises dictated that a delicate balance needed to be maintained between slave and "free-soil" states.

On December 29, 1845, U.S. President James Polk signed legislation making Texas the 28th state. War between Mexico and the United States broke out soon after, with the outcome of that conflict defining the Rio Grande as Texas' new border with Mexico. The "Compromise of 1850" saw Texas give up approximately one-third of its land mass in exchange for ten million dollars to pay the state's immense public debts.

Texas would be the last slaveholding state added to the U.S., and also the very last to free her slaves. Some six "free" states (Iowa, Wisconsin, California, Minnesota, Oregon, and Kansas) would be admitted after Texas and before the Civil War. But down South, the eyes of many were on Texas. A peculiar, Southern-fried brand of Manifest Destiny was emerging. A vision for the future that included the conquest of new slaveholding lands throughout the Western Hemisphere. Land was there for the taking . . . if men, arms, and money could be combined with careful planning and bold action. A new empire, a new golden circle reaching from the border states of Maryland and Delaware down through the jungles of South America. . . .

With Texas as their model.

Look What We Found!

*Theodore Jones (l) and Henry Grob revealing their
treasure discovery in a 1930s newsreel.*

When Henry's mother first saw the gold, she was instantly frightened. Her initial impulse was to tell her son to take the coins back to wherever he had found them. Naturally, Henry wasn't going to do that, so he took the find to the second most trusted adults in his life — his older sister Gertrude and Gertrude's husband, Paul Eberhart. Paul was a U.S. soldier stationed at a nearby base. Conveniently for Henry, the couple lived in an apartment upstairs in the same building as Henry and Mrs. Grob.[1]

Eberhart's immediate concern was the recently passed Executive Order 6102, which outlawed most private ownership of gold by U.S. citizens. Owners of gold bullion and gold certificates were required to turn their hard asset savings into the U.S. Treasury for the fixed price of $20.67 per troy ounce. If gold "hoarders" did not accept government cash for their gold, they could be subject to heavy fines and possible imprisonment. Although there were limited exceptions involving collector's coins and gold jewelry, the Eberharts were probably correct in that the boys were inviting arrest if they did not hand over their find to the authorities. The scenario of two poor neighborhood boys trying to swap mounds of gold coins for cash at a bank teller window was highly improbable. Better to bring the gold to the authorities then have the constabulary types catch wind of the discovery and come looking.[2]

Ironically, although the controversial ban on alcohol had just been lifted after the decade-long failed experiment that was

12

Prohibition, the U.S. had immediately turned around and slapped a new ban on the right of its people to own gold. This was contrary to Article 1, Section 10 of the Constitution which clearly forbids U.S. states from making anything but gold and silver coin "legal tender." Paper currency had long since become a fact of life in America, but removing the backing from currency, and forcing the citizenry to use "fiat" money, was certainly a new undertaking — especially the outright ban on private ownership of gold, a basic fundamental right of any free person.[3]

With the country's gold now in U.S. government coffers, and the public forced to accept cash in its place, President Franklin D. Roosevelt next devalued the dollar in 1934. He accomplished this by raising the official price of gold to $35 through the "Gold Act." Such was the cost of implementing the government's "New Deal." The United States government then set about constructing Fort Knox, and in 1937, shipped some 500 railcars of gold to the heavily guarded vaults there.[4]

Meanwhile, back in Baltimore, Paul Eberhart rounded up Henry, Henry's gold, then Theodore, and Theodore's gold, and proceeded to pay a visit to the Eastern Police Station which was not far away. But before they did, the boys and their families hedged their bet by withholding a sizable portion of the treasure trove.

"We've got $7,000 in gold pieces and would like to give them to you," the boys announced to the befuddled desk sergeant on duty.[5]

The police that night could scarcely believe their eyes. They helped to count the coins, some damaged, and many which remained stuck together. In total, they came to a total of $7,882 in face value, aside from the potential numismatic value of the coins, which all proved to be dated in the previous century (though not all dates were legible). After placing the coins in the station vault, and assuring the boys they would get their money after any legal issues were sorted out, the boys began to feel that perhaps they had done the right thing.

Henry and Theodore were so comfortable, in fact, that they invited the authorities back to the Joneses' modest apartment, where another pile of gold coins with a face value of $3,542 was relinquished into police custody.[6]

That second stash officially pushed the astounding treasure to $11,424 . . . an amazing number in an era when the average new house cost less than $6,000. Today, with gold well north of $1,000 an ounce — and given the rarity and age of some of the coins in the hoard, the present day 21st-century value would easily reach several million dollars.

Whether the boys and their families had, in fact, handed in *all* of the coins is still a topic of debate. Subsequent events, however, would favor the view that $11,424 represented but a portion of the 1934 Baltimore treasure trove. It is quite likely that a sizable number of the uncovered gold pieces never made it into official hands. But by any accounting, Henry and Theodore had stumbled across one of the greatest finds in the history of American treasure.

Where the gold had come from? What would become of it? These were the immediate mysteries that needed to be resolved.

Within hours, on September 1, 1934, the City of Baltimore would be waking up — to a serious case of gold fever.

The Voyages of Captain John

One of the persons who once owned the treasure house on South Eden Street, site of young Theodore and Henry's stupendous find, was a 19th-century Maryland sea captain name John J. Mattison. A lifetime Baltimore resident and a career mariner, Mattison would purchase the mystery home in 1855, living there at 55 S. Eden with his wife and family until sometime right before the beginning of the Civil War in 1861.[1] During the tumultuous Civil War years, Mattison would rent his house to fellow seafarer Captain John E. Stevens — before selling the property to a long-time neighbor, the candle company executive Andrew J. Saulsbury from nearby South Central Avenue (quite literally just around the corner). The sale to Saulsbury would occur almost immediately after the end of the Civil War in June, 1865.[2]

In the latter part of 1839, Captain Mattison would navigate his vessel *The Eliza Davidson* out of Baltimore Harbor, down the Patapsco River, out to the Chesapeake Bay, and into the open deep blue waters of the Atlantic Ocean. Once out to sea, Mattison would chart a course for due south and the sunny, familiar clime of Havana, Cuba.

That Mattison and his business partners, wharf owners James S. Corner and Thomas Corner, still possessed *The Eliza*

Davidson was something of a blessing. Just months earlier, their commercial vessel had been seized as part of a French blockade off the coast of South America. The resulting court fight over cargo insurance would make it all the way to the Maryland Court of Appeals.[3]

Apparently the Corner brothers and Mattison, who each owned a third of the brig *The Eliza Davidson*, had contracted with an Alfred Peabody to carry cargo from Montevideo, Uruguay to Corrientes, Argentina, where the brig would unload some of the goods taken on in Uruguay, and then add additional cargo at Corrientes. The American brig would then make the long charter voyage north to Boston, Massachusetts. Mattison had the good sense to insure the cargo with the Charleston Insurance and Trust Company, a cargo which included bales of dry goods and many barrels of wine and rum, before he left port in Montevideo. The cargo was insured by the captain for the sum of $4,000.

Trouble began soon after *The Eliza Davidson* arrived in Corrientes to complete the first leg of her journey. France had been in conflict with Argentina, and was in the process of blockading the port of Buenos Aires in order to bring about a successful settlement of that dispute. No official notification had been given that the French also intended to blockade Corrientes, a city in the northernmost province of Argentina.

On March 16, 1839, a French vessel of war, *The Perle*, appeared in port at Corrientes. Eleven armed sailors from *The Perle* boarded *The Eliza Davidson* and seized her, taking Captain Mattison's crew prisoner onboard the French corvette. Mattison protested to the French officer in charge, but his complaints fell on deaf ears. Things really went bad for *The Eliza Davidson* when the thirsty French sailors discovered the brig's shipment of wine and rum. In his later court deposition, Captain Mattison described how the French seamen, "*descended into the hold, and drew off a portion of wine and rum for their own use, being part of the cargo.*"

Now thoroughly inebriated, and their number growing to 20, the Frenchmen then attempted to get the brig under way, with disastrous results. In Captain Mattison's own words, "*In hoisting some casks of water on board, they spilled a large quantity on the goods in the hold, which caused considerable damage . . . they got the brig under way, cutting the running rigging and breaking many articles that came in their way; they also broached the brig's provisions, and used them without ceremony.*"

By March 18th, with *The Eliza Davidson* well on its way back to Montevideo as a French war prize, Mattison notes that, "*The French crew regularly drew from the cargo three buckets full of wine per day, and used the brig's provisions extravagantly.*" The captive captain was so troubled by the actions of the French sailors that he "*considered the safety of the vessel and his life in great danger.*"

By March 25th, *The Eliza Davidson* had limped into port at Montevideo in a great state of disarray. At this time, Mattison testifies, with "*the French crew still in possession of said brig and the greater part in a state of intoxication, having free access to the wine and spirits and provisions generally . . . Commodore Nicholson, in command of the U.S. Squadron, came along side of the brig, accompanied by the American Consul, and took the deponent on shore for the purpose of an interview with the French Admiral.*"

Once onshore, the U.S. admiral, the American consul, and Mattison were able to convince the French to release *The Eliza Davidson* into the captain's custody. Despite protests from the Americans, the French refused to pay for damages to Mattison's brig, leaving *The Eliza Davidson* in port for several days while the captain contracted with local workers to have the ship repaired. Mattison also contacted Alfred Peabody, who had chartered the brig, asking for full payment on the voyage. Peabody naturally refused to make payment since his cargo had not arrived in Boston and, more to the point, had been permanently lost. Peabody also officially canceled the charter, and the captain concurred. An arbitrator eventually awarded Mattison $1,200 for the Peabody cargo he had successfully delivered to Corrientes on the first leg of the charter — before the French seized his ship. However, angered over the loss of the bulk of his goods, businessman Peabody refused to pay even that reduced sum. Mattison and his partners received not a penny, and were burdened with costly and extensive repairs.

After a few weeks in Montevideo, and with *The Eliza Davidson* again seaworthy, Mattison was fortunate enough to book yet another charter for a shipment (supposedly of meat) going from Uruguay to Havana, Cuba. Mattison and the Corner Bros. would receive the extremely handsome charter sum of $5,000 . . . after which Mattison would head for home port in Baltimore.

The Maryland lawsuit came about when Mattison and the Corner brothers attempted to file a claim with the Charleston Insurance and Trust Company for the loss of the Peabody cargo. The plaintiffs had filed for the full $4,000 insured amount of the lost cargo.

Charleston Insurance and Trust denied the charter party's claim, citing the following reasons:

1. Mattison should have known about the French blockade, and that the captain had sailed with the insured cargo into a known war zone.

2. Mattison and the Corner Bros. had subsequently booked a charter that had earned them $5,000 — a greater sum for a shorter voyage from Montevideo to Havana (Boston being at a much greater distance from Montevideo).

3. Mattison had been awarded a partial $1,200 in arbitration on the Peabody shipment, even though Peabody had declined to abide by the ruling of the arbitrator. The plaintiffs were therefore attempting to recover a higher sum of money than their original interest in the insured cargo.

The lawyer for Mattison and the Corner brothers was able to successfully counter these assertions from the defendants. Both the lower court, and later the Maryland Court of Appeals, found in favor of the plaintiffs, ruling that Charleston Insurance and Trust (the defendant) was in breach of the insurance contract on *The Eliza Davidson's* cargo. Charleston Insurance was ordered to pay the plaintiffs' claim for loss of their freight.

The intriguing case of Charleston Insurance and Trust Company vs. James J. Corner and Thomas Corner, December, 1844, can be found summarized in the 1885 collection <u>Reports of Cases Argued and Adjudged in the Court of Appeals in Maryland</u>.[4]

So, in the fall of 1839 as Captain Mattison set sail for Havana, Cuba aboard his rescued and repaired *Eliza Davidson*, one would have expected Mattison and the Corner brothers to have exercised a greater degree of caution with their vessel on the high seas. Such was not the case, however, for this particular voyage would be *The Eliza Davidson's* last charter under Captain John Mattison's command.

Life at sea during the 19th century was hard, and the dangers many. This particular voyage greatly increased those risks, however, as *The Eliza Davidson* would be pressed into a most clandestine and illicit service. So clandestine and illicit that, once safely harbored in Havana, Captain Mattison would designate a replacement skipper to command his *Eliza Davidson* on the next and most dangerous leg of her journey — east across the Atlantic to the "dark continent" of Africa.[5]

It is known that Captain Mattison was in Havana by early November, 1839 because of an incident that came to the attention of the American Consul in that city. Three members of the crew of another American ship, the *Huron of Portsmouth*, had been jailed by local authorities for some offense committed while in port. Before the captain of that ship could intercede on behalf of his men, the captain fell ill and passed away, leaving no one to speak for the American sailors held prisoner in a foreign jail. The American Consul, J.P. Trist, sought the assistance of captains from other American ships in port. Captain John J. Mattison of Baltimore happened to be available and willing to help the American Consul. Mr. Trist[6] writes as follows:

CONSULATE OF THE UNITED STATES OF AMERICA,
Havana, November 28, 1839.

SIR: I beg leave to enclose a copy of a letter addressed by me, on the 2d instant, to Captain George C. Boardman, of the ship Huron of Portsmouth; the object of which, as you will perceive, was to obtain the testimony of some of our countrymen in regard to the state of health of the three American seamen therein named. In compliance with my request, a party was made up by Captain Boardman to visit the Cabaña, and an afternoon (that of the 5th instant) appointed for the purpose. He, however, became unwell on the previous night; and thus began a postponement, which, in consequence of his protracted illness and death, has ended in a total failure.

I avail myself, therefore, of your visit to the port, to request your attention to the subject. Any afternoon that it may suit your convenience, my clerk will accompany you to act as interpreter. If agreeable to you, I should wish that two or three of our merchant captains might be of the party. Captains Sturgis and Pike (who were selected by me, for the reason that, like their friend, the late Captain Boardman, they were commanders of American ships of the first class, casually here with large cargoes from Liverpool, and utter strangers to this port, as well as to myself) have both left here. Of those invited by Captain Boardman to accompany him,

Captain Mattison, of the brig Eliza Davidson of Baltimore, also now for the first time known to me, is still here. A more suitable selection could not, I believe, have been made. To him I would propose to add Captain David B. Barton of Warren, Rhode Island, master of the packet-ship Norma; Captain Morgan S. Gordon, of Portland, master of the barque Ellen, (two of the regular traders to this port from New York;) and Captain Charles M. Folger, of Nantucket, master of the brig Hope and Susan of Nantucket.

I am, sir, very respectfully, your obedient servant,

N. P. TRIST.

POSTSCRIPT.—The point specified in my letter to Captain Boardman, as that to which I wished attention to be particularly given, is, *the condition of the men as to health.* A second point, in regard to which I will request you to ascertain the truth as far as possible, is, *whether their treatment and condition have differed* (and, if yea, in what *particulars,* and to what *extent*) *from that experienced by the men of the ship William Engs,* who were confined in the same fortress, and whose confinement commenced about the same time with that of the present prisoners.

N. P. TRIST.

Whether Mattison was able to assist the American Consul in Havana and, whether they were eventually successful in bringing about the release of these sailors, is unknown. What is known is that Mattison had more pressing matters to attend to in Havana, and it involved a certain trading firm of dubious repute, the Havana house of Pedro Martinez and Co.

The following month, on December 16th, Captain Mattison struck the following bargain with Simon Perez de Teran, a senior partner at the Martinez Trading Company. The agreed upon charter party would allow Teran and Martinez to have exclusive use of *The Eliza Davidson,* of which Mattison was part owner (along with the Corner brothers), for a period of two years, in exchange for the sum of $8,500 dollars. An interim master of Mattison's choosing, Alexander Hanna of Baltimore, would command the ship under orders from Teran. At the conclusion of the two-year charter, the brig would be returned to its owners and/or agents at the vessel's home port of Baltimore. The ship would remain under her American colors during the charter.

John Mattison had been the master of *The Eliza Davidson* for some 11 years, since her construction in New York in 1828. December, 1839 would be the last time Mattison would ever see *The Eliza Davidson.* The vessel's cross-Atlantic voyage to Africa would be her last — at least under American colors.

20

On January 9, 1840, the aging brig set sail for Sierra Leone with Captain Hanna and a crew of 11 officers and sailors — seven Americans, two Englishmen, an Italian, and one mate from the island of Malta. There were no passengers, just cargo. The ship, still sailing under the United States flag, arrived off coast near the Gallinas River, Sierra Leone on February 26th.

First stop for *The Eliza Davidson* was the infamous slave factory of Jose Alvarez, located on the Gallinas, where most of the ship's Havana cargo was unloaded. At Gallinas, *The Eliza Davidson* unloaded her cargo from Havana, and then took on a new shipment which included dry goods, arms, and ammunition. Just before setting sail from Gallinas, the interim master, Captain Hanna, was seen rowing out to his ship in a canoe accompanied by two young African boys.

The ship's steward, Charles Knoff, cautioned the captain that bringing the boys aboard could mean trouble with the authorities. Captain Hanna brushed the steward's concerns aside, telling him the boys were to be his "apprentices."

The Eliza Davidson then headed for Shebar, where she took on 60 tons of rice for slave trader Jose Alvarez back in Gallinas. Next, the brig journeyed to the Plantain Islands, were she offloaded some of Alvarez' cargo and took on yet another 70 tons of rice for Alvarez. While docked at Shebar, a third boy had been brought aboard the American freighter.

During her return to the Alavrez compound in Gallinas, on April 4th, a British sloop *The Wanderer* intercepted *The Eliza Davidson*, upon which she was boarded by Her Majesty's officers and sailors. Captain Hanna had told the three boys to hide when he saw the British sloop approach — but the authorities found them anyway. A quick search of the brig turned up the enormous quantity of rice, the dry goods, tobacco, 240 Spanish doubloons, six cutlasses, 12 muskets, two pistols, and a box of ammunition. More interestingly, the British inspectors found an enormous quantity of water casks aboard *The Eliza Davidson* — far more water (some 2,000 gallons) than would be required for any normal, legitimate voyage. And, of course, the British found the three boys hidden aboard ship, and noted that the boys' presence onboard had been conspicuously absent from the ship's log.

Faced with such disturbing evidence, the British questioned Captain Hanna and accused him of slave trading. Hanna denied the accusation, saying there were no slaves aboard, and no slave equipment. He admitted to the 2,000 gallons of water, without offering an explanation. Hanna claimed the boys were put on board as a favor to Alvarez to learn English and to wait on tables. When asked if he knew that Jose Alvarez was a slave trader, Hanna guessed that he might be because the captain had seen a building at the Alvarez compound in which many blacks were being kept in chains.

Describing Hanna's version of events as both "lame and improbable," *The Eliza Davidson* and her crew were detained, and trial immediately scheduled in a joint English/Spanish mixed court of justice in Sierra Leone.

From the outset, Hanna's legal position was weak, and both the ship's steward and the three boys testified readily that the primary reason for *The Eliza Davidson's* voyage was to bring slaves back to the New World — to Havana most certainly and also to the United States.

During testimony, Hanna maintained his innocence, and that the three boys would have been returned to The Gallinas on the brig's return voyage from Shebar and The Plantain Islands with the cargo of rice for Alvarez. However, Hanna still had no answer as to why *The Eliza Davidson* had been outfitted to carry 2,000 gallons of water. Hanna also stated that he believed the true price paid for the vessel in Havana had been $12,000 . . . even higher than the price listed in the charter agreement between Captain Mattison and Simon Perez de Teran.

Hanna failed to mention the boys during courtroom testimony.

The subsequent testimony of the brig's steward, however, largely contradicted that of the captain. Charles Knoff related how the chief mate cautioned the master that the boys could get them in trouble, and how Hanna ordered the boys to stay out of sight before being boarded by investigators from the British sloop. Knoff explained how the captain said he would make the boys his apprentices, and bring them to his home (in Baltimore). Knoff also revealed that he believed the number of gallons of water on board to be far greater than 2,000 gallons — compelling evidence that the brig had been outfitted for human cargo.

But it was the testimony of the two boys from The Gallinas compound of slave trader Alvarez who put the verdict completely out of question. Their names were Enjahe and Wurrah, and they told the court how they were kept in a barracoon (enclosure) on Alvarez' property, waiting to be sold and placed on a ship. Enjahe further testified that both he and his mother were slaves, brought from the interior of the country, and purchased by Alvarez in exchange for rum, cloth, and cutlasses.

While at Gallinas, a Spaniard named Bongo was the headman in charge of about 30 slaves. Men were manacled and fettered, women wore iron collars, and the children did chores. Bongo had delivered Enjahe to Hanna, master of the brig. The entire barracoon was to be sent away on this vessel as soon as the master could obtain enough rice. Bongo had said he intended to sell them all to the American captain.

Wurrah then gave a similar deposition, corroborating the older boy's story. The third and youngest child, Caulker from Shebar, had little to add.

The ship's owners, identified as Captain Mattison and the Corner Brothers of Baltimore, where the vessel had been insured, did not bring any counter claims (it actuality it would have been impossible to reach them in the United Staes and Cuba in time for the trial).

The prosecution then summed up its case. *The Eliza Davidson* had been detained with actual slaves on board, and had been clearly outfitted as a slave ship. The slave boys had been conspicuously missing from the ship's log. Captain Hanna's testimony wasn't credible and, frankly, was preposterous. The Havana charter party was a sham transaction, a thin disguise for selling the brig as a "secret slave trader." The terms of the charter (two years for $8,500 . . . $12,000 according to Hanna) constituted an actual sale of the ship to Teran and his partner, Englishman Charles Tyng. The vessel, therefore, while flying the Stars and Stripes, was actually a Spanish ship whose port was Havana, and was property of the Havana trading house of Pedro Martinez, who had incurred an owner's responsibility. An outright purchase of a ship the age and class of *The Eliza Davidson* should have brought little more than $4,000 U.S. dollars. Teran and Tyng were known offenders to the court, and had been involved in cases with other ships. All 20-30 slaves at the Alvarez compound had been slated for sale to Hanna, Mattison's handpicked man in charge, once Alvarez could obtain enough rice to stock the slave ship — and also his Gallinas barracoon for the next batch of slaves from the interior. The vessel had been chartered by, and consigned to, well-known slave dealers, and was detained while returning to a most notorious slave-mart. The final destination for the slaves transported via *The Eliza Davidson* was to have been Havana . . . and possibly the United States.

The court put much weight on the testimony of the children, noting that they had no motive to deceive, and were not mature enough to concoct such a tale. The ship's steward had largely confirmed the boys' testimony.

In pronouncing sentence, the court noted that while it could not prove the youngest of the three children to have been a slave, the older two boys could not be considered anything *but* slaves. They were housed in a barracoon at the slave factory of the well-known Alvarez, and sold to the master of *The Eliza Davidson*. Parties transferred were dealt with as chattels, not as human beings. The Gallinas boys were considered and treated by the master and his chief officer as slaves, and not included in the ship's log. The exclusive employment of the *Eliza Davidson* "*in the haunts of the most notorious of slave-dealers*" proved that the vessel was employed in abetting the slave trade.

On April 18th, 1840 the mixed court of British and Spanish justice condemned Captain Mattison's brig of 11 years as a slave trader, and *The Eliza Davidson* was forfeit to The Two Crowns. The boys were set free and considered as "emancipated from slavery." In a separate trial, the vessel's English crew members were convicted of participating in the slave trade.

On April 24th, the English officers of the mixed court of justice made a report[7] to their superior, The Right Honorable Viscount Palmerston, who agreed with the determination. A copy of the proceedings was forwarded to the American Consul in Havana, N.P. Trist, who did not protest the outcome.

Sadly, the mixed court of justice in Sierra Leone also released the statement that, "*The slave traders of Havana are more embarrassed than discouraged by the difficulties*" posed by their court.

That Captain John J. Mattison of Baltimore was directly and undoubtedly involved in the slave trade ties directly to the gold coins that will be found underneath his (and later Andrew Saulsbury's) house in 1934. Consider the following information taken direct from page 6 of the 1861 book *The Authentic Exposition of the K.G.C., Knights of the Golden Circle, or a History of Secession from 1834 to 1861*, written anonymously by a secret member of that order.[8] The writer explicitly describes the early attempts of the Southern Rights Clubs of the 1830s to find a way to circumvent the existing ban on the African slave trade:

"The African slave trade being contrary to the laws of the United States, and to the laws of the whole civilized world, it was not hoped to carry it on in an open manner. The first efforts of the S.R.C.'s, therefore, was directed to the fitting out, manning, and equipping of secret slavers, which were to cruise around the African coast and kidnap negroes whenever a good opportunity was afforded. Between the years 1834 and 1840 it is presumed that at least six of these vessels were equipped and sent out. Some of them were successful, and filled the measure of their appointment, while others were captured by English and other fleets, to the great mortification of the S.R.C.'s and the discouragement of their enterprise. They did not, however, "give up the ship" in consequence of these discouragements, but continued their slave piracy with renewed vigor, whenever it seemed possible to conceal their maneuverings."

Mere coincidence? Mattison's brig was seized by the British in early 1840 and quickly condemned as a secret slaver — then forfeited to the English and Spanish crowns. Both the timing and the circumstances fit perfectly. Was *The Eliza Davidson* the final blow in 1840 that convinced the S.R.C.'s to change their subversive tactics?

It stretches credulity to believe that Captain Mattison and the Corner Brothers weren't knowingly involved in the slave trade. Mattison was a regular in Havana, and most certainly knew the reputation of Teran, Tyng, and the House of Martinez. The exorbitant fees charged to Teran to "lease" *The Eliza Davidson* certainly point to Mattison and the Corners being in on the game. The interim skipper, Hanna of Baltimore, was handpicked by Mattison — and his actions strongly suggest that Hanna intended to bring some of the Gallinas slaves back to the United States.

When seized by the French in 1839, *The Eliza Davidson* was carrying a large number of casks of wine and rum, of which the French mariners regularly partook. This vessel was *already* outfitted to haul large quantities of liquid cargo — be it wine, rum, or water. Remember, the inebriated French sailors destroyed a large number of dry goods in the cargo hold when they attempted to hoist several casks of water. There was so much water aboard Mattison's brig in Argentina that it was getting in the way of the mischievous French sailors. Apparently, the vessel seems to have been outfitted for the slave trade sometime *before* its two-year "lease" in Havana. Mattison received $5,000 for carrying "quintals of meat" from Montevideo to Havana, a relatively short voyage. One must wonder as to the type of "meat" Mattison actually carried to the Cubans on short notice — and if that "meat" was actually a euphemism for slaves delivered in chains to Teran, Tyng, and the infamous House of Martinez in Havana.

Then there is the matter of *The Eliza Davidson* being insured, in Baltimore, before she was "leased" in Havana. Although Mattison and the Corners received two and perhaps as much as three times *The Eliza Davidson's* value for the highly suspicious two-year lease, they were still technically the owners of that vessel. Can we assume they collected (or tried to collect) the insurance money once Teran, Tyng, and Hanna had lost their ship? That Mattison and the Corner brothers had previously attempted to collect full insurance payment on their partially lost Argentina cargo says that is a fairly safe bet.

Those 5,000 gold coins, later buried in Captain Mattison's cellar in 1856, make the bet a virtual lock.

A closer look at Mattison's business partner, James Corner, helps to give a more complete picture. Corner was known for being the owner of Buchanan's Wharf at Pratt Street, a short walk from the site of James Armstrong & Co. on Concord Street by the Pratt Street Bridge. The Pratt Street docks were heavily involved in the legal 19th-century U.S. slave trade, with the Port of Baltimore being a convenient central slave mart where human beings were regularly bought and sold. In a July, 2000 article in *The Baltimore Sun*, *A Bitter Inner Harbor Legacy: The Slave Trade*, columnist Ralph Clayton describes how, "*The major slave dealers, who came from Kentucky, Georgia, Virginia and Tennessee built their slave pens near Pratt Street, the major east-west connection to the wharves in the Inner Harbor and Fells Point.*"[9]

James Corner would also achieve notoriety in the 1840s by becoming the owner of the first trans-Atlantic packet line (passenger ship carrying mail and cargo) in existence, Baltimore to Liverpool.[10]

However, it is Corner's participation as a delegate to the Maryland Colonization Society that is the most interesting for our purposes. The first colonization societies appeared in New England around 1816, formed by Quakers who believed that the black race could never get a fair deal in North America — hence it was in the best interest of black people to be repatriated to the African continent where they might live in peace and (hopefully) with minimal interference. And since there was another James Corner in 1840s Baltimore, a free black man who was active in pressing for a better education for the black children of that city, I assumed it was the black James Corner who had been involved with the society.

A peek at the 1841 journal for The Maryland Colonization Society[11] quickly told me that it was indeed the white wharf owner who had been named as a delegate. By the 1830s and 1840s, the colonization movement had been largely infiltrated by Southern sympathizers as a way to deal with the growing numbers of free blacks in American society. And in 1840s America, no city boasted more free blacks than did Baltimore. To the 19th-century Southern mind, free blacks and Northern abolitionists represented a potentially volatile mix, and so the best way to deal with this threat was to fund the repatriation of freed American blacks back to their mother continent.

The Maryland Colonization Society's own chart showcases the demographics that concerned their members:

Population of Maryland in 1790, 1800, 1810, 1820, 1830 *and* 1840, *as shewn by the census taken in those years,*				
	White.	Slaves.	Free Col'd.	Agg. Col'd.	Total.
1790	208,649	103,036	8,043	111,079	319,728
1800	216,326	105,635	19,587	125,238	341,548
1810	235,117	111,502	33,927	145,429	380,546
1820	259,522	107,998	39,730	147,728	407,350
1830	291,108	102,994	52,938	155,932	447,040
1840	317,717	89,495	62,020	151,515	469,232

And to cast aside any doubt, the following excerpt from the 1841 Maryland Colonization Society Journal clearly demonstrates the hostility between the MCS and their northern abolitionist counterparts:

". . . what is known as modern abolition, which aims at the immediate extirpation of slavery, without any regard to the rights of property under existing laws, and with a blind recklessness of consequences, began to assume a defined shape and extensive organization; and as soon as the Colonization policy of Maryland was understood, it became the point of virulent and opprobrious assault: the leading publication on the subject being a pamphlet published in Boston, entitled 'The Maryland Scheme of Expatriation Examined' — the aim of which was to set Colonization in the position (which it indeed truly occupies,) of the antagonist of abolition, and as such, to consign it to public execration."[12]

It astonishes many persons today that President Abraham Lincoln, author of the 1862 Emancipation Proclamation, had been a member of the Illinois Colonization Society, which also sought to repatriate freed blacks to Africa. While strongly opposed to the institution of slavery, Lincoln held little hope that whites and blacks could live equally and peaceably in a shared society, and on numerous occasions had voiced such an opinion. In his message to Congress on December 1, 1862, Lincoln talked about his resettlement plan: *"That portion of the earth's surface which is owned and inhabited by the people of the United States is well adapted to be the home of one national family; and it is not well adapted for two, or more. I have urged colonization of the Negroes, and I shall continue. My Emancipation Proclamation was linked with this plan . . . I can conceive of no greater calamity than the assimilation of the Negro into our social and political life as our equal . . . We cannot attain the ideal union our Fathers dreamed, with millions of an alien, inferior race among us, whose assimilation is neither possible or desirable."*[13]

As for wharf and ship owner James Corner, besides Southern pride and culture there was also great financial incentive for participation in the movement towards colonization. The Maryland Colonization Society's own report on its ongoing efforts to repatriate blacks to its Cape Palmas colony in Liberia would have any 19th- century Baltimore shipping magnate seeing dollars signs:

28

Number of Expeditions dispatched by the Md. State Col. Society, since 1831.		
	Date of sailing.	No. of Emigrants.
Schooner Orion, . . .	Nov. 1831 .	. 31
Ship La Fayette, . . .	Dec. 1832 .	. 146
Brig Ann, ...	Nov. 1833 .	. 17
Schooner Sarah and Priscilla, .	1834 with supplies only.	
Brig Bourne, ...	Dec. 1834 .	. 57
Schooner Harmony, . . .	June, 1835 .	. 27
Brig Fortune, ...	Dec. 1835 .	. 39
Schooner Financier, . .	July, 1836 .	. 15
Brig Niobe, ...	Oct. 1836 .	. 32
Brig Baltimore, . . .	May, 1837 .	. 55
Brig Niobe, ...	Nov. 1837 .	. 85
Schooner Columbia, . .	May, 1838 .	. 36
Brig Oberon, ...	Nov. 1838 .	. 52
Brig Boxer, ...	Dec. 1839 . .	. 32—624

To grasp Corner's full participation in the slave trade, one must realize that he profited by involving his ship in the highly illegal African slave trade, profited additionally by collecting on the legal domestic slave traffic passing through his wharf on Pratt Street, and then, finally, sought to profit in the scheme to ship freed American blacks back to Africa.

One might suspect that Baltimorean James Corner and Louisiana slave trader Jim Bowie matriculated at the same school of underhanded business.

Not coincidentally, one of the requirements for membership in the secret Confederate society the Knights of the Golden Circle (KGC) was to take an oath to oppose the allowance of free blacks in American society, as has been noted by David C. Keehn in Knights of the Golden Circle.[14]

After their loss of the aging brig *The Eliza Davidson* to its condemnation and forfeiture as an illegal African slave trader, the Corner Brothers and Captain Mattison did do business for a time in the early 1840s operating a new vessel, the bark *Ann Eliza*.

Shipping records indicate that Mattison and the Corners were involved in further South American charters. In March, 1841, Mattison and *The Ann Eliza* transported an immigrant French family of four by the name of Argenteer (or Argintier) from Rio de Janeiro, Brazil to their new home in Baltimore, where they were sworn in as U.S. citizens.[15]

Captain Mattison seems to have dropped from the mid-1840s shipping records, however. Perhaps he had a falling out with the Corner brothers, and parted ways with them. Litigation and subsequent appeals concerning *The Eliza Davidson's* lost South American cargo dragged on through 1843.

Mattison would reappear by the late 1840s, at the helm of a new ship, the bark *Maria*, on which he would sail to new destinations. First, Mattison would serve the lucrative California Gold Rush, and later the Hawaiian Islands (then known as the Sandwich Islands), presumably to transport New England missionaries — although many adventurers from Hawaii also participated in the gold rush because of the islands' direct shipping route to California.

The California Gold Rush, touched off in 1848 with the discovery of gold at Sutter's Mill near Sacramento, would result in the incredible recovery of some 12 million ounces of placer gold from 1848 through 1853. Some 300,000 people from the United States and around the globe would ultimately flock to America's newest state in a mad dash for new found riches. The sleepy settlement of San Francisco would explode from a population of just 200 in 1848 to 36,000 by 1852. Of the approximate 300,000 fortune seekers about half of that number would arrive by sea. In the days before the construction of the Panama Canal, East Coasters would have to sail around Cape Horn at the bottom of South America to reach the West Coast — an arduous voyage of several months.

Captain Mattison, who took on passengers from ports such as Baltimore, Philadelphia, New York, and New London, would be mentioned in at least two books and a collection of letters written about the experience of the legendary "49ers":

Palmer, Robert H. *A Voyage Round Cape Horn* Philadelphia: William S. Young, 1863. Pages 1-18 contain an account of the voyage, August 7-December 13, 1849, from Philadelphia, Pennsylvania to San Francisco, California in the bark *Maria* under the command of Captain Mattison.

Schultz, Charles R. *Forty-niners 'round the Horn* Columbia: University of South Carolina Press, 1999. This is an account of the thrilling, and at times harrowing, maritime adventures of fortune hunters who sailed from the east coast of America around Cape Horn to California during the gold rush of 1849.

La Motte Family. Letters, 1849-1872. Bancroft Library, University of California, Berkeley, California. # C-B 450. The library has both original letters and typescript copies. Six of the letters by Robert and Harry La Motte to their family contain details of their voyage from Philadelphia, Pennsylvania to San Francisco, California in the bark *Maria* under the command of Captain John J. Mattison. At least two of the letters are in journal form and contain entries for several days.

Merchant ships fill San Francisco in 1850-51.

The following shipping record survives from Captain Mattison's 1851 voyage from New York to Honolulu to San Francisco. It was recorded in port at Honolulu, and includes a detailed tally of the cargo carried by his bark *Maria* on that long voyage:

```
SHIP:  MARIA
TYPE:  Barque                          FROM:  New York
ARRIVED:  May 18, 1851                 CAPTAIN:  Mattison
PASSAGE:  144 days from New York.
CARGO:  Pork, 101 kegs butter, 100 doz. candles, varnish, pails,
        mackerel, 20 small anchors, paint and assorted goods.
                       Passengers
              A. Narring      F. Narring
              - - - - -
```

Among the items listed are 100 dozen candles. The men involved in collecting the 5,000 gold coins which would be buried under Captain Mattison's Baltimore home in 1856 were involved in the manufacture and sale of candles on a wholesale basis. And like Mattison and his business partner, wharf owner James Corner, they were also involved in the cause of "Southern rights" and the promotion of the American slave trade. Their cause would ultimately lead to the secession of the Southern states from the Union and the deaths of hundreds of thousands of Americans.

The seizure of Captain John J. Mattison's brig *The Eliza Davidson* in 1840, and its condemnation and forfeiture as a slave vessel, were intimately and *directly* connected to the burial of the 5,000 coins beneath the treasure house on South Eden Street.

Let the Circus Begin

To say that Henry Grob and Theodore Jones became *overnight* Baltimore celebrities is almost an understatement. The press loved the story . . . and why not? Two fatherless boys — one whose mother took in laundry[1] and subsisted on the public dole, the other whose mother picked tomatoes on Maryland's Eastern Shore for grocery money[2] — finding a fortune in precious metal beneath a crumbling tenement house. Such was a storyline bound to catch on anywhere and anytime. And nowhere would the story resonate more strongly than in the Depression-era America.

Henry and Theodore had hit the big time . . . *The Baltimore Sun, The Baltimore Evening Sun, The Maryland Daily Record* . . . even the national papers had picked up the unfolding treasure tale. The boys are photographed with each other, with police, at the police station, with the treasure, in the cellar, with their mothers, and, of course, holding the axe that had split open the pot of golden treasure.

Well-wishers began to stop by the boys' home, offering congratulations and lots of advice. Visitors, of course, usually asked to be shown the now-famous cellar. One caller well known to the boys was plumber Robert King. King had been contracted by the property manager to repair water pipes in the cellar — pipes that had run tantalizingly close by the treasure.[3]

At night, lights could be seen emanating from the cellar windows of nearby homes as neighbors explored ancient row-house cellars in the hopes golden lightening might strike twice. No further treasure discoveries were reported.[4]

Baltimore police posted a short-term guard at the treasure site, and even conducted their own hunt for more uncovered treasure. But the police search came up empty, and the guard was quickly pulled.[5]

Soon fan mail started to arrive at both the Grob and Jones residences. The two formerly bored teens occupied their time by reading the letters the postman dropped off each day.[6]

In an effort to identify and count all the gold coins from 132 S. Eden St., Baltimore police officials soaked the antiquated hard money in a mixture of coal oil and vinegar — and then used a knife to pry apart any pieces that had become cemented together through years of concretion. Their primary mission seems to have been an accurate accounting of the treasure, not a careful preservation of the find. Gold is soft and easily scratched. Young Theodore Jones and Henry Grob had already done enormous damage to the numismatic value of the coins by hacking them out of the earth with an axe and a corn knife.[7] Some reports also described the boys' use of a hammer, an image designed to illicit involuntary winces from coin aficionados everywhere.

Early speculation on who might have buried the cache centered on a long-dead sea captain named Donaldson. Donaldson had been involved in the Latin American coffee trade, and had pre-deceased two sisters.[8] The three siblings had lived together for many years on Eden Street. However, it would soon be confirmed that the sea captain and his sisters had occupied the home *next door* to the treasure home. Formerly known as 55 S. Eden during most of the 19th-century, the treasure site's street number had been eventually changed. All of the numbers on that block had been redone, only adding to the confusion in determining whose family members and ancestors had lived in which house.

Curious coin collectors and concerned numismatists inquired as to whether they might be allowed to inspect the mystery coins, but their requests were denied. Baltimore's aggravated chief of police, Charles Gaither, called the fuss over the coins "so much nonsense."[9] It seems the intense interest generated by the coins was beginning to interfere with normal police department business. No numismatic examination of the coins would be undertaken until the coins were transferred to the circuit court.

On the legal front, the Jones and Grob families hired one of Baltimore's biggest legal names, Harry O. Levin. A former Maryland politician and well-known champion of the underdog, Levin was a natural choice to represent the boys in their quest to secure clear title to the gold. As Levin had immediately anticipated, the court battle ahead would prove fierce, with multiple parties stepping forward to file their claim.[10] Anybody with any prior or current connection to the treasure house, no matter how tenuous, was a potential litigant. And with so much found money at stake, the claims would likely be coming from all directions — the current owners of the treasure property, former owners of the treasure property, current residents, former residents, and the heirs and descendants of persons associated with the Eden Street home going back well into the mid-1800s. The courts had set a 90-day deadline for claimants to file.

Levin would work on a contingency basis. Any recovered gold or money would be split three ways between the Grobs, the Joneses, and Levin.[11] While Levin's fee might seem excessive considering the fortune in gold at stake, it must be realized that Levin risked months or even years of contentious litigation — and wouldn't get reimbursed a cent if his young clients lost.

On September 11, a photo of Bessie Jones, Theodore's mother, appeared in an edition of the *Baltimore Evening Sun*.[12] Unnerved by noises she had heard around the Jones apartment, including someone apparently jiggling her apartment door, Mrs. Jones was photographed waving a loaded pistol. The caption for this startling photo announced *"Prowlers Beware!"* to Baltimore readers. The treasure boy's mom had a pistol and was prepared to use it.

Meanwhile, barely two weeks after the chance discovery, on September 15, Henry Grob got into trouble with the law. It would not be the last time the boys would find themselves in hot water. While hanging out at the Broadway Pier nears Fells Point, young Henry and a companion began to do damage to pier property. A pier supervisor intervened, and the confrontation became physical.[13] Henry and his friend would be hauled in front of a local magistrate and fined $5. Unable to pay the fine, Henry remained in police custody overnight, but was released the next day. Charges were later dismissed.

Theodore Jones, meanwhile, was invited to visit the clothing store of one Morton "Uncle Mort" Blum, a downtown Baltimore merchant.[14] "Uncle Mort" fitted young Jones with a new suit and slipped the lanky teen some pocket money. Theodore then spent the next several days meeting and greeting curious potential customers in front of the Blum store. It was reported that Jones earned $3 a day for this most unusual promotional effort.

The golden duo was also interviewed by a Baltimore radio station concerning the circumstances of their amazing treasure find.[15]

Although a veritable flood of litigants is expected, the field of claimants is held to the relatively and surprisingly small number of ten. Based on their chance discovery of the gold, the boys' legal position is a strong one. Lawyer Harry O. Levin is happy to take their claim on a contingency basis[16], since the chance of recovery is high. Other claimants on less solid legal footing will be forced to pay hourly legal fees in a case that will more likely approximate a courtroom marathon than sprint. Filing a claim to the gold would be one thing . . . but prosecuting that claim to an expensive finish would be entirely another.

One of the first claims comes from the estate of Harry Chenven, a recently deceased former jeweler who had lived in the third-floor rear apartment of the treasure home since 1927 — but who had passed away just days before the gold discovery. Chenven, an immigrant from Russia, had once owned a jewelry store on South Broadway Avenue, just a few blocks east of Eden Street.[17] But mental health difficulties had cost Chenven both his family and his business, and saw Chenven institutionalized for a time in a mental health facility. Upon Chenven's release, he sells newspapers on the streets of Baltimore, but never returns to his once lucrative profession — or to his wife and young son. Chenven's jewelry business had specialized in purchasing scrap gold from the citizens of East Baltimore, melting down that gold, and selling the raw material to the Philadelphia Mint some 90 miles to the north. In exchange, the mint sent Chenven U.S. gold coins of recent mintage.[18] Chenven's ex-wife figures her crazy husband must have been burying his gold coins all these years — even though he appeared destitute and survived only with the financial help of a sister and intervention of a long-time friend named Gammerman. Chenven, whose rear third-floor apartment is the least desirable at 132 S. Eden, did not even have a working toilet. The recluse would simply use a chamber pot . . . throwing the contents of that pot out the window, and in the process soiling Theodore Jones' bedroom window directly below.[19]

The next claim comes from the grandson of a wealthy candle and soap maker, Andrew J. Saulsbury. Reuben Foster, the grandson, obtains a court order to become the administrator of his long-dead grandfather's estate. Some eleven different Saulsbury family members will be represented by Foster, who hires attorney Charles F. Stein to argue the Saulsbury family's consolidated case.[20] The claim, on surface, appears to be a strong one. Andrew J. Saulsbury had purchased the house (from sea captain John Mattison) when it was known as 55 S. Eden Street, just after the end of the Civil War in 1865. The Eden Street neighborhood had been more prosperous then, attracting merchants, craftsmen, small business owners, and successful mariners to its spacious row homes facing a pleasant city park. Saulsbury had been a man of considerable wealth, and was known to hand out gold coins as presents on holidays.[21] The house had been in the Saulsbury family for almost a quarter of a century. Even more importantly, this prosperous businessman had died relatively young and quite suddenly. There had been no time for Saulsbury to draft a will. Of all the former owners of the property, Saulsbury looked far and away the best bet to have buried the coins.[22]

The final and most troubling claim from the boys' standpoint came from the current owners of the treasure house, sisters Mary Pillar Boyd Findlay and Elizabeth H. French. The Findlay/French sisters had inherited the "ground rent" from their father, Charles Findlay, a Baltimore businessman who made his money through iron and lumber. In fact, the "ground rent" on the Eden Street property had been in the Findlay family since 1851.[23] In certain real estate markets, ownership of a property is divided between the homeowner and the underlying landowner. The homeowner pays an annual fee, or ground rent, to the landowner. Earning "ground rent" is usually a stable, hassle-free way to invest in real estate, since it comes without the burden of many of the usual headaches associated with being a landlord, namely repair and maintenance. That is, until the home-owning tenant stops making the annual ground rent payment. Such became the case with the treasure home on Eden Street in 1932.[24]

Since 1919, the house at 132 Eden Street had been the property of a Russian immigrant couple named Schapiro. Despite repeatedly mortgaging their home, the Schapiros managed to make the annual ground rent payment to the Findlay/French sisters. However, Mr. Schapiro passed away, and soon after his widow, Ida Schapiro, died in 1931. The Schapiro estate made its initial ground rent payment for 1932, but in 1933 missed making the annual fee payment to Findlay/French. According to court records, the property had fallen into a state of near total disrepair, and apparently became the target of squatters. Faced with a downwardly spiraling situation, the Schapiro estate seems to have simply abandoned their ownership claim to the treasure home. It was a move they would soon come to regret. [25]

The widow Mrs. French contacted her son, Henry Findlay French, who contacted his attorney, C. Arthur Eby, to begin ejectment proceedings.[26] With the Schapiro representatives ignoring their court summons and failing to appear before the judge, the outcome was a mere formality. Judge Samuel K. Dennis awarded full ownership of the treasure house to the elderly sisters.[27] With title now secured, Henry Findlay French hired property manager Benjamin Kalis to bring the dilapidated property up to code, and to begin filling its rooms with paying tenants.[28] Kalis hired a crew of ten contractors and spent several hundred dollars making the necessary repairs. The treasure home at 132 S. Eden Street would never be returned to its 19th-century glory — but would be again passable by the standards of its hardscrabble immigrant neighborhood. Kalis resumed collecting payments from the hangers-on such as old man Harry Chenven, the crazy ex-jeweler from the third-floor rear apartment.[29] And, property manager Kalis was also successful in quickly renting out the temporarily vacant spaces. He would rent the second floor space directly under Chenven to a public assistance recipient named Bessie Jones, recently arrived from Pittsburgh with her adolescent son, Theodore.[30] The whereabouts of Bessie's husband were unknown, and she had recently changed her last name and Theodore's last name to Jones from Sines.[31] Mrs. Jones was so short of cash that, according to Treasure in the Cellar author Len Augsburger, Kalis had to put the $5 deposit for the power company under his own company name to ensure that the Jones would have electricity.

Upon his arrival in January, 1934, newcomer Theodore would be bullied by some of the local boys for being an outsider. But when Henry Grob from nearby Caroline Street interceded on

Theodore's behalf, the two soon became good friends. Later court documents[32] would describe the boys as "constant companions." And when the hot summer weather came to Baltimore, the cool, dark cellar under Theodore's tenement house would make an excellent spot for the bored teens to "kill time." And so the "Rinky Dinky Doos Boys Club" was formed. And when Henry and Theodore would go looking for a spot to bury their club's cigar box containing club dues, they would accidentally uncover the buried dues of one of the world's largest and most daring of boys' clubs, the Knights of the Golden Circle.

Meanwhile, attorney Harry O. Levin now knew who his competition would be. Jennie Zimmerman, niece to Ida Schapiro and the hard-luck representative for the Schapiro estate, had made noises about filing a claim, but the sad fact for the Schapiros was they didn't have a legal leg to stand on. By not making their $60 ground rent payment to Findlay/French in 1933, the Schapiros had forfeited a chance at the golden windfall. The property had since been legally titled to the Findlay/French sisters. No smart lawyer would take the Schapiro case without a hefty, up-front retainer. Despite threats from Ms. Zimmerman, the Schapiros were out of the running.[33]

That left the Chenven heirs, the Saulsbury heirs, the Findlay/French sisters, and the boys. Either the Chenven or Saulsbury heirs would have a legitimate chance if they could provide tangible evidence of ownership of the gold. But proving ownership of a treasure that had been buried for decades was destined to be extremely difficult, if not near impossible. The Findlay/French claim rested on the simple fact that the sisters owned both the land and the row home that rested on that land. The gold had been found in their cellar.

Henry and Theodore, of course, had discovered the treasure trove. Would finders-keepers rule the day?

That the gold was "treasure trove" was not in doubt. Buried for decades, its original owner was probably dead and not coming back. The coins had neither been mislaid nor accidentally lost, they had been purposely concealed . . . perhaps for some illegal and/or illicit purpose.

Maryland, however, had no particular statute pertaining to treasure trove. Precedent from other jurisdictions would weigh heavily on the judge's decision.[34] Levin, while doing his legal homework, found that ancient Roman law favored a 50/50 split between discoverer, and landowner. English common law had originally favored a "finders-keepers" mentality . . . but then had switched to the custom of having all "treasure trove" being awarded to the crown. Only problem was, with 100% of the treasure trove reverting to the crown, the peasants' only motive for turning in the gold was fear of getting caught. In more recent times, the English had instituted a more sensible, compromise policy. Today, treasure trove goes to the state, which then sells the treasure to a museum and reimburses the finder for the hoard's cash value. Everybody wins . . . except possibly the landowner. But in a country where 2000-year old Roman and Anglo-Saxon treasure hoards surface from time-to-time, and often in the hands of amateur archaeologists and even farmers or ordinary citizens, England's modern treasure trove laws make good sense.

While researching American case precedent, Levin would find only a handful of relevant and analogous finds.[35] A contractor digging a basement for a homeowner and coming across a mason jar of buried coins; a pair of young brothers paid to clean out a dilapidated henhouse who discovered a rusted can containing gold coins. In these few and far between incidents, the legal system had awarded the treasure trove to the finders, not the property owners. Unless the owner of a property could also prove ownership of the buried treasure, the treasure had been awarded to its finder. In America, ownership of the land did not equate with ownership of the treasure. Being the actual finder of a treasure was, literally, golden.

This was great news for Henry and Theodore. Levin felt confident. Only one small, remaining detail could prevent Henry and Theodore's ultimate triumph. . . .

Did Henry and Theodore have a right to be in that cellar? Or, had Henry and Theodore trespassed on the Findlay/French cellar?

If so, thousands of gold coins would slip through the boys', and Levin's, collective fingers.

Opening testimony in the case of the Baltimore Gold Hoard was set for December 11, 1934 in Baltimore's Circuit Court. Eugene O'Dunne, an old warhorse on the bench, would be the presiding judge.[36]

Judge O'Dunne ordered that the coins be transferred from police jurisdiction to control of the circuit court. He further ordered that the coins be locked away in a safe deposit box . . . but not a *bank* safe deposit box.[37] Judge O'Dunne realized the coins had value far and above their nominal face value. O'Dunne also knew that the feds had gotten wind of the hoard, and didn't want them marching into some bank, flashing their badges, invoking the Gold Act, and walking out with the entire cache.

The case of the Baltimore gold hoard would be a case for Baltimoreans to decide . . . and the proceeds would go to the litigants with the strongest case.

Birth of the KGC

The Knights of the Golden Circle in secret ceremony.

Thomas Jefferson, the Founding Father famous for penning the Declaration of Independence, and who would become America's third President, was also a Virginia plantation owner and the owner of hundreds of slaves throughout his lifetime. Nevertheless, Jefferson had a firm vision of an America without the institution of slavery, and spoke out for much of his life against the practice:

"Nothing is more certainly written in the book of fate than that these people are to be free."
"I can say with conscious truth that there is not a man on earth who would sacrifice more than I would to relieve us from this heavy reproach in any practicable way."
"This abomination must have an end. And there is a superior bench reserved in heaven for those who hasten it."

According to the Monticello Foundation as well as other sources, Jefferson had included strong anti-slavery wording in his original draft of the Declaration of Independence, but other delegates lobbied Jefferson to remove it.[1]

The Founding Fathers proved far too preoccupied with the birthing of a nation from a fragile coalition of 13 original colonies to deal with the potentially fractious subject of slavery. Instead, they chose to punt, leaving a more stable and expanding 19th-century America to face society's ultimate dilemma . . . that of a continuing blatant contradiction, both vile and undeniable, to the very ideals supposedly held to be "self-evident" in that treasured Jeffersonian declaration of 1776. The United States would never be a truly "free" country until the odious practice of slavery had been fully stamped out.

The vast majority of Jefferson's fellow Southern slaveholders, unfortunately, folks who had been born, lived, and died as members of the slaveholding class, did not share Jefferson's hope that slavery would one day be abolished. Rather, they saw slavery as part of the natural order of things, much the same as the ocean tides, the seasons, and the daily rising and setting of the sun. To slaveholders, owning human property was perceived as a God-given right, part of the natural social order, and furthermore, they believed, a right protected and guaranteed under the original Constitution of the United States. They had zero intention of ever giving it up, and could scarcely imagine a world without slaves performing chores and working their vast fields of crops. The abandonment of a more than 200-year tradition which had economically enriched the Southern elite (and some Northerners) enormously was wholly and entirely unthinkable.

In 1807, the United States passed the Act Prohibiting Importation of Slaves (signed by President Jefferson), which took effect in 1808, the earliest date permitted under the U.S. Constitution. The new federal law denied the importation of any new slaves into the country. This legislation, however, was not always rigorously enforced. Also, the American domestic slave trade continued unabated, and actually began to increase near mid-century as King Cotton demanded the use of more slave laborers in the Deep South.[2] During the antebellum days, more than a million U.S. slaves would be forcibly transferred from the Upper South to states such as Mississippi, Alabama, Louisiana, and Georgia.[3] Until the Civil War in 1861, the domestic U.S. slave trade had been alive, well, and in fact, growing. . . .

In the North, where all states had abolished slavery by 1804, the Abolitionist movement began to take hold. The white abolitionists, social reformers, and members of several religious sects opposed to slavery on the basis it was both criminal and sinful, began to speak out for change.[4] Horrified Southerners worried that these meddling Northern abolitionist "do-gooders" were fomenting slave uprisings and rebellions. In one such 1831 uprising, scores of white Virginians would be brutally slain, causing concern for further violent incidents throughout the South.[5] Some of the more strident members of the Southern elite naturally looked for ways to push back.

According to the anonymous author of The Authentic Exposition of the Knights of the Golden Circle or a History of Secession from 1834 to 1861, the actual organization known as the KGC did not come about until 1854 or 1855. It, however, was preceded by earlier like-minded underground organizations:

"About the close of the year 1834, there were to be found, in Charleston, New Orleans, and some other Southern cities, a few politicians who earnestly desired the reestablishment of the African slave-trade and the acquisition of new slave territory. . . . These men formed themselves into secret juntos, which without any particular form or ritual, were called S.R.C.'s (Southern Rights Clubs). . . .

"The African slave-trade, being contrary to the laws of the United States, and to the laws of the whole civilized world, it was not hoped to carry it on in an open manner. The first efforts of the S.R.C.'s, therefore, were directed to the fitting out, manning, and equipping of secret slavers, which were to cruise around the African coast and kidnap negroes whenever a good opportunity was afforded. Between the years 1834 and 1840 it is presumed that at least six of these vessels were equipped and sent out. Some of them were successful, and filled the measure of their appointment, while others were captured by English and other fleets, to the great mortification of the S.R.C.'s and the discouragement of their enterprise . . . but continued their slave piracy with renewed vigor, whenever it seemed possible to conceal their maneuverings."[6]

The most well-known and widespread SRC was The Order of the Lone Star, founded in 1834. As its name suggested, the OLS sought not only to reestablish the African slave trade, but also to expand — starting with Texas — Southern slaveholding territory deep into what they observed to be a weak and chaotic Latin America populated by "bastard" races. According to author David Keehn in *Knights of the Golden Circle: Secret Empire, Southern*

Secession, Civil War, the Order of the Lone Star "*also had chapters in northern port cities including Baltimore and New York.*"[7]

It seems likely that Baltimore's secret slaver, Captain John Mattison, would have been involved with the Baltimore chapter of the OLS . . . as would his business partner, James Corner, a listed Baltimore City delegate for the Maryland Colonization Society.[8] After all, what is the chance of their ship having been seized by the English off the coast of Sierra Leone in 1840 and forfeited for the crime of slave trading *without* Mattison and Corner having been involved with the OLS, the direct forerunner of the KGC? The dates and the circumstances involving their loss of *The Eliza Davidson* all mesh perfectly with the Baltimore-Havana-Sierra Leone setup having been an undercover operation by the OLS.

By the early 1840s, having already aided in the armed takeover of Texas, the Order of the Lone Star, as well as other lesser Southern Rights organizations, continued to look southward for potential "filibustering" operations that could result in the annexation of additional new slave territories. Cuba and Mexico were the two obvious and favored targets. The anonymous author of *The Authentic Exposition of the Knights of the Golden Circle or a History of Secession from 1834 to 1861* suggested that, by 1844, the primary focus of the SRCs shifted from circumventing the African slave trading ban to the acquisition of new slave territory.[9] The SRCs felt emboldened by the growing friction between Washington, D.C. and the government of Mexico. The SRCs reportedly did all in their power to inflame the U.S. government against both Spain and Mexico, in the hopes that a war would result in newly absorbed southern U.S. lands.[10]

These early Southern Rights Clubs were heavily influenced by the political rhetoric of John C. Calhoun, a U.S. senator from South Carolina who also served as Vice-president under John Quincy Adams and Andrew Jackson. Calhoun was a strong supporter of slavery, states' rights, limited government, and free trade. While other Southern politicians explained away slavery as a "*necessary evil*," Calhoun instead maintained a position that the institution of slavery was a "positive good."[11] His view of sub-Saharan African peoples was entirely paternalistic, reasoning that they were better off under the supervision of white Europeans.

In a speech delivered on the floor of the U.S. Senate, Calhoun maintained that "*Many in the South once believed that it [slavery] was a moral and political evil; that folly and delusion are gone; we see it now in its true light, and regard it as the most safe and stable basis for free institutions in the world.*"[12]

In fact, according to author Irving H. Bartlett in his 1994 book *John C. Calhoun*, the senator was *"firmly convinced that slavery was the key to the success of the American dream."*[13] The societal standing of a man, it seemed, could be gauged by the number of slaves at his disposal.

Calhoun, who *Rebel Gold* authors Getler and Brewer call *"the intellectual father of the KGC,"*[14] would have his name spelled backwards (Nuohlac) used by KGC members as the secret group's original password.

In late 1845, Texas was finally admitted into the Union, and the much anticipated war between the U.S. and Mexico followed soon after. Lasting from 1846 until 1848, the Mexican American war resulted in New Mexico (including much of present-day Arizona) and California being added as U.S. territories, and the revised Texas border with Mexico being established down along the Rio Grande. The South, which had supplied most of the men to do the fighting, and which had wholeheartedly backed the campaign against Mexico, was naturally nonplussed when Washington and the Northern politicians resisted the addition of these territories as new slaveholding states. California, where large quantities of gold would be found in 1848, was quickly added into the Union, but as a free state. New Mexico was also added — as a free state. Not one slaveholding state would be admitted to the Union after Texas.

Southern politicians and their wealthy backers viewed these events as a political conspiracy. With each new "free state" grafted onto the nation, the South saw itself being marginalized, its power in Washington, D.C. ever decreasing.[15] At this current rate, the mighty North and its abolitionist busybodies could someday conceivably try to legislate the Southern way of life out of existence.

That, the South would not stand for. It would either fight, secede — or both.

One of the U.S. heroes of the Mexican-American conflict was a fiery 33rd-degree Freemason named John A. Quitman, who was both the former and future (10th & 16th) Governor of Mississippi.[16] In 1846, at the beginning of the war, Quitman was made a Brigadier General of Volunteers, and would command a brigade under Zachary Taylor in northern Mexico. Following the successful Battle of Monterey, in which Quitman's Volunteers and the Texas Rangers combined to defeat Mexican forces, Quitman next joined General Winfield Scott's expedition that would end in the "Siege of Veracruz." Quitman would subsequently be promoted to Major General in the U.S. Regular Army. Quitman led his troops on to several major victories, culminating ultimately in the surrender of the citadel in Mexico City. After the Mexicans had conceded their capital to Quitman, General Scott would name Quitman as the Military Governor of Mexico City, a post the Mississippian would hold for the duration of the American occupation. Quitman would be the only American ever to rule from Mexico's National Palace.

After the war, Quitman was again elected as the Democratic Governor of Mississippi and became, on the side, involved in private "filibustering" efforts to conquer new Latin American territory, especially Cuba.[17] According to Rebel Gold co-authors Getler and Brewer, Quitman was the owner of several plantations and more than 400 slaves, and was the leading Freemason — the Grand Master — in his state (and a friend, no surprise, to Albert Pike, the eventual Grand Master of Arkansas who will play a significant part in this story).[18] Quitman was a political disciple of South Carolina's John C. Calhoun, and would also accept leadership of the main SRC at the time, the Order of the Lone Star. By 1850, Quitman would be pushing for secession as well as potential Southern "filibustering" expeditions to Cuba and Central America that were clearly in direct violation of U.S. laws on neutrality.

Quitman was approached by filibusterer Narciso Lopez in 1850[19] to head a takeover expedition of the island of Cuba, but would decline direct involvement on the grounds such a commitment would conflict with the office of Governor of Mississippi. Quitman did, however, offer to help assist Lopez in obtaining men and arms. Lopez would stage an undermanned 1851 attempt without Quitman's on-site leadership. According to David Keehn in *Knights of the Golden Circle*, Lopez launched an invasion with a band of some 450-based American insurgents, but Lopez and his men would be surrounded and captured by Spanish-led defenders after the raid's expected Cuban backers failed to come to the invaders' assistance. Lopez was quickly executed by his Spanish captors.[20]

Birth of the KGC

With both Cuba and Mexico on high alert for Northern mercenaries hatching schemes of private conquest, representatives of those countries put the word out that soldiers of fortune captured during such missions would be shown no mercy. A swift and unceremonious death would be their certain fate. Given the enormous potential rewards for success, certain elements of American society remained undeterred, and therefore the decade of the 1850s featured no less than <u>five</u> failed filibustering expeditions into Northern Mexico alone. The most spectacular of those disasters, according to Keehn, involved the 1857 foray into Sonora, Mexico led by California state senator Henry Crabb.[21] Crabb and his company of 1,000 California soldiers of fortune would be taken prisoner by the Mexican Army and systematically executed.

Serial filibusterer William Walker, probably the most prolific and successful of the 1850s "freebooters," would lead private military expeditions into Mexico, Costa Rica, and Nicaragua.[22] Walker's early victories would see him installed at the 1st President of the Republic of Lower California, the 1st President of the Republic of Sonora, and the President of the Republic of Nicaragua. He was a popular and heroic figure to many Americans in the South and Southwest. Walker's luck would finally run out in 1860, however, when he was executed by firing squad in Honduras.

It seemed a repeat of the Republic of Texas was proving much more difficult than most had anticipated.

By 1851, the messy political fallout from the failed Lopez filibuster would lead to Quitman's resignation as Governor of Mississippi. Charges against Quitman (left) were eventually dropped as the result of three hung juries. Not long after, Quitman and the Order of the Lone Star would again turn their attention back to Cuba. The authors of <u>Rebel Gold</u> maintain that Quitman, along with his slavery expansion-minded companions Caleb Cushing and Jefferson Davis, would promote their mutual friend Franklin Pierce as the Democratic Party candidate for President. There was hope for a while that incoming Democrat President Franklin Pierce might simply purchase Cuba from Spain.[23] That acquisition, however, did not materialize. Quitman, ever-mindful of Lopez' cruel fate, vowed that any subsequent Cuban filibuster would not be attempted unless it was well planned, adequately funded, sufficiently armed, and that enough boots could be landed on Cuban soil to ensure success. According to Robert E. May, author of Manifest Destiny's Underworld: Filibustering in Antebellum America, by 1853 Cuban exiles in New York City were soliciting Quitman's help for another crack at Havana.[24] Quitman quietly approached President Pierce (later publicly accused of being a Knight himself), who offered his encouragement for his loyal supporter's expedition. With the help of fellow filibusterer Mansfield Lovell (Lovell would later rise to the rank of general in the Confederate Army), Quitman set out to raise and equip his expedition force.

By early 1854, Quitman, Lovell, and the OLS had several thousand recruits ready to go, according to author Robert E. May.[25] Southern newspapers announced that Quitman was in New Orleans, preparing to sail for Cuba within the month. Quitman, however, delayed his planned departure until the following month . . . and then again until the month after that, sweating every detail. In the process, Quitman and his Order of the Lone Star lost much of their momentum. Antsy volunteers, who had been ready for weeks on end to go at a moment's notice, began to drop out as fast as the OLS could sign on and train new recruits. Meanwhile, the Spanish protested loudly to Washington that filibusterers were recruiting and drilling openly on U.S. soil in flagrant disregard of American neutrality laws.[26]

Then, the sudden passage of the 1854 Kansas-Nebraska Act changed the political dynamics completely. The 1854 act, brainchild of Lincoln adversary Stephen A. Douglas, the Democratic U.S. Senator from Illinois, effectively repealed the Missouri Compromise of 1820 — which for 34 years had barred slavery in Kansas. Douglas' legislation allowed for the white males of each U.S. territory — including Kansas — to vote on whether to allow slavery in those territories. Many Northerners, most especially the Abolitionists, were furious. They figured rich Southern slave owners would simply buy up Kansas, fill the land with Southern sympathizers, and turn it into yet another slave state. President Pierce, a Northern Democrat, feared that the uncompromising Abolitionists were, in fact, the biggest threat to national unity.[27] The last thing the President needed now was Quitman and The Order of the Lone Star grabbing Cuba and proclaiming it for the U.S. — as another slaveholding territory seeking admittance into the United States. Had Pierce allowed that to happen, the cheese might have come sliding off the Union's cracker right then and there in 1854.

Quitman was subsequently "invited" to Washington to receive a lecture on the new facts of life. Quitman could expect zero help from Washington. Neither the President nor his Secretary of State would be relaxing the U.S. Neutrality Laws of 1794 anytime soon. And besides, Cuba was already preparing against an invasion, reinforcing their defenses on a continuing basis. . . .

The Pierce Administration would add a final exclamation point to its blunt directive by seizing one of Quitman's vessels.[28] Spanish Cuba would be apparently safe from an American invasion until 1898, when Teddy Roosevelt would arrive with his Rough Riders to charge up San Juan Hill in the defining battle of the Spanish-American War.

By early 1855, a frustrated John Quitman would resign from his leadership roles in both the aborted Cuban filibuster and his coast-to-coast SRC, The Order of the Lone Star.[29] He would seek public office again and be elected to the U.S. 34th Congress, and remain in Congress as a pro-slavery, states' rights Southern Democrat until his passing in 1858.

Meanwhile, in Lexington, Kentucky less than a year before Quitman exited the OLS, five men would be called together for a July 4th meeting in a hotel room. Their purpose? The formation of yet another Southern Rights Club, this one being called "The Knights of the Golden Circle."[30] From this entirely inauspicious beginning with but a handful of original and little-known members, the KGC would grow to become the Union's worst nightmare, a group of radical secessionists, uncompromising on the subject of slavery, who sought to annex new slave territory through filibustering expeditions and political intrigue. This secret, underground society would resort to espionage, infiltration, disinformation, outright insurrection, and even treasonous plots to achieve its stated objectives.

As with other secretive societies of the nineteenth century, the K.G.C. was shrouded in elaborate rituals complete with codes, signs, and passwords allegedly borrowed and modified from Freemasonry.

The K.G.C.'s leader was an enigmatic, eccentric fellow named "General" George Washington Lafayette Bickley. According to historians such as David Keehn in <u>Knights of the Golden Circle</u> and Ollinger Crenshaw in his 1941 *American Historical Review* article, "*The Knights of the Golden Circle: The Career of George Bickley*," the Virginia-born Bickley suffered from an unhappy childhood and subsequently ran away from home at age 12 to seek excitement and adventure on the open road.[31] He would eventually find a great deal of adventure — as well as all the expected troubles and misadventures often associated with leading such a restless, unconventional, and at times wholly reckless lifestyle.

Many of Bickley's detractors refer to him as a crank, a crook, and most especially as an unsavory "con man."[32] To be sure, Bickley was long on style but glaringly short on substance. As both a dreamer and a schemer, the K.G.C. leader took shortcuts, and made rash boasts and predictions that an optimistic and over-reaching Bickley could not usually back up with action or results.

To borrow an old Texas phrase, "General" Bickley could usually best be described as being someone who was "*all hat and no cattle*."

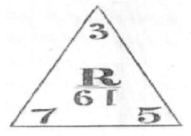

But whatever Bickley *wasn't*, and for all of his numerous and well-documented shortcomings, he definitely *was* a skilled propagandist, networker, orator, writer, and superb salesman. The man, as they say down South, could "*talk a dog off of a meat wagon*."

Bickley was a man who inspired confidence in other men . . . an individual they would believe at face value and follow.

As a youngster out in the world on his own, according to David Keehn in *Knights of the Golden Circle*, Bickley would get by "*on the strength of his glib tongue and good looks*" while toiling at a series of nondescript odd jobs.[33] He would return a decade later to Russell County, Virginia to study medicine under a local physician. Bickley, after the apprenticeship, would open his own medical office at a Virginia hotel in nearby Tazewell. The aspiring physician billed himself as a "phrenologist," which meant he studied the contours of the human skull and tried to predict the mental faculties and character of a person based on the conformation of the individual's head.[34] Although considered to be a valid science at that time, according to the "*History of Phrenology*" at www.phrenology.org, the practice was often "subject to the abuse of con men." It has been since relegated by the modern world to the realm of "voodoo science."

While still practicing phrenology in Tazewell, Bickley founded a local historical society, and wrote a manuscript on the *History of the Settlement and Indian War of Tazewell County, Virginia* — a reference work that would be used for many years.

As was George Bickley's way, he was able to parlay his limited medical training as a country doctor into a professorship at the Eclectic Medical Institute in Cincinnati, Ohio. The school taught a form of alternative medicine that used botanical remedies along with other exotic substances, combined with rudimentary physical therapy practices. Bickley secured the position on the basis he was an 1842 graduate of the University of London, and had studied under the renowned English physician John Elliotson. Bickley's "credentials" were published in the March, 1853 issue of the *Eclectic Medical Journal*. Only problem was, Dr. Elliotson had resigned from the University of London in 1838, and the school had no record of Bickley having ever attended that institution of higher learning.[35]

As a teaching professor who was supposed to be an authority on physiology and scientific botany, Bickley showed little interest in his students, preferring instead to expend his energy in publishing new medical papers and texts.[36] He published the *Principles of Scientific Botany* along with several works pertaining to pseudo-science, *as well as Adalaska; Or, The Strange and Mysterious Family of the Cave of Genreva*, a work of fiction based on the premise of Manifest Destiny. Manifest Destiny was a contemporary and much romanticized political subject with which Bickley would grow increasingly enamored.

Luck came Bickley's way in 1853 when he married a wealthy Cincinnati widow, Rachel Dodson, apparently to gain access to her substantial wealth. Once in the marriage, Bickley, for a while, "*freed himself from the mundane need to earn a living*," according to K.G.C. historian David Keehn.[37] Bickley moved onto his wife's family farm, taking a leave from the Eclectic Medical Institute, and began to engage himself in a series of whimsical ventures including, but not limited to, real estate speculation, investing in Caribbean coal mines, exporting farm implements to Russia, and the formation of paramilitary drill companies.[38] He also did some newspaper editing, and published a "Manifest Destiny" journal that he christened *Bickley's West American Review*. In the journal, "Dr." Bickley recommended that the capital of the United States be moved south to the Ozarks because "*the circle of our limits*" will soon include "*a part of the British possession, the West Indies, and Mexico.*"

For a time, Bickley would also dabble in nativist American Party "Know-Nothing" politics, same as Freemason Albert Pike (and later John Wiles Booth). Bickley was fascinated and instinctively drawn to the mystique surrounding the era's numerous "secret societies."[39]

Bickley's lavishly funded playtime would be permanently curtailed, however, once his wealthy wife discovered he had been trying to convert her substantial assets to his own name. As per Frank L Klement in his book *Dark Lanterns: Secret Political Societies, Conspiracies, and Treason Trials in the Civil War*, the self-absorbed phrenologist was subsequently run off of the farm by his wife's indignant relatives, and was forced to return to the Eclectic Medical Institute in Cincinnati to once again earn a regular paycheck.[40]

Before Bickley's abrupt departure from the moneyed Dodson banking family, one of Bickley's entrepreneurial schemes had involved the July 4th, 1854 Lexington, KY formation of the Knights of the Golden Circle. Growing such an organization from a limited base of five members was hard work, and Bickley had already involved himself in multiple projects such that the K.G.C. had initially remained little more than a grandiose romantic notion. That would change with the official departure of John Quitman from the vastly larger, well organized Order of the Lone Star.

Details are sketchy, but somehow, in the mid-1850s, George Bickley was able to pull off a major coup of the most stunningly improbable proportions. The now supposedly leaderless OLS purportedly consented to "merge" with Bickley's embryonic Knights of the Golden Circle, which had been centered primarily in the cities of Lexington and Cincinnati, and was largely the product of "Doctor" Bickley's fertile imagination and excessive ego.[41]

Better yet, the newly merged organizations would now operate under the banner of The Knights of the Golden Circle — and not under the nationally recognized "brand" of the 20-year old OLS — the same OLS which had reportedly played a hand in the nearly miraculous annexation of Texas. Furthermore, George Bickley, the fake professor who had practiced the voodoo "science" of phrenology, was named as the organization's leader and commanding officer. The now "General" George Bickley found himself, with the stroke of a pen, suddenly in charge of thousands of paying volunteers across large swaths of the country.

David Keehn in his *Knights of the Golden Circle* describes Bickley's gift promotion in the following fashion:

"During his sojourn across the South, George was somehow able to convince the leaders of a preexisting southern society called the "Order of the Lone Star" (OLS) to merge with his Knights. This had truly an exponential impact since the OLS had more than fifteen thousand members in at least fifty chapters spread across ten southern states with large concentrations in Mississippi, Louisiana, Texas, and Alabama. It also had chapters in northern port cities including Baltimore and New York, where it operated out of Tammany Hall and the Empire Club. The merger with the OLS suddenly transformed Bickley's nascent KGC into a truly powerful force with far-flung members and prestige." [42]

This begs the *big* question — was George Bickley's meteoric rise to the pinnacle of America's SRCs entirely attributable to his impeccable timing and "glib tongue and good looks" . . . or was something else afoot? Bickley may have been behind the KGC, but who was now behind Bickley and pushing him to the fore?

To help raise funds for the KGC, Bickley began selling dubious bonds for a Bickley enterprise known as the "American Colonization and Steamship Company."[43] Says writer Dane Phillips in his 2013 article *All War is Debt Funded*, *"Financial support for the KGC came from the American Colonization and Steamship Company in Veracruz, Mexico, which was capitalized for $5 million despite the fact that Bickley had no visible personal fortune. Who were Bickley's benefactors?"*

Phillips elsewhere in this same article basically answers his own question when he states, *"Comprising mostly local*

Freemasons, the society patterned itself on Masonic lodges in its organization and its rituals. Initiates were sworn to secrecy."[44]

Bickley's benefactors were apparently wealthy, pro-South, pro-slavery, states' rights Freemasons who needed a vehicle for opposing Northern abolitionism and the unwanted intrusion into Southern affairs.

Interestingly, according to author Robert E. May in his book *John A. Quitman: Old South Crusader*, more than $500,000 in funds collected for Quitman's planned invasion of Cuba were never returned to the donors.[45] May speculates that the money may have instead found its way into KGC coffers. The OLS had for years operated a large chapter in Baltimore, which would have been converted around this time to a KGC "castle." Could the coins found under the Eden Street cellar have been funds collected originally for Quitman's aborted Cuba operation (Havana being one of "secret slaver" Captain John Mattison's favorite trading destinations), but later converted into KGC assets? Certainly the timing (1855-1856) would have been absolutely correct.

In 1858, Bickley became the editor of a publication called the *Scientific Artisan*, which covered the world of inventions and patent law. According to Marquette University's Professor Frank Klement, an author of three books and 40 articles about the Civil War, a Bickley co-worker at the *Scientific Artisan* would later recall Bickley as "*an ignorant pretender, as restless and scheming as he was shallow, very vain of his person, exceedingly fond of military display, and constantly engaged either in devices to borrow money and crazy schemes of speculation, or in debaucheries even less creditable than his swindling.*"[46]

Absolutely charming! Does Bickley sound to you like the solid, responsible person you might want running your 15,000-member organization? Or rather, does he sound like a pompous, overly self-confident windbag who would make an excellent candidate to take the fall should something go horribly wrong?

OLS head John Quitman had been forced to resign the governorship of Mississippi when a hastily-prepared Narciso Lopez-led filibustering expedition to Cuba ended in abject failure. He had escaped prison only by the grace of three hung juries.[47] Might Quitman, once he was elected to Congress, have wanted to run the OLS from a distance, using someone such as Bickley as his proxy? If so, it would make perfect sense to change the organization's name so as to further remove Quitman from any potential quagmires. The so-called "merger" with Bickley (his proxy) and the K.G.C. (whose catchy name would give the well-known OLS a fresh coat of paint) would have provided Quitman with double protection, along with the important legal tool of plausible deniability.

Maryland's Masonic "Grand Master" of this same period, Charles Webb, would organize and back the candidacies of top Democratic pro-slavery, secessionist politicians in his state, leaving them to stand up to the eventual wrath of President Lincoln and his Union Army while Brother Webb operated largely untouched from the political shadows.

Still, had Quitman really remained the brains behind the O.L.S. - K.G.C. during the late 1850s? Some researchers say no, that Quitman's friend and fellow Freemason, Grand Master Albert Pike of Arkansas, was now at the reigns of America's most notorious secret society.[48]

What we know for sure is that John Quitman was no longer in charge of the K.G.C. after July 17, 1858 — because on that date the Mississippi Congressman would pass away at his Natchez, MS plantation after a very protracted and mysterious illness. Wikipedia lists the cause of death as "National Hotel Disease" which Quitman supposedly contracted during the inauguration of President James Buchanan.[49] Rumors, however, have persisted for more than 150 years that Mr. Quitman succumbed as the result of poisoning, providing the situation with an air of intrigue.

In the biography *John A Quitman: Old South Crusader*, author Robert E. May paints the following scenario:

"Quitman made no secret of his interest in being Buchanan's secretary of war. But all is known for sure is that Quitman became ill after some time spent at the hotel (the National Hotel), and that he blamed his ailment entirely upon what he stigmatized as the 'National Hotel poison.' Perhaps he gave credence to rumors circulating in Washington that abolitionists had tainted the hotel's food in a plot to eliminate Democratic leaders. Such would be a likely construction for his attributing the 'effect of the poison' to arsenic." [50]

Congressman Quitman had been in line to become the Freemasons' Sovereign Grand Commander of the Supreme

Council of the Southern Jurisdiction. That, of course, never happened. Instead, according to Bob Brewer and Warren Getler in their book *Rebel Gold*:

"Pike, who would emerge as the world's most powerful Freemason, joined the Scottish Rite in Charleston in 1853. He revised its rituals between 1855 and 1857, and became a thirty-third degree member later that year. Elected to the Supreme Council of the Scottish Rite's Southern Jurisdiction in July, 1858, he ultimately became the Sovereign Grand Commander in January, 1859. . . . Coincidentally, Pike's confirmation as a Supreme Council member came a few days after the mysterious death — possibly the result of a slow-acting poison — of prominent Supreme Council member John A. Quitman in Mississippi." [51]

Brewer and Getler also observe that, *"As an unabashed apologist for slavery, Pike saw to it that key supporters of the Southern cause were corralled into the Supreme Council's ranks by the fall of 1859. Most significant among his appointments to the Council in 1859 was that of Kentuckian John C. Breckinridge, who was then Vice President of the United States under James Buchanan."* [52]

According to the anonymous author of the *Narrative of Edmund Wright*, Breckinridge was a no-doubt-about-it member of the Knights of the Golden Circle who would *"flaunt the emblems of treason under the nose of an imbecile president. . . . John C. Breckinridge was, and still is, one of the great lights of the K.G.C.*[53] *He is indebted to the Order for his nomination at Cincinnati on the Buchanan ticket, and for subsequent political advancement. While Breckinridge was vice-president of the United States, he publicly wore, in the City of Washington, the emblematic jewelry of this traitorous Order thus — shamelessly parading his treason to the Government of which he was one of the principal officers."*

And as the Civil War was about to commence, Sovereign Commander Pike would change the name of his *Supreme Council of the Scottish Rite's Southern Jurisdiction* to simply the "Supreme Council for the Confederate States of America."

The web site knightsofthegoldencircle.webs.com, which operates as a clearing house for knowledge concerning this shadowy underground organization, says boldly that, "*Strong evidence suggests that Albert Pike (1809-1891) was the genius behind the influence and power of the Masonic-influenced K.G.C., while Bickley was the organization's leading promoter and chief organizer for the K.G.C. lodges, what they call 'Castles' in several states.*" [54]

Brewer and Getler, in <u>Rebel Gold</u>, add emphasis to the point that Bickley was little more than a *"front-man"* for the rapidly growing Knights:

"*Northern commentators, including those writing in Continental Monthly, fingered 'brutal and arrogant' Albert Pike —* in contrast to the 'miserable quack' George Bickley — *as the dark genius behind the Masonic-influenced, hidden Confederacy, the KGC.*" [55]

And true to script, when the federal government finally came looking for someone to arrest in connection with the clandestine activities of the underground Knights of the Golden Circle, it would be Commander-in-Chief "General" George Bickley of the so-called Knights of the "American Legion" who would be hauled off to prison in Fort Warren located at the entrance to chilly Boston Harbor.

Albert Pike, the "dark genius" behind the operations of the K.G.C. and other treasonous Confederate plots, would seek asylum for a while in Canada at the close of the Civil War — but soon return to the U.S. and never spend a day in jail.

However, KGC "front man" or not, as the 1850s came to a close, George Bickley was nevertheless commanding his share of the national press.

From the 7/20/1859 *Southern Broad-Axe* in West Point, Mississippi: *(emphasis added)*

A New Filibustering Expedition.—The New York Tribune gives an account of what is styled a new filibustering expedition, now organizing, and to be called the "Knights of the Golden Circle." It consists of two legions—one in the United States, and one in Cuba. The Tribune, which contains its information from a printed circular, says:

Each legion is to consist of ten thousand men and their officers, besides commissary, surgical and conveyance departments. The American legion is to include a regiment of cavalry, a regiment of mounted riflemen, a regiment of artillery, five regiments of infantry, and a reserved guard. **The headquarters of this recent military organization appears to be the city of Baltimore,** *and the central authority seems to be bested in a war board, composed of a commander in chief and of brigadier generals, appointed or to be appointed one for each of the ten regiments. From this board emanates the selection of colonels. The colonels select their own inferior officers, who must, however, be approved by the colonels. The colonel is also to select for himself a lieutenant-colonel and two majors, and the four together are to agree upon some suitable person for a brigadier-general, to be commissioned and placed on the general staff.* **The chief business of the colonels and their inferior officers appears to be, at present, the enlistment of men and the raising of funds.**

The members are each to pay one dollar initiation fee, and also a weekly tax of ten cents. A fund for the purchase of arms, ammunition and general outfit is to be raised by the sale of scrip, in which all the subordinate officers are to be employed. This scrip is issued in sums of five, ten, twenty, fifty, or one hundred, or one thousand dollars, and is to be paid for either in cash, *in powder, lead, iron, cotton cloth, red or blue flannel, tobacco, train oil, shoes, blankets, spades, etc., or partly in promissory notes of short dates.* **The soldiers who may enlist in this expedition, are promised each a grant of six thousand four hundred acres of land, also seven dollars a month in specie and seven in scrip; arms, ammunition, uniforms, etc., to be furnished by the board of war before leaving American soil. The men, it is stated, can pursue their ordinary business till November.** [56]

And, from the 8/16/1860 *Old-Line Democrat* in Little Rock, Arkansas: **(*emphasis* added)**

Knights of the Golden Circle.—General Bickley has published an address to the Knights of the Golden Circle, requesting them to repair to their Texas encampment by the 15th of September. He declares the object of the association to be to Americanize and Southernize Mexico. The Knights will go to Mexico as emigrants, under the sanction of the Mexican government. **The order is said to number fifty thousand** *members, with a capital of one million of dollars.* Texas has subscribed nearly half a million of dollars, and a general call is made upon other States to donate liberally, as the object is to establish a Southern confederacy. [57]

The Knights were garnering much press, and that press in turn helped to fill the KGC's growing coffers. But you can't exactly go into a bank and open up an account under the name of a subversive organization bent on opposing the will of the mighty federal government. Instead, the "hard money" funds of this expanding "underground" organization, by necessity, needed to go underground — in many cases, quite *literally.*

That seems to be exactly what happened in the politically volatile city of Baltimore, the so-called *"headquarters"* of this *"recent military organization."*

The fortune hidden away in the dark cellar on Eden Street was Knights' gold.

Baltimore and the Slave Trade

By the mid-19th century, Baltimore had become uniquely positioned in the Southern slave trade. For decades, many planters in Maryland, Virginia, and Delaware had been setting slaves free. The need for slave labor had begun to diminish in the Border States.[1] And, as the number of slaves in Maryland slowly declined, the number of free blacks began to rise. By 1860, approximately half of Maryland's black residents were free,[2] and almost 90% of blacks living in Baltimore were free.[3] Baltimore had, at the time, more free blacks than any other U.S. city.[4] However, Baltimore still remained a thriving center for the legal domestic slave trade, with thousands of blacks being auctioned off and "sold south" to the Cotton States.

The following U.S. census numbers tell the story:

Total Slave Population in Maryland 1790–1860

Census Year	1790	1800	1810	1820	1830	1840	1850	1860
All States	694,207	887,612	1,130,781	1,529,012	1,987,428	2,482,798	3,200,600	3,950,546
Maryland	103,036	105,635	111,502	107,398	102,994	89,737	90,368	87,189

Although the first African slaves arrived in Maryland in 1642, slavery was slow to take hold in the colony. The preferred method of acquiring cheap labor was to take on indentured servants from Europe, particularly England. Tobacco would rapidly change that dynamic. By the 1755, African slaves represented fully 40% of Maryland's population.[5] The vast majority of Maryland slaves labored to harvest and process tobacco, now far and away the state's dominant cash crop.[6]

During the 19th century, as the need for slave labor subsided in Maryland, a new cash crop came to the fore . . . the slaves themselves. The cotton gin had revolutionized agriculture in the Deep South, creating a voracious need for more slaves on its huge cotton plantations. According to one historian, between 1790 and 1859 more than a million slaves were "sold south" . . . most from Virginia and Maryland.[7]

Baltimore's bustling Inner Harbor became a focal point for this shameful commerce.

Baltimore and the Slave Trade

Ralph Clayton, a Baltimore librarian and author, in the July 12, 2000 *Baltimore Sun* writes, "*The major slave dealers, who came from Kentucky, Georgia, Virginia and Tennessee built their slave pens near Pratt Street, the major east-west connection to the wharves in the Inner Harbor and Fells Point.*"[8]

The slave pens were basically downtown slave jails complete with bars and guards,[9] located near the Baltimore docks. They were primarily used by the slave dealers to house slaves until they could be sold . . . or shipped to Southern ports such as New Orleans for auction. They were also used to warehouse slaves whose owner was away on business, or the slaves of travelers who were staying over in Baltimore. Problem slaves such as habitual runaways could likewise be housed there until sold.[10]

Out-of-town dealers would stay at the Barnum or Fountain Hotel, placing newspaper advertisements announcing they had cash and were willing to buy. According to *Baltimore Sun* reporter Scott Shane, a dozen or more local Baltimore dealers operating from harbor-side storefronts along Pratt Street displayed banners such as "5,000 Negroes Wanted" and "Negroes! Negroes! Negroes!"[11]

At the appointed time, slave sellers would empty a slave pen and march their shackled merchandise down Pratt Street to auction, or to the waiting ships in the Inner Harbor and at Fells Point. One Georgia dealer named Slatter, put off by the constant complaints of those having to witness the sad spectacle of human beings coffled like animals, began to hire carriages and omnibuses to transport sold slaves to the waiting ships. Slatter was always sure to follow closely on horseback to prevent escapes.[12] Other dealers simply marched their manacled slaves in the middle of the night when decent citizens were likely to be home in bed.

Slatter charged owners 25¢ per day to feed and house their slaves, promising to "make good all jail-breaking or escapes from my establishment."[13] The Georgia businessman also assured both customers and naysayers that he would never break up slave families. But records since found by researchers prove this to have been a boldfaced lie.

In Baltimore City directories, slave dealers were listed between "Silversmiths" and "Soap." Even though few Baltimoreans owned slaves, the business of slave dealing was a fixture in the local economy. Famed abolitionist Frederick Douglass, who grew up in 1820s Baltimore, remembered the dark days. *"I lived on Philpot Street, Fells Point, and have watched from the wharves, the slave ships in the basin,"* Douglass recounted. *"The ships with their cargoes of human flesh, waiting for favorable winds to waft them down the Chesapeake. In the deep still darkness of midnight, I have often been aroused by the dead heavy footsteps, and the piteous cries of the chained gangs that passed our doors."*[14]

Owners of the slave ships preferred to dock their vessels further out in the harbor for added protection, in case the city's free blacks such as Douglass got any ideas about intervening.[15] Baltimore was just a short train ride from the Mason Dixon line and the Northern abolitionists. Also, the state's Methodists, Quakers, and various other religious sects had taken an increasingly dim view of such nefarious, sinful activity. Maryland was also the last leg of the journey north for many of those seeking illegal freedom by means of the Underground Railroad.

This volatile mixture of free blacks, abolitionists, slave dealers, slave ships, the Underground Railroad, and the nearby Mason Dixon line might help to explain the hardline stance taken by so many Southern-leaning Baltimoreans as the 1860s approached. Perhaps the winds of change were not yet in the air in Charleston, Atlanta, Montgomery, or New Orleans — but these winds were beginning to threaten the Monumental City in general, and Pratt Street in particular.

John Brown's shocking 1859 anti-slavery raid at Harpers Ferry, Virginia underscored that threat. In the wake of Brown's failed attack and subsequent martyrdom, some of the Maryland and Virginia slaveholders and their supporters began to form local militias.[16]

Still, the procession of chained prisoners being marched down Pratt Street continued. Today, a statue of the legendary Baltimore-born slugger Babe Ruth stands at the corner of Eutaw and Camden Streets, which in 1860 was the exact site of trader Joseph S. Donovan's slave pen just a short walk from the Baltimore docks.[17]

Charles McKay, who visited Baltimore from Scotland just before the outbreak of the Civil War, was appalled by what he witnessed. Wrote McKay, *"In states like Maryland, slavery exists in its most repulsive form; for the owner, having no use for the superabundant Negroes, seems to acknowledge no duties or responsibilities towards them, but breeds them as he would cattle that he may sell them in the best market. . . . The owners have little compunction in selling the wife without the husband, or both without the children, according to the caprice or wants of the purchaser.*"[18]

In July, 1862, President Lincoln offered a near $30 million federal buyout of Maryland slaveholders at $300 per emancipated slave.[19] Maryland politicians balked at the proposal, a decision they would later regret. Maryland remained a slave state throughout the war. Lincoln's Emancipation Proclamation of 1863 did not affect Maryland as she was exempt based on her decision (though coerced) not to secede from the Union.

Meanwhile, out in Baltimore's Harbor, the competing but money-hungry slave dealers would consent to ship their human cargoes together on the same barks, brigs, packet ships, and schooners. New Orleans was the favored destination.[20]

Slaves

One of those wharves directly off Pratt Street was Buchanan's Wharf, owned by Maryland Colonization Society delegate James Corner.[21] Corner had made Baltimore history in the 1840s by owning the fastest trans-Atlantic packet line in the world, Baltimore to Liverpool. And one of Buchanan's Wharf's best-known sea captains was the secret slaver himself, Captain John J. Mattison.

Captain Mattison's house on S. Eden Street, just off E. Pratt Street, stood but a short walk from the Inner Harbor. And under Mattison's house lay buried a fortune in U.S. gold coins.

Between the docks at the Inner Harbor and the Mattison treasure house, on Concord Street by the Pratt Street Bridge, stood the factory building that housed the James Armstrong & Company soap and candle manufacturing firm.[22] The firm was run by executives Charles Webb, James Webb, Thomas Armstrong, and Andrew J. Saulsbury.[23] From the factory's windows the tallow chandlers could look out across the Inner Harbor at the ships and the wharves . . . and also at the chained slaves being marched down Pratt Street to Fells Point as they were doomed to be "sold south" to Louisiana.

New Orleans was a regular port of call for Captain Mattison, as was Havana, Cuba and Rio de Janeiro[24] . . . all slave trading meccas. Mattison was also in the habit of carrying large quantities of candles aboard his ship, most likely candles from the brick factory building by the Pratt Street Bridge. Mattison would one day serve on the board of directors of a related James Armstrong company . . . a company insuring vessels in the Port of Baltimore — and their cargoes.[25]

Candle executive Andrew J. Saulsbury, a neighbor of Mattison's from S. Central Avenue, the next street over from Eden, was a well-known, outspoken Southern sympathizer.[26] He was an ardent proponent of Baltimore's slave trade and its infamous slave pens along Pratt Street. Surely he knew Captain Mattison . . . if not from the Armstrong umbrella of Baltimore enterprises, then certainly from their tree-lined row-house neighborhood.

In 1865, tallow chandler Saulsbury would buy Captain Mattison's Eden Street treasure home for $3,200 [27] — buried golden hoard included. He would move his young family all of one block. The sea captain would move himself and his wife a few blocks east to South Broadway Avenue, still within comfortable walking distance of the Pratt Street wharves.[28]

The purchase of the treasure house at 55 S. Eden St. was no ordinary real estate transfer.

During the war, Saulsbury had become so incensed by the Union occupation of Baltimore his public utterances in support of secession would cause his entire family to be threatened by Union soldiers.[29] After the South's defeat, Saulsbury would decorate his new Eden Street parlor with paintings of Confederate heroes Robert E. Lee and Stonewall Jackson.[30]

And in the cellar of Saulsbury's home, buried in the dark recesses by a brick wall under shovelfuls of hard-packed dirt and oyster shells, rested the gold coins in an old copper pot wrapped inside a man's boot.

The coins, the paintings, the slave pens, the slave ships, the rebellion, the over 600,000 dead, even Lincoln's assassination,

they were all somehow connected, all part of a greater picture —
of a grand conspiracy.

On July 24, 1863, just weeks after the Battle of Gettysburg,
Colonel William Birney of the United States Colored Troops would
help to liberate "Cam-liu's slave pen" on Pratt Street near the
harbor. Writing to his commanding officer, Col. Birney would
report, "*In this place I found 26 men, one boy, 29 women, and
three infants. Sixteen of the men were shackled and one had his
legs chained together by ingeniously contrived locks connected by
chains suspended to his waist.*" The soldier would describe how
the slaves were confined in sweltering cells or in the bricked-in
yard where "*no tree or shrub grows and the midday sun pours
down its scorching rays.*"[31]

Among those freed that July day were a four-month old boy
born in the jail, and a 24-month old toddler who had entered the
pen at age one month.[32]

The brutal slave pens of Baltimore would finally, thankfully, be
no more.

Sworn Testimony

Baltimore Courthouse and Battle Monument

In the opening days of the "treasure" trial, Theodore Jones and Henry Grob appeared before Judge O'Dunne to retell their experience of uncovering the mysterious copper pot filled with gold coins. It was a tale that had already been told many times in the press, and there was little if anything new to their story that the boys could add. Neither Theodore nor Henry had any idea who buried the fortune in the cellar or why.

Theodore, when asked by Judge O'Dunne how old he was[1], answered that he was "sixteen." In fact, though he looked sixteen, Jones was only fourteen. Otherwise, the boys' testimony appeared to be truthful. No doubt the teens were coached and well prepped by their very capable lawyer, Harry O. Levin.

Theodore made a point of getting it on record that, "*Ever since I have been in Baltimore, him and I have been pals. We always went around together.*"[2] The boys had maintained their solidarity, making it clear that anything they were rewarded would be split 50/50.

The attorney for Harry Chenven's estate, the recently deceased jeweler who had lived in the apartment above the Joneses, tried to get Theodore to speculate on whether the old recluse could have buried the gold. Was Chenven a miser? Could the copper pot have belonged to the eccentric loner? Theodore could only offer that he didn't know the man well at all, except that he liked to come home late and dump the contents of his chamber pot out of his third-floor window — sometimes soiling the boy's window directly below.[3]

C. Arthur Eby and Emory Niles, representing the Findlay/French sisters, owners of the property, asked Theodore if he had ever gotten permission from Mr. Kalis, the property manager, to play in the rear of the cellar. Theodore admitted he had not.[4]

Henry's testimony, elicited by Levin, centered on how the boys had spent time that summer playing in the front part of the Eden Street cellar, where the tenants' storage lockers were situated. Later in the summer, the boys had expanded their domain to include the rear portion of the cellar.[5]

The attorneys for the Findlay/French team showed Henry photos of the cellar, including the partition between the front and back sections of the cellar. The photos showed a padlocked door. Henry agreed there was a door to the rear portion of the basement, but indicated that it had never been locked during the summer.[6] Henry described how he and Theodore had previously used the rear of the cellar to chop wood for Theodore's mother.

Lawyers for the Saulsbury heirs questioned Henry about the boot that had been wrapped around the corroded copper pot, and also the many oyster shells that had been found on and around the pot when the boys had been digging.[7]

Testifying for the Chenven estate were Harry Gammerman and Zachary Chenven. Gammerman, Chenven's friend and caretaker, told the court how he had known Chenven in the "old country." How the Jews were persecuted in Russia at that time, of how rights were systematically deprived, and Jews eventually forced to live in the "Jewish Pale of Settlement." Gammerman, his friend Harry Chenven, and many others emigrated to the United States after the turn of the century, with Gammerman and Chenven sailing to America in 1908. Gammerman described his friend's career as a Baltimore jeweler, and his later mental health troubles that caused him to lose his family, leave the jewelry business, and for a time become a reclusive street peddler of Baltimore newspapers.[8]

Zachary Chenven, Harry's son who lived in New York, described his visits with his father, and how Harry Chenven had promised to put his son through medical school. That is, if young Zachary came to live with his father. This was a curious promise for a man who seemed to live in perpetual poverty with no recent visible means of support.[9] Had the senior Chenven actually been a miser, hoarding gold from his days as a jeweler? If so, Harry Chenven would not have been the first eccentric, mentally troubled individual living in squalor who actually had secreted away a golden nest egg.

Mr. Schonfield, the Chenvens' attorney, argued that since Mr. Chenven had lived at 132 S. Eden for years before his death, and the former jeweler had repeatedly sold old scrap gold to the mint in exchange for gold coins, and because he was planning to put his son through medical school, Chenven must have been the source for the coins buried in the cellar.

Judge O'Dunne did not agree.[10] There was no evidence that Harry Chenven had buried the gold in the copper pot. The corroded, ancient pot had obviously been placed in the ground many decades before Chenven had stepped ashore in his new country. And the dates on the coins, 1834 -1856, suggested that the coins had probably been buried _before_ Chenven had even been born.

The judge dismissed the Chenven claim, leaving the Saulsburys, the Findlay/French sisters, and the Rinky Dinky Doo boys still in the running.

But just when it appeared the Baltimore gold hoard field was narrowing, another claimant to the coins appeared in Judge Eugene O'Dunne's office. Agent George Almoney of the U.S. Secret Service requested that the Baltimore City Circuit Court hand over the gold in exchange for U.S. currency, at $20.67 per ounce, so that the coins would "cause no more trouble."[11] O'Dunne refused, and would not reveal to Almoney the location of the hidden safety deposit box. O'Dunne admonished the federal agent for not recognizing the numismatic value of the coins, which when sold would be expected to command an amount far in excess of the gold content. Reluctantly, Agent Almoney agreed to allow the court to oversee the sale of the coins with the proceeds going to the winning claimant(s).

With the federal threat averted, and the Chenvens out of the running, Judge O'Dunne asked the remaining parties if they would be willing to settle out of court.[12] Harry Levin, counsel for Theodore Jones and Harry Grob, offered who he thought was the boys' strongest competition, the Findlay/French sisters, a settlement of 25%. The attorneys for the sisters turned down Levin's offer, holding out for nothing less than 50%.

And so the trial continued.

The Saulsbury team brought in a coppersmith to give expert testimony that the copper pot was at least 50 years old, and probably older.[13] The old pot exhibited a large amount of verdigris, the green pigment that results from copper having been exposed to the elements over a considerable length of time. James Kavanagh, the expert witness, offered that it was a style of pot not manufactured since the previous century, and most likely made overseas. Harry Levin tried to shake Kavanagh's testimony by getting the expert to admit even he couldn't pinpoint the exact year of burial. But Kavanagh stood by his testimony that the pot was at least fifty years in the ground and probably more. Combined with the mid-19th century dates on the coins, the coppersmith's testimony helped to narrow down the approximate decade in which the coins had been hidden in the cellar.

Reuben Foster, grandson of Andrew Saulsbury, produced for the court an 1859 gold dollar, passed down for years within his family.[14] The coin was said to have belonged to his grandfather, who kept gold coins at the Eden Street address and gave them to friends, family, and servants as holiday gifts.

The remaining Saulsbury daughters, now in their 70s, recalled that their childhood had been idyllic, and how their father had been a well-to-do businessman of considerable wealth. The girls had been particularly fascinated by the desk in their parents' bedroom . . . and especially the desk drawer in which the candle maker had kept a ready supply of gold, silver, and copper coins. Their father, a staunch supporter of the Confederacy, had been in the habit of throwing oyster parties at the Saulsbury home for his many gentlemen friends. And the Baltimore City councilman had odd boots made to accommodate a bad foot that caused a noticeable limp.[15]

Elizabeth Saulsbury Audoun, born in 1859 to Saulsbury's first wife who had passed away just before the war, testified as to when the Saulsbury family had moved to Eden Street from neighboring Central Street. Although property records clearly showed that Andrew Saulsbury had purchased the Eden Street residence in 1865 from sea captain John J. Mattison, city directories did not have the family living on Central Street until 1867. Mrs. Audoun told the court that she remembered moving to Eden Street at age six — in 1865. That still left a nine-year gap between the most recently dated coin (1856) and the earliest time the Saulsburys could have occupied the treasure home, in 1865.

Mrs. Audoun, who appeared frail and somewhat confused during her testimony, would pass away just a few months after the trial.

The Saulsbury lawyers summed up their case by appealing to Judge O'Dunne's logic. The person who had buried the coins could only have been someone of considerable wealth, who lived at the Eden Street house or had regular access to the property, was in the habit of collecting gold coins of mostly smaller denominations, and who had met with a sudden demise. Andrew Saulsbury was clearly the only individual who met all these parameters.[16] Therefore, Saulsbury was the only person who could have buried the gold under that pile of hard-packed dirt and oyster shells, wrapped in an old boot.

Judge O'Dunne, however, was having difficulty in accepting the Saulsbury claim. He believed the coins had been buried sometime during the Civil War — before the Saulsburys had occupied the house. O'Dunne also surmised that Captain Mattison was not likely to have moved to nearby Broadway Street while leaving a fortune in gold behind. Likewise, Mattison's tenant for much of the war period, Captain John E. Stevens[17], had moved to E. Baltimore Street after leaving Eden Street, and was also quite unlikely to have left thousands of gold coins in the cellar if, in fact, the coins had been his.

Neither O'Dunne nor anyone else ever suspected that Mattison, Saulsbury, and perhaps even Stevens were part of a conspiracy to collect, hide, and watch over the gold for some later purpose.

In Elizabeth Saulsbury Audoun, the judge saw a senior citizen whose recollection of events nearly 70 years in the past could not be considered as reliable evidence. The year 1856 was the last mint date on the coins, and the Saulsburys could not firmly establish occupancy of the treasure house before 1867. Those eleven years represented a very long and very troubling gap.

Indeed, according to author Len Augsburger, grandson Reuben Foster had taken his aunts for a tour of Eden Street to verify that the treasure home in question had most assuredly been their childhood home. The late nineteenth-century renumbering of houses on that block had already caused considerable confusion amongst potential litigants in the case.

"*It has greatly changed,*"[18] observed one of Foster's aunts, no doubt shocked at the wholesale decline of Eden Street during the intervening 50+ years since the daughters had moved away. It is a common refrain heard amongst visiting former city dwellers that have spent a lifetime away from "the old neighborhood."

The coins could have been buried by anyone between 1856 and 1867. Judge O'Dunne was just as inclined to believe that an associate of Captain Stevens, someone who perhaps was subsequently killed in the war, could have deposited the coins in the cellar before going off to battle.

In his summary, Judge O'Dunne wrote that, "*I find in support of the Saulsbury claim nothing more than a plausible possibility falling far short of legal proof of ownership.*"[19]

With a few stokes of O'Dunne's pen, the 11 Saulsbury heirs were ruled out of the running. The fight for the gold was now down to the Findlay/French sisters and the two teenaged pals who comprised the Rinky Dinky Doos Boys' Club.

The crucial question that now took front and center stage was whether the boys had committed an act of trespass by entering the rear portion of the cellar.

The Findlay/French lawyers put Benjamin Kalis on the stand. Mr. Kalis, owner of the American Realty Company, had been employed by Henry Findlay French to act as property manager for his mother and aunt's rental property on Eden Street.[20] Kalis was the individual tasked in late 1933 with getting the dilapidated house renovated and its six rooms rented out.

Under oath, Kalis testified as to how he hired and supervised a crew of workers to do the rehab. Kalis also had the power company install electrical service, which included meters mounted in the rear portion of the cellar for each unit. Because he didn't want anyone back there where the meters were located, Kalis said he mounted a door on hinges to deny access to the rear portion of the cellar, and then padlocked the door.[21]

However, under cross-examination, Kalis could provide neither a specific date nor an itemized record which included that particular door having been installed. Moreover, although Kalis testified he visited the Eden Street property on a weekly basis, he admitted that he rarely went into the cellar — but that the last time he was down there, the door had been locked. Kalis' carpenter and plumber both agreed with their boss, saying that they each used a key for the times they needed to access the rear section of the cellar. But since Kalis and his contractors worked on dozens of similar Baltimore properties, remembering minute details about every location, and keeping meticulous repair ledgers for each building, was not a realistic expectation. [22]

Harry Levin, representing the boys, countered by putting several of the Eden Street tenants on the stand. Each tenant testified that the door to the rear section of the cellar was almost never locked. They talked of having ready access to that area for the purpose of storing coal or chopping wood. Bessie Jones, Theodore's mother, even told the court that for much of 1934 there had been no door whatsoever separating the front and rear portions of the cellar. Worse for the Findlay/French team, a second floor Eden Street tenant testified that the door and lock in question were not installed until *after* the boys' treasure discovery.[23] The inference was that the landlords had repaired the door and installed a padlock *after the fact* in order to make it appear that the boys had trespassed. Doing so certainly would have gone a long way in nullifying Levin's contention that the boys had been "lawfully engaged in a joint enterprise."

Courtroom photos of the treasure cellar[24] seemed to lend credence to the idea that the partition guarding entrance to the treasure site had been more recently installed than other doors at the property.

At this point in the trial, Judge O'Dunne had heard enough. The testimony of all parties was concluded, and the judge would now retreat to his office to consider the evidence and write his opinion.

The elderly sisters, the Jones and Grob families, and much of Baltimore now awaited Judge O'Dunne's verdict.

His Honor would not keep the interested parties waiting long.

A Band of Brothers

JAS. ARMSTRONG & CO.

MANUFACTURERS OF

ALL KINDS OF SOAPS

AND

Hard Pressed Tallow Candles,

CONCORD ST.

CHAS. WEBB.
THOS. ARMSTRONG.

BALTIMORE.

To understand how those 5,000 gold coins came to be buried under the treasure house on South Eden Street, one first needs to understand the men behind the firm of James Armstrong & Co.

As its name implies, the company was founded by James Armstrong . . . along with partner Samuel Cairns. Armstrong and Cairns operated a factory at 115 Concord Street in Baltimore near the Pratt Street Bridge. The firm specialized in the manufacture of soaps and candles — candles being an important household staple in the days preceding the invention of the electric light bulb. In 1852, James Armstrong associated itself with another company, Charles Webb and Sons, located several blocks north on Ensor Street. With founder Charles Webb having passed away a few years prior, the Ensor Street firm found itself in the control of the Webb sons, Charles, Jr. and James (now DBA as Charles & James Webb & Company). After the association was formed with James Armstrong, however, both the Concord and Ensor Street locations would eventually be conducted under the sole name of James Armstrong & Company.[1]

By 1855, things begin to happen. Original partner Sam Cairns withdraws, and founder James Armstrong admits his nephew, Thomas, to the firm.[2] Thomas Armstrong's soon-to-be best friend, Andrew J. Saulsbury, has already been on board as an executive with James Armstrong & Co. since the early 1850s. We can guess this because Saulsbury's first-born son, named James Armstrong Saulsbury, according to Maryland census data was born in 1854. Saulsbury will one day own and occupy the treasure house on South Eden St. But for now, after 1853, it is the veteran sea captain John J. Mattison, along with his wife and

74

children, who occupies the treasure property on South Eden. Saulsbury and his growing family live just around the corner from Captain Mattison at 138 South Central Avenue.

Saulsbury appears to have grown up in the neighborhood. Municipal records indicate that the Saulsbury family operated a grocery and paint store on the southwest corner of Montgomery and Light Streets, close by the Baltimore waterfront. City directories going back to Saulsbury's birth in the late 1820s list the Saulsbury store at that location. The enterprise seems to have suffered a bankruptcy in 1849 (when future Maryland governor William Pinkney Whyte bringing action against Andrew Saulsbury, Sr. in chancery court). Subsequent to the bankruptcy proceeding, the grocery concern is reorganized for a time, and does business as Andrew J. Saulsbury & Son in the early 1850s. It is likely this son, Andrew J. Saulsbury, Jr., who eventually joins James Armstrong & Co.

In court documents related to the 1935 trial concerning the disposition of the treasure trove, remaining Saulsbury family members identify the candle executive as having been an "ardent Southern sympathizer."[3] So ardent, in fact, that the Saulsbury family is supposedly threatened on at least one occasion by the Union troops who occupy Baltimore for the duration of the Civil War.[4] Two paintings are said to adorn the Saulsbury parlor after the close of the war — those of Confederate military heroes Robert E. Lee and Stonewall Jackson.[5]

Saulsbury's hot-blooded political views, it is said, are made well aware "to everyone that knew him."

In 1858, James Armstrong also withdraws from the eponymous firm he once helped to build with founding co-partner Sam Cairns. Armstrong leaves the candle and soap enterprise in the hands of its remaining partners, Charles Webb, Jr., James Webb, and nephew Thomas Armstrong. James Webb is put in command of the Ensor street factory, while Charles Webb and Thomas Armstrong remain at the Concord Street headquarters[6] just a few minutes walk from South Eden Street and South Central Avenue. The firm's partners are assisted by their young but experienced executive, Andrew J. Saulsbury. We can speculate that the nearby Saulsbury family grocery business was likely a purveyor of Armstrong candles.

Saulsbury and Thomas Armstrong become such close friends that Saulsbury will one day have a grandchild named "Thomas Armstrong Saulsbury."[7]

This band of brothers, this "candle cabal" — Charles Webb, James Webb, Thomas Armstrong, and Andrew Saulsbury, are exceedingly well connected in the City of Baltimore.

Charles Webb and James Webb are both longstanding Freemasons.[8]

Charles is allied with the "reform" mayor, George William Brown, who will come to power with the promise to clean up the violence, corruption, and thuggery that had persistently bedeviled 1850s Baltimore politics.[9] Charles is also a former Whig Party member, later a staunch Southern Democrat, and director for the Baltimore & Ohio Railroad. Later in life, he will be appointed tax collector by the late 1870s Mayor of Baltimore, George Proctor Kane, an appointee of Brown's in 1860 and a key figure in Baltimore's bloody and tumultuous Civil War days.[10]

MARYLAND CONTESTED ELECTION.

LIST OF VOTERS—Continued.

Ward.	Name and residence.	Voted.	Did not vote.	Reasons for not voting. Violence.	Reasons for not voting. Intimidation.
20	Hiram Woods, sr., 167 Garden street	1			
3	A. J. Saulsbury, 138 Central avenue	1			
9	Thomas Armstrong, Fountain Hotel	1			
7	Archibald Wilson, 168 Orleans street		1		
	H. Reynolds, 156 Bond street		1		
4	James Kelmailin, Slimmer alley		1		
7	P. Correcan, 66 Dallas street		1		
8	P. McMahon, 5 Abrehan street	1			
11	Lawrence Clarke, Richmond street	1			
4	R. Sandorf, 41 Lombard street		1		
9	John Lutz, 17 Fish Market space		1		
	Joseph Kiser, 9 Fish Market space		1		
7	Maxwell Connor, 91 Bethel street		1		
	T. McCluney, Caroline street, near Mulliken		1		

James Webb is a member of the Baltimore City Council,[11] as well as treasurer of the Maryland Central Railroad.

Andrew Saulsbury will also become a member of the Baltimore's City Council.[12]

And James Armstrong, the firm's founding partner? When James Armstrong "withdraws" in 1958 to leave his factories in the hands of younger men, he does so not with the intention of retiring. Instead, the senior Armstrong leaves to found an entirely new firm in a wholly unrelated business. And on the Board of Directors of this new firm will sit Freemasons Charles and James Webb. . . .

. . . and also *John J. Mattison*, ship's captain and secret slaver from years past.[13]

Captain John Mattison, the man who has 5,000 gold coins stashed under his house before the beginning of the Civil War.

Yes, the same Captain Mattison, who, in 1865, will sell his house with 5,000 gold coins in the basement to Andrew Saulsbury, the "ardent" Southern sympathizer and James Armstrong & Co. executive.

You see, when Mattison sells his house to Saulsbury, the two men are far from being strangers. In fact, they are more than mere neighbors. This secret slaver and this fiery Confederate candle executive? They share much more than a chance real estate transaction. They are brothers to a cause. Saulsbury and Mattison are almost certainly Knights of the Golden Circle.

And so, apparently, is Thomas Armstrong.

Thousands of gold coins will be found in a tin box buried under a hotel in which Thomas Saulsbury resides.[14] And, a mere mile away from that hotel, thousands of coins buried under a home owned alternately by Captain Mattison and Andrew Saulsbury?

All three men engaged as executives or board members of two companies founded by a single individual, James Armstrong?

With two politically connected Freemasons, the Webbs, on the board of directors of each company?? And with these Freemasons being connected to some of the most influential secessionists in the city on the eve of the Civil War? Secessionists who will be jailed by Lincoln?

Mere coincidence you say??? A fortune in buried gold says not.

We say the coins were buried as part of a conspiracy . . . a conspiracy to cause the South to break away from the North.

A Band of Brothers

A conspiracy to invade Mexico, Cuba, Nicaragua . . . and other lightly guarded Latin American fruits ripe for the plucking.

A conspiracy to create a vast slave empire that would make a select few people rich for generations to come. A conspiracy conceived by the Order of the Lone Star, later merged into the Knights of the Golden Circle.

Saulsbury, the Armstrongs, the Webbs . . . they all had knowledge of the treasure. And they all knew the ultimate purpose for the coins.

Unfortunately for this band of brothers, this Candle Cabal, the best laid plans of mice and men . . . .

Evolution of a 19th-Century Candle and Soap Dynasty

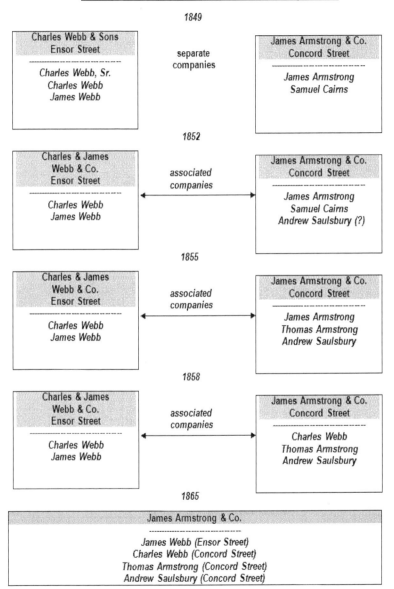

1849

| Charles Webb & Sons | separate | James Armstrong & Co. |
Ensor Street	companies	Concord Street
Charles Webb, Sr.		James Armstrong
Charles Webb		Samuel Cairns
James Webb		

1852

| Charles & James Webb & Co. | associated | James Armstrong & Co. |
Ensor Street	companies	Concord Street
Charles Webb	←→	James Armstrong
James Webb		Samuel Cairns
		Andrew Saulsbury (?)

1855

| Charles & James Webb & Co. | associated | James Armstrong & Co. |
Ensor Street	companies	Concord Street
Charles Webb	←→	James Armstrong
James Webb		Thomas Armstrong
		Andrew Saulsbury

1858

| Charles & James Webb & Co. | associated | James Armstrong & Co. |
Ensor Street	companies	Concord Street
Charles Webb	←→	Charles Webb
James Webb		Thomas Armstrong
		Andrew Saulsbury

1865

James Armstrong & Co.
James Webb (Ensor Street)
Charles Webb (Concord Street)
Thomas Armstrong (Concord Street)
Andrew Saulsbury (Concord Street)

The Captain Comes Home

MARIA	18501227	18510517	-58	225	59	335	142	4105321	51	01 JOHN J. MATTISON NEW YORK		SAN FRANCISCO
MARIA	18510704	18510815	-35	237	33	286	43	2201991	4	01 JOHN J. MATTISON SAN FRANCISCO		VALPARAISO
MARIA	18510824	18510921	-57	277	-25	319	29	2201911	4	01 JOHN J. MATTISON VALPARAISO		RIO DE JANEIRO
MARIA	18511014	18611110	-23	306	9	326	28	2201921	4	01 JOHN J. MATTISON RIO DE JANEIRO		NEW ORLEANS

Shipping records for Captain Mattison and *The Maria*.

Once the lucrative "round the horn" voyages to San Francisco and the California gold fields began to peter out — in tandem with the overall decline in the diggings — Captain John Mattison seems to have returned to more familiar ocean routes. During the 1850s, Mattison and his barque, *Maria*, could usually be found sailing to ports throughout the Gulf of Mexico, Central America, and South America.[1]

The life of every sailor is a tenuous one. A mariner lives with the ever-present knowledge that each voyage may be his last. Storms, faulty ship construction, accidents, piracy — all were occupational hazards that threatened a 19th-century life spent at sea. Becoming "lost at sea" without even a body for loved ones to bury was a fate that befell thousands. The modern treasure hunting company, Odyssey Marine, earns it keep by using sophisticated technology to scoop up gold, silver, and other precious artifacts from shipwrecks that litter the ocean floor. The publicly traded Odyssey Marine grosses millions of dollars annually.[2]

During one particular passage from Valparaiso, Mexico to Rio de Janeiro, Captain Mattison, however, came face-to-face with a danger that was most unusual and terrifyingly bizarre. Mattison, quite unknowingly, had taken aboard the *Maria* one of history's most evil and vicious serial killers.

We will never know how close Mattison may have come to having his throat cut and his body dumped overboard for the sharks and other various sea scavengers. If fate had taken a different turn, Mattison might have never returned to Baltimore to bury those 5,000 gold coins in the Eden Street cellar.

The monster's given name was Albert W. Hicks,[3] but often went by the alias William Johnson. Born in Rhode Island, Hicks could have just as easily been birthed in Hell by the devil himself. At age 15 he tires of chores on the family farm, and runs away to avoid hard work. The teen supports himself by stealing valuables at a local train station. Soon caught and jailed, Hicks escapes but is quickly recaptured. Upon his eventual release, Hicks signs on with a New England whaling vessel and begins a life of crime at sea. He attempts to foment mutiny and other troubles onboard various whaling ships, and is confined and beaten by one ship's captain. Vowing revenge against the world, Hicks soon begins to rob and eventually murder victims in various ports. One rampage occurs on Oahu in the Sandwich Islands (today known as Hawaii). Taking on a sidekick from Boston with the moniker Tom Stone, this diabolical duo team up to create mayhem in port cities across the Western Hemisphere and beyond. While today's serial killers use the mobility afforded by the automobile and modern highway systems to commit homicides in various jurisdictions, Hicks and Stone use the 19th-century ocean trade routes to achieve the same effect. Whenever local scrutiny becomes too uncomfortable, these psychopaths sign up for another voyage and are transported hundreds or even thousands of miles from the scene of their latest crimes.

Hicks and Stone are successful in some of their attempted mutinies, and even succeed in commandeering a Spanish vessel by drawing pistols on their fellow crew members and captain, forcing them into a small boat on the high seas. Hicks and Stone then scuttle the ship and make off with a fortune in precious metals, leaving the ship's crew to a horrendous fate.

Mutiny is only one of this pair's criminal specialties. During the California Gold Rush, Hicks and Stone stalk the mining camps, robbing and killing unsuspecting miners for their nuggets and bags of gold dust. According to the 1860s account of Hicks' escapades, The Life, Trial, Confession, and Execution of Albert W. Hicks, the Pirate and Mutineer.[4] Hicks and Stone may have committed as many as 97 murders in the California goldfields.

Moving from California to Mexico, Hicks and Stone turn their attention to the mule trains hauling silver ore from that country's rich silver mines. In between robbing these transports of a fortune in silver, Hicks and Stone commit innumerable highway robberies. And when pickings on the highway grow slim, these marauders resort to home invasions — generally at the cost of the inhabitants' lives. Man, woman, child . . . it makes little difference to Hicks and Stone.

When the pair finally leave Mexico, they do so by signing on for a voyage aboard Captain Mattison's vessel, The Maria. They dig up their buried silver and unload it for $15,000 — an enormous sum in the 1850s. In Hicks' own words:

"We returned to Valparaiso and took passage aboard the bark Maria, of Baltimore, Captain Mattison, bound to Rio Janeiro. Nothing of particular interest occurred during our voyage to Rio, and staying there six or seven weeks, and spending nearly all our money in gambling and debauchery, we took the road between Rio and Montevideo, where we robbed all worth robbing, and murdered all who resisted us.

"There is many a whitened skeleton bleaching by that roadside now. . . . If I should travel that road now I should have plenty of ghostly company." [5]

Hicks and Stone next travel south to Argentina, where they continue on with their murderous ways, and later back to Rio for a repeat of many of their earlier scenes. *"The bar-room, brothel, and Monte-table were the only attractions for us,"* explains Hicks. *"We led the life of demons."* [6]

For a time, the murderous conspirators actually try to invest their ill-gotten fortune in legitimate businesses. They own, alternately, a boarding house, a hotel, and a bowling alley. But with their only real aim in life the continuance of their debauchery, Hicks and Stone eventually leave their businesses behind and hit the road in a spree of new robberies and killings.

When Hicks survives a ship's sinking at sea, but Stone perishes, Hicks takes on a new partner in crime, a brute named Lockwood. Lockwood proves nearly as adept at mayhem as the former sidekick, Stone. Hicks and Lockwood continue the macabre ocean roadshow through South America, Africa, the Mediterranean, and then back to the Caribbean. Finally, when Lockwood is lost to yet another marine disaster, Hicks sails back to the United States — first to New Orleans, and then on to New York.

Incredibly, while in New York City, Hicks marries and fathers a child. He appears to settle down, and be (at least superficially) devoted to his wife and the baby. For some four years, Hicks leads an apparent double life — that of a loving father and husband at home, and murderous bandit away from the city. Hicks (now going by the alias William Johnson) is careful not to commit any criminal offenses in his immediate environs.

Albert W. Hicks, 19th-century serial killer.

Eventually, and inevitably, the psychopathic Hicks makes a fatal mistake. Signing on as a deckhand aboard the Virginia-bound oyster sloop the *E.A. Johnson*, Hicks soon slaughters the captain and two fellow crew members with an axe, and dumps their bodies overboard. Gathering the captain's money, silver pocket watch, and all other valuable and useful items aboard the sloop, Hicks attempts to make his escape using the ship's yawl (a small sailboat). However, during his attempt to depart, and with no one at the *E.A. Johnson's* wheel, the oyster sloop collides with a passing schooner, causing considerable damage. Help is quickly summoned, and the crew of the schooner watch as the madman on the sailboat heads for Staten Island. Once on board the sloop, the authorities are confronted with a horrific scene of violence and treachery, the *E.A. Johnson's* decks being "awash with blood." Hot on the suspect's trail, investigators learn of the name "William Johnson" and of the sailor who had just a day earlier signed on with the oyster sloop. Within hours the detectives have discovered Hicks' rented room, his wife and son, and soon learn the true identity of the man they desperately want for the three murders aboard the *E.A. Johnson.*

Now running for his life, Hicks heads straight for familiar territory . . . Providence, Rhode Island. But this time the police are fast closing in on the fiend's trail, and when Hicks books temporary lodging at a Providence rooming house, the police zero in and arrest Hicks fast asleep in his bed, without incident. The serial killer is then transported back to New York City and held in the infamous "Tombs" to await trail. Authorities find in Hicks' possession a slain crew member's overcoat, the slain captain's silver watch, and a money bag containing five hundred dollars. At first Hicks claims to have been "shanghaied" by the captain of the oyster sloop. But then realization of the hopelessness of his situation sets in, and the psychopath comes clean with a full confession. Sideshow entrepreneur P.T. Barnum visits Hicks in jail, and agrees to give Hicks a box of cigars and send $25 to his wife and son in exchange for a plaster bust to be made of the prisoner's head and shoulders — to be exhibited at Barnum's "museum."

In a trial lasting six days, Hicks is convicted by a jury of twelve for the offenses of murder and piracy on the high seas. On July 13, 1860, in front of a crowd of onlookers estimated to be north of ten thousand (both on shore and in boats anchored offshore in New York Bay), the murderer and pirate Albert W. Hicks is hung from the gallows on Bedloe Island.[7] The ghastly affair had been advertised in New York newspapers with refreshment vendors and tour boat operators doing a landmark business on the day of Hicks' execution.

Never heard of Bedloe Island? That's because you know the island by a different name today. The gallows there once stood on what we now call Liberty Island, and at the approximate location for the future site of the Statue of Liberty.

A reading of Hicks' confession today seems surreal, and begs the question as to how a man could murder and rob so many victims in so many countries for so many years yet escape detection. Was Hicks elaborating? Boasting? Fantasizing? One throwaway comment, however, makes Hicks' confession all the more plausible. It is the trivial description of the Hicks and Stone taking an early 1850s voyage from Valparaiso, Mexico to Rio de

Janeiro, Brazil aboard the bark *Maria* with a Captain Mattison from Baltimore. Ship records from that period show that Captain Mattison did indeed make that same trip aboard the *Maria* on multiple occasions. Once safe and back in Baltimore, Mattison will purchase the treasure house on Eden Street in 1853. While Captain Mattison owns the house from 1853 until its sale to candle merchant Andrew Saulsbury in 1865, ownership of the underlying ground will be retained by a Baltimore businessman named Charles Findlay.[8] Mattison and all subsequent owners of the treasure house will be required to pay annual "ground rents" to Findlay . . . and subsequently to Findlay's two daughters upon the lawyer's demise.

We also know that Captain Mattison, like Saulsbury, was involved in real estate speculation in the Baltimore property market. Legal records show that in 1854 Captain Mattison foreclosed on a vacant lot on Wolfe Street near Fells Point when the buyer failed to make the agreed upon payments.

And in 1856, the captain buries 5,000 gold coins in the cellar of 55 S. Eden St.

So what did Mattison do in later years . . . during the Civil War and after? Mattison and his bark, *The Maria*, seem to disappear from the voyage records after the mid-1850s.

In an 1868 issue of *The Baltimore Underwriter*, the following ad appeared for the American Fire Ins. Company of Baltimore: [9]

The insurance company, founded in 1858 by James Armstrong, the same entrepreneur responsible for **James Armstrong & Co.**, manufacturers of fine soaps and candles, listed the following individuals on their Board of Directors:

The Board of Directors, with **James L. Armstrong** as president (also shown in directories during that time period as James S. Armstrong), featured the familiar names of **Charles Webb**, 33rd degree prior Grand Master of Maryland Freemasonry,[10] and his brother, **James Webb**, also a leading Baltimore Freemason and co-member of Baltimore City Council — along with Charles Webb, James Webb, and Andrew Saulsbury are all longstanding executives at James Armstrong and Co., with the Webb bothers and Thomas Armstrong being partners of that soap and candle firm.

Also listed as a director at American Fire Insurance in none other than the secret slaver himself, lifelong mariner Captain **John J. Mattison**. Mattison's inclusion is a natural, since he knows much about vessels in port and their cargoes, having had the French Navy seize one of his ships and their thirsty sailors empty the casks of wine — while soon after having the British Navy seize the same Mattison vessel for the illegal transportation of slaves from West Africa to the New World.

There can be no doubt that Captain John J. Mattison was well-acquainted with all the executives of James Armstrong and Co. When Mattison sold the treasure house at 55 South Eden Street to Andrew Saulsbury at the close of the Civil War in 1865 [11] he was not selling his home to some unknown stranger. No, Mattison sold the treasure house on Eden Street to a longtime friend, neighbor, and trusted colleague. The ship's captain and the candle maker were members of the same inner circle . . . along with both Armstrongs and certainly both Webb brothers. When Mattison sailed the ocean blue bringing boxes of candles to exotic ports of call, he was likely selling James Armstrong and Co. candles.

And when Mattison turned the treasure house over to Saulsbury in 1865, he was also turning control of the gold over to Saulsbury as a fellow operative of the Knights of the Golden Circle. The 5,000 gold coins in the cellar belonged to neither Mattison nor Saulsbury *personally*. The coins were the secret property of the KGC. Mattison had acted as the initial sentinel or keeper of the coins from 1856 — when they were buried — until the early 1860s when fellow mariner Captain John E. Stevens[12] occupied the house (still owned by Mattison), and became the interim sentinel watching over the coins. Then, after 1865, the task fell to Saulsbury.

Sure, there were likely practical considerations involved in Saulsbury's purchase of the Eden home from Mattison. Mattison was some 24 years older than Saulsbury, his children having grown and left by 1865 . . . leaving just Mattison and his wife. Saulsbury, on the other hand, has now married for a second time and finds himself with a growing family and two live-in maids.[13] Saulsbury needs a bigger house, and Mattison is looking to downsize.

But the timeframes for occupancy of the treasure house are key:

♦ **Captain Mattison** — 1853 to 1861 (pre-Civil War)
♦ **Captain Stevens** — approximately 1861 to 1865
(Civil War)
♦ **Andrew Saulsbury** — June 1865 until 1873
(after Civil War)

The beginning and the end of the Civil War determines who moves from Eden, into Eden, and when.

Captain Mattison moves to South Broadway Avenue, just a few short blocks to the east of the treasure house.[14]

Captain Stevens moves just a few short blocks north to East Baltimore Avenue, a mere stone's throw from the treasure house.[15] And Andrew Saulsbury moves into the treasure house from just around the corner, his former home being around the block at 138 South Central. Saulsbury has already been a neighbor of Mattison's for years.

No one moves farther than a short walk. *When* they moved is just as important as *where* they moved, and perhaps even more so. The moves occurred at the beginning of the Civil War and immediately after the end of the Civil War, in the years 1861 and 1865.

Sea captain John J. Mattison watches over the coins while plans are being made for the KGC to invade Mexico, Cuba, and other vulnerable targets for Southern expansion. Once the War Between the States commences, Captain Stevens watches over the house for Mattison. Then, once the war ends and the dust settles, Andrew Saulsbury moves his family from around the corner and into the treasure house.

So, who buried the coins?

In his book <u>Treasure in the Cellar</u>, Len Augsburger admits there is a colossal problem with the timeframe for his theory that Saulsbury — and Saulsbury alone — buried the treasure. Here is Augsburger's cogent analysis of this dilemma:

"The 1856 date made no sense. The banking panic of 1857 was at least a year off, and the beginning of the Civil War four years beyond that. The distribution of the dates (on the coins) suggested that the hoard was pulled from circulation entirely in 1855 or 1856. Had the coins been collected over time, the dates might have been represented in closer proportion to their original mintages (since the hoard was very underweight in coins minted in 1856) . . . Andrew J. Saulsbury would have had to quickly assemble the coins sometime in 1856, and then have moved it from his Central Street home to Eden Street in 1865 or later. Did Saulsbury bury gold at 138 S. Central as well? It was hard enough to prove he buried it at 132 S. Eden, let alone a previous residence." [16]

Exactly! The evidence does not suggest that Andrew Saulsbury buried the coins after 1865. In fact, it suggests that Saulsbury likely did not bury the coins at all.

The evidence points to Captain John J. Mattison as having buried the coins — with the knowledge of some of his KGC friends at James Armstrong and Co., most notably Andrew Saulsbury.

The sequence of probable events surrounding the treasure can only be understood through the prism of the Knights of the Golden Circle. The coins were not the property of a single individual. Captain Mattison did not personally own the coins. Neither did Saulsbury, the Webb brothers, nor the Armstrongs. The coins belonged to the KGC, and were collected under their name, and to be used expressly for their purposes — to fund a planned invasion of Cuba, Mexico, and other high-probability targets for Southern expansion. The date of 1856 makes <u>perfect</u> sense in KGC terms. The Southern Rights clubs had been around for decades, pushing their pro-South, pro-slavery agenda, and financing "secret slavers" such as Captain Mattison and his *Eliza*

Davidson to circumvent the international 19th-century ban on slave trade coming from the African continent. Pitchman George Bickley would come along in 1854 and merge these various Southern Rights clubs under the single banner of the Knights of the Golden Circle.[17] The newly formed KGC would be on the move in the mid-1850s, forming new chapters (known as castles) and signing up recruits (read mercenaries) looking for adventure and fortune south of the U.S. border.

It is the date of *1865* or after that makes no sense for the burial of the gold at the treasure house at on South Eden Street. There simply was not enough hard currency in circulation to amass such a large quantity of gold coins. Again, coin expert and author Len Augsburger makes the point abundantly clear in his Treasure in the Cellar:

> *"Hard money had been scare ever since the Civil War, when the Union authorized 'legal tender' in 1862 to finance the campaign. One hundred and fifty million dollars of greenbacks were printed, and unlike previous currency issues, these were not redeemable in gold. . . . Salmon Chase, the Treasury Secretary, attempted to stem the tide by selling U.S. Treasury gold on the open market, to little effect. Gold, silver, and copper coins all disappeared from sight. . . . Hard money would not return into normal circulation until the 1870s."* [18]

This means that gold coinage wasn't even commonly available in everyday circulation for Saulsbury to have collected the gold in the late 1860s. The time when gold coinage was readily available was during the 1850s — as gold began to flow back East from California and other Western goldfields. Saulsbury did not bury the gold, Mattison buried the gold. And he buried the gold in 1856, just as the evidence suggests. But he did so under the auspices of the KGC, and almost assuredly with the knowledge of the Armstrongs and the Webbs. When Andrew Saulsbury bought the house from Mattison in 1865 for $3200,[19] he knew exactly what was buried in the cellar, because it was now his turn as the keeper of the KGC gold.

So why was Mattison's cellar chosen in 1856 for hiding the gold? Because, Mattison had already served the clandestine organization (originally The Order of the Lone Star) for nearly 20 years. First as a secret slaver, and later almost certainly as a spy.

Mattison was a man who could be trusted. Mattison's occupation as a sea captain would undoubtedly prove invaluable to an organization such as the KGC. Mattison sailed freely from port to port from Boston, New York, Philadelphia, and Baltimore down to Mexico, the Gulf of Mexico, Cuba, most of South America, and even up to California[20] — a KGC hotbed of activity in the early days after that state's annexation from Mexico after the 1846-1848 Mexican-American War. Mattison's profession took him to nearly all of the countries inside the intended Golden Circle. The intelligence Mattison would have been able to gather for his KGC brethren would have been extremely important. All the while his quiet Baltimore home on Eden Street, watched over by his wife, would have been the perfect sanctuary for 5,000 buried gold coins. Mrs. Mattison would, of course, have had absolutely no knowledge of the fortune buried beneath the property . . . for such knowledge could have placed her in potential danger. Loose lips sink ships, and the sea captain's wife did not have a "need to know" concerning KGC business — quite the contrary.

Although Mattison almost certainly buried the coins, he almost certainly did not collect them. The coins would likely have represented initiation fees and dues owed by KGC members.

According to Warren Getler and Bob Brewer in Rebel Gold, "*Tens of thousands of supporters from a cross-section of society (doctors, judges, craftsmen, editors, lawyers, clergymen, laborers, etc.) were reported to have secret oaths and joined such castles. For a fee of $1, $5, or $10, for the first three degrees of initiation, respectively, as well as payment of a prorated property tax, initiates became rank and file members.*"[21]

Make no mistake that when initiates paid those fees, they were paying them in gold coin. The KGC, understandably, had an aversion to paper money — especially the paper money being issued by the United States federal government, their main obstacle to "Southern rights." Paper money is also not ideal if wealth needs to be buried for any length of time, since it is easily damaged by the elements. Gold is much better suited to the task.

The 5,000 gold coins in the copper jug buried beneath 55 S. Eden in 1856 represented fees and property taxes collected from a KGC castle in Baltimore, tucked away in reserve for the coming planned invasion of Mexico, an invasion which Southern newspapers were reporting on by 1858 and 1859.[22]

Although Mattison's quiet home would have proven perfect as the hiding spot for the treasure, Mattison's frequent voyages meant he was away far too often to have conducted regular KGC meetings from his home. The coins would have almost certainly been collected elsewhere. But where, and by whom? Any of the insiders at James Armstrong and Co. could be considered likely suspects. They all live in the immediate neighborhood, with senior partner Charles Webb living more in the direction of downtown Baltimore. Freemason and Baltimore City Council member James Webb lives on Aisquith Street not far from the Ensor Street soap and candle factory. James Armstrong lives close by on Dallas Street. And his nephew Thomas Armstrong resides at The Fountain Hotel, which will become a hotbed of Confederate activity during the approaching war.

But the most likely candidate as source of the coins was Andrew J. Saulsbury, who lives but a two-minute walk from the treasure house in the 1850s. His daughter's testimony at the 1935 trial concerning the disposition of the treasure hints at Saulsbury's involvement with the KGC . . . and also his apparent function in the organization.[23] Augsburger was actually somewhat close to the truth when he wrote that, "*Saulsbury would have had to quickly assemble the coins sometime in 1856, and then have moved it from his Central Street home to Eden Street in 1865 or later.*"[24]

The point that cannot be stressed enough is that the coins found beneath Mattison's house (Saulsbury's eventual home after June, 1865) are directly tied to Saulsbury's description as an "*ardent Southern sympathizer.*" The coins in the cellar and the paintings of Southern heroes on his parlor walls are no mere coincidences.

In an 1866 anonymously written book entitled History of the Plots and Crimes of the Great Conspiracy to Overthrow Liberty in America (sometimes referred to simply as The Great Conspiracy), the author makes the following claims about the 1859-1860 induction of John Wilkes Booth into the KGC:

"*The high-strung thespian took the vows of the KGC in a room adorned with portraits of Confederate leaders Jefferson Davis and Stephen Douglas, and a bust of John C. Calhoun.*

"*Booth swears to risk all to help Southern independence, as well as to end Yankee domination.*"[25]

The Captain Comes Home

Sound familiar? After the war, on 55 S. Eden St., the Saulsbury home features two paintings, one depicting General Robert E. Lee, and the other General Stonewall Jackson. It is easy to imagine those portraits of Davis and Douglas hanging on the Saulsbury wall at 138 S. Central just a few years earlier — at the dawn of the Civil War.

"He was an ardent Southern sympathizer. That everyone knew," stated one Saulsbury daughter in 1935.[26] So was John Wilkes Booth, who had grown up on North Exeter Street just three short blocks (4/10th of a mile) from the Saulsbury home.

Author David Keehn, in his 2013 book <u>Knights of the Golden Circle: Secret Empire, Southern Secession, Civil War</u> directly points to John Wilkes Booth as being a member of the KGC:

> *"At least one active castle of the Knights was operating in Baltimore by early 1859, when Bickley arrived. It existed in the south central neighborhood near St. Vincent's Church, where Wilkes Booth had grown up in a townhouse on Exeter Street. Among the castle's members were Samuel Street, a schoolmate of Booth, and the O'Laughlen brothers. Michael O'Laughlen, a close friend of Booth, would later become one of the conspirators Booth enlisted in his Civil War plot to abduct the sitting president, Abraham Lincoln. It is likely that Booth became affiliated with this castle when he returned to Baltimore from his acting stint in Richmond."* [27]

Keehn goes on to say that, *"Over the next few years, Wilkes Booth would rise to become a prominent leader in the Knights."* [28]

In the 1866 <u>Private Journal and Diary of John H. Surratt, The Conspirator</u>, written by Surratt and edited by Dion Haco, Surratt describes how he was introduced the Knights of the Golden Circle by another knight, John Wilkes Booth, and inducted into the mysterious KGC on July 2, 1860 at a castle in Baltimore.[29] Surratt, an accomplice in President Lincoln's 1865 assassination, revealed details about the Knights' secret ceremonies, and noted how actors, cabinet members, congressmen, judges, and other politicians were in attendance for his swearing in ritual.

Was Saulsbury's home at 138 S. Central used for KGC induction ceremonies after the Saulsbury children had been tucked into bed? And, for added security, the coins brought to neighbor Captain John Mattison's home just around the corner for safekeeping? With that much gold being collected, along with a steady stream of visitors (and a few possible spies or persons bent on larceny), it would certainly make sense to store the money _away_ from the Saulsbury home located at 138 S. Central. Was the active castle of the Knights located in Booth's south central Baltimore neighborhood in fact the home of Andrew J. Saulsbury at 138 S. Central? Were the Webbs, Armstrongs, and Captain Mattison present for many of that castle's secret meetings?

Saulsbury's daughters would mention that their father was in the frequent habit of giving "oyster parties" to his gentlemen friends.[30] The treasure at 55 S. Eden had been stored in a copper jug or pot, wrapped in a man's boot. Saulsbury was known to walk with a limp, and was known to have odd boots made to help alleviate his uneven gait.[31]

What if Saulsbury's frequent "oyster" parties morphed into KGC induction ceremonies late at night? The money then transferred to the out-of-the limelight Mattison home, where it would eventually be buried in the cellar. Captain Mattison no doubt wore boots as the skipper of commercial shipping vessels. And oysters would have been a natural for a man whose life revolved around the nearby Baltimore Harbor. The boot and oyster shells strongly suggest Captain Mattison as the person who buried the coins at 55 S. Eden . . . and the dates on the coins prove it. Not a single coin in the thousands that were uncovered was minted after 1856. Saulsbury did not buy the treasure house until 1865.

Might Saulsbury have helped Mattison to bury the coins? That is for sure a possibility. But the coins belonged to neither man — all signs point to this being strictly gold that was property of The Knights of the Golden Circle. Even the copper pot in which the coins are unearthed is symbolic of the Knights of the Golden Circle. KGC members in the Northern and Border States were often referred to as "Copperheads." Many would wear a large 1850s copper cent affixed to their jackets as a show of loyalty and allegiance.[32] The Masonic-influenced KGC was steeped in ciphers, code, and symbolism.

If the gold had belonged to Mattison, and was being hoarded by the sea captain for his own purposes, we would have expected to see numerous Spanish and Latin American gold and silver pieces in that pot. Mattison traveled and traded extensively in

Cuba, Mexico, Brazil, and other Latin American countries. Yet there was not one single foreign coin in the lot. Not one! On May 29, 1865, the new President of the United States, Andrew Johnson, offered a general amnesty to Confederate troops.[33] Johnson did this barely six weeks after Lee's surrender at Appomattox and Booth's subsequent assassination of Lincoln. Within *days* of Johnson's offer of amnesty, Saulsbury purchases the treasure house from Mattison. With the war over and the immediate pressure now off, ardent Southern sympathizer and tallow chandler Andrew Saulsbury moves into the treasure house and becomes the new keeper of the KGC gold. The dates fit perfectly; they are not mere happenstance.

To quote Augsburger in <u>Treasure in the Cellar</u>, *"The earliest that Saulsbury could have buried it (the coins) would have been in June 1865, and the conflict was over and the White House occupied by a president whose political views were closer to his own."*[34] Precisely! Augsburger is questioning why Saulsbury would bury the coins <u>*after*</u> the war when his "ardent Southern sympathizer" views were less likely to attract the kind of official scrutiny that they did during the war. (Saulsbury's daughter would later recount how Union soldiers had threatened the Saulsburys[35] on more than one occasion while Baltimore was under the grip of martial law and patrolled by federal troops.) Of course, Saulsbury never buried the coins, *Mattison* had done so almost a decade before. What is really going on is that with official hostilities now at an end, the KGC feels more comfortable moving Saulsbury into the treasure home as the new sentinel in charge of the treasure property. To have done so during the war would have been far too risky, given Saulsbury's tendency towards being both brash and outspoken.

Captain Mattison and his wife have already moved just a few blocks east to a smaller home on South Broadway. Captain Stevens, Mattison's tenant, moves to East Baltimore Avenue. The era of Reconstruction had begun. And the aging sea captain, Mattison, would trade his post at his ship's helm for a seat in the boardroom of James Armstrong's American Fire Insurance Company.[36] This is the same James Armstrong who had long been a benefactor to candle executive Andrew Saulsbury. Also the man for whom Saulsbury would name his first-born son — James Armstrong Saulsbury.[37] Saulsbury and Mattison had more than just the treasure house in common. They both knew James

Armstrong, formerly of James Armstrong and Company . . . as well as James Webb and his brother, 33rd-degree Freemason Charles Webb.

All coincidence you still say?

Those 5,000 buried gold coins buried for 78 years in the Mattison/Saulsbury cellar say not.

So, did Saulsbury ever actually see the coins in his cellar? I believe he must have checked on them . . . if only just once. It would have been human nature for Saulsbury to want to verify with his own eyes that Brother Mattison had left the coins as agreed, and in the location that Mattison had described. The first hint that Theodore Jones and Henry Grob got that something was afoot during their 1934 Rinky Dinky Doos dig was that lone $20 gold piece . . . located in the dirt a few inches _above_ the copper treasure pot which was wrapped in a man's boot split lengthwise.[38] When Mattison buried the coins, he would have almost certainly filled the pot upstairs with the treasure, where the captain could naturally see what he was doing. He would have also split the man's boot and wrapped it tightly around the pot _upstairs_, where he could work with adequate lighting and adequate space. Once the coins were secured in the pot, Mattison would have then carried the pot down to the dark, cramped rear cellar for burial. If the odd coin had popped out while lowering the vessel into the hole, it would have likely fallen to the bottom of the hole and been _underneath_ or perhaps beside the pot. This, however, is not what happened.

The stray $20 gold piece found by the boys above the treasure pot is more likely the result of someone — Andrew Saulsbury — uncovering the pot at a later date, very possibly 1865 when the soap and candle executive purchased the Eden Street house from Mattison. Digging down just deep enough to gaze upon the top of the boot, Saulsbury would have probably poked a couple of fingers inside the tightly wrapped and still mostly buried copper vessel . . . enough to feel the coins underneath the split in the leather, and to deftly extract a sample specimen. Satisfied with the $20 gold piece in his hand, Saulsbury must have tossed the gold piece back on top of the boot and quickly filled in the hole.

No one would lay eyes on the treasure again until August 31st, 1934.

Here Comes the Judge

Judge Eugene O'Dunne

In coming to a decision to award the treasure to either the owners of the property at 132 S. Eden Street or the boys who had uncovered the treasure on that property, Judge O'Dunne had two primary considerations:

1. Had Henry Grob and Theodore Jones trespassed on the rear portion of the cellar at the treasure house?

2. In the absence of a Maryland treasure trove law, what other legal precedent existed for awarding the treasure?

Technically, in the very strictest of terms, Henry and Theodore had probably committed an act of trespass when they entered and explored any part of the Eden Street cellar that did not specifically involve the Joneses' storage unit. Storage for the Eden Street tenants was located in the front of the cellar. The boys had originally kept to the front of the cellar, but by late summer had begun to spend time in the rear portion of the cellar.[1]

Whether the rear portion of the cellar had been locked before the boys discovered the treasure was highly doubtful. The Findlay/French lawyers could provide no conclusive proof that the cellar partition was always locked, as had been their claim. The cellar was simply not checked on any consistent basis by the property management team employed by the Findlay/French family.[2] Even more troubling, multiple witnesses who resided in the building testified that the door was almost never locked. One resident went so far as to say the padlock had not been installed until *after* the treasure had been discovered[3] — giving rise to the suspicion that Mr. Kalis or someone else employed by the Findlay/French sisters had attempted to manufacture evidence of trespass.

In reality, Bessie Jones was a paying tenant who lived with her son at the Eden Street address. Henry Grob was an invited guest of the Jones family. For the adolescent Jones and Grob boys to explore common areas of the property would not have been entirely unexpected. Although the boys had not requested specific permission from Mr. Kalis to play in the rear portion of the cellar, no sign had been displayed telling them to KEEP OUT! And it was doubtful that a lock had been placed on the partition door before Grob and Jones had entered the rear portion of the cellar . . . or that the boys had done anything to damage or remove a lock. It was not even 100% clear that any partition yet existed on August 31, 1934[4] when the boys made their highly improbable and miraculous discovery.

So, in practical terms, Grob and Jones had apparently done nothing wrong. In forming their Rinky Dinky Doos Boys' Club, and in endeavoring to bury the cigar box "assets" of said club, resident Theodore Jones and his guest, Henry Grob, were, as lawyer Harry Levin had claimed, "engaged in a lawful enterprise."

So, the teens were in the clear regarding the issue of trespass.

Precedent was an entirely different matter. The Findlay/ French team had naturally argued that as legal owners of the property, the Findlay/French sisters should be entitled to all, or at least part, of any treasure trove discovered on their property. In fact, since the Findlay family interest in the Eden Street address dated back to 1851[5], prior to when the coins could have first possibly been buried (in 1856), who besides the Findlay/French sisters had a better right to that treasure?

Justinian law, as it so happens, backed up the Findlay claim.[6] In ancient Rome, the owner of the property would have the right to demand a 50/50 split with the discoverer(s) of treasure. But English law in more modern times saw treasure reverting to the state — however, with finders receiving monetary compensation commensurate with the value of the treasure discovery. Thus, items of archaeological and historical value would generally be confiscated by the state, with the state then selling those valued artifacts to a museum, and using the funds received from the museum to reward the discoverer(s). In this way, the public would be granted access to see the artifacts on display, the discoverers would be encouraged to come forward with their find and be compensated by the state, and the state could receive income tax assessed against that compensation. Under such guidelines, everyone — except the property owner — would benefit.

Property owners, under English law, were required to prove ownership of the treasure itself. If they could prove ownership, then the discovery would cease being treasure trove. It would be returned to the land owner(s) as simply lost or misplaced property.

The Findlay/French team had offered no evidence that the gold coins were ever property of the Findlay family. For most of the Eden Street property's existence, the family had simply collected an annual ground rent. Someone else had obviously buried the Eden Street treasure.

Scant precedent existed in American legal proceedings regarding the dispensation of treasure trove. But what O'Dunne was able to uncover (with the assistance of the boys' attorney, Harry Levin, who was only too happy to provide the judge with treasure trove precedent), clearly favored the idea of "finders keepers."

Perhaps the most similar case on record involved an 1894 discovery in Oregon by two young farm brothers named Danielson, ages eight and ten.[7] The Danielsons were hired by their neighbors, a Mr. and Mrs. Roberts, to clean out an ancient, trash-filled henhouse on the Roberts' property. The Danielson boys agreed to perform this manual chore for five cents. The brothers used shovels to scoop up the refuse, hauling the trash away by means of a sled. While scooping out the piles of ancient junk, the older Danielson's shovel struck something hard. Calling his younger brother for help, the boys uncovered a rusted, half-gallon can. The can proved too heavy to lift with a shovel, and its lid was too rusted for the children's fingers to pry open. Grabbing a pick, the ten-year old then chopped open the container, revealing a pair of musty, old tobacco sacks.

The boys figured the tobacco sacks were filled with rocks. But when they opened the sacks, they instead spotted gleaming piles of gold coins.

The Danielsons knocked on the Roberts' door, and explained to Mrs. Roberts what they had found. *"Well, let's have it,"* Mrs. Roberts demanded. The boys dutifully scooped up the coins, brought them to the house, and then went back to finish cleaning out the hen house.

Later, upon completion of the job, the Danielsons returned to the Roberts' house for their five cents. Curious about what they had found, the boys asked Mr. Roberts how much money had been in the rusted can.

"Over seven thousand dollars," answered Mr. Roberts. Most adult workers at the time brought home about $400 per year — roughly 22¢ per hour.

"We put the money there some time ago," Mrs. Roberts told the boys. *"We were going to buy something with it. Don't say anything about it, and the Lord will bless you."*

But the boys did say something about it. They told their family, who hired a lawyer and sued the Roberts for the boys' fair share of the treasure.

The case of the Oregon gold coins would make its way through the court system for most of a decade before reaching the Supreme Court of Oregon. In 1904, at which time the Danielson brothers had grown into young men, the court awarded the entire golden treasure trove to the Danielsons, citing old English common law. The judges opined that since the rusted tin can had obviously pre-dated the Roberts purchase of the property, the 40-year old henhouse had pre-dated the Civil War, and that several other parties had owned the property in the interim, the gold coins represented lost treasure. Buried treasure, according to the Oregon lawmakers, should be awarded to its finders — *not* the landowners.

In summary, the judges concluded that, *"Owners of the soil acquire no title to a treasure trove by virtue of their ownership of the land."*

Decisions in other "treasure trove" cases[8] in Maine, Indiana, and once again in Oregon seemed to square with the outcome of

Danielson vs. Roberts. In the United States, when discoverers of treasure trove had committed no transgressions, "finders-keepers" was the rule of the land.

The Findlay/French sisters could not prove ownership of the gold, nor had they ever claimed ownership of the gold. There was also no evidence that their deceased father, Charles Findlay, from whom they had inherited the Eden Street ground rent, might have had any involvement with the buried coins.

The Findlay/French sisters, by sole reason of their ownership of the Eden Street treasure house, did not have a right to the lost gold, which according to the presented evidence constituted treasure trove.

The Rinky Dinky Doos had been engaged in a lawful enterprise at 132 S. Eden Street. They had not trespassed, and so far as the court knew, had done nothing wrong.

Judge Eugene O'Dunne of the Baltimore City Circuit Court was ready to render his decision.

Mobtown USA

Scene from movie *The Gangs of New York*, which
featured 19th-century sectarian violence
similar to Baltimore.

During the mid-nineteenth century, thousands of European
immigrants began flooding through America's port cities. Boston,
New York, Philadelphia, and Baltimore were the main focal points
for this dramatic influx. The newcomers arrived from Ireland,
Germany, Italy, and a mix of other European nations, including
Great Britain.

Baltimore's position in the process of immigration was
particularly unique: According to the *Encyclopedia of American
Immigration* from the Salem Press:

*"Most southern slave-holding states had very low immigration
rates during the first half of the nineteenth century. Their slave-
based economic systems did not offer the same economic
opportunities that the industrializing, non-slave states of the North
could offer to immigrants. However, Maryland, one of the
northernmost southern slave states, was home to an estimated
59,500 immigrants in 1850. This was the largest number of
foreign-born people in any southern state except Louisiana, and it
accounted for nearly 12 percent of Maryland's entire free
population. As in Louisiana, Maryland's early foreign-born*

population was primarily the consequence of mid-nineteenth century immigration from Germany and Ireland; Germans constituted 55 percent of all Maryland immigrants in 1850, and Irish immigrants constituted one-third.

"Maryland's immigrants were heavily concentrated in the port city of Baltimore, where Germans had begun to arrive during the eighteenth century. Irish immigration had been stimulated by Ireland's great potato famine of the 1840's and was supported by job opportunities on the Baltimore-based B&O Railroad. Southwest Baltimore, in particular, became an Irish community during the nineteenth century. Indeed, so great was the railroads' need for immigrant labor that the B&O Railroad itself opened piers for immigration at Locust Point in 1868 that made Baltimore a primary point of entry for immigrants to the United States." [1]

By the 1850s, Baltimore already had more free black residents than any city in the country. Add to that demographic a city now bursting at the seams from European immigration, a city growing in just 30 years from 80,000 to over 200,000[2] — with nearly 25% now foreign born and Catholic.

American-born Baltimoreans naturally began to feel a bit besieged.[3] Poverty was on the rise. Overcrowding, crime, and other social problems had dramatically increased, putting a strain on municipal budgets. Also, the newcomers were usually willing to take increasingly scarce jobs at lower and lower wages. Many politicians catered to the immigrant influx as a source of new votes, resulting in increased corruption and political patronage. Certain classes in the native population began to look upon themselves as being systematically dispossessed and marginalized.

> *"Give me your tired, your poor,*
> *Your huddled masses yearning to breathe free,*
> *The wretched refuse of your teeming shore."*

The sentiments expressed on the famous 20th-century plaque at the Statute of Liberty (not erected until the 1880s) were not exactly embraced by many Baltimore nor American citizens in general during the height of the great mid-19th century influx. One prominent Baltimorean recoiled at the *"horrible multiplications of robberies, and drunkenness, and murders,"* that accompanied the waves of unwashed, uneducated, and largely unwanted peasant immigrants.[4] Francis Walker's contemporary commentary on the situation was even more blunt, observing, "*The new immigrants are beaten men from beaten races, representing the worst failures in the struggle for existence.*" [5]

Such sentiments did not make for a mellow political scene. Predictably, out of this this increasingly confrontational situation was born a new political party, the nativist American Party. The party arose from within a series of secret societies that had sprouted nationally, America-first clubs with names such as the Order of the Star Spangled Banner and the Order of United Americans. Members took a solemn oath to oppose immigrants and to block further immigration. Rank and file was almost exclusively limited to American-born, white Protestant males.[6]

The 1850s demise of the Whig Party and the country's prevailing two-party system created a power vacuum, enabling the American Party to siphon off alienated, frustrated voters. The American Party functioned as a semi-secret organization . . . so secret that when members were asked by outsiders about the group's activities, they answered with the canned response, "*I know nothing.*" The phrase caught on with the general public, which began to refer to the anti-Catholic, anti-foreigner American Party as the *Know Nothings.*[7]

Abraham Lincoln, who during the mid-1850s would abandon the faltering Whigs for the newly formed Republican Party, wrote in an 1855 letter to a colleague his thoughts concerning the increasingly influential American Party:

I am not a Know-Nothing. That is certain. How could I be? How can anyone who abhors the oppression of Negroes, be in favor of degrading classes of white people? Our progress in degeneracy appears to me to be pretty rapid. As a nation, we begin by declaring that "all men are created equal." We now practically read it "all men are created equal, except negroes." When the Know-Nothings get control, it will read "all men are created equal, except Negroes, and foreigners, and Catholics."[8]

No city in America would muster more support for the Know-Nothings than Baltimore. Maryland would come to have a Know-Nothing governor, Thomas Holliday Hicks — and Baltimore would have a Know-Nothing mayor, Thomas Swann. During the 1856

U.S. presidential election, the Know-Nothing candidate, former President Millard Fillmore, would take 21% of the vote nationwide. He would carry only one state, Maryland,[9] due mostly to overwhelming support from Baltimore.

Baltimore's own rising theatrical star, John Wilkes Booth, was said to have dabbled in Know-Nothing politics in his youth.[10]

The Baltimore Know-Nothings would reign from 1854 through 1860. Their grip on power was ensured by gangs of politicized street thugs who patrolled polling stations with an eye towards keeping Catholics, the foreign-born, and other Know-Nothing opponents from casting ballots. Emanating from the local taverns, volunteer firehouses, and assorted hangouts, the nativist gangs sported colorful names such as the Plug Uglies, Rip Raps, Black Snakes, American Rattlers, Tigers, and the author's personal favorite, the Blood Tubs.[11] All of these gangs had been imbued with the idea that immigrants in general should go back where they came from, and that Catholics in particular had been sent here as part of a Papist plot to seize control of their country.

Unfortunately, during the 19th-century, the U.S. voting process did not involve any real level of secrecy. Voters came to the polls, ballot in hand, brightly colored to indicate the party of their choosing. The Know-Nothing ballot was garishly striped, making it easy to spot at a distance. Any voter brave enough — or stupid enough — to approach an American Party-controlled voting facility in a nativist gang stronghold risked harassment, a beating, or worse. Stabbings and shootings were not uncommon. Election riots occurred almost every year during 1850s Baltimore. In 1856 alone, the year Buchanan bested the Republican, Fremont, and the Know Nothing candidate, Fillmore, some 30 Baltimoreans were killed in election-day violence, with over 300 injured.[12] The police, who were often sympathetic to the gangs' anti-immigrant proclivities, or were just plain frightened, conveniently weren't on hand to intervene. Fillmore easily carried Baltimore.

In response, the young men in some of Baltimore's ethnic neighborhoods were quick to form their own highly politicized gangs. Chief among these were the Bloats, the Bloody Eights, and the Buttenders.[13]

Gang members wearing stovepipe hats were not only quick to use their fists, clubs, bricks, and paving stones during a melee . . . but also knives, pistols, and rifles. It was reported that some nativist gangs even towed around the occasional mini-cannon.

The best known and probably most feared of these gangs, the Plug Uglies, were fond of strapping on sharp, needle-like shoemakers' awls and kneeing opposition voters — with the business end of an awl — who might dare to approach a poll carrying the wrong-colored ballot. The group gleefully carried a sign that teased, *"Come up and vote, there is room for awl!"*[14]

Not to be outdone, another Baltimore gang's signature warning was to take a torch to the beards of immigrant men attempting to exercise their constitutional right.[15]

The Blood Tubs, a group of butchers and slaughterhouse workers, delighted in splashing opposition voters with pigs' blood. It was a terrific deterrent to other immigrants who might see a fellow neighbor just returning from the polling place covered in blood and gore.[16]

In their quest to swing election-day tallies in their favor, the Baltimore gangs were not simply content to keep opposition voters away from the polls. Voter fraud was rampant. The most extreme and bizarre form of this was a practice known as "cooping." Days before an election, gang members would patrol the streets looking for Catholics and other immigrants going about their daily business. The gangs would snatch these men, often in broad daylight, and hustle them to a waiting cellar or shed. There the victims, often imprisoned a dozen or more at a time, would be beaten and then forced to consume large amounts of alcohol or drugs. On Election Day, the gangs would cart around their stupefied victims from polling place to polling place, forcing them to repeatedly turn in the Know Nothing Party's striped ballot.[17]

Some researchers believe that famed horror author Edgar Allan Poe may have been the victim of an election week "cooping." In the fall of 1849, the 40-year old Poe was found unconscious in a Baltimore gutter — on Election Day — never to reawaken. This American literary giant would pass away four days later in an institution located only a few short blocks from Eden Street. Poe had been on his way to be married, taking a train north from Richmond with a stopover in Baltimore. Poe, known for his fondness of drink, disappeared after having patronized a Baltimore tavern. The popular storyteller was reportedly spotted in various parts of town, wearing unfamiliar clothing and looking befuddled and confused. Members of Poe's family certainly suspected he had been slipped a mickey and "cooped."[18] The celebrated master of the suspenseful short-story was buried in Baltimore. For several decades, a mysterious "Poe Toaster" appeared every year at Poe's gravesite in the early morning hours of January 19th, Poe's birthday, dressed in black with a white scarf and wide-brimmed hat. The elusive figure would pour a glass of cognac, raise a toast to the literary master, and then vanish into the darkness, leaving behind an unfinished bottle of cognac and three red roses.[19]

By the end of the 1850s, the citizenship of Baltimore was done with the thugs, the violence, the fear, and the sham elections. An investigation was ordered after the "contested" 1859 election, which included a survey of individual Baltimore voters on their experience at the polls. The following registered responses from that survey are part of the U.S. Congressional record: [20]

"Cooped in the 2nd Ward and made to vote four times."
"Knocked down and beaten."
"Ruffians tore up my ticket."
"Made to vote the Know-Nothing ticket."
"Pulled away by the neck often."
"Driven from polls."
"Ruffians in full possession of polls and protected by police."
"Forcibly taken from home and compelled to vote against sentiments."
"Ticket torn up after being passed through window."
"Forced to vote the American ticket though not a citizen."
"Unwilling to make an attempt."
"Four balls put in my house. Afraid."
"Election a mockery."
"Useless."
"Wounded."
"Stabbed."
"Beat away from polls."
"Polls obstructed."
"Immediately driven off."
"Papers taken away."
"Prevented."
"Permission not granted."
"Dare not attempt."
"Compelled to vote against will."
"Struck with awl."

"Cooped from Saturday till Wednesday, forced to vote American ticket."
"Confined to house with 215 others."
"Forced to vote against sentiments with pistol pointed at him."

In some wards, the 1859 voting appears to have proceeded in relative normalcy. People either voted with no difficulty, or were simply absent on Election Day. In other city Baltimore wards, 20, 30, and sometimes 40 consecutive surveyed voters check off either "violence" or "intimidation" as their reason for not having cast a ballot.

Clearly, wholesale change was need in Baltimore — and change is what they would get, with help from the Maryland state legislature.

By 1860, a reform ticket was organized by a "Committee of Twenty" concerned influential Baltimore citizens. This Democratic committee put forth a new mayoral candidate, George William Brown, whose job it would be to take back City Hall. And a new marshal, George Proctor Kane, whose job it would be to take back the streets from the hooligans.

The reform movement was spearheaded by Charles Webb,[21] past Grand Master of the Maryland Freemasons . . . and a senior partner at the soap and candle manufacturing firm of James Armstrong & Co.

But by 1861, with George William Brown and Marshal George P. Kane at the helm only a few short months, Baltimore's public enemy number one would no longer be the Plug Uglies, the Rip Raps, nor the Blood Tubbers. The brewing War Between the States would take precedence over all other civic matters. And the new public-enemy number one in the Monumental City would be a bearded, menacing, stovepipe hat wearing individual of an altogether different variety — President-elect Abraham Lincoln from Illinois and his band of meddling Northern "Black Republican" abolitionists. For this upstart Baltimore public enemy came equipped with the awesome might of the United States federal government and its powerful Union army.

Would Maryland bow to federal pressure and stay with the Union? Or would she secede like her fellow Southern states and join the rebel Confederacy of Jeff Davis?

Soon, the city known as "Mobtown"[22] would be thrust front and center into the national spotlight. The future of Maryland —

and of all America — would be partially determined by the actions of the "Know-Nothing" Governor Thomas H. Hicks, Baltimore's Mayor George William Brown, and Marshal George P. Kane. And all three men were associated with soap and candle manufacturer Charles Webb of James Armstrong & Co. — whose fellow candle executives Andrew Saulsbury and Thomas Armstrong will each come to have a fortune in gold coins buried beneath their respective residences.

Mobtown, where for years there had been *room for awl*, was about to get a taste of an unexpectedly different brand of 19th-century violence.

Harpers Ferry

John Brown, militant abolitionist.

In a society that permits slave ownership, one of the greatest fears of the masters is slave insurrection . . . of slaves rising up and taking arms against the slave owners. The United States of the nineteenth century was no exception.

During a late 1700s debate in the Continental Congress over how to tax slaves, one South Carolina delegate and slave owner challenged the notion that his slaves should be taxed at a different rate from his other property . . . such as land, sheep, cattle, and horses. Ben Franklin, both a Quaker and an abolitionist, wryly replied that, "*Slaves rather weaken than strengthen the state, and there is some difference between them and sheep. Sheep will never make an insurrection.*"[1]

Franklin's observation would prove horribly true for many of the French slaveholders in the Caribbean sugar-producing colony of Saint-Domingue, today the Republic of Haiti. The slaveholders of that land used brutal repression to keep control over their African slaves, who outnumbered their masters more than 10:1. On the heels of the French Revolution, in 1791, some 100,000 of the island's slaves rose up against their well-armed but badly outnumbered owners. Within weeks, approximately 4,000 French citizens would be slaughtered in what Jack R. Censer and Lynn Hunt in Liberty, Equality, and Fraternity would describe as revenge through "*pillage, rape, torture, mutilation, and death.*"[2]

Maximilien de Robespierre would subsequently abolish the institution of slavery throughout the French Empire. However, when Napoleon Bonaparte seized power, he would attempt to reinstitute slavery in Saint-Domingue — but fail. By 1804, the slaves were fully in control, resulting in one last violent purge of the remaining "blancs." The Haitian Revolution was history's only slave revolt that led to the actual founding of a new state. For more than a century, whites would not be permitted, by law, to own land in the Republic of Haiti.[3]

The largest American slave insurgency occurred in the Territory of Orleans in 1811.[4] Approximately 100 enslaved men, armed mostly with hand tools, marched from the countryside towards the city of New Orleans. Along the way they were joined by other slaves, their number growing quickly to as many as 300-500. After two days of burning crops and plantation houses, the marchers were stopped by a hastily formed militia. Some 95 participants were either executed after trail or killed in the confrontation with the armed defenders. Dozens more insurgents were hunted down and shot in the following weeks. Two militia members were also killed.

The bloodiest, most shocking United States uprising occurred in Virginia in 1831.[5] A former runaway slave named Nat Turner, nicknamed "The Prophet" because he gave frequent biblical readings, took a solar eclipse as a sign from God to begin a revolt. Gathering up dozens of local followers, the conspirators silently crept from plantation house to plantation house, killing 60 Virginians of all ages with the use of knives, hatchets, axes, and clubs. Before he was hung, Turner admitted he had wanted to spread "terror and alarm" amongst whites. He was so successful in his goal that the Virginia legislature briefly considered the possibility of abolishing slavery. Instead, the limited freedoms of all Southern blacks, slave or not, were severely curtailed as the South grew increasingly more vigilant with regards to insurrection.

The increased activity of the Underground Railroad only served to further enrage Southern slaveholders. Free blacks, escaped slaves, and white abolitionists colluded to guide runaway slaves north to freedom. Harriet Tubman, after escaping to Philadelphia with her family, would return to Maryland's Eastern Shore on numerous occasions to guide some 70 people across the Mason-Dixon line[6] — hiding by day in woods or in safe houses, and traveling at night by moonlight. Tubman, nicknamed "Moses" for leading so many people to freedom, was aided by her friend, Baltimore's Frederick Douglass, and by white abolitionists such as Quaker Thomas Garrett in Delaware and newspaper editor William Lloyd Garrison.

Out west, famed detective Allan Pinkerton would go to work for Chicago abolitionist leaders. Pinkerton's Dundee, Illinois log cabin was used as a stopover for the Great Lakes region's Underground Railroad.[7]

When the South was successful in getting the odious 1850 Fugitive Slave Laws passed, which legally obligated Northerners to return runaway slaves, the Underground Railroad simply extended its routes up to Canada.

The more that signs appeared signaling changes were coming, the more the slaveholding states resisted.

In 1854, with the nation expanding westward, the Kansas-Nebraska Act called for the Kansas Territory to decide through "popular sovereignty" whether it would become a free soil or slave state.[8] That meant settlers would decide the issue by popular vote. Soon, proslavery forces from bordering Missouri, known as the Border Ruffians,[9] began flooding into Kansas in order to sway the vote. Northern abolitionists countered by sending their own "free-state" men armed with Sharps rifles.[10] Amongst the abolitionists was a man named John Brown, who had come at the urging of his grown sons, who had preceded Brown in Kansas and had written to their father in Ohio asking for assistance. The free-state men were being outnumbered and intimidated by the Ruffians. On May 21, 1856, the Border Ruffians burned the free-state town of Lawrence,[11] destroying newspaper offices and ransacking businesses and homes. The raid would become known as the Lawrence Massacre as well as "Quantrill's Raid." A few days later, Republican Senator Charles Sumner took to the Senate floor where he lambasted his pro-slavery colleagues for what he described as "The Crime Against Kansas." Shortly thereafter, Sumner was nearly beaten to death for his speech by cane-wielding South Carolina Congressman Preston Brooks.[12] News of the violence in both Kansas and in Congress shook the country.

On the evening of May 24, 1856, longtime abolitionist John Brown gathered his sons and a small group of followers armed with broadswords. At the small proslavery settlement along the Pottawatomie Creek, Brown's group began dragging pro-slavery men from their cabins . . . and hacked five of the Southerners to pieces. The "Pottawatomie Massacre"[13] would escalate the regional violence into a nearly all-out war, prompting *New York Tribune* editor Horace Greeley to coin the term "Bleeding Kansas."[14]

In retaliation, Major General John Reid of Missouri would cross into Kansas with 300 armed recruits, heading for the free-state settlements at Osawatomie. After the Missourians had killed one of Brown's sons and a neighbor, Brown organized a counterattack despite having only 40 fighters. Caught by surprise, Reid suffered heavy casualties, including 20 killed and many more wounded. The Missourians eventually chased Brown's men away and sacked their settlement. Despite losing their outpost, the outgunned Osawatomie men were hailed as heroes to many Northerners, and John Brown became the fighting champion of the nation's abolitionists.[15]

In September 1856, another bloody showdown between Brown's free-state men and the Border Ruffians was averted when the new territorial governor offered clemency to all combatants on both sides. Brown and his three remaining sons used the ceasefire as a chance to head back East, with Brown seeking more funds and arms from sympathetic Northern abolitionists.[16] Brown, his sons, and his participating followers were never charged with the murders of the five Missourians.

The territorial dispute in Kansas would drag on until 1861, when Kansas would finally be admitted into the Union as a free state. One of the primary pro-slavery belligerents was the Missourian William Quantrill, a reputed member of the Knights of the Golden Circle.[17] Quantrill was also the leader of a feared guerilla band known as Quantrill's Raiders. During the Civil War, Quantrill's Raiders, led by Quantrill and his lieutenant, "Bloody" Bill Anderson, would "bushwhack" Union forces as well as several pro-Union settlements. They were best known for the infamous

"Lawrence Massacre" of 1863, during which many pro-Union men were executed in front of their families.[18]

One of Quantrill's young guerilla fighters was a Missouri teen named Jesse James.[19] James would use Quantrill's guerilla tactics to rob trains, banks, and stagecoaches after the war. The motives behind James' life of crime are still the subject of much debate.

Back in the North, the increasingly militant John Brown got busy working his wealthy abolitionist backers for support. Although many of these men professed to believe strictly in non-violence, Brown had done a good job convincing the pacifists that conflict with the South was, unfortunately, inevitable — and that allowing slavery to continue was intolerable. They reluctantly agreed, sometimes not wanting to know the particulars of the kind of tactics John Brown had in mind.[20] Simply talking about the problem had gotten America nowhere. John Brown was willing to do more than just talk . . . much more.

In 1858, Brown made one final journey back to Kansas. At first Brown accompanied another free-soil leader who had been making retaliatory raids into Missouri. Then, Brown organized his own border incursion into Missouri, freeing 11 slaves, taking two white slavers prisoner, and looting the Border Ruffians' horses and wagons in the process.[21] Later, Brown would guide the 11 now fugitive slaves to freedom in Ontario.[22] While passing through Chicago on his journey northward, Brown met with Allan Pinkerton, private eye and fellow abolitionist. Pinkerton arranged and paid for the illicit group's ferry ride to Canada.[23]

1n 1859, and now funded by a wealthy "Secret Six" cabal of the nation's preeminent, moneyed abolitionists,[24] Brown plotted his next move — a raid on the federal arsenal at Harpers Ferry, Virginia. Brown was ready to bring the fight to the South's home turf. With the weaponry stolen from the arsenal, Brown would attempt to lead a slave uprising that would force the South to abandon, once and for all, the shameful institution of slavery.

Using the alias Isaac Smith, Brown rented a farmhouse just across the Potomac in nearby Washington County, Maryland. Brown was joined by 20 of his fellow raiders, 15 white and five black. The Northern abolitionist donors quietly sent 198 breech-loading Sharps carbines. Brown, meanwhile, contracted to have nearly 1,000 pikes manufactured for the cause.[25] Longtime friend Frederick Douglass of Baltimore backed out, warning Brown that an attack on a federal installation would "*array the whole country against us.*" Harriet "Moses" Tubman, hiding out in Montreal, was unable to participate for health reasons.[26]

Brown believed that with the nearly 100,000 muskets and rifles they would steal from the arsenal, the group could march south through the countryside striking fear into the hearts of slaveholders. He fully expected the revolt to "go viral" with hundreds of slaves joining the insurgents within the first 24 hours,[27] and new armed bands being dispersed daily throughout the South to make guerilla warfare on the slaveholders.

On Sunday evening, October 16, 1859 the raiders struck. They grabbed some hostages in town and from surrounding areas, most notably Colonel Lewis Washington, a great-grandnephew of George Washington. The raiders also confiscated the first President's swords and pistols, as Brown believed the possession of such sacred objects would give his group divine protection.[28]

Seizing the lightly-guarded armory was easy. The raiders were also careful to cut the telegraph wires to prevent early news of the raid from bringing federal reinforcements.

Things began to go wrong when Brown's men stopped a B&O train passing through Harpers Ferry. When the train's baggage handler unexpectedly confronted the raiders, he was shot dead. The first casualty of the conflict, this duty-bound railroad employee, had ironically been a free black man.[29]

The train was able to continue, and soon the conductor had alerted nearby authorities to a robbery in progress. Townspeople from Harpers Ferry, including local militias from both Virginia and Maryland, began to take up arms against the attackers. By morning, several nearby gun-toting farmers had joined the armed townspeople and the local Virginian and Maryland militias. Once the militias were able to secure the bridge leading back across the Potomac River into Maryland, Brown's avenue of escape vanished. He quickly moved his hostages and remaining men inside a small adjoining fire engine house, where the raiders wasted no time in barricading themselves securely inside. What had begun as a raid had now morphed into a no-win siege.[30]

Brown eventually sent out one of his sons, Watson, and another man to negotiate with militia leaders. Although the pair came waving a white flag, the men were met with gunfire. Watson was shot and killed, and the other raider wounded and placed under arrest.[31]

Later, when one of the raiders attempted a daring escape, he was shot and killed while swimming back across the Potomac. Another firefight then broke out, and yet another Brown son, Oliver, was mortally wounded. The militia men then succeeded in breaking into a guardhouse and freeing some of the hostages. But Brown, his men, and the remaining hostages still remained holed up inside the engine house.[32]

When news of the attack reached President Buchanan at the White House, Buchanan immediately called out the U.S. Marines. In one of history's great ironies, the officer selected to lead the rescue of the federal arsenal was Virginia's Colonel Robert E. Lee. Lee arrived with a detachment of some 88 Marines. He instructed his lieutenant to offer John Brown the option of surrendering peacefully so that Brown's remaining men might be men spared.[33] Brown, having already watched two of his sons die, defiantly refused.

Soon after, Lee and his men used a long wooden ladder to break down the doors to the engine house. Within a few short moments, all of the remaining raiders were either killed or captured. John Brown was taken alive, although badly wounded as the result of being struck with a saber.[34]

The abolitionist threat now had a face . . . the stern, bearded, unforgiving face of old John Brown. To the majority of abolitionists, Brown was a hero. To the South, he was the bogeyman, the encroacher, the embodiment of evil, and everything they feared.

Not all abolitionists, however, immediately supported Brown's extreme action. Some agreed with Frederick Douglass' pre-raid assessment that the attack on Harper's Ferry, essentially a suicide mission, would *"array the whole country against us."*[35]

William Lloyd Garrison, editor of the abolitionist newspaper *The Liberator*, a co-founder of the American Anti-Slavery Society, and a stalwart voice calling for the immediate emancipation of all slaves, harshly denounced the operation as "misguided, wild, and apparently insane."[36]

The rising anti-slavery Republican politician from Illinois, Abraham Lincoln, seemed entirely bewildered by the incident. *"John Brown's effort was peculiar,"* Lincoln observed. *"It was not a slave insurrection. It was an attempt by white men to get up a revolt among slaves, in which the slaves refused to participate."* [37]

But essayist and philosopher Henry David Thoreau, defending Brown, wrote, "*I think that for once the Sharp's rifles and the revolvers were employed in a righteous cause . . . he (Brown) has the spark of divinity in him.*" [38]

Allan Pinkerton, himself a man of action, heaped accolades on Brown and his war on slavery. Supposedly Pinkerton told his son, Willy, to "*Look well upon that man . . . he is greater than Napoleon, and perhaps just as great as George Washington.*" [39]

Opinion across the nation was extremely and bitterly divided. According to Bill Friedheim at the Borough of Manhattan Community College, "*Depending upon the viewpoint, editorials (at that time) used the partisan vocabulary of 'saint,' 'crusader,' 'martyr,' 'madman,' 'devil,' 'lunatic,' and 'murderer.'*" [40]

Predictably, old man Brown used his trial as a platform to point an accusatory finger at slavery. "*Now, if it is deemed necessary that I should forfeit my life for the furtherance of the ends of justice and mingle my blood further with the blood of my children and with the blood of millions in the slave country whose rights are disregarded by wicked, cruel, and unjust enactments — I say, let it be done!*" [41]

During a jailhouse interview given to a reporter, old John Brown would warn, "*You had better — all you people at the South — prepare yourselves for a settlement of this question, that must come up for settlement sooner than you are prepared for it. The sooner you are prepared the better. You may dispose of me very easily, — I am nearly disposed by now; but this question is still to be settled, — this negro question I mean; the end of that is not yet.*" [42]

Brown, of course, would be convicted and sentenced to hang. On December 2, 1859, the date on which Brown would be brought to the gallows, the abolitionist would make one final prediction . . . more bloodshed.

"*I John Brown am now quite certain that the crimes of this guilty land will never be purged away, but with Blood. I had . . . vainly flattered myself that without very much bloodshed, it might be done.*" [43]

John Brown became a national martyr on that day in 1859. And as the old abolitionist had predicted, the settlement of the question came up sooner than the South, or the rest of the nation, was prepared for. And it was settled with far more bloodshed than perhaps even old Brown himself could have imagined. By early

1861, scarcely more than a year after John Brown was hanged by the neck until he was dead for the crimes of murder and treason, Union troops would be marching into battle to the tune of *John Brown's Body.*

John Brown's body lies a mouldering in the grave,
John Brown's body lies a mouldering in the grave,
John Brown's body lies a mouldering in the grave.
His soul's marching on!

Chorus.

Glory Hally, Hallelujah! Glory Hally, Hallelujah! Glory
Hally, Hallelujah!
His soul's marching on!

One of the added stanzas the Union soldiers would sing would include reference to hanging Confederate leader Jeff Davis from a tree. Fellow abolitionist Julia Howe, upon hearing Union soldiers singing the *John Brown* song, would pen her immortal words to *The Battle Hymn of the Republic,* which are still sung to the same melody as *John Brown's Body.*[44]

Meanwhile, Virginia authorities, concerned about a last-minute abolitionist attempt to free John Brown, ordered exceedingly tight security for Brown's execution. No civilians were allowed to attend. Some 1,500 armed soldiers and militia men were ordered to stand guard against any desperate move to rescue the old man.[45]

No last-ditch attempt was made. In the South, people rejoiced. Up North, solemn church bells tolled.

"He done more in dying than 100 men would in living," observed Brown's friend, Harriet Tubman. *"I could live for the slave,"* added Frederick Douglass. *"But he could die for him."* [46]

One of the attendees to John Brown's hanging was a young actor named John Wilkes Booth. Since, for security reasons, only military personnel were in attendance, it has been speculated that Booth had signed on for a brief stint with the Virginia militia — or had signed on as a volunteer with the paramilitary Richmond Grays.[47] Booth had been a member of a Richmond actors' group at that time. Others have postulated that Booth simply talked someone into letting him borrow a uniform.

Regardless, John Wilkes Booth was undoubtedly present for the execution. He was spotted close to the gallows, standing nearby Major Thomas Jonathan Jackson — soon to become renowned as General "Stonewall" Jackson.[48]

Initially, Booth celebrated the execution of Brown, the arch-enemy of all pro-slavery Southerners. From Booth's own diary, as quoted in John Brown Abolitionist: The Man Who Killed Slavery, Sparked the Civil War, and Seeded Civil Rights by David Reynolds, *"I looked at the traitor and terrorizer with unlimited, undeniable contempt."*[49]

But upon reflection, Booth's view of Brown softened as he considered Brown's zeal, commitment, and ultimately his courage in the face of death. Later, according to James Cross Giblin in Good Brother, Bad Brother: The Story of Edwin Booth and John Wilkes Booth, the actor would tell his sister, Asia, *"(John Brown) was a brave man; his heart must have been broken when he felt himself deserted at the gallows."* [50]

Although Brown and Booth could not have been further apart on the political spectrum, Booth must have sensed a kindred spirit in the old martyred warrior. Both men were unabashedly outspoken, fiercely passionate in their beliefs, and seemingly unwilling to compromise. Certainly both were quick to anger, quick to confront, and ultimately willing to use deadly violence if their cherished causes were threatened.

After Brown's execution, Booth remained in Charles Town, site of both the trial and hanging. Further proof of Booth's growing fascination with John Brown would surface when Booth befriended Major Lewis Washington, who had been taken hostage by Brown and his men. For when Booth finally left Charles Town several days later, he did so in possession of John Brown's own pike, a gift from Colonel Washington.

According to Nora Titone in My Thoughts Be Bloody, *"This descendant of a founding father — who survived his kidnapping by John Brown — presented young Booth with the murderous spear Brown had used when making his last stand. Asia (Booth's sister in Philadelphia) saw the inscription 'Major Washington to J. Wilkes Booth' inked on the weapon's wooden shaft. . . . The youth who had played in the Maryland forests with a lance from the Mexican War now had his own memento of military service. Asia leaves a sad account of John exaggerating the details of his service with The Grays. He let his sister believe he had been 'one of the party going to search for and capture John Brown,' not simply a guard* at the hanging." [51]

John Brown had taken Major Lewis Washington hostage, partly so he could gain possession of George Washington's pistols and swords, which he considered talismans that might help protect his ill-fated raid of Harpers Ferry. After Brown's hanging, young Booth — Lincoln's eventual assassin — then acquirers the martyred crusader's spear as a talisman of Brown's own courage and power.

Historians generally agree that John Brown's raid on Harpers Ferry was a major catalyst, a prelude — perhaps even the opening act — to the American Civil War.

Little more than five years later, the nationally acclaimed stage performer, Baltimorean John Wilkes Booth, would provide the shocking grand finale to the most terrible of wars in United States history.

The nagging question which will always haunt the events of April 14, 1865 is this . . . just how much help did Booth have from his fellow Confederates?

And, just how high up the chain of the rebel command did the conspiracy go?

Grand Masters of the 33rd Degree

Baltimore's 19th Century Masonic Temple.

In 1810, Charles Webb, Sr. emigrated from Portsmouth, England to Baltimore and soon after went into the business of manufacturing soap and candles. When Webb emigrated, little did he know that in just four years, he'd be helping to defend his adopted country against his native country . . . Webb was stationed at Fort McHenry during the bombardment by the British Fleet in 1814.[1]

Webb's soap and candle factory, located on Ensor Street in Baltimore, was enlarged and expanded over the years. Webb would eventually bring his two sons, Charles, Jr. and James, into the family business, which became known as Charles Webb & Sons.[2]

In 1816, Brother Webb was made a Mason in St. John's Lodge, No. 34. By 1821 he would be elected Master of that lodge, serving in that position for several years. According to The History of Freemasonry in Maryland by Edward Schultz, the senior Webb was an active and zealous Mason. [3]

Not only did the Webb sons follow their father into the soap and candle business, inheriting the factory upon their father's passing in 1849 — but they also followed Charles Webb, Sr. into a lifelong association with Freemasonry. Both were made Masons at their father's lodge, St. John's No. 34 of Baltimore.[4]

Son James would also rise to the position of Master at Lodge No. 34, as well as Fidelity Lodge No. 137. James Webb would, in addition, become involved in the public affairs of the City of Baltimore, and at various times "was appointed to positions of honor under the city government."[5] One of those positions happened to be as a member of the Second Branch of Baltimore City Council, a position also held by friend and fellow tallow chandler, Andrew J. Saulsbury.

But it is the other Webb son and candle magnate, Charles Webb, Jr., who would experience an unprecedented, meteoric rise through the ranks of Maryland Freemasonry. According to John Thomas Scharf's late 19th-century book The History of Baltimore City and County, Maryland, Charles Webb, Jr. . . .

". . . has held several positions of important trust, among them that of director in the Baltimore and Ohio Railroad, to which he was elected by the Reform Council of 1860. In 1845 he became a member of St. John's Lodge of Freemasons, and shortly after his admission he was elected to one of it chairs. He continued to ascend in regular order until he reached the highest office which the lodge could confer upon him. In 1853 he was chosen Grand Master by the Grand Lodge of Maryland, and held that position until 1858, when he declined a re-election. His advance in Masonry was more rapid than that of any man of his time. When the office of Grand Master was conferred upon him he was the youngest man who had ever filled the position, and the older heads feared he was too young for its responsible duties were agreeably surprised to find that he presided with firmness and dignity. . . .There has been no time when the assemblages of the Grand Lodge were more harmonious or the landmarks adhered to more rigidly than during his administration." [6]

Webb's political allegiances are also documented in The History of Baltimore City and County, Maryland. According to that publication, Webb's . . .

". . . earliest political affiliations were with the Old-Line Whig Party, but when that party allied itself with the Know-Nothing organization, Mr. Webb's ideas of the nature and destiny of this government were too broad to allow him to continue his connection with it, and he became its active opponent in the ranks of the Democratic Party. He believed that the State ought not to have any connection with religious sects, that both ought to be free from such entangling and perplexing alliances, and, moreover, that this country needed engrafted upon it a hardy foreign emigration, and should be the asylum for the oppressed of every nation."[7]

Elegant words for sure, but they are still meant to put a "spin" on the real circumstances surrounding the chaotic situation of 1856-1860 Baltimore and Mr. Webb's participation in that frenetic political mosaic.

The Whig Party was a 19th-century American political faction that strongly favored business interests, and looked to modernize the country through the employment of a market-oriented economy.[8] Four American presidents (William Henry Harrison, John Tyler, Zachary Taylor, and Millard Fillmore) were elected under the Whig banner. The Whigs, who saw themselves as the "anti-tyranny" party — "Whig" being a name patriots used to refer to themselves during The War for Independence — sought for government to whole-heartedly support rapid industrial and economic growth in the United States. They strongly believed in the value of the good, old-fashioned American "Protestant work ethic." It's not hard to see how a competitive business owner such as Webb would have been attracted to the go-getter ideals of such a party. Many of today's so-called "Tea Party" members would have been drawn to the Whigs if alive in that time period. The Whigs were often criticized for their "aristocratic pretentions" and their lack of empathy for the poor and those members of society who had proven to be less competitive.

Where the Whig party went the way of the dinosaur was during the tempestuous 1850s. The Whigs were blindsided by increasingly divisive national issues of prohibition, nativism, and most especially, the question of slavery.[9] The Compromise of 1850 brought the issue of slavery strongly to the fore. Most northern Whigs saw slavery as being incompatible with the ideal of a free-market, free-labor economy.[10] Most upper-crust, business-oriented Whigs from the South were, not surprisingly, slave owners. After a string of political defeats, the northern Whigs (such as Lincoln) began drifting towards the newly formed Republican Party, or even the Constitutional Union Party. The southern Whigs gravitated to the short-lived, nativist American Party . . . which also drew members from north of the Mason-Dixon Line.

The American Party, also known as the Know-Nothings, was a law-and-order party looking to clamp down on crime, alcohol, and the problems caused by the 1850s flood of immigrants, often Catholic, from countries such as Ireland and Germany.[11] The Know-Nothings sought to have only native-born Americans elected or appointed to office. They feared that immigrant Catholics had been flooding the polling places with non-citizens . . . mostly those who owned their allegiance to the Pope in Rome, and not to the President of the United States in Washington, D.C. The moniker "Know Nothing" originated with the party's secretive members who, when asked about their group's activities, had been trained to reply simply, "*I know nothing.*" The phrase soon stuck with those outside of the organization.[12]

Baltimore, a decidedly Southern leaning town in a slave-owning border state, was ground zero for the Know Nothing movement. The city, long a Catholic beachhead in the United States, had been the recipient of wave after wave of Irish and German immigration. In 1856, when former Whig President Millard Fillmore ran for re-election as the standard-bearer for the American Party, winning 23% of the popular vote nationwide, he carried only one state — Maryland — and soundly trounced all opposition within the Baltimore city limits.[13] During the late 1850s, Baltimore would have a Know-Nothing mayor, and Maryland a Know-Nothing governor. The mayoral elections of 1856, 1857, and 1858 would all be marred by voting-day violence, with Baltimore living up to its "Mobtown" reputation.

The Know-Nothing nativists, however, would eventually succumb to the same divisions as the Whigs . . . most notably on the subject of slavery.[14] Those from the South wholly supporting slavery, while party members from the North being largely opposed.

So when Grand Master Charles Webb of James Armstrong & Co. abandons the sinking Whig ship, he is invited to climb aboard the passing S.S. Know Nothing, but decides instead to book passage with the Democrats, there is strong logic behind his decision.

First, Webb cannot stomach the violence and corruption that seems to be endemic within the Know Nothing organization in Maryland . . . most particularly within Baltimore, as evidenced by their election-day use of the Plug Uglies and other assorted ruffians.

Second, when Webb bypasses the Know Nothings and joins the Southern Democrats he is backing the group that is most stridently pro-slavery, anti-abolition, anti-Republican, and most assuredly anti-Lincoln. Webb is throwing his lot in with the party of Stephen Douglas and Vice-president John C. Breckinridge.[15]

Specifically, in 1859-1860 and beyond, Grand Master Webb will be in league with the Baltimore secessionists. The History of Baltimore City and County, Maryland continues:

"Mr. Webb took an active part, therefore, in the reform movement of 1859 which resulted in the election of George William Brown mayor of the city of Baltimore, and was one of the celebrated committee of twenty, representing the Seventh Ward, who had charge of and managed that campaign to the successful result of re-establishing order and law in Baltimore."[16]

More to the point, law and order would be established by the newly installed reform chief of police, Marshal George Proctor Kane. Kane would soon report directly to Mayor Brown and also to the Democratic Reform Council in charge of straightening out the corrupt mess and the chaotic violence left by the previous administration — an administration which had been under the control of the Know-Nothing incompetents.[17]

As the nation stumbled headlong into war, Baltimore's two new leading political figures — Mayor George W. Brown and Marshal George P. Kane — had come to power largely thanks to tallow chandler/Masonic Grand Master Charles Webb and his fellow band of reform-minded kingmakers. Brown and most especially Kane would shortly become two of the most controversial figures in Baltimore history.

Charles Webb's rise to power in the Freemasons is most interesting, largely due to the connections and associations he would form as a result of that well-known but little understood fraternal group. At just 33, Webb would become the youngest Maryland Freemason to have assumed the title of Grand Master. A key figure in Maryland Freemasonry in the period of Webb's ascension to Grand Master (1845-1853) was the future Maryland governor, Thomas Holliday Hicks.[18] Hicks had been inducted into the Maryland Freemasons in 1826 . . . when Charles Webb, Jr. was just six years old. In 1849, Hicks would be named Maryland's Deputy Grand Master of Freemasonry.[19] Surely Hicks and the rising young star in Maryland Freemasonry, Charles Webb, were well acquainted.

Hicks, the future Governor of Maryland, would go down in history with Brown and Kane as three of Maryland's most controversial political figures. These three men — Hicks, Brown, and Kane — would have substantial influence upon Maryland's precarious national standing at the dawn of the Civil War. Grand Master Charles Webb of the firm of James Armstrong & Co. was associated with *all three* individuals.

But the most interesting association by far is the 1853 selection of one Albert Pike as a "companion" Mason to newly inducted Grand Master Charles Webb and the Maryland Freemasons.[20] By 1859, Albert Pike would become the Sovereign Grand Commander of the Scottish Rite's Southern Jurisdiction of the United States, a post he would hold for some 32 years. Pike was arguably the more influential, and perhaps the most controversial and enigmatic, Freemason of his time on the entire planet.

Albert Pike, in 1853 the Freemason Grand Master of Arkansas, travelled to Baltimore to be "anointed" as a companion Mason to young Webb and his Maryland grand lodge. Presumably, Webb would have presided over the ceremony that granted Pike his "companion" status. Perhaps the "old heads" who had been so worried about a 33-year old assuming the helm of the Maryland Freemasons figured Webb was going to need more than a little help. A total of six Masons were named as "companion" Masons in 1853. Only one, however — Pike — seems to have been recruited from out of state:[21]

LIST OF ELECTED GRAND OFFICERS

	GRAND MASTERS.	DEPUTY GRAND MASTERS	SENIOR GRAND WARDENS.
1841	Benjamin C. Howard	Charles Gilman......	William Denny......
1842	Charles Gilman.	Anthony Kimmell...	" " ......
1043	" "	" "	Thomas Hayward...
1844	" "	" "	" " ....
1845	" . "	Hugh Ely...........	J. R. W. Dunbar.....
1846	" "	" "	Daniel A. Piper......
1847	" "	John D. Readel.....	M. Topham Evans...
1848	" "	" "	Charles Goodwin....
1849	Charles H. Chr.	Thomas H. Hicks...	Enoch S. Courtney..
1850	" "	Simeon Alden........	Jacob H. Medairy....
1851	" "	John D. Readel.....	Charles Webb......
1852	John D. Readel....	John F. Hopkins....	Lawrence Sangston..
1853	Charles Webb.......	William Denny......	Edward T. Owens..
1854	" "	Edward T. Owens...	J. M. S. Maccubbin..
1855	" "	" "	George I. Kennard...
1856	James A. McKenney.	John S. Berry........	James Bruster........
1857	Charles Webb	Anthony Kimmel....	William McClymont.
1858	Charles Goodwin....	John J. Heckart.....	William Campbell...
1859	Anthony Kimmell...	John Coates.........	John L. Yeates .....
1860	John S. Berry........	Nicholas Brewer.....	Samuel M. Haller....
1861	" "	" "	W. L. W. Seabrook..
1862	John N. McJilton.....	W. L. W. Seabrook..	James Logue.........
1863	John Coates.... ...	" "	William J. Wroth....
1864	" "	John A. Lynch.	" " ....
1865	" "	Francis Burns........	Lawrence Sangston..
1866	" "	" "	" " ....
1867	" "	" "	" " ....
1868	" "	" "	" " ....
1869	John S. Berry........	" "	Lucius A. C. Gerry..
1870	John H. B. Latrobe..	" "	" "
1871	" "	" "	" " ..
1872	" "	" "	" " ..
1873	" "	" "	John S. Tyson........
1874	" "	" "	" "
1875	" "	" "	Charles E. Hayward.
1876	" "	" "	John M. Carter......
1877	" "	" "	...
1878	John M. Carter	John S. Tyson........	Edmund J Oppelt....
1879	" "	" "	Ferdinand J.S.Gorgas
1880	John S. Tyson.	Woodward Abrahams	Thomas J. Shryock..
1881	" "	" "	Albert Ritchie.......
1882	" "	" "	" " ....
1883	" "	" "	William M. Isaac....

List of top Maryland Freemasons from the mid-1800s.

As a matter of interest the names of the Companions since anointed are also given, viz:

1824.—Thomas W. Hall, Walter Ball, Oliver Holmes.
1825.—Alex. M. Anderson, Henry S. Keatinge, M. S. Baer, Wm. D. Bell, Archibald Dobbin, Jas. King.
1826.—Casper Quinn, Peter Galt, J. Smart, Elijah Stansbury, Jr., John Huzza, Thomas Salsbury.
1827.—George Earnest, Jr., T. C. Cochran, Jacob Baer, Samuel Keerl, G. W. Haller, George Earnest.
1828.—Philip Reigart, John D. Miller, Charles Howard, of John Eager, Otho H. Williams, Frisby Tilghman, John Ogston.
1829.—John H. B. Latrobe, Ephraim Larrabee, John B. Fitzgerald.
1830.—Ninian Beall, John Goshorn.
1831.—Jos. Robinson, Samuel Child, Jesse T. Peters, Ezra Williams, Horatio N. Steele, Jas. Stirrat.
1832.—David Atkinson, Wm. Bayley, Isaac Bartlett, John Hahn, Frederick J. Dugan, Thomas B. Griffith.
1833.—Joseph Helm, S. W. Woolford.
1834.—Robert Sims, Frederick Clarke.
1836.—Charles Gilman, Wm. Gwyn, Jr.
1838.—Thomas Hayward.
1840.—Robert Keyworth.
1841.—Hugh Devalin.
1842.—E. S. Courtney.
1844.—C. R. Hardesty.
1845.—Samson Cariss, John S. Marll.
1846.—D. A. Piper, Asa Child, C. H. Ohr.
1847.—B. B. French, Jas. B. George.
1848.—Oliver Whittlesey, R. C. Morse.
1849.—H. W. Heath.
1851.—Edward T. Owens, Charles Goodwin, Noah Rider.
1853.—Geo. M. Lamb, Jas. Logue, Wm. M. Smith, C. H. V. Levy, Albert Pike, B. Thrall.
1854.—W. S. Lucas, Robt. Clark, Wm. M. Smith.
1855.—Wm. H. Faulkner, Levin J. Drummond.
1856.—James Goszler, J. N. McJilton, John L. Yeates, Wm. Augustus White, James G. Smith.
1859.—James Bruster.
1860.—J. H. Medairy, Charles Webb.

According to the web site www.gospeltruth.net, "... *Freemasons with higher degrees are called companions, while in the lower degrees Masons address each other as brothers. After swearing to the same points contained in previously taken oaths, the kneeling candidate, with hands on the Holy Bible, proceeds:*

'I furthermore promise and swear, that I will aid and assist a companion Royal Arch Mason when engaged in any difficulty, and espouse his cause so far as to extricate him from the same, if within my power, whether he be right or wrong.'" [22]

Basically, to be anointed as a companion Mason at a lodge or chapter means to take an oath, possibly a blood oath, that you will back up your fellow Masons from this lodge or chapter in general — and to the Grand Master of this lodge or chapter in particular. And you will do so within your power whether they happen to be *right or wrong*. In 1853, Brother Pike had clearly sworn such an allegiance to young Brother Webb.

In 1860, after Webb had declined nomination to continue as Maryland's Grand Master, and therefore became a PGM (Past Grand Master), he was himself anointed as a "Companion Mason" to the grand lodge and the organization's new master, John S. Berry. [23]

Charles Webb   Albert Pike

It is interesting that, in 1853, Brother Pike travels all the way from Arkansas (or New Orleans, where Pike spent most of 1853) to participate in this fraternal Baltimore ceremony. A several hundred mile journey to Baltimore in the 1850s would not have been undertaken without some important purpose. But then, Albert Pike was a most interesting and purposeful man.

Born in Massachusetts in 1809 (the same year as Lincoln), Pike is accepted at Harvard as a young man, but cannot afford the tuition. Instead, he becomes largely self-taught, and for a while earns a living as a schoolteacher. Then, after traveling west to the hinterlands of the American frontier (Missouri and New Mexico, interestingly) to become a trapper, Pike winds up settling in Little Rock, Arkansas where he marries and takes over a Little Rock newspaper, *The Advocate* (with a little help from his wife's dowry).[24]

Pike, according to Warren Getler and Bob Brewer in <u>Rebel Gold</u>, was able to put together a "political machine" in Arkansas through the patronage of his longtime friend and mentor from Massachusetts, the enigmatic Caleb Cushing.[25]

A brilliant scholar who is reported to have spoken as many as seven languages, Pike will eventually pass the bar and become a Little Rock lawyer. *But not just any run-of-the-mill country attorney.* Pike will become a prolific author, especially on legal issues, and involve himself in Whig Party politics. He will also legally represent several of the "civilized tribes" of Native Americans such as the Cherokees, Creeks, and Choctaw. According to Warren Getler and Bob Brewer in <u>Rebel Gold</u>, Pike successfully lobbies in Washington, D.C. to obtain large sums on Indian claims filed against the federal government. It is said that Pike's settlements for the slave-owning "civilized" tribes sometimes reach as much as $500,000 [26]. . . a colossal payout by 19th-century standards. Pike would be aided in obtaining these enormous settlements by his friend and fellow Freemason, U.S. Vice President John C. Breckinridge, a loyal friend of the South. The total amount in personal fees supposedly earned by Pike in his representation of various Native American interests is a staggering $190,000 — much of that paid in gold coin.[27]

With the collapse of the Whig Party, Pike would dabble a while in Know-Nothing politics before eventually joining the so-called "states' rights" Southern Democrats. Pike's politics, as well as his meteoric ascendancy through the ranks of Freemasonry, match quite closely the personal history of Baltimore tallow chandler Charles Webb of James Armstrong & Co.

A staunch supporter and apologist for slavery, Brother Pike would first see military action during the Mexican-American War, serving from 1846-1847 with the rank of captain. But it was during the Civil War that Pike's political, Masonic, and Native American connections would propel him to the forefront of America's bloodiest conflict.

By 1859, Albert Pike had become the Grand Sovereign Commander for the Southern Jurisdiction of Scottish Rite Freemasonry. Once in power, Pike would make sweeping changes throughout the organization, including increasing the number of Masons serving on the Supreme Council from nine to 33.[28] Among the new Masons sitting on Pike's Supreme Council would be John Breckinridge, whose candidacy for the U.S. Presidency in 1860 would split the Democrat Party in two and usher Republican Abraham Lincoln into the White House.[29] By 1960, many in the K.G.C. leadership saw the Northern imposition of abolitionism as inevitable, and actually wanted the "Black Republican" from Illinois to be elected President, thereby giving the South an excuse to secede. Once free from the Union, The South could then be expanded into the newly acquired slaveholding territories of Mexico, Cuba, Nicaragua, and beyond. Basically, following the agenda set forth by the calculating Knights of the Golden Circle.

By 1860, following John Brown's shocking raid along with increasing political pressure from Northern abolitionists, not the least of which was the rise of Abraham Lincoln to national prominence, the Southern states' rights advocates, assorted Dixie "fire eater" politicians, the Cotton states' vast slaveholding interests, and certainly the KGC, were all spoiling for a fight.

At the start of the war, Pike would be accorded the rank of Brigadier General in the Confederacy. His longstanding personal and professional relationship with the "civilized" Indian tribes would prove invaluable to the South, as these tribes would remain loyal to their friend Albert Pike and the Confederate States of America. Pike was named, in March of 1861, to the post of Commissioner to the Indian tribes for the CSA.[30] Eventually, Pike's role would be expanded to Commander of the Department of Indian Territory (he spoke several native languages as well as Greek, Latin, and Hebrew). As Brigadier General, Pike would be placed in charge of Indian forces fighting under the Confederate flag.

At the 1862 Battle of Pea Ridge in Arkansas, Pike and Brigadier General Ben McCulloch (a known, high-ranking KGC member) would command Native American troops against Union forces.[31] McCulloch was a Texan who had fought with Sam Houston in 1836 against General Santa Anna, and also in the subsequent Mexican-American War. McCulloch, in 1861, headed a group of several hundred Texas volunteers, known as McCulloch's Rangers, including possibly some 150 KGC soldiers, who caused the federal military installations in San Antonio to surrender and be handed over to the rebel forces. During the battle in Pea Ridge, Arkansas, McCulloch would be killed by a sharpshooter, but McCulloch and Pike's troops would temporarily succeed in overrunning Union positions. During the fighting, it was alleged that a substantial number of Pike's men tortured Union soldiers and even scalped some of the bodies on the battlefield.[32] The scandal caused by this bloody and barbaric incident, along with some lingering charges concerning the mishandling of Confederate funds which had been leveled at Pike, resulted in Pike's resignation from the Confederate Army. The allegations of financial impropriety would eventually prove groundless, and Pike vehemently voiced his disgust and regret at the unfortunate conduct of his troops at Pea Ridge. However, with the damage already done, Pike retreated to his log cabin on a western Arkansas mountain retreat known as Greasy Cove. Pike would spend the rest of the war working in seclusion and penning his Freemason treatise, Morals and Dogma. Pike's Morals and Dogma [33] would become the official guidebook used and issued by the Scottish Rite Freemasons for most of a century.

Many sources claim that while George C. Bickley was publically the nominal head of the K.G.C., the true leadership and guidance of that Masonic-influenced organization came from none other than the Grand Sovereign Commander himself, Albert Pike.

And in 1853, when long-time Baltimore resident George Bickley was busy planning a nationwide organization for the promotion of "Southern rights" and the expansion of slaveholding territory, the enigmatic Albert Pike was travelling north to Baltimore to meet with the newly installed Grand Master of Maryland Freemasonry — candle and soap magnate Charles Webb.

Subsequent to the South's surrender in 1865 and the Knights of the Golden Circle purportedly going underground, it has been alleged that Albert Pike may have been one of the principals involved in the original founding of another secret, subversive organization — the Knights of the Ku Klux Klan.[34]

Although the connection between the K.G.C. and the Klan is tenuous, the name "Ku Klux" would appear to have been derived from the Greek word "kuklos" meaning circle. Certainly the early

Klan members may have patterned themselves, post-war, after the Knights of the Golden Circle. Whether they were a successor group to the K.G.C., or simply copied some of the K.G.C.'s outward appearances, is a matter for debate. What is known is that during the era of Reconstruction, while the Klan's influence was on the rise in the South, the K.G.C.'s profile was on the wane — or, as some suggest, the K.G.C. simply became invisible and went underground.

An early 20th-century historian, Walter Fleming, cited Pike as being "the chief judicial officer" of the Klan.[35] It is a charge hard to disprove more than a century later, and the topic tends to be very controversial with those involved in researching the history of the Freemasons in America.

What is known is that Pike's good fiend and protégée, Cherokee Chief Stand Watie, himself a 32-degree Mason, was the last Confederate general in the field to surrender.[36] Watie signed a peace treaty in June, 1865 with federal representatives on ground belonging to the Choctaw Nation, which today would be in Oklahoma.

According to Warren Getler and Bob Brewer, co-authors of Rebel Gold, Brewer had years before interviewed a 92-year old Arkansas woodsman whose family had once known Pike, and whose ancestor had actually been contracted by Pike to build his log cabin . . . and was paid for his services in gold coin.[37] Pike was known to keep a substantial amount of gold coinage at his Greasy Cove property. The knowledge of Pike's wealth did not escape Pike's neighbors, some of whom had favored the Union and had resented Pike's high-profile Confederate activities. At some point a plan was hatched to raid Pike's rural hideout and steal his gold. Tipped off by a Masonic friend who had heard rumblings about the plot, Pike fled hurriedly into the night by horse and buggy with his black servants, some hastily gathered clothes and belongings, and a trunk full of Masonic books and gold coins.[38]

The location of Pike's log cabin retreat is today the Albert Pike Recreational Area in the Ouachita National Forest.

Albert Pike in later years.

Triumph of the Rinky Dinky Doos

AWARDED FORTUNE IN BURIED GOLD

"Before attempting any discussion of the evidence, or of the law, may I be permitted to say that no case, within my years of service on the Bench, has been so full of romance or has been more ably presented, both on the evidence and the law, than has been this case." Judge Eugene O'Dunne, February 9, 1935.[1]

On February 16, 1935, Judge O'Dunne announced his much awaited decision. It was an outcome that would stun no one . . . except perhaps the feisty Findlay/French sisters and the 11 hopeful heirs of candle and soap executive Andrew Saulsbury.

O'Dunne's pronouncement was brief and got right to-the-point. "*I award the whole of the contents of the copper pot of some $11,427 face value, to the infant defendants as finders of treasure trove.*"[2]

It was apparently over. The Rinky Dinky Doos had won. Depression-era Baltimoreans, who had backed local boys Henry Grob and Theodore Jones as the sentimental favorites from the start, rejoiced.

Judge O'Dunne commented that he expected the gold hoard to be auctioned off for the princely sum of $30,000.[3]

The boys, however, had two immediate problems. First, neither would be awarded their share of the money until they had turned 21. And second, both the Findlay/French team and also the numerous Saulsbury heirs announced their intention to file appeals almost as fast as you can say "Maryland crab cakes."

This did not, however, stop Henry and Theodore from making public their plans for a suddenly brightened future. Said Henry Grob, in a scripted United newsreel short destined for movie theaters around the country, "*I'm glad that the decision of Judge O'Dunne is in our favor, because now I can complete my education, buy my mother a home, and help others in my family who are in need.*"

"*That's a swell idea,*" added Theodore. "*I think I'll do the same.*"

To local reporters, Henry boasted that, "*I'm going to get my mother a home out Canton way,*" referring to a neighborhood a bit more upscale than the Grobs and Joneses currently occupy. "*I told her once I was going to make her life easy.*"[4]

Mrs. Ruth Grob, however, offers that, after purchasing a small house, at least some of the money should be used to send Henry to college.[5] No such path is laid out for Henry's pal, Theodore, who according to some accounts has received little schooling since the second grade and is deemed "functionally illiterate."[6]

Bessie Jones, always wary, tells reporters that the Joneses "*are not counting on the money until we get it . . . a bird in the hand's worth two in the bush.*"[7] She also makes noises about paying back some of the money she and Theodore have received from Baltimore relief workers.

Theodore reiterates that he still just wants to buy his mom a washing machine.

Judge O'Dunne, meanwhile, turns the gold coins over to the care of Charles McNabb, deputy clerk of the court.[8] O'Dunne then authorizes a public auction of the coins to be held on May 2, 1935. The auction will proceed and the coins sold even though the appeals from the Saulsbury and Findlay/French claimants will almost certainly be in the process of ongoing litigation. After all, the proceeds won't be going anywhere until the "infant defendants" come of age. None of the litigants are opposed to the auction.

Finally, the court appoints Baltimore coin and stamp dealer Perry W. Fuller to conduct the auction.[9] Fuller gains access to the 19th-century coins and curates them. He boils the gold in a solution meant to clean the coins of any corrosive substances applied to them by the over-helpful Baltimore police, or otherwise. *"They're not polished,"* Fuller reveals, *"that would've ruined them. They are in unusually good condition. Many appear to have never been in circulation."*[10]

The auction is scheduled to take place at the luxurious Lord Baltimore Hotel, a world away from the urban jungle of City Springs Park, Caroline Street, and the slowly deteriorating 19th-century row homes along Eden Street.

On February 21, the Secret Service, which has been pestering Judge O'Dunne for months to hand over the golden treasure, officially announces they are at last dropping their interest in the Baltimore hoard.[11] The coins, bolstered by Perry Fuller's expert examination, have apparently qualified as "collector" coins and are thus exempt from the 1933 Gold Act.

The much anticipated May sale of over 3,500 gold coins at the Lord Baltimore Hotel will go on.

Bickley at the Border

General George W.L. Bickley of the
Knights of the Golden Circle.

The smooth-talking opportunist "General" George Bickley now found himself "large and in charge" of some 50 KGC chapters spread across at least 10 Southern and Southwestern states. His shadowy, wealthy Southern backers had funded the KGC-related American Colonization and Steamship Company of Veracruz with an eye-popping $5 million in capital[1] (something on the order of a half billion 21st-century American dollars). This was certainly an amazingly fortuitous turn of events for a marginally successful grifter who had just recently been kicked off his wife's farm for trying to lay his greedy hands on her family's substantial banking fortune.

Whether the more than $500,000 collected for the aborted 1854 Quitman expedition to Cuba had been added to the $5 million KGC war chest will never be known.[2] The 5,000 gold coins left under the cellar at Eden Street, possibly collected by the

Baltimore chapter of the Order of the Lone Star before its "merger" into the KGC, would seem to suggest not. With Baltimore having had one of the oldest, wealthiest, and largest OLS chapters in the country, donor totals in the range of $15,000 to $20,000 for this key chapter (50-100% above the national average) would have been expected for the Cuban operation. Remember, Baltimore was the second largest city in the United States at that time, and $15,000 - $20,000 would have been the approximate face value of the estimated five thousand or more gold coins unearthed by Henry Grob and Theodore Jones on Eden St. in 1934. The figure of 3,000 Maryland Knights mentioned in the anonymous 1861 <u>The Authentic Exposition of the Knights of the Golden Circle or a History of Secession from 1834 to 1861</u> offers further substantiation for the theory.[3]

While Mexican-American war hero John A. Quitman, the 10th and 16th Governor of Mississippi and later a Congressman from that state, was familiar with the halls of power in Washington, D.C. and the palatial governors' mansions of the South, General Bickley takes another approach to leading his Knights. Bickley, the quintessential outsider, enjoys speaking to groups of like-minded men in modest meeting halls and hotels across the South and up in the Border States. In the late 1850s, Bickley would go "on the stump" across the South, spreading the rebellious, expansionist message of the K.G.C., recruiting new members, and delivering speeches designed to "*fire the Southern heart.*"[4]

According to the Texas State Historical Society, Bickley and his K.G.C. "*proposed to establish a slaveholding empire encompassing the southern United States, the West Indies, Mexico, and parts of Central America. Centering on Havana, this empire would be some 2,400 miles in diameter — hence the name Golden Circle. Leaders of the K.G.C. argued that their empire would have a virtual monopoly on the world's supply of tobacco and sugar and perhaps cotton . . . and have the strength to preserve slavery in the South from constant attacks by northern Abolitionists.*"[5]

As with its predecessor, the OLS, Bickley's Golden Knights were organized in a hierarchical manner with three degrees — military, commercial/financial, and political. As author David Keehn explains in his <u>Knights of the Golden Circle: Secret Empire, Southern Secession, Civil War</u>, the military degree was at the bottom, "*and a fund raising benevolent degree above that. At the apex was the political degree, with the goal of supporting U.S. political candidates who would advance the society's filibustering and proslavery objectives. A supreme council (as with the Freemasons) governed the group's overall policy."* [6]

Only members in the political division — and especially those select KGC leaders sitting on the supreme council — were privy to KGC plans in their entirety. Members in the lower degrees were given information strictly on a need-to-know basis. As a group, they believed that KGC plans centered on the defense of Southern rights, especially as they pertained to domestic slaveholding interests. Only leaders in the upper echelons (Knights of the Inner Temple) actually knew that the real main objective of the K.G.C. was Latin American conquest. In fact, the identities of those K.G.C. bosses holding the coveted political degree were often kept secret from men in the lower ranks. This had the effect of forming a second, insulated secret organization within the larger underground structure. As per the anonymous author of The Authentic Exposition of the Knights of the Golden Circle or a History of Secession from 1834 to 1861 writes, *"In drumming for the Order, the agents took care to say nothing about the original objects for which it was framed, viz.: the re-establishment of the African slave-trade and the acquisition of slave territory. It was always represented to outsiders as a strictly 'anti-submission' Order, only designed aid in the securing of 'Southern rights;' and of course almost every Southern man is for Southern rights."* [7]

Author David Keehn goes on to explain that *"by the 1850s, the OLS was reputed to be a shadow organization within the Democratic Party; dedicated to expansionism and serving as a counterweight to the American or Know-Nothing Party."* [8] This is, of course, exactly what we see with candle and soap magnate Charles Webb, the Grand Master Freemason of Maryland getting involved in Baltimore politics in the late 1850s to ensure that the Know-Nothings are voted out, and replaced with hand-picked Democrat proslavery secessionists such as Mayor George Brown and Marshal George Kane.

There were also further class breakdowns within each KGC division. For example, according to the Texas State Historical

Society, *"the military division comprised the Foreign Guard, those men who wished to participate in the wild, glorious and thrilling adventures of a campaign in Mexico and the Home Guard, men who would support military efforts from home. Bickley created, on paper at least, an army of 16,000 men."*[9]

Interestingly, according to author David Keehn in his Knights of the Golden Circle, *"the KGC's higher degree members, while not necessarily expected to bear arms, are nevertheless officers."*[10] It seems the field of battle for many of the higher KGC ups, those with the most to gain by a military-styled invasion, would be a desktop. Their mighty weapon of choice, a quilled pen.

Bickley, according to the anonymous author of the pamphlet The Authentic Exposition of the Knights of the Golden Circle or a History of Secession from 1834 to 1861, *"having framed a constitution, by-laws, and ritual, and having effected thereby all the, to him, necessary changes and changes in the Order (formerly the OLS), he christened it with the highly chivalrous name Knights of the Golden Circle."*[11]

"Tens of thousands of supporters," according to Rebel Gold authors Bob Brewer and Warren Getler, *"from a cross-section of society (doctors, judges, craftsmen, editors, lawyers, clergymen, laborers, etc.) were reported to have taken secret oaths and joined such castles (3,000 in Maryland and Baltimore alone). For a fee of $1, $5, or $10 for the first three degrees of initiation, respectively, as well as payment of a prorated property tax, initiates became rank-and-file members."*[12]

And this, of course, matches quite well with the combined coin breakdown we see from the officially reported treasure totals coming out of S. Eden Street (whether the gold coins were collected as initiation fees and dues, donations towards the 1854 aborted Cuban invasion, or both):

Denomination	Number of Coins	Total Face Value
$20.00	317	$6,340
$10.00	81	$810
$5.00	255	$1275
$2.50	65	$162.50
$1.00	2789	$2,789
Total	**3508**	**$11,381.50**

The OLS/KGC "enlisted men" donated thousands of $1 coins, while the KGC "officers" of various degrees donated hundreds of more valuable, higher denomination gold coins. The breakdown is what we might expect from collected fees, dues, taxes, and donations to a hierarchal organization. New recruits were also asked to buy and wear the K.G.C. emblem.

In return, K.G.C. initiates could expect to share in the eventual spoils from a successful filibuster expedition, be that Cuba, Mexico, Nicaragua, Honduras, or some other exotic Latin American locale. According to the *Rules, Regulations and Principles of the K.G.C.*, a 60-page booklet penned by Bickley himself, *"Each enlisted man who improves and occupies the land . . . . is promised 640 acres with a sliding scale increasing by rank up to the commander in chief, who is promised 3,200 acres."* [13]

In particular, according to <u>The Authentic Exposition of the Knights of the Golden Circle or a History of Secession from 1834 to 1861</u>, *"The year 1856 gave the Knights a new impetus, and added many to their numbers, in the consequence of the very large growth of the anti-slavery sentiment in the North during the year. . . . It is now that the pro-slavery tree began to produce the buds of secession."* [14]

Knights, of course, are encouraged to purchase stock in the K.G.C. investment vehicle, the American Colonization and Steamship Company, and are told that General Bickley himself (broke, in debt, and hounded out of Cincinnati by creditors at the time he was founding the K.G.C.) has provided most of the working capital (millions of dollars) for the ACSC up to this point. Amazingly, the steamship company's alleged main asset, the real value backing the entire enterprise, is the thousands of acres they have yet to conquer from their next filibuster target! [15]

According to Knights of the Golden Circle historian David Keehn, the K.G.C. announces that it is seeking the, *"establishment of a separate and independent nation upon such basis as to render it subservient to the march of American Civilization."* [16] The Knights describe their operation as *"defensive colonization"* and estimate that, at a minimum, 16,000 men and $2 million in working capital (to be replenished on a monthly basis) will be required to stage a successful colonization in their Latin American country of choice.

That choice, according to Commander–in–Chief Bickley, will be Mexico. While the European power, Spain, still seems willing to fight for its Caribbean colony, Cuba, the independent nation of Mexico by the later portion of the 1850s had descended into chaos and outright civil war. In that chaos Bickley — and his invisible, behind-the-scenes handlers — see a major opportunity.

"*There is no reason . . . that can be advanced for the acquisition of Cuba, which is not ten-fold more cogent for our exercising control over Mexico.*"[17]

Previous American filibusterers had longingly set their sights on the four northernmost provinces of Mexico, desiring to break them off from their mother country into a new "Republic of the Rio Grande." These semi-autonomous Mexican states — Chihuahua, Coahuila, Nuevo Leon, and Sonora — were largely rural, underpopulated, and contained vast deposits of untapped gold and silver ore. Extracting that mineral wealth with the use of slave labor could be fabulously profitable.

Bickley and his unseen backers, however, had an ulterior motive in scheming to seize Northern Mexico. Besides the fabulous mineral wealth, the "Republic of the Rio Grande" could be broken down into smaller political units, and Washington lobbied to admit these new 15-25 slaveholding states into the Union,[18] thus throwing the balance of Congressional political power back to the South. Such a coup would prove checkmate for the abolitionists.

Meanwhile, Bickley continued to make inroads by signing up new members in new cities and in new states with new castles. Making Bickley's job easier was the growing acrimony between North and South, the situation being inflamed by saber-rattling Southern "fire-eaters" such as newspaper editor William Yancey and politicians Albert Brown, Senator Louis Wigfall, Edmund Ruffin, and William Porcher Miles. Bickley, who had experience working as an editor for Southern newspapers, new exactly how to go about getting his name and the name of his K.G.C. into Southern news columns. Often exaggerating the size and strength of his secret organization, Bickley used the friendly Southern press to both excite and anger Northern editors, who parroted Bickley's exaggerated claims in their own columns, thus propelling his Knights into the role of national bogeyman.[19] Later, Union intelligence reports would also use Bickley's published but unverified figures to underscore the K.G.C.'s looming threat to national security.

John Brown's failed 1859 raid on Harpers Ferry would give the loquacious Bickley an entire arsenal of new rhetorical ammunition.

By 1859, the K.G.C. is proudly announcing that, *"We have the invitation of four (Mexican) State Governors to come and shall receive their cooperation if we only take care of the people of those States."*[20] Soon after, General Bickley would also claim that he had reached an agreement with Liberal President Benito Juarez. Juarez had been opposing the ruling Conservative Party, whose main strength is centered in and around heavily populated Mexico City. Juarez' forces, meanwhile, hold sway in the Mexican hinterlands and coastal ports.

The years 1859 and 1860 would coincide with a tremendous explosion in the numbers of men joining the ranks of the K.G.C., men such as actor John Wilkes Booth in Baltimore in 1859, followed by Booth's friend John Surratt the year after.[21] In fact, according to historian David Keehn, Bickley had shifted his recruiting focus by 1859 to the Baltimore and Washington areas. Baltimore in particular, writes Keehn, *"was a key commercial center whose merchants supplied the South and generally had prosouthern leanings. Castles of the KGC were already formed in Baltimore, and Bickley had established contacts."* [22]

Bickley could now envision the actual invasion and conquest of Northern Mexico. *"Once Mexico is Americanized,"* boasted K.G.C. propaganda, *"the other states of the Caribbean and Central America will be invited to join . . . which will give us control of the Gulf."*[23]

One reporter writing for the *Arkansas True Democrat* on September 7, 1859, however, warns that he believes Bickley to be *"a most dangerous man, and if he is not stopped, he will do the whole country an incalculable injury. . . . He is playing with the most dangerous passions of the southern people."*[24]

The reporter, who had been personally introduced to Bickley, believed that President Juarez, in his desperation, could well look to the KGC for assistance . . . but that General Bickley *"is looking only to the extension of negro slavery."*

In order to cover all his bases for a successful expedition into Mexico, Bickley first needed to get the approval of the highly influential "George Washington" of Texas, the legendary Sam

Houston. Governor Houston at this time was reportedly considering entering his name as a candidate for President of the United States in the upcoming 1860 election.[25] And Bickley would also need to get the informal green light from the current Buchanan Administration up in Washington, D.C., so as not to run afoul of the existing federal neutrality laws.

Elkanah Greer, the Grand Marshall of the Texas KGC, was already lobbying hard for an invasion of Mexico, believing his powerful Texas Knights might be able to accomplish the job on their own. By the late 1850s the Texas Knights had more members than any other state, with an intimidating roster of 32 KGC castles and growing statewide. According to David Keehn in his Knights of the Golden Circle: Secret Empire, Southern Secession, Civil War, Gov. Sam Houston, alleged to have been a member of the Order of the Lone Star, was approached by Greer, who offered his "regiment of a thousand volunteers, ready to move at a moment's notice."[26]

Houston, himself a slaveholder who had presided over the convention of Freemasons that formed the Grand Lodge of the Republic of Texas,[27] was not opposed to an expedition into Mexico. Mexico had presented Texas with an ongoing security problem for some time, with violence and chaos reigning just across the border, Mexican bandits crossing the Rio Grande to prey upon well-heeled Texans, and runaway slaves disappearing across the border into a country where slavery had been made illegal. Creating a "buffer" zone by grabbing the lightly populated northern Mexican states would relieve Texas of much of this constant annoyance.

Some speculated that Governor Houston might even mount his own military incursion into northern Mexico, beating the KGC and other filibusterers to the punch.

Where Houston parted company with the KGC, however, was in the highly politicized subject of secession. Houston had fought long and hard to have his beloved Texas admitted into the Union, and was not so eager at this late stage to reverse course and see her forcibly separated from the U.S.A. From a practical standpoint, Houston also believed that the South was about to commit political suicide. In a speech made from his hotel window in Galveston to a gathered crowd of Texans, Houston made the following prediction that would prove both incredibly and tragically spot on:

"Let me tell you what is coming. After the sacrifice of countless millions of treasure and hundreds of thousands of lives, you may win Southern independence if God be not against you, but I doubt it. I tell you that, while I believe with you in the doctrine of states' rights, the North is determined to preserve this Union. They are not a fiery, impulsive people as you are, for they live in colder climates. But when they begin to move in a given direction, they move with the steady momentum and perseverance of a mighty avalanche; and what I fear is, they will overwhelm the South." [28]

By 1861, the Texas secession convention would replace Houston with his lieutenant governor, and eventually vote to secede from the Union. Houston would also wisely turn down President Lincoln's offer of 50,000 troops to prevent Texas's secession. Fearing the resultant bloodbath, Houston would reply simply, *"Allow me to most respectfully decline any such assistance of the United States Government."* [29]

Houston would explain his actions to his fellow Texans, saying *"I love Texas too well to bring civil strife and bloodshed upon her. To avert this calamity, I shall make no endeavor to maintain my authority as Chief Executive of this State."* [30]

The KGC and its fellow headstrong, fire-eating rebels would get their way and propel Texas headlong into the Civil War.

Bickley, meanwhile, was still trying in 1859-1860 to put much-needed filibustering assets in the field while holding off the impetuous Texas Grand Marshal, Elkanah Greer. Not knowing fully what to expect from Governor Houston, Bickley tested the political climate in Washington. Buchanan's December, 1859 annual message to Congress left the nation no doubt that President Buchanan was seriously concerned and disappointed with the deteriorating situation to the south of our country's border. According to historian David Keehn, Buchanan felt that while Mexico should be rich and prosperous and powerful, he wondered whether the commercial nations of the world would give Mexico up to *"anarchy and ruin."* Buchanan *"blamed General Miguel Miramon's Conservative regime for these barbarous outrages"* — and *"detailed a series of arrests, deprivations, and murders against the persons, property, and trade of U.S. citizens in Mexico."* Buchanan proclaimed, reports Keehn, *"it was the duty of the United States as a neighboring state to restore peace and order for the benefit of the Mexican people.*"[31]

Furthermore, President Buchanan sought authorization "*to employ a sufficient military force to enter Mexico for the purpose of obtaining indemnity for the past and security for the future.*"[32] With the help of the U.S., the constitutional government of Benito Juarez could "*soon reach the City of Mexico and extend its power over the whole Republic.*" Buchanan wished that the American-led military operation would be peopled by U.S. volunteers "*who sympathize with the sufferings of our unfortunate fellow-citizens in Mexico.*"

Strong stuff, basically a wink and a nod for the K.G.C. to commence filibustering operations — so long as the U.S. Congress was to go along with Buchanan's recommendation. Also, that Mexico's Liberal Party leader Benito Juarez would signal the Americans for their military assistance. To get around the restrictive neutrality laws, the Americans first had to be "invited."

Texas Grand Commander Greer, already interpreting Buchanan's message to Congress as an open invitation, announces that the K.G.C. should "*make haste to take the initiative in our grand and glorious undertaking.*"[33] Greer then asks for a March, 1860 K.G.C. rally to be held in New Orleans to raise the remaining required funds and to discuss "*matters of importance in connection with the enterprise.*"

Basically, concludes Keehn, Greer was putting pressure on Bickley to act, criticizing the smooth-talking General for his "apathy." For General Bickley, the time to "put up or shut up" was drawing near, whether his K.G.C. was fully prepared or not.

Understand that Bickley's career as a filibusterer was dogged by repeated accusations, especially from the Northern press, that he was an individual of questionable reputation and dubious credentials. David Keehn describes one typical press attack in June, 1859, when the New York correspondent for the *San Francisco Daily Evening Bulletin* sarcastically noted that "*the filibusters have got up a new dodge for raising the wind and filling their pockets with the products of other people's labor by starting a new association called the 'Knights of the Golden Circle.' The correspondent indicates that the KGC's headquarters appears to be in Baltimore and that the KGC proposes to raise a separate U.S. and Mexican legion of ten thousand men each to be headed by a Board of War. He observes that this looks like a scheme for putting money into the hands of the commander in chief by 'playing on filibuster credibility.'"* [34]

This is indeed uncomfortable coverage for a fake voodoo doctor masquerading as a commanding officer and handling enormous sums of incoming money as the front man for a clandestine society of greedy, scheming, hot-headed, and fantasy-prone adventurers and filibusterers.

Somehow, Bickley must have known that his days at the apparent helm of the K.G.C. would be numbered . . . unless he had actually started to believe his own press from the mostly KGC-friendly newspapers of the Deep South. Bickley was far more used to Southern editors singing his praises, and whipping up local interest for his traveling act, which, according to author Thomas G. Dyer, *"had all the trappings of a medicine show."* [35]

For example, in his book Secret Yankees: The Union Circle in Confederate Atlanta, Thomas Dyer describes how, *"After a brief stay in New Orleans, 'General' Bickley and a retinue arrived in Atlanta (hunting dues-paying members of the Knights of the Golden Circle). Local secessionists were eager to hear about the filibustering schemes and had orchestrated a well-attended meeting in the city hall on a Monday evening in mid-March 1860. A persuasive speaker, Bickley convinced his audience that he was a veteran of the principal battles of both the Mexican War and the Crimean War and that he was an expert on military affairs, bearing 'upon his bosom,' according to the Intelligencer, 'the emblem of his valorous deeds in that (Crimean) war.' Bickley had brought with him 'Major' Henry Castellanos, who 'enchanted the audience with the most finished, classic and thrilling strains of refined eloquence ever listened to.' 'The people of Atlanta are devoted to Southern interests and Southern rights,' The Intelligencer gushed, 'and whenever questions involving this subject are the topic of discussion the people of Atlanta always give an attentive hearing.' The Intelligencer declared the meeting a grand success. . . . Some of the most prominent of Atlanta's citizens . . . formed a committee to receive the donations and enroll new Knights."* [36]

Bickley may have been long on sizzle, and positively super at collecting donations, but some KGC members, especially Texas's Elkanah Greer, were wondering, "Where's the beef?"

When the promised get-together of KGC officials took place in New Orleans in early 1860, as had been requested by Mr. Greer, New Orleans newspapers were, according to historian

David Keehn, reporting that *"KGC leaders were maintaining hourly contact with hundreds of New Orleans citizens prepared to embark on the 'noble work' of placing 'the liberal' Juarez party in the full and peaceful occupation* of the City of Mexico." [37]

Obviously, thousands of members from dozens of castles were awaiting word that the 1860 invasion of Mexico would soon be a go. That military incursion, however, would never take place.

First, to the surprise and extreme disappointment of the other KGC leaders in attendance in New Orleans, especially the Texan Elkanah Greer, Bickley was forced to admit that not only did he not have the necessary additional funds required to underwrite the imminent invasion — but that he had also failed to bring forth his promised KGC army division.[38]

As had been the pattern with Bickley's entire vanity-driven life, the prevaricating "General" had grossly over-promised and under-delivered. Or, as they say in Texas, he was "all hat and no cattle."

Concurrent with Bickley's failure to live up to his end of the bargain, other factors were coalescing to thwart the scheme to conquer Mexico and seize it for the *"purposes of Christian civilization."*

First, as the success of Benito Juarez' armies had recently improved in the field, he became naturally reluctant to "invite" the Americans to cross the border — and especially the KGC — knowing full well the commensurate cost such "assistance" would necessarily require.[39]

Second, the Buchanan Administration began to, at the last moment, get cold feet regarding any private incursion into Mexico. As David Keehn explains in <u>Knights of the Golden Circle: Secret Empire, Southern Secession, Civil War</u>, *"But neither the U.S. Congress nor the Buchanan administration would approve federal funding for Sam Houston's proposed expedition. The U.S. Senate also refused to approve the negotiated Treaty of Transit and Commerce with Juarez, due to the growing U.S. sectional divide and concerns about mutual security entanglements. The Buchanan administration distinguished its objectives from the KGC's by noting that it advocated intervening in order to maintain, assist, and preserve Mexico as an independent republic, while the KGC proposed to occupy and annex Mexico a la Texas."* [40]

Basically, the 1960 Bickley expedition, which was being egged on by the Texas Knights and their state leader, Elkanah

Greer, with the tacit backing of Sam Houston, was now suffering the same last-minute fate as John Quitman's aborted 1854 invasion of Cuba. Promised governmental and political support had evaporated, leaving the filibusterers twisting in the wind.

The problem now for Bickley was that KGC troops were already massing along or within striking distance of the border with Mexico. Hundreds more were waiting for the expected call in New Orleans. Thousands, according to Keehn, from twenty different locations around the country (including Baltimore and even New York) had congregated in the town of Gonzales on the Guadalupe River. Many of these KGC fighters then left Gonzales to gather forces at the Rio Grande River. Thousands more volunteers had entered at Brownsville, Texas by April 12th . . . with more riding into town daily. The vaunted Texas Rangers also began arriving in force. Newspapers around the country were now reporting on the unusual troop activity, expecting an invasion to be imminent.[41]

Governor Sam Houston, however, knowing that the U.S. government was in the process of withdrawing all support for the Mexican operation, reluctantly issued a proclamation for the assembled Knights to disband. According to Texas KGC military leader Ben McCulloch, a letter of notification was posted on the wall at Gonzales city hall informing the "group of citizens" who had congregated in the town for the purpose of participating in a military incursion of Mexico that they *were without authority from the government of the United States or the State of Texas.*" [42]

The KGC volunteers could expect zero support from Congress, President Buchanan, Benito Juarez, or Governor Houston. The previously open door to Mexico had just been slammed shut.

Without proper funding, sufficient manpower, and official support, the leaderless KGC troops began to slowly disperse. There would be no invasion of Mexico. The doomed mission was officially called off. McCulloch attempted to change Sam Houston's mind, but to no avail.[43] The disappointed, empty-handed soldier Knights angrily disbanded and began their long, arduous trek home.

In New Orleans, the blowback from this sudden fiasco hit Commander-in-Chief George Bickley hard. The KGC's nominal leader was accused by several parties of being a charlatan, fraud, and an outright imposter. There were even accusations made, quoted in the *Charleston Mercury* and elsewhere, that Bickley had absconded with KGC initiation fees. Jeff Davis' own brother-in-law, the noted New Orleans filibuster leader Joseph Davis Howell, proved Bickley's loudest detractor, publicly apologizing to fellow adventurers for Bickley's outright "deceit." According to author David Keehn, Howell's charges were backed up by Samuel Lockridge, a veteran recruiter for filibusterer William Walker's Central American expeditions, who said that he had been led to believe by Bickley that President Buchanan and his cabinet had their "heart and soul" in the cause. However, after asking to see Bickley's war chest and his preparations for the venture, Lockridge *"found it was a humbug of the first order and that they had no means and never had the promise of assent by or from responsible parties."*[44]

Finding himself pinned on the ropes, Bickley tried to roll with these many punches, saying that those interested in a *"mere filibuster"* had forced him to act hastily and without proper preparation — and *"without a proper observance of the law."*[45] Bickley's nephew, Charles, put the blame on *"rowdies, gamblers, and other disreputable elements"* who had attempted to hijack the mission for their own purposes . . . possibly in an attempt to divide the organization.

Divide the organization it did. Many Texas and Deep South castles sought to go their own way, refusing to recognize General Bickley as their appointed leader. Other castles and their state and local leaders, especially from the northern Border States, rallied to Bickley's defense. The contentious schism threatened to widen, potentially splitting the organization irreparably apart.

Bickley soon called for a May 7th convention to be held in Raleigh, North Carolina, requesting an investigation of the charges being levied against him by dissident factions of the KGC.

In Raleigh, Bickley was able to prevail, though barely, using his networking and oratory skills to maintain a tenuous grasp on KGC leadership.[46] His position would be greatly diminished, however, as much power was ceded to state and local commanders such as Texas' Elkanah Greer and Maryland's Robert Charles Tyler. While Bickley still remained as the nominal "President of the American Legion," he would no longer serve as commander-in-chief of the KGC's armed forces.[47] Meanwhile, rumors were running rampant in Raleigh that, with the KGC in disarray, Texas Governor Sam Houston might himself take the Mexican bull by the horns and launch a Lone Star State-based expedition into northern Mexico. However, as the pivotal election of 1860 approached, attention would be increasingly drawn away from filibustering and towards holding off the Northern abolitionists and their continuing assault upon "Southern rights."

Not Cuba, not Mexico — but Abraham Lincoln, the "Black Republican," would soon become the focal point of Bickley's re-engineered KGC. Rather than increasing the size of its slaveholding territory, the South would soon be in a fight just to keep what it already had.

As news of Lincoln's impending election victory approached, KGC President Bickley granted a November 12, 1860 interview with the *Houston Telegraph* in which he was quoted as saying, *"If I learn that Mr. Lincoln has been elected, no movement of the K.G.C. will be attempted until it is determined by the Southern States whether they will submit or not . . . I believe it to be the duty of the members of this organization to lend their services to the Governors of their respective States."* [48]

In Washington, D.C., pro-South and suspected K.G.C.-affiliated members of the lame-duck Buchanan Administration were secretly conspiring to move arms and materials to Southern locales.[49] These arsenals would later be seized by K.G.C. paramilitary units to be used for the benefit of the Confederacy. As war dawned, Union military strategists would quickly come to the realization that they were facing a determined, prepared foe that already enjoyed a sizable head-start. Most key federal military positions were held, traditionally, by Southern officers. This trend had been accentuated during the Buchanan regime.

As described in John Hope Franklin's The Militant South, 1800-1861, John Floyd, the U.S. Secretary of War, had made sure by 1960 that all of the Cotton States had already received their full 1861 quotas of federal arms shipments. Rifles, muskets, and ammunition were disproportionately sent to Southern arsenals, to be subsequently turned against the Union. The Cotton States had made additional substantial pre-war purchases of war materials.[50] By early 1861, Southern newspapers were actually bragging that the South would have at its disposal some *one million* stands of arms once Texas and the Border States migrated to the Confederate camp. The rebels would be well-stocked with federal arms and ammunition, and led by federally trained career military men.

David Keehn in <u>Knights of the Golden Circle: Secret Empire, Southern Secession, Civil War</u> notes that a U.S. Army informer who had infiltrated the KGC's November, 1860 Council of War reported to his superiors that "*orders were given to seize Navy-Yards, forts, etc. while KGC members were still Cabinet officers and Senators.*"[51] Federal forts in the South were subsequently taken over by paramilitary troops "*likely related to the KGC.*" The informer specifically named Secretary of War Floyd, as well as Secretary of the Treasury Howell Cobb and Vice President John Breckinridge as being members of the Knights of the Golden Circle.

As the nation's capital prepared for President Lincoln's inauguration, and the capital still lay largely unguarded, plans for a Southern military move against Washington were apparently under consideration. Thomas W. Cutrer, in his book <u>Ben McCulloch and the Frontier Military Tradition</u>, cites documentation that reveals Texas KGC leader Ben McCulloch supposedly led 500 Texas Rangers and soldiers from Mississippi to Virginia for the purpose of raiding Washington and preventing Lincoln's inauguration.[52] For reasons unknown, the planned assault on D.C. never took place.

Newspaper editor Horace Greeley, in describing the nation's capital, would later give his readers the following famous, much-repeated 19th-century advice:

"*Washington is not a place to live in. The rents are high, the food is bad, the dust is disgusting and the morals are deplorable. **Go West, young man, go West** and grow up with the country.*"[53]

But in 1861, as the Southern states seceded and the nation slipped inexorably towards war, Greeley, a staunch abolitionist Republican and the owner of the *New York Tribune*, would publish the following angry missive to the American people, charging the KGC with outright treason:

"*Before the opening of 1861, a perfect reign of terror had been established throughout the Gulf States. A secret order, known as the 'Knights of the Golden Circle,' or as 'Knights of the Columbian Star' succeeding that known, six or seven years earlier, as the 'Order of the Lone Star,' having for its ostensible object the acquisition of Cuba, Mexico, and Central America, and the establishment of Slavery in the two latter, but really operating in the interest of Disunion, had spread its network of lodges, grips, passwords, and alluring mystery, all over the South, and had ramifications even in some of the cities of the adjoining Free States. Other clubs, more or less secret, were known as 'The Precipitators,' 'Vigilante Committee,' 'Minute Men,' and by kindred designations; but all of them were sworn to fidelity to "Southern Rights"; while their members were gradually prepared and ripened, wherever any ripening was needed, for the task of treason. Whoever ventured to condemn and repudiate Secession as the true and sovereign remedy for Southern wrongs, in any neighborhood where slavery was dominant, was henceforth a marked man, to be stigmatized and hunted down as a 'Linconite,' 'Submissionist,' or 'Abolitionist.'"* [54]

Ironically, when George Bickley had been earlier using his new wife's wealth to fund his various schemes and ventures, one of the more notable of his endeavors was the creation of a Southern-leaning newspaper to act as a Dixie counterbalance to Greeley's *Tribune*.[55] Bickley's publication failed after but a few short months, probably having escaped Greeley's notice altogether. Now, by 1861, Greeley was practically accusing the troublesome Bickley and his Knights of having precipitated disunion, secession, treason, and perhaps even the Civil War itself.

As the War Between the States quickly escalated into a conflagration of unfathomable proportions, the vast majority of KGC members signed on for duty in the regular Confederate Army. President Bickley did likewise, the fake voodoo medicine man offering his services as an army surgeon. Bickley would be captured in 1863 in Indiana by Union forces under suspicion of being a spy, and sentenced to an indefinite term in solitary confinement at Boston's Fort Warren.[56] On December 18th, 1863, Bickley would pen a letter of complaint to President Lincoln, criticizing him for the supposedly inept running of the U.S. government, and also describing Bickley's present circumstances *"in a cell seven by three and a half feet, which contains besides myself, a bed, a stool and water and urinal buckets, so that when everything is put up compactly I have left me for exer - a space of six feet by eighteen inches, about the size of a common coffin."* [57]

It is not known whether the President was so kind as to have offered Mr. Bickley new accommodations in one of the infamous slave pens that still lined Baltimore's Pratt Street by the Basin.

Without the silver-tongued Bickley, the increasingly underground KGC got reorganized under various names such as the Order of American Knights, and later the Order of the Sons of Liberty. Post-Bickley KGC leaders seem to have included Copperhead politician Clement Vallandigham, a pro-South, "states' rights" lawyer and Democratic Ohio Congressman with ties to the alleged "Northwest Confederacy." [58] Vallandigham was a shrewd choice to succeed Bickley because of his formidable political influence, and also because the largely underground wartime KGC was focusing on causing disunion and anti-war sentiment in both the Northern and Border States. Vallandigham would be jailed, however, for "*Publicly expressing, in violation of General Orders No. 38, from Head-quarters Department of the Ohio, sympathy for those in arms against the Government of the United States.*"[59] That order had been issued by one General Ambrose Burnside, made forever famous for the wearing of his distinctive "sideburns." Vallandigham was arrested for giving a speech in which he charged that the war was being fought not to save the Union, but instead to free the slaves by sacrificing the liberty of all Americans to "King Lincoln." Vallandigham would die in 1871 when, representing a client against the charge of committing a barroom shooting (the defense maintained the victim's wound had been self-inflicted), Vallandigham would accidentally shoot and kill himself while attempting to reenact the disputed incident.[60]

The anonymous author of the Authentic Exposition of the Knights of the Golden Circle or a History of Secession from 1834 to 1861 suggested, somewhat cryptically, that a "*Mr. V ——— , of Ohio, and a Mr. C ——— , of Massachusetts, were said to be about the only reliable members the Order claimed among the prominent Northern politicians.*"[61]

It has always been speculated that "Mr. V" was, in fact, Mr. Vallandigham, and that "Mr. C" was none other than Caleb Cushing, a longtime friend, confidant, and early mentor to the Freemasons' Grand Sovereign Commander, Albert Pike. Cushing had served as a foreign diplomat, a Congressman, and also as the 23rd U.S. Attorney General. Cushing, a "doughface" (Northerner with Southern sympathies), presided in 1860 over the Democratic Convention held in Baltimore. He subsequently joined the Southerners who seceded from the regular convention to nominate their own candidate, John C. Breckinridge, for the Presidency.[62]

Another leader of the post-Bickley organization appears to have been one Phineas Wright, a lawyer from St. Louis who appointed himself as "Supreme Grand Commander" of the rapidly fading Knights.[63]

The former KGC "founder" and president, George W.L. Bickley, would be released by the Union several months after the close of the war. He would die two years later in 1867, a sad and broken figure, in the then bustling City of Baltimore. . . .

Which brings us to the ultimate KGC question, aside from whether the Knights buried a fortune in gold and silver treasure in depositories across the country! The true mystery, the real controversy surrounding the Knights of the Golden Circle is this . . . did the organization survive the American Civil War in any meaningful way? Did the KGC go underground, waiting for the day when the South would rise again? Were the Knights planning a second round of rebellion against the hated North?

Some observers believe that is exactly what happened.

The 1861 Baltimore Plot to Kill Lincoln

Abraham Lincoln prior to growing his trademark beard.

Historians have long debated whether a real plot existed to assassinate President-elect Abraham Lincoln in February, 1861. Certainly the nation was already sliding headlong into conflict upon Lincoln's November 6, 1860 victory over a split field of three other candidates. Despite receiving less than 40% of the popular vote, Lincoln's triumph was nearly assured when the Democratic Party suffered a schism with the national Democrat Party running long-time Lincoln foe Stephen A Douglas, and the breakaway "Southern Democrats" nominating outgoing U.S. Vice-president John C. Breckinridge. Breckinridge was also a member of Albert Pike's Supreme Council for the Scottish Rite Freemasonry in Charleston, South Carolina.[1] The election picture was further clouded by the candidacy of Constitutional Union candidate John Bell of Tennessee.

The 1861 Baltimore Plot to Kill Lincoln

It has been said by David Keehn, Warren Getler, the anonymous author of the 1861 Authentic Exposition of the K.G.C., and other K.G.C. observers that the organization had hoped that Breckinridge would win the South, Douglas the North, and that the election would then be thrown into the House of Representatives, where the "states' rights" candidate Breckinridge would prevail.[2] And if the Breckinridge strategy were to backfire, and if the "abolitionist" Lincoln were elected, then the Southern states would simply secede. In fact, it has been postulated that many members of the Knights of the Golden Circle actually wished (and secretly worked for) for Lincoln's election so as to force the issue of secession.[3]

The more "ardent" Southern sympathizers, by 1960, had had enough of the Northern abolitionists and their political machinations.

Breckinridge did his part, winning some 11 Cotton and Border states with nearly 20% of the popular vote. Despite garnering 30% of the popular vote, Douglas only managed to take one state (Missouri), and John Bell three states (Kentucky, Tennessee, and West Virginia). With Lincoln winning 17 states and 180 electoral votes, the election was never decided in Congress. Lincoln automatically became the President-elect of the United States. He would become the new 16th President on March 4th, 1861 — provided he could make it to Washington, D.C. alive.

Of the 30,000 votes cast in Baltimore during the 1860 presidential election, barely 1,000 had been for Mr. Lincoln. Police Marshal George Kane, according to Michael Kline in The Baltimore Plot, described the paltry 3% popular vote for Lincoln as having been cast "from the very scum of the city."[4]

Six Southern states would secede before Lincoln was to leave home for his inauguration, and Texas would be added to that list before he set foot in the White House to preside over a nation already badly divided. Maryland was yet another state teetering precariously "on the bubble," as was neighboring Virginia.

On February 11, 1861, the "Lincoln Express" inaugural train embarked from Springfield, Illinois for a whirlwind, two-week whistle-stop tour through Illinois, Indiana, Ohio, New York, New Jersey, Pennsylvania, and finally Maryland — before arriving in Washington, D.C. on February 23 in advance of Lincoln's March 4 inauguration. The circuitous route would see Mr. Lincoln transported across some 18 different rail lines through approximately two dozen major cities and many more small towns. The President-elect was determined to give a speech at every stop, and to let the crowds get a good look at their newest Commander-in-Chief. Lincoln would become hoarse and completely exhausted well before arriving in the nation's capital.[5]

Every stop but one before arriving in Washington, D.C. was situated above the Mason-Dixon Line in regions that had largely supported Mr. Lincoln. Only one stop, the last stop before D.C., lay decidedly in hostile Southern territory. President-elect Lincoln was scheduled to spend February 23rd in the City of Baltimore.

Even before Lincoln's special inauguration train departed from Springfield, rumors began circulating that there could be trouble along the route in Maryland, particularly that secessionist hotbed of Baltimore.[6] Although there would be several senior military men on board the train, as well as Lincoln's advisors, high-

ranking politicians, assorted dignitaries, personal assistants, and Lincoln's wife and three sons, the entourage would be lightly armed and rely heavily on local police protection for their safety.

Lincoln allies General Winfield Scott and Senator William Seward were so uneasy at the prospect of him traversing Baltimore that they enlisted the help of New York Police Superintendent John Kennedy to send a team of detectives to Baltimore well in advance of Mr. Lincoln's arrival. These spies would gather intelligence on potential threats to Lincoln and his entourage.[7]

Separate from General Scott and Senator Seward, railroad president Samuel Felton also had concerns. Depending on the final schedule, the Lincoln Special might be riding his Pennsylvania, Wilmington, and Baltimore (PW&B) Railroad route to Baltimore, and Felton was loathe to have an incident occur on his tracks — especially since one of the circulating stories involved the derailment of the Lincoln Special north of Baltimore and the subsequent indiscriminant murder of parties on board.[8]

That public sentiment was almost entirely against Mr. Lincoln in Baltimore was underscored emphatically by the following editorial run in *The Baltimore Sun* before the inauguration:

Had we any respect for Mr. Lincoln, official or personal, as a man or as a President-elect of the United States, his career and speeches on his way to the seat of government would have cruelly impaired it. . . . As it is, no sentiment of respect of whatever sort with regard to the man suffers violence on our part, at anything he may do. We do not believe the Presidency can ever be more degraded by any of his successors, than it has been by him, even before his inauguration; and so, for aught we care, he may go to the full extent of his wretched comicalities. We have only too much cause to fear that such a man, and such advisers as he has, may prove more capable of infinitely more mischief than folly when invested with power. A lunatic is only dangerous when armed and turned loose; but only imagine a lunatic invested with authority over a sane people and armed with weapons of offense and defense. What sort of fate can we anticipate for a people so situated? And when we reflect that fanaticism is infested with like fears, suspicions, impulses, follies, flights of daring, and flights of cowardice common to lunacy itself, and to which it is akin, what sort of a future can we anticipate under the presidency of Abraham Lincoln? [9]

The editorial writer for *The Baltimore Sun*, writing in early 1861 could have, of course, scarcely imagined a future with hundreds of thousands of Americans killed at the hands of fellow Americans, slavery abolished, the South in ruins, the painful era of Reconstruction, and Mr. Lincoln with his portrait on the U.S. $5 note and one-cent coin.

Southern politicians and newspaper editors weren't the only ones rattling sabers and issuing threats during this period. Pennsylvania Senator Simon Cameron, as quoted by *The Pittsburgh Gazette*, scoffed at the possibility that Maryland might be bold enough to secede and block the Lincoln Special from delivering the President-elect for his inauguration. "*Sir, the old Keystone has 300,000 fighting men. Should that little craft (Maryland) fall into the hands of pirates, one broadside from the Pennsylvania four-decker will clear the road to Washington and . . . guarantee him a safe passage to the White House!"*[10]

With the anger of Baltimoreans rising with the daily approach of the Lincoln Special, Superintendent Kennedy dispatched his team of undercover agents to the Oriole City, where they ensconced themselves in and around The Fountain Hotel near Light Street in search of rebel terrorists. Of course, entirely unknown to Mr. Kennedy, General Scott, and Senator Seward, the PW&B's Mr. Samuel Felton was also bringing in his crack team . . . a detachment of operatives from the Pinkerton Detective Agency, led by none other than the famed "private eye" Allan Pinkerton himself. Pinkerton would disperse his agents throughout downtown Baltimore, and assign himself the cover identity of newly arrived Southern stockbroker "John H. Hutcheson."[11]

Pinkerton as "Hutcheson" would open his newly established brokerage office at 44 South Street . . . just a few doors from the offices of the Eden "treasure" home's ground rent recipient, Charles Findlay, who was in the iron business. Pinkerton had also established himself on the same downtown block as James Armstrong's American Fire Insurance Company of Baltimore, a firm with which sea captain John J. Mattison and candle and soap makers Charles and James Webb would be associated.[12]

Pinkerton's spies would include America's first female detective, Kate Warne, who would go by the code name "Miss Cherry."[13] Warne's role would be to pump the ladies of Baltimore for information regarding a possible plot.

The Pinkertons subsequently added a second lady detective, Hattie Lawton, who posed as agent Timothy Webster's wife. The danger inherent in the Baltimore operation would be underscored just a year later when Agent Webster would be found out as a Union spy in Richmond. Webster's punishment was to suffer hanging — twice. The first attempt to execute the prisoner failed when the hangman's noose malfunctioned. As they led Webster to the gallows a second time, the condemned man blurted out, "*I suffer a double death!*" This time, the rope held. Timothy Webster, 40, was the first spy on either side to be executed during the Civil War.[14]

Once set up in Baltimore, Pinkerton and his team achieved almost immediate results. Buying drinks for several ardent "pro-Southern" sympathizers at local bars, Pinkerton was regaled with plans for Lincoln's demise on the streets of a hostile Baltimore. Kate Warne was also able to obtain valuable intelligence by posing as a flirtatious Southern belle at the Barnum Hotel bar.[15]

While patronizing the bar at Barnum's Hotel, the undercover Pinkerton (as Mr. Hutcheson) overheard a disturbing piece of news uttered from the lips of none other than Marshal George P. Kane. While in Pinkerton's presence, Baltimore's top cop boasted that there would be no police presence in Baltimore to guard Mr. Lincoln and his guests upon their arrival.[16] Pinkerton soon grew to suspect that Marshal Kane was either in on the plot to assassinate Lincoln — or was prepared to turn his back and allow the unspeakable crime to happen. Pinkerton began to keep close tabs on Kane, whom he labeled in his reports to railroad executive Samuel Felton as being a *rabid secessionist.* Harry Ezratty, in his Baltimore in the Civil War, says that the Pinkertons *"implicated Police Chief Kane"* in the plot, and indicated that Kane *"would be pleased to see Lincoln out of the way."* [17]

Pinkerton's political views on this subject are worth mentioning, as he was not exactly a detached professional without some "skin" in this high-stakes game. A fiercely committed abolitionist, Pinkerton had aided the "underground railroad" in its quest to smuggle runaway slaves to their freedom north of the Mason-Dixon Line.[18] He did so in direct defiance of runaway slave laws on the books that compelled Northerners to respect the personal property rights of Southern slave owners. It has been said Pinkerton despised slavery even more than Abraham Lincoln himself, and once described the murderer and martyr John Brown as a *"great American . . . possibly even greater than Napoleon, and as great as Washington himself."*[19]

In fact, it is known that Pinkerton on at least one occasion helped fund one of Brown's "underground railroad" operations across the border into Canada (then known as British North America).[20]

In the anonymous <u>1861 An Authentic Exposition of the "K.G.C." Knights of the Golden Circle or a History of Secession</u>, written by a "member" of the order, the author proposed a scene similar to what Superintendent Kennedy's spies were reporting back from Baltimore. The communications to Kennedy, which were relayed to General Scott and Senator Seward, described a massive plot with a crowd of large numbers of belligerent Southern fanatics lying in wait for Lincoln in and around Baltimore's Calvert Street Station.

"The inauguration of Lincoln being near at hand," wrote the anonymous presumed member of the K.G.C. *"some of the K.G.C. bethought themselves that it would be a very fine idea to assassinate him, and capture Washington, inasmuch as such a thrilling movement would strike terror to the hearts of the "Abolitionists," afford an opportunity to rob the National Treasury, and thus secure the entire field in advance. . . . Now, had it not been for the encouragement from Northern quarters (the so-called Copperheads), the Southern Castles would never have matured the plan for the Capital's seizure as far as they did.*

"The plan alluded to, of which the people of the country generally had several hints, was as follows: About one thousand men, armed with bowie knives and pistols, were to meet secretly at Baltimore, where they were to secure the services of the Plug Uglies. Thence they were to proceed to Washington, on the day previous to the inauguration, and stop at the hotels as private citizens, after which their leader was to reconnoiter and select the most effective mode of operations on the succeeding day. This scheme was not encouraged by Jeff Davis, as he was not yet quite crazy enough to think that a few dozen of his 'chivalry' could terrify the whole world by one demonstration. (Texas senator and K.G.C. sympathizer Louis) *Wigfall, however, thought it a 'capital' idea, in more sense than one, and urged its vigorous prosecution. Fortunately, the plot was discovered, to some extent, in time to give Gen. Scott an opportunity to present some very forcible, and,*

with the K.G.C., decisive arguments against it. I know the Governor of Maryland (Thomas H. Hicks) tried to make it appear that no contemplated plan for the assassination of the President elect existed; but he really knew about as little of the matter as Mr. Lincoln himself, and had he known it, would doubtless have done all in his power to conceal the matter, when he saw the preparations being made to prevent it, in order to preserve the fair fame of Baltimore." [21]

K.G.C. historian David C. Keehn agrees that the inauguration conspiracy involved not only the assassination of Lincoln, but the subsequent complete takeover of the nation's capital.

Says Keehn in his <u>Knights of the Golden Circle: Secret Empire, Southern Secession, Civil War</u>, *"The respected judge George Paschal, who had confronted (K.G.C. President George) Bickley at the October 1860 KGC meeting in Austin, similarly warned a friend in Washington City that the South was virtually in arms and moving northward with the objective of seizing the capital. He said that the Texas KGC leader Ben McCulloch would lead the assault. Rumors separately circulated that Ben McCulloch was encamped in northern Virginia with a force of five hundred Texas Rangers who would sweep into Washington and prevent Lincoln's March 4 inauguration."* [22]

That assumes, once again, that Lincoln would still be alive to be inaugurated. Baltimore loomed larger and larger as the Lincoln Special made its way east — and then south towards the Mason-Dixon Line.

Keehn goes on to say that, *"Wigfall also helped convert the Breckinridge and Lane Clubs in Baltimore and Washington City into paramilitary organizations that could assist in a takeover."* [23]

Washington, D.C., in the days leading up to Lincoln's swearing in, had been left woefully unguarded. Senator Seward was already advising the President-elect to seize the capital *before* the rebels.[24] The plan to assassinate Lincoln, coupled by an organized uprising to seize Washington D.C., seems to have had a window of opportunity for success. The mob was angry and waiting for Lincoln in Mobtown, U.S.A. The question was, how many committed assassins might be lurking in that raucous crowd?

The U.S. Congress, alarmed by growing rumors that secret organizations "hostile to the United States" might attempt to disrupt the inauguration and do harm to Mr. Lincoln, ordered witnesses to appear before a hastily convened "Select Committee." Two of the most important witnesses to be interrogated were Thomas Holiday Hicks, Governor of Maryland, and Cipriano Ferrandini, a Corsican immigrant and hair stylist who operated a barbershop in the basement of Baltimore's Barnum Hotel.[25]

Governor Hicks, the "Know Nothing" chief executive of that state, testified before the legislators that while he believed there had been a plot to assassinate Lincoln, the threat no longer existed. Hicks, a pro-South slave owner but nevertheless resistant to secession, was himself rumored to be a target for the assassins. According to author Michael J. Kline in The Baltimore Plot, Hicks had received much intelligence, including news articles and numerous "anonymous" letters, warning of an assassination plot and of rebel intent to burn Maryland bridges to prevent Union access to Washington, D.C. [26] He neglected, however, to reveal much of this to the Select Committee, instead choosing to snip the signatures from the signed letters and hand them over to suspected conspirator Marshal Kane! Hicks' testimony, writes Kline, was not the whole truth; at worst, it was an outright lie.

More startling was the testimony of Mr. Ferrandini (left), who freely admitted his allegiance to the South and his preparedness to help prevent Union troops from passing through Baltimore on route to wage war against Southerners. Within two months, Ferrandini and like-minded Baltimoreans would be given such an opportunity. The barber, however, denied any knowledge of a plot to disrupt the inauguration or to specifically do harm to Mr. Lincoln.

According to Harry Ezratty in his Baltimore in the Civil War, committee members took special note of the fact that Ferrandini had acquired special military training in Mexico, which was sponsored by the secessionists. Upon returning to Baltimore the Corsican immigrant had seemingly been given the rank of "captain" and would thereafter be addressed as "Captain Ferrandini." [27]

The Pinkertons had also uncovered the volatile Ferrandini during the course of their covert surveillance. Pinkerton agents, under the guise of Confederate sympathizers, met with "Captain" Ferrandini at both a hotel and a bar. While at the bar, agents claimed Ferrandini told them that *"Lincoln surely must die"*[28] and that he, Ferrandini, was *"willing to give his life"* for his adopted country. The barber would eventually be arrested but was quickly released. The detectives learned that Ferrandini and his alleged co-conspirators belonged to a group of shadowy reactionaries who called themselves the Baltimore Society of the Knights of Liberty. The KGC was known to operate under such various names as the Order of Sons of Liberty, Order of American Knights, and the Knights of Liberty — to list just a few.

The alleged co-conspirators of Ferrandini included Baltimore businessman William Byrne, the head of a paramilitary group known as the National Volunteers whose main mission in early 1861 was to prevent Lincoln's inauguration. According to the authors of Come Retribution: The Confederate Secret Service and the Assassination of Lincoln, Byrne was also a suspected high-ranking member of the KGC. [29] His "National Volunteers" were said to meet in the basement of the Barnum Hotel, the same location as Ferrandini's barber shop. Cipriano Ferrandini was also highly suspected of being a "captain" in the KGC, as his self-given rank implied.

Another member of Ferrandini's inner "circle" was Otis K. Hillard, a man who wore the symbol of secession, the "Palmetto Cockade" of South Carolina, proudly on his chest. Hillard was simultaneously thought to be a member of three secret societies, the Palmetto Guard, Byrne's National Volunteers, and the KGC. When testifying in front of the Congressional Select Committee, Hillard denied there was a plot to harm Lincoln, and refused to name any members of the National Volunteers. According to a report submitted by Pinkerton operative Harry Davies (see Norma Cuthbert's Lincoln and the Baltimore Plot), Hillard did privately admit that he was involved in a plot against the President-elect.[30]

John Wilkes Booth regularly frequented Barnum's Hotel,[31] as obviously did Marshal Kane. Ferrandini ran his barber business from the basement of the hotel, a favored spot for smugglers and Confederate sympathizers. Says Harry Ezratty, *"there has been much speculation about whether Ferrandini and Booth actually met and in engaged in conspiracy at Barnum's in 1861."*[32] Some four years later, Booth would meet his 1865 co-conspirators for drinks at this very same hotel — while plotting the successful 1865 assassination of President Lincoln at Ford's Theater.

According to author Michael J, Kline in The Baltimore Plot, "*It is certainly possible that in late 1860 and early 1861 that while Byrne, Ferrandini, Hillard, and others were fomenting hatred of all things North in secret Baltimore conclaves, J. Wilkes Booth was right there with them, reciting passages from Julius Caesar to inspire and incite.*"[33]

Barnum's Hotel was scarcely more than a city block away from The Fountain Hotel, another Baltimore hotbed of secessionist intrigue and Confederate covert activity. This included the later handling and packaging of clothes from yellow fever victims meant for resale or donation to unsuspecting citizens in the North — so as to create a pandemic and resulting panic behind enemy lines and disrupt the Union's ability to prosecute the war. The Fountain was also the residence of Thomas Armstrong, an executive at James Armstrong & Co. and a close friend of Andrew Saulsbury.[34]

Saulsbury, much like Byrne, Ferrandini, Hillard, and Booth was vociferous about his diehard support of the South. "*He was an ardent Southern sympathizer*," testified his daughter in 1934. "*That everyone knew.*" [35]

Some of Kennedy's New York detectives had booked rooms at The Fountain where, disguised as Southern agitators, they never lacked for company.[36]

Meanwhile, as the Lincoln Special traveled through Northern cities and towns, with the President-elect speaking to large, enthusiastic crowds, it was noted that a particular individual seemed to be stalking the inaugural party. Appearing first in

Cincinnati, this same man would be seen at many venues along the east-bound route. He was subsequently identified as George N. Sanders (left), a political radical and an "avowed advocate of political assassination." He was also, according to Michael J. Kline in The Baltimore Plot, "*no fan of Republicans.*"[37]

More ominously, Sanders would be identified as a "*future confidant*" of assassin John Wilkes Booth. In October 1864, when John Wilkes Booth would travel to Montreal to present his original plan for kidnapping President Lincoln to George Kane and the Confederate Secret Service agents, Booth would be seen in the regular company of George Sanders and blockade runner Patrick Charles Martin at the St. Lawrence Hotel.[38]

Otis Hillard, while in his cups, would eventually confide to undercover Pinkerton operatives Charles D.C. Williams and Harry Davies that Hillard and his group had their own operatives shadowing the Lincoln party along the route, who were reporting back to Baltimore via telegram.[39] This was strong corroboration that the suspicious appearance of George Sanders at multiple Lincoln speeches and whistle stops was no mere accident.

As other undercover Pinkerton detectives plied boastful secessionists with alcohol at downtown Baltimore watering holes, particularly Barnum's, the outline of the 1861 plot against Lincoln began to take shape. Meanwhile, unbeknownst to the Pinkerton agents, New York Superintendent Kennedy's men, operating from rooms at the nearby Fountain Hotel, were gathering much the same intelligence. New York detectives Eli Devoe and Thomas Sampson, posing as action-seeking Southern secessionists, managed to join one of the Baltimore paramilitary groups in order to get the disturbing inside scoop.[40]

Author Michael J. Kline believes that the man entrusted with drilling the paramilitary group that agents Devoe and Sampson had infiltrated, a sombrero-wearing Texan named Captain Hays, was actually non-other than pro-secessionist Texas Senator Louis T. Wigfall.[41]

Apparently, the primary plan involved creating a diversion at the Calvert Street Station where Lincoln and his party were scheduled to arrive on the afternoon of February 23rd. Young toughs would be stationed at critical positions in and around the train depot, mixing with the large and noisy crowd.[42] Upon being given a predetermined signal after Lincoln stepped off the train, the ruffians would create some diversionary disturbance to distract Kane's police, who would then chase after the miscreants — leaving the exposed President-elect temporarily unguarded or certainly under-guarded. At that precise point the assassins would strike. Otis Hillard allegedly related to Pinkerton agent Harry Davies that he would be given the first shot, using a revolver hidden under his coat.[43] Several others, however, would also be poised to take aim at Lincoln in the event that Hillard failed or was somehow thwarted.

According to Kline in The Baltimore Plot, James H. Luckett, a fellow stockbroker who had introduced Mr. Hutcheson (Allan Pinkerton in disguise) to "Captain" Ferrandini and several other members of the conspiracy, divulged that Kane's police were in on the plot. The police, said Luckett, were to pretend to fall for the planned diversionary tactic, leaving Lincoln exposed for the kill. After the shooting, they would only make a plausible show at attempting to apprehend the assassins, who would — by design — escape amidst the panic and mass confusion.[44]

According to Norma B. Cuthbert's Lincoln and the Baltimore Plot, Luckett also informed Pinkerton as Southern stockbroker "Mr. Hutcheson" that Ferrandini would not allow Lincoln to get through Baltimore alive — and that Governor Hicks better soon agree to secession or he himself would be hung.[45]

The conspirators were said to have a backup plan in effect, in case the primary assassins were not afforded a clear target at Calvert Street Station. This involved an attack on Lincoln's open carriage as it left the Calvert Street depot and rode through nearby streets.[46] There was even a Plan B in the event Lincoln arrived instead from Philadelphia at the President Street Station a couple miles to the east,[47] and not from Harrisburg at the Calvert Street depot (as was ultimately scheduled). The Lincoln advisors were now being warned of these preparations not just by Pinkerton or Superintendent Kennedy, but also by Vermont's Lucius Chittenden, a Republican "Peace Conference" delegate trying to broker a solution to the growing North-South tensions. Chittenden had met with Republicans in Baltimore who had managed to gain inside knowledge of the conspirators' plans.[48] What Chittenden was told by the Baltimoreans greatly alarmed him.

If Lincoln chose to ride along Pratt Street in an open carriage, the conspirators reasoned that shooting him would be relatively easy. However, Lincoln's team, possibly tipped off to the raucous, hostile crowd awaiting them in Baltimore, might have instead elected to keep President-elect Lincoln inside his railroad passenger car for added protection. Since railroad travel wasn't permitted in downtown Baltimore, passenger cars were routinely unhooked at the President Street Station and carted by teams of horses along the Pratt Street tracks to Camden Street Station, just over a mile away. At the Camden Street depot the Lincolns and their guests would be hooked to another engine and transported to Washington, D.C. along the Baltimore and Ohio rail line.

As Chittenden related in his memoir <u>Recollections</u>,[49] Plan B involved the rebels dumping some large obstruction onto the tracks at the point Lincoln's rail car crossed over Jones Falls at the Pratt Street Bridge. A team of knife-wielding attackers would be ready to storm the presidential rail car as it slowed to a halt. The dozen or so assassins would race through the enclosed car, stabbing the president and anyone else who resisted. They would flee through a nearby rum shop and onto a waiting schooner docked at The Basin — today known as Baltimore's Inner Harbor. Given such a head start amidst the chaos, the killers would sail to safe haven in Virginia, untouched and unidentified.

Two aspects of "Plan B" are quite significant. First, the designated "kill spot" on Pratt Street at the Jones Falls bridge crossing just happened to be almost at the very doorstep of James Armstrong & Company, Baltimore's manufacturers of fine soaps and candles . . . operated by Charles Webb, James Webb, Thomas Armstrong, and Andrew Saulsbury. The Armstrong executives would apparently have full view of the event from their office windows.

Second, the schooner positioned behind the rum shop off Pratt Street would have been at or nearby the wharf where Captain John J. Mattison had docked his ships for decades. Could the aging captain and former secret slaver have been part of the assassination plot? Other potential candidates would have included Patrick Charles Martin, a Baltimore liquor dealer originally from New York with ties to Marshal Kane and ultimately the Confederate Secret Service in Canada.[50] Martin, sometimes referred to as "Captain" P.C. Martin in Civil War records and reports, would become a blockade runner for the Confederacy, smuggling badly needed contraband from Canada to rebel forces in the South. Martin was certainly more than capable of piloting the schooner. Finally, we should not forget Captain John E. Stevens, Mattison's mystery tenant on Eden Street during the war years. Not much is known about Stevens except that he moved to nearby East Baltimore Street after the war . . . upon Saulsbury's purchase of the Eden Street treasure house from Mattison. There was a Captain John E. Stevens from New York City in the period leading up to the Civil War, and one record lists him specifically as a yacht captain.[51] Someone with experience sailing high-performance yachts would have made an excellent getaway skipper for Lincoln's killers. Perhaps liquor salesman Patrick Charles Martin, a known Kane associate in Canada during the war and originally from New York, recruited Stevens for the job from New York City.

Allan Pinkerton and his subordinates seem to have also obtained intelligence regarding this part of the plot. According to Pinkerton, *"A captain of the roads reported that there was a plot to stab the President-elect. The alleged plan was to have several assassins, armed with knives, interspersed throughout the crowd that would gather to greet Lincoln at the President Street station. When Lincoln emerged from the car, which he must do to change trains, at least one of the assassins would be able to get close enough to kill him."*[52]

Regardless of the particulars, it seems that if Lincoln had taken Pratt Street to get to Camden Street Station on the afternoon of February 23rd, 1861, a deadly trap had been prepared for that contingency. Otherwise, Otis K. Hillard and his merry men were prepared for the kill shot over at the Calvert Street depot, with the assistance of several street thugs scattered throughout the crowd waiting for the their cue to create a diversion.

Apparently, the killers had devised *multiple plans* involving each Baltimore rail station. Lincoln was to be targeted no matter what his route or itinerary.

Cipriano Ferrandini, as Mr. Luckett had boasted to Pinkerton while the alcohol flowed freely, would not allow Lincoln to pass Baltimore alive. *"Lincoln,"* Ferrandini had personally promised Pinkerton, *"shall die in this city."*[53]

Not surprisingly, of all the cities Lincoln visited on his lengthy two-week route, Baltimore was the only one that had not extended the President-elect a formal invitation. Mayor George Brown, an avid secessionist who'd been backed by candle and soap magnate Charles Webb's "reform" committee, did not extend a public invitation to Lincoln. Neither did Baltimore's City Council, the pro-South Maryland state legislature, nor the "Know Nothing" Governor Thomas Hicks. Lincoln's only welcome in the Monumental City was provided by a smattering of private Republican citizens.[54]

Officially, Lincoln had been rudely and completely snubbed.

Now, Lincoln's scheduled train route through Maryland was being published in the newspapers, and the hour and location of his arrival in "Mobtown" made known to all. A passenger on the Lincoln Special, Captain George W. Hazzard, concerned about Lincoln's safety, had earlier written to the President-elect to warn him about Baltimore. Said Hazzard, in a letter that is now part of the Abraham Lincoln Collection at the Library of Congress, "*I have for many years known Col. George P. Kane, the Chief of the Baltimore police . . . I have but little confidence in Col. Kane's abilities and less in the integrity of his character. Independent of this there are men in that city who, I candidly believe, would glory in being hanged for having stabbed a 'black republican president.*"[55]

Freemason Charles Webb's fervently secessionist, handpicked reform mayor was leaving Lincoln's protection entirely up to Webb's "rabidly" secessionist handpicked reform marshal — who then decided to provide, at best, only nominal, token protection.

With the Lincoln Special progressing towards New York City, Philadelphia, Harrisburg, and then Baltimore, the President-elect was being looked after by the likes of lawyer Norman Judd and Judge David Davis, both close political advisors from Illinois, and personal assistant Ward Hill Lamon, a hulking figure with a brace of pistols who doubled as the chief executive's personal bodyguard. Aging Colonel Edwin Vose Sumner also accompanied the new President. Colonel Sumner, selected personally by General Winfield Scott to protect Lincoln, was the ranking military officer in the approximate 40-person entourage. He was sworn, same as Mr. Lamon, to protect Mr. Lincoln at any cost for the duration of the trip.[56]

As details of the Baltimore plot emerged, Allan Pinkerton began to send cryptic, partially coded telegrams to scheduled stops along the route, meant for Lincoln's chief advisor, Norman Judd. At first, Judd kept the alarming information entirely to himself. Pinkerton would then see fit dispatch Kate Warne to intercept the Lincoln Special and Mr. Judd in New York City, so that Judd could be apprised of the situation in Baltimore.[57]

Likewise, the independent reports from Superintendent Kennedy's on-site team, which corroborated the Baltimore "boots on the ground" information from the Pinkertons, began to reach the likes of Lincoln associates General Scott and Senator William Seward.

The alarm bells were finally starting to go off.

As the various insiders surrounding Lincoln grew increasingly concerned, the new President pressed wearily on. He greeted local dignitaries, gave speeches to the large, boisterous crowds at every stop, and ate at several grand banquets per day, each prepared in his honor. A distracted and tired Abe Lincoln, a constant slave to the Lincoln Special's demanding, marathon schedule, remained blissfully unaware of the deadly reception awaiting him in the Oriole City. No one had yet told Honest Abe. Lincoln's closest friends and advisors were all busily debating, in private, about exactly what to do.

By the time Lincoln was scheduled to arrive in Philadelphia, on February 21, Allan Pinkerton had already decided, with his client Samuel Felton's knowledge, to leave Baltimore for Philadelphia to demand an audience with the President.

That night, in downtown Philadelphia, one of Pinkerton's agents slipped Norman Judd a note requesting an immediate and urgent meeting. The already nervous Mr. Judd agreed. Pinkerton and his agent then summoned Mr. Felton to the detective's room at the St. Louis Hotel. Soon after Felton arrived in Pinkerton's room, so did Mr. Judd.[58]

Pinkerton had devised a plan. Neither the President nor his advisors would be the least bit thrilled at the prospect of carrying out Pinkerton's scheme. But what Pinkerton had in mind could well save Mr. Lincoln's life, and deliver him to the White House to begin serving his term.

The only way to rid the nation of slavery, abolitionist Pinkerton well knew, was to see Mr. Lincoln safely to Washington. Pinkerton was steadfastly determined, at all costs, to fulfill his self-appointed mission. The fate and future of America depended on it.

As detailed in Norma B. Cuthbert's Lincoln and the Baltimore Plot, Pinkerton laid out the results of his investigation, with PW&B CEO Sam Felton solemnly backing his story.[59] The rebels had amassed a team of assassins in Baltimore, complete with elaborate preparations for Lincoln's demise, including backup plans for various contingencies. The President-elect would be either shot, stabbed, or his rail car derailed if necessary with fireballs and/or hand-grenades used to finish the job. Plotters

Hillard and Ferrandini were specifically mentioned, as well as Pinkerton's assertion that the Baltimore police, led by Marshal Kane, were disloyal and would provide the Lincoln party with no assistance.

Pinkerton summed up his presentation with the stern warning that if the Lincoln Special were to proceed through Baltimore as planned, Pinkerton "*did not believe it was possible he (Lincoln) and his personal friends could pass through Baltimore in that style alive.*" Mr. Felton heartedly concurred.[60]

Judd would later recall, as recounted in Henry Clay Whitney's Lincoln the Citizen that, "*From their representations I became satisfied that a well-maintained plot did exist to kill Lincoln in Baltimore, and I then saw that something must be done.*"[61]

Pinkerton advised Judd that Mr. Lincoln's route needed to be secretly altered. Judd agreed, but felt the proud and stubborn Lincoln would never acquiesce to such a maneuver.

At this point, the great man himself — exhausted, overfed, and sleep-deprived — trying fitfully to get some rest in his suite at the Continental Hotel, had to be notified. Such a terrible secret could no longer be kept from the boss.

Pinkerton wanted the President to skip his planned Harrisburg stop altogether and travel directly (undercover) through Baltimore that night on the 11 p.m. train out of Philadelphia. He had barely an hour left to meet Lincoln and convince him of the prudence of this course of action. Pinkerton and Judd hurried to Judd's room over at the Continental, and immediately sent a messenger to request Lincoln's presence for an urgent meeting.

Soon the haggard figure of Lincoln appeared. Judd introduced the famous Pinkerton, who really needed no introduction, since he had met the President on previous occasions. Lincoln remembered the detective, whom he liked.

Judd and Pinkerton then presented their case to the President, as detailed in Allan Pinkerton's own History and Evidence,[62] stressing the seriousness of the would-be assassins, the depth of the intelligence that had been collected, and of Marshal Kane's boast at the Barnum Hotel that no police protection would be afforded to the Lincoln Party. Hillard, Ferrandini, and others in the cabal were described, their participation in the plot outlined.

Lincoln listened intently. He took the evidence being presented seriously. However, he balked at Pinkerton's suggestion to leave directly on the 11 o'clock train that evening for Baltimore and, ultimately, Washington, D.C.

"*No, I cannot consent to this,*" argued Lincoln firmly, as related in Cuthbert's <u>Lincoln and the Baltimore Plot</u>. "*I shall hoist the flag on Independence Hall tomorrow morning . . . and go to Harrisburg tomorrow. . . . (Once) I have fulfilled all my engagements . . . I shall endeavor to get away quietly from the people at Harrisburg tomorrow evening and shall place myself in your (hands).*"[63]

Later that evening, Mr. Lincoln sat alone in his hotel room pondering the startling developments that had earlier necessitated his last-minute change of plans. Was the Baltimore plot real? Could he afford, as the nation's new President, not to greet the crowd in Baltimore? Should he call off Pinkerton's subterfuge and emerge from the rail car at Calvert Street Station on the afternoon of the 23rd as planned?

Just then, at 11 p.m., the hour at which the late-night Philadelphia to Baltimore train was leaving the station, Lincoln received one last surprise visitor. It was Fred Seward, son of Senator William Seward. Young Seward proceeded to show Mr. Lincoln a series of unsettling reports and letters, summing up Superintendent Kennedy's investigation into the Baltimore plot. Apparently, the wholly separate investigation by the New York detectives sent to Baltimore had reached much the same conclusion as the Pinkerton detectives. The result of three weeks of undercover activity by Union spies was that "*there is serious danger of violence to and the assassination Mr. Lincoln in his passage through that city should the time of his passage be known . . . there are banded rowdies holding secret meetings, and . . . threats of mobbing and violence.*"[64]

The danger to the President and the Presidential party was deemed "imminent." Once more, the recommendation of the undercover operation so ordered by Senator Seward and General Winfield Scott was that, "*All risk might be easily avoided by a change in the travelling arrangements which would bring the Mr. Lincoln and a portion of his party through Baltimore by a night train without previous notice.*"[65]

Two separate, independent investigations with no knowledge of each other's existence had uncovered the same terrifying information while recommending the same radical course of action — that Abraham Lincoln should secretly slip through Baltimore at night completely unnoticed.

Next morning, after Mr. Lincoln had addressed the Philadelphia crowd and hoisted the flag at Independence Hall, the Lincoln Special headed west to Harrisburg. At the Jones House in Harrisburg, some excitement occurred when the President-elect realized he could not find a copy of the inaugural address, a speech Lincoln had been honing since before they had all left Springfield, Illinois. Son Robert Todd Lincoln had misplaced his father's gripsack which contained the speech. To Lincoln's relief, the gripsack (with top-secret speech inside) was recovered in the hotel's baggage room where it had been set aside by a hotel clerk.[66]

The President made his scheduled speeches in Harrisburg, all six of them, although he apologized for their brevity on account he was feeling a bit unwell. Lincoln also met with various local dignitaries, including Pennsylvania Governor Curtain, and ate more banquet food.

That evening, back at Harrisburg's Jones House, Norman Judd dropped the bombshell on the rest of the Lincoln Special insiders. For his own protection, Mr. Lincoln would be secretly leaving that evening to pass quietly through Baltimore at night. He would arrive in Washington D.C., while skipping all appearances in Baltimore.[67]

A heated debate broke out amongst the men as Lincoln listened. The President's political advisors, like Judd, generally approved of the plan. The military men, however, saw Lincoln's decision in a far different light.

"*That proceeding,*" huffed Colonel Sumner, according to Cuthbert's <u>Lincoln and the Baltimore Plot</u>, "*will be a damned piece of cowardice. . . . I'll get a squad of Cavalry and cut our way to Washington, Sir.*"[68]

Mr. Judd reminded Colonel Sumner that such action, even if successful, would likely cause the President to be late for his own inauguration.

Ward Hill Lamon, Lincoln's linebacker sized personal assistant and unofficial bodyguard, offered his boss a revolver and a Bowie knife. Pinkerton protested Lamon's offer. Says Cuthbert in <u>Lincoln and the Baltimore Plot</u>, Pinkerton, "*would not for the world have it said that Mr. Lincoln had to enter the National Capitol armed.*"[69]

This would not be the only head-on clash between Messrs. Pinkerton and Lamon. In later years, Pinkerton would accuse Lamon of being an ignorant, loudmouthed drunk whose behavior threatened the success of this most crucial undercover operation. Lamon, for his part, never believed there had been a credible threat to the President's life. He saw the "charade" as a chance for Pinkerton to curry favor with the new Administration and to gain notoriety for his growing detective agency. [70]

In the end, the men turned to Lincoln for his explanation.

"*I've thought the matter over fully,*" Mr. Lincoln said calmly, as recorded in Henry Clay Whitney's Lincoln the Citizen, "*and I reckon I had better do as Judd says. The facts come from two different and reliable sources, and I don't consider it right to disregard both.*"[71]

So, the matter was settled.

As darkness fell over Harrisburg, the 16th-President of the United States changed clothes, then emerged from a quiet back exit at the Jones Hotel, where he was secretly whisked away in a horse-drawn carriage to the train depot. A special engine and train car was already waiting and at the ready. Pinkerton saw to it that all of the telegraph lines leading south to Baltimore were cut — just in case any rebel spies had been somehow tipped to Mr. Lincoln's change in itinerary.[72]

As the night proceeded, Lincoln's secret ride rumbled east at top speed back towards Philadelphia. This evening, Mr. Lincoln would arrive in time to catch the late-night train from Philadelphia to Baltimore. He was accompanied by Allan Pinkerton, Kate Warne, and personal bodyguard Ward Hill Lamon.

The top executives at the Pennsylvania Railroad, on whose tracks the secret, shades-drawn Presidential train raced to Philadelphia, had been in on the scheme. So, of course, was Samuel Felton of the Philadelphia, Wilmington, and Baltimore (PW&B) Line, which would carry these four passengers to Baltimore. The decision had been made, however, that the executives of the Baltimore & Ohio Railroad could not be trusted which such highly sensitive information.[73]

According to Summers in The Baltimore and Ohio in the Civil War., "*John Work Garrett, president of the B&O Railroad, had, the previous winter, declared his railroad to be a 'Southern line' and asked rhetorically was it not right that 'Baltimore should declare her position in the irrepressible conflict' threatened and urged by Northern fanaticism."*[74]

Charles Webb, past Grand Master of the Freemasons and senior executive at James Armstrong & Company, was also a director at the B&O Railroad.

Once in Philadelphia, Mr. Lincoln, disguised in an ordinary sack overcoat and "Kossuth" hat (a kind of Scottish cap) while being coached to slump and crouch to conceal his true height, was quickly transferred from the special Pennsylvania rail car to the sleeper car aboard the PW&B night train. For the rest of his surreptitious journey Lincoln would play the part of a reclusive invalid traveling with the assistance of family.

Along the route through northern Maryland to Baltimore, Pinkerton had placed agents at the major bridge crossings, who were instructed to continually flash a lantern at their boss on the approaching train to signal possible trouble ahead. Just one quick flash to Pinkerton gave the lead detective the "all clear" sign.[75]

In Baltimore's President Street Station in the dead of night, the railcar carrying the "sick and invalid" Mr. Lincoln, a watchful Mr. Pinkerton, a well-armed Mr. Lamon, and a sleepless Ms. Warne was unhooked from the PW&B train. Once free, it was then pulled by a team of horses along the tracks of a deserted Pratt Street just past 3 a.m. as all of Baltimore — including the conspirators — slept undisturbed. Before the lone, inconspicuous rail car reached Camden Street Station for the final leg of the journey south to Washington, D.C., the sound of clopping horse hooves would have momentarily broken the silence as the rail car passed by the corner of Concord and Pratt Streets and the darkened factory and offices of James Armstrong & Company on the right, and the gently lapping harbor lined with docked sailing ships, including Captain Mattison's vessel, on the left.

By morning, after a nerve-wracking 45-minute layover at Camden Street Station followed by an uneasy but uneventful ride in the back berth of a B&O sleeper car, Mr. Lincoln and his three-person escort arrived safely in the nation's capital. Pinkerton and Lamon had been on the ready at each stop, riding shotgun at the door to the last car's rear platform in case anyone tried to approach the railcar. Sam Felton had seen to it that undercover security was provided for the front of the train. In the flickering candlelight, the passengers slept away peacefully, blissfully unaware of Mr. Lincoln's presence behind his berth's curtain and of the President's highly unorthodox secret security arrangements.[76]

By morning, the President-elect was by stealth delivered to Willard's Hotel via carriage and checked into his luxury suite most of a day ahead of schedule.

According to Pinkerton's subsequent report, as told in Cuthbert's Lincoln and the Baltimore Plot, "*Mr. Lincoln was cool, calm, and self-possessed — firm and determined in his bearing. He evinced no sign of fear or distrust, and throughout the entire night was quite self-possessed.*"[77]

Kate Warne, who had zealously guarded the President throughout that long night, from Harrisburg to Philadelphia to Baltimore, and who had made most of the arrangements for the hastily scheduled plan to smuggle Lincoln into Washington (posing as Lincoln's sister), had validated Pinkerton's decision to hire her as the country's first female detective. It has been said that Warne, who "*did not sleep a wink*" throughout that fateful evening, was Pinkerton's inspiration behind his agency's soon-to-be famous slogan "*we never sleep.*"[78]

With Lincoln safely resting in his room at Willard's Hotel, three blocks from the White House, the much relieved Allan Pinkerton fired off a final coded telegram to his client Sam Felton in Pennsylvania. . . .

"*Plums delivered nuts safely.*"[79]

Elsewhere in the elegant Willard Hotel, the so-called "Peace Conference" of Northern and Southern politicians was meeting in the grand ballroom in an apparent attempt to come to a solution to the ongoing secession of Southern states and the threat of civil war.

The meeting was soon interrupted, however, by whispered rumors that Lincoln had already arrived at the hotel.

Vermont's Lucius Chittenden, a pro-Union delegate who had been privy to the Baltimore Republicans' knowledge of the Baltimore assassination plot, happened to be seated between two fiercely pro-secessionist delegates. As the conference was called to order, a slave owned by Virginia's pro-secessionist James Seddon approached his master and handed over a note. Seddon read the note, blinked, and reached past Chittenden to pass the note to Missouri's Waldo Johnson, also an uncompromising secessionist. As revealed in Chittenden's Recollections, "*Mr. Seddon glanced at it, and passed it before me to Mr. Johnson, so near to my face that, without closing my eyes, I could not avoid reading it. The words written upon it were LINCOLN IS IN THIS HOTEL! The Missourian was startled as by a shock of electricity. He must have forgotten himself completely, for he instantly exclaimed 'How the devil did he get through Baltimore?' There was no reply, but the occurrence left the impression on one mind that the preparations to receive Mr. Lincoln in Baltimore were known to some who were neither Italian assassins nor Baltimore Plug-Uglies. Mr. Johnson was not the only delegate surprised by the announcement of Mr. Lincoln's presence in Washington. . . ."[80]*

By the following year, James Seddon would become the Confederate States' Secretary of War for the duration of hostilities — a post to which he was appointed by CSA President Jefferson Davis.

On the afternoon of February 23rd, 1861, a crowd of thousands stood disappointed at the Calvert Street Station in Baltimore as Abraham Lincoln failed to make his scheduled appearance. The train from Harrisburg had been purposely halted several blocks north of the Calvert Street depot at North Charles and Bolton Streets to allow Mrs. Lincoln and the Lincoln sons to disembark and be escorted to a private reception at the Gittings mansion on Mt. Vernon Place. They would be spared from the raucous mob awaiting the Lincolns at Calvert Street Station.

Mrs. Lincoln and sons would be whisked to their quiet engagement by none other than Marshal George Kane, who assumedly was notified of the last-minute change of plans only after Mr. Lincoln had been smuggled through the city the previous evening.

Once it was made clear that Mr. Lincoln would not be showing his craggy, angular, and now bearded visage in Baltimore, the huge crowd at the depot eventually began to break up and disperse. During this time, a curious event was observed by several onlookers . . . the presence of eggs. Broken eggshells on the ground, yolk seeping from broken eggs inside the pockets of young toughs, and the smell of egg permeating the tense downtown air.[81]

For example, *The Philadelphia Inquirer*, in its February 25, 1861 column *The Story About Baltimore*, would write, "*There were many reckless boys and dissolute young men in the crowd, who had eggs and other missiles in their pockets, which, as is presumed, they designed throwing at somebody."*[82]

Since the "somebody" who didn't show was Mr. Lincoln and his party, and the eggs and other missiles remained un-thrown on the afternoon in question, a conclusion here is easily drawn. The real question is, were these *"reckless boys and dissolute young men"* merely local troublemakers looking for kicks? Or, were they part of an organized plot to divert the attention of the underwhelming number of men assigned to Marshal George Kane's Calvert Street police detail?

Not surprisingly, the new President was lampooned in newspapers across the country, where both his good judgment and intestinal fortitude were loudly and sometimes rudely challenged. These included even some solidly pro-Republican publications. The harshest, most vile criticism came from, not unexpectedly, the hometown *Baltimore Sun:*

"Had we any respect for Mr. Lincoln, official or personal, as a man . . . the final escapade by which he reached the capital would have utterly demolished it, and overwhelmed us with mortification. He might have entered Willard's Hotel with a 'head spring' and a 'summersault,' and the clown's merry greeting to Gen. Scott, 'Here we are!' and we should care nothing about it personally."[83]

Needless to say, this was tough stuff, and would have been bitter medicine for a proud man such as Mr. Lincoln to swallow.

Headlines in other cities read *"Lincoln's Panic and Flight," "Terrible Conspiracy to Assassinate Abraham Lincoln: Or a Prodigious Hoax,"* and *"Flight of Mr. Lincoln from Harrisburg in Disguise."*

Newspaper cartoons of the 1860s ridiculing Lincoln's late-night ride to Washington, D.C.

It was a most inauspicious way for the 16th President of the United States to begin his term. The *New York Tribune* summed up this most unusual turn of events by writing, *"It is the only instance recorded in our history in which the recognized head of a nation . . . has been compelled, for fear of his life, to enter the capital in disguise."*[84]

Thankfully, President Abraham Lincoln survived to be inaugurated on March 4th, 1861 in Washington D.C. For the swearing in ceremony he was aptly guarded. Though Lincoln was temporarily safe and ensconced in the White House, Washington, D.C. and the nation were still under imminent threat. The 16th President of the United States would be afforded no early days "honeymoon." Lincoln would need to act boldly, decisively, and with due speed. Surrounded by the hostile, pro-South states of Virginia and Maryland, the nation's capital was in need of immediate military reinforcement.

And Baltimore? Lincoln would deal with that problem in due time. He would not likely soon forget the indignity and humiliation of having to sneak through that rebel-controlled metropolis in cheap disguise and under cover of darkness.

The President and the nation stood teetering on the edge of a precipice. Was a war between the states inevitable? Lincoln strove mightily to prevent that outcome. But his first and foremost goal was to preserve the Union. If the South proceeded with her madness, Abe Lincoln was prepared to do the unthinkable — use military force against fellow Americans — to prevent the ultimate breakup of the country.

Less than two months after his inauguration, the first blood of the Civil War would be spilled. The violence began not on some far away battlefield between opposing armies, but rather in an anti-Union riot that flared dangerously out of control on the busy streets of downtown Baltimore.

Much of that red American blood would be splashed on Pratt Street by the Basin, today's touristy Inner Harbor. Some of that blood would fall onto the cobblestone roadway just past the Pratt Street Bridge that spanned Jones Falls. From there it would run into the gutter at the bottom of the road that housed the offices of James Armstrong and Company, longtime purveyors of fine soaps and candles.

Some 16 people — four Union soldiers passing through town and about a dozen local civilians — would die on April 19th, 1861. Marshal George Kane and Mayor George Brown would be front and center stage in that historic, deadly melee.

At least 600,000 more fellow countrymen would die in the resulting aftermath. . . .

The United States of America would never again be remotely the same.

Baltimore at War

Painting depicting the Pratt Street, Baltimore riot of April 19, 1861.

The first shots fired in the Civil War occurred during the Confederate siege, bombardment, and eventual takeover of Fort Sumter, South Carolina by Brigadier General P.G.T. Beauregard (a suspected Knight)[1] and his rebel troops from April 12 through April 14, 1861. However, the Confederates managed to wrestle the fort from federal control with no loss of life. The first actual *casualties* in the War Between the States would be suffered just days later, on the streets of Baltimore, in what would become known as the "Pratt Street Riot."[2]

With seven Southern states announcing their plans to secede from the Union, and subsequent military force being used by Southern authorities to seize federal property, the young presidency of Abraham Lincoln faced an immediate and serious challenge. Since the nation's capital, Washington D.C., was surrounded by the Southern slave states of Maryland and Virginia, Lincoln realized his first order of business was to protect an unguarded and potentially vulnerable seat of federal power. In response, the President sent out a call for immediate federal troop reinforcements to move south into Washington. With the insurrection still in its infancy, Lincoln asked for 75,000 volunteers to serve for 90 days.[3] While many Northern states quickly met the call to supply troops, other less compliant states balked at Lincoln's request. Governor Clairborne Jackson of Missouri replied that, *"Not one man will the state of Missouri furnish to carry on any such holy crusade."*[4] Governor Magoffin of Kentucky's retort was equally harsh. *"Kentucky will furnish no troops for the wicked purpose of subduing her sister Southern states."*[5]

On April 17th, Virginia formally voted to secede from the Union. Might Southern-leaning Maryland with its pro-Confederate legislature be next? If the emboldened rebels were to launch an all-out assault on an encircled and lightly guarded Washington, D.C., their chance of seizing the capital and placing Lincoln under arrest was high. Rumors had already been circulating that KGC-affiliated Ben McCulloch from Texas was in Virginia raising an army for this very purpose.[6]

Only the weak, vacillating, Know-Nothing governor of Maryland, Thomas Holiday Hicks, stood between the rebels and their goal of tipping Maryland into the secessionist fold.

For President Lincoln, an already bad situation was rapidly growing worse. With Virginia announcing its move to the Confederate camp, time was of the essence. The time to act was now.

As Frederick Seward wrote in his book <u>Seward at Washington, 1846-1861</u>, *"The people of the District are looking anxiously for the result of the Virginia election. They fear that if Virginia resolves on secession, Maryland will follow; and then Washington will be seized."*[7]

The Massachusetts troops of the state's 6th Regiment were put on a southbound train out of Boston the evening of the same day Virginia seceded.[8]

The problem for any troops arriving from the North was traversing Confederate-leaning Maryland — and especially the dangerous city of Baltimore with its well-earned 19-century "Mobtown" reputation. Union soldiers would face the same intimidating threat Mr. Lincoln himself had faced just two months earlier in his attempt to reach Washington for his March 4th inauguration. All trains headed south to the capital were forced to pass through Baltimore. There was simply no other solution to quickly and efficiently transport such a large number of soldiers. The troops needed to travel by rail; therefore, that required dangerous travel through the very heart of the "Charm City."

The first troops to reach Baltimore — at the Bolton Street Station near Howard Street — were some 400+ volunteers from Pennsylvania's 25th Regiment, who had ridden on trains headed south from Harrisburg. The volunteers were met in Baltimore on April 18th by regular Army units being redeployed from out west on the nation's frontier. The largely unarmed Pennsylvania volunteers, wearing civilian clothes, would march or ride in carriages to catch the Baltimore & Ohio train at Camden Street Station to complete their journey south to Washington. Meanwhile, the regular Army units would march or catch local transportation to nearby Fort McHenry to help bolster that military installation's defenses in light of the escalating tension between North and South.[9]

The sudden influx of Union troops on April 18th that were heading south or reporting for assignment at Fort McHenry caught the citizens of Baltimore by surprise. No one, including the mayor nor the police, had been informed of their arrival. There were some minor incidents reported, mostly taunting and name-calling from the locals, but the troops all reached their destinations practically unscathed . . . though there were scattered reports of a few stones and bricks being hurled, and of one Yankee soldier suffering a minor head wound.[10] These first Union troops went through downtown Baltimore quickly, and they did so without confronting and provoking the jeering street protestors.

The following day, April 19th, would prove an entirely different matter. With news of Union troop arrivals spreading by the hour, the anti-war and pro-secessionist elements of the city would now be prepared to resist the blue-coated Yankee aggressors. The Union forces' element of surprise had come and gone. Still, they had their orders, and were fully intent on carrying them out.

Colonel Edward F. Jones of the 6th Massachusetts regiment, which had departed from Boston on the evening of the 17th, and had arrived in Philadelphia on the 18th, had been warned by railroad personnel of impending trouble in Baltimore. While on route to that city, Colonel Jones went through the PW&B railcars, telling the men to load their weapons, and gave the following order:

"The regiment will march through Baltimore in columns of sections, arms at will. You will undoubtedly be insulted, abused, and, perhaps, assaulted, to which you must pay no attention whatever, but march with your faces to the front, and pay no attention to the mob, even if they throw stones, bricks, or other missiles; but if you are fired upon and any one of you is hit, your officers will order you to fire. Do not fire into any promiscuous crowds, but select any man whom you may see aiming at you, and be sure you drop him."[11]

This directive would prove frightfully difficult to carry out, based largely on the antiquated muskets the Massachusetts soldiers had been issued. Reloading these one-shot weapons was a drawn-out, tedious process . . . making the muzzle-loaded long guns entirely unsuitable for the up-close and personal job of urban crowd control.

The first seven companies of the 6th Massachusetts had their rail cars pulled quickly along the tracks from President Street to Camden Street Station, a total distance of about 1.5 miles, before the crowds of Baltimore rowdies began to swell and grow menacingly angry.

Suddenly, a group of men and boys jumped out to barricade the street at Pratt and Concord, just over the Pratt Street Bridge at Jones Falls and within easy sight of the James Armstrong & Co. building. A ship's anchor from the harbor and other heavy objects were dragged onto the tracks, rendering them unpassable. The 6th's regimental band and four other companies of soldiers were left stranded, their rail cars surrounded by angry Baltimoreans. If there was ever any doubt that Lincoln might have been in trouble on February 23rd had he kept to his scheduled itinerary, what happened to the armed Massachusetts 6th Regiment should dispel those doubts. Dismounting the blocked rail cars that had, until now, afforded them "iron-clad" protection, the soldiers marched double-time on foot westward toward Camden Street Station. They did so under an almost continuous barrage of stones, bricks, oyster shells, and other hurled garbage. The Massachusetts men followed the lead of their courageous ranking officer, Captain A.S. Follansbee.[12]

The armed Union troops were now fully out in the open, exposed to the same Pratt Street "kill zone" that had once been prepared for the hated Mr. Lincoln. And again, executives at

James Armstrong & Company offices were being afforded a bird's eye view. As the crowd pursued the main body of Union troops westward on Pratt Street, the troops broke out into a run towards Camden Street station, firing wildly over their shoulders at their pursuers.

In the confusion, scores of uniformed Massachusetts soldiers at the very rear turned, broke rank, and ran back towards the President Street Station, looking for sanctuary, while some of the troops not dressed in uniform attempted to duck off the street and blend in with the crowd. To make matters worse, unarmed recruits of the Pennsylvania 26th were just arriving at the President Street Station from Philadelphia, and found themselves immediately trapped and under threat of assault at that depot.[13]

On Pratt Street, one brazen rioter began dancing ahead of Captain Follensbee's marching soldiers while contemptuously holding aloft a rebel flag. A Union officer wrestled the Stars and Bars away from the protestor, while someone in the crowd used the momentary opportunity to snatch a Yankee's musket.[14] It would not be the only musket grabbed and turned against its owners during the melee.

Over at Camden Street Station, Marshal Kane arrived with a detachment of about 50 police. Kane and his men had their hands full keeping the mob away from Colonel Jones and his troops as they boarded the B&O train cars headed south out of Baltimore.

Meanwhile, the mob busied itself with piling up yet another formidable barricade, this one further along the tracks at the intersection of Pratt and Gay Streets. This seemed a deliberate attempt to box in the remaining four companies of the 6th Massachusetts, led by Captain Follansbee, which were now being blocked from either retreating to President Street or advancing to Camden Street.[15]

More than a quarter of a century after that tragic day, the former Baltimore Mayor George William Brown (right) would describe the hellish chaos on Pratt Street in the chapter "The Fight" from his memoir, Baltimore and The Nineteenth of April, 1861.[16] Brown, a staunchly pro-secessionist politician handpicked by

Charles Webb's Democratic reform committee, had been working at his office when he was informed by a messenger sent by Marshal Kane of the trouble boiling over on Pratt Street.

"I immediately hastened to the office of the board of police, and found they had received a similar notice," recalled Brown. *"The Counsellor of the City, Mr. George M. Gill, and myself drove rapidly in a carriage to the Camden-street station. The police commissioners followed, and on reaching the station, we found Marshal Kane on the ground and the police coming in squads. A large and angry crowd had assembled, but were restrained by the police from committing any serious breach of the peace.*

"After considerable delay seven of the eleven companies of the Massachusetts regiment arrived at the station, as already mentioned, and I saw that the windows of the last car were badly broken. No one to whom I applied could inform me whether more troops were expected or not. At the time an alarm was given that the mob was about to tear up the rails in advance of the train on the Washington road, and Marshal Kane ordered some of his men to go out the road as far as necessary to protect the track. Soon afterward, and when I was about to leave the Camden-street station, supposing all danger to be over, news was brought to Police Commissioner Davis and myself, who were standing together, that some troops had been left behind, and that the mob was tearing up the track on Pratt street, so as to obstruct the progress of the cars, which were coming to the Camden-street station. Mr. Davis immediately ran to summon the marshal, who was at the station with a body of police, to be sent to the point of danger, while I hastened alone in the same direction. On arriving at Smith's Wharf, foot of Gay street, I found that anchors had been placed on the track, and that Sergeant McComas and four policemen who were with him were not allowed by a group of rioters to remove the obstruction. I ordered the anchors to be removed, and my authority was not resisted. I hurried on, and, approaching Pratt-street bridge, I saw a battalion, which proved to be four companies of the Massachusetts regiment which had crossed the bridge, coming towards me in double-quick time.

"They were firing wildly, sometimes backward, over their shoulders. So rapid was the march that they could not stop to take aim. The mob, which was not very large, as it seemed to me, was pursuing with shouts and stones, and, I think, an occasional

pistol-shot. The uproar was furious. I ran at once to the head of the column, some persons in the crowd shouting, 'Here comes the mayor.' I shook hands with the officer in command, Captain Follansbee, saying as I did so, 'I am the Mayor of Baltimore.' The captain greeted me cordially. I at once objected to the double-quick, which was immediately stopped. I placed myself by his side, and marched with him. He said, 'We have been attacked without provocation,' or words to that effect. I replied, 'You must defend yourselves.' I expected that he would face his men to the rear, and, after giving warning, would fire if necessary. But I said no more, for immediately felt that, as mayor of the city, it was not my province to volunteer such advice. . . .

"The column continued to march. There was neither concert of action nor organization among the rioters. They were armed with only such stones or missiles as they could pick up, and a few pistols. My presence for a short time had some effect, but very soon the attack was renewed with great violence.

"The mob grew bolder. Stones flew thick and fast. Rioters rushed at the soldiers and attempted to snatch their muskets, and on at least two occasions succeeded. With one of these muskets a soldier was killed. Men fell on both sides. A young lawyer, then and now known as a quiet citizen, seized a flag of one of the companies and nearly tore it from its staff. He was shot through the thigh and was carried home apparently a dying man, but he survived to enter the army of the Confederacy, where he rose to the rank of captain. . . . The soldiers fired at will. There was no firing by platoons, and I heard no order given to fire. I remember that at the corner of South street several citizens standing in a group fell, either killed or wounded. It was impossible for the troops to discriminate between rioters and by-standers, but the latter seemed to suffer most, because, as the main attack from the mob pursuing the soldiers from the rear, they, in their march, could not easily face backward to fire, but could shoot at those whom they passed on the street. Near the corner of Light street a soldier was severely wounded, who afterward died, and a boy on a vessel lying in the dock was killed, and about the same place three soldiers at the head of the column leveled their muskets and fired into a group standing on the sidewalk, who, as far as I could see, were taking no active part. The shots took effect, but I cannot say how many fell. I cried out, waving my umbrella to emphasize my words, 'For God's sake don't shoot!' but it was too late. The

statement that I begged Captain Follansbee not to let the men fire is incorrect, although on this occasion I did say, 'Don't shoot.' It then seemed to me that I was in the wrong place, for my presence did not avail to protect either the soldiers or the citizens, and I stepped out from the column. . . . At the moment when I returned to the street, Marshal Kane, with about fifty policemen (as I then supposed, but I have since ascertained that in fact there were not so many), came at a run from the direction of the Camden-street station, and throwing themselves in the rear of the troops, they formed a line in front of the mob, and with drawn revolvers kept it back. This was between Light and Charles streets. Marshal Kane's voice shouted, 'Keep back, men, or I shoot!' This movement, which I saw myself, was gallantly executed, and was perfectly successful. The mob recoiled like water from a rock. . . ."[17]

    The soldiers broke into a run for Camden Station, sometimes still firing wildly into the crowd. The police assisted the soldiers onto the southbound B&O train cars, but an angry mob followed the train south for nearly a mile, attempting to drag more heavy objects, including logs, onto the tracks leading from the city.[18]

    Of the nearly 1,800 Union troops, some 130 were missing. To add to the chaos, more federal troops were still arriving at both the Calvert Street and President Street stations. Some stranded soldiers were sent by police north to Havre de Grace or Philadelphia. A few actually walked for days to make it back into Pennsylvania.[19]

    Later that day, Maryland officials, including Kane, Brown, and Governor Hicks who had come quickly from Annapolis on news of the trouble, demanded of Washington that no more Union troops be allowed to travel through their state. The telegrams flew hot and heavy, with the Marylanders protesting that more violence would certainly be the result, and that Lincoln and his administration needed to get their troops to the capital via some other less confrontational and antagonistic route.[20] Maryland officials were holding the President accountable for the chaos in Baltimore. Some four soldiers had already been killed, along with at least three dozen Union men wounded. A dozen Baltimorean lives had been lost, with an unknown number injured. Historians have place the number of Baltimore citizens wounded at upwards of 100.

President Lincoln, under pressure to defend Washington before it was too late, told a peace delegation from the YMCA that *"union soldiers were neither birds to fly over Maryland, nor moles to burrow under it."*[21] Like it or not, Mr. Lincoln was determined to send more troops south to Washington, D.C. by rail, and if the people in Baltimore couldn't behave themselves, they would soon be dealt with by a very displeased President with the power of the entire federal government and its massive military might at his disposal.

A frustrated Marshal Kane, already no fan of Mr. Lincoln and *"the very scum of the city"* who had voted for the President (Kane's own words), had by this time reached his breaking point. Kane's contacts at the B&O Railroad had passed along a dispatch from the Pennsylvania Railroad warning of more Union troops heading south for Baltimore. The officials at the PRR duly noted *"that it was impossible to prevent these troops from going through Baltimore."*[22] More unwanted Union troops, more rioting, more death. Late on April 19th, a livid Marshal Kane would fire off the following controversial telegram to Virginia militia leader Bradley T. Johnson in Frederick, MD:

"Streets red with Maryland blood; send expresses over the mountains of Maryland and Virginia for the riflemen to come without delay. Fresh hordes will be down on us tomorrow. We will fight them and whip them, or die." [23]

For all of Kane's demonstrated bravery on April 19th protecting the lives of both Union soldiers and his fellow Baltimore citizens, it would be Kane's incendiary telegram asking for protection from the Virginia militia that would make Marshal Kane a marked man in the White House and in Washington's corridors of power.

Mayor George Brown would issue his own public call to arms, advising that *"All citizens having arms suitable for the defense of the city, and which they are willing to contribute for the purpose, are requested to deposit them at the office of the marshal of police."*[24]

Maryland officials, including Kane, Brown, and Governor Hicks would all vociferously demand that no more Union troops be allowed to travel through the state. Their urgent requests would fall on deaf federal ears.

The American Party's "Know Nothing" Governor Thomas Holiday Hicks, in an attempt to quickly get a handle on the volatile situation, checked into a hotel room at the downtown Fountain Inn and set up temporary office in that longtime Baltimore establishment. Hicks then sent word for Brown, Kane, and a few other available officials to see the governor for an emergency meeting at The Fountain.[25]

As news of the Pratt Street tragedy spread first through Maryland, and then across an apprehensive nation, word came to former Baltimore native James Ryder Randall who was teaching English literature at a Louisiana college. Randall also soon received word that a close friend had been slain on Pratt Street by members of the 6th Massachusetts Regiment. Believing that Maryland was about to secede from the Union, the staunchly pro-Confederate Randall defiantly penned the following poem:

> *The despot's heel is on thy shore,*
> *Maryland! My Maryland!*
> *His torch is at thy temple door,*
> *Maryland! My Maryland*
> *Avenge the patriotic gore*
> *That flecked the streets of Baltimore,*
> *And the battle queen of yore,*
> *Maryland! My Maryland!!* [26]

As to the identity of Randall's "despot" whose heel is on Maryland's shore, there can be no doubt. Randall's despot is President Abraham Lincoln. Later sung to the tune of *Lauriger Horatius* (better known as the Christmas song "*O, Tannenbaum*"), Randall's turgid poem turned to song became popular throughout the South, and was eventually adopted as the Maryland State song in 1939. Efforts to have the words to "*My Maryland*" changed or replaced by a different song have all since failed. "*My Maryland*" remains the official song of Maryland to this day.

Meanwhile, at the Fountain Hotel on the evening of April 19th, a nervous Governor Hicks appeared to be growing increasingly paranoid by the minute. The hotel, known to be patronized by a legion of secessionists and outspoken Southern sympathizers, was proving to be inhospitable territory for a pro-Union governor who had been refusing to call a session of the Maryland state legislature so that a vote on the subject of secession could be taken.

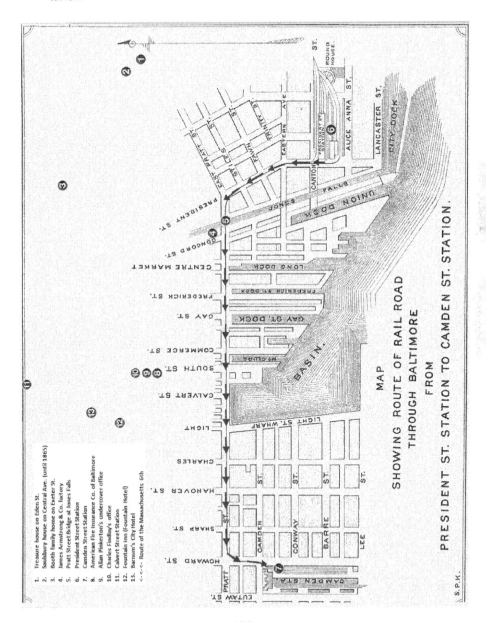

1. Treasure house on Eden St.
2. Saulsbury home on Central Ave. (until 1865)
3. Booth Family home on Exeter St.
4. James Armstrong & Co. factory
5. Pratt Street Bridge at Jones Falls
6. President Street Station
7. Camden Street Station
8. American Fire Insurance Co. of Baltimore
9. Allan Pinkerton's undercover office
10. Charles Findlay's office
11. Calvert Street Station
12. Fountain Inn (Fountain Hotel)
13. Barnum's City Hotel
<<< Route of the Massachusetts 6th

MAP

SHOWING ROUTE OF RAIL ROAD THROUGH BALTIMORE FROM PRESIDENT ST. STATION TO CAMDEN ST. STATION.

S.P.K.

Hicks, who had been openly threatened by Northern politicians with armed invasion if his state dared secede, was now facing the increased possibility of being strung up by the neck by some of his more strident constituents if indeed Maryland *failed* to secede. The culturally pro-South yet politically pro-Union governor was caught between that proverbial rock and a hard place . . . and the atmosphere at The Fountain with freshly spilled blood still staining nearby Pratt Street was anything but mellow.

Sometime that evening, a thoroughly terrorized Governor Hicks fled The Fountain "*apparently out of fear for his life,*" according to George Radcliffe's work <u>Governor Thomas H. Hicks</u>.[27] Hicks sought refuge in the downtown home of Mayor George Brown, with the emergency meeting being reconvened at the mayor's house. Hicks, now completely unnerved, reportedly did not want to come out of his guest bedroom, forcing the Maryland decision makers to hold their strategy session there.

Attending the bedroom meeting with the governor were Mayor George Brown, Marshal George Kane, Mayor Brown's brother, and former Maryland Governor Enoch Lewis Lowe. The mayor's bother and the former governor were present largely in an advisory capacity, and also to act as witnesses to what was to transpire.

The three primary decision-makers in those confined bedroom quarters were Mayor Brown, Marshal Kane, and Governor Hicks. It is important to understand that Charles Webb of James Armstrong & Co. was closely acquainted with all *three* men, who at that crucial point in history held the fate of all Maryland in their hands. Webb had spearheaded the 1859 push by the pro-slavery Democratic Reform Committee to have the corrupt American Party administration of Thomas Swann removed. Webb's political allies Brown and Kane were then installed to clean up the mess left by the departing Know-Nothings, and to once again instill the public's trust in both the mayor's office and the beleaguered police department, which had been criticized for its ineffectual service during the city's "Mobtown" days. That rebuilding process had been slowly underway until April 19th, 1861, when it suddenly seemed the wheels were threatening to come off Baltimore's entire municipal wagon.

Mr. Webb was also well known to Governor Hicks through the politician's membership in Maryland's influential Scottish Rite Freemasons.[28] In the year 1849, at a time when Webb was the rising star in Maryland Freemason circles, Thomas Holiday Hicks served as the Deputy Grand Master of the society's statewide organization. Webb would be elected to the post of Senior Grand Warden in 1851, and then Grand Master in 1853 — with Arkansan Albert Pike named as one of Webb's six "companion" masons. There can be little doubt that Webb would have been on a first-name basis with Hicks for years prior to their late-night April 19th meeting at the home of the mayor.

From the start of the meeting, Brown and Kane badgered Hicks for permission to burn the railroad bridges north of Baltimore. This highly radical and dangerous move seemed the only option available to prevent further troops from passing through an already highly agitated city. Hicks, at first, respectfully refused, wanting no part of such blatantly criminal action. Secessionists Brown and Kane continued to insist. In theory, the legal authority of the mayor and the police marshal ended at Baltimore's city's limits. Governor Hicks, on the other hand, had executive dominion over the entire state. The bridges several miles north of Baltimore were the structures that needed to be incapacitated. President Lincoln had to be thwarted, else more blood would surely be spilled in Baltimore. It was ugly business, for sure, but Brown and Kane felt they were trying to do what was best for Baltimoreans, as well as their Southern brethren who might well become the next targets for the invading Yankee boys in blue.

Gradually, the mayor and the marshal wore the governor down, who could not readily disagree with their prediction for more street violence. Finally, Hicks relented and told Mayor Brown he could "*do as he pleased*" according to George Radcliffe's Governor Thomas H. Hicks.[29]

Such an answer was not good enough for Mayor Brown or Marshal Kane. The perpetrators knew they needed specific and express consent from the governor. As Michael J. Kline says in his book The Baltimore Plot, "*. . . but Brown was not seeking tacit permission in the form of Hicks' offer to look the other way, to wash his hands of the responsibility like some Pontius Pilate. Mayor Brown was seeking an order to act, or at the least, the governor's express consent — his agreement to engage in the plan. Mayor Brown was a lawyer who well knew the elements of conspiracy. If he and others were ultimately to be charged with conspiring to torch bridges, Brown wanted Governor Hicks in on it.*

The Union government might not think twice about arresting a pro-secession mayor and police chief, but the apparently pro-Union governor of a state as vital as Maryland? Surely, Brown must have figured, the governor's sanction would demonstrate to Washington the legitimacy of the act and save them all."[30]

Although Brown would later deny it, he finally relented and gave his consent, as was later supported by all others present in the room. Brown would attempt to weakly explain his actions by saying that, *"The Mayor could act as he pleased . . . I had no power to interfere with his designs. If this be consent to the destruction of the bridges, then I consented. If this be complicity in an unlawful act, then I was accessory."* [31]

"The admission by Hicks," points out author Michael J. Kline in <u>The Baltimore Plot</u>, *"is an astounding one for a governor to make. At best, it demonstrates a total abdication of responsibility. At worst, no matter whether his role in the conspiracy is termed inaction, tacit consent, or active participation, Hicks conferred state authority where previously there was none."* [32]

Said Mayor Brown of the matter, *"Governor Hicks was first consulted and urged to give his consent, for we desired that he should share with us the responsibility of taking this grave step. This consent he distinctly gave in my presence and in the presence of several others, and although there was an attempt afterward to deny the fact that he so consented, there can be no doubt whatever about the matter. He was in my house at the time, where, on my invitation, he had taken refuge, thinking that he was in some personal danger at the hotel where he was staying."* [33]

"Like Nero who fiddled why Rome burned," added Kline, *"Hicks did nothing, while railroad bridges so vital to his state and to his nation — the Union he so ardently claimed to love — literally went up in smoke."* [34]

Meanwhile, about the time Marshal Kane, Mayor Brown, Mayor Brown's brother, and the former Governor of Maryland, Enoch Lewis Lowe, were meeting by candlelight with the badly frightened Governor Hicks in the mayor's guest bedroom, the Virginia militia, summoned earlier by telegram by the volatile Marshal Kane, came galloping into town from the west, arriving to fight and whip the fresh Yankee hordes that would assuredly be descending upon the city in the morning. Yes, they would whip the invaders, according to Kane, or <u>die</u> trying. The chances of avoiding all-out war were dwindling with each passing hour.

The very first place the militia men would stop and dismount was at the Fountain Hotel near downtown Baltimore. The militia leaders were anxious to meet at once with Mayor Brown, Marshal Kane, and Governor Hicks so they could be updated on the situation and carry out their orders to defend the City of Baltimore. To the militia's surprise, none of Maryland leaders were present at The Fountain, as had been expected, with Governor Hicks having apparently fled that hotbed of secessionist activity hours earlier — out of fear for his immediate safety.[35]

It was a fluid situation if there ever was one. The mayor and the marshal, with Hicks' reluctant consent, now fine-tuned their daring alternate plan. If their revised scheme was successful, the militia would not have to resort to fighting those damned Yankees in the streets of Baltimore come sunrise on April 20th. If the Yankees were to be prevented from ever reaching the city, then an immediate crisis of catastrophic proportions might be averted.

Very late into that night, under cover of darkness, two teams of men were sent north on the roads out of Baltimore.[36] They were under the command of one Colonel Isaac Trimble of the Maryland Militia, who would later gain fame as General Trimble, the leader of a Confederate division at Gettysburg's "Pickett's Charge." Trimble would lose a leg at Gettysburg, be captured, and subsequently become a federal prisoner at Johnson Island north of Sandusky, Ohio on Lake Erie.

One crew was dispatched to burn and destroy key bridges along the route of the Northern Central Railroad that connected Baltimore to Harrisburg. The other crew, a group comprised largely of Baltimore police, was led by Marshal Kane. Kane's squad was given the task of wrecking the bridges along the route of the P. W. & B. railroad that connected Baltimore to Wilmington, Delaware and Philadelphia. *"Each squad,"* according to Thomas Scharf's History of Maryland, *"was equipped with picks, axes, crowbars, and a good supply of turpentine."* *"Soon,"* according to Michael J. Kline in The Baltimore Plot, *"telegraph lines were cut and the bridges north of Baltimore on the Philadelphia, Wilmington, and Baltimore and the Northern Central Railroad lines were ablaze."*[37]

After a few short hours of officially sanctioned sabotage, Washington was completely cut off from the North. Anecdotal evidence suggests that two of Kane's fellow bridge-burners included future Kane associates Patrick Charles Martin, a

Baltimore at War

Baltimore liquor salesman and soon-to-be Confederate blockade runner — and also a young, promising stage actor, Johns Wilkes Booth, who after April 14th, 1865 would require no introduction.[38]

Marshal Kane's efforts at resisting the Union forces did not end with the burning of the railroad bridges. As a Ms. Helen M. Linscott would years later write to President Lincoln (letter found in the Abraham Lincoln Papers at the Library of Congress) that, *"I arrived in Baltimore on the 14th of March, 1861, and remained there several weeks. I was there at the time of the riot, and was personally acquainted with Marshal Kane. It was on Sunday, April 21st that Kane was making preparation to march out and attack the Federal troops that were encamped in a wheat field a few miles from the city — that I entered the room where his ammunition was stored, and wet as many procussion caps, rifle powder, etc. as I could conveniently reach."*[39]

Supposedly, while Marshal Kane was busy raising an armory of muskets, shotguns, pistols, and ammunition, Colonel Trimble was organizing an army of 15,000 "temporarily enrolled" volunteers to defend the city.

The bridge-burners had done their jobs well. A furious President Lincoln was forced to reroute the bulk of his volunteers through Annapolis (they arrived there by steamer via the Chesapeake), while placing that capital city of Maryland under federal control. Governor Hicks and the mayor of Annapolis both protested, but this time the Union forces would not be turned away. When Union General Benjamin Butler requested permission to land his 8th Massachusetts troops at Annapolis on April 20th, his request was initially denied. Butler told the governor and the mayor his troops *must* be allowed to land, because they were hungry. According to John Lockwood and Charles Lockwood in their Siege of Washington: The Untold Story of the Twelve Days That Shook the Union, when Hicks and the mayor told Butler that no one would sell them anything, Butler made it very clear that hungry troops with weapons could simply take what they needed if it wasn't offered for sale. Butler was then given permission to land his Massachusetts regiment, along with the 7th New York. By April 25th, these soldiers would arrive in Washington to help secure the capital.[40]

With Annapolis under martial law, and Baltimore still in an uproar, Governor Hicks acquiesced to calling a session of the Maryland State legislature for the purpose of voting on the subject of secession. Hicks cleverly arranged for the vote to be held in the western Maryland town of Frederick, where the Union enjoyed much greater support than in either Baltimore or Annapolis. On April 29, Maryland voted not to secede. It did, however, vote not to reopen the rail links with the North, and requested that the President remove the ever-increasing number of federal troops now being stationed in Maryland.[41] Governor Hicks must have breathed a tremendous sigh of relief — although his publicly stated stance, according to Michael J. Kline in The Baltimore Plot, had been *"that if the people of Maryland, through special elections, wanted to secede, he would not interfere."*[42]

The secessionists, eager for a second bite at the apple in June, would never get the chance. Once President Lincoln had secured Washington, D.C. to his satisfaction, his attention turned almost immediately north to the 'rebel" bastion of Baltimore. The President had been humiliated by having to travel through Baltimore in the dead of night under disguise, and afterwards by the reckless, bold-faced opposition of Brown and Kane when the President had summoned badly needed troops to defend Washington from possible attack.

Soon the Massachusetts 6th Regiment would be called back to Baltimore, only this time its soldiers wouldn't simply be passing through. This time, the Massachusetts 6th would bring many, many friends along for the return trip. Their mission would be to clamp down hard on "Mobtown" for the remainder of the war, and to deal swiftly and severely with any insurrectionists.[43]

Lincoln ordered no less than an occupied Baltimore. Southern sympathizers and those suspected of treason would be imprisoned without trial, sparking protests from newspaper editors, judges, lawyers, mayors, and members of the state legislature. Some of the more vociferous of these dissenters would also find themselves thrown behind bars without due process.[44] In the eyes of the South, this only confirmed Lincoln's status as a despot and a tyrant bent on destroying Southern rights.

When a member of the Maryland militia was detained at Fort McHenry for anti-Union activities, Baltimore's Judge Giles issued a writ of habeas corpus . . . basically, an order that the militia man be brought before the local court so as to prevent his illegal and wrongful imprisonment. However, Major W.W. Morris, the commander at Fort McHenry, instead of delivering the suspect to local authorities, wrote the following letter to Judge Giles:

"At the date of issuing your writ, and for two weeks previous, the city which you live, and where your court has been held, was entirely under the control of revolutionary authorities. Within that period United States soldiers, while committing no offense, had been perfidiously attacked and inhumanly murdered in your streets; no punishment had been awarded, and, I believe, no arrests had been made for these crimes; supplies of provisions intended for this garrison has been stopped; the intention to capture this fort had been boldly proclaimed; your most public thoroughfares were daily patrolled by large numbers of troops, armed and clothed, at least in part, with articles stolen from the United States; and the Federal flag, while waving over the Federal offices, was cut down by some person wearing the uniform of a Maryland soldier. To add the foregoing, an assembly elected in defiance of law, but claiming to be the legislative body of your State, and so recognized by the Executive of Maryland, was debating the Federal compact. If all this be not rebellion, I know not what to call it. I certainly regard it as sufficient legal cause for suspending the privilege of the writ of habeas corpus.

"If, in an experience of thirty-three years, you have never before known the writ to be disobeyed, it is only because such a contingency in political affairs as the present has never before arisen." [45]

The opinions of the members of the Maryland state legislature had been rendered moot. Any such member of that political body who advocated secession would now find themselves whisked off — without benefit of trial — to a federal prison. And any newspaper editor or judge who protested the action would soon find themselves bunking with their legislator.

America's bloodiest war would go on for four more years . . . but it would do so largely without the participation of Maryland — and more specifically, without interference from Baltimore.

After Governor Hicks' term expired in 1862, Hicks' successor appointed him to the U.S. Senate to represent Maryland upon the death of Senator James Pearce. In 1864, while campaigning for reelection to the Senate (though ill), Hicks heartily endorsed President Lincoln's own reelection. Senator Hicks succumbed to his illness in February, 1865, with his funeral being held in the U.S. Senate Chamber. One of those in attendance to pay respects was a war-weary, haggard-looking President Lincoln. Mr. Lincoln, the avowed abolitionist, and Hicks, the slave-owning, anti-immigration American Party standard bearer, couldn't have held more politically disparate views. But the two men had found common cause in their allegiance to the Union, and in their shared commitment to settle differences within the laws that hold our Union together.

Just weeks after attending Mr. Hicks' funeral, the President himself would begin experiencing a recurring late-night premonition of his own impending demise and state-sponsored funeral. Sadly, Mr. Lincoln's vivid nightmare would soon prove to have bordered on clairvoyance.

Auction Day

The Lord Baltimore Hotel

Coin expert Perry Fuller did not have a great deal of time to put together an auction for more than 3,500 rare collector coins. Judge O'Dunne had handed down his decision on February 16th, 1935 to award the proceeds of the treasure to teenaged pals Henry Grob and Theodore Jones. The public sale was scheduled for May 2nd. There was some consideration for New York City as the logical site for such a large auction.[1] But the coins were discovered in Baltimore, and it would be in ballroom of the 23-story Lord Baltimore Hotel in downtown Baltimore where the treasure would be sold to the highest bidders.

Fuller divided the approximate 3,508 coins into 438 lots, then had some 3,000 16-page catalogs printed and sent to numismatists, coin dealers, and major coin collectors around the country.[2] Fuller also withheld 50 of the one-dollar pieces, paying two dollars apiece for those coins. According to Leonard Augsburger's 2002 article "*The 1934 Baltimore Gold Hoard*" published in the November/December issue of *Rare Coin Review*, some of these gold pieces would be kept for Fuller's own use, with others being set aside as auction souvenirs.[3]

The auction would receive requests for catalogs from almost every state in the union.[4]

While Judge O'Dunne had predicted the sale would bring $30,000 or more, Fuller's more conservative estimate was $25,000. He claimed to have received almost $20,000 in private bidding prior to the date of the auction.[5]

Coins from the low production and long defunct New Orleans Mint were said to be the most coveted by coin aficionados. The lots were available for pre-auction viewing, by appointment and under armed guard, at the First National Bank of Baltimore, just around the corner from the Lord Baltimore Hotel on West Baltimore Street.[6] First National Bank was located at Redwood and Light Streets, coincidentally the very same intersection that was once dominated by The Fountain Hotel, an establishment that played a significant role in the 19th-century intrigue surrounding the origins of Baltimore's golden treasure trove.

Here is a breakdown of the coins listed in Perry Fuller's April, 1935 auction catalog: [7]

Denomination	Number of Coins	Total Face Value
$20.00	317	$6,340
$10.00	81	$810
$5.00	255	$1275
$2.50	65	$162.50
$1.00	2789	$2,789
Total	3508	$11,381.50

Meanwhile, back in court, round two of the legal drama was being rehashed by the eight appellate judges. Lawyers for the Saulsbury and Findlay/French teams submitted hefty briefs to the Court of Appeals describing how Judge O'Dunne had been in error when he awarded the treasure to the boys. Harry Levin, counsel for the boys, submitted his own brief outlining why O'Dunne had been right.[8]

The Saulsburys argued how O'Dunne's theory that the coins had been buried during the Civil War was faulty, and that the wealthy Andrew J. Saulsbury was the one and *only* person who could have hidden the coins in the Eden Street cellar.[9] Since only Saulsbury could have buried the treasure, the treasure should be the rightful property of the Saulsbury heirs. Since the gold was simply lost property, and not actual treasure, the rules pertaining to treasure trove simply did not apply.

The Findlay/French team held that none of the treasure trove case precedents O'Dunne had relied upon were applicable because none had dealt with the central issue of trespass.[10] Although the boys' forays into the rear portion of the cellar may have been innocent enough, they still had no right, nor any legitimate reason, to go back there. Trespass was trespass. And the common law of treasure trove did not apply — Maryland was obviously devoid of any treasure trove statute.[11] Once more, the sisters announced they were tired of their growing public reputation for being a pair of greedy old ladies. They wanted it known that their plans had always included a substantial reward for the boys . . . even in the event the court awarded the sisters 100% of the treasure.

Levin praised Judge O'Dunne for his courage and his wisdom.[12] He opined that the Saulsburys had presented far from conclusive proof that tallow chandler Andrew Saulsbury was responsible for burying the coins. After all, why would a shrewd businessman such as Saulsbury bury money in the ground that would pay no interest or dividends? Saulsbury the corporate executive, city council member, and building association investor bore little resemblance to the stereotypical reclusive miser. Levin, like O'Dunne, believed the coins had been buried *before* the Saulsburys moved in. Why else would there be no coins dated after 1856 . . . at least nine years before the Saulsburys were known to have set foot on the property?

Concerning the French/Findlay sisters, Levin maintained not only had there been no realistic evidence of trespass by Henry and Theodore[13], but there existed the possibility that someone in the French/Findlay camp had attempted to manufacture false evidence of trespass sometime after the treasure had been discovered. The boys had done nothing wrong. Tenants had routinely chopped wood or stored coal in the rear portion of the cellar. Certainly Theodore Jones, a tenant, could innocently enter that space with an invited guest, Henry Grob. Treasure trove law most certainly did apply, and the Findlay/French sisters did not have a right to the treasure solely based on their ownership of the house. Judge O'Dunne's decision had been both fair and correct, and should not be reversed.

On April 30th, the same week as the auction, the Court of Appeals began to hear oral arguments.

On May 2nd, Henry and Theodore arrived late at the auction and left early. They sat at the back of the ballroom, looking uncomfortable in their suits and ties, and fiddled with one of Fuller's auction catalogs.[14] Levin arranged to get them a few souvenir gold dollars from the auction's organizer as mementos of their August 31, 1934 discovery.

Both O'Dunne's and Fuller's predictions concerning the final auction tally would prove too high. After three cautious hours of bidding, with many bids having arrived by mail, the 438 lots of 3,508 coins brought in just over $19,000 dollars.[15] A rare 1856 $20 double eagle from New Orleans went for $105. However, most coins sold for little more than their gold content, just under two times face value. 1935 was still solidly within the grasp of Depression-era dynamics, and cash was undoubtedly king. Hungry, fearful, out-of-work people did not flock to auctions for collectibles. Perry Fuller, himself a casualty of the times, would ultimately be forced to file for bankruptcy.[16]

The proceeds of the auction were turned over to deputy clerk court Charles McNabb, pending outcome of the appeal.

Fuller submits a bill for use of the ballroom and his auction services of nearly $1,100.[17]

On July 2nd, the Maryland Court of Appeals announces that by a split vote of 4-4, they are upholding Judge O'Dunne's February 16th ruling. *"The Court being equally divided in the opinion on the question arising in the above cases, it is ordered this second day of July 1935, that the decree be and it is hereby affirmed."*

The treasure proceeds still belong 100% to Levin, Jones, and Grob. They are practically home free.

By now, the Saulsburys have decided to cut their losses, withdrawing from further expensive litigation. Not so for the Findlay/French sisters. Perhaps encouraged by the 4-4 split amongst the appellate judges, they ask for a re-argument before the court.[18] Their request is something akin to football's "Hail

Mary" pass, but the sisters have already come this far, and decide to explore this one final opportunity. They are nearly out of appeals.

All Henry Grob and Theodore Jones apparently have to do now is wait about five years, until after 1940, before they come of age.

But strange events are beginning to take place on Eden Street at the treasure house. Since the auction at the Lord Baltimore Hotel, Mrs. Bessie Jones has married a ne'er-do-well by the name of Philip Rummel. Rummel, a World War I veteran, is a simple, affable, relatively harmless man. However, Rummel also possesses a somewhat spotty work history[19] along with an apparent fondness for drink. Bessie takes in laundry to earn pocket change, and Rummel works part time hours — when he can get them — as a city street cleaner. But their meager combined income is hardly enough to support a family of three. And young Theodore, meanwhile, is drifting . . . with little ambition except to collect his "finders keepers" windfall upon reaching the age of 21. He is no longer employed by "Uncle" Mort Blum's clothing store as a special guest attraction — step right up, meet the lucky kid who discovered the pot of gold.

The promised, expensive $50 washing machine that will make Theodore's mother's life easier? It has mysteriously arrived a full five years earlier than would have been expected.

Soon the upstart Rummels are also enjoying a new radio. And, a spiffy new coffee maker.[20] Also, other modern gadgets of convenience, luxury items not commonplace during the bleak 1930s. Not bad for poor folks in the depths of the Great Depression who were, until very recently, scrapping by on relief. Talk about keeping up with the Joneses.

Visitors from outside the neighborhood are now dropping by to discuss business with Mr. Rummel, Mrs. Rummel, and young Theodore.[21]

A new car is seen parked in front of the treasure house. Sometimes young Theodore is seen driving the shiny, late-model automobile.[22] Neighbors are beginning to take notice. There is the inevitable gossip.

Something is clearly afoot on Eden Street . . . and it won't be long before everyone in the City of Baltimore knows.

Once again, those plucky treasure kids are about to make front page news.

2,000 Gold Coins in "The Fountain"

Fountain Inn, Baltimore

The Fountain Hotel just before its demolition in 1870.

One of the more historic sites in "old" Baltimore was the Fountain Hotel, located at the intersection of Light and East Redwood Streets just south of East Baltimore Street. Built during the 18th-century, the Fountain Hotel, originally known as the Fountain Inn, was famous for its old-style charm and roster of celebrity guests. During the War Between the States, it was also the site of much political intrigue.

President Washington had stayed at the Fountain on several occasions, and the inn was fond of boasting how it had been Washington's favorite lodging establishment.[1] President Thomas Jefferson was also an honored guest, although he suffered the misfortune of losing his horse to a stable fire there.[2]

In September, 1814, Baltimore attorney Francis Scott Key finished penning his *Star Spangled Banner* in one of the Fountain's rooms.[3] Just days earlier, Key had been an accidental witness to the bombardment of Fort McHenry by the British navy. Key was caught onboard a British warship during the surprise attack — he'd been negotiating an exchange of prisoners between the British and the Americans. By October, Key's instantly popular poem would be set to music by Charles Durang, a member of the Pennsylvania regiment . . . and first sung in public to a gathering of soldiers at nearby MacCauley's Tavern by Durang's brother, Ferdinand. The Durang brothers of Philadelphia are ancestors of the author of this book.

Other famous visitors to The Fountain included General Lafayette, Andrew Jackson, Charles Dickens, Edgar Allan Poe, and scores of 19th-century senators, governors, and even U.S. Presidents. The colorful history of The Fountain was the subject of a 1948 book, The Fountain Inn Diary, written by Matthew Paige Andrews.[4]

However, in addition to famed luminaries such as Washington, Jefferson, Key, Lafayette, Jackson, Dickens, and Poe, The Fountain Inn Diary neglects to mention perhaps the Fountain Hotel's most *infamous* visitor — presidential assassin John Wilkes Booth. That Booth had been familiar with The Fountain Hotel comes as no surprise, as the hotel stood just 7/10th of a mile west of the Booth family home on Exeter Street. In his 2008 book The Baltimore Plot, author Michael J. Kline describes The Fountain as "an old boyhood haunt" of Booth's. Kline cites 1855 correspondence between Booth and fellow conspirator Michael O'Laughlen — an Exeter Street neighbor of Booth's — as evidence of Booth's long familiarity with the Baltimore hotel.[5]

A more obscure figure connected to The Fountain Hotel was candle and soap executive Thomas Armstrong of James Armstrong & Co. According to the 1859 Baltimore contested election survey, Armstrong listed The Fountain as his primary *residence*. Placing Armstrong at The Fountain[6] on the eve of the Civil War lends further credence to the position that Armstrong, the Webb brothers, and Andrew Saulsbury were all active in the secession movement, and quite likely members and/or associates of the Knights of the Golden Circle. Saulsbury's vociferous support of the South is a matter of public record as a result of the 1934 court testimony of his daughters. Charles Webb was a supporter of two of Baltimore's most prominent secessionists, Mayor George Brown and Marshal George Kane. The political position of secret slaver Captain John J. Mattison should be self-evident.

From the very beginning of hostilities in Baltimore in April, 1861, The Fountain Hotel became a focal point of heightened rebel activity — much of this clandestine.

On April 19th, 1861 rooms at The Fountain Hotel had been commandeered by the Know Nothing, slave-owning governor of Maryland, Thomas Holliday Hicks, who left his Eastern Shore home and made his way to Baltimore upon news of the Pratt Street Riot. Governor Hicks would establish his makeshift emergency headquarters at The Fountain.[7] And when Marshal George Kane fires off his infamous "*We must fight them and whip them, or die*" telegram requesting military assistance to block Lincoln's southern-bound troops, it is to the Fountain Hotel where the Maryland militia first rides.[8]

In Daniel Stashower's 2013 book The Hour of Peril, about the Baltimore plot to kill Lincoln prior to his inauguration, the author mentions the experience of two New York detectives, Thomas Sampson and Ely Devoe, who are sent early on to Baltimore as Union spies:

"By their own admission, Sampson and Devoe played their roles with gusto. 'As soon as we reached our destination we assumed the role of Southern sympathizers and mixed freely with the secessionists,' Sampson recalled. 'We were well supplied with money, very swaggering and loud-mouthed, and soon made friends with a certain class of Southerners whose talk was fight to kill. We stayed at The Fountain Inn and for some weeks had a good time. By degrees we worked our way into the confidence of our new friends.'" [9]

That detectives Sampson and Devoe know right where to go in Baltimore for intelligence on secessionist activities is not surprising, as they were being directed by New York Superintendent John A. Kennedy — originally a Baltimore native.

Later during the war, towards the end 1864 and into early 1865 when circumstances had grown most dire for the Confederacy, The Fountain Hotel would play a role in one of the most nefarious schemes in the history of modern warfare. Desperate Southern sympathizers would concoct a plan to bring biological terrorism to the North, and run part of their diabolical operation from a room at The Fountain.[10]

The terror plot would begin with a Mississippi governor and a Southern doctor with career experience in combating outbreaks of yellow fever throughout the South. Kentucky-born Luke Pryor Blackburn had shown much skill and courage in controlling the fever, and in preventing its further spread. After Dr. Blackburn offered his services to the Confederacy as the General Inspector of the Hospitals and Camps, but was turned down, the Mississippi governor enlisted Dr. Blackburn as a civilian agent. Blackburn made his way to Toronto, Canada, a haven for many Confederate operatives looking to attack and harass the Union from the north. It was in Toronto that Dr. Blackburn is alleged to have conceived his plot to commence bio-terror upon the Union.[11]

Waiting for another outbreak of yellow fever, Dr. Blackburn soon got his chance, as news of an outbreak in Bermuda filtered back to Canada and the warring states. Blackburn set sail for Bermuda — under the guise of helping to quell the contagion — but had an ulterior motive in mind. While administering to the sick and dying, Dr. Blackburn began collecting clothes worn by victims of the island's yellow fever outbreak.[12] Blackburn selected the best quality clothes he could obtain and packed them into eight steamer trunks, which he then paid to have shipped to Halifax, Nova Scotia. Once he had returned to Toronto, Blackburn began recruiting agents for his plot to release the deadly disease on the North. He offered one such agent, a man who called himself Harris — but whose actual name was Godfrey Joseph Hyams — the princely sum of $60,000 to spread viral terror across Union cities.[13] Blackburn confided in Hyams that the Confederate government had bankrolled the effort with $200,000 in seed money.

According to the May 29, 1865 edition of *Halifax Morning Call*, while in his room at the Queen's Hotel in Toronto, Blackburn told Hyams, "*You want to serve the Confederacy? I can tell you how you can do more than to join Lee's army with 100,000 men — can add more fame to your name than General Lee.*"[14]

Blackburn then asked Hyams if he could be trusted, and if he were a Freemason. When Hymans agreed that Blackburn could trust him, but that Hyams wasn't a Freemason, Dr. Blackburn replied, "*Well I am. Here is the right hand of friendship of a Freemason, which will never degrade or betray. Will you accept it in friendship?*"[15]

The physician then went on to explain to Hyams that, "*I want you to kill and destroy as many of the Northern army or the people of the place you go to as you can. It is to consist of cases of goods, shirts, and pants. They will have yellow fever in them.*"[16]

Hyams was instructed to use camphor and cigar smoke to protect himself when handling the contaminated items. The plan involved offloading as many of the wares as possible to used-clothing establishments in the targeted cities.

The agent set about retrieving the steamer trunks from Nova Scotia, and importing them into the United States. Targeted cities included Boston, New York, and, of course, Washington, D.C. To expedite the spread of the yellow fever, Hyams contracted out some of the work to a fellow agent, a man named Myers from Boston. Myers was given some expense money, and instructed to sell the goods to used clothing stores . . . and to then forward the proceeds to Hyams at The Fountain Hotel in Baltimore. In his room at The Fountain, Hyams attempted to sort out his own contaminated stock and to "*smooth them out so they might sell better.*"[17]

At one point during his mission, Hyams ran low on funds, and arranged to meet Dr. Blackburn in Niagara Falls. Accompanied by other Confederate sympathizers and agents, Blackburn gave Hyams $100 in gold and then returned across the border to Canada.[18]

In early April, 1865, upon completion of his assignment, Hyams once more travelled to Toronto to seek payment from Blackburn. According to Hyams, Blackburn "*laughed in his face*" and refused to hand over the money.[19] Infuriated, Hyams went to Canadian officials with his story, and Dr. Blackburn was later arrested in Montreal.

It was during this time that Lee surrendered at Appomattox. The war was over, and the cause of the Great Rebellion had been lost.

In the end, Blackburn's bio-terror attack was a complete and utter failure. Although Blackburn had amassed considerable knowledge on how to fight the dreaded yellow fever (known for causing liver failure and the resulting yellow jaundice), he and other 19th-century doctors didn't realize that yellow fever couldn't be spread by simple contact with contaminated clothing. The spread of the disease is limited to the bite of an infected mosquito that transmits the virus from victim to victim.

Yellow fever, as we now know, originated from the continent of Africa. Ironically, it's spread to South America and ultimately to North America was a direct result of the African slave trade.

Although charged by the Canadians, Dr. Blackburn was never successfully prosecuted. His complex, largely circumstantial case involved a maze of conflicting jurisdictions — Ontario, Quebec, Nova Scotia, Bermuda, and the United States. Ultimately, all charges against the physician were dismissed . . . but Dr. Blackburn would remain in Canada until 1873, still fearful of U.S. prosecution. Dr. Luke P. Blackburn would eventually return to his homeland, summoned upon the news of yet another outbreak of yellow fever. He would be elected to the governorship of Kentucky in 1879.[20]

In later years, Governor Blackburn would categorically deny his involvement in the Great Fever Plot that was largely operated out of Baltimore's Fountain Hotel. He would characterize the plot as *"too preposterous for intelligent gentlemen to believe."*[21]

A curious footnote to the "Great Fever Plot" however, involves the timing of Dr. Blackburn's arrival in Montreal, which was known as the "Richmond of the North" because of the number of Southern spies and sympathizers who had gravitated there. On October 18, 1864, Dr. Blackburn registered as a guest of Montreal's St. Lawrence Hotel — on the very same day John Wilkes Booth checked into The St. Lawrence looking for fellow Baltimorean George Kane.[22] It is also alleged that Booth was later seen in Boston in the company of Blackburn's chief conspirator, Godfrey Joseph Hyams, the man who would soon use The Fountain in Baltimore as a base of operations for spreading the yellow fever throughout the North.[23]

As we have seen, Baltimore's Fountain Hotel had long been a haven for Southern sympathizers both before and during the Civil War. And the old hotel would continue to serve the South in the immediate aftermath of hostilities. According to Randolph Abbott Shotwell, whose papers have been published by the North Carolina Historical Commission, the well-known Fountain Hotel functioned, at the close of the Civil War, as a *"free lodging place for penniless ex-Rebels going home."*[24]

Fountain historian Matthew Paige Andrews describes the predicament of the once successful Fountain Hotel during the tumultuous 1860s:

2,000 Gold Coins in "The Fountain"

"The war period, however, saw the increasingly rapid decline of the famous old hostelry; and shortly after the close of hostilities, it was felt that the career of the ancient Inn should be brought to an end. The decision of the stockholders having been made, the plans for a new building were advertised in the local press of December 3, 1869, and the committee appointed for the purpose of reconstruction obtained a charter for the formal incorporation of 'The Fountain Inn Hotel Company of Baltimore.'" [25]

But as demolition got underway in 1870 to make way for the new Carrollton Hotel, something most unusual occurred. As the following blurb from the September 7, 1870 edition of the *New York Times* reveals:

*"**A lucky laborer, named Murray, while excavating upon the site of the old Fountain Hotel, Baltimore, a few days since came upon a tin box, which was found to contain 2000 gold coins.**"* [26]

Or, as Matthew Paige Andrews describes in his 1948 The Fountain Inn Diary:

*"**The disappearance of the Fountain Inn was not without a flurry of excitement, however, for workmen discovered in its ruins a box containing several hundred dollars in gold and silver coin.**"* [27]

Coins buried in a tin box beneath the Fountain Hotel? Less than a mile from the Booth family's Baltimore townhome — and barely a mile from the Mattison/Saulsbury treasure house at 55 S. Eden?

Let's take a look once again at the following excerpt from the 1860 voter survey taken as a result of the 1859 contested election, which was marred by violence at the polls: [28]

20	Hiram Woods, sr., 167 Garden street	1		
3	A. J. Saulsbury, 138 Central avenue	1		
9	Thomas Armstrong, Fountain Hotel	1		
7	Archibald Wilson, 168 Orleans street		1	
	H. Reynolds, 156 Bond street		1	

What are the chances of having two individuals, Andrew Saulsbury and Thomas Armstrong, listed adjacent to each other in this voter survey — and with both men subsequently having a fortune in gold coins discovered beneath their respective residences? In 1960 Saulsbury doesn't yet own the treasure home at 55 S. Eden, which is just around the corner from his 1860 home at 138 Central — but he will own that house by 1865. And likewise what are the chances that treasure home owner and Armstrong Company business associate John Mattison's "secret slaver" activity is unconnected to the coins, or the ardent Southern sympathies so forcefully voiced by candle maker Andrew J. Saulsbury? How can this all be mere coincidence?

Mattison is the owner of 55 S. Eden in 1860, and also appears in the same contested election survey: [29]

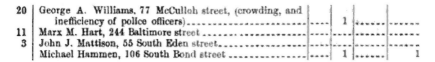

20	George A. Williams, 77 McCulloh street, (crowding, and inefficiency of police officers)		1		
11	Marx M. Hart, 244 Baltimore street				
3	John J. Mattison, 55 South Eden street				
	Michael Hammen, 106 South Bond street		1		1

Thomas Armstrong, Andrew Saulsbury, and Captain Mattison are all associated with companies founded by James Armstrong, the uncle of Thomas Armstrong. Saulsbury and Thomas Armstrong are candle and soap company executives at James Armstrong & Co. located by the Pratt Street Bridge. Mattison, whose ships have long docked at nearby Buchanan's Wharf off Pratt Street, at some point joins the board of directors of the American Fire Insurance Company of Baltimore, whose president is James Armstrong. Also serving on the board of directors of the insurance company, along with Captain Mattison, are Freemason brothers Charles and James Webb. The Webbs, of course, are co-workers and fellow executives at the candle and soap firm along with Thomas Armstrong and Saulsbury.

Saulsbury is so personally indebted to the Armstrongs that he names his first-born son *James Armstrong Saulsbury*, and that son would ultimately name his first boy (Saulsbury's grandson) *Thomas Armstrong Saulsbury*. Saulsbury named his second son after himself (*Andrew J. Saulsbury, Jr.*), and third son *Wilson Webb Saulsbury*. Another Saulsbury grandson would be named *Charles Webb Saulsbury*.[30]

2,000 Gold Coins in "The Fountain"

When Saulsbury purchases the treasure house from Mattison in 1865, he is not purchasing that property from a stranger. Saulsbury is buying the home at 55 S. Eden from a neighbor, friend, business associate, and longstanding brother to the cause of Southern rights. The gold coins, buried in 1856, stay buried under the house because they belong to this clandestine group of Southern sympathizers. They do not belong to Mattison or Saulsbury *personally*. The gold coins, mainly in small denominations, were most probably the dues and OLS/KGC initiation fees collected in anticipation of the aborted invasion of Cuba. Mattison had been, pre-Civil War, the original caretaker of the golden cache. His associate and tenant, mariner John E. Stevens, occupied the treasure house during the war (whether Stevens actually knew the coins were buried there we can only guess — the important thing is Mattison retained ownership of the house). Immediately after the war, when Mattison sells the house to Saulsbury, it is the fiery, outspoken, secessionist candle maker who becomes the new caretaker of the golden stash.

Likewise, the coins in the tin box buried on the grounds of the Fountain Hotel were almost assuredly derived from K.G.C. business . . . or at the very least were connected somehow and in some way with the rebel effort. We know that the old hotel was a veritable hornet's nest of Southern sympathizers and clandestine activity.[31] Although there is not much to go on regarding this second batch of coins, there are nevertheless a few things that may be logically deduced:

First, like the coins found a mile away at 55 S. Eden, the Fountain Hotel coins are almost undoubtedly American. Andrews characterizes them as amounting to several hundred "*dollars.*" The *New York Times* article just refers to them as *2,000 gold coins*. We can assume that if they were foreign coins, this might have been unusual enough to mention. Whether there were silver coins mixed in with the gold coins, or just gold coins as mentioned in the 1870 news article, the inclination is to go with the newspaper article version of 2,000 gold coins. The newspaper article appeared just days after the find in 1870, while Andrews' description of the coins some 78 years later in 1948 is much more likely the result of a "whisper down the lane" story handed down and corrupted over time. Two thousand gold coins, most likely in small denominations, and buried in a tin box, sounds suspiciously similar to the 5,000 gold coins, mostly in small denominations, buried in a copper pot — under a house within comfortable walking distance of The Fountain.

Second, although no mintage dates are given on the Fountain Hotel coins, we can assume that the dates on these coins would not have been very ancient. If the dates had not been fairly contemporary to 1870, that would have been a detail that would have gotten into one of the narratives. So, with no mention of dates or older mintages, along with no mention of foreign coins (and a specific reference to "dollars"), we can assume these to have been U.S. coins of a relatively recent mintage.

Third, based on the history of U.S. gold coin mintage, gold coins became much more common in everyday circulation after the discovery of gold in California in 1849. The greatly increased gold supply translated directly into the increased mintage of gold coins during the 1850s. Likewise, the upheaval surrounding the outbreak of the Civil War, and the resultant government printing of unbacked paper money to cover the war effort, meant that hard money was quickly pulled from circulation by the public and hoarded after 1861. Indeed, the mintage of gold coins dropped precipitously after 1861. To quote numismatist Len Augsburger, author of Treasure in the Cellar, "Hard money had been scarce ever since the Civil War when the Union authorized 'legal tender' in 1862 to finance the campaign. . . . gold, copper, and silver coins all disappeared from sight. . . . Hard money would not return into normal circulation until the 1870s."[32]

So, by the time gold and silver coinage circulated freely once again in the U.S. economy, The Fountain would have only existed as a memory. With the Fountain hoard having been discovered in 1870, nearing the end of the period when gold and silver coins had disappeared from circulation, logic says that the coins must have been buried prior to 1862.

For example, there were 1,361,355 Indian Princess gold dollars minted in Philadelphia in 1861. In 1862 only 6,200 were minted. No year from 1862 through 1870 saw a mintage higher than 10,500.[33] Unless someone robbed the mint, those thousands of coins buried in the tin box on the grounds of The Fountain must have been collected, and stashed away, prior to 1862. And, since gold coins weren't produced in the smaller $1 denomination until the year 1849, and The Fountain coins were apparently of smaller denomination (the only way to bridge the gap between The New York Times' 1870 mention of 2,000 gold coins vs. Matthew Paige Andrews' subsequent 1948 description of several hundred dollars in gold and silver coin), logic dictates that the hotel coins were plucked from circulation and buried sometime *after 1849.*

A search of the Baltimore contested election survey records shows that out of the 33,552 listed registered voters in Baltimore as 1860 dawned, only six — including candle and soap executive Thomas Armstrong — were identified as being residents of the Fountain Hotel.[34] The vast majority of the Fountain's clientele would have been short-term guests, not permanent boarders who had actually registered to vote from the hotel. Burying some 2,000 coins in a tin box on the premises would not be something a hotel guest just passing through is likely to have done. But a permanent boarder involved in the era's political intrigue that was engulfing The Fountain — the very neighborhood, boyhood haunt of John Wilkes Booth? That scenario seems much more highly plausible.

The rapid decline of the hotel in later years makes it a low probability that any cash-strapped owner/operator of the fading Fountain Hotel would have a fortune in gold coins buried on site.

Of the following six permanent residents of The Fountain in early 1860, only one resident bothered to vote — and had the apparent confidence for his safety to vote:

- ◆ M.F. Cabell
- ◆ James Kernan
- ◆ James B. Lanfer
- ◆ B.R. Pem
- ◆ Peter Ostara
- ◆ **Thomas Armstrong (voted)**

Armstrong had proudly cast his ballot along with his co-workers, the politically connected Baltimore councilmen, James Webb and Andrew Saulsbury. The vast majority of the intimidated Baltimore electorate had stayed home . . . and many more were beaten or harassed before they could cast their ballots — excepting those who had been "cooped" so they could vote multiple times at the behest of their captors!

The 1934 discovery of the 5,000 gold coins beneath Saulsbury's Eden Street home, buried in a copper pot and wrapped in a boot, makes Fountain Hotel resident and fellow candle executive Thomas Armstrong the best suspect as the source of the 2,000 or so gold coins found in a tin box under The Fountain Hotel in 1870.

Otherwise, this is just one coincidence — amongst a string of amazing coincidences related to our story in its entirety — that is very difficult to swallow.

Confederate *007*

1860s newspaper depiction of
Marshal Kane's arrest on June 27, 1861.

During the early morning hours of June 27th, 1861, Marshal George Kane was awakened at his Baltimore home by General Banks and a phalanx of Union troops. The marshal would be quickly whisked away under heavy guard to a cell at historic Fort McHenry.[1] Later that same day, President Lincoln would order martial law imposed over Baltimore and much of the state of Maryland. This emergency state of affairs would exist for the next four years, much to the resentment of a vast majority of Baltimoreans.

Just a month earlier, a similar scene occurred when a lieutenant from the Maryland Militia, John Merryman, was seized and detained in much the same fashion.[2] Merryman had been suspected of being a participating member of the clandestine crews tasked with the late-night April 19th burning of railroad bridges to prevent the passage of additional Union troops through Baltimore. The troops, on order from Lincoln, had been making their way south to defend Washington, D.C. from possible rebel attack. Marshal Kane had allegedly been the "crew captain" of the demolition team assigned the duty of sabotaging the Philadelphia, Wilmington, and Baltimore line. A second, different group of men had simultaneously dismantled the tracks heading south into Maryland from Harrisburg.

Anecdotal evidence suggests that John Wilkes Booth may have been one of the helping hands under the direct supervision of Marshal Kane. Certainly Booth, a native Baltimorean like Kane, had a life-long penchant for being where the action was. According to Baltimore Republican leader Worthington G. Snethen, in an interview given to the *Boston Commonwealth* on April 22, 1865, while Booth was still on the run for assassinating Lincoln, Snethen identified Booth as one of the bridge burners of 1861. According to Snethen, not only did Booth participate in the "bridge-burning" party under the direction of Kane — but young Booth was also one of the ringleaders. *"John Wilkes Booth, to whom all the evidence thus far points as the murderer,"* said Snethen, *". . . raised a company of desperadoes in April, 1861, and led them out to burn the bridges running northward."*[3]

Roger B. Taney, Chief Justice of the United States Supreme Court, and a Marylander by birth, ruled in the famous case *"Ex parte Merryman"* that President Lincoln had acted illegally when he ordered the suspension of habeas corpus in the involuntary Fort McHenry detention of John Merryman.[4] When a citizen is detained by the police or some other authority (such as the military), a court can issue a writ of habeas corpus and demand that the detaining authority show proper cause for its action — for example, by filing criminal charges against the person they have in custody. Otherwise, the detaining authority is compelled to release the detainee. The problem for the President and his officers at Fort McHenry was that no court in Maryland would have convicted Merryman or any other rebel suspect from the events of April 19th.

Taney subsequently issued an order that General George Cadwalader, the commanding officer at Fort McHenry, appear in his court with Mr. Merryman. Habeas corpus is Latin for "*you should have the body.*" But Cadwalader, on orders from Washington, D.C., ignored Judge Taney's summons. When an officer of the court was sent to Fort McHenry, that person was refused admittance. The law may have been on Merryman's side, but the armed Union soldiers at Fort McHenry were not heeding the law. Merryman was being detained indefinitely without being charged.

The subsequent arrest of Marshal Kane was so sensitive and high profile that the soldiers were instructed to temporarily detain any Baltimore police or other citizens spotted along the early morning route back to Fort McHenry.[5] Like Merryman, Kane would now be imprisoned with no formal charges being filed.

Union authorities were especially motivated to go after George Kane after General Banks and his men had seized a city warehouse under Kane's control, finding inside a prodigious quantity of stockpiled weapons. According to author Orville J. Victor in <u>The History, Civil, Political, and Military of the Southern Rebellion</u>, the cache consisted of "*fifteen dray loads of carbines, flint-lock muskets, and pikes.*"[6] Union authorities suspected Kane of not only burning railroad bridges in defiance of Lincoln, but now also of trafficking weapons for the rebels.

Many more arrests would follow, including that of Mayor George Brown (detective Allan Pinkerton would be afforded the "honor" of arresting the city's pro-Confederate mayor). The Baltimore police commissioners were suspended, and then subsequently imprisoned at Fort McHenry. General Banks then appointed a new police board, fired the entire police force, and organized a new roster of pro-Union officers who served directly under the occupying Union authorities. The Union police force was then paid out of Baltimore municipal funds, a move that further humiliated and angered the town's pro-South citizenry.[7]

Other Marylanders imprisoned included members of the Maryland General Assembly suspected of holding Southern sympathies, the Baltimore City Council, and even pro-Southern newspaper editors and owners.

Prisoners were processed at Fort McHenry, and then transferred away at the earliest convenience to remove them from the Baltimore area . . . usually to Fort Lafayette, New York, and then onto Fort Warren in Boston.

Basically, the entire slate of "Reform Party" pro-secessionist Democrats who'd been swept into office after ousting the Know-Nothings in 1860 found themselves in jail by late 1861.[8] According to researcher Matthew Kent, at Fort Warren, the Baltimore police commissioners wound up living in one of the upper rooms of the casemates of the fort, while Kane and Mayor Brown shared a nearby room.[9] Brown and Kane shared a history together that went back to their youthful days in the Independent Grays, a volunteer paramilitary organization from Maryland similar to the Richmond Grays which was later joined by John Wilkes Booth.

Deprived of his revolver and his hidden arsenal, Marshal Kane resorted to carrying on the fight with a pen. At Fort Lafayette, Kane wrote the following letter in September, 1861 to President Lincoln:

"*Whilst suffering great agony from the promptings of nature and effects of my debility I am frequently kept for a long time at the door of my cell waiting for permission to go to the water-closet owing to the utter indifference of some of my keepers to the ordinary demands of humanity.*" This from Maryland Voices of the Civil War, author Charles W. Mitchell.[10] The debility to which Kane refers is his claim to have contracted malaria while in confinement.

President Lincoln, preoccupied with early Union defeats in 1861 and the deaths of thousands on battlefields strewn across the nation's countryside, apparently did not have the time to address Kane's lack of lavatory privileges. Getting no response from the President, Kane next wrote to Secretary of State William H. Seward in October, 1861. Kane requests from Seward a speedy trial, and writes that conditions were so bad at Fort Lafayette that Kane required medical care for "*an affliction of the heart which I attribute to the nature of my confinement at Lafayette,*" as recorded in Robert Nicholson Scott's 1894 work The War of Rebellion by the United States War Department.[11]

Considering the subsequent events of April, 1865, these letters from Kane are important because they show more than just a general antipathy towards the Union and its abolitionist policies. For the slave owning Marshal Kane, they hint at a growing personal grudge against the individual men directly responsible for his 14-month imprisonment under harsh conditions and without due process under the law.

In a subsequent publicly printed outburst at Seward, Kane wrote that, *"In this imprisonment I am understood to have been the special victim of Mr. Secretary Seward, who in concert with his hired minions has omitted no occasion to heap upon me accusations which he knew to be false and therefore dared not bring to the ordeal of a public trial . . . I can only promise that in due time and upon a proper occasion Mr. Seward shall hear from me."*[12]

Kane, of course, wasn't the only one issuing threats concerning his controversial imprisonment. While rehearsing for a play in New York, members of John Wilkes Booth's acting company got into a discussion as to whether Secretary of War John Stanton should be shot for the arrest of Marshal Kane and the Baltimorean's subsequent imprisonment at Fort McHenry. According to one onlooker, recounts Gordon Samples in Lust for Fame — The Stage Career of John Wilkes Booth, *"Yes you are right!"* It was Booth's (voice). *"I know George P. Kane well; he is my friend, and the man who could drag him from the bosom of his family for no crime whatever, but a mere suspicion that he may commit one some time, deserves a dog's death."* One observer to Booth's tirade later wrote that, *"It was not the matter of what he said; it was the manner and general appearance of the speaker, that awed us. . . . He stood there, the embodiment of evil."*[13]

Upon his late 1862 release, Marshal Kane promised Union officials he would head south. Instead, Kane does just the opposite, making his way north to Montreal, Canada. Up in officially neutral Canada, the Confederate government in Richmond was funding satellite offices staffed with intelligence and espionage agents in the cities of Toronto, St. Catherines, and Montreal. Montreal came to be known affectionately as "Little Richmond" with rebel activities there centered at the upscale St. Lawrence Hotel, also known as St. Lawrence Hall.[14]

Two of the most active Confederate agents in Montreal were Baltimoreans Patrick Charles Martin and Marshal George P. Kane, now known because of his recently acquired military rank as "Colonel" Kane. Kane and Martin were assisted by Kentuckian George N. Sanders, described by author William Tidwell of Come Retribution as *"fanatical in his Southern sympathies."* Sanders, another Confederate operative, *"looked upon Lincoln as a bloody tyrant . . . and had a history of advocating political assassinations."*[15]

St. Lawrence Hall in Montreal, circa 1870.

The Confederates in Canada were tasked with wreaking havoc along the Union's border with Canada, diverting Union soldiers and supplies from the battlefields in the South. They also encouraged so-called "copperheads" or Southern sympathizers in the Great Lakes states of Ohio, Indiana, Michigan, Illinois, and Wisconsin to resist Union authority and to create as much trouble as possible for the U.S. federal government in that region. The Confederacy as well hoped to solicit the support of the Canadian citizenry and their supposedly neutral government.

According to the CIA's online library, in February, 1864 the Confederate Congress passed a bill authorizing a campaign of sabotage against "*the enemy's property, land and sea.*" The bill established a Secret Service fund of $5 million U.S. to finance the sabotage. Of that money, some $1 million was specifically earmarked for use by agents in Canada, overseen by Confederate Commissioners Clement Clay and Jacob Thompson.[16]

In 1864, in response to continued clandestine rebel activity in the Great Lakes area and along the porous northern border with Canada, a controversial report was authored by Joseph Holt, the Advocate General of the United States Army. Although today this document is simply known as "*The Holt Report*," its official title during the war was "*Order of American Knights or Sons of Liberty: A Western Conspiracy in Aid of the Southern Rebellion.*"[17] The premise of Holt's report to the federal government was that a secret pro-South, pro-slavery organization that went by various names (today best known as the Knights of the Golden Circle) was behind a reign of coordinated subterfuge and terror in the country's Northwest (in 1864 this meant the region around the Great Lakes, not the Pacific Northwest which was yet to be settled). Holt's critics have labeled his report as grossly exaggerated. If the South had been able to successfully complete just a fraction of the activity Holt claimed, they would have likely won the war.

However, though undoubtedly overhyped, there was nevertheless a great deal of truth in the Holt Report. The Confederacy was definitely active in Canada and The Great Lakes region. And in Montreal, a.k.a. Little Richmond, the face of Confederate espionage was aptly represented by fellow Baltimoreans Kane and Martin, along with Kentucky's George N. Sanders.

Evidence to their complicity exists in the papers of Jefferson Davis, edited by Lynda Crist. Two weeks after the disastrous Battle of Gettysburg in July, 1863, Kane writes to Davis in Richmond to offer his services from Montreal. Colonel Kane's "services" include "*organizing an expedition against Chicago, Milwaukee, and Detroit.*" Supposedly, Kane's plan was "*to destroy all shipping, thus paralyzing the lake commerce.*"[18]

Patrick Charles Martin, who had moved his family to Montreal, played host to Kane there, and ran a successful blockade-running business during the war. Martin, sometimes referred to as Captain P.C. Martin, would ship contraband goods along the St. Lawrence Seaway and then out to Halifax, Nova Scotia. From Halifax, cargoes would be sneaked through ports in Atlantic islands such as Bermuda until they reached their final destination in Dixie.

A native New Yorker, Martin had operated as a Baltimore liquor salesman before the war. The Union War Department had a file on Martin, describing him as "*an uncompromising rebel of the April 19th variety.*"[19] This would indicate that the feds believed that Martin had played a part in the April 19th Baltimore uprising later known as "The Pratt Street Riot." It also suggests that Martin likely aided Marshal Kane and Mayor Brown in the burning of the railroad bridges on late-night April 19th. Baltimorean John Wilkes Booth was said to have accompanied them.

Nearing the end of 1863, Colonel Kane would get a chance to see his plan to "*destroy all shipping, thus paralyzing the lake commerce*" put into action. The Canadian Confederate agents devised a scheme to hijack a few of the smaller steamers on Lake Eerie, and then through diversion and an "accidental" collision with the *U.S.S. Michigan*, board that warship with armed soldiers and put her under the Confederate flag. Kane was to help arm the nearly 180 raiders with Colt revolvers. The ship's heavy guns would then be trained on Johnson Island, with the ultimatum that all 2,000 Confederate prisoners there be released. The prisoners at Johnson Island, according to author Michael J. Kline of The Baltimore Plot, were given advance notice of the raid through coded messages hidden in personal advertisements published in local newspapers.[20]

Colonel Kane and Patrick Martin's efforts to free the prisoners at Johnson's Island are detailed in a report given by Confederate Captain Robert D. Minor, CSN, to Admiral Franklin Buchanan:

"*Finding Marshal Kane and some of our friends in Montreal, we set to work to prepare and perfect our arrangements, the first object of the plan being to communicate with the prisoners on Johnson's Island, informing them that an attempt would be made to release them. This was effected through a lady from Baltimore, a Mrs. P.C. Martin, then residing with her husband and family in Montreal, and whose husband did all in his power to aid us in every way. She brought a letter from Baltimore, which General [J.J.] Archer (who, with Major-General [I.R.] Trimble, was a prisoner at Johnson's Island) had sent there to Beverly Saunders, Esq., telling us to communicate with him through the personal columns of the New York Herald.*"[21]

Unfortunately for the Confederates, a double agent was in the process of tipping off Union authorities. Warned of the raid, Secretary of War Stanton alerted the captain of the *U.S.S. Michigan*, sent immediate reinforcements, and the rebels were forced last-minute to abort their elaborate plans and fade back into Canada.[22]

Had "Little Richmond" succeeded in seizing the *U.S.S. Michigan*, the rebels could have not only freed 2,000 prisoners — including Isaac Trimble, Kane's co-leader in the 1861 Baltimore bridge burnings — but they might very easily have inflicted heavy damage to coastal towns, military installations, and lake shipping. The *U.S.S. Michigan* was the only Union warship patrolling the Great Lakes in 1863 and was unmatched in her firepower.

According to Kline, *"the failure of the Johnson Island raid would have been a demoralizing blow to the Confederacy's secret operations force. Reportedly, over $100,000 had been expended to procure the necessary equipment for the raid."*[23]

His daring plot thwarted, in November, 1863 Colonel Kane must then write to Jefferson Davis to inform the commander-in-chief of the group's failure at Johnson Island.

In their book Rebel Gold, Warren Getler and Bob Brewer write that, *"According to the consensus history, the failure of those 'Northwest' raids to achieve their intended results sent the KGC into rapid decline. . . . The KGC's nominal public 'leaders' — George Bickley, Sons of Liberty head Clement L. Vallandigham and the Order of American Knights' Phineas C. Wright — were all at some point arrested and thrown into jail for their seditious activities, along with numerous other KGC associates."*[24]

In early 1864, Colonel Kane left Montreal, ran the Union blockade at great risk to his life, and reported for duty in Richmond.

William Tidwell in Come Retribution describes Kane's journey south:

"On 25 January 1864, the U.S. counsel at Halifax reported that former police marshal of Baltimore George P. Kane, Dr. Blackburn, and Major Wistor or Wister (an escapee from Johnson's Island) were expected to arrive in the next two or three days. He said they were planning to run the blockade and all of them had been involved in the Johnson's Island "rescue plot." Blackburn was presumably on his way to Havana to collect "infected" clothing, but Kane was on his way to Virginia. On 15 February he was being serenaded by well-wishers at his hotel in Richmond."[25]

One of Kane's stateside assignments was to help Marylanders form their own militias. With Maryland firmly under

Union military control, more than 60,000 citizens either signed up or were drafted into Lincoln's armies. Barely 20,000 Marylanders fought for the Confederates, and the vast majority of these had to circumnavigate Union lines to reach rebel held territory to enlist.

Civil War draft records show that a young man named Andrew J. Saulsbury was drafted for service by Union forces from his home at 179 S. Central Avenue in Baltimore. The candle and soap executive Andrew J. Saulsbury — then living at 138 S. Central — was too old to have been this individual, and his second son, also Andrew J. Saulsbury, was too young. Judging from the name and address, it is a high probability that the individual drafted into the Union army from the S. Central Avenue row house was either a cousin or nephew to the James Armstrong & Co. executive. With the city under occupation and the federal government drafting local boys to fight against the South, this would have no doubt made staunch secessionists such as Saulsbury, Webb, Brown, Mattison, and their friend George P. Kane incredibly angry.

By July, 1864 the *Charleston Mercury* is reporting that Colonel Kane is "*about to cooperate with our forces near Baltimore, with 15,000 Maryland recruits.*"[26] Whether Kane was able to recruit anywhere close to that number of volunteers is doubtful (curiously, 15,000 is an exact match for the number of National Volunteers who were supposedly on call in 1861 to disrupt Lincoln's Baltimore visit, and later the passage of Union troops through Baltimore). What is not in doubt is that from July, 1864 onward Baltimore would not be under serious threat from Confederate troops. Still, Kane pushes on, later trying to organize a heavy artillery corps comprised of Marylanders. Even as late as March, 1865, Colonel Kane is instrumental in procuring fresh uniforms for Marylanders serving in the Confederate Army.

At some point in the latter half of 1864, Colonel Kane made one last trip up to Montreal. Around this time another aborted raid was planned on Fort Douglas, a major holding area for Confederate prisoners. That raid was thwarted when Union Colonel Benjamin J. Sweet realized that "*Chicago is filling up with suspicious characters, some of whom are escaped prisoners, and others who are here from Canada.*"[27] According to the CIA's files under "*Intelligence in the Civil War: Conspiracy in Canada*," Sweet planted his own spy amongst the rebels, and thus succeeded in gaining knowledge of his enemy's plan. With the aid of Union agents, Sweet arrested the raid's leaders and Sons of Liberty (a later name for the K.G.C.) officers, along with "*106 bushwhackers, guerillas, and rebel soldiers.*" Union agents seized some 142 shotguns, 349 revolvers, and thousands of rounds of ammunition at the home of a suspected rebel collaborator. The surprised Union authorities immediately increased the military guard on Chicago.[28]

The operation to free Confederate prisoners from Fort Douglas was allegedly masterminded by Confederate Secret Service agent Thomas Hines from the rebels' offices in Canada. Interestingly, Hines sought help from the Yellow Fever Plot organizer, Dr. Luke Blackburn. According to Nancy Disher Baird in Luke Pryor Blackburn: Physician, Governor, Reformer, "*Blackburn's activities during the remaining months of the war are a mystery, but it is likely that he was involved in more than one of the various schemes concocted by his Confederate associates in Canada . . . Hines authored an elaborate plan to set off a massive insurrection in the northwest and burn several northern cities to draw attention from the Chicago area, where he and local Copperheads (antiwar and pro-Confederate residents of the North) would aid the escape of military prisoners at Chicago's Camp Douglas. Blackburn was to lead diversionary forces against Boston. An inebriated rebel prisoner revealed the plan, and troops were moved into Boston, thus thwarting Blackburn's part of the scheme. Hines, who expected to lead the prison break, owed his escape from Federal authorities in Chicago to Mary Morris, Blackburn's sister, who was married to a local judge.*"[29]

Ms. Baird's assertion about Blackburn is corroborated by John W. Headley in his 1906 work Confederate Operations in Canada and New York. Headley writes that, "*Confederates had been selected to be in Chicago, under command of Captain Hines, and endeavor to carry out plans for the release of the prisoners at Camp Douglas and Rock Island in Chicago. . . . Colonel (Jacob) Thompson advised us that detachments under Captain Churchill in Cincinnati and Dr. Luke Blackburn in Boston would set fire to those cities on Election Day.*"[30]

Other rebel plots involved the destruction of Union infrastructure, including the attempted derailment of trains in upstate New York. But perhaps the most daring and bizarre rebel plot of all was the Montreal-run operation to burn down New York City. Again, from the files of the CIA:

"Commissioners Thompson and Clay authorized the boldest operation yet: the torching of New York City by eight agents. The agents were to set the fires with containers of 'Greek fire,' the general name, dating to antiquity, for incendiary substances. The 1864 version of Greek fire was developed for the Confederacy by a Cincinnati chemist who mixed phosphorous with carbon bisulphide. Exposed to the air, the mixture bursts into flames.

"In New York, the leader of the saboteurs went to a certain basement where an old man with a beard handed him a valise containing twelve dozen sealed, four-ounce bottles. Each man checked into a series of hotels, then went back to each one, opened a bottle in the room, left, and locked the door. They had set fires in 19 hotels, a theater, and P.T. Barnum's American Museum. The fires did not amount to much. There was no panic. There was no uprising."[31]

Kane's Confederate host in Montreal, Patrick Charles Martin, was one of those saboteurs. According to author Matt Herzfeld in his article *John Booth Lived Here: How Montreal Fell for the Confederacy*, *"The Confederates in Montreal were a shambolic bunch. One of them, P.C. Martin, thwarted his own plan to burn New York City to the ground when, afraid of being found out, he closed the door of the hotel room in which he had begun the blaze, cutting off the fire's oxygen supply so that it burned little besides the room itself. He would later sink with a ship in the St. Lawrence and never be seen again."*[32]

Not all of the Confederate plots failed, however. On October 19th, 1864, the Canadian Confederates struck, of all places, in the sleepy upstate Vermont town of St. Albans. Confederate Lt. Bennett H. Young led some 22 rebels south from Canada to infiltrate the town. The Confederates arrived two and three at a time in order to avoid suspicion. At the appointed time, the soldiers produced weapons and stormed into three of the town's banks — The St. Albans Bank, Franklin County Bank, and The First National Bank of St. Albans.[33]

Reportedly, the rebels decided to rob these Northern banks in retaliation for Union atrocities committed in Southern cities. They were also trying to fund their clandestine operations, plus divert Northern troops into defending the country's Canadian border and away from the main battlefields.

"*I take possession of this town in the name of the Confederate States of America!*" announced Lieutenant Young of the Confederate Service. At the St Albans Bank, tellers and bystanders were forced at gunpoint to "*solemnly swear to obey and respect the Constitution of the Confederate States of America.*"[34]

According to www.stalbansraid.com, a web site dedicated to telling the story of the northernmost land action of the American Civil War, the Jesse James-styled operation netted the bandits approximately $208,000 in cash, gold, and silver. More precious metals were left behind when they proved too heavy to carry, and in their haste the rebels also overlooked a substantial amount of cash.[35]

Before riding north, the Confederate guerillas rounded up the town's horses so that armed pursuit would be delayed. Lt. Young also ordered St. Albans to be burned. But the vessels of "Greek fire" the rebels tossed about failed to do their job, and damages were limited to the burning down of a single shed. One townsperson was shot and killed, however, and others were wounded.

The rebels made Canada before any posse could reach them. Embarrassed Canadian officials ordered that the bandits be arrested, and most were. Some $88,000 of the stolen loot was returned to Vermont banks, leaving some $120,000 unaccounted for. Ultimately the rebels were released on the grounds they were not bandits, but rather soldiers acting on orders from their commanding officers, namely Clement Clay and Jacob Thompson. Canada was trying its hardest to remain under a strict policy of neutrality. The raid, however, turned many sympathetic Canadians against the Confederacy.[36]

It is said that the Confederate Secret Service agent in Montreal who called upon his Canadian connections and worked diligently behind the scenes to get the raiders released was George Kane's close associate, George N. Sanders,[37] the Lincoln inauguration train's multi-city stalker back in 1861. Sanders had apparently been coordinating his activities with "Captain" Cipriano Ferrandini, a card-carrying member of the K.G.C. who had sworn to kill Lincoln in Baltimore before the March 4th inauguration.

In The Trial: The Assassination of President Lincoln and the Trial of the Conspirators (edited by Edward Steers), witness Henry G. Edson testified in federal court as to his participation in the judicial investigation of the St. Albans Raid. Edson, an attorney, was in Canada to represent the interests of the Vermont Banks and the United States. Said Edson, *"I saw there George N. Sanders, Jacob Thompson, Clement C. Clay, and others of that circle of rebels. I heard a conversation between George N. Sanders and other parties at St. John's, in regards to movements in the States contemplated by the rebel authorities. . . . In speaking of the so-called St. Albans Raid, George N Sanders said he was ignorant of it before it occurred, but was satisfied with it. He said that it was not the last that would occur; but it would be followed up by the depleting of many other banks, and the burning of many other towns on the frontier, and that many Yankee sons of — (using a course, vulgar expression) would be killed. He said that they had their plans perfectly organized, and men ready to sack and burn Buffalo, Detroit, New York, and other places, and had deferred them for a time, but would soon see the plans wholly executed. . . . He made other statements in connection with the case . . . that he had employed twenty or thirty counsel in Canada. Sanders claimed to be acting as an agent of the so-called Confederate Government."* [38]

Sanders, according to <u>Rebel Gold</u> authors Warren Getler and Bob Brewer, had once been the leader of the territorial-expansionist "Young America" movement which *"attracted the likes of Pike and Bickley."* He was a *"former colleague of Caleb Cushing in the Pierce administration and comrade of* [KGC operative Thomas] *Hines in running KGC operations in Canada."* [39]

In fact, along with Jefferson Davis, George Sanders would be named as "one of the top ten" Lincoln assassination plot co-conspirators identified from the May, 1865 trial that was prosecuted by Major Henry Lawrence Burnett. The following excerpt was extracted from "The Lincoln Conspirators" section of the 1917 book <u>American State Trials</u> edited by John D. Lawson:[40]

> What is the evidence, direct and circumstantial, that the accused, or either of them, together with John H. Surratt, John Wilkes Booth, Jefferson Davis, George N. Sanders, Beverly Tucker, Jacob Thompson, William C. Cleary, Clement C. Clay, George Harper, and George Young, did com-

bine, confederate, and conspire, in aid of the existing rebellion, as charged, to kill and murder, within the military
department of Washington, and within the fortified and in-
trenched lines thereof, Abraham Lincoln, late, and, at the
time of the said combining, confederating, and conspiring,
President of the United States of America, and commander-
in-chief of the army and navy thereof; Andrew Johnson,
Vice-President of the United States; William H. Seward,
Secretary of State of the United States, and Ulysses S.
Grant, lieutenant general of the armies thereof, and then in
command, under the direction of the President?

In the 1954 book Confederate Agent: A Discovery in History,
James D. Horan lays it out plain and simple when he writes that
Sanders was one who seemed to be "*pulling wires . . . to
manipulate the actions of the Confederate agents.*"[41] Agents, of
course, such as Dr. Luke Blackburn, Patrick Charles Martin,
George Kane, and one John Wilkes Booth.

One day prior to the St. Albans Raid, on October 18, 1864,
the hotel record shows that two men checked into the St Lawrence
Hall in Montreal. One was Dr. Luke Blackburn, the man who
would later be accused of spreading clothes infected with deadly
yellow fever virus throughout Northern cities . . . some of those
clothes being prepared for shipment out of the Fountain Hotel in
Baltimore by accomplice Godfrey Joseph Hyams, a.k.a. Mr. Harris.
The other individual was actor John Wilkes Booth, who checked
into Room 150.[42] Upon arrival, Booth immediately began looking
specifically for Colonel George P. Kane, whom he seemed most
anxious to meet. Kane, however, had just recently left to run the
Union blockade and report to Richmond for duty there. According
to witnesses at the hotel, Booth was visibly agitated on learning
that he had missed Kane. He would later settle in, however, for a
game of cards with Dr. Blackburn.[43]

According to William Tidwell in Come Retribution, "*there is
solid evidence that Booth was in personal contact with two Confederate agents during his Montreal visit. They were Patrick C.
Martin and George N. Sanders. . . . George Sanders was staying
at the Ottawa Hotel in that city. The two must have met promptly.
Various people saw them together frequently.*"[44]

Booth is also supposed to have spent much time at the
Montreal residence of Patrick Martin. According to Edward Steers,

Jr. in <u>Blood on the Moon</u>, *"Martin may have also given Booth the partial means to finance his recruitment efforts. When Booth returned to Washington from Montreal, he carried not only Martin's letter, but also a draft for $1,500 that he deposited in Jay Cooke's bank. While the source of Booth's funds cannot be positively established, Patrick Martin seems to be a reasonable source. Booth's income from acting was drying up, and his losses in the oil fields (on investments) had been substantial ($6,000* according to some sources). *When the Confederate agents set up operations in Canada in May of 1864 they received a million dollars in gold from Confederate Secret Service funds to finance their operations against the United States. Some of this money may have been given to Booth in Montreal to help underwrite his scheme to capture Lincoln. The fact that Booth returned from Canada and made a deposit in Cooke's bank within a week suggests that Martin had provided the funds. The amount of money was not trivial. In today's market, $1,500 is the equivalent of approximately $16,000 in current dollars* (the author of this book argues the amount would be much higher). *Booth disbursed all of this money between January 7 and March 16, the most active period of his recruitment activities, which further supports the notion that the funds were to support his capture plan."*[45]

In <u>John Wilkes Booth: Day by Day</u>, Arthur F. Loux writes that *"On his last day in Montreal, accompanied by Patrick C. Martin, with whom he had been staying for several days, [Booth] deposited $455 in an account at the Montreal branch of the Ontario Bank. He also exchanged $300 in gold for a bill of exchange . . . and told the teller he was going to run the blockade."*[46]

The official reason Booth gave for his Montreal trip was to arrange for shipment of his theatrical wardrobe back to the States. Martin booked this equipment transport via Halifax and Bermuda on one of his ships. Booth told a fellow guest at the St. Lawrence Hotel, a Mr. John Deveny, who had recognized the famous actor, that he was in town merely "for pleasure."[47] It does not take ten days to arrange for the shipment of a few trunks of garments and stage accessories. We can assume that whatever Booth's business in Montreal with Kane, Martin, Sanders, and Blackburn it probably did not concern canoeing or trout fishing. Compared to the likes of Kane, Martin, Sanders, and Blackburn, by October, 1864 Booth is a mere choir boy. He has only voiced his continued displeasure at the President, and smuggled some much-needed medicines back to the Confederacy. Meanwhile, Booth's Montreal companions have been involved in privateering (or piracy, depending on your outlook), train derailments, armed bank robberies, planned prison breaks, sabotage, hijacking, biological warfare, and the attempted arson of entire towns and cities, including New York City.

That, of course, will all change on the evening of April 14, 1865 . . . a date for which John Wilkes Booth will go down in eternal infamy.

Little is factually known about what actually transpired when Booth visited Montreal for ten days in October, 1864. However, Clayton Gray, in his book *Conspiracy in Canada*, offers the following quote from Booth, by way of St. Lawrence Hall owner Henry Hogan. Apparently, Booth had been drinking at the hotel bar, and subsequently involved himself in a friendly game of billiards when the subject of the American national election arose. Said Booth: *"It makes little difference, head or tail, Abe's contract is near up, and whether re-elected or not he will get his goose cooked."* [48]

During the trial of Booth's co-conspirators in May, 1865, a resident of Boston testified that he overheard Confederate agents discussing the coming assassination of President Lincoln. Henry Finnegass, once an officer in a Massachusetts regiment, said that he had been in the St. Lawrence Hall in Montreal on February 14th or 15th. According to author William Tidwell in April '65, Confederate Covert Action in the American Civil War, Finnegass told the court he had overheard a conversation between George Sanders and William Cleary (another Confederate operative in Canada). In that discussion, Cleary allegedly said, *"I suppose they are getting ready for the inauguration of Lincoln next month."* Sanders replied, *"Yes. If the boys have any luck, Lincoln won't trouble them much longer."* Cleary then asked, "Is everything well?" Sanders then said, *"Oh, yes! Booth is bossing the job."* Finnegass went on to explain that he had been in Montreal for eleven days and that he had left on February 17, 1865. He had not met either Cleary or Sanders but knew them both by sight; Sanders had been pointed out to him by the clerk of the hotel, and he had seen both testify at the trial of the St. Albans raiders. Supposedly, Mr. Finnegass overhead the conversation from a distance of about ten feet. [49]

Booth is bossing the job . . . but certainly not without help.

According to a *New York Times* article on April 28, 1865, subsequent to Booth's capture and slaying at the Garrett barn in northern Virginia, the newspaper reported that "*Booth had on his person a draft for sixty pounds drawn by the Ontario Bank of Canada on a London banker. The draft was dated in October last.*"[50]

In <u>Jesse James' Secret</u>, James researcher Ron Pastore makes the case that the Knights of the Golden Circle "*was a secret spy ring that operated for the South during the Civil War. This group went by various other names including the Confederate Secret Service, for one. . . . It was spearheaded by a close-knit group of people working through the Southern Secret Service.*"[51]

Piracy, train derailments, armed bank robberies, planned prison breaks, sabotage, hijacking, biological warfare, the destruction of bridges, the attempted arson of entire towns and cities — and the murder of the President of the United States.

If it walks like a duck, and quacks like a duck . . . then it's probably a duck.

Marshal George Kane and John Wilkes Booth —
rebel birds of a feather.

The activities of Colonel George Kane, George Sanders, Patrick Charles Martin, Dr. Luke Blackburn, and yes, John Wilkes Booth, all hint strongly at their involvement in the KGC.

When Booth's alleged granddaughter, Izola Forrester, compiled her 1937 groundbreaking work This One Mad Act, Forrester quoted Booth family associates as saying her actor grandfather was a member of the KGC castle in Baltimore. Forrester sums up her literary effort with the words, *". . . after forty years of ceaseless research to find new material and verify reports and rumors, I have come to the following conclusions . . . that Lincoln's assassination was instigated by men high in the order of the Knights of the Golden Circle, said to have been a branch of Freemasonry, flourishing in the North as well as the South."*[52]

That KGC castle in Baltimore almost certainly included the likes of Mayor George Brown, Booth's longtime friend and associate Marshal George Kane, past Masonic Grand Master Charles Webb, his brother James Webb, secret slaver Captain John Mattison, and close friends and business associates Thomas Armstrong and Andrew J. Saulsbury — twin keepers of the KGC's gold.

The same Baltimore castle, of course, would have also counted eventual Lincoln assassin John Wilkes Booth amongst its membership. The Booth family townhome was less than half a mile from Saulsbury's Central Ave. home, certainly close enough to have been considered *"in Booth's Exeter Street neighborhood."*[53] Booth, of course, would never survive to face charges in a courtroom. According to K.G.C. author and expert David Keehn, Booth was definitely a sworn member of the Knights of the Golden Circle. Incredibly (as per Keehn), after his violent demise at the Garrett farm, Booth's remains were temporarily storied in the same Green Mount Cemetery family vault where KGC founder George Bickley would be buried after his 1867 death — in Baltimore.[54]

The Candle Merchant of Eden Street

1870 federal census record for Andrew J. Saulsbury and family at the 55 S. Eden treasure house.

Andrew Jackson Saulsbury was born in Baltimore in 1927. It is believed his family operated a grocery and paint store at the corner of Montgomery and Light Streets, close by the harbor and only a few blocks south of the current location of Baltimore's National Aquarium. The distance between the Saulsbury family store and the site of the treasure house on Eden Street is only 1.3 miles, and the James Armstrong & Co. candle factory on Concord Street would have been less than a mile away. City directories list the Saulsbury store from the late 1820s until the early 1850s. In 1849, the estate of Andrew Saulsbury, Sr. was declared bankrupt, and the grocery business was reorganized, continuing on for a few years after 1849 as Andrew J. Saulsbury & Son.[1]

Exactly when Andrew Saulsbury joined the soap and candle firm of James Armstrong & Co. is not known, but we do know he named his first son, born in 1853, James Armstrong Saulsbury — so it can be assumed that Saulsbury had become part of the firm during or prior to 1853. Armstrong candles were likely retailed from the neighborhood Saulsbury corner store. Young Saulsbury, an extrovert with a keen business mind, would have been easily recognized as a born salesman with management potential. Both Samuel Cairns and James Armstrong, the original founders of the company, were still active at the Concord Street facility, and probably mentored their neighborhood protégée. In 1852, James Armstrong & Co. aligned itself with a former Baltimore competitor, the firm of Charles and James Webb & Co., located several blocks north on Ensor Street. The Webb Brothers had inherited their firm from their father, Charles, Sr., who had passed away in 1849.[2]

In 1855, when Samuel Cairns retired from the Concord Street business, James Armstrong immediately promoted his nephew, Thomas, to the position of partner in the firm.[3] Thomas Armstrong and Andrew Saulsbury had quickly hit it off as friends, with Saulsbury's eventual grandson being named "Thomas Armstrong Saulsbury."[4]

In 1858, James Armstrong left the firm he had built to venture into an entirely new business,[5] opening the American Fire Insurance Company of Baltimore on South Street. With the older man removed from the day-to-day activities of the Concord Street facility, Charles Webb would be called on to assist at Concord Street, with his brother, James, remaining at the Ensor Street building.[6] Charles Webb would now work on a daily basis with both Thomas Armstrong and Andrew Saulsbury at the combined company's main plant near the Pratt Street Bridge.

After the birth of James Armstrong Saulsbury in 1853, Saulsbury and his first wife would have two more children, both daughters. Julia would be born in 1855 or 1856, and Elizabeth in 1859. During this period, the family would make their home at 138 South Central Avenue, the brick townhome being just a short 4/10ths of a mile walk from the Concord Street candle factory near Pratt Street by the wharves.[7] The house sat on a street paralleling Eden Street, home of veteran sea captain John J. Mattison.

It has been reported from multiple sources that the actor John Wilkes Booth was inducted into the Knights of the Golden Circle in either 1859 or 1860, at a Baltimore KGC castle in the vicinity of his boyhood home at 62 North Exeter Street. The castle was described as being a private residence "*in the neighborhood*" that featured a bust of fiery Southern rights Senator John Calhoun, and portraits of two other national friends of the Southern cause,[8] possibly Lincoln adversary Stephen Douglas and President Buchanan's young, pro-slavery Vice-President, John C. Breckinridge, who was only 36 when he assumed that office. Breckinridge, a close friend of Albert Pike, would soon be serving in the Confederate Army as a general. It is said that many actors, businessmen, military men, and high-up Baltimore politicians were in attendance for Booth's swearing-in ceremony.[9] At only 4/10ths of a mile from Booth's family home on Exeter Street, the Saulsbury residence on South Central can certainly be described as *"in the neighborhood."*

Booth home at 62 N. Exeter St.

Booth's initiation fee — likely a gold dollar — would not have gone into the pot buried under the Mattison home just around the corner. The last of the Eden Street coins were minted in 1856 — and buried sometime in 1856 judging by the low number of 1856 coins in that hoard. If Booth's initiation coin went anywhere, it probably went into the tin box that would be found a decade later buried on location at Thomas Armstrong's residence, The

Fountain Hotel. If the Saulsbury home was indeed the site of Booth's alleged induction into the KGC — as the gold coins beneath the Mattison/Saulsbury and Armstrong residences would strongly indicate — then Thomas Armstrong would likely have been in attendance . . . along with the Webb Brothers and possibly even Charles Webb's secessionist political allies, Mayor George Brown and Marshal George Kane, amongst others.

Just before the beginning of the war, in 1861, Saulsbury's first wife would pass away.[10] The widower and father of three, however, would soon remarry — to a young woman 16 years his junior. They would not have a child together until 1865, the end of the Civil War, with the couple ultimately producing a total of four more children — in 1866, 1868, 1869, and 1873.[11] These dates bear testament to the enormous effect the war must have had on the lives of ordinary people in cities on the bubble, such as Baltimore, Maryland.

After losing his first wife in 1861, the 1862 death notices seem to indicate that Saulsbury would lose another family member in short order — his father, Andrew, Sr. Military records also show that a young man by the name of Saulsbury, from 179 S. Central, was drafted into the Union Army in 1863. If this young Saulsbury had been a nephew or cousin to the candle executive, there is little doubt Andrew Saulsbury would have been enraged. To an outspoken Confederate supporter such as Saulsbury, it was bad enough that the Union had imposed martial law on the city and replaced the Baltimore police force with federal troops — while imprisoning Mayor Brown, Marshal Kane, and scores of other civic leaders without trial and with no charges. But later, to draft young Baltimoreans to fight against their very own people? No wonder Saulsbury's daughter, Elizabeth, would recall years later that the family had been "*threatened on more than one occasion by Union troops.*"[12] Saulsbury was not a man to hold his tongue, although with a wife and young children to feed and protect that might have been the safer course of action.

"*He was an ardent Southern sympathizer, that everyone knew,*" the Saulsbury daughters would recall in 1934.[13]

The treasure home on Eden Street is practically within shouting distance of the former South Central home, and an easy under ten-minute walk to the Concord Street candle factory off Pratt Street. The Pratt Street wharves where Captain Mattison for years docked his merchant ships would have been visible from the windows of James Armstrong & Co.

Just as Saulsbury would waste little time in taking a second wife during the early months of the Civil War, the chandler would close on a new home almost immediately upon cessation of hostilities in 1865. With three children and now a fourth on the way, perhaps more square footage was in order. Perhaps Saulsbury also felt confident that business would quickly return to normal with the surrender of General Lee at Appomattox. In June, 1865 Saulsbury would purchase the larger home of neighbor John J. Mattison at 55 S. Eden Street for the sum of $3,200 . . . paid in cash.[14] According to Baltimore coin hoard historian Len Augsburger, Saulsbury never carries a mortgage on the property. He does, however, have to pay "ground rent" to Baltimore commodities broker and attorney Charles Findlay, Esq., since Saulsbury owns the house — but not the underlying property.[15]

Interestingly, Charles Findlay is somewhat connected to James Armstrong, with both men having served as committee members for the First Presbyterian Church of Baltimore. And while Armstrong's insurance company, The American Fire Insurance Company of Baltimore, is listed at 6 South Street, the directories of the day list Findlay's company (he is both treasurer and secretary), Rowlesburg Lumber & Iron, at 30 South Street. The possibility these two powerful individuals were acquainted is obviously quite high . . . it is no secret that people in the lumber business always need fire insurance.

The treasure house on Eden Street was actually two three-story brick boxes, front and back, connected at the first floor by a passageway with a kitchen and bathroom.[16] The structure in front filled the entire width of the lot, and faced east across a well-kept city park that featured a fountain and pleasant footpaths. The rear structure was smaller, allowing space for a side walkway that joined a small, hidden courtyard between the buildings to the alleyway behind the rear building that ran south down to Pratt Street. Entrance to the cellar was through a Bilco door and submerged stairway in the courtyard.

During the 1934 court proceedings, Saulsbury's daughters would remember an idyllic childhood, one where all the children were well-dressed, well fed, and well cared for.[17] Their father kept a well-stocked library, and was in the habit of giving out gold, silver, and copper coins as presents during holidays. Two black

maids, who lived in the rear portion of the house — perhaps
Theodore and Mrs. Jones' eventual room — assisted Mrs.
Saulsbury with looking after the children and the running of the
household. The home itself was furnished with feather beds,
clocks, overstuffed chairs, plush rugs, and was by all accounts a
"beautiful" home.

Andrew Saulsbury was fond of decorating the walls of his
Eden Street home with several paintings, including a
commissioned portrait of himself. The two most prominently
displayed paintings, however, were of Confederate generals
Robert E. Lee and Thomas "Stonewall" Jackson.[18] It was
remembered that Saulsbury liked to entertain his gentlemen
friends in the evening, and that many an oyster was served to his
numerous visitors. Could the *post-Civil War* portraits of Lee and
Jackson at 55 S. Eden have been replacements for the *pre-Civil*
portraits of popular Southern-rights politicians that perhaps had
graced the walls of 138 S. Central? Had John Wilkes Booth and
other Confederate-leaning adventurists been inducted into the
expanding Knights of the Golden Circle at a ceremony in the
Saulsbury residence on Central Avenue? Had those coins been
kept for a time at the Saulsbury residence, and then, for security
reasons, relocated and buried around the corner in the cellar of
the much quieter and far less conspicuous home of "secret-slaver"
John Mattison? Did Saulsbury assume stewardship of the
treasure at the end of the war when he purchased the long-time
home of Captain Mattison?

Those 5,000 gold coins didn't bury themselves in 1856, and Captain Mattison lived at his Eden Street home until the 1860s, later moving two blocks east to South Broadway and renting the treasure home to fellow mariner Captain John E. Stevens during the war — and before selling the treasure property to Saulsbury in 1865.

The fact that Mattison left the coins behind in Saulsbury's possession is prima facie evidence of a conspiracy. The very size of the hoard itself is suggestive of group conspiracy. Augsburger had said in his Treasure in the Cellar that the apparent timing of the burial of the coins, in 1856, "made no sense."[19] Yes, it absolutely makes no sense if you are assuming the pot of gold coins was the product some Silas Marner or Ebenezer Scrooge type individual, a stingy lone miser counting and socking away coins out of sight from the world late at night. But Mattison, a wheeling-dealing crusty old mariner, had sailed the seven seas, and also had a ship seized for illegal slave trading in an apparent Southern Rights operation to do an end run around the international slave trading ban.[20] Saulsbury was an extroverted entrepreneur who made no effort to conceal his "ardent" Southern sympathies — to the point of endangering his own family's safety by drawing the ire of federal troops patrolling Baltimore after Lincoln had imprisoned the city's secessionist leaders. Those secessionist leaders, particularly George Brown and George Kane, had gained office due in no small measure to the efforts of Maryland Freemason Grand Master Charles Webb.[21] And all three men, Webb, Mattison, and Saulsbury, were directly connected through intimate business relationships involving companies under the control of founder James Armstrong.[22] Webb, Mattison, and Saulsbury were all well acquainted, and were brothers-in-arms to the same ill-fated Southern cause of foreign conquest and domestic rebellion. The coins in the pot were collected to further the clandestine plans of The Knights of the Golden Circle — plans cut short and ultimately dashed by the Civil War and its resulting abolitionist outcome.

The timing of the burial of the coins, in the year 1856, makes *perfect* sense in the context of KGC (and predecessor OLS) planning and strategy for the late 1850s. And what we know about Messrs. Webb, Mattison, and Saulsbury all fits with their being willing and active participants in a conspiracy to aid and abet the

Knights of the Golden Circle — and the resultant Southern
Rebellion against President Lincoln and the Union.

If it walks like a duck and quacks like a duck . . . then what we
have is most likely a duck. And if it lays 5,000 gold coins, then it is
almost assuredly a golden duck. This is especially true when
there are eventually 2,000 *more* gold coins discovered beneath
the residence of James Armstrong's nephew and fellow Concord
Street tallow chandler, Thomas Armstrong — discovered in a tin
box but a mile from the treasure house.[23]

The date of closing on the treasure house is June, 1865. Lee
surrenders to Grant in April, 1865. Booth assassinates Lincoln at
Ford's Theater five days later. Booth himself is hunted down and
killed two weeks after his final "mad act." In late May, President
Andrew Johnson offers a blanket amnesty to all Confederate
combatants . . . so Johnny Reb can come marching home. The
era of Reconstruction has begun. In June, Saulsbury buys the
treasure home from Mattison, the coins safely buried beneath a
pile of dirt and oyster shells in the far corner of the rear portion of
the basement. By early July, four of the eight convicted Lincoln
conspirators are hung by the neck until they are dead at Fort
McNair in Washington, D.C.

Although the city directors continued to list Andrew Saulsbury
at 138 S. Central until 1867, it is reasonable to assume that the
Saulsburys moved there soon after purchasing the treasure house
in 1865. First, the Saulsburys would have been in need of a larger
home with child number four on the way. Second, Elizabeth
Audoun Saulsbury, who was born in 1859, testified in court that
the family had moved to Eden Street when she was six . . . in
1865, not 1867.[24] Because of her frail sate in 1935, the judge did
not believe her recollection to be credible. But two things would
have indelibly marked 1865 in Elizabeth's mind. First, 1865 would
have likely been the year she began her schooling, and people
always remember where they lived when they started school.
Second, with the Lincoln assassination and the end of the Civil
War, 1865 was a most memorable year. Rather, what probably
happened was the Saulsburys moved to Eden Street in 1865, as
the daughter had testified, and Andrew Saulsbury likely rented out
the Central Avenue property for a while until he could sell it.
Saulsbury was known to put his money in real estate, and was
well enough off not to have to carry a mortgage on his primary
residence. More than likely the Saulsburys did, in fact, move to

the treasure house immediately after the war, and the city directories did not catch up with the change until two years later. Mattison's tenant Captain Stevens had moved from the treasure home to E. Baltimore Avenue before the 1865 sale, and since no one was listed as living in the treasure home until the Saulsburys during the latter portion of the 1860s, it is reasonable to assume that the directories had simply not yet gotten caught up (they would have been in disarray since publication had ceased during the war). And most obviously, neither Mattison nor Saulsbury would have left the property to sit vacant with a fortune in gold coinage hidden there.

Once at his new home on Eden Street, Saulsbury begins to dabble in local politics, perhaps at the urging of fellow candle executive and politician James Webb. Saulsbury joins the second branch of the reinstated Baltimore City Council, where he finds his services needed on the highway commission.[25] The Baltimore mayor and police chief had been imprisoned for much of the war, and the police force and city council disbanded. Now with city government restored into the hands of Baltimoreans, Saulsbury goes to work tending to issues such as road paving, street grading, highway widening, the installation of city gas lamps, storm drain repair, and the construction of much needed city sewers.[26] He manages to get a much-sought sewer constructed down the street from his home, at Eden and Pratt Streets. Saulsbury also manages to get new stepping stones installed at the street corner — and sees to it that the permit for James Armstrong & Co. to expand its place of business is approved. Overall, as numismatist Len Augsburger notes, Saulsbury is generally conservative with the city's money but also very pro-business in his council activities[27] — not surprising for someone who has spent a lifetime in private industry. There is nothing, however, relating to Saulsbury's routine and largely mundane functions on Baltimore City Council that would even remotely hint at any reason for 5,000 gold coins to become buried in his cellar. Because Saulsbury joined City Council after the war, and the coins were buried some five years prior to the war, Saulsbury's years of service would seem to bear little or no connection to the treasure hoard.

Those paintings of Lee and Jackson, and Saulsbury's outspoken Southern sympathies, however, are an entirely different matter altogether.

By the very early 1870s, Andrew Saulsbury had spent nearly half of his life in the soap and candle making business. But at some point the real estate bug had bitten Saulsbury — he was a moonlight consultant on the formation of building associations and had begun to dabble in local real estate.[28] Suddenly, the busy father of seven had a looming life decision on the horizon.

Would it be soap and candles . . . or brick and mortar? The relative safety of working for Charles Webb at James Armstrong & Co. — or the exhilarating chance to be his own boss and stamp the Saulsbury name on his own firm?

True to his temperament, the hot-blooded, extroverted Andrew Saulsbury would not take forever in coming to a decision.

A Thief in the Night

So the lucky Rummels of Eden Street apparently have a new set of wheels, a Plymouth.[1] Also the new washing machine, a radio, and even a coffeemaker. [2] Problem is, the Rummels still live on Baltimore's rapidly declining South Eden Street. As with the Clampett clan made famous by the sitcom *The Beverly Hillbillies*, it's time for Philip, Bessie, and young Theodore to "move away from there." They

initially choose Overlea, a small, charming community on the periphery of Baltimore, annexed by the city in 1919. On the evening of Labor Day, September 2, 1935, the Rummels journey from Eden Street to Overlea to inspect a house they are interested in purchasing.[3]

Upon their return to Eden Street, the upstart Rummels are in for a rude surprise. In their absence, their second floor rear apartment at the treasure house has been burglarized. Someone apparently climbed the fire escape at the back of the property, broke into the dwelling through a window, and made off with the Rummels' "life savings."[4]

The thief — or thieves — leave behind only a mangled, empty strong box.[5]

Someone had apparently been watching the family's movements, waiting for a window of opportunity. This, despite the previous year's dramatic newspaper photograph[6] showing Bessie Rummel (then Bessie Jones) waving a pistol in front of 132 S. Eden Street, vowing to protect their little apartment from any misguided intruders.

Shaken and in disbelief, the Rummels hike over to the Eastern Police Station to report the incident. Eastern happens to be the very same station house to which the boys delivered their golden surprise in a cigar box just a year earlier.

Mr. Rummel tells the disbelieving officers that a total of $3,100 in U.S. currency and some $500 in gold coins have vanished. Baltimore's finest are skeptical that a part-time, lowly paid street cleaner and a woman who takes in laundry could manage to save $3,600.[7] Might this rather have something to do with that famous pot of gold?

A Thief in the Night

Under interrogation, Mr. Rummel comes clean. There were
no "life savings." Rummel's stepson had convinced his stepfather
to lie to the police. As suspected, the stolen $3,600 had been part
of Theodore and Henry's treasure adventure. But not, however,
the September, 1934 headline-making discovery. No, seems this
latest gold came from a _second_, previously undisclosed, mid-1935
dig in the magical cellar.[8] Incredulously, a completely distinct and
separate bonanza the boys uncovered just after the Lord
Baltimore Hotel coin auction, and upon the conclusion of Henry's
school year.

As the boys put it, they decided to have "_another go_" at the
cellar. And although the property at 132 S. Eden had already
been thoroughly searched by Baltimore authorities — and anyone
else bold enough to surreptitiously gain access to the site, Henry
and Theodore claimed they had dug in the only portion of the
entire cellar that had somehow remained unexplored.[9]

Again, the boys had discovered an ancient buried pot . . . by
one account a large oyster can. And again, the container had
been chock full of highly prized 19th-century gold coins.

As before, they decided to split the proceeds. Henry kept
half, and Theodore the other half. The boys never bothered with
an exact tally.[10] The alleged $3,600 in cash and gold stolen from
the Rummels consisted entirely of Theodore's split of the new
recovery — or at least the portion that hadn't already been spent.

Henry, meanwhile, had hidden his coins inside in a tin can
under his mattress. But while horsing around, as teens do,
Henry's brother, John, had leapt onto Henry's bed, landing directly
on top of the hidden container of coins. Brother John then told
their mother, Ruth, who investigated and confiscated Henry's new
stash.[11]

This time, with the original discovery proceeds still tied up in
courtroom litigation, and in the possession of a court-appointed
trustee, neither the Grobs nor the Rummels went running to the
authorities to announce the latest find. This "second" pile of gold
would be kept secret — that is, until the night of the infamous
Eden Street burglary in early September, 1935.

The authorities seem particularly puzzled by the broken glass
found _outside_, and not inside, the window of the Rummels'
apartment.[12] And, they are most especially troubled by the boys'
assertion about "_having a second go_" at the cellar. The Eden

Street property had been searched and searched again by professionals. Not a single additional gold coin had been found.

How could Henry and Theodore have possibly scored a second can holding yet another fortune in gold? Their story seemed most unlikely, the scene at the rear of the second floor apartment suspicious.

However, the skepticism shown by Baltimore's men in blue is mild compared to that of the utter disbelief professed by the legal eagles on the Findlay/French team.

"We think the fantastic tale of a second find is altogether unbelievable," scoffed Emory Niles, Esq.

Not surprisingly, despite their appeal having been denied, the Findlay/French team now files an immediate petition to have the civil suit reopened. And, based on the shocking news of a "second" treasure find kept entirely hidden from the authorities, Judge Eugene O'Dunne is left with no choice but to grant a new hearing.

Round Two of the legal drama is scheduled for September 20th, 1935.

A rejuvenated Findlay/French team can smell victory. Either the "second" find will turn out to be coins simply withheld from the court after the original discovery . . . or, the boys reentered the rear cellar without permission and made an unlikely second, most incredible find. According to the lawyers for the elderly sisters, this is now an open-and-shut case of either fraud or trespass . . . take your pick. Henry and Theodore have unwittingly placed themselves and attorney Harry O. Levin in some legal hot water. Levin, who has been representing the boys for a year on a contingency basis, without yet receiving a dime, is quick to announce his total lack of knowledge of any subsequent treasure find.[13] Levin says he is just as surprised as everyone else, seems his young clients and their families never mentioned a word of this to him.

Meanwhile, the Findlay/French sisters engage the services of a private eye.[14] The Grobs and Rummels maintain that most of the coins from the so-called "second discovery" have already been sold, mainly to a pair of gold-buying brothers named Eli and Yale Merrill. Judge O'Dunne orders an immediate halt to the disposal of any more coins or cash connected to the case.[15] O'Dunne wants to sort out this most untidy of situations within the confines of his downtown courtroom.

On the first day of testimony, Judge O'Dunne clears the courtroom. He wants the witnesses to testify one-by-one, and not in front of other witnesses waiting to take the stand. Will those involved be able to keep their stories straight?

Theodore tells the court the boys uncovered the second pot of gold several feet *south* of their original find, and points to the spot on a diagram of the cellar. Henry then testifies that they discovered the second pot several feet *west* of the original gold-filled copper can.[16]

Neither boy can pinpoint an exact date of discovery, nor do they know the number of coins and the total face value contained in the second pot. And regarding the second pot, no one can say where the actual container now is. It may have been an oyster can, or some other copper container, or even a galvanized container, and yes, it did look much the same as the first pot. But, we don't know what happened to it, sorry.

According to Bessie and Philip Rummel, several persons had knocked on their Eden Street door inquiring if they might have any gold coins for sale.[17] Bessie testifies that she sold $1,000 face value coins to a nameless "older, shabbily dressed man" for $1,250. Then brothers Yale and Eli Merrill showed up, asking to buy in larger quantities. After checking out the brothers and their business cards (Yale was an advertising man, and Eli worked in a pawn shop), the Rummels do a series of deals to sell $2,500 face value coins to the Merrills for about $3,000. The coins could fetch at least $4,000 at auction, perhaps more.

Other coins had been given to George and Frances Rummel, Philip's brother and sister-in-law.[18] George Rummel had been hurt in an accident and unable to work, so George and Frances had badly needed the money. So, Philip and Bessie had kindly obliged them.

When the Merrill brothers inquire about purchasing even more collectible coins, the Rummels point them to the Grobs' residence on nearby S. Caroline Street.[19]

Ruth Grob testifies that yes, she sold coins to gold a buyer who had shown up unannounced on S. Caroline Street. Got $3,400 in currency for $3,400 face value in coins.[20] A bad deal, son Henry had told her, but there were bills to pay and things the Grobs desperately needed to buy. Unlike the poor Rummels, robbed of everything, Ruth had the sense to put her newly acquired cash in the bank. Then she paid for expensive dental

work, bought new furniture, and much-needed new clothes.[21]
Plus, a used Ford and, oh yes, a modest brick home in Canton.
Henry's older sister and brother-in law, Paul and Gertrude
Eberhart, had recently moved in with them.

The Merrills arrive in court with their high-priced hired gun,
attorney Simon Sobeloff. Sobeloff arrives with the gold coins
purchased from the Rummels by the Merrills.

"*The worst has happened,*" quips Judge O'Dunne. "*The
lawyers have them already!*"[22]

The Merrills tell the court they have done nothing wrong. It is
perfectly legal to buy collector coins from a willing seller. The Gold
Act expressly excludes collectible numismatic coins from the
general ban on buying gold. The brothers have broken no laws,
and have complied with the summons to appear in court . . . along
with the coins they legally purchased from a willing seller.[23]
However, the clandestine way in which the Merrills purchased the
coins, along with their request for the Rummels "not to tell anyone"
about the transactions, is evidence they knew they were operating
in a grey area . . . a very murky grey area. No one hires a legal
eagle like Simon Sobeloff if they think they are in the free and
clear. And nearly everyone in Baltimore had knowledge of the
courtroom drama regarding the fight for ownership of the treasure.
The Merrills certainly read the newspapers — the news articles
were admittedly what sparked the brothers' idea to pay a call on
132 S. Eden Street in the first place.

An inventory of the Merrill coins[24] purchased from the Jones-
Rummel clan (allegedly from the "second" treasure find) shows the
same approximate spread of denominations and dates exhibited
by the first pot: 1834 – 1856. However, the "second" pot of gold
seems to have contained more coins with earlier mint dates from
the 1830s and 1840s. A breakdown by denomination is as
follows:

$20	$10	$5	$2.50	$1
15	37	138	18	1,092

The inventory included none of the coins Bessie Rummel had
sold to the nameless, elderly, "shabbily dressed" buyer who had
appeared at their apartment door, none of the coins stolen during
the Labor Day burglary, and of course none of the coins kept or
sold by the Grob family.

A Thief in the Night

The thief or thieves who supposedly robbed the Rummels took some $3,100 in cash and another $500 in face value gold coins. And that is after the Rummels' notorious spending spree ($800 for the new Plymouth, $50 for a washing machine, radio, coffeemaker, etc.). Nor does it include the coins gifted to George and Frances Rummel. The Grobs allegedly banked $3,400 from the sale of their coins[25] . . . and very likely spent more cash that was never deposited.

With these figures in mind, when added to the original documented hoard of 3,358 gold coins, the actual combined number of coins from pots one and two is very conservatively in the *5,000 to 6,000* range.

Harry O. Levin, attorney for the Grobs and Rummels, has to be worried he might never realize his contingency fee of 1/3 share of either pot. Privately, you know Levin just has to be fuming at the Grobs and the Rummels.

And, what looked like a risk-free sweet deal for the Merrrills has become an expensive legal quagmire. The brothers have no assurance their $2,500 investment won't be suddenly confiscated by the court.

The hopeful but ultimately hard-luck Saulsbury heirs have now lost their chance at not only one, but *two* pots of gold. Gold they are certain Andrew Saulsbury once buried under his home for some mysterious reason they can only guess.

The Rummels, whose share of the second pot has already been allegedly ripped off by a person or persons unknown, now fear that Theodore's rightful share of the first pot may be forfeited. Bessie Rummel, already mistrustful of the system, harbors suspicion that the Baltimore police may have been somehow involved in the Labor Day burglary.[26] Since the Labor Day break-in, the Rummels have already moved away from Eden Street.

Mrs. Grob, dogged by the Findlay/French investigator, and tired of all the legal maneuvering and wrangling, is also concerned that her dreams of a college education for son Henry may disappear along with the auction proceeds from the first pot. Not only is Ruth Grob suspicious of the police, the court system, and the Findley/French attorneys, but she is also second-guessing the motives of her son's own lawyer, Harry O. Levin. Unhappy and unnerved, Henry's mother begins to seek out other legal representation.

All eyes are on Judge O'Dunne.

Bessie Rummel, near the end of the proceedings, produces an old copper pot, telling the court she later remembered it got dumped in the yard behind the front and around back of 132 S. Eden Street.[27] Everyone who sees the "second" pot agrees it looks much like the first. But is it the real deal, or had Bessie simply gone out and searched antique stores until she came across a similar old-looking container?

The Findlay/French lawyers make their final argument based on the evidence, appealing to Judge O'Dunne's common sense. The idea that the boys could find a second buried pot of gold, almost nine months after uncovering the first pot, when even Henry himself had admitted the authorities had left the cellar looking as if "a plow had gone though" it, was preposterous. The boys couldn't get their stories straight, and the adults' testimony was chock full of discrepancies and contradictions.[28] The entire Grob/Jones/Rummel story was, frankly, a fabrication lacking any credibility.

The Findlay/French side also accuses the Merrill brothers of being speculators, rather than collectors, who stood to reap a quick profit by flipping the coins to real coin aficionados.

However, to the French/Findlay team's stunned disbelief, Judge O'Dunne plays devil's advocate with the disputed evidence and conflicting testimony. Rather than seeing the numerous discrepancies as proof of fabrication, O'Dunne instead sees the incongruous stories as actually lending credibility to the argument for a second find. The witnesses, reasons the judge, had not simply gotten together to get their stories straight. Anyone attempting to fabricate such a tale would certainly have more closely compared notes.[29]

In announcing his decision, once again, in favor of the treasure kids, O'Dunne tells the court, "*I find that there was a second find in these premises, 132 South Eden Street, on or about May 27th.*"

While O'Dunne agrees that "*not all of the contents of the first pot,*" had been turned over to the authorities, he chooses to write that off to human nature. Most folks, O'Dunne believes, would have withheld at least a few coins under the circumstances. No harm, no foul.

In closing the proceedings, O'Dunne imposes an injunction on any of the interested parties in disposing of any of the coins or proceeds from the second discovery, made on or about May 27th,

1935.[30] The appeals for a re-argument of O'Dunne's February, 1935 decision are still pending . . . and the judge fully expects his latest ruling to be likewise appealed.

On this one, final point O'Dunne and the French/Findlay lawyers have ultimately found some common ground. The French/Findlay team is madder than hell and has every intention of appealing — again. They are convinced that Henry and Theodore first committed trespass, then committed fraud upon the court, and as reward are now set to collect a fortune at age 21 . . . a nest egg that rightfully belongs to two senior landowners in the twilight of their unassuming lives. They were robbed first by the boys, and now by the court. . . . Perhaps the elderly French/Findlay sisters are not familiar with the old Mexican curse, the one that says, "*May your life be filled with lawyers.*"

But as events surrounding Baltimore's gold hoard continue to unfold, some observers will come to believe that it is those mysterious, alluring coins from the cellar that are truly cursed.

The Night They Drove Old Dixie Down

Locomotive for train used by Confederate President
Jeff Davis to flee Richmond in April, 1865.

Virgil Caine is the name and I served on the Danville train.
'Til Stoneman's cavalry came and tore up the tracks again.
In the winter of '65, we were hungry, just barely alive
By May the tenth, Richmond had fell
It's a time I remember, oh so well.

The night they drove old Dixie down
And the bells were ringing.
The night they drove old Dixie down
And the people were singing
They went, "Na,na,na . . ."

The Band, 1969[1]

John Wilkes Booth and Marshal George P. Kane had somehow failed to connect in Montreal in October, 1864. Booth had arrived there on October 18th *specifically* requesting to see Kane, but the former Baltimore Marshal of Police had already left to run the Union blockade and report for duty in Richmond. It is strongly suspected that Booth was in Canada to present his daring plan to Kane and other Confederate agents there such as Patrick Charles Martin and George Sanders.[2] Booth was prepared to kidnap President Lincoln, remove him to Confederate territory, and to demand the release of several thousand CSA prisoners in exchange for the President's safe return.

Mighty bold stuff. . . .

George Kane had possibly been involved in the alleged 1861 "Baltimore Plot" to kill President-elect Lincoln, had participated in the movement to force Maryland to secede, had directly participated in the burning of railroad bridges to thwart Lincoln's plan to send more federal troops through Baltimore, had summoned the Virginia militia to "whip" the "fresh hordes" of Yankee troops "or die," had done time in a series of Union prisons for his treasonous activities, and upon his release, headed north to Canada to conspire to perpetrate further plots against the Union — most notably the aborted raid to free some 2,000 Confederate prisoners from an island in Lake Erie near Sandusky, Ohio.[3]

Booth had spent the war years earning a fortune on stage, often in front of admiring audiences across the North. Off stage, he made verbal assaults and threats against the Union in general and President Lincoln in particular. Booth's sole known contribution to the Southern cause, besides possibly having been involved in the April 19th, 1861 bridge burning escapade, had apparently been to smuggle the occasional stash of quinine to the Confederacy for use on rebel soldiers afflicted with malaria.[4]

Back in Richmond, George Kane was assigned to work under General Winder, whose main task was the defense of the Confederate capital, along with overseeing the CSA's military prisons.[5] Winder reported to Secretary of War James Seddon, and had previously been Jeff Davis' instructor at West Point. As a member of the Confederate Special Services, Kane regularly passed along intelligence concerning enemy troop movements in Virginia. Kane seems to have reported surveillance information directly to Winder, to General Lee, and near the end of the war even to CSA President Jeff Davis himself.[6]

In June of 1864, General Lee mentioned Kane specifically while writing to Jefferson Davis about a plot to liberate and arm Confederate prisoners held in southern Maryland. *"Great benefit,"* writes Lee, *"might be withdrawn from the release of our prisoners at Point Lookout if it can be accomplished. The number of men employed for this purpose would necessarily be small, as the whole would have to be transported secretly across the Potomac. . . . With relation to the project of Marshal Kane* [who had already been working with his superior, General Winder, on some unknown project involving Maryland], *if the matter can be kept secret, which I fear is impossible, should General* [Jubal] *Early cross the Potomac he might be sent to join him."* [7]

Kane's "project" that Lee references might have had to do with Kane's ongoing efforts to organize Confederate militias of Marylanders inside that occupied state. Or, it could have been related to the Confederate plan (never undertaken) to raid Point Lookout, a plan similar in nature to Kane's aborted raid on the Johnson Island military prison at Lake Erie. But there is also the possibility that what Lee was alluding to were the South's early-stage plans for the kidnapping of the "abolitionist" president and Yankee aggressor, Abraham Lincoln.

General Lee, however, in the same correspondence, also writes to President Davis that, *"I can devote to this purpose* [the raid on the military prison at Point Lookout] *the whole of the Marylanders of this army, which would afford a sufficient number of men of excellent material and much experience, but I am at a loss where to find a proper leader."* [8]

Since Kane already seems to own this special project which Lee fears can't be kept a secret, but Lee is *"at a loss"* to find a leader for the Point Lookout prison raid, we can conclude that Kane's project and the Point Lookout raid were likely wholly separate operations. And Kane's efforts to recruit Marylanders to join the Confederate armed forces would have been accomplished largely under the radar — not with General Jubal Early and his men crossing the Potomac to join Kane in Maryland. Again, Lee seems to be referring to some entirely separate mission altogether.

The only operation that fits Kane's secret project — one so sensitive and high-profile that Lee and Davis not dare to spell it out on paper — would be the planned kidnapping of President Lincoln for the purpose of exchanging him for Confederate prisoners.

To have armed Confederates crossing the Potomac to aid the conspirators in transporting the kidnapped president through southern Maryland and into Virginia would probably have been a necessity for such a daring plan to have succeeded.

John Wilkes Booth had already been recruiting a squad of conspirators as early as September, 1864.[9] He then went to Montreal in October to see fellow Baltimorean and — by Booth's 1861 description — friend, George Kane, to present his plans for kidnapping Mr. Lincoln.[10] Kane seems to have been selected in early 1864 to oversee this desperate action, with Booth later being recruited or having volunteered to carry out the actual assignment.

One must not forget the bitter personal animosity George Kane held towards Union Secretary of State Seward, Union Secretary of War Edwin Stanton, and particularly President Lincoln for the marshal's nearly 14-month long incarceration without trial. Also, the ongoing destruction and loss experienced by the South. There is motive aplenty to explain Kane's participation in a strike against Lincoln.

That the Confederates would dare to target President Lincoln personally may have been instigated by a controversial event known as "The Dahlgren Affair."[11] On March 2, 1864, some gung-ho Union soldiers participated in a bungled raid on Richmond, Virginia. The failed attack was led by Colonel Ulric Dahlgren, who was killed near the King & Queen County courthouse. Allegedly, on the commanding officer's body, papers were discovered that included signed orders on Union Army stationery that pointed towards a plot to assassinate Jeff Davis. According to one part of the instructions, "*The men must keep together and well in hand, and once in the city it must be destroyed and Jeff. Davis and Cabinet killed.*"[12] The plot was purportedly authorized by Union Brigadier General Judson Kilpatrick, with the blessing of Edwin Stanton.

The papers were soon turned over to an alarmed Jeff Davis, his Secretary of State, Benjamin Judah, and Secretary of War, James Seddon. Transcripts of the orders were subsequently published in Southern newspapers, and quickly denounced by the North as forgeries. The North claimed the papers were faked in order to discredit the increasingly successful Union war effort.

Today's historians are split over whether the papers authorizing the raid were fabricated or genuine. Since Edwin Stanton is thought to have destroyed the documents after the

Union confiscated them from Richmond at the close of the war, the original papers have not survived for the benefit of modern forensic analysis. However, Civil War scholars such as Stephen W. Sears and author Edward Steers (<u>Blood on the Moon</u>) have concluded that the Dahlgren documents were indeed authentic — and thus the raid on Richmond and assassination plot against Davis real.[13]

Sears succinctly summed up the impact of the Dahlgren Affair, connecting it directly to the assassination of Abraham Lincoln in the following year:

"Judson Kilpatrick, Ulric Dahlgren, and their probable patron Edwin Stanton set out to engineer the death of the Confederacy's president; the legacy spawned out of the utter failure of their effort may have included the death of their own president."[14]

With the failed assassination of CSA President Jeff Davis in March, 1864, President Lincoln became fair game for the South — and all the more so as the course of the war proved increasingly disastrous for Richmond. Detective Allan Pinkerton strongly believed that Marshal George Kane had been involved in the 1861 "Baltimore plot" against then President-elect Lincoln. By 1864-65 Kane's personal animosity towards the "abolitionist President" would have undoubtedly multiplied several-fold. Kane had been directly involved with the 1864 Confederate scheme to commandeer a Union warship and to use that warship to free CSA prisoners from Johnson Island on Lake Erie.[15] Kane may also have been party to a similar plot to free Confederate prisoners from Lookout Point, Maryland. By late 1864 it had likely become apparent that the kidnapping of a single man, the lightly guarded President Lincoln, could be accomplished with a surgical strike by a small team of operatives . . . and it could be executed more easily than a direct and highly complicated assault (and resulting prison break) at a heavily guarded military penal facility behind enemy lines.

The Union's decision in 1864 to cease prisoner exchanges with the South, already chronically short of men to fight the numerically superior North, put further pressure on the Confederacy to act. General Ulysses S. Grant defended the Union's draconian action with the following August 18, 1864 statement:

"It is hard on our men held in Southern prisons not to exchange them, but it is humanity to those left in the ranks to fight our battles. Every man we hold, when released on parole or otherwise, becomes an active soldier against us at once either directly or indirectly. If we commence a system of exchange which liberates all prisoners taken, we will have to fight on until the whole South is exterminated. If we hold those caught they amount to no more than dead men. At this particular time to release all rebel prisoners North would insure Sherman's defeat and would compromise our safety here."[16]

"Hard" does not even begin to describe conditions at places such as Andersonville, Georgia where thousands of confined Union troops died of starvation, disease, abuse, and neglect.

By late 1864 and into early 1865, Booth's plan to snatch Lincoln and rescue the Confederacy was moving forward. He spent approximately $10,000 — an enormous sum in an era of $300 average annual salaries — to arm and outfit his cabal of kidnappers (with items including carbines, pistols, ammunition, daggers, and two sets of handcuffs purchased in New York).[17] Although Booth was a wealthy man, he had for many months been neglecting his lucrative acting career in the furtherance of his obsession to take action against Lincoln. The amount of $10,000 invested in this project strongly suggests that Booth had substantial financial backing . . . most likely from the Confederate underground, whether in Montreal, Richmond, or both. Booth held planning sessions as far away as Boston,[18] seeking hardline Southern supporters wherever he could find them. One of the alleged attendees at an early Booth meeting in Boston (July, 1864) was non-other than Godfrey Joseph Hyams (alias J.W. Harris), the Confederate operative allegedly hired by Dr. Luke Blackburn to distribute clothing tainted with yellow fever to vital areas within Union territory.[19] Hyams is said to have hatched part of the bio-terror plot from his room at Baltimore's Fountain Hotel, a known center of secessionist activity, the listed residence of candle executive Thomas Armstrong, and a longstanding neighborhood hangout of Booth's.

From Adam Mayers' 2003 book Dixie and the Dominion (Canada, the Confederacy, and the War for the Union), *"In July, Booth was in Boston and made his first Canadian connection. Godfrey Hyams, Thompson's courier and a double agent, had been sent to Boston as part of a plot devised by Dr. Luke Blackburn. . . . In what became known as the Yellow Fever Plot, Blackburn infected clothes with the disease and shipped the trunks to Boston and other Northern points, where Hyams was to collect them and deliver them to Union hospitals as a deadly act of charity. At the last minute Hyams had a crisis of confidence and refused to deliver the trunks. But Hyams met Booth there, and a check of hotel registers found that Booth had stayed at the Parker House in Boston along with Hyams, a man registered as H.V. Clinton, and two others giving false names and Canada as their address. "H.V. Clinton" was also registered at the St. Lawrence Hall in May and August. The Hall by then had become a rendezvous for Confederate agents."*[20]

Booth's initial game plan involved grabbing Lincoln from his box at Ford's Theater and lowering the president to the stage using ropes. The image of the towering chief executive being incapacitated and lowered to the stage in front of a very large and stunned audience — who would sit meekly by and do nothing — was so preposterous that some of Booth's early cohorts either threatened to back out or actually did excuse themselves from active participation.[21] Some of these early meetings with Booth's boyhood pals Sam Arnold and Michael O'Laughlen were held over drinks at Baltimore's Barnum Hotel,[22] where possibly Marshal Kane, known KGC member Cipriano Ferrandini, and other Confederate sympathizers were alleged to have hatched the plot to assassinate President-elect Lincoln in 1861. Later clandestine meetings with Booth in charge were held at restaurants and hotels in Washington, D.C. or at Mary Surratt's boarding house in the district.

Sam Arnold, keeper of the weapons purchased by Booth in New York, was so petrified at Booth's seemingly insane plan that he told the actor, "*You can be a leader of the party, but not my executioner.*"[23] Arnold, incidentally, would reveal years later that Booth's plan to snatch Lincoln was conceived some *six weeks* before Booth traveled to Montreal in October, 1864.

Finally forced to admit to the total unworkability of kidnapping the President from his box at Ford's Theatre (a stage upon which the actor had often performed), Booth revised his scheme to one in which the participants would snatch Lincoln somewhere away from the White House and Ford's Theatre. Preparations were made to whisk the President through southern Maryland and then across the Potomac River into Virginia. Co-conspirator John H. Surratt is said to have purchased a boat meant to be used for this purpose.[24]

Historian William A. Tidwell, author of <u>Come Retribution</u>, the story of the Confederate Secret Service's involvement in the Lincoln assassination, maintains that Booth's escape route through southern Maryland coincided with known lines of Confederate underground communication — a network of rebel agents who employed a system of flags and torches to relay news of enemy movements. Booth and accomplice David Herold received food, shelter, and assistance from a number of individuals during their post-assassination flight from Ford's Theater.[25] They had even pre-arranged to have a doctor available along the route in case Lincoln or one of the conspirators became injured during the operation. In late 1864 in Montreal, a Confederate operative and suspected KGC member named Patrick Charles Martin, who had played host to Marshal George Kane in Canada, provided Booth with a letter of introduction.[26] That letter was to Dr. William Queen, an elderly physician who lived near the southern Maryland swamp in which Booth would later seek refuge. The letter asked Dr. Queen to set up a meeting between Booth and Dr. Samuel Mudd, the medical doctor who would later set Booth's broken leg while the assassin was on the run for his life.

Despite Mudd's later protestations to the contrary, he certainly knew who Booth was, and according to Tidwell and other historians, Booth and Mudd had met on multiple occasions prior to April 15, 1865. Dr. Mudd, to no surprise, had also harbored strong anti-Union, pro-secessionist sentiments. In a subsequent affidavit, Mudd admitted to his meetings with Booth in both Washington and Charles County, MD, and even stated that the actor had made him an offer to purchase Mudd's land in southern Maryland (affidavit of Samuel Mudd in Clara E. Laughlin's <u>The Death of Lincoln</u>).[27]

On March 4, 1865 Booth actually attended Lincoln's second inauguration as a guest of Lucy Hale, the daughter of a U.S. ambassador. Later, Booth would write in his diary, "*What an excellent chance I had, if I wished, to kill the President on Inauguration Day.*"[28]

But despite his hatred of Lincoln, Booth's mission in early March was to kidnap Lincoln, not assassinate him. A dead Lincoln could not be exchanged for thousands of Confederate prisoners.

By mid-March, 1865 Booth's extensive planning was ready to be set into motion. Initially, Booth's new plan was to grab Lincoln from his "summer" residence, the Old Soldiers Home located just three miles from the White House. It would be a daunting task, perhaps only marginally easier than accosting the President from his box at the crowded Ford's Theatre. But then, the conspirators learned of a far better opportunity. On March 17th, President Lincoln was scheduled to attend a play at the Campbell Military Hospital, not far from the Old Soldiers Home. Booth and his men would endeavor to set upon Lincoln as he was driven in his carriage — out in the open on a local, little-used road. At the appointed time, the kidnappers took their positions along Lincoln's route . . . but the President never showed.[29] At last moment, Lincoln had a change of plans, deciding instead to attend a reception at the National Hotel in downtown D.C. Ironically, Booth had been staying at this very same hotel while he stalked the chief executive and waited for the presidential carriage that never came.

Many of Booth's co-conspirators dropped out as various kidnapping plots were either delayed or aborted. And the names of several of Booth's early-stage associates have been lost to history. However, as April, 1865 neared, Booth's hardcore inner group included himself, David Herold, George Atzerodt, Samuel Arnold, Michael O'Laughlen, John Surratt, and Surratt's mother, Mary. Confederate sympathizers along the escape route, such as Dr. Mudd, would be in place to assist the participants as they transported their prized captive to Virginia and into the heart of the Confederacy.

But time was quickly running out on the Confederacy. Richmond would fall, and General Lee would surrender to Grant at the Appomattox courthouse before Booth's team could pull off a successful kidnapping attempt.

By April 1, the Union Army has finally succeeded in its attempt to outflank the Confederate defenders of the Southern capital. General Ulysses S. Grant's troops are able to collapse the end of Lee's lines around Petersburg. Richmond will soon be cut off from its supply routes and encircled by hostile forces. Lee tells General George Pickett to "hold Five Forks at all hazards" . . . but Union General Philip Sheridan's forces overrun Pickett's position.[30] General Lee has no choice but to advise President Jeff Davis that an evacuation of Richmond needs to proceed immediately. It is now checkmate for the die-hard South.

The Night They Drove Old Dixie Down

On April 2, 1865, food riots break out in Richmond as mobs loot city stores. President Davis orders the rioters to stop, and even flings pocket change to them from atop his wagon, threatening to have the trouble-makers arrested.[31] That evening, under cover of darkness, Jeff Davis and his Confederate leaders flee the capital. The Confederate Army follows close behind. As they prepare to retreat southward, the rebels take the Confederate treasury with them, along with at-risk gold and currency from the vaults of several Virginia banks. The next morning, Union troops enter Richmond and occupy the city.[32]

On April 9th, General Lee's Army of Northern Virginia surrenders. Davis, in full flight, wants the other rebel armies in the field to reorganize and fight on. But Davis' advisors and the military leaders accompanying him through Virginia and North Carolina are pressing him to end the carnage. All hope of victory is now lost. The writing is on the wall, whether a bitter Jeff Davis cares to read the message or not.

Two days later, on April 11th, the now seething John Wilkes Booth attends a White House speech given by the victorious Lincoln. The President, who has already been elected to a second term under the banner of ushering in the 13th Amendment, which abolishes of slavery and involuntary servitude, now openly reveals his plans to "enfranchise" former slaves.

"*That means n*g**r citizenship!*" fumes Booth after the speech. "*Now, by God, I'll put him through. That is the last speech he will ever give.*"[33]

Three days later, Booth would be true to his word. He would attempt to decapitate the U.S. government in one fell swoop, bringing chaos to Washington, D.C. based on the actor's desperate and misguided hope of rallying his cherished, dying, secessionist Confederacy.

Booth, who had promised his mother he would not sign up for military service, had recently written to her that, "*I have begun to deem myself a coward and to despise my own existence.*" On the morning of April 14th, 1865, the despondent actor writes in his diary that, "*Our cause being almost lost, something decisive and great must be done.*"[34]

Around noon on that fateful day, Booth by happenstance learns that President Lincoln and Ulysses Grant would be attending a play at Ford's Theatre. Quickly assembling his team, Booth spells out the shocking new plan. They will not try to kidnap the President . . . instead, Booth will kill him. And Vice-president Andrew Johnson, General Grant, and Secretary of State William Seward will all be murdered simultaneously. Desperate times require desperate measures.

Booth begins the hasty preparation by ordering all of the group's weapons stored at the Surratt tavern in Surrattsville, Maryland to be transported to Washington and be made ready. Thespian Booth, with his unfettered access to Ford's Theater, sneaks upstairs and drills a small peephole for spying into President Lincoln's box.

When the conspirators learn last-minute that Grant has declined the invitation to attend the play, but will instead be traveling by train to Philadelphia, Michael O'Laughlen is sent to follow Grant. However, the general and his wife subsequently travel north in a guarded private rail car.[35] O'Laughlen is therefore unable to carry out his hastily improvised part of the attack.

At seven o'clock that evening Booth meets with his fellow conspirators one last time to finalize the operation. Booth will kill Lincoln with a concealed derringer (though he has apparently already lost the opportunity to murder Grant with a knife). Lewis Powell will kill the bedridden Seward at his home, with David Herold assisting with the getaway and subsequent rendezvous with Booth. And George Atzerodt is given the assignment to kill Vice-President Andrew Johnson at the V.P.'s downtown hotel, the Kirkwood House. The multiple slayings would take place at or near ten o'clock. Atzerodt, naturally terrified by the bloody, seemingly deranged last-minute assignment, argues with Booth he has agreed to help with a kidnapping, not the performance a murder. Booth, who simply won't take no for an answer, informs the shaken Atzerodt it is far too late to back out now.

Atzerodt, however, completely backs out, and spends the next several hours drinking in the Kirkwood House bar, where he arouses suspicion by pestering the bartender with questions about Johnson's stay at the hotel.[36]

Lewis Powell (a.k.a. Lewis Paine) goes to Seward's home, guided by David Herold. Seward is convalescing in bed after a recent serious carriage accident. On the pretense of bringing the Secretary of State some medicine, the hulking Powell demands to be brought to Seward's side. An argument ensues, followed by a struggle, and Paine pulls a gun and knife on Seward's sons, a military nurse, and another family visitor. Powell succeeds in stabbing the elder Seward repeatedly, but his blade is deflected by the injured Seward's jaw splint. Practically everyone is injured in the blood-soaked, wild melee, and the waiting Herold, upon hearing the loud commotion and resultant screams, flees the scene without Paine.[37]

At Ford's Theatre, Booth waits for an opportune moment, storms into the President's box, shoots Lincoln in the back of the head, stabs Lincoln's guest Major Henry Rathbone, and leaps from the box onto the stage, yelling "*Sic semper tyrannis!*"

Thus always to tyrants. . . .

Whether the assassin broke his leg by leaping down upon the stage, or later when his horse fell on top of him, has long been a matter of historical debate.

Meeting up with co-conspirator Herold, the pair flees the capital and rides south through the night. Early next morning, they arrive at the southern Maryland home of Dr. Mudd, who sets and treats Booth's injured leg. From there Booth and Herold dodge capture until April 26th, hiding out in the swamps of southern Maryland, receiving help from numerous rebel sympathizers, all while being pursued by the biggest manhunt in U.S. history. An astonishing price of $100,000 1865 dollars had been placed upon Booth's head. After successfully crossing the Potomac by rowboat, Booth is shot and killed at the Garrett farm just inside in Virginia, and Herold taken captive.

Four of Booth's accomplices (Powell, Herold, Atzerodt, and Mary Surratt) would be hung less than three months later for their crimes. Four others (Dr. Mudd, Samuel Arnold, Michael O'Laughlen, and Ford Theater getaway lookout Edman Spangler) would do prison time for their roles in the conspiracy.

For our purposes, the big question is, "What was Marshal George P. Kane doing while John Wilkes Booth & Company are setting in motion their plan to bring Lincoln down? What was Kane doing while Richmond fell to Grant's Union forces?"

We know that Kane was on special assignment to General Winder in Richmond, and that Kane regularly reported on Union troop movements in Virginia. So he was an intelligence agent who scouted and spied for the Confederate brass back in the rebel capital.[38]

But in 1876, while preparing his run for the office of mayor of Baltimore, Marshal Kane attempted to answer nagging questions concerning his role in the waning days of the Civil War — and his personal relationship to the assassin J.W. Booth. On March 22, 1876, the following amazing interview with Kane was published in *The New York Daily Graphic*:

> *"Towards the end of the war, in March or April, I was resting, out of the way, in the Valley of Virginia. While there a letter dated the previous December was received by me from Martin in Montreal. It said across the face, after the family and friendly matter in it was complete: 'What do you know of John Wilkes Booth? He has been here and stopped at my house. He expressed great disappointment at not finding you, and said he had expected to meet you here. What is his character? He became intimate at my house with my wife and daughter. Has he a good reputation in Baltimore?*
>
> *"This part of the letter," continued Kane, "was a mystery to me. I had never known Wilkes Booth, if I had ever heard of him, and I doubt that I had ever heard of him. The host of the house where I was lodging came to me just after I received this letter and said: 'Colonel Kane, Stoneman is raiding up the valley. His scouts are close on you and you will be arrested if you stay here.' I placed the letter inside of the lining of my traveling bag, mounted a horse with the bag, and rode through the woods and broken country to Danville, where I arrived nearly dead with fever and fatigue. Just after I arrived there Mr. Davis and his party, flying from Richmond to Charlotte, came along and I rode with them in the car to Greensboro, where I had to stop off. While lying there, hardly in my senses, after some days had elapsed, the man of the house said to me: 'Colonel Kane, we have a part of a torn New York newspaper here which contains some startling intelligence. A man named Wilkes Booth has assassinated President Lincoln.' "I endeavored," said Colonel Kane, "to recall where I had heard that name. I rose up almost delirious and tapped my forehead, muttering, 'Wilkes Booth. Who is he? How is he connected with me?' Then in a few minutes I cried to the man, 'Bring me my satchel!' I tore out Martin's letter and read it again. And," concluded the Colonel, "although I never knew Booth, that letter might have cost me my life if it had been found secreted in the satchel at that time."[39]*

According to Michael J. Kline in The Baltimore Plot, "*Kane's story, though entertaining, seems full of holes and flavored with fabrication.*"[40]

Kline's characterization of Kane's explanation as "entertaining" is an understatement. Kane almost certainly knew Booth personally . . . and could scarcely not have known who Booth was. Booth was one of the most famous, most highly paid stage actors on the continent. The noted thespian from a famous stage family often listed himself or referred to himself as being from Baltimore. Kane, in his youth, once held aspirations of a career in the theater. In fact, Kane owned a part interest in Baltimore's Olympic Theatre at Charles and Baltimore Streets — a venue at which Booth had performed! [41]

Anecdotal evidence suggests that Booth may have participated with Kane in the burning of the railroad bridges north of Baltimore in April, 1861 to prevent more Union troops from passing through the city.[42]

Upon hearing of Kane's June, 1861 arrest by Union forces occupying Baltimore, Booth was described by fellow actors as having flown into a wild rage, declaring that Kane was a "*friend*" and stating that the persons responsible should "*die a dog's death.*"[43]

Then there was the eyewitness evidence that Booth had specifically sought out an audience with Kane in Montreal in October, 1864 — supposedly for the purpose of presenting Kane Booth's plans for kidnapping President Lincoln. Booth was said to have been visibly disappointed to have learned that Kane had departed and was already on his way back to Richmond.[44]

Booth certainly seems to have believed he knew fellow Baltimorean Marshal George P. Kane.

William A. Tidwell, in Come Retribution, explains the phenomenon of what was going on with people such as Marshal Kane in the post-Civil War years:

"With the Union victorious, there was no Confederate government to defend individuals who had carried on clandestine activities. Some of these people who had been involved with Booth in one way or another and were afraid they would be tried by peacetime standards for what they had done in the war . . . a strong attempt was made to hide questionable activities or to reinterpret wartime experiences to fit innocent explanations. . . ."[45]

Innocent explanations . . . even Kane admits in his interview that had Martin's letter about Booth been discovered in his satchel, that it could have very well cost the marshal his life.

Let's examine the text of this incredible interview, and try to determine what is really going on behind George Kane's "innocent explanations" of his wartime service.

Remember, this is a man who burned bridges leading into Baltimore and defied Lincoln personally. A man who went to prison for that defiance. And who, when released, led a reign of espionage and insurgency against the Union from "Little Richmond" in Quebec. Kane personally championed a recruitment effort to sway more of his fellow Marylanders to register with the rebel armed forces.[46] He was given special, top-secret projects by the Confederate high command. We might even dare say that Kane's role appears to have been something of a "James Bond" for the Confederacy.

First, what was Kane doing "resting" out in the Valley of Virginia (Shenandoah Valley) during the Confederacy's final desperate hour of need? Richmond is being surrounded and faces imminent threat, Booth is preparing to kidnap Lincoln, yet one of the Confederacy's top special agents is resting out in the country? Hardly believable.

If we substitute the words "*waiting*, out of the way" for the words "*resting*, out of the way" then Kane's actions here begin to make more sense. The colonel's assignment was to go to a designated, pre-arranged, secluded location and wait for someone important. But who was Kane waiting for?

Given the time frame, March or early April 1865, an educated guess would be that Kane is waiting for Booth, Booth's co-conspirators, and a drugged, incapacitated, trussed-up Abraham Lincoln. It is Booth's mission to deliver Lincoln to Kane so that the captive President may be used as a bargaining chip in negotiations with the North. Deliver Lincoln to Kane, an angry man who had taken his imprisonment without trial very personally, and who had written Lincoln from his jail cell complaining of his unfair treatment. Turnabout, to George Kane, would have seemed deliciously fair play.

"*I can only promise that in due time*," Kane had threatened from prison, "*and upon a proper occasion, Mr. Seward shall hear from me*."[47]

It has always been assumed that Booth, had he kidnapped the President, would have delivered him into the arms of the Confederate hierarchy in Richmond. But Richmond, the crowded capital city, is exactly where the Union would have expected Lincoln to be taken. The North had worked hard to infiltrate Richmond with spies, and the Yankees would have offered a huge reward for information on the whereabouts of their kidnapped chief executive. So, on retrospect, a crowded, intrigue-filled Richmond would not have been the best, most logical place to hide Lincoln.

Too many spies, too many eyes.

"*Out of the way*" in the country would have been much more practical. But why the Valley of Virginia, today more commonly known as Shenandoah Valley?

John Wilkes Booth was known to own property in rural Virginia. Booth had purchased a farm near Harper's Ferry from a friend, and was also known to keep his "wife" Izola D'Arcy Mills Booth out in the Shenandoah Valley.[48]

According to W.C. Jameson, author of <u>John Wilkes Booth: From Beyond the Grave</u>, one of the detectives frantically searching for Booth after Lincoln's assassination, Luther Potter, thought Booth was actually headed towards Shenandoah Valley. Says Jameson, "*Luther was convinced that Booth left his diary behind on purpose in order to lead pursuers to believe he was escaping in a southerly direction. Luther Potter reasoned that Booth's original intention was to escape to Canada. He decided that the road west from Fredericksburg (not far from where Booth was eventually shot in the Garrett barn) was a logical route to depart into Shenandoah Valley and thence northward and across the international border.*"[49]

Izola D'Arcy Mills

Canadian newspaper columnist Matt Herzfeld, writing in the *The McGill Daily* on January 26, 2012, echoes the opinion that Canada was Booth's ultimate destination in April, 1865. In the article "*John Booth Lived Here: How Montreal Fell for the Confederacy,*" Herzfeld takes a quote from Booth's correspondence: "*I must post myself in Canuck airs,*" said John Wilkes Booth, the man who assassinated Abraham Lincoln. "*For some of us . . . may have to settle here shortly.*"[50] Booth had been making brief visits to Montreal for some time, and he planned on fleeing to Canada after shooting Lincoln. He never made it back north. . . .

Although many historians question whether Booth was actually married, records have shown that a wedding ceremony was performed in 1859 in Connecticut, when Booth married an actress named Izola Mills (This One Mad Act, Izola Forrester).[51] Whether the marriage was technically void because Mills was still legally married to someone other than Booth is largely irrelevant. Supposedly the marriage was kept secret to further Booth's career, since he believed his box office attraction remained strong so long as his numerous female fans still considered him to be an eligible bachelor. Regardless, Booth and Izola supposedly had two children, a boy (Jerome) and a girl (Ogarita).

Again, from Jameson's book, "*After the marriage to Izola, John continued acting, mostly in Richmond, and his wife continued to live in the Shenandoah Valley. In time, she moved onto Booth's farm near Harper's Ferry. On October 23, 1859, Ogarita, the mother of author Forrester (*This One Mad Act *by Izola Forrester about her family and supposed grandfather, J.W. Booth), was born to John Wilkes and Izola.*"[52]

If Jameson's information is accurate, then Booth had owned multiple properties in the Shenandoah Valley — one near Harper's Ferry, technically at the far northern end of the valley, and also elsewhere farther south in the valley. And in late March/early April 1865, it is likely Marshal Kane may be waiting for Booth at one of these properties in the valley. The timing coincides perfectly, since Booth's kidnapping scheme initially went into effect in mid-March.

Booth's other close connection to the Shenandoah Valley, aside from attending the hanging of John Brown in 1859, was a man named Beall. John Yeates Beall was raised in Jefferson County (then Virginia but today West Virginia) at the northern end of the Shenandoah Valley. Beall and Booth were supposedly college friends who had together attended the University of Virginia. More likely, they met at John Brown's hanging while Beall was a member of the local Virginia militia. According to John W. Headley in Confederate Operations in Canada and New York, Beall became a privateer during the war with two boats and some 18 men under his command active in preying upon Union shipping on the Chesapeake Bay and Potomac River.[53] Baltimorean Patrick Charles Martin was allegedly involved in the same activity on the same waterways. Beall was captured in 1863, jailed at Fort McHenry, but later released in 1864 as part of a prisoner exchange. As with Colonel Kane, Beall headed north to Canada, where he plotted to launch privateers on the Great Lakes. Also like Kane, Beall became involved in yet another aborted scheme, overseen by Confederate boss Jacob Thompson, to seize a vessel (the *Philo Parsons*) and use it to board and capture the U.S. gunboat *Michigan*. Later, on December 16, 1864, Beall participated in the derailment of a passenger train in upstate New York as part of an attempt to free Confederate officers. Beall was arrested in Niagara, tried, and ultimately sentenced to death by hanging. Many appeals were sent on Beall's behalf, asking for leniency.[54]

In Lloyd Lewis' book <u>Myths After Lincoln</u>, Lewis tells of a longstanding legend that John Wilkes Booth had personally approached the President, asking Lincoln to show mercy by sparing Beall's life. Lincoln agreed, but was later pressed by Secretary of State William Seward to go on with the execution because Beall had presented such a clear and present danger to Seward's home state of New York. Lincoln changed his mind again and signed the death warrant for Beall, who was executed at Fort Columbus, Governors Island, NY on February 24, 1865. "*This is murder,*" protested Beall on his way to the gallows. "*I die in defense of my country.*"[55]

When news of Beall death reached Booth, he became absolutely enraged and vowed revenge against both Lincoln and Seward. In less than two months, Booth would have his revenge. Lincoln would be dead, and Seward nearly so.

While in Montreal in October, 1864, Booth had apparently arranged for <u>two</u> letters of introduction from "Little Richmond" verifying his loyalty to the Southern cause. The first, the better known letter of introduction from Patrick Charles Martin for Dr. William Queen and ultimately designated for Dr. Samuel Mudd. Booth was already planning his escape route through southern Maryland, and knew he might need the assistance of a doctor if either Lincoln or a member of Booth's team were injured while making their hasty getaway. Little did Booth realize that it would be his own broken leg that Dr. Mudd would set.

In his interview with the *New York Daily Graphic*, it appears as if Kane is explaining how he himself was being asked by Patrick Charles Martin for a reference or second letter of introduction regarding Booth.[56] The exact contents of Martin's letter will never be known, because we only have Kane's word on the subject. Martin's blockade running vessel, the *Marie Victoria*, was lost at sea shortly after Martin penned his letter to Kane. Martin supposedly went down with his ship in the Gulf of St. Lawrence — along with Booth's theatrical wardrobe stowed aboard.[57] So, Martin was dead, and Booth would be dead soon after, leaving Kane as the sole person who knew what Martin's letter actually contained. And Kane apparently destroyed the incriminating correspondence knowing all too well that it "*may have cost me my life.*"[58]

The logical conclusion is that both letters of introduction coming out of Booth's October, 1864 meeting with Confederate agents in Montreal had to do with planning the Booth gang's escape route for the kidnapping of Lincoln. This includes Martin's letter to Kane, although it would be odd that Martin would write and send a letter of introduction for Booth, and then subsequently write to Kane asking for more information about the temperamental actor. What is Kane not telling us? Was the other letter of recommendation for Booth written by Martin, but with the actual seal of approval coming from Kane?

We know that Kane scouted for Generals Winder, Lee, and even Jeff Davis near the end of the war. But he is not scouting at the time he is "resting" out of the way in the Valley of Virginia. It is supposedly the "owner of the house" who comes to warn Colonel Kane that "*Stoneman is raiding up the valley. His scouts are close on you and you will be arrested if you stay here.*"[59]

Rather, what more likely happened is that a Confederate courier arrived at the Shenandoah Valley hideaway and relayed the following message to Kane. "*Sir, Richmond is being evacuated, President Davis and his cabinet are retreating south, and Stoneman's forces are in pursuit. Your current mission is canceled. Proceed at once to Danville and report there to President Davis and Secretary of War Breckinridge.*"

In the New York newspaper interview, Kane describes his meeting with the "Davis party" as somehow accidental, as if he rode day and night through the woods and open country of Virginia to, by happenstance, bump into the Confederate high command — as it was "flying from Richmond to Charlotte" with the Confederate treasury and the gold of six Virginia banks in tow.

Again, how convenient . . . but hardly believable! Kane did not ride blindly south and meet with, by pure chance, the Confederate train fleeing Richmond. No, this was a *rendezvous* on order from the Confederate supreme high command. Kane's new assignment was to provide security and intelligence for the southward bound "Davis party" and its precious fortune in gold and silver coins and bullion.

Whether Booth failed to get the memo that "Kane's special project" to capture Lincoln for ransom and exchange him for Confederate prisoners was off will never be known. Either a furious John Wilkes Booth changed plans after Lee's surrender at Appomattox on April 9th, and decided to go rogue and kill Lincoln on his own . . . or the Confederate high command actually sanctioned a last-ditch effort to dispatch their counterparts in the Union high command, thereby decapitating and paralyzing the entire U.S. government. Did Davis and company actually order the simultaneous assassinations of Johnson, Seward, Grant and Lincoln on the night of April 14, 1865? We will likely never know for sure. But one thing is certain, and that is Booth was no crazed, mentally ill lone gunman. He had help, and plenty of it.

Either way, with the long-planned kidnapping of Lincoln now off the table, the arrival of a drugged and trussed up "abolitionist president" would no longer be awaited in Virginia — whether out in Shenandoah Valley or down in Richmond. Kane's "special project" had been aborted, and now the special-ops colonel was suddenly needed "stat" down south in Danville. He arrived just in time, despite his alleged fever and an arduous journey on horseback, to meet his fleeing rebel bosses.

Whether Kane actually *"rode with them in the car to Greensboro, where I had to stop off,"* is extremely, highly debatable. Kane claims that he stayed behind in Greensboro to recover from his illness, and after some days had elapsed, *"while lying there, hardly in my senses,"*[60] was told about the assassination of Lincoln carried out by a man named Wilkes Booth. Naturally, Kane maintains the fiction that he never knew anyone named Wilkes Booth, and is puzzled as to why his Montreal host, Martin, a suspected KGC operative, is writing and asking him for a recommendation on Booth's character.

Nonsense! This is pure misdirection and fabrication.

According to Marshall P. Waters, PhD, in his 2007 paper *"Confederate Treasury — the Final Disposition,"*[61] records indicate that the "Davis party" left Danville quickly on or about April 6th (with General Stoneman and his army nearly cutting them off and capturing the rebel leaders before they could depart). The rebel supreme command arrived in Greensboro on April 7th, and then in Charlotte on April 8th. Captain William Parker, tasked with guarding the treasury, supplied these same dates from his records. And where was Colonel Kane during this time? On April 8th, Kane was reporting to Davis (taken from Jefferson Davis' own published papers) from his position just 15 miles from *Danville* as he was spying on Union troop activity.[62] Hardly the man who was nearly dead from fever and fatigue, as he claimed in the 1876 *New York Daily Graphic* interview. Here is the dated record in question taken from Jeff Davis' own papers:

Apr. 8 From George P. Kane (LNT, LHA Davis Papers, r26, f246–47); printed in *OR*, ser1, v47, pt3, 772–73: sent at 4:30 P.M., fifteen miles from Danville; met three of Wheeler's officers while looking for part of Early's train, which was in advance of Kane; officers reported morning fight at Henry Court House, confirmed by another account that 600 U.S. troops were holding the town and that Wheeler's men had killed 100 but were falling back.

It is this author's contention that Kane never left Danville for Greensboro. Or, if he did accompany the Davis party to Greensboro, he quickly doubled back and returned immediately to Danville, which was already falling into enemy hands. Why? Colonel Kane had one final duty to perform in Danville, an undercover assignment he would keep a closely guarded secret for the rest of his life.

Obviously, just as Kane had not been "resting out of the way" in Shenandoah Valley at the time Booth was attempting to kidnap Lincoln, Kane was also not "*lying there*" in Greensboro, "*hardly in my senses, after some days had elapsed.*" Kane's highly classified assignment was one he dared not divulge to the press, even 11 years after the fact. Colonel Kane would take this highly guarded Confederate secret to his grave.

As the Confederacy quickly crumbled around them, the Davis party continued southward, from Virginia to North Carolina, and then North Carolina to South Carolina, and then back and forth between South Carolina and Georgia. Switching from train to wagons, and then from wagons back to train. Jeff Davis was essentially running his vanishing empire from a railroad boxcar. The sun was setting swiftly on the dying Confederacy.

Meanwhile, as some of the rebel treasury's funds were paid out to rebel officials, officers, and rank-and-file soldiers for their service, other monies were buried along the route to keep them from falling into the hands of advancing Union forces. Slowly but surely, the $500,000 Confederate treasury dwindled away to nothing . . . except, of course, that which might have been hidden along the way. The approximately $450,000 in assets of the six Virginia banks, however, remained largely or wholly untouched.[63]

Although Jeff Davis expressed regret over the assassination of Lincoln, Lincoln's successor, President Andrew Johnson, put a $100,000 price on Davis' head, same as Booth. Davis was now a wanted criminal on the run. On April 26th, Booth would be shot and killed in a Virginia barn. Davis, if not careful, would surely be next.

Meanwhile, Union officials would interview General George Bickley in his prison cell, trying to get information on the K.G.C.'s possible connection to and involvement in the assassination. Front-man Bickley would steadfastly disavow any knowledge of such a plot, which was probably the truth.[64]

On May 4th, Davis met with his Confederate cabinet for the last time in Washington, Georgia at the Georgia Branch Bank Building . . . with only 14 fanatical, diehard members present.[65] On that day, Jefferson Davis officially and forever dissolved the beleaguered Confederate government, and the group dispersed, with Davis fleeing even farther south. Five days later, Davis and his wife would be arrested by Union forces in Irwinville, Georgia. The Confederate president was said to have approximately $3 on his person at the time he was searched and placed in restraints. Obviously, the wealth of the Confederacy and of the banks of Virginia had traveled elsewhere.

The next day, May 5th, Union troops entered Washington, Georgia. In a December, 2009 article "*The Missing Confederate Gold*" published in *The Surratt Courier Newsletter*, historian Dr. Marshall Waters describes how, "*Captain Lot Abraham USA and two companies of the Fourth Iowa Cavalry arrived in Washington. By just one day they had missed the Confederate President Jefferson Davis, Secretary of War John C. Breckinridge . . . and* *what remained in the treasury. Not all was lost to the Fourth Iowa Cavalry, however, because for weeks Washington had become a supply depot with munitions, rations, and sundry other supplies stored there. Confederate property was scattered everywhere as Confederates retreated further south through Washington. In the name of the U.S. Government, Captain Abraham impounded, seized, and/or confiscated everything including the $450,000 silver and gold coin at the Bank of Georgia Branch.*"[66]

So the bank gold and silver had fallen into Yankee hands, though deep inside Confederate territory. The Virginia bank officials immediately protested that their bank assets were private bank funds, and therefore not subject to seizure and forfeiture as were the monies in the Confederate treasury. Union officials allowed the Virginia bank employees to ride with the seized gold and silver. The Union officers' first concern was in getting the bank assets back to Virginia and out of the current chaos of a war zone. Only then could Union courts and politicians decide the ultimate fate of the Virginia bank assets.

Some say the money was destined for Abbeville, South Carolina where it was to be shipped back to Richmond by rail. Others say it was headed for Savannah, Georgia and ultimately Napoleon III in France, to whom the South was financially indebted.[67]

Either way, the money never got there. . . .

For several days, the small contingent of Union soldiers guarding the $450,000 tried to take some less-traveled country back roads in order to maneuver their vulnerable wagon train to safety. The last known location of the Virginia bank assets would be near the sleepy crossroads of Chennault, Georgia. The location is not far from the Savannah River and the South Carolina state line. Here, the rebel money trail would end abruptly.

On the evening of May 24-25, the wagons of gold and silver coin and bullion rested approximately 100 yards from the plantation house of Dionysius Chennault, an elderly planter and Methodist minister. The loot had all been packed into socks and stored inside wooden kegs. The party's wagons were driven by teamsters, and lightly guarded by only a handful of weary Union soldiers. Still riding the wagon train were the nervous Richmond bank officials and also the Assistant Secretary of the Confederate Treasury, Judge William Wood Crump. The wagon train was given permission to spend the night in Chennault's corral. As midnight fell, all was quiet.

Suddenly, out the darkness, 20 armed men rode up and began robbing the wagons. As author Bill Yenne writes in his 1999 book Lost Treasure: A Guide to Buried Riches, the *"persons unknown struck and took much — but not all — of the gold. As witnesses, apparently including Reverend Chennault told it, there were remaining gold coins in piles that were ankle deep."*[68]

The surprise confiscation was so fast and so silent that Chennault family members inside the plantation house initially knew nothing of what was happening. Many in the party accompanying the bank assets were caught preparing for sleep — some already in their nightgowns. However, in the bandits' haste to transfer and cart away the loot, a large quantity of gold coinage was spilled on the ground. Also, one of the highwaymen apparently had a hole in his rucksack or saddlebag, causing even more gold to be dropped along the trail. According to Bill Yenne, "there are any number of stories that the gold is buried within a five- or ten-mile radius of Washington."[69]

According to Dr. Waters, on the day following the heist, bank officials reported $251,029.90 stolen, although some of the spilled coins were recovered from the roadway and also from Chennault area residents. Still, bank officials estimated that robbers netted about $179,000 for their brazen efforts.[70] Speculation as to the identity of the perpetrators has always centered on either rogue, marauding Yankee troops or hungry and desperate returning rebel soldiers. Another possibility, of course, is that with the implosion of the Confederacy, the Knights of the Golden Circle swooped in to claim the gold that otherwise had little chance of returning safely to its rightful owners in Richmond and/or Paris. The KGC would never have trusted the honesty of the hated Union constabulary, especially not with $450,000 in gold and silver coin.

Union authorities apparently did not have the gold, because they spent much time interrogating and at times torturing members of the Chennault family and their neighbors — with no satisfactory results.[71] The nearly $200,000 in gold and silver coins remain missing and unaccounted for to this day, having become yet another part of cherished Confederate folklore.

And Colonel George P. Kane? He remained in Danville . . . for the next several years. But *why*?

Included on the train ride from Richmond to Danville were 39 wooden kegs of Mexican silver dollars or "eight reale" coins.[72] These coins had been paid to the Richmond government for cotton sold to Mexico. The problem was, the silver hoard weighed over 9,000 pounds. The average automobile today weighs between 3,500 and 4,000 pounds. Such a cargo was slowing down the "Davis party" train, endangering the safety of all on board. One rebel commander referred contemptuously to the treasury in general, and the silver in particular, as a "cumbersome elephant."[73] Later, when traveling by train was no longer an option and the retreating rebel leaders were forced to switch to wagons, transporting the silver would not have been practical, and perhaps even impossible.

The silver was loaded onto the train in Richmond, but was no longer with the "Davis party" in Charlotte when the next accounting of the treasury was taken.

Neither, of course, was the shadowy Colonel Kane.

While in Danville, the gold and silver sat heavily guarded in a separate boxcar left sitting for three entire days (April 3-6) on a side rail.[74]

It was almost certainly during this time that the bulky kegs of silver were offloaded and buried. Legend has always centered on a particular Confederate burial ground, Greenhill Cemetery, situated nearby the railroad tracks within Danville city limits. To this day, the town of Danville, which owns the cemetery, has forbidden anyone to dig for the treasure.

Historian Dr. Marshall Waters, whose family comes from the area in Wilkes County, Georgia through which the rebel gold passed and then vanished, has spent a lifetime studying the mystery of the lost Confederate treasure.

In a television appearance filmed at the Museum of the Confederacy in Richmond, Waters told investigators from Brad Meltzer's History Channel program "*Decoded*" that the silver had been buried in Danville, and was likely still there.[75] The folks from "*Decoded*" next called in famed Confederate treasure hunter Bob Brewer of Arkansas to explore the Danville cemetery. Although Brewer and his hosts from *Decoded* weren't permitted to dig, Brewer did find various Confederate treasure signs and symbols on an old tree in Greenhill Cemetery. Brewer described the carved signs as clues to the direction and distance where buried treasure lay hidden for nearly 150 years. Brewer concluded that the archaic rebel symbols were pointing towards a location near the railroad tracks. *"It smells like money to me,"*[76] Brewer commented. Brewer had previously used similar tree and rock carvings to uncover old mason jars of 19th-century gold and silver coinage at locations in other states. Brewer attributes those treasure signs and associated caches to the activities of a post-war KGC.

Authors Wesley Millett and Gerald White, known for their love story <u>The Rebel and the Rose</u>, which is set against the backdrop of the fall of Richmond and the retreat south, also weigh in on the subject of the Mexican silver in their scholarly, nonfiction article *"Mystery of Lost Confederate Gold."*

"One treasury clerk — in particular, Micajah Clark — provided a detailed accounting of the disposition of the funds.

"An aspect of the treasure that Clark omitted concerned the fate of 39 kegs of Mexican silver dollars. These were coins that the Confederacy received through the sale of cotton to Mexico. The Mexican coins had been transported to Danville, Virginia, and when the Davis party was forced to move further south, primarily by wagon, the more than 9,000 pounds of silver would have considerably slowed down the procession. For this reason, the coins were almost certainly buried in Danville, and evidence suggests, they remain there today."[77]

Millett and White also explain why they believe the Danville silver was never recovered.

"Danville became an encampment for the Union army. With enemy soldiers occupying the town, any effort to dig up the some 160,000 8-reale coins would have certainly been seen."[78]

Millett and White go on to argue that, *"The evidence is strong that no one else managed to dig up the silver either, quite possibly because of where it was buried… in a cemetery area. Then too, given the volume and weight of the silver, the digging would have certainly been noticed by soldiers and townspeople, whether during the day or at night under the glow of kerosene lamps. Possibly, the fact that almost 1,400 Union soldiers, former prisoners warehoused in the town, had died of smallpox, dysentery, and other diseases and were buried nearby, could also have discouraged random digging.*"[79]

Millett and White conclude that, *"With the technology of today, why does the specie remain buried? For one reason only. The coins are buried on city-owned land, and Danville officials, concerned about disturbing graves, continue to refuse all requests to dig, even test holes. Perhaps the city will ultimately change its mind and enrich its coffers with the largest portion of the estimated $16 million in value.*"[80]

Obviously, neither Dr. Waters nor Messrs. Millett and White knew about the secret Danville involvement of Colonel George P. Kane, the "Agent 007" of the Confederate underground. When Kane, in his interview with the *New York Daily Graphic*, talked about arriving in Danville just as Davis and his party came "flying" through from Richmond to Charlotte, and how he stopped off at Greensboro and spent many days there recovering from illness, none of this was true. The Confederate train, Davis, his cabinet, the soldiers, and the Confederate treasury remained in Danville for three days. The treasury sat in a boxcar on a side rail for three days. The train left Danville on April 6, arrived in Greensboro April 7, and then in Charlotte April 8. Meanwhile, on April 8th,[81] Kane was not "lying there, hardly in my senses" in Greensboro, but instead is sending military reports to Davis from outside of Danville.[82]

Even the *007* of the Confederacy can't be in two places more than 40 miles apart at the same time!

Kane's entire deception is based on drawing the interviewer and subsequently the reader's attention away from Danville, to grossly understate the importance of Danville, and most specifically Kane's personal involvement with Danville.

Why? Because Kane was apparently assigned to bury (or help to bury) the over 9,000 pounds of Confederate silver in or around Danville. Why else would Kane want everyone to think he was laid up in Greensboro, when he was really healthy and involved in Confederate business back in Danville?

When President Andrew Johnson offered a general amnesty to Confederate combatants in May, 1865, Kane might have easily gone home to his native Baltimore and resumed his comfortable career in public service. As a Confederate war hero and the man who had risked everything to prevent Yankee troops from passing through Baltimore, Kane could have "written his own ticket" in the

Monumental City. The lifelong Baltimorean had walked the walk and had valiantly risked his life in defense of his city. Baltimore had remained virtually unscathed by the war, and Kane's life, wife, friends, substantial political connections, and career were all back there waiting.

But no, Colonel Kane decides to stay in sleepy Danville for the remainder of the decade, purportedly going into the "tobacco manufacturing" business.[83] But Kane's real business in Danville was acting as the patient sentinel for the over 9,000 pounds of Mexican silver dollars buried right under the noses of the Yankee occupiers of Danville and the strategic rail line and train depot located there. "Fresh hoards" of Union soldiers encamped in Danville, without a clue of what lay buried beneath their feet. Kane could no longer think about "whipping them or die," that contest had been decisively settled, but he could remain undercover until the 39 kegs of buried silver could be dug up and moved. Even if the hated Yankees stayed for years in that encampment as the slow and difficult period of "Reconstruction" unfolded.

Working in the tobacco business was simply Kane's way of supporting himself and providing a cover until his task of moving the Mexican silver out of Danville was completed. Of course, he named his business the Roanoke Tobacco Works [84] and not the Danville Tobacco Works, further distancing himself from that town. Then it was "adios" and back to his beloved Baltimore to resume his political ambitions.

I believe when Bob Brewer and the crew from Brad Meltzer's *Encoded* went poking around in 2010 for signs of silver in Danville's Greenhill Cemetery, they were hunting a dry hole. Colonel Kane remained in Danville until at least 1869[85] before he returned to Baltimore to resume his public service career. Kane would not have left until his final assignment was finished, and the 39 kegs of silver were delivered safely into unofficial Confederate — or *KGC* — hands.

Once back in Baltimore, Kane was appointed to the Jones Falls Commission on January 31, 1870.[86] Charles Webb of James Armstrong & Company would almost certainly have had a hand in Kane's initial political appointment. Jones Falls is the body of water located directly beside the site of the Armstrong & Co. soap and candle factory on Concord Street. It flows directly under the nearby Pratt Street Bridge, scene of one of the violent Pratt

Street Riot skirmishes on April 19, 1861, and empties into the nearby Inner Harbor, formerly known as The Basin. The powerful and politically connected Webb was a good friend to have in Baltimore. The Freemason grand master had backed Kane before the Civil War, and would strongly support his ally again after the war.

Also serving on the Jones Falls Commission with Kane, according to historian John Thomas Scharf, was non-other than fellow 1861 bridge-burner "General" Isaac R. Trimble.[87] Trimble had lost a leg at Pickett's Charge during the Battle of Gettysburg, was captured, and imprisoned on Johnson Island where he and other fellow Confederate inmates had been the subject of an aborted rescue plan devised by Colonel Kane. Now, post war, Kane and Trimble were trying to figure out a plan to prevent Jones Falls from routinely flooding Baltimore's harbor district.

George P. Kane, Mayor of Baltimore, Maryland, 1877–78

Their engineer on the project was one Benjamin Latrobe. Once an approved plan was in place to deepen, clean, and wall off Jones Falls, Kane and Trimble were replaced on the commission by another close friend and associate of Charles Webb — fellow candle maker and keeper of the Eden Street golden treasure pot, Andrew J. Saulsbury.[88]

By 1873, Kane's fortunes were on the rise as he was elected Sheriff of Baltimore City.[89] In 1877, Kane's Baltimore comeback was completed as he was elected Mayor of Baltimore after winning his party's nomination from fellow Democrat Ferdinand Latrobe.[90] Latrobe's father, John H.B. Latrobe, had become the Grand Master of Maryland Freemasonry a few years after Charles Webb's mid-1850s reign as state grand master.[91]

One of Kane's first duties as mayor was to appoint his good friend Charles Webb of James Armstrong & Co. — Saulsbury's boss — to the position of city tax collector.

The History of Baltimore City and County, Maryland records that "*Mr. Webb had always declined political office until the position of city collector was tendered him by Mayor Kane."* Apparently, the bond between Webb and Kane was so tight that Kane was the one individual to whom Webb could not say "no." This tome on Baltimore history also states that *"Mr. Webb's administration of his office has been of the most distinguished character, and he has won golden opinions from all sorts of people. The energy with which he has followed up and brought into the treasury the delinquent revenues of the city has been as marvelous as it has been gratifying."*[92]

So the relationship between the two friends and colleagues had come full circle. In 1859-1860, Webb, his reform committee, and Mayor Brown had tapped Kane to become marshal so that he might clean out the corruption and also the violence perpetrated by such notorious riff raff as the Plug Uglies, American Rattlers, and Blood Tubs. Now, in 1878, Kane was turning to his friend Charles Webb to bolster the flagging revenues of a long mismanaged city.

But Kane's occupancy of the mayoral office would be short-lived. On June 23, 1878, Mayor Kane passed away at his home from Bright's disease,[93] a debilitating kidney ailment. Charles Webb stayed on to help Kane's successor, Kane's former opponent, Ferdinand Latrobe, during Latrobe's first term. Latrobe would go on to serve seven terms as Mayor of Baltimore, dominating city politics for the rest of the nineteenth century.

However, what Mayor Kane lacked in political longevity, he certainly made up for in political intrigue and drama. Although Kane failed to finish out both his terms as marshal and as mayor, George P. Kane served Baltimore during some of the most tumultuous and pivotal days in the city's nearly 350-year history. Kane is no doubt one of the most colorful and controversial characters the Monumental City has ever produced. His connections to Charles Webb, John Wilkes Booth, the Baltimore Plot against Lincoln, the April 19th Pratt Street Riot, the Confederate intelligence underground, the Confederate lost treasury, and the mysterious Baltimore gold hoard on Eden Street only add to this man's powerful and enduring mystique.

The Candle Goes Out

In 1871, after nearly two decades of service at James Armstrong & Company, tallow maker and chandler Andrew J. Saulsbury decided to go solo and open his own Baltimore real estate office.[1] It must have been a weighty decision for the 44-year old father of seven (there would eventually be eight). He had a wife, those many young children, a large household, and two live-in maids to support. As a self-made man growing up in his father's paint and grocery business, Saulsbury would have been no stranger to hard work, self-sacrifice, and deprivation. The bankruptcy of his father's store in 1849[2] when Saulsbury was only 22 would have undoubtedly remained a painful memory. Saulsbury had not been born with a silver spoon in his mouth, and knew what tough times were like. His decision to leave a comfortable executive position at the candle and soap firm, where he had been employed for nearly half his life, must have been a monumental decision for this business-savvy Baltimorean.

No one would have been prepared for what happened just two years later, in 1873, with Saulsbury still in the prime of his life.

According to one of Saulsbury's daughters, although her father did suffer from bouts with asthma[3] and walked with a noticeable limp, he was by no means a weak or sickly man. So when one particular November week her father came down with what appeared to be either a bad cold or the flu, no one grew especially alarmed. The end, unfortunately, would come quickly.

During the 1934 courtroom battle over the disposition of the coins, a Saulsbury daughter recounted how her father's death had been completely unexpected. *"I don't remember him being confined to the bed in that illness. He sat in a chair,"* she recalled nearly 62 years after her father's passing.[4]

The description of Saulsbury remaining in a chair, especially if he slept there, might actually have been a tipoff to the seriousness of his condition. Persons experiencing chronic obstructive pulmonary disease (COPD), emphysema, pneumonia, black lung disease, or other types of life-threatening lung illnesses are known to prefer sleeping while sitting up, as such a position helps them to avoid shortness of breath.

Andrew J. Saulsbury died at home on Friday, November 28th, 1873.[5] The cause of death was most likely pneumonia, exacerbated by an underlying asthmatic condition. In keeping with the custom of that time, and for obvious practical reasons, both the wake and funeral services for the candle maker were held in his home at 55 S. Eden.[6] As Saulsbury's body was transported north to Green Mount Cemetery by funeral wagon, a long line of fellow Baltimoreans followed to pay their respects to this well-known Baltimore councilman, business executive, entrepreneur, family man, and loyal son of the Confederacy.

Fellow candle and soap executives James Armstrong, Thomas Armstrong, and James Webb would serve as Saulsbury pallbearers.[7] The 46-year old's body was laid to rest that Sunday, November 30th, in the very same cemetery where John Wilkes Booth, Michael O'Laughlen, and Samuel Arnold — all conspirators to the original 1865 plot to kidnap President Abraham Lincoln — were also laid to rest. Booth, of course, had been killed two weeks after he assassinated the President. O'Laughlen would die in federal prison in 1867 at Fort Jefferson on the desolate island outpost of Dry Tortugas just west of the Florida Keys. O'Laughlen succumbed to the yellow fever epidemic that swept the prison and those mosquito-infested islands. Fellow inmate Dr. Samuel Mudd, infamous for having set Booth's broken leg after the assassin's escape from Ford's Theater, attempted to treat the stricken O'Laughlen but could not save him.[8] Both Mudd and Arnold would later be pardoned from Fort Jefferson by order of President Andrew. Johnson.

According to <u>Treasure in the Cellar</u> author Len Augsburger, while the minister preached upstairs at S. Eden beside the body of the deceased tallow chandler, reading the passage from the Book of Revelation which describes how the streets of heaven are paved with pure gold,[9] almost no one in that crowded room would have been aware of the fortune in gold coin buried somewhere just below their feet. That is, of course, all except for perhaps the Armstrongs and James Webb.

For their own protection, certainly Saulsbury's wife and the children obviously knew nothing about the 5,000 gold coins in the cellar. Mrs. Saulsbury would later retrieve her husband's rainy day stash of gold and silver coinage in their bedroom chest, using the money to pay for a fitting headstone for the dearly departed.

It soon fell to Saulsbury's good friend and fellow councilman, James Webb, to handle the affairs of the Saulsbury estate.[10] Not only did Saulsbury leave behind a young widow, eight grieving children, two maids, and his fledgling real estate business . . . he also left his family a considerable inheritance. It is here that Augsburger has done yeoman's work in digging up long-forgotten records at Baltimore City Hall.

As administrator, James Webb would list, amongst Saulsbury's many holdings, his fully paid home at 55 S. Eden, dozens of other investment properties scattered throughout the immediate neighborhood, some $17,000 in U.S. government bonds (a rather surprising investment for an ardent Southern sympathizer), and a considerable interest in a local building association. In total, Saulsbury's impressive portfolio of assets would top the $100,000 mark — several million dollars would be a fair present-day equivalent.[11]

Webb, however, would never live to fully probate the Saulsbury estate. Saulsbury's friend, co-worker, and fellow Baltimore councilman would pass on just two years later in 1875 — as would Captain John J. Mattison. The eponymous founder of James Armstrong & Co. would die soon after, leaving the remaining partners Charles Webb and Thomas Armstrong fully and 100% in charge of the soap and candle enterprise.

In fact, Saulsbury's dealings were so far-flung and inadequately documented that his assets kept popping up for decades after his demise. The book would not be fully closed on the Saulsbury estate until 1898,[12] some nine years after the death of his second wife, Margaret, in 1889.

As for PGM (Past Grand Master) Charles Webb, the powerful Freemason had for years declined all invitations to official public service. However, in 1878, Webb would receive a personal request from an old political friend and cherished associate — a request the prominent Freemason could not decline. The new mayor of Baltimore would call on Webb's business, organizational, and financial acumen to become the city's new tax collector, with Baltimore in dire need of new sources of revenue.

According to the 1881 <u>History of Baltimore City and County, Maryland</u>, *"Mr. Webb had always declined political office until the position of city collector was tendered him. . . . Mr. Webb's administration of his office has been of the most distinguished character, and he has 'won golden opinions from all sorts of people.' The energy with which he has followed up and brought into the treasury the delinquent revenues of the city has been as marvelous as it has been gratifying, and it is no reflection upon previous officials to say that no former city collector has ever been so successful in the collection of taxes. Mr. Webb's efficiency in this position has largely been due to his long business experience and to the careful and systematic habits secured by early training."*[13]

The new Baltimore mayor who personally reaches out to the candle magnate for help? He is none other than George Proctor Kane, formerly Marshal Kane.[14] Yes, the very same George P. Kane who had boastfully offered no police protection to President-elect Lincoln on Lincoln's way through Baltimore to his inauguration. The same George Kane had been arrested and imprisoned on orders from President Lincoln because of his secessionist activities and his infamous "*we must fight them and whip them, or die*" telegram. The same George Kane who headed north to Canada upon his release from prison, and who became part of the Confederate "secret service" plotting war upon the Union from the country's northern borders. The same Charles Kane who had desperately written to C.S.A. President Jefferson Davis two weeks after the Battle of Gettysburg, offering to organize a Confederate attack on the Great Lakes cities of Chicago, Detroit, and Milwaukee in order to destroy all shipping, thus "*paralyzing lake commerce.*" The same Charles Kane who plotted to attack a federal installation with the intent to free some 2,000 Confederate prisoners. And most definitely yes, the same George Kane who, in 1864 while in Montreal with other rebel plotters, was specifically sought out by his old "friend" John Wilkes

Booth to discuss and review the mad actor's plans to kidnap President Lincoln.

"I know George Kane well," Booth had ranted upon hearing of Kane's arrest in June, 1861. *"He is a friend, and the man who could drag him from the bosom of his family for no crime whatever but a mere suspicion deserves a dog's death."*[15]

Apparently Webb, who was instrumental in seeing Mayor George William Brown and Marshal Kane installed to power in 1860, would return the favor to Kane in early 1878, drawing upon all of his long experience as a Masonic organizer and captain of Baltimore industry to bolster Baltimore's flagging revenues.

But Webb would not report to Kane for long, as Mayor Kane would die suddenly in office in June, 1878, barely a year after his election.[16] Kane's successor was a man named Ferdinand Clairborne Latrobe, who would eventually serve a total of seven terms as Mayor of Baltimore. If the name Latrobe sounds familiar, it should. John H.B. Latrobe was Ferdinand Latrobe's father, and the Freemason who succeeded Brother Charles Webb in 1870 as the latest Grand Master of Maryland.[17] In 1859, Webb would be recognized as a "companion" Mason to the order — basically, swearing his allegiance to Maryland Freemasonry in general, and Brothers John Berry and John H.B. Latrobe in particular.[18]

John H.B. Latrobe, of course, had doubled as the president for Maryland's Colonization Society,[19] which advocated for the "voluntary" removal of free blacks from both the state and the nation.

One of Ferdinand Latrobe's first acts as the new mayor was to reappoint Charles Webb as the city tax collector.[20] Soon after, in 1880, the Maryland Freemasons bestowed upon Brother Webb the honorary title of *"Freemason for Life."*

In 1889, Margaret Saulsbury, widow of Andrew Saulsbury, would pass away, and the treasure house at 55 S. Eden (soon to become 132 S. Eden) would be sold and pass into a succession of unfamiliar hands. Mrs. Saulsbury was almost certainly oblivious to the golden fortune that had been secreted beneath her home more than three decades earlier.

In 1891, upon the recent deaths of three of their most celebrated PGMs (Past Grand Masters), the Maryland Freemasons recognized their departed leaders in a solemn ceremony at the grand lodge in Baltimore. During the proceedings, Grand Master Thomas J. Shryock, *"After presenting a full record of his official acts, and thoughtful and timely recommendations, turns his thoughts to the vacant seats once occupied by the three Grand Masters, John S. Tyson, Charles Webb, and John H.B. Latrobe. Beautiful tributes are paid to their memories, and he closes his address with Brother Albert Pike's beautiful poem, "Every Year."* Portraits of Latrobe and Webb appear at the proceedings.[21]

Albert Pike, the former suspected leader of the Knights of the Golden Circle, Brigadier General in the Confederate Army, and the Grand Sovereign Commander of the Southern Jurisdiction of Scottish Rite Freemasonry, would himself pass away in 1891 at the age of 82.[22]

With the rest of the entire "candle cabal" now all gone, Thomas Armstrong tries to go it alone at the firm he now calls James Armstrong & Co. Soaps. But by 1898, the financial hardships have become too great. Subsequent to a lawsuit filed by a New England investor, a Maryland court pronounces the half-century old firm to be insolvent.[23]

With the early 1900s death of Thomas Armstrong, the man likely responsible for the stash of coins found on site at The Fountain Hotel in 1870, no one is left who was originally involved with the burial of the coins in the cellar at the treasure house on South Eden. The banking panic of 1907 comes and goes. *The Titanic* sinks in the North Atlantic. World War One devastates Europe. Prohibition is declared in the U.S. The Roaring Twenties ushers in an age of excess and rampant stock market speculation. Baltimore's native son, George Herman "Babe" Ruth revolutionizes the game of baseball by launching 60 home runs in a season. The Crash of '29 heralds the beginning of the Great Depression. Proclaiming that we have "nothing to fear but fear itself, President Franklin D. Roosevelt unveils his plans for a New Deal to help the country out of its malaise.

And in a declining inner-city neighborhood not far from the sometimes rough-and-tumble Depression-era Baltimore docks, two bored adolescent boys formulate their plan for a local "Rinky Dinky Doos" club. The only question that remains, where to bury the cigar box containing their newly formed club's secret holdings. . . .

Henry and Theodore's Long Wait

1935 Plymouth

Henry Grob celebrated his 16th birthday on May 12, 1935 — not two weeks after the coin auction at the swanky Lord Baltimore Hotel. Henry would subsequently drop out of school,[1] joining his good pal Theodore Jones as a teenager with too much time on his hands.

Henry and Theodore each had over six thousand dollars being held for them in trust by the clerk of the Baltimore Circuit Court. The boys, however, were able to collect regular interest payments earned on their accounts.[2]

If one can believe Judge Eugene O'Dunne's October, 1935 decision, the boys had uncovered an amazing "second" pot of gold coins on or around May 27th, knowledge of which had been withheld from the authorities. The Grobs and Jones/Rummel families had been busy converting the latest coins to cash, selling their gold at near face value to buyers who came calling unannounced at their homes.[3]

To his credit, Henry was able to obtain regular employment at the packing company where his brother-in-law worked. Henry earned approximately $16 per week toiling in the mayonnaise department of the Panzer Packing Company.[4]

Meanwhile, the Grob family had purchased a home in suburban Canton, as well as a used Ford automobile. They would soon upgrade to a newer and better Ford model. The Jones/Rummel household had purchased many new conveniences, a used Ford, and then splurged on a brand new 1935 Plymouth for approximately $800[5] — or Philip Rummel's annual income as a part-time Baltimore streets department laborer. None of this was made public, of course, until after the mysterious 1935 Labor Day break-in at the Rummel residence. Now, both of Judge O'Dunne's decisions regarding the disposition of the 'first" and "second" pots of coins were in appeal.

Free time, extra money, no school, and access to fast cars are a recipe for trouble when it comes to teenaged boys. Henry and Theodore were no exception . . . especially the adventurous, street-wise, more spontaneous Theodore.

Theodore's first brush with traffic court came in July, 1935[6]. . . the very same month Bessie Jones had wed Philip Rummel. Theodore was stopped and arrested by Baltimore police for driving without a license. The boy's new stepfather had to go to court to have Theodore released on parole and into Mr. Rummel's custody.

Apparently, Theodore did not learn from this experience. In January, 1936, the teen became involved in a much more serious road incident.[7] This time, the boy was not only driving without a license or registration, but also observed driving recklessly at high speed. According to the Baltimore authorities, Theodore nearly hit a policeman and a milk wagon, and then turned off the Plymouth's headlights in order to evade his pursuers. The magistrate suspects the teen had been drunk. Bessie Rummel tells the court she plans on selling the car, so Theodore will be without wheels[8] — however, the magistrate figures Theodore has already gotten off lightly once before, so he's had his chance and blown it. No kid gloves this time around. Theodore is sentenced to four months at The Maryland Training School for Boys, a juvenile detention center in North Baltimore.

Mr. Rummel, having experienced the daring burglary of his family's hidden loot, and now the forced confinement of his new stepson, observes that the golden hoard has thus far brought them *"nothing but bad luck."*[9]

Bessie, undaunted, hires a new lawyer, Henry Siegel, who discovers that the boy was improperly sentenced.[10] Theodore, now sprung from reform school, comes home to his mother, stepfather, and the waiting 1935 Plymouth — which Bessie has somehow neglected to sell, despite her solemn promises in court.[11]

In April, 1936, the Baltimore Court of Appeals announces that they are upholding Judge O'Dunne's decision regarding the original, 1934 gold discovery.[12] In assessing the testimony and the evidence, the court rules that O'Dunne had committed no judicial error in arriving at his February, 1935 "finders keepers" decision — and that the attorneys for the Findlay/French sisters had not presented any new substantial, convincing evidence to warrant overturning O'Dunne's ruling.

The boys and their attorney, Harry O. Levin, still own the proceeds of pot number one. However, since the injunction against disposing any of the gold or money connected to pot number two still stands, the Merrill brothers are forced to sit on their $2,500 golden investment[13] pending the outcome of further litigation.

With the official proceedings surrounding the original 1934 discovery now concluded, attorney Harry Levin petitions the court to have his 1/3rd contingency fee released to him.[14] The court agrees. After deducting for auction expenses, taxes, and administrative fees, Harry Levin, Esq. at last receives a hefty $6,200 payout from the City of Baltimore for find number one. Levin's big gamble has finally paid off, and quite handsomely.

Deputy court clerk Charles McNabb, however, is still riding shotgun on the boys' 2/3 share of the 1935 coin auction proceeds.[15] All Henry and Theodore have to do is stay out of jail, stay alive, and reach the age of 21 . . . the piles of cash are there waiting for them.

But on October 7, 1936, Baltimore's finest once again bust young Theodore Jones. The charge? Speeding without a license through East Baltimore, this time with sidekick Henry Grob along in the passenger seat. Jones has been denied a license because of his previous reckless driving conviction. But he still has the 1935 Plymouth, almost certainly purchased from money obtained from the sale of gold coins derived from the "second" discovery in the cellar at 132 Eden Street. The Plymouth has proven to be far too much of a temptation for this bored youth. This time the court throws the book at hard-luck Theodore, sentencing the boy to three months incarceration.[16] Worse yet, because Baltimore's most famous juvenile delinquent has maintained the fiction that he is two years older than his actual age, the judge in traffic court sentences Jones to serve his time in an *adult* penal facility. Only 16, and hoping to cash in and collect his $6,200 a full two years early, Theodore is sentenced as if 18 and an adult.

Henry and Theodore's Long Wait

Young Theodore Jones has apparently been too clever for his own good.

Bessie Rummel takes the news philosophically, thinking this tough-love experience in an adult institution may finally convince her wayward son to walk the straight and narrow.[17] Superstitious Phillip Rummel, however, still believes nothing but bad luck has followed the Jones-Rummel clan since the day the Rinky Dinky Doos struck gold beneath the dark cellar at 132 S. Eden.

The Baltimore courts, meanwhile, have yet to render a final decision concerning the disposition of the supposed treasure from pot "two" . . . or at least what still remains of the controversial, so-called second discovery.[18] The Grob portion has been mostly spent, and the Jones/Rummel half mostly stolen. But the Merrill brothers still have a sizable number of those coins purchased on the sly with a wink and a handshake. Their substantial $2,500 investment, however, still remains in a court-imposed legal limbo.

And, unfortunately for all others concerned, the crack legal team hired by the elderly Findlay/French sisters is like a frenzied terrier that refuses to let go — no matter how many times they've been seemingly kicked to the curb. These much aggrieved Findlay/French folks are still out for satisfaction, blood — and money. At this stage of the legal game, they are looking for someone, anyone, doesn't much matter who, to go after and seek their teeth into. They seem determined, at all costs, not to go home empty-handed.

Someone is going to have to throw the four-fisted, sue-happy Findlay/French sisters a bone. Else, the costly legal shenanigans surrounding the coins may never, ever come to an end.

Mystery of the Coded Due-Bill

In 1875, two years after Andrew Saulsbury's sudden demise, the following business math problem was published in the textbook New Practical Arithmetic compiled by Henry Bartlett Maglathlin. The text was published by the Yankee publishing firm of Robert S. Davis & Co. of Boston. The publishing company also maintained subsidiary offices in New York, Philadelphia, St. Louis, and Chicago. The book, loaded with examples of how to accomplish mundane examples of everyday business mathematics, is about as dry and straightforward as a workbook of this type can get.

New practical arithmetic

Henry Bartlett Maglathlin

However, near the bottom of page 76 of New Practical Arithmetic,[1] what may be the strangest and most bizarre piece of evidence put forward in Knights' Gold suddenly appears:

2. Baltimore, Nov. 16, 1866. James McClintock owed Andrew Saulsbury for 110 bu. of corn, at 75 cents a bushel,

---

What is an Account? What party is the Debtor? The Creditor?
What is required in the settlement of an account? What is a Due-Bill?

UNITED STATES MONEY. 77

bought Oct. 1; 3 bbl. of flour, at $7.50 a barrel, bought Oct. 7; and 62 bu. of oats, at 43 cents a bushel, bought Nov. 5; and Mr. Saulsbury owed him for 6 thousand of extra shingles, at $6 a thousand, delivered Oct. 5; for cash $60, paid Nov. 1; for bill of labor, amounting to $8.66, rendered Nov. 10. The account was settled Nov. 16 by giving due-bill, amounting to $27, for the balance due A. S. Make out the account, and settle it in your own name for Andrew Saulsbury.

The answer to the problem can be found later, at the back of the workbook:

(2.)   BALTIMORE, Nov. 16, 1866.

MR. James McClintock,

          To ANDREW SAULSBURY,   *Dr.*

Oct. 1.	For 110 bushels of corn, at .75,	$82.50	
" 7.	" 3 bbls. of flour, at $7.50,	22.50	
Nov. 5.	" 62 bushels of oats, at .43,	26.66	
			$131.66

                                              Cr.

Oct. 5.	By 6 M. extra shingles, at $6,	$36.00	
Nov. 1.	" Cash,	60.00	
" 10.	" Bill of labor,	8.66	
" 16.	" Due Bill,	27.00	
			$131.66

          Réceived payment,

                                    _____ for

                              ANDREW SAULSBURY.

The obvious question is, what in the world is this example doing in this book? And how did it get there?? And how did Andrew Saulsbury's name ever get involved???

Saulsbury is a real, live, flesh-and-blood person in 1866 living and doing business in post-Civil War Baltimore. By November 16, 1866 Saulsbury has almost certainly moved his family from 138 Central Ave. to 55 S. Eden just around the corner. The paintings of Stonewall Jackson and Robert E. Lee now hang in the parlor at 55 South Eden.[2] In 1866 the fortune in buried gold lies undisturbed beneath the Saulsbury cellar at 55 S. Eden. And now, some two years after his sudden death in 1873, some Boston publisher is using Andrew Saulsbury of Baltimore as a math example in their mundane math textbook.

The example doesn't belong there. It makes no earthly sense. As _Treasure in the Cellar_ author Leonard Augsburger himself once commented, on first being notified of this discovery, "_It certainly doesn't belong there — but nevertheless there it is._"[3]

Adding to the mystery is Saulsbury's known occupation at the time of November, 1866. Saulsbury is employed as an executive in the manufacture of candles and soap at James Armstrong & Co.[4] What would Saulsbury be doing selling someone 110 bushels of corn, three barrels of flour, and 62 bushels of oats? And what is he doing receiving 6,000 extra shingles in return? Sure, bartering was a more common form of transaction in the 1800s than it is today. And perhaps Saulsbury could have used shingles to repair the roof on one of his rental properties, since we know that part of Saulsbury wealth was apparently derived from his ongoing real estate speculation.[5] But a wagon load of agricultural products in exchange for shingles, labor, and cash? This is undoubtedly one very strange transaction. And it in no way squares with Saulsbury's life and employment situation in 1866. Clearly, something else would seem to be afoot.

It is true that Saulsbury, in his younger days, had been employed at his father's grocery store at the corner of Montgomery and Light Streets. Such a transaction might have some practicality for a 19th-century grocer. But no listing for that store can be found in the Baltimore directories after 1855-1856, when it was known in its later days as Andrew Saulsbury & Son. An 1862 death notice in Baltimore for one Andrew Saulsbury would lead us to believe that Saulsbury's father had passed away during the Civil War, some four years prior to this transaction. Obviously

Saulsbury's deceased father and the now defunct family grocery cannot be the source of this mysterious due-bill.

So what in the devil is going on here? And who is James McClintock?

"*All war is deception*," writes Chinese military general Sun Tzu in his book on military tactics, The Art of War.[6] From its start, in its campaign against a bigger and better equipped North, subversion and misdirection were the rules of engagement for the KGC. Confederate agents regularly communicated using encrypted waybills, church documents, personal diaries, ciphers, secret handshakes and signals, as well as encoded messages.[7] Northern KGC "copperheads," operating behind enemy lines, were known to pass information via coded classified advertisements in Northern newspapers.[8] When KGC President George Bickley was arrested as a spy in Indiana by Northern forces in 1863, a number of incriminating KGC documents were found in his briefcase. These included the *Rules, Regulations, and Principles* handbook for the Knights of the Golden Circle, as well as the key to a Confederate cipher. Additional seals and documents were found hidden in undergarments worn by Bickley's wife who had accompanied her husband on the mission.[9] Bickley was jailed without trial and never charged with a crime, all the while protesting his innocence. He would die penniless just a few short years later, in 1867, while in Baltimore.

That Saulsbury may have been communicating with another KGC operative by means of a coded due-bill should not be surprising. Union troops had supposedly threatened the candle maker and his family during their wartime occupation of Baltimore.[10] Saulsbury, according to court testimony in 1934, had never been one to tone down his fervent support for the South's cause.

And it is also not surprising that post-war Union agents, with Saulsbury on their watch list, might have intercepted a coded missive about corn, flour, and oats being exchanged for "*extra shingles.*"

No listing can be found for merchant named James McClintock in post-Civil War Baltimore. But a quick search of known Confederate operatives yields a tantalizing possibility. One of the South's leading weapons technology experts was a man named James McClintock.[11]

A primary reason for the Confederate defeat was the Union's ability to impose a smothering blockade on all Southern ports. A lack of much needed supplies from allies in Europe squeezed both the South's civilian population as well as her armies in the field. Businessman, lawyer, inventor, and Southern plantation owner Horace Hunley took up the challenge in 1862, bankrolling an ambitious scheme to develop the world's first successful attack submarine.[12] According to fellow Confederate inventor Frances Smith, "*From the Chesapeake to the mouth of the Rio Grande, our coast is better fitted for submarine warfare than any other in the world.*"

In New Orleans, Hunley enlisted the help of ship engineers McClintock and Baxter Watson. The trio drew up plans and set about constructing the South's newest secret weapon. The Confederate sympathizers first built a small, crude submarine named *The Pioneer*, and tested the craft in the Mississippi River and on Lake Pontchartrain.[13] But when Union forces threatened Louisiana, the men scuttled *The Pioneer* and headed east for Mobile, Alabama. With the help of some new team members and machinists in Alabama, inventors Hunley, McClintock, and Watson were able to construct a second submarine, *The American Diver*.[14] Although the trio attempted to use both electromagnetic and steam propulsion systems on their highly experimental craft, they eventually decided to go with a more simple hand-cranked model. Time was quickly running out. After an unsuccessful February, 1863 attack against a Union blockade, *The American Diver* sank to the bottom of Mobile Bay during a storm.

Hunley, McClintock, and Baxter then set about building their third and final "fish boat" which they dubbed "*The Hunley.*"[15] This sleek, more modern looking metallic weapon featured ballast tanks, hand pumps, two watertight hatches, and a pair of conning towers with portholes. Almost 40 feet in length, *The Hunley* would be manned by a crew of eight: one to steer the sub and seven others to sit on a bench while operating the hand-cranked propeller. The business end of *The Hunley* sported a long "spar" torpedo, giving the craft a marlin-like appearance. At the point of the wooden spar was affixed a copper cylinder containing some 90 pounds of black gunpowder. The plan was to approach an enemy vessel from under the waves, then ram the point of the spar into the enemy ship's hull. Beating a hasty retreat, and leaving the explosive charge embedded in the target ship, a connected line would play out and subsequently be tripped once the retreating sub reached a safe distance some 150 feet from its intended victim. The system, though crude by today's standards, would eventually prove effective.

By July of 1863, *The Hunley* was ready for service. During a demonstration for the Confederate Navy, the submarine successfully attacked a coal flatboat in the waters of Mobile Bay. The CSA military took control of the vessel and shipped her by railroad to Charleston, South Carolina where General P.G.T. Beauregard was defending the city from both Union land and naval attacks.[16]

On August 29, 1863, while preparing to make a test dive, *The Hunley* was accidentally and prematurely launched with her hatches still open. The vessel sunk instantly, killing five members of her volunteer crew of eight. The surviving crew members barely escaped with their lives.[17]

After being successfully salvaged, the Confederate Navy recommenced with test operations. On October 15th, 1863, The *H.L. Hunley* failed to surface while performing a mock attack. The time the entire crew of eight would be lost — including inventor Horace Lawson Hunley, who had insisted on being aboard after the initial fatal mishap.[18]

General Beauregard (who, according to KGC historian David Keehn, was accused of trying to form a KGC castle at West

Point!)[19] ordered the sub to be once again salvaged by a dive team. This time, modifications were made to *The Hunley's* design that would cause her to surface at the time she began her attack — the underwater approach having proven far too dangerous.

Although badly shaken by the loss of 13 crewmen in two fatal mishaps, Beauregard was desperate to break the Union stranglehold on Charleston. A new volunteer crew of eight was chosen, commanded by Lieutenant George E. Dixon.[20] Dixon, a veteran who had previously fought under Beauregard at the Battle of Shiloh in 1862, faithfully carried a lucky 1860 $20 gold piece that had been given to him by his sweetheart. Dixon had been struck by a Union bullet at Shiloh, suffering a serious wound to his thigh. But the $20 golden charm in his trouser pocket had taken the brunt of the bullet's force, saving Dixon's leg and quite possibly his life.[21]

On February 17, 1864, *The Hunley* slipped into Charlestown Harbor, unseen by Union forces. Before the tragic day was over, the vessel would make naval history. *The U.S.S. Housatonic*, a 1,240-ton steam-powered enemy ship, sat guarding the entrance to Charleston Harbor. *The Hunley*, approaching underwater, quickly surfaced and jabbed its barbed spar into the Housatonic's hull. As the 'fish boat" hastily backed away, making its escape, the deadly torpedo exploded. *The Housatonic* and her crew of five sank to the bottom of the harbor in minutes.[22]

The Hunley had become the first combat submarine in the history of warfare to successfully sink an enemy warship.

After the successful attack, the *H.L. Hunley* failed to return to her base, and all hands on board were lost. For over 130 years, various theories were put forth to explain the submarine's disappearance. In 1970, famed diver and underwater archaeologist Dr. E. Lee Spence is said to have first pinpointed the location of this most unusual wreck. Then, in April 1995, a dive team led by popular adventure novelist Clive Cussler "rediscovered" the lost sub just 100 yards from the remains of the Housatonic. The craft lay in 27 feet of water, buried under many feet of silt. *The Hunley* lay in an almost perfect state of preservation.[23]

On August 8, 2000, *The Hunley* was raised after nearly 136 years underwater, and transported back to the Warren Lasch Conservation Center in Charlestown — site of the old navy yard.[24]

Mystery of the Coded Due-Bill

While the mystery of the *H.L. Hunley's* demise remains uncertain, the leading suspected cause was the premature detonation of the 90 pounds of black gunpowder encased in the sub's torpedo. Some experts have also speculated that the sub was damaged by artillery fired from *The Housatonic* — or accidentally rammed by a rescue vessel responding to *The Housatonic's* plight.

Inside the dark hull of that ancient and historic submarine, reclamation specialists came across a most unusual and awe-inspiring artifact — an 1860 $20 gold piece. The soft, deformed coin, damaged from a Union rifle ball, was sanded down smooth on the obverse side. It contained a most haunting inscription, one that read

Shiloh April 6, 1862
My life Preserver G.E.D. [25]

On April 17, 2004, the remains of the third and final crew of the *H.L. Hunley* were laid to rest with full Confederate honors with the Second Confederate national flag at Magnolia Cemetery in Charleston. A crowd of several thousand attended the solemn ceremony, including thousands of Civil War re-enactors and civilians wearing period clothing.[26]

Late 1850s photo of James McClintock.

After the Civil War, inventor and designer James McClintock tried shopping his submersible technologies on the open market.[27] Sources say that he eventually went to Canada during the late 1860s and early 1870s. Ultimately, McClintock tried to do a deal in Nova Scotia . . . his designs for a new, improved submarine in exchange for being granted British citizenship. According to Brian Hicks and Schuyler Kropf, authors of Raising the Hunley, McClintock felt that his work on *The Hunley* had gone largely unrecognized, although McClintock to this day is credited as being the historic submarine's chief builder, with Horace Hunley having provided the funds and original vision.

In 1879, while testing new contact mine prototypes in Boston Harbor, marine inventor James McClintock was killed in an explosion.[28] Some observers at that time had labeled McClintock's death as "suspicious." McClintock was a member of Masonic Lodge #40 in Mobile, Alabama.

Did the U.S. federal government deem James McClintock to be a loose cannon, an embittered and dangerous individual prone to selling new and potentially threatening technologies on the open market . . . and to the highest bidder without regards to consequences? And did they take steps in 1879 to eliminate this possible threat?

Did Andrew Saulsbury, the ardent Southern sympathizer, try to purchase weapons technology for the K.G.C. in 1866 from engineer James McClintock? Were they financing some new, secret research in search of a wonder weapon? And did federal spies intercept a coded-due bill between Saulsbury and McClintock? A due bill that was later used in an innocuous business math book published in Boston in 1875? Was the inclusion of that coded due-bill in The New Practical Arithmetic a way of telling the cagey K.G.C. "we are watching everything you do" . . . you can never outsmart us?

What other explanation could logically be put forward to explain the facts? How did the transaction wind up as an example for writing out a proper due-bill in a Boston math textbook? Was it simply pure happenstance? Could the due-bill showing the strange bartering transaction between Saulsbury and a James McClintock actually have some innocuous basis in reality? Did Andrew Saulsbury (not by any means a common name) of Baltimore, a relatively obscure candle and soap company executive, really trade large quantities of oats, corn, and flour in exchange for shingles, labor, and cash? Was there actually another James McClintock involved in the 1866 transaction who was not the secret Confederate designer of cutting edge war technology?

Perhaps there really is a logical explanation, and the publication of this due-bill was just a mere coincidence.

But those paintings of Robert E. Lee and Stonewall Jackson in Saulsbury's Eden Street parlor — plus the 5,000 gold coins buried in his cellar, argue that the publication of this most unusual due-bill in Maglathlin's The New Practical Arithmetic in 1875 was no random accident.

The coded due-bill was likely intercepted by federal agents, and the K.G.C.'s attempt to purchase new, cutting-edge weapons technology was probably foiled. As a result, the buried gold at 55 S. Eden Street would remain undisturbed for decades under a layer of loose soil and some discarded Chesapeake Bay oyster shells.

The Sisters Finally Cash In

Mary Pillar Boyd Findlay and Elizabeth Hollingsworth Findlay French may have lost all hope at winning a share of the "original" discovery, but the contested treasure from pot number two was still very much up for grabs.

Although the Findlay/French sisters had grown up knowing prosperity, having come from a genteel background, their financial circumstances as early 20th-century senior citizens were modest at best. The sisters' only saving grace in this legal marathon was that their lawyers, same as Henry O. Levin for the boys, had agreed to take their case on a contingency basis.

The Findlay/French team had lost out on Judge O'Dunne's original "finders keepers" decision in February, 1935. Then the sisters lost again in the Court of Appeals in July, 1935. Judge O'Dunne had also denied their motion to review the original case. And now, in late 1935, Judge O'Dunne had ruled that Henry and Theodore did indeed make a second treasure find in the cellar,[1] and again had awarded the prize to the boys — although most of that "second pot" money was already stolen or spent by the time the authorities were made aware.

C. Arthur Eby and Emory Niles, lawyers for the elderly sisters, have already filed an official request for a rehearing of the 4-4 tie vote on their appeal.[2] They argue that the twin questions of treasure trove law and trespass have yet to be adequately addressed. Now, they are also appealing O'Dunne's decision that denied a review of the case, citing evidence based on knowledge of a "second" and new treasure find. Eby and Niles, of course, don't believe for a second there ever was a "second" find. They maintain the "new" coins are simply holdbacks from the one and only discovery on August 31, 1934.

Simon Sobeloff, representing the Merrills, and Harry Levin for the boys, both argue that there simply isn't enough evidence for the Findlay/French team to bring an appeal.[3] They say O'Dunne has already awarded the treasure to the boys, and ruled that there were two separate though improbable gold discoveries. Levin adds that since the uncovering of a second pot nine months later constituted a second event, it is deserving of separate litigation.

Hearings on the Findlay/French twin appeals are scheduled to begin in January, 1936. The Court of Appeals, appropriately, decides to consolidate all outstanding legal actions regarding the "Baltimore Coin Hoard" and to hear them as one case.[4]

Meanwhile, Theodore Jones, the prized 1935 Plymouth, and the undisciplined boy's inability to stay clear of both traffic court and subsequent incarceration, threaten to delay progress of the Baltimore Coin Hoard legal proceedings.

Simon Sobeloff maintains his temporary possession of the gold coins purchased by the Merrill brothers.[5]

By April, 1936, the Maryland Court of Appeals announces it has reached a partial decision. Regarding the original treasure discovery, the court upholds Judge O'Dunne's decision, finding no reason to overturn the February, 1935 verdict. They also concur with O'Dunne's later finding that the boys made two distinct and separate treasure recoveries. In upholding O'Dunne's rulings, the court simultaneously denies both outstanding Findlay/French appeals.[6] But in backing O'Dunne's subsequent finding of two separate treasure recoveries, the court also agrees with Harry Levin that separate litigation will be required to sort out legal ownership of pot number two. The sisters and their lawyers aren't quite out of the running just yet.

The Findlay/French attorneys begin to sue anyone and everyone with remaining assets connected to the second pot.[7] This includes the Jones/Rummels, Grobs, the Grobs' banks, and the coin buying Merrill brothers. Counselors Eby and Niles claim that if there was some doubt the boys trespassed in September, 1934 there can be no doubt the teens trespassed in May/June, 1935. They have their legal sites squarely trained on the proceeds from pot number two.

Levin, working entirely on a contingency basis, is awarded his 1/3 cut of pot number one.[8] Eby and Niles, also working on a contingency basis, are keen for a payout from pot number two.

Simon Sobeloff, a high-priced attorney on the fast track, will one day become the solicitor general for the United States. Sobeloff is charging the Merrill brothers by the hour, and those hours are starting to add up.[9] The boys' families got the Merrill brothers' cash, which is long gone, and now Sobeloff has the Merrill brothers' coins. If the Findlay/French team prevails, the Merrills will likely be left with neither the cash nor the coins. All the while, that hourly legal meter keeps running.

By summer's end, the Merrills finally wave the white flag. Negotiations between Eby, Niles, and Sobeloff commence. An agreement is hammered out by which the Merrills will pay the sisters $500 in exchange for dropping the brothers from the suit.[10] The Merrills' coins, purchased for $3,050 or just over face value, could fetch $4,000 or more at auction. Minus the $500 settlement plus Sobeloff's fees, Eli and Yale Merrill can exit the game of legal roulette while still slightly ahead.

With the settlement papers signed, the Merrills are off the hook, and are free to keep and/or sell their "second pot" coins as they please.

In October, 1936, the Findlay/French attorneys waste no time in filing an amended complaint, minus the exiting Merrill brothers.[11] The sisters are still looking to collect from the boys and their families.

Judge Edwin Dickerson is named as the person responsible for handling the Baltimore Circuit Court case involving the second pot of coins. Almost immediately, Harry Levin tries stalling the court. Then, in April 1937, Levin swings for the fences, and asks for a dismissal.[12] Dickerson denies the motion for a dismissal, and instead gives the boys and their attorneys (the Grobs, not trusting Levin, have retained a new lawyer) just 30 days to give the court a full accounting of their second treasure find. By May the boys and their representatives comply, and again request that the case be dismissed. Once again, Judge Dickerson denies the request. The case of the Baltimore Coin Hoard continues to drag on, now approaching three long years.

By mid-1937, Judge Samuel Dennis, the very same judge on the bench for the 1933 ejectment proceedings which saw control of 132 S. Eden St. pass from the Schapiro estate to Mary Findlay and Elizabeth French, takes over for Edwin Dickerson.[13]

The Findlay/French sisters, tired of their portrayal by the press as a couple of old, money-hungry, sue-happy busybodies, reveal that their intention had always been to share part of the Eden Street treasure with Henry and Theodore. When Judge O'Dunne is made aware of this new information, he is quoted as saying that if he had known the sisters were willing to share (they had previously turned down a Harry Levin settlement offer of 25%), that his 100% finders-keepers rulings in this case might have been different.[14] O'Dunne's curious admission indicates that his decisions regarding the Baltimore Gold Hoard may have been influenced by factors other than the exact letter of the law.

Final arguments in the matter resume in November, and by December, 1937 Judge Samuel Dennis is set to render the last and final verdict in this long, grueling, and hotly contested landmark case.

In reaching his decision to award the "second" pot to Henry and Theodore, Judge Dennis finds there had basically been no difference between treasure pots one and two. The landlords' agent, Mr. Benjamin Kalis, had still not put up any "KEEP OUT" sign for the rear section of the cellar. He had temporarily installed a lock on the rear cellar door, but evidence showed that had been quickly removed to allow tenant access to replace blown electrical fuses. In Dennis' opinion, both cases feature *"the same landlords, the same tenant, the same agent, the same (basically nonexistent) lease, the same boys, the same pseudo-cellar, the same barrier between the regular and pseudo-cellars and . . . the same right of entry."*[15]

In summary, Judge Dennis adds how the second pot has been lost through *"folly, inexperience, extravagance, and theft."*[16] The boys could keep the gold and the money, which had largely been stolen or already spent.

Harry O. Levin then petitions the court for $1,000 as payment for his services in litigating the disposition of the contents of pot number two. The request was granted and the money paid.[17]

The sisters could certainly try for a third appeal . . . but their legal chances were slim and none, with none being the odds-on favorite. Mary Findlay and Elizabeth French were going to have to settle for $500 minus expenses. They and their esteemed lawyers had fought the good fight, and still believed in the sisters' ultimate right to the gold coins buried on the property they legally possessed. But in the end, their persistent efforts went largely for naught. For the elderly sisters, this was the end of the line for their involvement with the legendary coin hoard.

As for the boys and their families, the December, 1937 verdict turned out to be largely a hollow, empty victory. Their "second pot" money had already disappeared or was misspent. And fate, by 1937, had chosen to intervene in a cruel and most unexpected way. Henry Grob and Theodore Jones, like many inner city youth, had already led fatherless lives filled with idleness, delinquency, deprivation, and much disappointment. The discovery of the gold, although briefly, seemed to have had changed all that. Unfortunately, over the long run, such was not the case. It was as Philip Rummel had previously warned . . . the gold continued to bring "*nothing but bad luck.*"

In 1937, the lives of these two Depression-era underdogs would take a turn for the worse . . . much worse. And this time, neither all the king's men nor all the gold in newly-built Fort Knox could help our young anti-heroes. Henry and Theodore had only to reach age 21, and the waiting fortune from pot number one was theirs to withdrawal.

Sadly, one of these best pals would never live to see that happy day.

Jesse James is Gone With the Wind

Jesse James as a young Confederate guerilla.

Who was Jesse James? Was he a simple bandit, gang leader, bank robber, and cold-blooded murderer? A larger-than life Wild West Robin Hood who stole from the rich and gave to the poor during the era of Reconstruction? Or, perhaps a front-line soldier in an underground army, conducting a campaign of terror against Union occupiers in a bid to revive the "Lost Cause" of the South?

Where history ends and legend begins is often a blurred line in the incredible story of Jeremiah "Jesse" Woodson James.

What we do know is that James was born in Clay County, Missouri in 1847. His older brother, the more reserved and studious Alexander Franklin "Frank" James, was born in 1843. The James boys' parents, Robert Sailee James and Zerelda Elizabeth Cole James, were Kentucky-born farmers who relocated to Missouri to build a log cabin and grow tobacco. Robert James also served the community as a Baptist minister. The James family prospered in Missouri, and, according to Ted Yeatman in Frank and Jesse James: The Story Behind the Legend, is said to have owned as many as six slaves at one time.[1]

When gold was found in California, Robert James was asked to accompany a wagon train of prospectors to Placerville, California to act as the party's chaplain. The senior James took on this challenge, an odd choice given his responsibilities back in Clay County. James' wife, Zerelda, also known as Zee, was left in charge of the boys, their baby sister Susan, the family slaves, and the farm. Before year's end in 1850, Robert James would be struck down by cholera, a deadly killer out in the remote gold fields of central California. [2]

The widow Zee James soon remarried, but her second marriage would end quickly in divorce. Zerelda's third and final marriage was to a kind, local physician named Dr. Archie Reuben Samuel, who came to be the James boys' stepfather. Dr. Samuel taught Frank and Jesse how to ride and shoot. With help from the slaves, Frank and Jesse worked the family farm, and by most accounts led a normal childhood. Frank read his stepfather's many books, and Jesse passed his spare time drawing pictures.[3]

As childhood turned to adolescence, all pretense of normalcy would quickly fade with the approach of the American Civil War. Although Missouri's economy was closely tied to the North, a majority of Missouri's settlers traced their recent roots to the South. And the most Southern-cultured of all Missouri counties was Clay County, known affectionately in the "Show-Me" state as "Little Dixie."

The James' farm, located in what is today known as Kearney, Missouri, lies just northwest of present-day Kansas City — barely 20 miles from the border with "Bleeding Kansas." Clay County was rife with Missouri "Border Ruffians" seeking to infiltrate Kansas and drive the Yankee abolitionists out of that state . . . so the remaining pro-Southern citizens of Kansas could cast a majority vote for slavery.[4]

The so-called Border Ruffians were itching for a fight, and men such as Old John Brown and his sons were willing to accommodate them. Brown would commit his infamous "Pottawatomie Massacre" in response to a bushwhacker atrocity that took place on Kansas soil.

Jesse James is Gone With the Wind

On May, 4 1861, big-brother Frank James joined the Missouri State Guard, fighting on the side of the Confederacy.[5] Frank saw action in the Battle of Lexington, in which the victorious Confederates seized control of southwestern Missouri. While taking leave to go home to the family farm, Frank James was arrested by a Union militia, and forced to sign a statement of allegiance to the Union before being released. Frank had other plans, however, and soon joined the infamous Quantrill's Rangers, a band of rebel guerillas using hit-and-run tactics to attack regular Union troops as well as local pro-Union militias.[6] Quantrill's Rangers were quite active in the Border War, staging several bloody incursions into nearby "Bleeding Kansas."

Allegedly, according to Bob Brewer and Warren Getler in Rebel Gold, cousin Jesse Robert "Dingus" James was also riding under Quantrill — and trigger-happy Captain "Bloody Bill" Anderson, as they bushwhacked the hated pro-Union Jayhawkers. [7]

In August, 1863 William Clark Quantrill — head of the KGC's Knights of the Iron Hand — along with his KGC-affiliated band of some 300 guerilla fighters descended upon the "free-sate" town of Lawrence, Kansas. Although Jesse James would later brag of his involvement, it is thought that only big brother Frank actually participated, along with future James Gang member Cole Younger . . . whose father had been murdered by a Jayhawker raiding party. After four hours of sheer mayhem and brutality, Lawrence, Kansas had been reduced to smoking ruins, and some 180 Kansas Jayhawkers lay dead.[8]

In response to the horrific border violence that stunned the nation, Washington, D.C. sought to crack down.

One day while young Jesse was working on the family farm, federal troops appeared, looking for big brother Frank. Somehow, the Union soldiers had been tipped to Frank's participation in the ongoing guerila attacks. The federals demanded to know Frank James' whereabouts, and they weren't taking no for an answer. Word was that Jesse was bullwhipped, but still refused to give up his brother. The worst treatment, however, was reserved for Jesse's stepfather, the mild-mannered Dr. Samuel. In front of his family, the respected physician had a rope strung around his neck and he was hoisted from a nearby tree.[9] With the defenseless man writhing and gasping for air, the soldiers would then lower Dr. Samuels to the ground, allowing him to recover — only to repeat the terrifying process, over and over again. Jesse's stepfather somehow survived the ordeal, but not without permanent brain damage. Soon after, the infuriated young Jesse rode away to join brother Frank and his fellow rebel outlaws.

In the book Jesse James Was One of His Names, authors Del Schrader and Orvis Lee Howk quote rebel bushwhacker and eventual James Gang member J. Frank Dalton on how the Confederate bands operated. In the final two years of the war, the raiders roamed the frontier hitting Union supply lines, trains, and even boats. *"We go behind Union supply lines,"* explained Dalton, *"capture and bury Union payrolls, figuring unpaid soldiers would become demoralized. And we'd grab and run with medicines, blankets, guns, ammunition, quinine . . . horseshoes, nails, sugar, hams."*[10]

And if the opportunity presented itself, the guerillas not only stole — they massacred. According to author Jim Feazell in "Jesse James" A Supernatural Thriller, the Confederate raiders *"murdered civilian Unionists, executed prisoners, and scalped the dead. Union forces enforced martial law with raids on homes, arrests of civilians, summary executions, and banishment of Confederate sympathizers from the state."*[11]

Frank James wintered in Texas with Quantrill's Raiders in 1863-'64, returning to Clay County Missouri in the spring with a group led by commander Fletch Taylor. This is when little brother Jesse finally teamed up Frank James, says William Settle in Jesse James Was His Name, or Fact and Fiction Concerning the Careers of the Notorious James Brothers of Missouri.[12]

Later, after Taylor was severely wounded, the James boys rode with Bloody Bill Anderson. In 1864, Jesse himself was seriously injured, but quickly recovered.[13]

In September, 1864, both James brothers reportedly took part in the ultra-violent Centralia Massacre as the rebel fighters mounted an invasion into northern Missouri, with an eye towards capturing St. Louis. During this incursion, Bloody Bill Anderson's men held hostage the small Missouri town of Centralia, with a population of about 100. The rebels harassed civilians, killed one man who resisted them, and robbed and set fire to many of the town's stores. During the rampage, a stagecoach arrived and was promptly held up at gunpoint. But what the raiders were really after was the scheduled train set to pass through Centralia. The rebels boarded the train, dragged off 24 wounded and unarmed

Union soldiers, and murdered the men in front of the horrified townspeople. Anderson's crew then set fire to the train depot, and sent the train along unmanned — which soon jumped the tracks, crashed, and burned.[14]

The Union cavalry quickly arrived to pursue the guerillas. However, the rebels set a trap, and ultimately ambushed and defeated the regiment, which was armed with the old-school muzzle-loading Enfield rifles. The Northern troops were no match for the revolver-toting Confederates. Of the 155 Union men involved in the battle, some 123 were killed. Most disturbing, some soldiers were said to have been slaughtered while attempting to surrender. According to writer William Settle, the guerillas scalped and dismembered some of the Yankee dead.[15] Frank James would later claim that Jesse killed Major Johnson, the Union officer in charge. As a result, Union authorities ordered the James Family relatives to leave Clay County. They temporarily resettled in Nebraska.[16]

Frank and Jesse, unfortunately, remained on the warpath. After Bloody Bill Anderson was eventually killed, the James boys split up. Frank again rode with Quantrill, and Jesse headed south to Texas with trusted Anderson lieutenant Archie Clement.[17]

Despite the disruptive mayhem inflicted by the rebel guerillas, the South's military fortunes were fast fading. In the spring of 1865, Clement's men encountered a Union cavalry on patrol near Lexington, MO. For the second time in his young life, Jesse would be shot and seriously wounded — this time while attempting to surrender.[18]

The South soon went down to defeat, and the era of Reconstruction began. While Jesse recuperated in Nebraska, his beloved South lay in shambles.

Soon after the war, Jesse married his first cousin, Zerelda "Zee" Mimms, who was ironically named after Jesse's own mother. There are stories that say Jesse tried to go straight, working for a time as a bounty hunter, but for Jesse the war would never truly be over.[19] He soon rejoined Archie Clement, whose band of now ex-rebel guerillas continued to attack the symbols of Yankee authority. Their first alleged bank robbery came in February, 1866, when they hit the Clay County Savings Association, reportedly owned by Republicans and former Union militia officers. An innocent bystander lost his life during the holdup. The desperadoes would make off with a hefty $60,000 in their first post-war bank heist.[20]

The State of Missouri countered by organizing a militia to go after the ex-rebels, who were now, by all appearances, acting simply as rogue outlaws, thieves, bandits, and murderers. Gang leader Archie Clement would soon be shot dead.[21]

But Clement's embittered gang continued on — Frank and Jesse James included. They would claim being forced into a life of crime because they and their families were being persecuted by the victorious North.[22] Frank and Jesse became the outfit's new leaders, which included their close friends, the Younger Brothers, and other revenge-minded ex-Confederates. The James-Younger Gang would rob some eight more banks and also other lesser targets before robbing their first train . . . arguably the first rail robbery in history. With beefed up security at the banks, moving trains and stagecoaches were becoming the new convenient targets of choice.

The date was July 21, 1873 when the James/Younger Gang learned of a Rock Island Railroad train passing through Iowa that contained a $75,000 shipment of gold. The shipment was delayed, however, and the bandits only managed to carry away a fraction of the heavy loot after successfully derailing the train near the town of Adair.[23] The Rock Island Railroad express, the world's earliest known robbery of a moving train, would be the first of many for the James/Younger Gang.

In October, 1897, a 16-year old Iowa boy digging for worms on little Beaver Island in the Mississippi River would make an incredible find — one to match or even exceed that of Henry Grob and Theodore Jones nearly 37 years later. According to newspapers of that era, Adolph Johnson's shovel struck something metallic, which soon proved to be a hastily buried iron box. Upon opening the box, the teenager was amazed to find approximately $50,000 in gold and paper money staring back at him.[24] While speculation initially centered on a Swedish nobleman who had lived on Beaver Island for many years, the James/Younger Gang would later become possible suspects as to the source of this buried treasure.

According to Jesse James expert Ron Pastore, author of Jesse James' Secret and star of the History Channel documentary Jesse James' Hidden Treasure, the James/Younger Gang probably stole as much as $1.5 million or more during their legendary "career." In today's dollars that would be something approaching the $100 million mark, a truly staggering sum.[25] What did they do with all that loot?

As the brazen bank, train, and stagecoach robberies mounted, the James/Younger Gang began to catch the attention of newspaper editors nationwide. Easterners couldn't get enough of the tales of pistol-packing outlaws and brazen bandits roaming the lawless American West. But it was a man named John Newman Edwards, an editor for the *Kansas City Times*, who would write news stories and "dime novels" that elevated Jesse James to the level of cult status.[26] James was, according to Edwards, a romantic figure in the mold of Robin Hood, continuing to fight on for the lost cause of the South, while robbing from the rich to give to the poor.

In one famous Jesse James tale, Jesse and some members of the traveling James/Younger Gang are offered a meal by the widow of one of their departed colleagues. After the meal, Jesse notices the woman in her kitchen, crying, and asks her if there is anything the matter. The widow explains to Jesse how the bank is ready to foreclose if she can't pay the several hundred dollars owed — by tomorrow. With the loss of her husband, the poor woman is practically destitute. This may be the widow's last night under her own roof. The bank's officer is intending to stop by the house next day at a pre-arranged time.

Jesse and his men pool their money, and are barely able to come up with the payment . . . it is just about all the money they have. Jesse presents the startled widow with the cash and some very specific instructions — to be absolutely sure to get a receipt tomorrow from the banker for the payoff amount.

The following day, the widow does exactly as instructed, and the irritated banker has no choice but to sign a receipt for the money. He had actually been looking forward to foreclosing and picking up the widow's property at pennies on the dollar.

While he is riding back to the bank, Jesse and his men step into the road, hold up the banker at gunpoint, and relieve him of the money they had lent to the widow the previous night. They save the widow's home, all while turning the tables on the greedy, predatory banker.[27] The tale is classic Jesse James.

Despite this colorful story, there is scant evidence that the James/Younger Gang ever robbed from the rich to give to the poor. But there is also not much evidence they spent these enormous sums of ill-gotten gains on themselves.[28]

So, where was all the money going? The strongbox on Beaver Island, Iowa discovered by the boy digging for worms may have provided a clue. Was much of the James/Younger Gang loot buried for a greater purpose? To help fund a planned second uprising against the hated North — and their despised, draconian policies masquerading under the Orwellian name of Reconstruction?

During the first half of the 1870s, the railroads and express companies were eager to put an end to the James/Younger Gang and their hit-and-run guerilla antics. So they turned to the one outfit uniquely equipped to deal with these so-called "Robin Hood" bandits of the Wild West.

The railroads and stage coach operators hired Allan Pinkerton and his famed Pinkerton Detective Agency.[29] The boss there took it as a personal challenge to see that the famous Jesse James would be hunted down, arrested, jailed, tried, and dispatched at the end of the hangman's noose . . . the very same Pinkerton who had earlier reported to his federal clients that Baltimore's Marshal George P. Kane was a "rabid secessionist" most likely involved with the 1861 plot to kill Lincoln. The very same Illinois ex-lawman who had assisted Old John Brown and the illegal underground railroad in defiance of the odious but legal Fugitive Slave Act, sometimes referred to as the "Bloodhound Law" after the dogs used to track fleeing slaves. These pre-war slaves, by law, whether in Alabama or New Hampshire, were considered to have been the righteous, legal property of their Southern masters. Anyone giving them aid and safe harbor was considered to have been a lawbreaker.

So, when fervent abolitionist Allan Pinkerton takes on the case involving Jesse James of the James/Younger Gang in 1874, he is not only out to capture an American outlaw, gang leader, bank robber, train robber, highwayman, and murderer. Pinkerton is just as importantly gunning for one of the few remaining potent symbols of the fallen Confederacy and their pro-slavery ideology.

According to T.J. Stiles, author of <u>Jesse James: Last Rebel of the Civil War</u>, James and his men had worn Ku Klux Klan masks during at least one of their robberies.[30] It is also said that James publicly threatened, after the war, to shoot any free black person he saw in Missouri not performing in the traditional role of subservient slave.

Also according to Stiles, the Confederate guerilla band Jesse had ridden with during the war essentially operated as a "death squad."[31] The James Boys, it seems, had functioned as guerilla hit men. KGC guerilla hit men, to be more specific. Ralph Ganis, a Jesse James researcher and author of the book Uncommon Men: A Secret Network of Jesse James Revealed, has commented on the History Channel that the Confederacy had the Knights of the Golden Circle create an underground movement, and "the guerillas were the militant wing of the KGC."[32]

During one of the James Gang's most infamous robberies, the holdup of the Daviess County Savings Association in Gallatin, MO, James shot and killed the cashier, Captain John Sheets. He did this specifically because he mistook Sheets for Samuel P. Cox, the militia officer who had tortured and killed James' fellow Civil War guerilla, William "Bloody Bill" Anderson.[33] And, says historian T. J. Stiles, James also targeted certain banks, railroads, and stagecoach companies because of their political affiliations.[34] Cole and Bob Younger, longtime gang members, later admitted under interrogation that the First National Bank of Northfield had been purposely targeted because it was associated with the Reconstruction Republican politician Adelbert Ames and Ames' father-in-law, General Benjamin Butler.[35] General Butler, of course, was the same Union commander who, in 1861, had invaded Baltimore with a force of 1,000 men and heavy artillery. He subsequently placed those heavy guns in strategic locations overlooking downtown Baltimore, and then imposed martial law across the city. Butler's "heavy-handed" takeover of the civil government of Baltimore was the causal factor for Mayor George Brown, Marshal George Kane, many other Democratic officials, and several hundred police officers all losing their jobs. It also contributed to the arrest and imprisonment of both Brown and Kane, and the subsequent harassment of newspaper editors, public figures, and everyday Baltimoreans such as Andrew Saulsbury and family who were characterized as Southern sympathizers and potential troublemakers.

But despite Allan Pinkerton's best efforts, he soon discovers that the well-insulated James boys have lots of friends in Clay County, Missouri. Pinkerton's efforts to infiltrate the Kearney, Missouri community eventually result in the murders of some of

Pinkerton's best agents . . . but not before one of the Younger Brothers is shot and killed by a Pinkerton detective.[36] One of the Pinkerton dead will soon include agent Jack Ladd, who was secretly posing as a field hand at work on a neighboring farm.

Thoroughly frustrated, some of Pinkerton's agents resort to the extreme measure of actually trying to smoke Frank and Jesse out of their mother's farmhouse. One day, Ladd gives the signal to other Pinkerton agents, believing he has seen Frank and Jesse James slip onto Zerelda James' homestead. But actually, Zerelda's infamous sons are many miles away. Later that night, the armed Pinkerton men surround the home, and toss an "incendiary" device through the window. Inside the home are Zerelda, the James Family matriarch, her incapacitated husband, Dr. Archie Samuel, and Jesse's half-brother, little Archie, who is a mere child. Although varying accounts have described the controversial device as everything from a smoke bomb up to a mortar shell, there is no doubt as to its horrendous effect. The resulting explosion kills little Archie, and mangles Zerelda's arm so badly that it is later amputated below the elbow.[37]

Upon hearing the news, Frank and Jessie gallop home to a scene of utter devastation. Not surprisingly, they vow vengeance on the perpetrators in particular, and all representatives of Union authority in general. Soon after, Pinkerton agent Jack Ladd is found murdered execution style, as is the owner of the adjacent farm who allowed the Pinkertons to use his property as a base for their spying operation.

The Pinkertons would never again get close to Frank and Jesse James in Clay County's "Little Dixie."

News of the bombing fiasco instantly brought forth public sympathy and even support to the James Boys. There were even calls for amnesty for the entire James/Younger Gang.[38]

But while as the Pinkertons were trying and failing to reign in the James/Younger Gang, it was a disastrous bank robbery gone bad up in the north country that would nearly prove to be the gang's undoing. On September 7, 1876, the most famous outlaw band in American history traveled to far away Minnesota to raid the First National Bank of Northfield, owned by Adelbert Ames and Union General Benjamin Butler. From start to finish, the daring operation did not go as planned.[39]

First, the two cashiers on duty resist. The acting cashier, even with a knife held to his throat, tells the robbers the bank's safe is on a time lock. It isn't, and the cashier is beaten with the butt of a gun for his trouble — and later dies. Meanwhile, the assistant cashier attempts to flee and is wounded in the shoulder. The heist, already taking far too long, is now becoming nightmarishly messy and complicated. Outside, the James/Younger lookouts grow increasingly nervous. So do passing townsfolk, who begin to realize something is amiss inside their bank. And, by the way, who are all these shifty strangers hanging around? The gang's jumpy lookouts, mindful of the unwanted attention, fire their weapons in an attempt to clear the street. This works . . . except many of the townspeople duck inside brick buildings, some of which contain handy firearms. Within minutes, the exposed and outnumbered gang members find themselves being shot at from surrounding windows and doors. Grabbing what loot they can, the gangsters leave the cashier lying mortally wounded, and try to beat a hasty retreat out of town. By the time the James/Younger party have shot their way out of trouble, two raiders have been killed, and a second Northfield resident lies dead.[40]

Outside of Northfield, Frank and Jesse split off from the others and make a beeline for Missouri. A local militia is soon on the gang's trail, and when the manhunt finally concludes, gunman Charlie Pitts is dead, and all of the Younger Brothers are captured.[41] Except for the lucky, slippery James Boys, the most feared outlaw band of the Wild West is now out of business.

Frank and Jesse laid low for a couple of years, but eventually returned to what they knew best. They recruited new gang members, then resumed their temporarily interrupted crime spree. Problem was, their new colleagues weren't the same battle-tested ex-Confederates of yesteryear.[42] The

replacements were largely just impressionable young guns out to make a buck, who lacked the fierce loyalty of the Youngers, Charlie Pitts, Clell Miller, Bill Chadwell, and the other original guerilla-trained members.

One new, relatively untested James Gang member, Bob Ford, would prove to be Jesse's undoing. By the early 1880s, the authorities turned up the heat on the effort to capture America's most wanted outlaw, Jesse Woodson James. The reward reached the incredible figure of $10,000 [43] — roughly 30 times the average working man's annual salary. That was $5,000 for Jesse's apprehension, and another $5,000 upon a successful conviction, which seemed like a foregone conclusion. Brother Frank James had a similarly high price placed on his own head.

Frank and Jesse also had additional private bounties on their persons, courtesy of the railroads they had repeatedly victimized.

The end was nearing for the outlaws Frank and Jesse James.

However, the law was also breathing down the necks of young gun Bob Ford and his brother, Charley. Unbeknownst to Jesse, the Fords had already surrendered themselves to the Clay County sheriff. Sheriff James Timberlake and Missouri Governor Thomas Crittenden offered the Ford Brothers a tempting backroom deal . . . deliver Jesse Woodson James to us and you'll both receive full pardons — plus the official reward money![44] The Fords were hardly in a position to refuse.

Bob Ford figured they stood little chance of bringing Jesse in alive, and was therefore willing to forgo the second half of the $10,000 prize for James' conviction. However, depending on the circumstances, if they killed Jesse in cold blood, the Fords would be open to a charge of murder.[45] Bob and Charley Ford did not want to collect their $5,000 reward from a jail cell. So, with Timberlake's help, Governor Crittenden reluctantly allegedly agreed to pardon the Fords if they murdered Jesse James, although Crittenden would have preferred that the West's most famous outlaw be taken alive.

On the morning of April 3, 1882, the Ford Brothers sat in the rented home of Jesse Woodson James in the town of St. Joseph, Missouri. James was living in St. Joseph with his wife and two young children under the assumed name of Tom Howard. James and the Ford Brothers were supposedly meeting to plan their next bank heist.

Bob and Charley Ford, of course, had other ideas.

April 3rd was an apparently warn spring day, and at some point Jesse James, a.k.a. Tom Howard, took off his jacket and gun belt, laying them both aside. During their strategy session, James took a break, and while walking around the room, happened to notice that a painting hanging on a wall was quite dusty. Supposedly, the world-famous outlaw moved a chair into place, grabbed a feather duster, and stood up on the chair to clean off the picture.

Seeing his golden opportunity, Bob Ford pulls out his gun, creeps up behind Jesse, and fires a single slug into the back of Jesse's skull. Jerimiah "Jesse" Woodson James, age 34, was dead before his body hit the floor.[46]

The stunning news traveled fast, and soon a crowd of curious onlookers had gathered in St. Joseph. The body was taken from the scene of the killing by local officials to be photographed and autopsied. Soon, Clay County's Sheriff James Timberlake arrives to take possession of the body.[47] Only problem was, St. Joseph wasn't exactly within Timberlake's jurisdiction, since that town lies over in Buchanan County. Timberlake supposedly wanted to take the body back to the James Farm in Kearney, Clay County for burial, which he does, despite protests from the authorities in charge. The sheriff had brought some deputized men along with him from Kearney to help with the transport and later act as pallbearers in the burial of Jesse James. Some of the men deputized by Timberlake just happened to be major members of the James Gang. And, perhaps not coincidentally, Timberlake himself had apparently served as a Confederate guerilla during the war.[48]

Two weeks later, Bob and Charley Ford were indicted for first-degree murder, pled guilty, were sentenced to hang, and then granted a full pardon by Governor Crittenden — all on the same day![49] After collecting but a fraction of the reward money, Bob and Charley Ford flee Missouri in fear for their lives. Sherriff Timberlake and Marshal Henry H. Craig would conveniently pocket the bulk of the reward money for themselves . . . over and above their official lawman's pay.[50]

But the outlaw Jesse James was finally dead and buried . . . or was he?

Ron Pastore, author of <u>Jesse James' Secret</u>,[51] has long suspected massive fraud in the supposed April 3rd, 1882 killing of Jesse Woodson James. To put it bluntly, Pastore says James' death was faked, and another criminal's body substituted in his place. The law had been closing in, and the real Jesse James needed to disappear —permanently. Jesse, Frank, and the Knights of the Golden Circle, says Pastore, came up with a plan to make this happen.[52]

The plan apparently worked to perfection.

Timberlake was almost certainly in on the ruse . . . and perhaps even the governor had knowledge.[53]

Before becoming sheriff, James Timberlake had served in a Confederate Army cavalry division under one of the most feared generals of the Civil War, Joseph Orville "Jo" Shelby.[54] Before the war, Shelby had initially commanded a group of Missouri "Border Ruffians" involved with terrorizing abolitionists in "Bleeding" Kansas. During the war, Captain Shelby led his "Iron Brigade" of Missouri volunteers on what would become known as "Shelby's Great Raid." In the fall of 1863, Shelby's deadly brigade traveled some 1,500 miles across Missouri and inflicted over 1,000 casualties against federal troops. Shelby's Great Raid would also capture or destroy approximately $2 million in Union property and supplies.

At the Battle of Pea Ridge in Arkansas, 1862, Captain Jo Shelby led his Lafayette County Mounted Rifles of the Missouri State Guard into the fray. Also present at Pea Ridge was former Texas Ranger Benjamin McCulloch, a close friend of Texas patriarch Sam Houston. After Texas had seceded on February, 1861, it was Ben McCulloch who had led a force of some 550 men to surround the federal arsenal at San Antonio, which surrendered to McCulloch without bloodshed. According to David Keehn, author of <u>Knights of the Golden Circle: Secret Empire, Southern Secession, Civil War</u>, about 150 of those men under McCulloch were active Knights of the Golden Circle from six different Texas KGC castles.[55] For his service in Texas, McCulloch would be appointed to the position of brigadier general by CSA President Jefferson Davis.

McCulloch was placed in command of Indian Territory by Jeff Davis, and with the help of fellow brigadier general Albert Pike, McCulloch was able to build important alliances for the Confederacy with the Cherokee, Choctaw, and Creek nations.[56]

During the fighting at Pea Ridge in 1862, McCulloch would suffer a mortal wound when shot out of his saddle by a Union sharpshooter from Illinois. Shortly after Pea Ridge, Brigadier General Albert Pike constructed Fort McCulloch, the main Confederate fortification in southern Indian territory. Pike named the fort for his late commanding officer and fellow Knight of the Golden Circle, Ben McCulloch.[57]

This is, of course, the same Albert Pike who was simultaneously Grand Sovereign Commander of the Southern Jurisdiction of the Scottish Rite Freemasons. The same Albert Pike who, in 1853, had been named as a Companion Mason to Baltimore's Charles Webb, the youngest grand master in the history of Maryland Freemasonry and a fast rising star in Pike's burgeoning Masonic empire. And it is also the same Albert Pike who had to resign from the Confederate Army when a number of allegations against him surfaced, not the least of which was that Native American soldiers under his command at Pea Ridge had tortured and scalped fallen Union soldiers on the battlefield.[58] Pike went into self-imposed seclusion at his rural Arkansas cabin for the rest of the war to write Morals and Dogma, Pike's grand collection of 32 essays that provided a philosophical rationale for the degrees of the Ancient and Accepted Scottish Rite of Freemasonry.[59]

Jo Shelby, meanwhile, would survive Pea Ridge, and later help to turn back a Union advance on Arkansas by destroying or capturing Union supply trains, and also seizing a Union tin clad (lightly armored gunboat), the USS Queen City.[60] Shelby would distinguish himself in many other battles before the war's end. And with the help of his trusted second lieutenant, James Timberlake, Shelby would go on to capture many towns from their Union garrisons, including Boonville, California, Lexington, Potosi, Stockton, and Waverly, Missouri.

Curiously, Shelby's adjutant and right-hand man, John Newman Edwards, would later become the editor of the Kansas City Times, where he would write romantic stories and dime novels about Jesse James' exploits as the anti-hero and Robin Hood of the Wild West.[61]

In mid-1865, as the war wound down and the Union declared victory, General Jo Shelby would refuse to surrender! Shelby instead led his troops — his "Iron Brigade" — south into Mexico, officers Edwards and Timberlake included, and offered the services of his remaining 1,000+ unit to Emperor Maximilian as a Confederate foreign legion.

The South immortalized Shelby and his men as "the undefeated." Just like Frank and Jesse James, they refused to admit the war was over, and that the Union had triumphed. A later verse applauding Shelby's defiance was added to the post-war Confederate anthem "*The Unreconstructed Rebel.*" There is no mistaking the sentiment:

> "*I won't be reconstructed, I'm better now than then.*
> *And for a Carpetbagger, I do not give a damn.*
> *So it's forward to the frontier, soon as I can go.*
> *I'll fix me up a weapon, and start for Mexico.*"[62]

Maximilian declined the Confederates' offer of military assistance, but did grant them Mexican land on which to live. Most of the self-exiled Americans soon drifted back to the U.S. however, no doubt encouraged by President Johnson's offer of amnesty. Timberlake would return to Missouri to resume farming, and then later embark on a career in law enforcement.[63] Edwards settled in at the *Kansas City Times* where he would soon help to reinvent Jesse James as a romanticized American icon. And, by 1867, Shelby himself would return to a life as a Missouri farmer, his departure from Mexico no doubt hastened by the overthrow and execution of Maximilian, and the revocation of the Maximilian land grant to the ex-Confederates. Before Maximilian was killed, he tried to smuggle a disguised wagon train of vast treasure north through Texas so it could be secretly shipped back to Europe. The treasure never made it. The wagons were attacked on the trail by, surprise, ex-Confederates, and everyone in the Mexican caravan killed. Maximilian's lost fortune has never been found.[64]

And Jesse's brother, Frank? Tired of life on the run, the more low-key, more intellectual Frank James would turn himself in to Governor Crittenden some five months after his brother's "death." Handing his holster to the governor, Frank said, "*I've been hunted for 21 years, have literally lived in the saddle, have never known a day of perfect peace. It was one long, anxious, inexorable, eternal vigil.*" He then ended his statement by boasting, "*Governor, I haven't let another man touch my gun since 1861.*"[65]

Supposedly, Frank James' only condition for surrender was that he not be extradited to Northfield, Minnesota on charges related to the infamous 1876 botched bank robbery, murders, and subsequent shoot-out and rampage. He would be tried for only two of the robberies/murders committed by the James/Younger Gang with Frank and Jesse's participation. Despite overwhelming evidence of over two decades of serial robbery, violence, and mayhem, Frank James would be exonerated of all charges and set free.[66] No further charges would be brought, and James would never be extradited to Minnesota to face justice there. Frank James would live until 1915, working at a variety of jobs that included shoe salesman, telegraph operator, and theater ticket taker. In later years he would give tours of the James Family farm in Kearney for 25¢.

During the high-profile trial of Frank James, the defense placed on the stand a most interesting witness on James' behalf. The judge, jurors, and onlookers were no doubt wowed by the critical testimony given by General Joseph O. "Jo" Shelby,[67] the "Unreconstructed Rebel" who refused surrender to the Union and quickly became an enduring symbol of Southern pride and Confederate defiance.

After the trial and acquittal of Frank James, with his reputation supposedly tarnished over the conspiratorial way in which Jesse James had been killed, James Timberlake moved to New Mexico where he and his brother reportedly operated a number of ranches.[68] Later, after the James controversy had calmed down, Timberlake returned to Missouri where Governor Crittenden reappointed him deputy U.S. marshal for the Western District of Missouri.[69] And, can you guess who would become marshal for the same district? Well, Jo Shelby, of course.[70]

With lawmen such as these, it's a wonder the James Gang had to pack it in after only 17 years. It was much like having the fox guarding the henhouse . . . with John Edwards at the *Kansas City Times* on scene as the "investigative" reporter.

When historian Ron Pastore finally was able to retrieve the original files of the Jesse James autopsy and inquest, he was stunned by what he uncovered. Nothing about the official findings matched the much-reported story of Bob and Charley Ford killing Jesse James with a single pistol shot on the morning of April 3, 1882. The body appeared to have been dead for several hours, with death likely having occurred the evening before. There was a round ball still inside the victim's skull, even though Bob Ford's single bullet had supposedly passed through Jesse's head and lodged in the wall near the hanging painting, where it was dug out and recovered. The ballistics were a total mismatch. Also, there were suspicious wounds on the victim consistent with a struggle at or before the time of death.[71]

Most disturbingly, the photos of the dead man did not appear to sync with known photos of Jesse James. The victim was apparently shorter, heavier, wore a beard, and had darker hair than the normally clean-shaven, sandy-haired Jesse Woodson James.[72] There were just too many discrepancies that needed to be explained . . . but weren't. Jessie James was dead, and all of officialdom was satisfied.

In his book Jesse James' Secret, Pastore reveals that artifacts kept hidden within the extended James clan for decades have provided startling clues to the mystery of who was actually buried in Jesse James' grave. During the last part of the 20th-century, while cleaning out the old Kansas homestead of a deceased family member, James descendants found a hidden, covered-up closet filled with ancient newspaper clippings, documents, photographs, and family mementos. An inspection of those belongings, tucked away for most of a century, would lead to the conclusion that Jesse Woodson James did not die in 1882, but rather lived until 1935 in rural Kansas under the assumed name Jere Miah "Jerry" James.[73]

But then who the devil was buried at the James' farm in Kearney, Missouri?

Pastore's investigation led him to believe that there were actually three men named Jesse James within the large, extended James clan. All were ex-Confederate guerillas, post-war bandits associated with the James/Younger Gang, and first cousins. The famous outlaw was Jeremiah "Jesse" Woodson James, a.k.a. Tom Howard. His cousins were Jesse Robert "Dingus" James, a.k.a. J. Frank Dalton, and Jesse Mason James.[74]

Pastore posits that with the heat on from authorities, gang members had tried to lay low during the early 1880s. However, cousin Jesse Mason James ignored the group's consensus agreement, continuing instead to commit freelance robberies under the "Jesse James" brand. With the noose tightening and the reward money from authorities and the railroads growing monthly, something needed to be done. A plot was therefore hatched to kill renegade troublemaker Jesse Mason James in place of Jesse Woodson James, probably with Sheriff Timberlake and even Governor Crittenden's knowledge.[75]

On the evening of April 2, 1882, the gang met at the home of "Tom Howard" with the presence of cousin Jesse "Mason" James requested. The cousin was lured to another part of the St. Joseph, MO property, perhaps the barn, where an argument and fight ensued. Jesse Mason James was beaten, pistol whipped, and then shot in the head. His lifeless body was stored in the barn overnight.[76]

Next day, the second phase of the audacious plan went into effect. The cousin's body was carried into the James' rented home and placed on the floor. A scarcely plausible story was cooked up about Jesse removing his guns and then climbing onto the chair to dust the painting. A slug from Bob Ford's gun was then fired into the wall to complete the staged scene . . . explaining why there were two bullets left behind, one in Jesse's skull, and the other lodged in the wall. Bullets that were an obvious and outright ballistics mismatch.[77]

This is likely why Timberlake was in St. Joseph so soon after the shooting, demanding to take the body back to Kearney for a fast and proper burial. And why Timberlake saw the need to deputize several James Gang members as his temporary helpers to complete the task.

Pastore says that the known photographs of cousin Jesse Mason James closely match the death photographs from April 3rd, 1882. And that modern facial recognition technology, used now to track and identify drug kingpins and international terrorists, has positively matched known photos of Jerimiah "Jesse" Woodson James to a man later named Jere Miah "Jerry" James . . . an individual who lived to the ripe old age of 88 in rural Neodesha, Kansas.[78] A positive match right down to the lumpy scar on the interior of the subject's left eyebrow.

See for yourself:

If these three faces belong to the same individual — and modern technology says they do according to Ron Pastore — then Pastore has set the history of the American West on its ear. And in the process, he's also revealed the true hidden power and ingenious deception of the Knights of the Golden Circle, the most insidious and successful home-grown terrorist organization the United States has faced to date.

It is truly inconceivable that Jesse James, Frank James, and many of their criminal associates could rob banks, trains, and stagecoaches for 17 years post-war without being apprehended and facing a judge. The only possible explanation is they had help, and lots of it . . . including assistance from sympathetic Southern-leaning friends in high places. The James/Younger gang was more than just a band of gun-toting murderers and thieves riding an amazing lucky streak. These men were part of a much bigger movement, as the assistance of Edwards, Timberlake, Shelby, and numerous others would strongly suggest.

Regarding Jesse's death, author Ted P. Yeatman writes that "*Jesse's death had been reported at least as early as late 1879, when a hoax was perpetrated by former gang member George Shepherd, who claimed he had killed the bandit in a shootout in southwest Missouri.*" Authorities wanted to be sure they had their man. In fact, on April 4, the day after the shooting, the *Los Angeles Times* raised the doubts in an editorial comment. "*Jesse James is like a cat; he has been killed a great many times, only to as often enjoy a resurrection.*"[79]

It seems doubts about Jesse's demise were raised immediately . . . this is not just some Johnny-come-lately, hare-brained 21st-century conspiracy theory.

Not convinced? Read Pastore's entertaining but well-researched <u>Jesse James' Secret</u>. The photographic evidence, presented both in the book and online at Pastore's web site, is alone quite convincing.

Pastore has also starred in the History Channel's documentary *Jesse James' Hidden Treasure*.[80] Using clues obtained from the James Family, the Jesse James Museum, documentation on KGC and Confederate codes, and his knowledge of cave systems in the rural Midwest marked with strange carved glyphs and drawings, Pastore narrows his treasure search to an undisclosed out-of-the-way canyon somewhere in Kansas. While explaining the true story of Frank and Jesse James and their involvement with the KGC, Pastore conducts his treasure hunt while attempting to decipher the archaic 19th-century symbols and rock etchings that, frankly, would be dismissed by most people as pointless doodles and ancient cowboy graffiti.

By show's end, Pastore and his team have unearthed a broken mason jar with approximately two dozen gold and silver coins from the mid-to-late 1800s. Pastore explains that his find is a KGC "paycheck" or buried payment for an ex-Confederate sentinel entrusted with guarding a much bigger treasure nearby. The baffling, faded codes scratched onto the canyon wall tell Pastore where to look. A second, rusted Mason jar lid unearthed in the vicinity hints at another "paycheck" long ago cashed.

Pastore does not locate the main cache, buried somewhere deeper in the wilderness in hopes of the day the South was to rise again. But he has vowed to return with heavy equipment to continue his search. Perhaps this Kansas mother lode will rival the strongbox full of cash and gold found by that Iowa boy digging for worms[81] — or Theodore Jones and Henry Grob's pot of gold in Depression-era Baltimore.

The $64 million dollar question is not whether another fortune lies buried in a remote canyon in Kansas, or even if our larger-than-life outlaw Jesse James died or didn't die in 1882. No, the really important question is, if Jesse and the James/Younger Gang were actually fighting a 17-year underground war of retribution against the North, and stockpiling buried treasure to finance a second go at the Yankees, then from whom were they taking orders? Who was calling "the shots" so-to-speak, and keeping the James Boys out of harm's way?

Was it Sheriff Timberlake? General J. O. Shelby, the "Unreconstructed" Rebel?

Or, maybe, just maybe . . . perhaps someone even bigger???

Golden Dreams

Shortly after news of the 1934 gold bonanza, Ruth Grob reported that her son, Henry, had been suffering with sleep difficulties. Henry was apparently beset by a series of magical dreams about gold and fabulous treasures.[1] The boys had become instantly famous, and folks looked upon Henry and Theodore as if they were the luckiest two kids in all of Baltimore — if not the entire U.S.A. But the unknowing boys had let the buried golden genie out of its copper vessel, and that all-powerful genie seems to have had a mind and will of its very own.

Soon the realty of the legal circus had set in. Henry and Theodore were in this titanic courthouse battle for the long haul. And even when boys emerged as winners in the contest for proceeds from the original 1934 discovery, the courts were determined to hold their money for years . . . until the best friends reached the legal age of 21. Discovery of the improbable "second" pot of gold, proceeds from which were spent surreptitiously, only served to further complicate an already complex courtroom drama. The Labor Day, 1935 break-in at the Jones/Rummel apartment, which exposed the existence of gold having been withheld from the authorities, had set off a new round of motions, filings, appeals, and requests for re-arguments.

With both boys having dropped out of school,[2] no need for education since a pot of cash awaited them at the end of the rainbow, Henry and Theodore drifted aimlessly. While Henry at least brought his family the much needed $16 per week[3] from the Panzer Packing House, Theodore continued his obsession with the Jones/Rummel's 1935 Plymouth . . . his license-less joyrides resulting in serious brushes with the law and, ultimately, months of confinement.

But by 1937, things were looking up. Theodore was out on parole, and the Findlay/French sisters were slowly running out of legal challenges. Eli and Yale Merrill had already paid off the property-owning sisters to the tune of $500 in exchange for being excused from the case. Harry O. Levin was doggedly pressing Judge Edwin Dickerson for a dismissal. But first, Dickenson demanded an accounting of assets derived from the disputed second find,[4] which the Grob and Jones/Rummel families provided, despite most of the treasure having been allegedly sold off, spent, or stolen.

The boys were nearly home free. Mid-year, Dickerson handed the courtroom reins over to Judge Samuel K. Dennis, who would by year's end rule that the questionable 1935 "second" recovery of gold coins also belonged to Henry and Theodore, same as the original 1934 discovery.[5]

However, Judge Dennis' long-sought December, 1937 decision brought little happiness or comfort to the Grob and Jones/Rummel clans.

In August, Henry Grob had come down with a bad summer cold. The now young man of 18 had been advised by a physician to refrain from swimming until fully recovered. Feeling invincible, Grob went swimming anyway, jumping into the harbor waters off Canton's Boston Street — near the Elliott Street home purchased with cash from the sale of coins from the boys' "second" pot of gold.[6]

Soon Henry's cold worsened, morphing into full-blown pneumonia. In 1937, doctors did not yet possess the medical magic bullet of powerful antibiotics. By the time Henry Grob was admitted to Baltimore's South General Hospital, there was little the hospital staff could do. Henry quietly slipped away on August 24th.[7]

A grief-stricken Ruth Grob petitioned the Baltimore Circuit Court for an emergency release of funds to bury her son. Although poor in life, Henry received a first-class funeral. Services were held in the family parlor, with many friends and neighbors attending.[8] A newspaper photo of Henry and Theodore smiling in front of piles of gold coins was prominently displayed. Henry's sister, Gertrude, fighting back tears, commented how, "*That picture is just about all Henry ever got out of it.*"[9]

Andrew J. Saulsbury, the man believed to be the most likely person to have collected and buried the coins, had likely passed away from pneumonia in 1874 at the Eden Street home — with the 5,000 gold coins still buried in the cellar. Now one of the boys responsible for uncovering the pot of gold had also died from pneumonia.

Henry Grob was interred in Baltimore's Oak Lawn Cemetery beneath a handsome granite headstone. Ruth Grob appealed to the court for an additional release of $200 for living expenses, listing herself as the sole heir of Henry's estate. The court graciously granted Mrs. Grob's request.[10]

In April, 1938 the court released the remainder of Henry's money to his "destitute" mother. After taxes, trustee commissions, trustee expenses, legal filings, court costs, funeral bills, Henry's hospital bills, the lawyer's bills, and the money previously paid to Ruth for emergency living expenses, Mrs. Grob received just over $3,600[11] of the nearly $5,800[12] that had been originally set aside for Henry at the Savings Bank of Baltimore.

Also in 1938, Theodore "Jones" got married and began to settle down. Theodore was married using the name given to him on his birth certificate, Theodore Krik Sines.[13] It was under the relatively anonymous name of Theodore Sines that Theodore began to slowly create distance between himself and the lingering tale of the Baltimore Gold Hoard. In May, 1939, with the court still believing him to be two years older than he really was, Theodore collected his several thousand dollar payout from the court, his share of the proceeds from pot number one.[14]

Sines served for a while in the U.S. Army, then came home to Baltimore, where he gained employment as a shipyard mechanic for Bethlehem Steel. Theodore would spend his entire working life, spanning four decades, at the shipyard. According to Leonard Augsburger, author of <u>Treasure in the Cellar</u>, Theodore led a modest, hardworking life, was a solid family man and a good provider, and seems to have spent his early-life bonanza rather wisely. Diagnosed with lung cancer in his later-50s, Theodore (Jones) Sines passed away in 1977.[15]

Theodore's stepfather, World War I veteran Philip Rummel, who always believed the Eden Street bonanza had brought the two families nothing but bad luck, died tragically soon after

Theodore collected his big payout, in 1940. Rummel, while intoxicated, stumbled and fell beneath the deadly steel wheels of a Baltimore City trolley car.[16]

The thousands of Baltimore Gold Hoard coins auctioned off at the Lord Baltimore Hotel in 1935 have been dispersed far and wide. The whereabouts of only a select few of these coins is today known. Most have passed from generation to generation, and from collector to collector. Since they can't be traced back to the auction, their provenance can no longer be determined.[17] But the legend, though growing dim, lives on.

The case, which during the hard economic times of the 1930s sparked so much fanfare and notoriety, has understandably faded into obscurity in the intervening decades. Mr. Augsburger's 2008 book did help to bring some renewed attention to this absolutely mesmerizing treasure story, especially amongst his fellow coin collectors.

Suspicion has always fallen upon Andrew Saulsbury, or some other unnamed 19th-century miser, as the source of the gold. It has never been suspected — until now — that the Rinky Dinky Doos Boys' Club, with a grand membership of two, while attempting to bury a cigar box of its meager club assets, accidentally unearthed the treasure chest from the Baltimore chapter of the country's largest and most subversive "boys'" club in history . . . the shadowy Knights of the Golden Circle.

Certainly the story of the Baltimore Coin Hoard should go down as one of the most improbable, inconceivable, unbelievable, and frankly bizarre events in the long history of this nation. The truth concerning this most unlikely of treasure discoveries is undoubtedly far, far stranger than fiction.

No one could make this stuff up.

The South Shall Rise Again

In 2005 an enormously important paperback book was co-authored by Bob Brewer and investigative journalist Warren Getler. The book, <u>Rebel Gold</u>, was originally released in hardback under the title <u>Shadow of the Sentinel</u>.[1] This most unusual book covers the life story of Bob Brewer, born in rural western Arkansas circa 1940 in the Ouachita Mountains. Young Brewer begins life as a Navy brat, but by age nine his father moves the family back from San Diego, California to Hatfield, Arkansas. Bob, now being raised in a proud, extended country family of modest means, begins to realize that a few elderly male members of his clan are hiding and guarding some dark secret of monumental importance. That secret has something to do with the surrounding woods and mountains. Two older men on Bob's mother's side, Will "Grandpa" Ashcraft and Odis "Uncle Ode" Ashcraft are in the habit of going deep into the countryside to "patrol" the land against unseen outsiders, which they call "cowans." There is talk of one outsider, a Mexican, having been killed and buried near a local stream some decades earlier.

Slowly, the men bring young Bob into their confidence, revealing tidbits of information that at first make little sense to the boy.

"Bobby, see the ol' beech there along the creek? That's a treasure tree. It's got carvings on it that tell where the money is buried." [2]

Whenever the curious youngster begins to ask probing questions, however, the old-timers quickly dummy up or deftly change the subject. Their plan seems to be to bring the young boy along slowly, pointing out clues and isolated tidbits from some giant, overarching puzzle . . . the overall picture which they are — as of yet — refusing to reveal to their young pupil.

The boy is made familiar with old rock drawings, tree carvings, and other subtle clues left in the woods as directional markers for those in the know. But markers to where, and for what? And left by *whom*?

Young Bob is shown strange rock formations, deformed trees with oddly shaped limbs, and faintly marked tree blazes easily missed. The carvings and drawings contain a blizzard of pictographs featuring animal forms such as turtles, snakes, turkey tracks, and horses. There are scrawled names, initials, numbers, Bible passages, and other coded signals that would mean absolutely nothing to the uniformed outsider. But to Grandpa (actually Brewer's great uncle) and Uncle Ode this ancient graffiti holds supreme meaning, and is connected to whatever they are guarding in the lonely and remote Ozark Mountains.

Bobby Brewer likens the entire situation to a scavenger hunt without rules. What is his family really up to? Why all the secrecy and fuss?

One day, a now teenaged Bob Brewer is in the rugged hill country with his Uncle Ode, who is riding upon his favorite stallion, Rebel. Suddenly the older man makes a startling revelation. Pointing his rifle up a steep ridge, Odis blurts out, *"There is more money buried on that mountain then you could ever spend in a lifetime."* [3]

Startled, Bobby naturally asks his mentor why he just doesn't go and dig up all the gold. After all, none of these hardscrabble backwoodsmen are wealthy by any means. In fact, the Brewers and the Ashcrafts are barely scraping by, living day-by-day off the land. Odis Ashcraft grinds out a meager living as an Arkansas lumberjack.

"Because it belongs to somebody else," warns Uncle Ode. *"And <u>nobody</u> can touch it."* [4]

Later, when Bobby accidentally finds an empty, partially buried old Wells Fargo strongbox in the woods, he brings the oddity to Uncle Ode for an explanation. The strongbox was recovered on a remote trail that locals say was once used by Jesse James and the James Gang as a getaway route after having robbed a stagecoach near Hot Springs, Arkansas in 1874.

"Put it back where you found it and leave it alone," barks Brewer's uncle.[5]

Soon after, Uncle Odis is killed in a freak accident by a felled tree. The Ashcraft family patriarch, "Grandpa" Will, is deeply shaken by the sudden loss of his favorite son, Odis, and begins making fewer and fewer patrols into the Ouachita Mountains. Likewise, Bobby Brewer's visits to Grandpa Ashcraft's cabin would become less frequent. Upon graduation from high school, Brewer embarks on a 20-year career in the Navy, following in the footsteps of his father. Brewer's naval career soon takes him far away from the backwoods of western Arkansas. Meanwhile, "Grandpa" Ashcraft would eventually pass away at age 92, apparently taking the mysterious family "backwoods" secret to the grave.

Fast-forward twenty years to the late 1970s . . . Bob Brewer now has a wife and family of his own. With his naval career behind him, Brewer decides to move back to Hatfield, Arkansas. First taking a job as an apiary (beekeeper) inspector, and then as a utilities superintendent, Brewer's civil service jobs allow him to travel around rural Polk County on a regular basis. They also afford him an opportunity to scout the land and be on the lookout for new treasure signs.[6]

At the local coffee shop in Hatfield, Brewer is struck by how often talk amongst the old-timers meanders into the realm of treasure hunting, buried Spanish gold, and mining claims. Bob finds the talk of mining claims particularly odd, since Arkansas has no history of successful commercial gold mining — the native geology simply not being supportive of the production of precious metals. There is an old diamond mine in Arkansas that is now a state park where visitors can hunt for diamonds . . . but there's no substantial gold. Rumors of "Spanish" gold buried by the wandering conquistadores who may have passed through Arkansas in the 16th and 17th centuries were only slightly more plausible. Sure, the Spaniards had discovered lots of gold throughout Mesoamerica, but why bury that gold in the remote, hilly, often forbidding backwater of Arkansas? That made no sense.

Determined to discover some answers, Brewer begins to photograph and catalog the old blazes, rock carvings, and tree markings of his youth — and then to scour the backwoods in search of more. Leaning heavily on the lessons of Uncle Ode and Grandpa Ashcraft, Brewer's trained eyes quickly come across additional signs throughout the forest.

Using a topographical map, the Arkansas man next begins to plot his significant finds by location. As his inventory of treasure signs, symbols, and markers grows, and the locations noted on the topo map, Brewer begins to sense some overarching pattern to the once-seemingly random code placements.

Bob's next step is to purchase a decent, late-model metal detector, and to canvas the wooded areas where the mysterious treasure signs are most concentrated. Bob's wife looks askance at his new, time consuming hobby . . . and at times Brewer himself ponders his growing obsession. Is he chasing phantoms? Can there really be anything more to the markings and signs in these woods than just some old hillbilly graffiti?

Certainly Uncle Ode and Grandpa Ashcraft had gone about their business as if those carvings and clues had been of extreme importance.

But important how . . . and why? Who had put them there . . . and for what reason? Brewer felt like someone sent on a surreal Easter egg hunt with strange, unexplained ground rules and no clearly defined boundaries. Bob isn't even sure exactly what types of eggs he is supposed to be looking for.

The metal detector quickly begins to pay dividends. Brewer is soon finding buried metal objects deep in the woods. Objects where logic said they didn't belong. Rusted plow points, broken horseshoes, metal rods . . . even rifle barrels and old pistols. Was there really this much trash just lying about deep in the Arkansas backwoods? Was Bob just imagining all this?

Brewer stayed the course, doggedly pinpointing the locations of the buried iron and steel objects on his topo map. To his amazement, he realized there was symmetry and a yet undisclosed method to the locations of the signs and the buried objects. They had been intentionally placed along a series of lines — lines that crossed and intersected. And that many of the objects and above-ground signs were purposely oriented to point towards further clues.

The Hatfield resident would spend much of his free time during the 1980s using his detector to find and record additional buried metal objects. Brewer eventually realized that a standard 19th-century compass could also be used to locate the metal pieces, which were usually buried at a depth of no more than a few inches. When walking over a buried piece of iron, the needle point on the compass would gyrate. Someone had been leaving invisible breadcrumbs in the forest, grid markers for an unseen trail that led to an unknown location. The coded messages on the trees and rocks were subtle signposts.

But signposts to where . . . and what?

By April, 1991 Brewer finds a spot deep in the woods triangulated by three important treasure signs — a blazed tree, an arrow-shaped rock, and a buried axe head. If Brewer's theory is correct, he realizes something of importance must be buried at this site. Swinging his detector, Bob gets to work, and the faithful detector soon registers a hit.

Carefully pinpointing and excavating his find, Brewer unearths a mason jar filled with gold and silver coinage. All the coins date to the mid-1800s, and are of U.S. mintage. There is some $400 in face value gold, and $60 of silver. But the precious metal content is easily 50-70 times the 19th-century face value . . . not to mention its historical and numismatic significance.

It would be the first big find of Brewer's treasure-hunting career — but not his last. Bob would go on to use his metal detector, his growing knowledge of KGC treasure signs, and the buried iron makers in the KGC's unseen geometric grid system to pinpoint the location of other relics and buried fruit jars filled with coins. It is believed these jars, known as paychecks, were stashed as a payment system for KGC sentinels entrusted with guarding the main KGC depository at the center of the web-like grid system that extended over many rugged miles.

Further research by Brewer reveals an old *Mena Star*, AR newspaper article with details of the James Gang's 1874 Hot Springs, Arkansas stagecoach robbery.[7] To Brewer's surprise, a map detailing the James Gang's getaway route has the bandits first traversing General Albert Pike's old property, named Greasy Cove — and afterward Grandpa Ashcraft's homestead a few miles to the west — before the gang escapes pursuers by fleeing into Oklahoma Indian territory. That territory was home to some of the Indian tribes once befriended and represented by lawyer and Washington D.C. insider, Albert Pike.

During the Civil War, Pike rose to the rank of Brigadier General in the Confederate Army, but resigned after Native Americans under his command at the Battle of Pea Ridge participated in the scalping of Union soldiers in the field. Pike, facing arrest, escapes to his cabin in the hills of rural Arkansas, where he spends much of the remainder of the war penning his Masonic tome <u>Morals and Dogma of the Ancient and Accepted Scottish Rite of Freemasonry</u>.[8] First published in 1872, Pike's work would be used a guidepost for Freemasonry for the next 100 years, and was regularly reprinted until 1869.

<u>Morals and Dogma</u> has been described as "a collection of thirty-two essays which provide a philosophical rationale for the degrees of the Ancient and Accepted Scottish Rite."

And yes, this would be very same Albert Pike who, in 1853, became a Companion Mason to young Charles Webb, the newly elected Grand Master of Maryland Freemasonry[9] and a candle and soap executive for the James Armstrong & Company. By the end of the 1850s, Pike would rise to the position of Sovereign Grand Commander for the entire Southern Jurisdiction of Scottish Rite Freemasonry and its Supreme Council. He was, for decades arguably, the most influential Freemason in the world, one who revised and revamped the order's elaborate rituals. And according to many, Pike had also become the unofficial head of the shadowy

Knights of the Golden Circle. He is also known to have written the lyrics to the Confederate version of the popular tune "*Dixie*."[10]

Pike, notes the authors of <u>Rebel Gold</u>, was "*an unabashed apologist for slavery*" and saw to it that key supporters of the Southern cause were corralled into the ranks of the Freemasons' Supreme Council.[11] Explains author Thomas P. Kettel in his 1866 <u>History of the Great Rebellion</u>, "*The Knights of the Golden Circle, having for its primary objective the extension and defense of slavery, was organized; and several degrees, as in the Masonic order, were open to the aspirant for high rank in it. To the initiated of the highest rank only was the whole plot revealed. . . .*"[12]

Albert Pike, the Freemasons, the war between the states, Confederate guerillas, stagecoach robberies, Jesse James . . . now Brewer began to understand the proliferation of Polk County rock carvings etched with a peculiar double **J**, sometimes almost in the shape of a ship's anchor:

JJ or J,

The Hot Springs stagecoach robbery, the pursuit across western Arkansas into Oklahoma Indian territory, buried loot. . . . these carvings were the telltale signs of Jessie James and the James-Younger gang. The James Gang had been robbing Union banks, Union stagecoaches, Northern companies, and wealthy individual Yankees not just out of spite, but also to build up a new nest egg for a future resumption of Confederate action. And the KGC, with their "dark prince" Albert Pike, were in the forefront of that clandestine effort.

Bob's treasure wasn't an accident . . . a random treasure the result of some miser who had buried a life savings on his farm or nearby patch of woods and never lived to make the withdrawal. These mason jars of coins had been buried deep in the forest, well out of the way — and Brewer had found them by deciphering the codes and following the trail of buried pistols, gun barrels, plow points, tools, and other seemingly innocuous pieces of metallic debris. It seemed almost like madness — but there was a clever, planned logic to all of it.

Getler and Brewer, in <u>Rebel Gold</u>, maintain that "*Some ten months after the war, a group of ex-Quantrill men — led by Cole Younger — hit the Clay County Savings Association in Liberty,*

Missouri. In that audacious daylight raid the outlaws took some $70,000 in gold, currency, and bonds. In pulling off the heist, they set a marker for their postwar operations. Still, the most famous KGC outlaw of them all was 33rd-degree Scottish Rite Mason, Jesse Woodson James. A former rebel guerilla conducting hit and run raids during the Civil War, Jesse W. James would become the KGC's master field commander. Consider: James and the Younger brothers never became a rich gang; they never used the booty they had stolen for personal gain. So what did they do with their plunder? The answer, which is only now emerging, is that they systematically buried it — under a masterful grid likely devised by Pike, (Caleb) Cushing, and others. The system employed complex cipher, precision surveyor's techniques, cryptic-Masonic-linked inscriptions on trees and rock faces, and a handful of bewildering coded maps. The hidden caches had to be protected. They had to be guarded by lifelong sentinels watching over them."[13]

Lifelong sentinels such as Will and Odis Ashcraft and the Confederate family members and trusted rebel insiders who had come before them.

Again, from <u>Rebel Gold</u>, these rebel sentinels *"had protected the layout for decades under supervision from unnamed higher-ups. All this, it appeared, was part of a KGC master scheme initially sketched out by Albert Pike, Caleb Cushing, and other powerful behind-the-scenes men of intrigue.*"[14]

Men of "intrigue" such as Pike's fellow Masonic Grand Master and "Companion Mason" Charles Webb of Baltimore, who would likely have overseen the collection of KGC gold at Andrew Saulsbury's KGC castle on S. Central Avenue, and its burial under the home of secret slaver Captain John Mattison just around the corner on S. Eden St. Also, of course, the second cache of Baltimore gold buried on the grounds of the nearby rebel hangout, The Fountain Hotel, home of Saulsbury confidant Thomas Armstrong. Armstrong and Saulsbury, of course, both reported directly to Webb at the soap and candle firm on Concord St., while Captain Mattison sat on the board of directors of the Armstrong-controlled fire insurance company — along with none other than Charles Webb and his brother and high-ranking Mason, James Webb.

So, we have Bob Brewer finding buried jars of coins in Arkansas amidst a forest of tree and rock carvings and buried iron signposts. Ron Pastore digging up more fruit jars of old coins and dore bars in Kansas alongside and nearby canyon walls covered in archaic glyphs and the initials **J.J.** Understand that Pastore digs up some of these artifacts even while the television cameras are rolling during the filming of the History Channel special *Jesse James' Hidden Treasure!*[15]

Also, realize that the "dark prince" Albert Pike didn't just direct the burial of vast treasure . . . he apparently buried some himself! In an earlier chapter, we left off with Pike and his servants fleeing his rural Greasy Cove property in Western Arkansas after being tipped off about an imminent attack from pro-Union locals. Yes, Pike was able to dodge his pursuers and load his wagon with books, personal items, and whatever gold and currency he had readily available in his cabin retreat. Pike got away safely and would live until a ripe old age.

But the big gold Pike had seemingly *buried* on his property was, of necessity, left behind. . . .

According to Brewer and Getler, Arkansas legend has it that one of Pike's servants had also tipped off the raiders as to the location of some of Pike's buried gold. The raiders found those gold coins, stashed under a rock near the Pike cabin in a large iron wash pot, just as Pike's servant had claimed. The find was subsequently confirmed to Brewer by an elderly Hatfield area man whose great-uncle had participated in the raid.[16]

Further evidence of even more Pike gold appeared in a fall, 1970 article from *Old West* magazine, written by J. Mark Bond, titled "*One Black Pot with a Yellow Fortune.*"[17] The article describes how a family from the Greasy Cove area, years after Pike's death, dug up a buried iron wash pot containing as much as $100,000 in gold coins. The article talked about beech trees with numerous carvings, arranged in a triangle . . . "*all you have to do is locate three beech trees in a triangle.*" The site was allegedly located just a few miles north of Pike's out-of-the-way cabin. And supposedly, it was found with the help of a mysterious waybill connected somehow to Pike.

A Greasy Cove local named Arthur Porter explained in the article that this second big recovery of gold around Pike's property had been in 1907 or 1908. Porter, just a youngster in the early 1900s, had been on hand for the discovery. "*I could see a little of one side of the rusty wash pot. It didn't take the men long to expose the rusty top. It was covered with an old piece of sheet iron or some kind of sheet metal.*"[18]

Incredibly, the *Old West* magazine article went on to relate how the waybill had hinted at yet another wash pot in the immediate vicinity containing as much as $80,000 in coins. No one knows if that cache has ever been uncovered.

Brewer goes on to describe how, using the information from the magazine article, he was able to locate the spot with the three triangulated beech trees and the now empty depression that once held a fortune in gold likely deposited there by Masonic Supreme Grand Commander Albert Pike. Today this land is part of the Albert Pike Recreational Area in the Ouachita National Forest.

Although Brewer was unsuccessful in uncovering more gold on Albert Pike's Greasy Cove property, a new lead would send Brewer off in another direction, causing him to expand his search area exponentially.

A fellow treasure hunter lent Brewer his copy of the 1975 book <u>Jesse James Was One of His Names: The Greatest Cover Up in History by the Famous Outlaw Who Lived 73 Incredible Lives</u>, written by one-time *Los Angeles Herald Examiner* columnist Del Schrader, along with Orvus Lee Howk, a.k.a. Jesse James III.[19] The central question explored by the book is whether Jesse Woodson James was the head of a criminal gang, or was he in actuality a chief member of the Knights of the Golden Circle who directed activities of a Confederate underground army in preparation for the coming of a second Civil War? According to Schrader and Howk, "*One of the deadliest, wealthiest, most secretive and efficient spy and underground organizations in the history of the world was The Knights of the Golden Circle, which operated over the globe for 65 years (1851-1916). . . . Some of the craftiest, finest brains in the South directed the Knights of the Golden Circle. The group was heavy on ritual, which was borrowed from the Masonic Lodge.*"[20]

Schrader and Howk added that during Reconstruction, "*a hidden Confederacy based in Nashville, Tennessee had buried enormous caches of gold, silver, and arms for the South to rise again. The stockpiled caches, ranging from those that could be dug up by shovel to those that required enormous mechanical lifts, were hidden in a complex, cross-border depository system. The symbols are not always arrows, turkey tracks, snakes, and birds, but sometimes they are the old Confederate Army code.*"[21] Howk, who was allegedly the grandson of Jesse James, described how some of the caches were relatively small. Some were buried in metal milk cans, as reportedly was the case when several hundred thousand dollars in KGC treasure — including double-eagle gold coins — was found in the 1960s near Troy, Ohio by the great-grandson of a former KGC associate of Jesse James.[22] However, much of the KGC money and arms was hidden in elaborate, deep underground vaults or chambers.

In Arkansas, one of Bob Brewer's best finds would be an old tea kettle filled with 19th-century gold coins . . . located by following the coded signs and iron markers on a KGC treasure grid.

Jesse James Was One of His Names basically conveys what J. Frank Dalton, allegedly Jesse James the famous outlaw, told Howk, his grandson. The authors (Schrader and Howk) supposedly relied on diaries, correspondence, affidavits, and photographs of Dalton-James to patch together the book.

In order to run a super-secret underground organization such as the KGC, James needed to be declared legally dead. Howk

J. Frank Dalton

says that the man in the coffin who was buried as Jesse James was actually rival Charlie Bigelow,[23] who bore a passing resemblance to James. The James gang bumped off Bigelow, had him placed in a wooden coffin, and saw to it that the James family and other Clay County locals went along with the scheme, willingly or unwillingly. Governor Thomas T. Crittenden was allegedly in on ruse, promising full pardons to gang members Bob and Charley Ford soon after the cold-blooded slaying. Bigelow had been committing copycat robberies under James' name, and so Bigelow's death as Jesse James solved multiple problems at once for Jesse. This is why the county coroner found so many anomalies, including the fact the body had apparently been dead since the previous evening — much longer than a couple of hours, as the killing was supposed to have occurred earlier on that same day.

Ron Pastore, author of Jesse James' Secret,[24] largely agrees with the Howk/Dalton scenario, except he maintains that it was a

James cousin, the troublesome Jesse *Mason* James, who was killed in place of Jesse Woodson James, and not the hapless Charlie Bigelow. Pastore identifies J. Frank Dalton as yet another Confederate guerilla and extended James family member, Jesse *Robert* James — but not "the" Jesse James.

Now legally dead and with the heat off, Jesse Woodson James was left free to pursue other activities. According to <u>Jesse James Was One of His Names</u>, the KGC's leadership was a well-organized, hidden Confederate cabinet. Their headquarters would later be moved from Nashville to Texas, and Jesse Woodson James, under an assumed identity, would take control in 1883-84.[25] The KGC employed blood oaths, cryptic passwords, and handshakes among its co-conspirators, and used cipher, signs, and symbols to communicate. It was all male. Women were kept in the dark for their own protection.

This is precisely why Margaret Saulsbury, Andrew J. Saulsbury's wife, had no knowledge of the vast fortune in gold buried under her Eden Street home in Baltimore. The gold was strictly KGC business.

Howk and Schrader also claimed that James was a 33rd degree Freemason.[26] Because only those selected by Pike's Supreme Council could have attained this highest possible degree in U.S. Freemasonry, the claim suggests a direct connection to Grand Sovereign Commander Albert Pike. Jesse James, Pike, and, of course, Grand Master Charles Webb of Baltimore, a companion Mason to Pike, would all have belonged to the same elite inner circle. If this startling claim about Jesse James is true, then all three men were fiercely pro-South, pro-Confederacy, operating at the very highest echelons of Freemasonry, and involved in the burial of gold for clandestine purposes.

According to <u>Jesse James Was One of His Names</u>, among the KGC's postwar higher-ups were Jesse James, Nathan Bedford Forrest, General J.O. Shelby, Cole Younger, and even Jefferson Davis.[27] They operated from Nashville, Texas, Colorado, and also had a network of affiliated leaders in Canada, Mexico, and England (generally those Confederate leaders living in exile and not covered by President Johnson's general amnesty, such as Colonel George Kane's Confederate Secret Service boss, Jacob Thompson, who allegedly skipped out of Montreal with some $200,000 in CSA funds).[28] The KGC leadership placed moles inside telegraph operations, insurance companies, and rail companies (some owned outright by the KGC) — each providing exquisite inside information for raids against trains, federal stagecoaches, banks, and other targets.[29]

Charles Webb and Thomas Armstrong were each on the board of directors of separate rail companies, and the American Fire Insurance Company of Baltimore, which insured valuable cargoes, featured Charles and James Webb, James Armstrong, and Captain John J. Mattison on its board. Charles Webb and Andrew J. Saulsbury were also connected to some of the East Coast's largest financial institutions. James Webb and Andrew Saulsbury were, of course, members of Baltimore City Council. George Kane and Charles Webb would eventually operate out of the Baltimore mayor's office.

A 1961 book written by Henry J. Walker, <u>Jesse James "The Outlaw"</u>[30], lends credence to many of Howk and Schrader's substantial claims. Walker was also convinced that the elderly J. Frank Dalton was really Jesse James. Also, that Dalton/James had been "*a high-ranking member of a secret society for the Southern cause.*"[31] Walker had interviewed Dalton and his remaining associates, all in their advanced age. Walker wrote that Jesse Woodson James and KGC and Confederate guerilla leader William Quantrill were "*high-degree Masons*" and were members of an unnamed militant secret order "*controlled by men in the high Confederate wing of the Democratic party of that time.*"[32] Walker quotes J. Frank Dalton as saying "*Quantrill was a 33rd degree Mason. We were all Masons, and attended Masonic Lodge meetings in various towns, using assumed names, of course.*"[33] The KGC had gone around the country burying gold and other treasure for the cause. States Walker, "*. . . the robberies and escapades they took part in were not actually of their own planning, nor the plans of their bands of outlaws. The James brothers were only a small part of a large movement of members for a 'lost cause' of the South. Some of these members were even elected to government positions; some were employees of express companies, and this secret organization was financed mostly by a foreign government to make regular espionage reports on the United States outpost forts. . . .*"[34]

To quote Brewer and Getler in <u>Rebel Gold</u>, this "*could explain why all the fabulous wealth reportedly stolen by the everyday criminal enterprise (the James Gang) remains almost entirely unaccounted for . . . for it was buried in the coffers of political combatants, in the coded depositories and weapons stockpiles of an underground post-Confederate terrorist network.*"[35]

Del Schrader also mentions that not only James, but other high-degree Masons were members of the Knights of the Golden Circle . . . and that John Wilkes Booth (friend and associate of Marshal George P. Kane), was a lower-ranking member of the KGC.[36]

If J. Frank Dalton were a mere crank, say Brewer and Getler, and if Del Schrader and Orvus Lee Howk were mere dupes, then at least one of them and perhaps all three certainly possessed an amazingly vivid and detailed sense of much-neglected, or deliberately concealed, chapters in U.S. history.[37] Howk revealed there were two Jesse James, each with two brothers who went by the name "Frank." They were first cousins Jesse Woodson James, and Jesse Robert "Dingus" James. James historian Ron Pastore claims three Jesse James: Jesse Woodson James, Jesse Robert James (alias J. Frank Dalton), and Jesse Mason James (shot and buried as Jesse James in 1882). Along with some copycat robberies, these multiple Jesse James would explain the large number of holdups attributed to the James/Younger Gang over a span of 17+ years, including two jobs pulled on the same day some 600 miles apart . . . not possible when limited by 19th-century modes of transportation.

Armed with information gleaned from <u>Jesse James Was One of His Names</u> and other sources, including a formerly indecipherable treasure map known as the "Wolf" map,[38] Bob Brewer soon realizes that the KGC network of depositories extends well across the South and into the American Southwest . . . Arkansas, Oklahoma, Kansas, Texas, New Mexico, and even as far away as Arizona.

Brewer is also able to complete the basic outline of the treasure grid design, which

KGC treasure grid over map

consists of a concentric circle and intersecting lines within a larger circle set against a square.[39] Its geometric symmetry is, of course, highly suggestive of Freemasonry and Masonic symbolism. The grid is not unlike the original design for the layout of Washington, D.C., a city planned, surveyed, mapped, and built by Freemasons.

Brewer would subsequently learn that a California treasure hunter named James J. Woodson had previously deciphered the KGC model as early as 1990. In an article entitled *"Knights of the Golden Circle"* in the newsletter *Treasure Hunter Confidential,* [40] Woodson had discussed his drawing that showed a tilted square superimposed on a circle. Dotted lines connected various opposing points within the circle and square. There was also an inner circle. Basically, here was the master pattern on which Brewer had spent countless hours doing an independent confirmation. The drawing showed shaded boxes and shaded circles within the treasure zone. The boxes were large caches, and the circles smaller caches. The boxes would be located along the circumference of the circle at the ends of the designated north-south and east west axes — *and at the precise center of the pattern.*

Amongst the many documents, materials, and artifacts contained in the Howk-Dalton collection from the Jesse James days was on old waybill with a cryptogram describing a "King Solomon's Treasure." The waybill included a specific reference to the Knights of the Golden Circle.[41]

The scale for the diagram was one inch per mile, but did not give a specific location or even a suggestion as to the state in which King Solomon's Treasure could be found. The illustrated waybill, complete with a symbolic KGC turtle, states:

"The Confederate Government leaders were powerful, rich influential men of the deep South who saw that the War Between the States did not settle all the issues or problems of that era. So finances were raised, Gold Bars, Gold Nuggets, Gold Dust, coins, silver, platinum, diamonds were hoarded in what they termed to be Military-Strategic locations all over North America. . . .

The bulk treasure was said to hold a few tons of gold, plus over $1,000,000 in old coins — Buried less than 30 feet deep. Twelve other treasures of less value represents 13 Southern states of USA — Those sympathetic toward the cause of the Old

South. . . . These treasures were hauled into this wild area between the years 1869-1890.

The survey pattern fits in with USGS maps of this particular area. . . .

We learned that there was no North door in King Solomon's Temple. So to enter the secret chambers of the secret workmen, we should by any and all means commence in the South and work our way towards the Northwest. Jesse James saw to it that dead folk are on guard — watching over these great treasures.

The Worshipful Master sits in the East. The Senior Warden sits in the West." [42]

Brewer's big break came when he realized his biggest find in the Ouachitas, a large iron tea kettle with $20 double eagles, was found at a spot that coincided with a family story about the shooting of a massive buck. Once again, it seems Grandpa Ashcraft had been speaking in code. The buck represented the tea kettle full of gold, which was found near the upended Wells Fargo strongbox, placed there to give searchers the impression that any treasure once there was now long gone. A search of Will Ashcraft's belongings produced photographs of the area which held further clues to buried treasure.

As Brewer and Getler explain in <u>Rebel Gold</u>, *"Methodical fieldwork eventually led Bob to the location of the Solomon's Temple layout."*[43] And to Bob's surprise and amazement, that fieldwork led him to his remote corner of the Ouachitas and Hatfield, Brushy Valley, and Greasy Cove. King's Solomon's Temple and his Ouachita treasure grid had been part of the same overarching complex!

"The unraveling of the Ouachita KGC treasure grid was almost magical — indeed, automatic — from that point on. The properly aligned template indicated about a dozen spots where treasure caches would be buried, some along the key centerline indicated by the deer photo. At each indicated spot in the forested hills, all now on government property, Bob found an unmistakable burial marker. These were all but invisible to the untrained eye; yet he knew exactly what they were. Each time, it was almost as if he recognized the scribbled signature of family." [44]

One of the central legends in Masonic lore concerns Hiram Abiff, the mythical architect and builder of Solomon's Temple, later guarded by the medieval Knights Templar. *"Those secreting the treasure left nothing to chance or coincidence,"* write Brewer and Getler in Rebel Gold. *"After all, 'the Worshipful Master sits in the East,' and none other than Albert Pike, the world's highest ranking Mason for decades, had lived due east of where the two men* [Brewer and his treasure hunting helper] *now stood."*[45]

Yes, a fortune in rebel gold, with Albert Pike to the East, and Senior Warden Jesse Woodson James to the West.

You'll have to read Rebel Gold to find out what Bob Brewer decides to do with the Confederate mother lode in the backwoods of Western Arkansas.

Rebel Gold, Jesse James' Secret, they are not just wonderful books about the uncovering of lost treasure. They are also keys to understanding why 5,000 gold coins came to be buried under a Baltimore house in 1856. Why Captain John Mattison and Andrew Saulsbury kept those coins hidden, and why Saulsbury's fellow candle and soap executive Thomas Armstrong had 2,000 more gold coins secreted away under the Fountain Hotel just a mile away. Why Baltimorean John Wilkes Booth and Marshal George Kane remained close associates from the April, 1861 bridge burnings up until Lincoln's assassination in April, 1865. And why Kane's friend and political ally, Freemason Charles Webb, who likely directed the KGC activities of Mattison, Saulsbury, and Armstrong, became a Companion Mason to Albert Pike in the early 1850s. Albert Pike, the dark prince, who would bury a fortune of gold at his Greasy Cove property in Arkansas, and oversee the burial of the King Solomon's Treasure depository with "senior warden" Jesse Woodson James.

Yes, Jesse Woodson James . . . the same man who was hunted by the famous detective, Allan Pinkerton.

But Bob Brewer wouldn't get all the Confederate gold — or silver. When he went hunting for those 39 kegs of Confederate silver buried at the Danville Cemetery,[46] he was nearly 140 years too late. The sentinel for that treasure, Colonel George Kane, Charles Webb's longtime ally, had stayed in Danville under cover until the KGC could move the bulky rebel fortune somewhere else.

But where?

Yes, George P. Kane . . . another man who'd also been watched and investigated by none other than an undercover Allan Pinkerton.

Coincidences, coincidences, coincidences. . . .

Victorio Peak and Beyond

Victorio Peak in New Mexico's San Andres Mountains.

In 1937, a man named Milton "Doc" Noss allegedly stumbled onto a treasure of enormous proportions, hidden inside a deep cavern underneath a remote New Mexico hillside. Noss, his wife, Ova, and friends were said to be deer hunting near a spring in the San Andres Mountains. Doc Noss decided to climb the hillside to get a better view of the countryside, when he was interrupted by a sudden, heavy rainstorm. Doc scrambled for refuge up on the hillside's rocky outcrop. While looking for a place to ride out the storm, Noss spotted a large rock that appeared as if it had been 'worked" by someone. Curious, Noss rolled over the heavy rock, exposing a small opening that led down to into what seemed to be an old abandoned mining shaft.[1]

Back at camp, Noss whispered to his wife that he had found an old, hidden mining shaft deserving of exploration. The couple would come back later equipped with flashlights and some rope. Doc, who was younger than his wife, and in better physical shape, would descend into the hillside alone. Ova, also known as Babe, stood guard at the entrance. Lowering himself through the musty darkness, Noss found that the shaft and connecting tunnel eventually led to an enormous natural cavern many hundreds of feet below the peak. And in a side tunnel off the main cavern, Noss, who supported he and Ova as a chiropodist (an unlicensed country foot doctor), found a hidden room with swords, antiquated helmets and armor, Wells Fargo strongboxes, jewelry, coins, documents, heaps of what Noss believed to be dusty, old iron ingots shaped like bricks — and several human skeletons trussed up with rope.[2]

With difficulty, Noss was able to make the arduous climb up out of the cavern, bringing a few samples up out of the narrow hole to show Ova. Doc and Ova could scarcely believe their good fortune. The couple would build a small shack at the foot of the hillside, with Doc making several descents into Victorio Peak to recover gold and silver coins, jewelry, and some of the more unusual artifacts found stacked inside the treasure room.

One evening, doc mentioned the strange piles of "pig iron" ingots he had seen in and around the deeply hidden treasure room. "There must have been a real market for pig iron back in them days," Doc said.[3]

Ova asked her husband to bring out a bar. "No," said Doc, "too heavy." But Ova insisted, wanting to see one of these mysterious 'iron" bars for herself. On the next trip down, Doc managed to find one bar that was smaller and lighter than the others, although the effort to bring even that smaller bar to the surface was excruciating.

"Here," said Doc, dumping the heavy bar on the hillside. "That's the last one of them babies I'll be bringing out."[4]

The bar proved too heavy for Ova to lift. Borrowing Doc's hunting knife, she managed to roll the dirt-encrusted bar over. The sun glinted off a spot on the bar where it had struck some loose gravel. Ova spotted a yellow gleam through the grime.

"Doc," asked Ova, "How many of these bars did you say was down there?"

"Oh, piles," Doc replied. "They're stacked up like cordwood down there."

"Well, Doc," said Mrs. Noss, "This bar is yellow. I think it's gold."[5]

Doc picked up the ingot and stared. *"Well Babe, if this is gold, and all that other down there is gold, then we can call Rockefeller a tramp."*

Thus, the legend of Victorio Peak was born. Most of a century later, treasure hunters are still trying to get at any gold that might still remain buried under tons of rubble. There's just one big catch . . . since the 1950s, Victorio Peak has sat within the highly restricted White Sands Missile Range.

For nearly two years after their incredible find, Doc and Ova Noss labored to take more heavy bars from the depths of Victorio Peak. According to David Leon Chandler, author of the 1978 book 100 Tons of Gold, the couple extracted at least 88 bars weighing some 40 or more pounds each. Some of these Doc Noss sold on the black market. But most bars Doc reburied at various locations in the desert. The more gold he brought out, the more paranoid Doc became. [6]

As per David Leon Chandler, a friend of Doc Noss from Gallup, New Mexico, attorney Melvin Reuckhaus, witnessed Noss trying to sell a bar of gold to a local pawn shop owner named Jack Levick. In a letter, Reuckhaus recalled how *"Levick was reluctant to deal with Doc, and Doc gave him my name as a reference. Levick called me, and I was curious enough to go down to the pawn shop and witness the transaction. Levick's gold license as a pawnbroker allowed him only to purchase a limited amount, so I suggested Levick buy a small piece. Doc took a hunting knife out of his pocket and cut a slice off the bar. Levick used a karat tester and said that it was almost pure gold, something in the neighborhood of 23 karats."* [7]

Another Noss associate, B.D. Lampros, in a 1952 affidavit submitted to the Secretary of Defense, stated that *"I worked with Doc Noss to carry gold out of the mine. In 1939 I took one bullion bar to Douglas, Arizona and had Holly and Holly assayers test it, and it assayed to run over $5,000 gold per ton. . . . The bar was a regular Wells Fargo gold bar. I saw quite a few other bars of the same type."* [8]

Local teens Benny Samaniego and Jose Serafin Sedillo also attested to having entered Doc's cave and seeing the gold. Noss used the boys as laborers, and threatened them with harm if they ever tried to take any of the gold for themselves. Since Doc was always armed and was an excellent marksman, the boys took his threat seriously.

Then we have one-time cowboy and rodeo rider, Tony Jolley, a friend of Doc Noss during the 1940s. Jolley has stated, in an on-camera interview, that he helped Noss move and rebury 110 gold bars in the desert surrounding Victorio Peak.[9] How did Jolley know the bars were real? Some years after Doc's passing, Jolley obtained a metal detector and was able to revisit one of the burial sites and recover 10 of those gold bars. Jolley had the bars assayed, and sold them quietly for quite a bit of money.

According to Ova Noss, her husband brought five bars to the Denver Mint in 1938 and had them drill holes to assay the bars. The ingots allegedly assayed at 60% gold. Records from the Denver Mint for that period, unfortunately, have reportedly been lost.

However, according to Bill Yenne, author of Lost Treasure, A Guide to Buried Riches, Denver Mint records did show that in 1939 a man named Charles Usher from Santa Monica, California brought in a gold bar that he had obtained secondhand from a man he described as "*Doc Noss from New Mexico.*"[10]

Then there are the swords, antique jewelry, silver cups, and other exotic artifacts in possession of the Noss family. Much circumstantial evidence and eyewitness testimony points to the conclusion that Milton "Doc" Noss stumbled upon a remarkable treasure in 1930s New Mexico. [11]

The big problem for Doc and Ova Noss, however, was the same problem Theodore Jones and Henry Grob encountered just a few years earlier in Baltimore. Ownership of gold, especially in the bullion form, was against the laws of the United States, and subject to confiscation, fines, and penalties. Doc was having trouble both getting the gold out of the deeply buried and largely inaccessible treasure vault, and then selling it at his own risk on the black market — chiefly across the border in Mexico.

By 1939, Doc Noss has decided to settle at least one of his twin problems, that of reasonable access to the dangerously hidden treasure. Hiring a mining engineer, Noss and his contractor concocted a plan for using dynamite to widen the narrow entrance and vertical shaft that had made extraction so difficult. Noss and the consultant argued, however, concerning the size of the explosive charge needed to do the job. For a big entrance, the engineer said much dynamite would be needed. Noss, who had experienced the shaft, cavern, and tunnels first-hand, warned that the peak's interior was too unstable for such a large charge.

Doc would be proven correct. The resultant blast would cause a massive cave-in, sealing the treasure under tons and tons of rocks and dirt.[12] Now cut off from his source of funding, Doc Noss found himself back at square one. Digging down through the peak's blocked passageways would require an exhaustive, large-scale operation. Noss now needed lots of heavy-duty equipment, manpower, expertise, and money. For the next two years, Noss would sell his plan to interested investors and his local New Mexico business contacts. Part of Doc's pitch would involve showing a fake gold-colored bar made from brass and other non-precious metals.

In 1941, Doc formed the Cheyenne Mining company along with Ova, several friends, and investors.[13] A cadre of speculators from Texas reportedly offered Doc and his Cheyenne Mining Company a six-figure buyout on the Victorio Peak claim, but Doc and his crew refused the offer. In early December, 1941 Doc laid out his plan for getting back down to the gold. Later that same week, Japanese planes attacked Pearl Harbor.

War was on — and Doc's plans for the gold would have to be put on indefinite hold.

The war years proved stressful for Doc and Babe Noss. Without access to more gold, unable to legally sell the gold ingots Doc had reburied in the desert, and having spent much money on building a road to the peak and other structural improvements to their claim, the couple's finances were growing desperate.

The year 1945 brought hope that the war would soon be over. Nazi Germany had surrendered, and American forces were rapidly island-hopping across the Pacific towards the Empire of Japan. Then, on July 16, the United States detonated the world's first nuclear weapon, code-named Trinity. The horrendous blast and resulting mushroom cloud devastated the Alamogordo Bombing Range in New Mexico, and reverberated throughout the entire Jornada del Muerto Desert. Victorio Peak, the site of Doc Noss' discovery, is located on the eastern boundary of the Jornada del Muerto (Route of the Dead Man).

With Operation Paperclip now underway, the United States would import Wernher von Braun and many other former Nazi rocket scientists to continue their work in the New Mexican desert.[14] The military had its eye on more land for tests, and the remote Hembrillo Basin — including Victorio Peak — sat squarely in their sights. The Army was now asking for "exclusive use of the land for military purposes."

Meanwhile, Doc and Ova Noss divorced, with Doc remarrying — further complicating their New Mexican mining claim on Victorio Peak. By 1949, however, Doc Noss was ready to reclaim the treasure. Doc convinced Texas oil man Charley Ryan to invest $25,000 towards heavy equipment in exchange for some of Doc's remaining hidden gold bars.[15] Noss and Ryan argued over the proper disposition of the gold. Noss wanted to continue moving bars on the black market, while Ryan wanted to try the legitimate route and approach U.S. authorities. Then, when Ova staked her own separate claim to the treasure, Doc feared Ryan might back out altogether. Doc secretly arranged to hire a pilot and his Piper Cub airplane to move his gold bars down to Mexico. Tragedy struck when the plane crashed on approach to Hembrillo Basin.[16] Now worried that a crash investigation might interfere with his removal of gold bars from the desert surrounding Victorio Peak, Noss tapped his friend, rodeo rider Tony Jolley, to help dig up and rebury the bars before FAA accident investigators could arrive the following morning.

Meanwhile, when oil man Charley Ryan received word that Noss was in the desert reburying the gold, he immediately suspected a double-cross. The following day, when Noss went to meet with Ryan, he was confronted by the oil man, who accused Doc of being a confidence man. A heated argument ensued, which then turned physical. Suddenly, Noss ran outside, heading for his pickup truck where he had stashed a loaded weapon.

Noss never got there in time. Ryan quick grabbed his gun, followed, and shot first. When it was over, Doc Noss lay dead, slumped against the front bumper of his vehicle.[17]

Charley Ryan would later be acquitted on the grounds of self-defense.

With Doc gone, Ova Noss pushed forward in trying to work her claim, and hired workers to begin removing tons of rubble from the shaft's entrance. But by 1955, the Army had secured full possession of the Hembrillo Basin, now officially part of the White Sands Missile Range. Army brass steadfastly refused Ova's repeated requests to mine on Victorio Peak, treasure trove or no treasure trove. While the State of New Mexico recognized the Noss claim, arguing that the military had only been granted surface rights to the area, the Army countered by saying that Public Land Order 703 withdrew all "*prospecting, entry, location, and purchase*" under the existing mining laws.[18]

Ova Noss would no longer be allowed on Victorio Peak.

In 1958, dramatic new developments came to Victorio Peak. An Air Force jet pilot named Leonard Fiege, from the nearby Holloman Air Force Base, decided to explore Victorio Peak with fellow airman Thomas Berchett. Fiege allegedly discovered a narrow backdoor passageway that led down to the treasure chamber, where he too spotted the mounds of metal bars stacked up "like cordwood" and partially covered by fallen debris.[19]

Fiege decided to leave all the gold bars, concerned that any unofficial removal of the treasure could jeopardize his claim. He and Berchett spent time closing up the hole that had led them down to the cache. Years later, Fiege would state, on camera, that he had actually put his hands on the gold ingots. "*It wasn't fantasy,*" explained Captain Fiege, "*it was real.*"[20]

Fiege tried to go up the chain of command through the Air Force. Meanwhile, Fiege and Berchett formed a corporation and made formal application, through the Air Force, to perform a search and retrieval of the gold. It would take three years of military red tape before Fiege and Berchett would get their chance.

On August 5, 1961 Major General John Shinkle at White Sands, with the approval of the U.S. Mint, allowed Fiege, several military officers, a Secret Service agent, and more than a dozen military police to try to locate the gold.[21] However, this time Fiege was unable to penetrate the opening he had used in 1958. The general ordered a halt to the operation.

The military ordered Captain Fiege to take a lie detector test. Fiege passed.[22]

Soon, rumors began circulating in Southern New Mexico that the Army had commenced a large-scale mining operation at Victorio Peak. At some point Captain Fiege (as well as others) surreptitiously re-entered White Sands and found his former back entrance to the treasure filled in and blocked by a steel gate.[23]

In late 1961, Ova Noss filed a complaint with the state land office that the Army had been illegally mining her claim. The Army denied the accusation — until some of Ova's friends set up a clandestine watch and got names and license plate numbers of military personnel involved in the secret project. The Noss associates filed affidavits as to what they had witnessed. Not long after, the Army's people and heavy equipment were removed from Victorio Peak.[24]

Later, this August 10, 1961 memo would be discovered in the Secret Service's files: *"This operation has been carried as a Top Secret project; and the only persons at White Sands Missile Range who know the nature of the mission are [names censored]."*[25]

The Army would belatedly admit that the Secretary of the Army had given his approval for White Sands Missile Range to mine the peak.

By 1963, a compromise was reached with the Army that would allow the Museum of New Mexico and Gaddis Mining of Denver, Colorado (under contract with The Denver Mint) to explore Victorio Peak.[26] It would be revealed years later that Ova Noss had been closely working with Gaddis management.

After a few months of exploration, at a cost of $100,000 to Gaddis Mining (in exchange for 35% of any treasure found), some 218 feet of drilling produced only pottery shards and some ancient Indian arrowheads. When the Gaddis/New Mexico Museum permit expired, the group would ask for a 90-day extension, claiming that an additional 250 feet of drilling would be required to complete the search.

According to the Museum of New Mexico Report, March 11, 1965, "*The results of the exploration program conducted in 1963 proved the existence of a number of open caves within Victoria Peak, similar to those described by the individual who claimed to have been in the caves and seen the artifacts and treasure.*"[27]

The Army refused any extension, although the New Mexico Museum and Gaddis Mining would persist for years in trying to regain entry at Victorio Peak. Meanwhile, throughout the remainder of the 1960s, continuous rumors would circulate that high military and governmental officials were behind the ongoing removal of gold from the site, with gold being whisked away to Fort Knox, Zurich, and other places unknown.

In the 1970s, the Victorio Peak story heated up once again thanks to the efforts of famed attorney F. Lee Bailey. Bailey had agreed to represent a consortium of treasure hunters interested in yet another crack at Doc Noss' treasure.[28] Bailey, who had in his possession a sample from a Doc Noss ingot that assayed at over 60% gold, decided to circumvent the U.S. Army entirely by using his influence at the White House. Bailey phoned U.S. Attorney General John Mitchell, who agreed to set up a meeting between Bailey, his clients, and White House Chief Domestic Advisor for President Nixon, John Erlichman.

Mitchell would later relate this request to Nixon's chief counsel, John Dean III, whose testimony about the incident would later become part of the Congressional record during the contentious Watergate hearings. On June 25, 1973, Dean would testify, on national television, that "*John Mitchell told me that F. Lee Bailey had a client who had an enormous amount of gold in his possession and would like to make an arrangement with the government whereby the gold could be turned over to the government without being prosecuted for holding the gold.*"[29]

By 1975, Bailey would publicly accuse the Army of engaging in renewed mining on Victorio Peak.

Meanwhile, one of Bailey's clients, Fred Drolte of Dallas, reportedly was able to find his way down to the gold. Drolte had contracted with New Mexico treasure hunter Joe Newman, who was supposed to have access to Victorio Peak by way of a hidden arroyo that allowed Newman to take a jeep part of the way onto the base, while hiking the remainder of his clandestine, back-door route.

According to David Leon Chandler, author of <u>100 Tons of Gold</u>, Newman said that he and partner Kevin Henry, *"Found no skeletons, no river, nor anything that Noss described as seeing in the big cave. I think we either hit the place where Fiege went in or we found a brand-new place. We found some bars."*[30]

Newman gave one of the bars to Drolte as evidence. Newman and his people were nervous about bringing out the gold, because some of them had been caught at Hembrillo Basin previously and had been threatened with federal prosecution in the event they would be caught a second time. But Drolte calmed Newman's fears by promising that *"if we got caught by the ranger riders I was to ask for a certain colonel and use Fred Drolte's name. Then we'd be released with no questions."*[31]

Drolte, a one-armed former pilot who was once convicted of conspiracy to smuggle hundreds of Army carbines to revolutionaries in Mexico, had concocted a grand scheme to haul gold bars from the peak using a helicopter equipped with a net.

Drolte took the bar, sliced off a sample, and presented it to F. Lee Bailey, who in turn gave the evidence to New Mexico's governor.[32]

Later, though Newman and Drolte were supposed to be partners in the recovery of Doc Noss' gold, Newman went to see Drolte on his mining claim in the nearby Caballo Mountains. Drolte, who was surrounded by armed guards, nervously said to Newman, *"Joe, I haven't been up to Vicky Peak. Don't ask me about Vicky Peak."*[33]

Newman would quickly surmise that Drolte had somehow double-crossed him on their deal. *"I think maybe Drolte has worked a deal with the Army to sneak in there and carry something out."*[34]

A later discovered Department of the Army memo from July 26, 1974 would go a long way in corroborating Newman's suspicions. Wrote Marvin Lasser, director of Army research, *"Earlier this week a group was allowed to go into the area for forty-eight hours. They came out with a gold bar. Harold [Dr. Harold Agnew at the Atomic Energy Commission laboratory] has the bar and is analyzing it for age and content. . . . Harold said that because of all the problems with this governor of New Mexico, and other groups, that someone should be looking after the Army's interest."*[35]

Pressure from Bailey, the governor of New Mexico, and other political sources would eventually lead to the Army relenting to yet another highly publicized search of the hillside at Hembrillo Basin. The year was 1977, and the effort would come to be dubbed "Operation Goldfinder."[36] Operation Goldfinder proved to be more of a media circus than a legitimate hunt for the famous treasure of Victorio Peak.

Participants in the search included famed treasure hunter Norman Scott of Expeditions Unlimited, Joe Newman, Captain Fiege's group, Tony Jolley, Harold Beckwith (Doc Noss' stepson), Violet Noss Yancey (Noss' second wife), and, last but not least, 81-year old Ova "Babe" Noss. The event was covered by a bevy of news reporters, and featured on a segment of television's *60 Minutes* with Dan Rather.

Interestingly, Fred Drolte, who had earlier been so keen on getting a chance to penetrate the hillside, now declined an offer to participate in operation Goldfinder. He purportedly told Joe Newman and others that he had *"no interest in the expedition."*[37]

Try as they could, the searchers could not find another entranceway down to the treasure room hundreds of feet below surface. And given the two-week time limit, efforts to dig out the known caved-in passageways proved futile.

"No gold has been found," dryly announced an Army spokesperson to the assembled news media at the conclusion of Operation Goldfinder. *"The Army has always maintained there is no gold at White Sands Missile Range — but no doubt the legend will live on. . . . This area is now closed to further search!"*[38]

Ground penetrating radar surveys conducted by the Stanford Research Institute had once again verified the Noss claim of a huge cavern and a shaft sealed by a cave-in. *"Further exploration of the peak should be undertaken,"* observed Stanford's technicians.[39]

When asked for her comment on the disappointing results of Operation Goldfinder, Ova Noss offered a simple explanation. *"The goddamn Army has stole the gold!"*[40]

Leonard Fiege and others concurred. The gold had been stolen. Kevin Henry, who had allegedly helped Joe Newman to bring gold out of the mountain, claimed that the blasting the Army had done in the interim had *"changed everything."* Newman himself had previously presented New Mexico authorities with evidence of Army digging on the peak. The Army, of course, denied all charges . . . but the Army's own photographs, published in a December 18, 1975 *Rolling Stone* magazine article "*A Hundred Tons of Gold*" clearly showed the presence of bulldozers, trucks, and heavy equipment at Victorio Peak.[41]

In 1979, Ova Noss died without ever seeing another gold bar come out of her claim.

During the 1980s, Terry Delonas, grandson of Ova Noss, created the "Ova Noss Family Partnership," an organization dedicated to getting to the bottom of Victorio Peak to once-and-for-all solve the riddle of Doc Noss' fabled treasure. But the Army denied access to Delonas, same as they had done to his grandmother and several other interested fortune seekers. Finally, in 1989, the U.S. Congress passed a special act, granting Delonas and the Noss heirs access to Victorio Peak — so long as they cooperated with the military by not interfering in the missile tests.[42] The Ova Noss Family Partnership has failed to find anything of significance since their return to Victorio Peak.

According to writer Kathy Weiser on the "Legends of America" web site, many friends and members of the Noss family believe that the military exploited Babe Noss' claim, and that the treasure is gone. However, Terry Delonas is on record stating that, "*We are not accusing the military of stealing the gold, but I do feel the Department of the Army in the 1960s treated my grandmother unfairly. . . . However, we've worked hard over the years to establish a working relationship with the military, and we're certainly not going to jeopardize that by accusing them of theft.*"[43]

However, the working relationship between the Army and Delonas' "Ova Noss Family Partnership" eventually broke down. On March 15, 1996, the military evicted the Noss group from White Sands Missile Range.[44] he reason given for the eviction was that the treasure hunters had stopped paying into an escrow account to cover expenses incurred by the military. The partnership countered that the Army had never itemized its expenses, and sued the Army in federal court. Meanwhile, many thousands of dollars in equipment wound up being abandoned on Victorio Peak.

Of course, the million (or perhaps billion) dollar question has always been, who stashed a king's ransom in gold bars and other valuable artifacts in tunnels connected to a huge natural cavern at the bottom of a mine shaft deep inside a desolate New Mexico hillside?

The most popular candidate seems to be Padre LaRue, a late 18th-century missionary priest from France who, according to legend, was told by an old Spanish soldier of a great vein of gold in the San Andres Mountains. LaRue traveled north from Mexico, confirmed the existence of the rich deposit, then led his Mexican parishioners north to build a new village and mine the gold. When word of this find got back to the Church, LaRue was ordered to turn over the gold, but instead buried the smelted bars. LaRue and his helpers would later be tortured, but supposedly did not give up the location of their underground vault.[45]

A similar story involves Don Juan de Onate, who founded New Mexico as a colony of Spain in 1598. Onate, obsessed with finding Cibola — the legendary Seven Cities of Gold — is described as a brutal man who forced local Native Indians to submit to near slave-like conditions in his ambitious quest for wealth. Allegedly, Onate amassed a fortune in precious metals and jewels, which he hid before being ordered to return to Mexico City.[46]

The problem with the LaRue and Onate stories is they don't explain the late 19th-century artifacts reportedly found at Victorio Peak. The Wells Fargo chests are simply from a much later time period than Onate or even LaRue. And Doc Noss specifically mentioned boxes of documents which contained dates up until 1880 — again, wholly inconsistent with a treasure buried by either LaRue in 1800 or Onate in 1600. Unfortunately, Noss burned these documents in the presence of Ova Noss, saying he was concerned that descendants of people mentioned in the documents might step forward to claim the treasure.[47]

A better match from a time perspective would be the lost treasure of Emperor Maximilian of Mexico. An Austrian archduke appointed as Emperor of Mexico by Napoleon III of France in 1864, Maximilian and his young, spendthrift wife proved most incapable of ruling a country about which they knew frightfully little. By 1866, with the American Civil War now over, the United States made it clear that they would no longer tolerate French soldiers in Mexico. Entirely unpopular with his Mexican subjects, Maximilian realized that his days as "puppet" emperor under Napoleon III were rapidly growing short.

In an attempt to smuggle a large treasure out of Mexico, Maximilian hatched a scheme to disguise several wagonloads of gold, silver, and other valuables as a shipment of flour headed for Texas. Guarded by his Austrian henchmen, the wagonloads of Maximilian's treasure were supposed to be transferred onto a ship at a Texas port, destined for Europe.[48] Problem was, the wagons had to make it through miles of Apache and Comanche country before arriving at a Gulf of Mexico port. During transport, the Austrians encountered a band of ex-Confederates from Missouri, headed into Mexico, who told of Indians and assorted bandits on the trail ahead. The Austrians hired the Confederates as extra guns, and proceeded into Texas. Unfortunately for the Austrians, the wily Confederates soon realized that this most unusual wagon train contained something far more valuable than flour. Upon opening one of the barrels of "flour" late at night, the Confederates confirmed their suspicion of royal treasure. The Missourians massacred the Austrians and their Mexican helpers as they slept, and took possession of their wagons. But with there being more wagons than Confederates, the murderers soon realized they needed to bury the bulk of the treasure and burn the wagons. With this deed done, the men filled their saddle bags with gold and silver coins. They would come back later for the main treasure. But when one of the conspirators fell ill, and asked his companions to ride on without him, suspicion arose that this man had plans to circle back and remove more treasure. So, the others shot their ailing associate and left him for dead.

Soon after, the remaining Confederates were ambushed and killed by Comanches, who stole their horses and treasure-filled saddle bags. Later, the badly wounded Confederate who had been left behind survived just long enough to make it back to civilization and tell his story. Searchers found the slain Confederates where the Comanches had surprised them . . . but not the buried treasure.[49]

Maximilian's lost treasure is believed to be buried near the Pecos River, some 30-plus miles south of Odessa, TX.[50] Although the time period and supposed contents of this famous cache are somewhat consistent with Doc Noss' 1937 discovery, it is hard to see how the treasure would have ever gotten from West Texas up to the badlands of Southern New Mexico. The slain Confederate bandits had neither the time nor the manpower to get several wagonloads of treasure into the desolate San Andres . . . and down into the caverns below Victorio Peak.

A more probable theory regarding the treasure of Victorio Peak involves the Mescalero Apaches' feared leader, Chief Victorio, for whom the remote peak is named. Victorio and his warriors used the Jornada del Muerto as a base of operations against encroaching settlers, the United States Army, and the Mexican Army. The Apache raiders were fond of hit-and-run tactics, and often targeted stagecoaches for quick plunder. It is said that Chief Victorio stored his stolen loot in the bowels of Victorio Peak.[51] And since Chief Victorio was killed in 1880 by the Mexican Army — after having been chased across the border by United States troops — the chief's date of death coincides with the dates Doc Noss saw on letters and documents he took from the cave. These dates were all *prior* to 1880.

Some have even speculated that Victorio may have found the LaRue or Onate treasure, and then added his ill-gotten late-19th century spoils to the pre-existing treasure.[52] This scenario, however, stretches the bounds of credulity. And it seems improbable that any bandit, even one as skilled and fearless as Chief Victorio, could have amassed such a collection of gold bars, coins, jewelry, and valuable artifacts by simply preying upon the odd group of settlers or passing stagecoach.

The sheer size of the Victorio Peak treasure points to a large, clandestine organization — or perhaps even an embattled government.

During Dan Rather's *60 Minutes* piece on Operation Goldfinder,[53] a few seconds of footage was devoted to a man named Jesse James III. James, a.k.a. Jesse Lee James, real name Orvis Lee Howk, is the purported grandson of the outlaw Jesse James . . . and he traveled to Victorio Peak in 1977 to participate in the two-week frenzy in the desert. James' claim? That his grandfather, as a member of the Knights of the Golden Circle, helped to bury the gold at Victorio Peak "*against the day when the South would rise again.*"[54]

Jesse James, according to the historical record, was killed in 1882. Jesse James was, according to multiple sources, a suspected high-ranking member in the KGC. Jesse's participation in the KGC-influenced Quantrill's Raiders is a matter of historical fact. And it is unlikely that James' multi-decade post-Civil War crime spree could have been pulled off without the support of well-placed friends in positions of power: Scottish Rite Freemasons such as Albert Pike, Caleb Cushing, and John C. Breckinridge who had vehemently supported the South and had opposed the abolition of slavery.

Why New Mexico? It was near the KGC stronghold of Texas . . . but not in Texas. It was desolate. It was on the frontier, somewhat out of the reach and prying eyes of the U.S. federal government. Only two Civil War battles had been fought on New Mexican soil. And it was the scene of regular legitimate mining activity.

According to Warren Getler and Bob Brewer in Rebel Gold, KGC depositories were often disguised as mine sites.[55] But instead of ore coming out, treasure went in. Then the site was closed and sealed, making it appear "abandoned." Just an old mining shaft and some covered up, played out hole in the ground.

But curiously, despite the presence of an old mining shaft at Victorio Peak, no slag or mine tailings were ever found. A mining shaft built into a hillside that had never been mined? This is why some observers have always felt that the treasure at Victorio Peak came from somewhere else. Those bars of gold were never mined, processed, and smelted on that property. There is simply no evidence of mining.

Albert Pike was very familiar with New Mexico. Pike had lived in New Mexico before settling permanently in Arkansas. Pike worked in the western outdoors as a trapper. Once, when his horse got spooked and ran off, Pike had to walk 500 miles through the wilderness — to get to Taos, New Mexico.[56]

Victorio Peak fits all of the characteristics of a KGC depository. Gold bars, gold coins, and silver coins buried inside a remote location at the bottom of a sealed, fake mine site.

Whatever happened to the gold bars from the Virginia banks and the Confederate Treasury? Were the raiders who swooped down on the wagon train in Chennault, Georgia really KGC operatives? Was the daring midnight heist staged in such a way as to throw Union authorities off the scent? If so, the piles of gold coins spilled in the roadway were certainly a nice added touch.

And what about the 39 kegs of Mexican silver coins that were too heavy to make the trip south? Are they still buried somewhere near Danville, Virginia? Or did Confederate special agent George Kane, who acted as sentry for the 9,000 pounds of Mexican silver throughout the late 1860s, hand over the silver treasure to the

KGC before heading home to Baltimore in 1869-70 to resume his career as a Baltimore public servant?

Did those Confederate gold bars, gold coins, 39 kegs of Mexican silver dollars, and other assorted valuable artifacts wind up at the bottom of Victorio Peak to fund a possible new war against the North . . . a war that never came about?

Did the not-quite-dead Jesse James, along with fellow rebel conspirator "Sheriff" James Timberlake, travel to New Mexico in 1882 to deposit the James/Younger Gang's treasure in an underground KGC depository? Was Orvis Lee Howk, a.k.a. Jesse James III, correct when he said in 1977 that his grandfather had buried the treasure against the day when "*the South would rise again?*" Or, was Jesse James really killed in 1882, and did James Timberlake actually, coincidentally travel to New Mexico from Missouri that very same year to help his brother in the ranching business?

Doc Noss would not have been afraid that descendants of Spanish conquistadors, French priests, Mexican peasants, or long-gone Native Americans might file in U.S. courts to reclaim the treasure he had discovered at Victorio Peak. But Southern treasure buried by late-19th century Americans and accompanied by late 19th-century documents written in English would have posed an obvious problem. That would be especially so if the treasure had been buried by the likes of Jesse James and the Knights of the Golden Circle.

We will probably never know the true story of what Doc Noss discovered in 1937 hidden away hundreds of feet below that hillside. But the known facts suggest that a KGC/Confederate depository would have to be considered as one of the leading explanations for a colossal treasure that, for most of a century, has long fascinated the imagination.

Baltimore 2016

The lone remaining row house on today's 100 block of S. Eden St.

When, during the 1934-1935 legal battle over the coins, one elderly Saulsbury daughter returned to Eden Street after more than half a century's absence, she was taken aback by the decrepit state of her idyllic childhood neighborhood. *"It has been greatly changed,"*[1] she remarked, observing the burgeoning slum that was now home to the immigrant Grob and Jones (actual name Sines) families. *"The census taker . . . ,"* notes Len Augsburger in <u>Treasure in the Cellar</u>, *"in 1930 would have needed fluency in Russian, Yiddish, Polish, German, and Italian in order to easily converse with everyone he interviewed."*[2]

This had been the great fear of the mid-nineteenth century American Party, better known as the anti-immigrant Know-Nothings. They had foreseen the very fiber of American culture being torn asunder by waves of unwashed European immigrants coming to these shores and bringing with them disease, ignorance, an unfamiliar mother tongue, and a dangerous allegiance to foreign powers.[3]

During the 1800s, Baltimore had advanced to become America's second most populous metropolis (1830-1860), ranked only behind New York City. A tremendous amount of business and industrial wealth was created in yesteryear Baltimore, a fact attested to by the city's rich historical architecture. Blessed with a mild climate, central East Coast location, and a world-class seaport, Baltimore was very much a "happening" place.

Baltimore's population reached its zenith just after World War II. The **1950** census showed a population of **949,708**, with Baltimore still being the sixth largest city in the United States. Its number of citizens had increased nonstop, every single decade, since the 1790 tally of 13,503.[4] The post-World War II economy was dominated by steel processing, shipping, auto manufacturing, and transportation. The 1950 demographics show a Baltimore that was approximately 75% white, and 23.8 percent black.

Since 1950, Baltimore has gone in reverse, losing population every single decade. As of **2010**, Baltimore's total citizenry was officially listed at just **620,961**. The city is estimated to be 63% or more black, and barely 29% white.[5] Racial change was hastened by the devastating street riots of 1968, which occurred when Baltimore was still not yet 50% black. Many cities across America were hit hard in the wake of the assassination of Dr. Martin Luther King. Baltimore, unfortunately, was hit harder than most. What had begun as slow but steady "white flight" to the suburbs switched to a mad dash by the end of the 1960s.[6] Author and radio/television commentator Ray Suarez chronicles this insidious process in his 1999 ground-breaking book The Old Neighborhood: What We Lost in the Great Suburban Migration, 1966-1999. My own two works of historical fiction, Row House Days and Row House Blues, give a personal account of growing up in a "changing" neighborhood in 1960s Philadelphia, just 90 miles to the north of Baltimore. To say those days did not make for a mellow scene would be an understatement of monumental proportion.

Today, the highly paid industrial jobs of post-war Baltimore have mostly been replaced by the low paying wages of a tourism and service economy. According to Robert Moore's 2004 article "*A Brief Economic History of Modern Baltimore,*"[7] some 90% of Baltimore jobs today are part of the so-called service economy. A quarter of Baltimoreans live in poverty, including more than a third of the children.

Wikipedia reports that as of July, 2013, Baltimore ranked as the 26th most populous city in the United States, behind such places as Austin, Columbus, El Paso, Memphis, and Nashville. Oklahoma City and Louisville will soon likely be surpassing Baltimore as well.

Baltimore in 2016 is the legacy of slavery. The roots of its decline trace back to the slave pens on Pratt Street, and to the comfortable people who not only justified the existence of those slave pens, but who sought to resume the African slave trade — as well as spread this sort of economic, legal, and spiritual tyranny across our entire hemisphere.

While Andrew J. Saulsbury and Captain John J. Mattison would have scarcely recognized the Eden Street of the Great Depression, Henry Grob and Theodore (Sines) Jones would have been even more out of their element on the 21st-century streets of Baltimore. As the Baltimore of the 1930s was everything the Know Nothings feared, today's Monumental City is the absolute worst nightmare of the Knights of the Golden Circle. One can only imagine what President Abraham Lincoln, signer of the Emancipation Proclamation, would have to say upon touring present-day Baltimore with its graffiti, collapsed buildings, vacant lots, and dangerous drug corners.

Baltimore's modern urban pathology has been uniquely portrayed by authors David Simon and Ed Burns in their gritty nonfiction book The Corner: A Year in the Life of an Inner-City Neighborhood.[8] Simon and Burns follow the life of a poverty-stricken Baltimore family struggling to survive amidst the open-air drug markets at the corner of West Fayette and North Monroe Streets. The wealthy aristocrats and industrialists of 19th-century Baltimore interred at nearby Green Mount Cemetery must be turning in their graves.

The success of The Corner was followed by an even bigger blockbuster, the gritty award-winning HBO crime series *The Wire*[9] — adapted for television by David Simon (a former police reporter) and David Mills. *The Wire* depicted the underbelly of the violent Baltimore drug trade, as embodied by the colorful but sociopathic characters Avon Barksdale, Stringer Bell, Calvin "Cheese" Wagstaff, Felicia "Snoop" Pearson, Marlo Stanfield, Brother Mouzone, Omar Little, and "White" Mike McArdle. The dysfunction, however, wasn't limited to just the street criminals, but rather extended to all facets of Baltimore society, including impoverished one-parent families, schools, the besieged police department, the docks, newsrooms, and even city council and the mayor's office. In *The Wire*, the destructive influence of illegal drugs reaches into and permeates every conceivable layer of city life. As creator Mr. Simons warned viewers, "*We are not selling hope, or audience gratification, or cheap victories with this show. The Wire is making an argument about what institutions — bureaucracies, criminal enterprises, the cultures of addiction, raw capitalism even — do to individuals. It is not designed purely as an entertainment. It is, I'm afraid, a somewhat angry show.*"[10]

For those not content to get their facts from Hollywood, a 1992 research study conducted by the Alexandria, Virginia-based National Center on Institutions and Alternatives (NCIA) showed that an astounding 56% of African-American males in Baltimore between the ages of 18-35 were in prison, on parole or probation, were being sought on arrest warrants, or were awaiting trial on any given day in 1991.[11]

According to a September 1, 1992 column by Norris P. West in *The Baltimore Sun*, then Mayor Kurt L. Schmoke said he was surprised when he learned that more young blacks were under criminal justice supervision in Baltimore than in Washington. Schmoke said his own staff confirmed the 56% figure with its own follow-up study.

"*The report, in my opinion,*" stated Mayor Schmoke, "*describes not just a local problem but a national tragedy.*"[12]

No society can long survive, let alone grow and thrive, when 56% of its young men are flooding the criminal justice system. There will simply never be enough funds to build that many prisons. Some other solution is sorely needed.

The director and co-founder of NCIA, Herbert J. Hoelter, was quoted by *The Baltimore Sun* as saying, "*We couldn't believe the numbers in Baltimore. I sent our people back a second and a third time, and they came back the same.*"[13]

For an up-to-date assessment of the situation in the Charm City, we have the recently released (December, 2014) "WAVE" study conducted by the Johns Hopkins Department of Population, Family, and Reproductive Health. "WAVE" stands for *"well-being of adolescents in vulnerable environments."* Dr. Kristen Mmari, who headed up the study, had 2,400 teenagers surveyed from poor communities in Baltimore, Ibadan (Nigeria), Johannesburg, New Delhi, and Shanghai. Participants were asked to answer questions about health issues relating to the environment in their communities. In something of a surprise, Dr. Mmari found that the kids from impoverished neighborhoods in the richest two countries (the U.S. and South Africa) expressed much more negativity about their surroundings. One young Baltimorean described *"big rats going around in people's trash, vacant houses full of squatters, and needles on the ground."*[14]

Dr. Mmari noted that, *"How kids perceive their environments is really important. That's what is driving many of these behaviors."*[15] In Baltimore, the "behaviors" to which Dr. Mmari refers include substance abuse, mental health issues, sexual violence, sexual risk-taking, and teen pregnancy. Although Baltimore is located in the richest country per-capita on the planet, and only 40 miles from the U.S. capital, the exposure to pervasive violence and a lack of social support contributes to such a bleak outcome for young Baltimoreans.

In an interview with columnist Elizabeth Kulze, Dr. Mmari stated that kids in both Baltimore and Johannesburg are fearful. *"They don't feel safe from violence. This is something we didn't really see in other cities. In Shanghai, for example, there wasn't a great deal of violence. You'd ask kids about their safety concerns, and they would say something like, 'I'm afraid of crossing a busy street.'"*[16]

In today's Baltimore, busy city streets are low on the list of concerns for inner-city youth. These are children growing up in an environment that sees itself as set apart from the rest of America. They have become alien strangers in a strange land, immersed in what University of Pennsylvania sociologist Elijah Anderson calls the *"oppositional culture."*[17] It is a place, a state of mind, where the abnormal becomes the norm.

Says Anderson in his 1994 article *"Code of the Streets"* from *The Atlantic, "Of all the problems besetting the poor inner-city black community, none is more pressing than that of interpersonal violence and aggression. It wreaks havoc daily with the lives of community residents and increasingly spills over into downtown and residential middle-class areas. Muggings, burglaries, carjackings, and drug-related shootings, all of which may leave their victims or innocent bystanders dead, are now common enough to concern all urban and many suburban residents. The inclination to violence springs from the circumstances of life among the ghetto poor — the lack of jobs that pay a living wage, the stigma of race, the fallout from rampant drug use and drug trafficking, and the resulting alienation and lack of hope for the future. Simply living in such an environment places young people at special risk of falling victim to aggressive behavior."[18]*

Baltimore, like many big cities, has attempted to counterbalance what's happened in its surrounding neighborhoods by pouring money into its downtown area, especially around its famed Inner Harbor. HarborPlace, The National Aquarium, The Power Plant entertainment complex, The Walters Art Museum, Fort McHenry, Oriole Park at Camden Yards, USS Constellation, Maryland Science Center, Baltimore's Museum of Industry, The Star Spangled Banner Flag House . . . but venture just a few blocks away from downtown and the harbor, and the scenery turns ominously bleak in a big hurry.

Straddled between Baltimore's downtown, the glittering harbor, and the desolate urban brownfields of the surrounding communities lies Washington Hill, the former neighborhood of Henry Grob and Theodore (Sines) Jones.[19] All of the brick row homes on the 100 block of S. Eden are now gone, except for one lone survivor. The southern end of the block, where the treasure house at 132 was located, is dominated by a foundry, American Alloy, which does custom metal casting. North of the lone row house lies a couple of empty lots and then a fenced-in parking lot at the corner. The landscape is decidedly mixed-use, with shuttered garages, parking lots, weeded lots, tired 19th-century row homes, public schools, industrial buildings, retail outlets, various small businesses, and a huge public housing project. Graffiti adorns many of the exposed brick and cinder-block walls. On the eastern side of Eden St. still sits City Spring Square, a city park since 1818, but long-since stripped of any hints of Victorian pretensions and elegance. Washington Hill is decidedly 21st-century "*inner city.*"

The gleaming office buildings and convention hotels, visible on the western horizon, offer a hope of creeping development and gentrification. If Baltimore can reverse its 65-year downslide, Washington Hill will almost certainly become one of the main beneficiaries. Baltimore has gone through so many cycles, and the next go-around may indeed bring with it a much-welcomed upswing.

The many ghosts of Pratt Street, however, still linger. The stovepipe hatted Plug Uglies, the 1861 rebel rioters, the would-be Lincoln assassins, the wealthy downtown secessionists, the anything-for-a-buck slave traders and slave auctioneers, the heartless slave pen owners and operators, the nameless black people in chains waiting to be "sold South," the ship's captains and crews taking aboard their downcast human cargoes destined for deep Southern ports. . . .

Baltimore, like so many American cities, desperately needing to break free from its past without simultaneously forgetting all the history that has happened. A metropolis that learns from its many mistakes, missteps, and excesses. A shinning, forward-looking Baltimore again on the rise, destined to repeat its 19th-century successes — but this time without the heavy 19th-century cultural baggage.

A Baltimore where everyone respects the civil rights of other Baltimoreans, and just as importantly — cherishes and lives up to their own civil responsibilities. Where everyone feels as if they are part of the U.S.A., and that all of us are in this together, and have a mutual stake in how things turn out. For this would be the unearthing of the real golden treasure of historic Baltimore, the pride of Maryland and the Monumental City of America.

Update:

As this book was about to be finalized, widespread violence broke out in Baltimore over the April 19th, 2015 death of one Freddie Gray. Gray died after suffering a critical spinal injury while having been placed in the back of a Baltimore City police van subsequent to his arrest. During the ride to a police station, Gray began screaming, and as a result was placed in additional restraints. Despite being given medical attention soon after it was realized that Gray had suffered a serious injury, the shackled suspect slipped into a coma from which he would not recover. Six of the police officers involved would be charged with crimes ranging from misdemeanor assault to "depraved-heart" murder.[20] Gray's demise ignited several days of ugly citywide protests punctuated by rioting, fire-setting, and looting.

Metro homicides since that April, 2015 day have climbed at a record pace. *The Economist* reported near the end of 2015 that the already high Baltimore homicide rate was up a staggering 78% since the riots.

None of the police officers charged were convicted. One proceeding was declared a mistrial, a second officer was found not guilty, and all charges against the remaining individuals were dropped.

It would seem, most unfortunately, that the much-awaited Renaissance of Baltimore City has been put on an ignominious and perhaps indefinite hold.

Conclusion

As a former news reporter, I don't like coincidences . . . and neither should you. Critics of this book will say that it is filled with circumstantial evidence, speculation, and of course, a string of "mere" coincidences. To a certain extent, this is correct. It is impossible to go back in time to 1856 and place a camcorder in the cellar of the treasure house on Eden Street. Outside of some faded, yellowing documents retrieved from an archive or located through the Internet, hard evidence is extremely difficult to come by in a 160+-year old "cold" case.

But consider the large number of coincidences present in this case. Ponder the substantial amount of circumstantial evidence that has been gathered, piled up, and carefully analyzed. At what point do the coincidences and "circumstantial" facts begin to reach the magic threshold known as a "preponderance of evidence?"

I submit this threshold has been met and exceeded in Knights' Gold.

In 2010, I did not set out to write a book solving the mystery of who buried 5,000 or more gold coins beneath a 19th-century townhome not far from Baltimore's Inner harbor. Instead, I was embarking on an entirely altogether different project — a book for adolescent boys with the tentative title Treasure Kids. The concept was simple . . . 50 stories about *real* kids finding *real* treasure. Meteorites, dinosaur bones, bags of cash, lost jewelry, gold nuggets, ancient artifacts, arrowheads, a Civil War sword . . . those sorts of improbable discoveries that occasionally do occur. It's how I became both acquainted and mystified with the story of the "Treasure in the Cellar." Sure, the tale of Henry and Theodore finding the gold was compelling. But who buried such an incredible fortune, and why? That part really gnawed at me . . . who left behind all this treasure?

As author and numismatic expert Leonard Augsburger wrote in his 2008 book Treasure in the Cellar, the coins' burial "*made no sense*." Everything known about this case pointed to soap and candle executive Andrew J. Saulsbury as the individual responsible for hiding the golden fortune. Saulsbury had the necessary wealth, was in the habit of giving gold coins as presents, and he also died suddenly over one tragic weekend in that very same house. Problem was, Saulsbury hadn't moved around the corner to Eden Street until at least nine years after the coins had been buried.

And for the well-traveled Captain John J. Mattison? He owned and lived in the treasure house in 1856 when the coins were apparently buried. But what person would sell his house and move three blocks away while leaving a fortune in gold behind? That also made no sense.

Reading Treasure in the Cellar, I was every bit as stumped as Len Augsburger was. Yes, the 1856 date made no sense. I could think of no obvious explanation.

Then, about a year later, while channel surfing on my living room couch, I just happened to come across the show *Brad Meltzer's Decoded*. This particular episode followed the story of Arkansas treasure hunter Bob Brewer, who claimed to have found caches of gold coins buried during the 19th century by a subversive secret society known as the Knights of the Golden Circle. The Masonic-inspired "KGC" had been formed years before the Civil War to protect Southern rights and the "lawful" God-given institution of slavery. But the KGC also had a second purpose, a daring agenda known only to members of high standing — the invasion and overthrow of Central American and Caribbean countries for the purpose of turning those lands into additional Southern slave states. The formation of the Republic of Texas had shown how this could be done.

And, if the North tried to intervene and prevent these plans for expansion from becoming reality . . . and pushed to abolish slavery? Then, the South would secede.

For this purpose, the KGC collected gold coins from its membership in the form of dues and taxes, while burying substantial amounts of treasure and arms in anticipation of conquering and building a new country — a "Golden Circle" that would stretch over a vast swath of the Western Hemisphere.

After the war and the South's defeat, western elements of this conspiracy moved previously amassed treasure to the wild American frontier, largely out of the reach of Washington, D.C. They also added to those already substantial treasures by robbing Union banks, trains, and stagecoaches. Jesse James was reputedly a member of this group. During the era of Reconstruction, the KGC would lie in wait for the day "the South Would Rise Again."

And while the professed leader of the KGC had been an outspoken former newspaper editor named George Bickley, Brewer and his co-author of the book Rebel Gold, Ivy League educated writer Warren Getler, claimed that the Grand Sovereign Commander of the Southern Jurisdiction of Scottish Rite Freemasonry had been the real brains behind the KGC. That man's name? Former Confederate General Albert C. Pike.

This "Lost Confederate Gold" episode of *Brad Meltzer's Decoded* ended with Bob Brewer and the show's investigators traveling to Danville, Virginia to look for 39 kegs of Mexican silver dollars allegedly offloaded in Danville in April, 1865 after the Confederate government had fled their capital, Richmond.

Buried gold and silver coins? A secret, subversive Southern organization? A massive conspiracy pulled off by extremist Confederate sympathizers? Did that all really happen?

I immediately wondered whether there was a connection to those thousands of gold coins found beneath the treasure house in Baltimore. Retrieving my copy of Treasure in the Cellar, I reread the passages where it said how candle and soap executive Andrew J. Saulsbury had been an outspoken supporter of the Confederacy whose Eden Street home featured prominent portraits of Robert E. Lee and Stonewall Jackson. How the Saulsbury family had been harassed during the war by occupying Union soldiers. How Saulsbury was *"an ardent Southern sympathizer, that everyone knew,*" as his own daughter had testified during the hotly contested 1934-35 treasure trial.

Had Saulsbury been "ardent" enough to have been a member of the KGC? The anonymous author of the 1861 work <u>An Authentic Exposition of the Knights of the Golden Circle — A History of Secession From 1834-1861</u> had written that the KGC had recruited some 3,000 members in Maryland alone. KGC president George Bickley had ties to Baltimore, he had allegedly gone to school in Baltimore, and would eventually work, reside, and die in Baltimore. Was Saulsbury one of those invisible 3,000?

And what about Captain John J. Mattison? For the 1856 date on the burial of the coins to start making sense, Mattison would somehow have to be involved. There had to have been a conspiracy involving two or more people . . . Saulsbury, Mattison, and perhaps others. Mattison owned the house in 1856, but he left the coins in the ground in 1865 when he sold the property to Saulsbury. Both men had knowledge of the coins. Mattison was the original caretaker of the treasure, with Saulsbury taking over the job in 1865 — precisely at the conclusion of the war.

For my theory to be right, two things needed to happen. First, I needed to find some connection between Mattison and KGC activity. And second, I needed to find further evidence of a connection between Mattison and Saulsbury . . . otherwise, they were nothing more than the happenstance seller and buyer of the Eden Street treasure home.

Locating the first piece of evidence was easy. Using the Internet, I quickly found documents relating to the 1840 seizure of Mattison's brig, the *Eliza Davidson*, for participation in the illegal act of African slave trading. The British Navy presented substantial evidence showing that Mattison's brig had been specifically outfitted with numerous water casks for the purpose of transporting slaves to Cuba and Baltimore. Mattison was also shown to have connections with a notorious Cuban slave trader named Simon de Teran. And worse, Mattison's ship was seized with three African children aboard who testified that they had been sold into slavery and were about to be transported across the Atlantic. The children had no reason to lie.

Mattison's ship was thus forfeited, despite his position that the ship had been rented/leased to the Havana slave trader. The British court had demonstrated that Mattison's vessel had been an

American vessel flying under American colors. The children were, thankfully, emancipated and returned to their homeland.

The anonymous author of An Authentic Exposition of the Knights of the Golden Circle — A History of Secession From 1834-1861 specifically noted that during the late 1830s and into the early 1840s, his organization had attempted to send "*secret slavers*" to Africa for the purpose of trying to directly oppose the ban on African slave trading. This operation was temporarily halted, however, after multiple ships were seized and subjected to forfeiture. This organization considered this too heavy of a price to pay, and vowed to change tactics to obtain their objective through other means. Captain Mattison's brig appears to have been one of the organization's vessels seized and forfeited. Mattison's involvement in the illegal African slave trade directly ties him to the coins later buried under his house . . . and left under his house when he sold the property to Andrew Saulsbury in 1865. For this scenario to have been coincidental is extremely unlikely.

Furthermore, Mattison's business partner who had a partial ownership interest in Mattison's brig, the wharf owner James Corner, was a delegate to the Maryland Colonization Society. The MCS sought to send all former and freed American slaves back to Africa, purchasing land in West Africa for that purpose, and contracting with ship owners to transport freed slaves to Africa. Many African Americans, according to the MCS records, were put on ships for the return voyage. A basic tenet of the KGC's political ideology was that no black persons were to be allowed to remain free in the United States. Either they remained as slaves, or they were to be returned "home."

The president of the Maryland Colonization Society was Mr. John H. B. Latrobe, who also happened to be the Grand Master of the Maryland Freemasons after Charles Webb. Latrobe had publicly supported the plan to repatriate freed blacks back to Africa.

Alright, so we had connected sea captain Mattison to the illegal slave trade and very likely the precursor organization to the KGC, the Order of the Lone Star. But how was he connected to Saulsbury, besides having sold Saulsbury the treasure house in 1865?

This one was a bit more difficult, and required extra digging. Finally, however, I was able to locate a document listing the board of directors of the American Fire Insurance Company of Baltimore.

Conclusion

The insurance company had been founded around 1858 by James Armstrong, the original partner of James Armstrong & Company, maker of fine soaps and candles. Armstrong had been Saulsbury's employer for many years, and something of a benefactor to the young man. Armstrong's nephew, Thomas Armstrong, a partner in the soap and candle firm, was apparently a close friend to Saulsbury. And James Armstrong's successor as lead partner at the soap and candle firm was Charles Webb, whose company had previously merged with James Armstrong & Co. Charles' brother, James Webb, operated the company's satellite office on Ensor Street. James Webb would later act as the executor of Andrew Saulsbury's estate.

The board of directors of the American Fire Insurance Company of Baltimore featured the top three executives of James Armstrong & Company: James Armstrong, James Webb, and Charles Webb. Also listed as a director at AFICB was none other than John J. Mattison, our sea captain, secret slaver, and original owner of the Eden Street treasure home.

When Andrew Saulsbury bought the treasure home from Captain Mattison, the men were obviously anything but strangers. They had been nearby neighbors for years, and were both closely connected to the business empire of James Armstrong. A subsequent shipping document for one of Mattison's early voyages shows a large quantity of candles as part of his bark *Maria's* cargo (not the Eliza Davidson, as that vessel had already been seized as a "secret" slaver).

Understand that the Armstrongs and the Webbs were more than mere employers and co-workers to Saulsbury. This is evidenced by the fact that <u>every</u> James Armstrong & Co. executive had a Saulsbury male child named for them. Saulsbury's first-born son was James Armstrong Saulsbury. He named his second son after himself, Andrew J. Saulsbury. And his third and final son was Wilson *Webb* Saulsbury. And the first two Saulsbury grandsons? They were Charles Webb Saulsbury and Thomas Armstrong Saulsbury.

Now *that's* some loyalty and gratitude.

Yes, these men were more than mere co-workers. Even more than causal friends. They were joined-at-the-hip **blood brothers**. One can easily imagine that Captain John Mattison must have been "Uncle John" to the many Saulsbury children.

Realizing that Saulsbury's connection to Mattison was through the firm of James Armstrong & Co., I began to research Saulsbury's connections to the Armstrong executives. First was Thomas Armstrong, since Thomas and Andrew had worked there together the longest.

The sole hit seemed at first a disappointment . . . a voter survey from the contested 1859 Baltimore election. This was the election marred by violence, when many people stayed home out of fear for their safety. The City of Baltimore saw fit to survey each of the approximately 30,000 registered Baltimore voters to find out if they had been intimidated or assaulted at the polls, or had simply refused to attempt to vote because they were afraid. Listed immediately right next to each other in the city-wide survey (they were probably asked the survey questions together at work) were A.J. Saulsbury of 138 S. Central Ave. and Thomas Armstrong of The Fountain Hotel. I thought it curious that Armstrong listed his residence as a hotel. After consulting with a few people who were knowledgeable about 19th-century customs, I found that it was not unusual for a young, well-to-do bachelor to live at a hotel where he could have his bed made, his meals prepared, and also walk to work. This must have been a low-stress, carefree existence to be sure.

Still intrigued, I next did some research on the Fountain Hotel, and found it had been a center for rebel sympathizers from before the war. I was amazed to read about the details of the Yellow Fever Plot, possibly the country's first brush with bioterrorism, and how the operation had been run out of one of the hotel's rooms, where infected clothing had been prepared for shipment to Union cities and military installations . . . including to President Lincoln at the White House.

The really big surprise, however, came when I queried The Fountain Hotel + gold coins, and came across the story about the tin box of 2,000 gold coins having been discovered by a "*lucky laborer named Murray*" who had been excavating in the ruins of the old hotel.

Two men, two close friends, both longtime employees of the James Armstrong & Co., both with fortunes in gold coins buried under their respective residences? I looked at those two lines in the voter survey and wondered what the odds were of that? Fairly infinitesimal if you asked me — perhaps even more so than

Conclusion

Mattison's secret slaver past not being connected to the copper pot full of gold coins on Eden Street.

Looking next at James Webb, I could only find that he and Saulsbury had served on Baltimore's City Council together, and that James Webb had been both a pall bearer at Saulsbury's funeral, and the executor of his estate. But James had worked at the company's satellite office on Ensor Street, site of the former Webb Company's headquarters. It was on Concord Street near the Pratt Street Bridge where Andrew Saulsbury, Thomas Armstrong, and senior partner Charles Webb worked at the company's main building.

So what was the story behind Charles Webb, James Webb's brother?

This is where I began to hit more "pay dirt."

I quickly learned that Charles Webb had been a high-ranking Freemason. In fact, by the early 1850s, Charles Webb had been elected the Grand Master of all Maryland Freemasonry. Many authors and researchers had noted a connection between the Southern Scottish Rite Freemasons and the Knights of the Golden Circle. The KGC had borrowed heavily from Masonic ritual, and also Masonic symbols and symbolism. It has even been said that many Southern Masonic lodges doubled as "castles" or meeting places for the Knights of the Golden Circle.

Looking into the history of the Freemasons in Maryland, I noticed that Charles Webb was first elected as Grand Master in 1853. He would subsequently serve in that position in 1854, 1855, and 1857. Then, I saw something that really caught my eye . . . a very familiar name. In 1853, Webb's initial year as Grand Master, his "companion" Mason, the person who solemnly swore to have Webb's back as new Grand Master, happened to be none other than the controversial Albert C. Pike. Pike would advance in a few years to become the Sovereign Grand Master for the entire Southern U.S. Jurisdiction of the Scottish Rite Freemasons. Afterwards, he would serve as a Confederate General under confirmed Texas KGC leader Ben McCulloch. When Pike's Native American troops scalped some of their fallen Union adversaries, Pike would soon be forced to resign in disgrace and retreat to his rural Arkansas log cabin where he would write the classic Freemason tome, Morals and Dogma.

Some say that Albert Pike was arguably the world's most powerful and influential Freemason in all the 19th century.

Had Albert Pike traveled all the way from Arkansas to Baltimore to be present for the installation of young Charles Webb as the new Grand Master of Maryland? If so, that would have been a considerable journey to undertake in 1853. What was Pike's reason for connecting himself to this rising young Masonic star?

Pike became Webb's companion Mason in 1853, the same year he joined the Southern Jurisdiction's headquarters in Charleston, SC. The KGC was officially cobbled together in 1854 through the merger of existing "Southern rights" organizations. The KGC probably began recruiting efforts in Baltimore as early as 1855, relying on existing pro-slavery, Southern rights networks . . . mainly the Order of the Lone Star, which had long been active in Baltimore. The coins were subsequently buried on Eden Street in 1856.

Perhaps the dates on those coins really did make sense after all.

While Grand Master Webb, later bequeathed the honorific title of Past Grand Master (PGM) Webb, had always declined invitation to run for public office, he nevertheless remained very active in political circles. Rather than be the front man, Webb seems to have preferred the role of backroom kingmaker, moving chess pieces around the political chessboard.

During the troubled Baltimore election of 1859, when the Southern "pro-slavery" Democrats were battling the anti-immigration American Party "Know Nothings" for control of the city, Charles Webb rolled up his sleeves and went to work. The former Whig Party supporter, having seen enough of the corruption and violence brought forth by the incompetent "Know Nothing" regime of Mayor Thomas Swann, decided to back a handpicked slate of Democratic candidates for office. Webb, at the forefront of the so-called "Committee of 20" in the Civic Reform Association, spearheaded a drive by the city's wealthy elites to oust the Know Nothings. According to Baltimore researcher Matthew Kent, information gleaned from the contemporary *Baltimore Sun* leads one to believe that, "*Aside from pro-slavery ideals, the Reform party derived much of its support from popular reaction against the violence and corruption that permeated the Know-Nothing administration of Baltimore City after 1854. Leading up to the 1859 elections Know-Nothings utilized street gangs such as the*

Tigers, Plug Uglies, and Blood Tubs to intimidate Reform candidates and voters."[1]

The Reform Party, thanks in part to Grand Master Charles Webb, was able to elect George Brown as their new mayor in 1860. Upon taking office, Reform candidate Brown described the prior Know-Nothing administration of Baltimore as nothing less than a *"reign of terror."* The Democratic "Reform" Party, allied with pro-slavery Maryland legislature, soon enacted the 1860 "Police Act." The Reform Democrats then, according to Frank Towers in his article *Secession in an Urban Context: Municipal Reform and the Coming of the Civil War in Baltimore*, *"used the new law to install four new police board commissioners with pro-slavery, anti-Know Nothing views."*[2] According to Kent's research, new Police Board President Charles Howard *"maintained close connections with pro-slavery interests through his involvement in the American Colonization Society."*[3]

The Police Commissioners, with the blessing of the Reform Party and Grand Master Webb, then appointed George Proctor Kane as their Police Marshal. David Detzer, in <u>Dissonance: The Turbulent Days Between Fort Sumter and Bull Run</u>, describes Marshal Kane as *"a successful businessman and slave-owning Democrat."* Kane's first order of business, according to Kent, *"was cleansing the police force of political opponents, corrupt officers, and those who harbored pro-Union sympathies."* The newly appointed police force, says Detzer, *"reflected Kane and the Commissioner's social views, namely that they kept tabs on the city's African Americans and Irish immigrants, and sympathized with the city's pro-South activists."* In Mayor Brown's own later words penned in 1887, *"Through the Reform Party and the Legislature, the Democrats had succeeded in establishing a police force of almost 400 armed men that were for the most part ideologically aligned with the pro-slavery interests of Maryland."*[4]

Charles Webb had done his job well. The only problem was, as Baltimore's power structure was being stocked with pro-slavery officials beholding to wealthy pro-slavery business elites, President Abraham Lincoln was about to come to Washington as the new Republican "abolitionist" President. And to get to Washington, Lincoln had to go through Baltimore, quite literally, to attend his own inauguration.

With some states having already seceded before Lincoln ever reached 1600 Pennsylvania Avenue, the country was fast reaching its boiling point. In secession-minded Baltimore, rumors of a planned assassination attempt percolated, eventually reaching the ears of Lincoln friends, advisors, and the new administration officials. Two independent investigations confirmed that a Baltimore plot to kill Lincoln did indeed exist, and that radical elements of the "National Volunteers" and the Knights of the Golden Circle were likely involved. Famed detective Allan Pinkerton suspected Marshal Kane, who he called a "rabid secessionist," of being involved with the plot.

Because of the credible threat of danger to Mr. Lincoln, last-minute plans were put into effect that saw the President-elect whisked through the city of Baltimore at 3:00 a.m. by his personal bodyguard and Pinkerton undercover detectives. Lincoln was forced to sneak through Baltimore unannounced, under cover of darkness, in complete secrecy, and in a shabby, almost comical disguise.

The Pinkerton-inspired charade may have indeed saved Lincoln's life, and altered the course of American history. Had Lincoln traveled through President Street Station to Camden Street Station at the appointed afternoon hour (this being one of Lincoln's two possible routes through Baltimore), information developed about the assassination plot revealed that the likely kill zone would have been just west of the Pratt Street Bridge near the corner of Pratt and Concord Streets. Heavy objects such as logs and ships' anchors were to be thrown onto the tracks, obstructing the path of Lincoln's horse-drawn rail car. Mr. Lincoln would then have been murdered as he emerged from the protection of that rail car, or stabbed by a team of knife-wielding assassins who would corner Lincoln inside his car. The determined assassins seemed to have plans for every contingency.

Escape would have been pulled off by the assassins running onto a waiting nearby fast schooner harbored in the Basin . . . one that would speed them to safety down in friendly, secession-minded Virginia. The schooner would have been on standby at or near the wharf where Captain John J. Mattison had docked his ships for decades. Candidates for getaway skipper include Mattison's wartime Eden Street tenant, New York yacht captain John E. Stevens, Marshal Kane's longtime rebel associate, Patrick Charles Martin, a wartime blockade runner, or possibly even the aging, crusty mariner himself, Captain Mattison.

Conclusion

The assassination of Mr. Lincoln could have easily been witnessed from the office windows of the candle and soap firm of James Armstrong & Co., located near the corner of Concord and Pratt Streets. Advertisements for the candle and soap company sometimes listed the firm's location as nearby or next to the Pratt Street Bridge.

Had Lincoln been killed as planned just after crossing Jones Falls at the Pratt Street Bridge, the entire event could have been pulled off in view of executives Charles Webb, Thomas Armstrong, and Andrew J. Saulsbury from the windows of their comfortable corporate offices. Had Lincoln traveled through President Street Station, the assassination gone off as scripted, and had the plotters been identified, the corporate building of James Armstrong & Company may well have become the Texas School Book Depository of the 19th century. The corner of Pratt and Concord would have likely been seen as the Dealey Plaza of its day.

Coincidence you say? Perhaps . . . but if so, the Lincoln kill zone just west of the Pratt Street Bridge and practically in front of the candle company's offices is yet another amazing happenstance in an already growing list of such improbable occurrences.

Remember, the old news reporter in me doesn't like happenstance . . . and neither should you.

Less than two months later, when Lincoln called for 75,000 volunteers to defend the capital against the rebels, again Baltimore became the choke point for Northerners headed south to Washington. On April 19th, 1861 the brewing North/South conflict boiled over onto the cobbled streets of downtown Baltimore. Hard-line secessionists Mayor George Brown and Marshal Kane performed admirably that day, placing themselves in harm's way between the rioters and the Yankee soldiers, protecting members of both groups in the process. Although 16 people died as a result of the riot, with perhaps a hundred or more injured, the casualties could well have been far worse had it not been for the heroic action and quick thinking of both the mayor and the marshal.

Let it be noted that the spot at which the soldiers of the Massachusetts 6th had their rail cars halted by heavy objects, such as a ship's anchor dragged onto the tracks, and where the soldiers were initially pelted with stones and debris and even shot at with pistols when they emerged from those cars, was approximately at the corner of Pratt and Concord Streets. The Union troops, forced out of their rail cars and onto dangerous Pratt Street, where they are first attacked — immediately after coming over the Pratt Street Bridge — are having this mayhem inflicted upon them at the very same February 23rd kill zone intended for President-elect Lincoln. And again, it is all happening within sight of the corporate offices of James Armstrong & Company, purveyors of fine soaps and candles.

These armed companies of military men suffered 20 serious casualties (including four dead) before reaching Camden Station. What would have been done to the hated Mr. Lincoln, whose rail car was only lightly guarded? There were no apparent squads of assassins present on April 19th, which was largely a spontaneous event. This was not so on February 23rd when Mr. Lincoln had been expected, and the plotters had time to plan and coordinate.

And without Mayor Brown and Marshal Kane on the scene, the number of April 19th casualties would have been much worse. Marshal Kane, while at the bar of the Barnum Hotel, was overheard by an undercover Allan Pinkerton to boast that *no police protection* was going to be afforded to Mr. Lincoln, who had received a paltry 1,000 votes in Baltimore, and those from "*the very scum of the city*" according to Kane.

At least the armed soldiers of the 6th Massachusetts had been provided belated police protection, and were instructed by Mayor Brown to defend themselves if needed.

It is, however, what Mayor Brown and Marshal Kane did after the riot that revealed their true Confederate colors, and would push the nation one step closer to the eventual all-out-war that was to come.

When later that day pro-Union Governor Thomas Hicks sets up temporary emergency headquarters in the Fountain Inn, he is harassed by rowdy secessionists into fleeing the hotel out of fear for his safety. Mayor Brown offers Governor Hicks sanctuary in the mayor's home . . . whether this occurred by design or by happenstance is hard to say. But the outcome of Hicks' experience at the Fountain Inn is that he winds up in a bedroom at the mayor's house being browbeaten by Marshal Kane and Mayor Brown into authorizing the torching of railroad bridges connecting Baltimore to the North.

Within hours, Marshal Kane leads a team of saboteurs north of the city to burn the rail bridges for the tracks leading from

Philadelphia. A second team, led by Colonel Isaac Trimble of the Maryland Militia, does likewise to the bridges for the tracks leading from Harrisburg. The demolition also involves the destruction of some track, and the cutting of all telegraph wires leading to the capital. Anecdotal evidence suggests that one of Kane's saboteurs is an aspiring young Baltimore actor named John Wilkes Booth.

Not content with simply destroying transportation links with the North, Kane also fires off a telegram asking for Virginia and Maryland militia members to ride to the defense of Baltimore. *"Fresh hordes will be upon us in the morning,"* warns Kane. *"We must fight them, and whip them, or die."*

Meanwhile, Mayor Brown puts out a call to the citizenry of Baltimore, asking for a donation of weapons with which to defend the city. Donated weapons are to be dropped off at Marshal Kane's police headquarters.

Two days later, militia leader Colonel Trimble and Marshal Kane are trying to organize an army of thousands to attack an encampment of federal soldiers who have moved into position north of the city. Some of the Baltimore defenders were to be equipped with arms supplied by Marshal Kane.

A frustrated Abe Lincoln would be forced, however, to reroute his troops through Annapolis, where they arrive by ship. This unexpected detour leaves Washington, D.C. largely unguarded from rebel attack for several more agonizing days.

Once D.C. is eventually secured, the Lincoln administration turns its focus back to Baltimore. The unruly Baltimoreans had threatened violence upon Mr. Lincoln's person in February, and had staged an unprovoked attack on his armed federal troops in April. Baltimore, in the words of the commander of Ft. McHenry, was *"entirely under the control of revolutionary authorities."* Something had to be done, and Mayor Brown and Marshal Kane were at the top of the government's list of known troublemakers.

As expected, the very next month, on May 13th, General Benjamin Butler and Union troops that included the 6th Massachusetts entered the city at night, during a rainstorm, and placed Baltimore under martial law. They built earthworks atop Federal Hill and positioned several cannons so they pointed down at the city, threatening both downtown and the busy harbor. Many Confederate-leaning Baltimoreans were forced to move south. Others who stayed were arrested. One person who remained behind and was imprisoned, ironically at Fort McHenry, was a young newspaper editor named Frank Key Howard, the grandson of Francis Scott Key. Upon his release in 1863, Howard would tell about his days as a political prisoner at Fort McHenry in his book Fourteen Months in the American Bastille. Two publishers who dared to print and sell Howard's book were subsequently arrested.

Baltimore would remain under federal occupation for the duration of the Civil War.

On June 23rd, 1861, there came a late-night knock at Marshal Kane's door. Under heavy military guard, Kane was escorted to Fort McHenry, where he was held without trial and later transferred to federal prisons up north. Mayor Brown would follow, arrested by the ever-present Allan Pinkerton, and would soon be sharing a room with Marshal Kane at chilly Fort Warren in Boston.

When the subject of Marshal Kane's arrest comes up in discussion amongst members of the Richmond acting company to which John Wilkes Booth belongs, the volatile thespian nearly blows a fuse. Booth brings the tense conversation to a swift close with his outburst that, "*I know George P. Kane well; he is my friend, and the man who could drag him from the bosom of his family for no crime whatever, but a mere suspicion that he may commit one some time, deserves a dog's death!*"

Which begs the question, if Booth had been an active participant in Marshal Kane's squad of bridge-burning saboteurs, and had been known to be openly vocal against the federal government in general and Mr. Lincoln in particular, how had Booth managed to escape the Union dragnet?

Apparently, Booth had slipped through inadvertently during the wide-scale September arrests (when Mayor Brown was detained). According to Michael J. Kline in The Baltimore Plot, Booth may have been amongst several people arrested in Baltimore by Pinkerton. Kline cites a news article from that period that reveals one of those arrested, but subsequently released after swearing an oath of loyalty to the Union, was a man named John Wilkes. "John Wilkes" had been one of Booth's early stage aliases when he was trying to gain an acting reputation apart from the famous Booth family name. Baltimore Republican leader Worthington Snethen would later complain that Booth had escaped the punishment he deserved "*through mistaken leniency of the government.*"[5] Kline speculates that either Pinkerton or the federal authorities occupying Baltimore in late 1861 had let Booth slip though their grasp thanks to a Civil War era "catch and release" program.

Realizing that a number of references to John Wilkes Booth had appeared during my research of Charles Webb's political ally, George Kane, I became interested to find out more about Booth's ties to Baltimore. A little digging revealed that the Booth family townhome was located on N. Exeter Street, less than a half mile from the Eden St. treasure house. The Fountain Hotel had been a known Booth hangout during his adolescent days, and Booth was said to have met with his 1865 conspirators for drinks at the nearby Barnum Hotel, headquarters for the notorious Cipriano Ferrandini — and also the place where Pinkerton had overheard Marshal Kane boast that no police protection would be given to President-elect Lincoln.

Booth and his co-conspirator, John Surratt, were allegedly inducted into the Knights of the Golden Circle in 1859 and/or 1860 in a "castle" in or near Booth's Exeter Street neighborhood. The private home in which the initiation ceremony occurred featured a bust of Southern "fire eater" John C. Calhoun and portraits of Confederate heroes Jefferson Davis and Stephen Douglas.[6] Andrew Saulsbury's Central Ave. home was just a short walk from Exeter St., and Saulsbury was an "ardent" and outspoken Southern sympathizer same as Booth. Saulsbury's post-war home on Eden Street would later be described as being adorned with portraits of Confederate war heroes Stonewall Jackson and Robert E. Lee. Perhaps these portraits served as something more than simple private acts of political defiance, being used for ceremonial, swearing-in purposes. The 5,000 gold coins in the cellar would appear to be evidence of initiation fees and dues having been collected during KGC ceremonies. What was really going on during those night-time oyster parties when Saulsbury would invite his "gentlemen friends" over to his house?

The KGC initiation ceremonies were said to be attended by some of the highest-ranking members of society, including judges, industrialists, bankers, and top military men.[7] Through Charles Webb and James Armstrong & Co., Saulsbury (who would himself later become a city council member) would have been exposed to the leading secessionists in Baltimore . . . movers and shakers such as Mayor Brown and Marshal Kane. And Kane was, by Booth's own admission, a friend of the future presidential assassin.

Which begs the question, just how does a 20-year old actor who now mainly lives and works in Richmond become acquainted with the 40-year old police marshal of Baltimore? Besides radical secessionist politics, what else might they share in common?

Upon his release from federal prison in 1863, an embittered Marshal Kane would embark on a two-year campaign of terror against the Union. He would do so mainly as a liaison between Richmond and the Confederate Secret Service office in Montreal. From 1863 until the end of the war, Kane would be involved in the plot to raid the federal fort at Johnson Island on Lake Erie to secure the release of some 2,000 Confederate prisoners, including longtime Kane associate Isaac Trimble (now General Trimble) of Gettysburg fame. The Montreal office of the Confederate Secret Service would participate in repeated plots and attacks on the North such as the Jesse James-style raid on the banks of St. Albans, Vermont, the failed attempt to set New York City ablaze, the derailing of Union trains in upstate New York, and various acts of piracy in the Great Lakes region. Kane would himself contact CSA President Jefferson Davis with an offer to organize a raid on Chicago, Detroit, and Milwaukee in which he and his agents would destroy vessels in port, thus, as Kane described, "*paralyzing the lake commerce.*" Correspondence in 1864 between General Robert E. Lee and CSA President Davis makes reference to a special project being planned by Colonel Kane. The nature of this project can only be guessed at, although some researchers have speculated that Agent Kane's classified assignment may have been the kidnapping of President Lincoln.

On October 18, 1864, actor John Wilkes Booth checked into the St. Lawrence Hall in Montreal and immediately set out to find Colonel Kane of the Confederate Secret Service, whom he thought was staying at the hotel. To Booth's dismay, Kane had already left Montreal on orders to return to Richmond. Over the next 10 days, Booth, supposedly in Montreal to make arrangements to have his stage wardrobe shipped home, would be seen in the company of Confederate agents George Sanders and Patrick Charles Martin. Sanders was a known political extremist with ties to European revolutionaries . . . and an agitator who was fond of advocating political assassination as a means to effect change. Interestingly, Sanders as a foreign diplomat in the service of the Pierce Administration had also enjoyed close ties to Albert Pike's mentor, Caleb Cushing. Sanders was also the person who, in 1861, had shadowed President-elect Lincoln from Cincinnati to the Continental Hotel in Philadelphia — possibly under orders from known KGC officer Cipriano Ferrandini at the Barnum Hotel in Baltimore. Sanders would be overheard at St. Lawrence Hall in Montreal to say that after the 1864 election, Lincoln wouldn't be a problem anymore, and that "*Booth was bossing the job.*" Martin, at whose home Kane had stayed in Montreal, was a former Baltimore liquor salesman turned Confederate blockade runner. He was described in Union intelligence documents as a "*rebel of the April 19th variety*" and may have accompanied Kane and Booth on the night the bridges were burned north of Baltimore after the Pratt Street Riot.

Also checking into St. Lawrence Hall on October 18, 1864 was one Dr. Luke Blackburn, the person responsible for orchestrating the Great Fever Plot, quite possibly America's first act of bioterrorism. Blackburn, a Freemason and "ardent" Confederate sympathizer, was in charge of the plan to spread yellow fever throughout strategic military locations and population centers in the North through the distribution of supposedly infected clothing. President Lincoln and the White House were on the list of intended victims. While Blackburn orchestrated this madness from the relative safety of neutral Canada, his helper, Godfrey Joseph Hyams, helped to prepare and distribute infected clothing from a room at Baltimore's Fountain Hotel — a known hangout of Booth's, the residence of Thomas Armstrong of James Armstrong & Co., and also the site of the subsequent discovery of a hidden tin box containing 2,000 gold coins.

We also happen to know that on at least one occasion, Dr. Blackburn and Colonel Kane had travelled together while running the Union blockade. . . .

And, that John Wilkes Booth was seen playing cards with Dr. Blackburn in the hotel parlor on the night of his arrival at St. Lawrence Hall . . . soon after he discovered that Colonel Kane had already left to run the blockade once again and return to his duties in Richmond.

The chance all these extraordinary details were the result of mere "coincidence" would necessarily have to be ridiculously small.

Godfrey Joseph Hymans, who would later flip and become a federal witness at the trial of the Lincoln assassination conspirators, was supposedly present for at least one of Booth's early strategy meetings for the Lincoln kidnapping plot. Hyams, who had a wife and newborn to support, reportedly grew angry when Dr. Blackburn failed to pay him for services rendered during the Great Fever Plot. Having been double crossed by Dr. Blackburn, who allegedly laughed in Hyams' face when asked for the agreed upon money, Hyams then contacted authorities with his bizarre but apparently true tale. That Hymans had originally been a loyal Confederate agent, and not a double-agent for the Union, is evidenced by the fact his first-born child had been proudly named "Stonewall Jackson Hyams."[8]

Two days after Hyams gave his initial statement to federal authorities, John Wilkes Booth assassinated President Lincoln at Ford's Theater. Hyams would later testify against CSA President Jefferson Davis on May 29th, 1865. Federal authorities would also interview former KGC president George Bickley in his prison cell to ascertain whether the KGC had been part of the plot. With Bickley having been on ice for some two years at Fort Warren, either he didn't know — or wasn't talking.

In March, 1865, Colonel Kane seems to have been involved in an effort to obtain fresh uniforms for Marylanders serving in the Confederate Army.[9] At the end of the month, by his own admission in an 1876 interview given to the *New York Daily Graphic*, Kane would be *"resting out of the way"* in Virginia's Shenandoah Valley. He is apparently not scouting enemy troop movements, because the owner of the house comes and informs the colonel that *"Stoneman is raiding up the valley."* While *"resting out of the way"* in the countryside as Richmond is being surrounded and about to fall, Kane admits to receiving a letter from Patrick Charles Martin in Montreal asking whether Kane can give a reference for the visiting John Wilkes Booth, and whether Booth has a good reputation in Baltimore. Kane later claims that he is "confused" by Martin's request, because he surely has no idea who "Wilkes Booth" is. Considering Booth's growing national reputation as an actor, his performance at a Baltimore theater partially owned by Kane, his alleged participation in the April 19, 1861 bridge burnings under the supervision of Kane and perhaps also Martin, and his pronouncement that the persons responsible for Marshal Kane's subsequent arrest should *"die a dog's death"* all point to Kane having a long personal history with President Lincoln's assassin. Kane, during this 1876 interview while running for the office mayor of Baltimore, seems to have been doing a bit of "damage control" regarding his connection to the infamous Booth. Patrick Charles Martin's letter of introduction for Booth to Dr. William Queen was ultimately used to set up meetings between Booth and Dr. Samuel Mudd. Dr. Mudd, a reliable Confederate sympathizer and likely a member of the Confederacy's southern Maryland underground intelligence network, would later be charged with aiding and abetting Booth's escape by setting the broken leg pf possibly history's most wanted fugitive. Mudd claimed on the stand that he didn't know who Booth was when Booth and David Herold knocked on the door to his home outside of Bryantown, MD just hours after Booth had shot and killed the President. Historians now generally agree that Mudd had met with Booth on several occasions leading up to Lincoln's assassination. That Mudd lied during his testimony is understandable, since plausible deniability was apparently a factor in sparing the doctor the same fate as four other Booth co-conspirators — a July 7th, 1865 date with the hangman's noose.

A reasonable person might assume that if Martin's first letter concerning John Wilkes Booth was written to Dr. Queen to facilitate the President's abduction, then his second letter concerning Booth — the one sent to Colonel Kane — might also have been written to further the same conspiracy. That Booth went initially to St. Lawrence Hall looking for Colonel Kane, his apparent friend and fellow Baltimorean, adds credence to this line of thought. The Canadian bank draft found on Booth's body after his death[10] further points to Kane, Martin, Sanders, and their fellow Canadian-based agents of the Confederate Secret Service.

We don't know the actual contents of Martin's letter to Kane because Kane apparently destroyed it, latter admitting that its contents "*might have cost me my life.*" Since Martin and Booth died shortly after Martin wrote the letter, and the letter did not survive, we only have Kane's 1876 interview for insight as to its contents.

Might Kane have been "*resting out of the way*" in Shenandoah Valley in anticipation of Booth and his abduction squad bringing a trussed-up president Lincoln to Kane's country hideaway? Special Agent Kane would have certainly been the man for the job of receiving the captured President . . . and no doubt it would have brought the colonel a sense of satisfaction after his imprisonment without trial at the hands of Union authorities. George Sanders had been overheard to say that *"Booth was bossing the job,"* but was Colonel Kane once again bossing Booth, same as during their April, 1861 bridge-burning mission? Booth was reported to have owned a getaway cottage in the Shenandoah Valley, possibly near Charles Town, and perhaps even a second property somewhere farther south in the valley. Likewise, Kane's description of *"resting out of the way"* while the sun set on his Confederacy seems a bit preposterous. Kane was in the "Valley of Virginia" for a good reason, whether it was to receive a kidnapped Mr. Lincoln or for some other rebel matter of high importance. Was Kane's secret project as alluded to in the letter from General Lee to President Davis his *"bossing"* of Booth and the kidnapping of Mr. Lincoln? The company Kane kept in Montreal says probably yes.

The Confederate hierarchy certainly knew where Colonel Kane was in early April, 1865 when they dispatched a courier to a "resting" Kane with orders for him to meet the retreating President Davis and his CSA Cabinet at the rail hub of Danville, VA. Kane saddled up his horse and rode through the "woods and broken country" of Virginia to meet the *"Davis party"* as they were *"flying from Richmond to Charlotte."* Kane makes it sound almost as if the train simply slowed while going through Danville so he might somehow hop aboard. Actually, Jeff Davis and the Confederate train stayed in Danville for approximately three days, with the guarded Confederate treasury resting inside a designated box car on a side rail.

Confederate researchers and historians have long suspected that 39 kegs of Mexican silver coins, obtained through cotton sales to Mexico, were offloaded at Danville in early April, 1865 and hidden from the advancing Union armies. With the silver estimated to have weighed a hefty 9,000 pounds, this is a logical assumption. Many have searched for the legendary Confederate silver hoard, but apparently none have found it. Could that be because Colonel Kane, the likely sentinel for the 39 kegs of hidden silver, was successful in moving the silver to a safer location at a later date?

In his 1876 *New York Daily Graphic* interview, Kane told how he continued south with the Davis party to Greensboro, North Carolina, where he supposedly left the train because of illness and fatigue, seeking refuge at the home of a local resident. According to Kane, this stay would have been from about April 7th, when the

Conclusion

Confederate train reached Greensboro on its way to Charlotte, until sometime after President Lincoln's assassination on April 14th, which occurred just five days after Lee's surrender at Appomattox. Kane describes how the owner of the Greensboro house where he was a guest brought him a newspaper account with the *"startling intelligence"* of Wilkes Booth's killing of Mr. Lincoln. Kane then goes on to mention how the letter from Martin, secreted in his saddle bag, could have cost Kane his life even though he had never met nor known a *"Wilkes Booth."*

This is an interesting yarn to be sure, but certainly not one to be taken at face value.

Jefferson Davis' own papers include a summary of an April 8th, 1865 telegram received from Colonel Kane who is reporting on enemy troop movements around Danville![11] According to the telegram, Kane is not sick and lying nearly out of his senses in Greensboro, but rather is playing the role of CSA Secret Service agent back in Danville, serving his cherished Confederacy until the bitter end.

The Chinese have a saying that the palest ink is stronger than the sharpest memory. If so, then the Davis records indicate Kane never left Danville, and his tale about lying ill in a house in Greensboro is either mistaken or, more likely, an outright fabrication.

Not only did Kane stay behind in Danville after the Davis party headed south to Greensboro and then on to Charlotte — Kane stayed on in Danville for approximately *four years*! He started a business there called the Roanoke Tobacco Works.[12] Interesting how Kane locates the new business in Danville, but names it after a town 78 miles to the northwest. Do you get the impression that Kane was ever eager to distance himself from Danville and his real reason for being there?

After the war, the rail hub of Danville became an encampment for Union soldiers. Under these circumstances, it's easy to see how Colonel Kane, who likely would have had a hand in burying the 39 kegs of silver, would not have been able to unearth the 9,000 pounds of precious metal while the area is crawling with armed Yankees keenly suspicious of the local folk. So, Confederate 007 waits and, meanwhile, operates a business to generate some money for living expenses . . . no doubt also sending some funds home to his family in Baltimore.

Meanwhile, after the rebel silver is buried in or around Danville, the gold from the CSA treasury is subsequently robbed in a mysteriously suspicious midnight holdup at the edge of a plantation on the sleepy outskirts of little Chennault, Georgia. Was the heist pulled off by roving Union soldiers looking for plunder, disgruntled Confederate bandits, or by elements of the KGC who saw fit to step in at the time of the South's imminent collapse and loss of the gold? Although still accompanied by Virginia bank officers, the bank assets had already fallen under Union control in Washington, Georgia. The bloodless precision with which such a large quantity of gold was retaken suggests a staged KGC operation to wrest the treasure back from the Yankee invaders — and have the "theft" blamed on locals, Confederate deserters, or perhaps even Union soldiers gone rogue. Details of the robbery, however, are not suggestive of a band of amateurs.

By the late 1860s, Kane sells his "Roanoke" Tobacco Works[13] and heads back to Baltimore. He soon secures a position on the Jones Falls Commission, likely with the help of his former political backer, Charles Webb, whose James Armstrong & Co. plant is situated along Jones Falls by the Pratt Street Bridge. By 1873, Kane will be elected sheriff of Baltimore. And in 1877, George P. Kane will be elected as the new mayor of the Monumental City. This is quite a comeback for someone who, 14 years earlier, had languished in a federal prison with no specified release date.

Upon his election to mayor, Kane will call upon his old friend, Charles Webb, to step away from private life and assume the duties of Baltimore City tax collector in the Kane Administration. It was noted how Webb had previously turned down many previous offers of public office — but this time was unable to say no to his longtime associate, the now Mayor George Kane. Webb's reputation as collector of taxes was stellar, as it was said he greatly increased the much-needed tax revenues of the city, and was a refreshing change from some of his corrupt, dishonest, and/or incompetent predecessors. *"Webb's administration of his office,"* according to one observer, *"has been of the most distinguished character, and he has won golden opinions from all sorts of people."*

Sadly, Mayor Kane's reign would be a short one, as he would lose his battle with Bright's disease just months after taking office. Kane's successor, Ferdinand Latrobe, would reappoint Webb as the new administration's tax collector. Latrobe was the son of John H. B. Latrobe, Webb's fellow Past Grand Master of the Maryland Freemasons, and also the one-time president of the Maryland Colonization Society, which had sought to send all freed American slaves back to Africa, in line with longstanding KGC policy.

Upon the deaths of Charles Webb and John H.B. Latrobe in the early 1890s, the Freemasons honored their memory with a ceremony that featured a reading from Albert C. Pike, the Sovereign Commander of the Southern Jurisdiction of U.S. Freemasonry and the suspected mastermind behind the Knights of the Golden Circle. Future researchers would also link Pike's name to the founding of the Reconstruction era Ku Klux Klan, whose name is possibly an anglicized pronunciation of the Greek word "kuklos" or *circle (*Pike was something of a linguistic prodigy who spoke a long list of languages). His involvement with the early Klan has long been a subject of controversy, and the Freemasons' position is that it can neither be proven nor disproven.

That Pike publicly called for the formation of a secret organization to protect white Southerners during the era of Reconstruction is, however, not in doubt. Pike argued in an April 16th, 1868 *Memphis Daily Appeal* editorial that a "secret association" of some sort was required to protect the rights of Southern white citizens with the abolishment of slavery. Although many researchers later took Pike's words to mean either the KGC or the KKK, Pike made it clear that the KKK was not what he had in mind. *"We should unite every white man in the South,"* wrote the Freemason leader, *"who is opposed to negro suffrage, into one great Order of Southern Brotherhood . . . whose very existence should be concealed from all but its members. That has been the resort of the oppressed in all ages. To resort to it is a right given by God. . . ."*[14]

Pike would also announce on another occasion that he would quit the Freemasons if the society ever allowed blacks to join. Little did I know when I started this "Knights Gold" project, after viewing the *Brad Meltzer's Encoded* episode where KGC treasure hunter Bob Brewer goes looking for the lost Confederate silver in Danville, that I would be linking people associated with the Baltimore treasure in the Eden Street cellar to the legendary Confederate silver in Danville. But it was the enigmatic George P. Kane himself who led me there. Truth, as mentioned earlier, is often stranger than fiction. Mayor George Kane may very well have been connected to the Confederate treasures in both Virginia and Maryland.

The big question is, if George Kane was eventually able to get the silver out of Danville, then where did it go? Somewhere south and west most likely, same as the Confederate gold likely seized in Chennault, GA by special agents of the KGC.

Authors Warren Getler and Bob Brewer in Rebel Gold have speculated that the post-war KGC buried much treasure in anticipation of a future insurrection against the North — the much-longed for day when the South would rise again. Not only was such treasure collected before the war, but the stockpiles of arms, cash, and precious metals were added to *after* the war. The primary source of Reconstruction-era funds seems to have been the guerilla-style raids on Union targets such as banks, trains, and stagecoaches, typified by the improbable careers of Confederate-trained raiders Frank and Jesse James. That the James boys and their James Gang were able to prolifically pull off huge heists, almost with impunity, for some 17 years speaks to some level of cooperation on the part of sympathetic Southern authorities. The James Gang was apparently involved in something much bigger than acts of random theft and mayhem, for which the authorities of all political persuasions would have had zero tolerance. However, a low-level war of insurrection against the hated North would have been quite another story. That Frank and Jesse James were practically untouchable in Clay County, Missouri lends credence to this line of thinking. Even the tenacious Allan Pinkerton and his vaunted detective agency were forced to retreat from the James case, partly because their agents were being murdered, and partly because of their ill-advised and reckless fatal firebombing of the James family homestead.

Conclusion

An attempt was made in Clay County to indict eight of the Pinkerton detectives, including Allan Pinkerton himself, for the murder of little Archie Samuels. But no formal charges were ever filed, and no Pinkertons were ever arrested.[15] Despite the staggering size of the James Gang's heists by 19th century standards, the James boys did not live extravagant lifestyles. And the idea that Frank and Jesse James were modern-day Robin Hoods stealing from the rich Yankees to give to poor Southern folk has been largely debunked. Which begs the question, where did all the loot go? In 21st-century dollars, we are talking about a total haul possibly in the $100 million range or higher.[16]

Getler and Brewer maintain that Albert Pike likely masterminded the burial of enormous amounts of Confederate treasure in a series of underground depositories spread across the South and Southwest. Brewer claims to have discovered one such depository in western Arkansas, referred to as the "King Solomon's Temple" treasure, spread for miles across a designed geometric pattern, and marked by subtle Confederate treasure symbols. The western Arkansas depository was located in the area of Pike's 19th century Greasy Cove cabin and the surrounding rugged lands. Getler and Brewer point to documentation showing that after Jesse James robbed the Hot Springs, Arkansas stagecoach in 1874, he and his men escaped across land owned by Pike before fading into Oklahoma Indian territory[17] belonging to Native American tribes Pike had represented in successful Washington court battles for reparations. Getler and Brewer point to the large number of "double J" carvings and markings in the King Solomon's Temple forest as an indication of James' frequent presence. Getler and Brewer theorize that part of the missing James Gang loot was buried in western Arkansas at the direction of KGC leader Pike, the same man once selected to be Charles Webb's "Companion Mason" upon Webb's ascension to the status of Grand Master for the state of Maryland.

Each KGC depository allegedly features a geometric pattern with archaic treasure symbols and subtle clues placed at the intersection of surveyed gridlines, with those above ground clues (as well as magnetized underground clues) pointing to the location of buried treasure. Each depository consists of several smaller treasures, some being buried fruit jars (known as "paychecks") with coins meant to reward sentinels whose duty it is to check on the suspicious activity of strangers who intrude on the remote treasure grid. At the center point of each systematic grid lies the main, deeply buried, quite likely booby-trapped depository containing the so-called bonanza or "mother lode" of Confederate riches.

Brewer has shown off mason jars and a tea kettle containing 19th-century gold and silver coins that he says have been unearthed in the forest surrounding the Arkansas mother lode. Jesse James historian Ron Pastore filmed his similar discoveries at a rural Kansas site in the cable television documentary *The Hidden Treasure of Jesse James*. Could the James Boys have buried treasure from Arkansas to Kansas? Writer Warren Getler says he believes the Confederate depositories may stretch as far west as Arizona — and may possibly be guarded even to this day!

It seems like an utterly fantastic story, yet Brewer, Getler, and Pastore apparently have the recovered gold and silver to back up their claims.

Ron Pastore asserts that the real Jesse James was not killed in 1882, but rather that a former James Gang member who had been something of a loose cannon was instead sacrificed in his place. Pastore, in his book Jesse James' Hidden Secret, maintains that the James Gang actually contained three men who went by the name Jesse James, all of whom were first cousins. There was Jesse Robert "Dingus" James, Jesse Mason James (the troublemaker killed in Jesse James' place), and Jeremiah Woodson "Jesse" James who was the younger brother of Frank James and the person today recognized as the "one and only" true Jesse James. Pastore says that robberies committed close together in time, though hundreds of miles apart and all attributed to Jesse James and his gang, point to multiple individuals operating under the "brand name" of Jesse James.

According to researcher Pastore, gang members Bob and Charley Ford, Clay County Sheriff James Timberlake, and possibly even Missouri Governor Thomas Crittenden, had all conspired to fake the death of Jesse James because of the political heat the outlaw's fame had brought down upon them. The James Gang chose to bump off troublemaker Jesse Mason James the night before by summoning the James cousin for a meeting and then dispatching their victim in the barn at the James' rented home in St. Joseph, MO where the outlaw had been living under the alias "Tom Howard." Next day, a staged scene was arranged in the

Conclusion

James residence to make it appear that the Ford brothers had shot Jesse James in the back of the head, and in cold blood, in order to collect the reward money and to receive pardons for the Ford brothers' crimes.

Within a short period of time, Sherriff James Timberlake appeared in St. Joseph to collect the body of Jesse James. Supposedly, this was on special request to bring the body back to the James family homestead in Kearney, Clay County so that the outlaw's mother and family could give Jesse a "proper burial" in the James family plot. Timberlake, although St. Joseph was *not* in his jurisdiction of Clay County and the sheriff was accompanied by known members of the James Gang, was able to gain possession of the outlaw's body after a hurried coroner's inquest and autopsy were performed. James' body was brought back to Kearney for quick burial, and later results from the inquest and autopsy showed that several key statements made about the manner of James' death did not match the evidence that had been discovered.[19] First, the victim had apparently been murdered sometime during the night *before* the morning the witnesses said he was killed. Second, there were signs of a struggle on the victim's body, which was at odds with the Ford brothers saying James had been shot totally by surprise — in the back of his skull — while dusting a painting hanging on the wall. Third, the bullet in James' skull was the wrong type of bullet for the gun Bob Ford allegedly used to kill James. And the bullet in the wall above the painting did not square with a single shot having been fired . . . and with a slug having already been found inside the victim's skull. Either the single shot had passed through James' skull, or it had not. The bullet could not have come to rest in two very separate places.

Something was seriously amiss.

Stranger yet, the photo of James' dead body only faintly resembled the outlaw, who was taller, thinner, and had lighter colored hair than the body in the morgue photo. The photo of the dead man, however, did more closely resemble first cousin and "loose cannon" gang member Jesse *Mason* James.[20]

Critics have suggested that the outlaw Jesse James, while using the alias Tom Howard, would have disguised his appearance. True, he might have dyed his hair darker, but that doesn't account for the apparently broader frame and shorter stature.

Brothers Charley and Bob Ford did not stay around long enough to collect most of the promised reward money on Jesse James. Instead, they fled the county and the state, and would regret participation in the incident for the rest of their lives. The Ford brothers would never again know peace.

The bulk of the James reward would eventually be pocketed by Clay County Sheriff James Timberlake. Timberlake had himself been a former Confederate officer under the command of legendary Confederate General J.O. Shelby, the man who had refused to surrender to the Union and instead took 1,000 of his most loyal troops into Mexico. James Timberlake had been one of Shelby's storied rebels from the "Iron Brigade" who had left Texas and headed south into Mexico rather than surrender to Union troops. So had John Edwards, the Kansas City news reporter who had written articles and books depicting James as a "romantic Southern hero" that had elevated James to something approaching national cult status.

Most interestingly, after the "murder" of Jesse James, Timberlake took his reward money and left Clay County for most of a year. The official story was that Timberlake refused to run for re-election because of the bad publicity and hard feelings generated by the nature in which Governor Crittenden, Sheriff Timberlake, and the Ford Brothers had conspired to bring about the demise of Jesse James.

So where did Timberlake go? Out to desolate New Mexico, of all places, reportedly to help his brother who was in the ranching business.[21] However, by next year, Timberlake returns to Missouri and is promptly appointed to the position of Deputy U.S. Marshal for the Western District of Missouri. Governor Crittenden is the person who appoints Timberlake to that post. It is all so very convenient — especially for the conspirators.

Meanwhile, at the Missouri trial of Frank James, who had surrendered his guns peacefully to Governor Crittenden, the star witness for the defense is none other than General J. O. Shelby. Most of the jurors would have counted themselves as loyal Southerners, and to them Jo Shelby is a beloved folk hero. In case any of the jurors missed the point of Shelby's testimony, the fabled Confederate commander at one point stands up and offers the accused his hand, saying, *"Allow me, I wish to shake hands with my fellow soldier who fought by my side for Southern rights!"*[22]

But James wasn't on trial for his actions during the Civil War. He was on trial for post-war armed robberies that cost the lives of at least four railroad employees, bank tellers, and innocent bystanders. However, according to television's History Channel at History.com, General Joseph O. Shelby, who had known Frank James during his days as a Civil War guerilla, encouraged the jurors to see Frank James as a defender of the South against corrupt big businesses from the North. And the Missourians were already persuaded to think that way based on the stories printed by another former Shelby guerilla, Kansas City newspaperman John Edwards, who had portrayed the James Boys as *"heroes who took money from ruthless bank and railroad companies and redistributed it to the poor."* The Missouri prosecutor found it difficult to find jurors who were not prejudiced in Frank James' favor. Looking over the panel of potential jurors, he reportedly concluded, *"The verdict of the jury that is being selected is already written."*[23]

Good ole' General Jo Shelby must have surely wowed those 12 Missourians, because after nearly two decades of murder, arson, armed robbery, theft, terrorism, insurrection, and treason, Frank James walked out of the courtroom a free man. As per the outlaw's surrender agreement, Governor Crittenden never extradited James to Minnesota, where James would have easily been convicted. Jesse James' big brother would live to be an old man, trading off his name as a cultural icon and notorious Wild West outlaw. *"Come have your ticket punched by Frank James!"*[24] advertised one theater where Frank James worked to earn a meager living. Where had all the money gone?

Likewise, what had Timberlake really been doing in New Mexico? And if his actual motive in April, 1882 had been to protect the KGC-connected James rather than bring him to justice, could he have brought the real Jeremiah Woodson "Jesse" James with him to the Southwest under the guise of yet another alias? When accounting for the travel time to and from New Mexico, Timberlake barely had a year (if that) to help his brother in the ranching business. It seems hardly worth his effort to have made the long trip. And his quick appointment as western Missouri's deputy U.S. marshal in 1883 belies a Missouri reputation that was not nearly as badly damaged as the history books might lead one to think.

Had James Timberlake, J.O. Shelby, and Frank and Jesse James pulled off one of history's most incredible deceptions? Did both Frank and Jesse James live to be old men, free of further consequences from their past lives of horrific serial crimes?

Who says that fairy tales can't come true? All it takes is money, some sleight of hand, and a little political magic.

Modern DNA evidence has supposedly shown, by comparing the DNA of known James family descendants to the bones found in Jesse James alleged gravesite in Kearney, MO, that there is a very high probability that the bones in Jesse James' grave do indeed belong to Jerimiah Woodson "Jesse" James.[25] But what if the bone fragments in that grave instead belong to first cousin Jesse Mason James? As a James family member, a blood relative, couldn't the experts have been fooled? They were looking for James family DNA and got James family DNA. Could the tests have only proven that a James family member's remains were found in that grave, and not specifically the remains of one Jeremiah Woodson "Jesse" James? Remember, the results showed only a high probability of a match to Jesse James, not a 100% definitive match. Those are exactly the results one would have expected if another family member, a male approximately the same age as Jesse James, had been found at that burial site. A male said to have been born by the name Jesse Mason James, and said to have committed crimes under guise of the "Jesse James" brand?

This is all, of course, further muddied by a wary, rural-based James clan that tended to marry within itself. Jesse's mother was Zerelda "Zee" James. So was Jesse's wife. When you have first cousins marrying each other, your DNA tests start to become a little fuzzy and less reliable. All we know about the bones found buried in Jesse James' supposed grave vis-a-vis modern DNA testing is that the bones came from a member of the James family — not necessarily from Jerimiah Woodson "Jesse" James himself. Could the bones have actually belonged to first cousin Jesse Mason James? You bet. . . .

Meanwhile, back in Kansas, researcher Ron Pastore has obtained early 20th-century photos of the extended James clan. A photo of an elderly James family member named Jere Miah "Jerry" James, taken during a Depression-era family get-together, shows a person who bears an uncanny resemblance to the notorious outlaw Jesse "Woodson" James. The likeness of the old man, right down to the bumpy scar on the inside of the left eyebrow, reportedly is so close to the known photographs of the real Jesse James that, according to Pastore, photo recognition technology has declared them a likely match.[26]

Critics, of course, will say this is explainable because the old man in the photograph is more than likely a close blood relative of Jesse James. So what if James had kin that could pass for his double? That would not be surprising.

Problem still is, the known 1882 morgue photos of the "dead" Jesse James aren't a match for the confirmed photos of the living Jesse James. When taken into account along with the 1882 forensic data that indicate a staged crime scene, problematic ballistics, and a body dead far too long to have been shot that morning, there are obvious concerns.

Is the body of 88-year old Jere Miah "Jerry" James, buried in rural Kenodoshah, KS really the body of the outlaw Jeremiah Woodson "Jesse" James?

After the death of James Timberlake, U.S. Marshal for the Western District, the career lawman would be succeeded in that position by none other than the legendary J.O. Shelby. Oh, how I just *hate* coincidences. . . .

In 1937, on a desolate hill many miles from nowhere in a largely uninhabited quarter of New Mexico, country "foot doctor" Milton "Doc" Noss would accidentally stumble on perhaps the greatest treasure find in American history. Deep inside the bowels of that hillside, known as Victorio Peak, and at the bottom of an apparently abandoned and closed off mine shaft, Noss would discover piles of dusty stacked bars of gold, saddle bags and strong boxes filled with gold and silver coin, and other valuable treasures and artifacts that belonged somewhere other than deep inside a derelict mining property.

Several people have seen Doc Noss' gold, both inside Victorio Peak and the many samples he extracted from that mysterious location. His family still owns artifacts such as swords, jewelry, and a bejeweled crown that speak to the credibility of the find. Noss was known to have sold his "illegal" gold at various pawn shops, and possibly to gold buyers south of the border in Mexico. His efforts to expand the mine's entrance resulted in a catastrophic collapse of the mineshaft, and barred Noss' efforts to get at the remaining treasure. Doc Noss was subsequently killed in an argument with a business partner who suspected that Noss was moving and hiding gold in an effort to cheat the wealthy Texan on their partnership to reopen the shaft. Doc's wife, Babe, was left to try to cash in on the couple's claim to "mine" Victorio Peak. More than one later explorer claimed to have gained access to the treasure rooms through obscured, hidden side-entrance passageways. One was an Air-Force officer who subsequently passed a lie detector test. With the federal takeover of the Victorio Peak property after World War II, for the supposed purpose of including the area as part of the "Cold War's" White Sands Missile Range, Babe Noss and her family were unable to resume work at the site. Appeals made to the federal government and the military for the purpose of being able to work their valid New Mexico mining claim were denied.

Later evidence would come to light showing that the military had begun mining activity at the site,[27] a charge that would be officially denied. Photographic evidence and eyewitness testimony, however, strongly countered the military's denial.

That the U.S. military, President Lyndon Johnson, high-ranking members of the Nixon Administration, and high-profile attorney F. Lee Bailey all took a seemingly keen interest in the Victorio Peak treasure story speaks to its apparent veracity.

In 1977, the U.S. military, under increasing public and legal pressure to come clean on the subject of Victorio Peak, agreed to allow a limited exploration of the supposed treasure site. Several parties, including professional treasure hunters and Babe Noss and her family, were granted permission to explore Victorio Peak. The much awaited Victorio Peak search turned into more of a media event than an actual treasure hunt. Looking at the amount of earth moving and apparent mining activity performed by the military during the years the property had been off limits, a disgusted Babe Noss told all who would listen that the government had already stolen the gold.[28]

Despite the use of such techniques as ground penetrating radar, no treasure was found in 1977's "Operation Goldfinder." Trash and debris left in the shaft leading to the bottom of the hillside indicated that Victorio Peak had seen many visitors since Doc Noss' death in 1946. A search for hidden side entranceways was undertaken, but none were found. Before any serious searching could get underway, the military called a halt to the fiasco and asked everyone to pack up and leave. The military maintained that they had given all those invited to attend a fair chance at finding the supposed treasure, but that none had obviously ever existed. The military said the gold was nothing but a myth. The treasure hunters interpreted the actions of the military as part of the government's longstanding conspiracy to prevent any serious exploration of the site from occurring. A serious hunt, they claimed, would have taken heavy mining equipment on site and much more time than the military had allotted.

The 1977 Victorio Peak "dig" had morphed into little more than a public relations opportunity for the military, with no systematic, time-appropriate, heavy equipment operation having been allowed.

The story was covered by Dan Rather and *60 Minutes*, who obviously saw Victorio Peak as more of a curiosity piece and human interest story on the madness of "gold fever" instead of a worthy news opportunity. That there was ever any actual treasure once buried inside that hill never seems to have crossed the minds of the producers and editorial staff of *60 Minutes*.

Many of the colorful characters involved in the history of Victorio Peak were shown and given a brief chance to say a few words. Mr. Rather found particular humor in the man who identified himself as Jesse James III. James had told Mr. Rather that his grandfather had buried the treasure in anticipation of the day *"the South would rise again."*[29]

Jesse James III, a.k.a. Jesse Lee James, was actually Orvis Lee Howk, co-author with Del Schrader of the 1960s book Jesse James was One of His Names. Howk is most likely the grandson of Jesse Robert "Dingus" James, who was a rebel raider, James Gang member, and first cousin of Jeremiah Woodson "Jesse" James. Little did Dan Rather know that, some 15 years later, Bob Brewer in Arkansas would use a treasure map and other clues from this very same book to locate buried treasure in western Arkansas . . . treasure connected by rock carvings and a published robbery escape route to Jesse James.

We must consider the possibility that if the real Jesse James did not die from a gunshot wound in 1882, and that Sheriff James Timberlake was in on the scheme to bury another man in James' place, then Orvis Lee Howk's statement his grandfather buried the Victorio Peak treasure against the day "the South would rise again" may have some basis in fact.

   Did James Timberlake travel to New Mexico with the real, not-so-dead Jeremiah Woodson "Jesse" James to bury Confederate KGC treasure at Victorio Peak? Might this treasure have included the recovered Danville silver, the gold from the "robbery" of the Confederate wagon train in Chennault, Georgia — and also the remaining loot from many of the James Gang's robberies? The timing for such a scenario squares perfectly with the known facts. The Danville silver and Chennault gold disappeared during the last days of the Civil War. George Kane stayed on in Danville until the late 1860s, quite likely until the KGC was able to remove the silver to a safer intermediate location. The James Gang continued to plunder out west until the early 1880s, at which point the notoriety of Jesse James, as well as the sizable reward money being offered for his capture, dead or alive, required KGC action to be taken to remove the increasing governmental pressure. So, a troublesome cousin, Jesse Mason James, was selected to take the place of the real Jesse James. Sheriff Timberlake, accompanied by James Gang members, whisks the body from St. Joseph in Buchanan County to Kearney for a fast burial, out of "respect" for Zerelda James and the James family. Then, Timberlake declines to run for re-election for sheriff of Clay County, supposedly because of the fallout over the cold-blooded killing of Jesse James, arranged through the services of two James Gang members, Bob and Charley Ford.

   No further investigation is conducted as to why the forensics from the murder of Jesse James are at such odds with the story told by Bob and Charley Ford. There are no answers provided as to why the bullet in James' skull didn't match Bob Ford's gun. Why there was a bullet of a different caliber still lodged in the wall above the painting, a bullet that did in fact match the Ford gun. Why the body showed signs of a struggle, at odds with the supposed surprise execution from a quick bullet to the back of the head. And why the body incongruously appeared to have been dead since sometime the previous evening. Also, why the photos of the body only bore a passing resemblance to Jesse James, who was taller, thinner, and had lighter colored hair than the corpse being represented as himself. The death photos show no apparent exit wound in the front of the head, as would have been expected had the bullet passed from the back of the skull and exited out the front of the skull, only stopping after it had become lodged in the wall. The shot fired into the wall on the morning of

April, 1882 with Bob Ford's gun was apparently fired in an effort to help "stage the scene."

Timberlake went out of his Clay County jurisdiction — with members of the James Gang — to bring the body back to Kearney, where the gravesite could be keep under the watchful eye of James' mother . . . supposedly to keep curiosity seekers away.

Bob and Charley Ford are sentenced to hang, but pardoned by Governor Crittenden — who had likely conspired with Timberlake and the Ford Brothers to set up the victim — within two hours. The Fords are paid a few dollars for their trouble, and take the opportunity to flee Missouri. "Angry" that James was killed instead of apprehended by the Fords, Crittenden instead awards most of the James reward money to Timberlake, who soon after leaves for New Mexico — quite possibly with the real Jesse James.

Jesse and Frank in 1872

Meanwhile, Frank James surrenders to the Governor, and stands trial with J.O. Shelby, Timberlake's former commanding officer from the storied Confederate unit that entered Mexico rather than surrender, testifying for Frank James in order to sway the jury not to convict. The tactic works, and Frank James never spends a day in prison.

Minnesota journalist Don Shelby, the great-grandson of General J.O. Shelby, was interviewed by forensic geologist Scott Wolter on the cable television show *America Unearthed*. This particular episode was *Lincoln's Secret Assassins*, about the alleged KGC involvement in President Lincoln's murder. As Wolter and Shelby stood at the site in Eagle Pass, Texas looking across the Rio Grande where General Jo Shelby had led his soldiers into Mexico, Wolter asked Shelby a very direct question. *"Do you think your great-grandfather was in the KGC?"*

Mr. Shelby barely hesitated, answering, "*I don't see how he could've helped but to have been in the KGC.*"[30]

If it walks like a duck and quacks like a duck, then it's probably a duck.

Why had James Timberlake gone to such lengths for the kin of Jesse James? Why had J.O. Shelby taken such a bold step as to publicly testify for the defense of the notorious Frank James? Why did columnist John Edwards make the James Boys out to be American heroes? There can only be one logical answer . . . the James Brothers had been all along doing the bidding of the KGC. Their 17 years of high profile robberies of mostly Union targets had been accomplished under the auspices and protection of the Knights of the Golden Circle.

In an online conversation with David C. Keehn, author of the recent book Knights of the Golden Circle, I asked Mr. Keehn if he thought Marshal George Kane had also been a member of the KGC. Keehn, who sticks close to the facts uncovered by his research, and whose writings are not subject to much speculation, said, "*I do suspect that he (Kane) was a Knights leader in Baltimore and was tied in with the Lincoln abduction/assassination but haven't been able to establish either.*"

Keehn knows that George Kane walked like a duck and quaked like a duck . . . but has never been officially connected to this secret society of ducks. But Kane, Booth, and the KGC were all assuredly birds of a feather. . . .

Allan Pinkerton, the detective/abolitionist who once compared John Brown to George Washington, got himself involved in a case that saw him spy on Marshal Kane and "Captain" Cipriano Ferrandini, and arrest Charles Webb's friend Mayor George Brown in Baltimore. And then later Pinkerton was put on the trail of Frank and Jesse James in Missouri. Mere coincidence you say? Or was the abolitionist Pinkerton really picking and choosing his cases to go after the infamous KGC?

Marshall Kane and Charles Webb were close allies in Baltimore. Sovereign Commander Albert Pike was Charles Webb's "Companion Mason" in the Scottish Rite Freemasons. Albert Pike, as the alleged mastermind behind the KGC, would have overlooked the KGC activities of J.O. Shelby, James Timberlake, Jesse James, and Frank James. The James Gang supposedly buried loot in and around Pike's western Arkansas property, the escape route used after an 1874 stagecoach robbery (actually, they robbed the same stagecoach on two separate occasions).

Just more coincidence?

We have accounts of treasure buried on Pike's property. Treasure buried in a "Solomon's Temple" treasure grid just west of Pike's Greasy Cove property,[31] an area with numerous "double J" rock and tree carvings. Treasure buried under the home of John J. Mattison and Andrew Saulsbury, both whom are connected to Webb through the companies owned by James Armstrong. More treasure buried under the Fountain Hotel that is the residence of Thomas Armstrong, nephew of James and best friend of Andrew Saulsbury, with both men working directly under Charles Webb.

Yet even more coincidence?

Future presidential assassin John Wilkes Booth, confidant of George Kane, who is known to "hang out" at the Fountain Hotel, a center for rebel activity and location where an agent for Dr. Luke Blackburn sets up the nefarious Great Fever Plot operation to mail infected garments to the White House and throughout the North. Dr. Blackburn, who checks into the St. Lawrence Hall in Montreal on the very same day John Wilkes Booth checks in (and is later seen playing cards with the assassin), while Booth is seeking an audience with George Kane, probably to discuss plans for the abduction of Mr. Lincoln. Then there are George Sanders, stalker of President Lincoln, and Patrick Charles Martin, the Confederate blockade runner, who transports Booth's wardrobe and writes to Kane in Virginia asking for a reference for Booth. Meanwhile, both Sanders and Martin host Booth for the next ten days in Montreal and are supplying Booth with funds while Kane, the Confederate 007, slips back to Richmond to work on a "top secret" assignment. Booth, "bossing" the Lincoln job, while meeting in Boston with Godfrey Joseph Hymans, Blackburn's agent who sends the clothes infected with yellow fever from his room at the Fountain Hotel. And again, George Kane, our 007, running the Union blockade with bioterrorist Dr. Blackburn . . . .

And so it goes, around and around, birds of a feather, quacking and swimming circles in the very same rebel duck pond.

Milton "Doc" Noss was very clear about the papers and documents he found along with the immense treasure buried in the caverns beneath New Mexico's remote Victorio Peak. The last date on any of those papers and letters was just before 1880. Nothing was dated *after* 1880.

Many who have looked at the Victorio Peak treasure story have concluded that the date of 1880 points to the Apache, Chief Victorio, for whom the 500-foot hill is named, as being the source of the treasure. The loot was presumably gathered from Apache raids on settlers, stagecoaches, and passing wagon trains. Chief Victorio, whose braves had been fighting simultaneous skirmishes with both the U.S. Cavalry and the Mexican Army, was reportedly killed in 1880 by Mexican forces, which explained the lack of any subsequent Victorio Peak 'deposits" after 1880.

This is an interesting theory, except that the enormous size of the Victorio Peak treasure, especially the great number of gold bars "stacked like cordwood" would tend to rule out random New Mexico Indian raids as the source of the fortune.

The Victorio Peak treasure was found in caverns and carved out rooms near the bottom of an abandoned, fortified mining shaft. The Apaches did not build mining shafts. White men seeking gold and other valuable minerals build mine shafts. Except, this peculiar mine seems not to have been worked. There were no tailings found, no waste rock plied up as evidence that gold or silver ore had been extracted from the hill and processed. This was a very strange mine indeed, one in which someone seems to have deposited valuable treasure, not extracted it. This is exactly what author Warren Getler of <u>Rebel Gold</u> fame claims the KGC to have done when constructing their main "depositories."[32] They used the cover of ordinary mining activity to sink a shaft, deposit the valuables, and then cover up the entrance as if the mine had been "abandoned."

More to the point, Doc Noss was very apprehensive about the specific names of the folks mentioned in the letters and on the documents from the cave. He was afraid of being on the receiving end of trouble caused by the descendants of the people whose names appeared in those letters.

Not only did Apaches in 1880 not build mine shafts, they also did not write and save letters in English mentioning the names of people an individual such as Doc Noss would have recognized. Names such as Jefferson Davis, Robert E. Lee, Louis Wigfall, James Seddon, Thomas Crittenden, General J.O. Shelby, Sheriff James Timberlake, the Younger Brothers, and Frank and Jesse James.

Noss did not have to fear the descendants of long-gone Apaches who might have stolen and buried the treasure. But he certainly had reason to fear the descendants of the Confederate leaders, the KGC, and most especially the current members of the James Family. That is not a lineup to mess with! Names such as Jesse James, Frank James, and Cole Younger would have certainly given me pause! Perhaps that is why Doc Noss, as later reported by wife Babe Noss, put all the papers in a can and burned them, to his wife's apparent befuddlement.

Paperwork from the 1870s, written in English, with certain names that caused Noss to become nervous, would necessarily have eliminated long-dead Spanish priests and conquistadors as the source of the Victorio Peak treasure trove.

In their waning years, the James Gang had drastically scaled back its operations, and was likely just stealing what members needed to survive. By 1880, the feds had seriously turned up the heat. Many original James Gang associates were dead, and the new members were not of the same caliber as their battle-hardened predecessors. With the private and federal rewards on their heads ever increasing, the walls were closing in on the James Boys. A bold plan was needed for them to escape and ride off into the sunset.

The only way for Jesse James to escape was to fake his own death. Once "dead" and under a new identity, James could head west and re-bury the James Gang's accumulated loot, collected over 17 years to further the cause of the post-war KGC. New Mexico was Albert Pike's old stomping ground, and James Timberlake had a brother there in the ranching business. Desolate Victorio Peak, with warlike Chief Victorio now dead, was the perfect inaccessible spot for a KGC depository. From mid-1882 until sometime in 1883, they sank the mine shaft, carved out some rooms in the underground caverns, then closed the mine's entrance and "abandoned" it. Timberlake went back to Missouri where Governor Thomas Crittenden soon appointed him as Deputy U.S. Marshal of all of western Missouri. Jesse James, under the guise of Jere Miah "Jerry" James, headed back to a long, quiet, obscure, and finally peaceful life in rural Neodesha, Kansas.

Frank James, meanwhile, was getting off scot-free thanks to J.O. Shelby, and mother Zerelda stayed at the family homestead which looked out upon the grave site of the loose cannon, black sheep cousin Jesse Mason James, buried in Jesse Woodson

James' place. Zerelda is said to have kept an eye out for "souvenir hunters."

Perhaps "souvenir hunters" weren't the only folks who worried Mrs. James.

First cousin and James Gang member Jesse Robert James would assume the new identity J. Frank Dalton, and ride on to write a final chapter of notoriety with his newly named "Dalton Gang." In his later years (for Dalton is said to have lived to be over 100 years old), Dalton's immediate family would seek to cash in by billing their patriarch as the "real" Jesse James. Grandson Orvis Lee Howk, a.k.a. Jesse James III, would co-author the book Jesse James Was One of His Names with Los Angeles news columnist Del Schrader. While Dalton was privy to many of the James Gang's secrets, he was almost certainly "a" Jesse James but probably not "*the*" Jesse James.

This brings us to two final important questions. First, why was the treasure in Baltimore abandoned at the same time the KGC was building its "depositories" in the remote Southwest? And second, is there more treasure still out there waiting to be found?

The KGC, much like the Freemasons, was built through the founding of local chapters. The Masons called these local meeting places lodges, while the KGC called them "castles." Each of the KGC castles enjoyed a certain amount of autonomy . . . especially after the scandal involving controversial Commander-in-Chief George W.L. Bickley. In today's modern world, we talk about an underground group operating through a series of "cells." A cell in one city or country might not always know what the organization's other cells are doing. This makes the organization as a whole much harder to infiltrate.

The Baltimore cell, founded long before the war for the purpose of agitating for Southern rights, and also to prepare for the armed acquisition of more slave territory, was a far different group than the Civil War's Quantrill's Raiders and the subsequent post-war James-Younger Gang. The Baltimore chapter was built by wealthy, comfortable businessmen with dreams of a rejuvenated South, the resumption of the African slave trade, and the conquest of foreign territory for the expansion of the Southern slave empire. Lincoln and the Civil War brought a crushing end to those dreams, along with the added indignity of having Union troops occupy their city for the duration of the conflict. Not only were they unsuccessful in seeing that the institution of slavery was expanded, but their ill-advised attack on Mr. Lincoln and the Union actually served to bring about the premature end of slavery. The KGC, far from being Dixie's savior, had actually helped to sound the South's death knoll by forcing a showdown with the North. Sam Houston's vision of Southern calamity precipitated by secession had proven eerily spot on.

Lincoln's Emancipation Proclamation put an end to the Old South forever, although it took much of a century for the Old South to realize this fact. In Baltimore, further direct resistance to Washington, D.C. and the North would have been futile. Instead, the modus operandi became the salvaging of Southern culture and social order. With slavery now out of the question, plantation slaves became sharecroppers. House slaves became lowly paid domestic servants. Once the Northern intruders and carpetbaggers had drifted back north one-by-one, any meaningful change could be thwarted by restricting the right of blacks to vote, and the imposition of segregation and a clearly-defined two-tier society. Say hello to Jim Crow.

The more things change, the more they stay the same.

Men such as the Armstrongs, the Webbs, Saulsbury, and Kane sought to hold the line on real change by becoming politically active. They became city council members like James Webb and Andrew Saulsbury, or the city tax collector such as Charles Webb, and even Mayor of Baltimore such as George Kane and Ferdinand Latrobe. The Armstrongs, Webbs, and Mr. Saulsbury also kept their businesses, concentrating wealth and further exercising political control over the city.

Dr. Luke Blackburn would return to Kentucky and become that state's governor.

These were fantastically powerful and wealthy men who did not need the gold coins they had collected as officers in the Knights of the Golden Circle. In fact, using any of the gold for personal reasons would have been considered a horribly shameful and dishonorable act, and would have exposed them to retribution had other Knights learned of such unforgiveable behavior. Giving the money back was not practical, since so much had transpired and so many of the rank and file members had been killed in the war.

The unexplained coded due bill with Andrew Saulsbury's name, published in that New England math textbook, is yet one more bizarre coincidence that defies reason. Did Saulsbury, in 1866, try to pay Confederate submarine and explosives expert James McClintock for new state-of-the art technology that might enable the KGC to once again take on Washington? Did federal agents publish the coded due bill in the math textbook as a way of letting the KGC know they were being watched? Was McClintock, who offered to sell his marine war technology to the British Empire, blown up in Boston Harbor because he had become a potential danger to the United States?

And the coincidences go on and on.

By 1870, it seems apparent that the older, wealthier Baltimore KGC members had abandoned any hope that the South might rise again. They were more interested in keeping control of their city and in maintaining the social order. The gold must have been a constant reminder of their colossal failure. They couldn't employ the treasure for what it was designed. They couldn't give it back. They couldn't honorably keep it. They couldn't even personally use it. So it just remained, buried where it was, because when it stayed where it was, in some way the dreams of their Golden Circle would not officially die, and there would always remain some last, faint, romantic glimmer of hope. The gold had become an albatross hung around their wealthy, Confederate, aristocratic necks. Perhaps they were a bit relieved when, in 1870, the Fountain Hotel was torn down and a lucky laborer named Murray walked away with a tin box containing some 2,000 secreted gold coins.

The curse of the golden genie had finally been passed onto someone else.

Western frontier men such as Jesse James, Frank James, and the Youngers were, however, quite a "different breed of cat" from the Baltimore stuffed shirts who had largely fought their war in boardrooms and behind closed doors while sipping Kentucky bourbon and smoking top-shelf cigars. For some of the western KGC guerillas, who had tasted and dished out incredible violence from a very young age, the war against Northern aggression would not soon end. Jesse James was reportedly shot some 22 times as a Confederate guerilla, including while trying to surrender. For men such as the James and Younger Brothers, this ongoing, seemingly unfinished conflict was deeply personal. They had known nothing but war. And the long reach of the federal government was often not quite long enough to extend into the outlying badlands of the Wild West.

Baltimore, obviously, was a different story altogether.

For 17 more years, the rebel guerillas continued to ride, now under the guise of outlaws and train robbers, exacting revenge and plundering for the KGC. Colonel Kane, who shared much in common with the western guerillas (the war had proven deeply personal), was stuck for almost a half a decade in Danville, acting as KGC sentinel for the 39 kegs of Confederate silver. Kane would not return to Baltimore until right before the Fountain Hotel was demolished and the coins buried on that property discovered. And Andrew Saulsbury, sentinel for the Eden Street cache, would die suddenly soon thereafter, leaving those coins securely hidden under the home of his widow. Perhaps the remaining Baltimore members "in the know" would leave the coins under the Eden Street house in case they could be later used. But James Armstrong, James Webb, and Captain Mattison would die shortly after Saulsbury, and Kane would die not long after them. That left only Charles Webb and Thomas Armstrong, who were busy running their soap and candle empire. Webb was also doubling as city tax collector under Mayor Ferdinand Latrobe.

One by one the wealthy, powerful conspirators grew old and died. The coins remained on Eden Street, slowly being forgotten — long out of sight, and now out of mind, buried so many decades ago in the far corner of that innocuous dirt floor basement. Eventually, everyone connected to the coins was dead, and the KGC disbanded. Same with the fortune secreted away beneath Victorio Peak, just that the process for this post-war hoard began later and took far longer. But eventually, Victorio Peak was forgotten as well . . . until by happenstance Doc Noss came along in 1937, caught accidentally on "Vicky Peak" by a driving rainstorm, looking for a temporary place to shelter.

Until now, no one had ever connected the Eden Street coins to the Baltimore KGC. The Baltimore KGC and coins to Marshal Kane, and the possible conspiracies to kidnap or kill Mr. Lincoln. Webb to Kane. Kane to the Danville treasure. Webb to Albert Pike. The Danville treasure to Victorio Peak. Jessie James and Albert Pike to Victorio Peak.

It's now, as they say, a whole new ball game.

Can there possibly be more treasure still buried out there across North America? The answer to this big question would seem to be a definite **yes**! Some KGC treasure has already been found (by Bob Brewer, Ron Pastore, Henry Grob and Theodore Jones, and quite possibly Milton "Doc" Noss). Other treasure has almost certainly been found but never reported. Some had been recovered long ago by KGC sentinels collecting on "paychecks." And some has been lost forever, bulldozed or flooded or built over, never to be recovered. But there is almost certainly more loot out there, still accessible, waiting for the right person or persons to come along and grab it. KGC treasure in Baltimore, Georgia, Arkansas, Oklahoma, Texas, New Mexico, perhaps even up in neighboring Canada. After 150 years, it won't be even remotely easy — but then again, neither will it be impossible, provided the gold and silver still exist. Perhaps it will be found by a professional treasure hunter. Or, by boys digging for worms, or even perhaps burying their club's secret papers in an out-of-the-way spot left untouched for several generations.

Serendipity. . . .

The Baltimore Gold Hoard was discovered by the perhaps city's smallest boys club ever, the Rinky Dinky Doos, whose membership consisted of Henry Grob and Theodore Jones. What they uncovered, totally by accident, was from the golden treasury of what had been the city's largest, most secretive, and most dangerous boys' club in history — the Knights of the Golden Circle, formerly the Order of the Lone Star.

Truth is stranger than fiction, and there is yet another pot of gold out there not at the end of some rainbow, but rather hidden by the shadowy men of the KGC with hopes you would never find it.

Good luck. . . .

My own treasure has been in telling you this incredible, almost unbelievable, yet very true story. It's my personal pot of gold at the end of that ever-shifting rainbow.

Notes

1. SERENDIPITY

1. Ann McGinley-Bok, *Family Remembrances* (California: Pathfinder Publishing, 2006), p.198.
2. The People History web site at www.thepeoplehistory.com.
3. *Baltimore Evening Sun*, 9/1/1934, p.3.
4. Leonard Augsburger, *Treasure in the Cellar* (Baltimore: Maryland Historical Society, 2008), pp.20-21.
5. Ibid., p.17.
6. Ibid., p.21.
7. Ibid., p.22.
8. Testimony of Theodore Jones and Henry Grob, BCCC#2, docket A-579, 1934.
9. Leonard Augsburger, *Treasure in the Cellar* (Baltimore: Maryland Historical Society, 2008), p.27.

2. THE REPUBLIC OF TEXAS

1. www.historyguy.com. "Mexican-American War."
2. Lee Stacy (editor), *Mexico and the United States* (Singapore: Marshall Cavendish Corp., 2002), p.487.
3. www.pbs.org. *"New Perspectives on the West — Tejas."*
4. www.pbs.org. *"New Perspectives on the West — Antonio López de Santa Anna."*
5. www.freedomdocuments.com. *"The Text of Travis' Alamo Letter."*
6. www.wikipedia.com. *"William B. Travis."*
7. Richard R. Sherman, *In the Right Place at the Right Time: Twenty-six Prominent Americans* (iUniverse, 2008), p.41.

8. David F. Marley, *Wars of the Americas: A Chronology of Armed Conflict in the Western Hemisphere — Second Edition* (ABC-CLIO, Inc., 2008), p. 723.
9. J.R. Edmondson, *Jim Bowie: Frontier Legend, Alamo Hero* (The Rosen Publishing Group, 2003), p.35.
10. Graeme Donald, *Loose Cannons: 101 Myths, Mishaps and Misadventures of Military History* (Osprey Publishing, 2012), in the section "Kentucky 'Fraid Chicken?"
11. Gail Selinger with W. Thomas Smith, Jr., *The Complete Idiot's Guide to Pirates* (The Penguin Group, 2006), p.330.
12. Victor South, *Remember the Alamo: Americans Fight for Texas 1820-1845* (Mason Crest, 2013)
13. Mary L. Scheer (editor), *Women and the Texas Revolution* (University of North Texas Press, 2012), p.129.
14. Mark M. Carroll, *Homesteads Ungovernable: Families, Sex, Race, and the Law in Frontier Texas* (The University of Texas Press, 2001), p. 33.
15. www.wikipedia.com. *"Republic of Texas."*
16. Robert E. May, *Slavery, Race, and Conquest in the Tropics* (Cambridge University Press, 2013), p.36.

3. LOOK WHAT WE FOUND!

1. Leonard Augsburger, *Treasure in the Cellar* (Baltimore: Maryland Historical Society, 2008), p.27.
2. Ibid., pp.27-28.
3. *Forbes*, "Governments Still Heavy-Handed 80 years After FDR's Gold Confiscation" by Adrian Ash, 4/5/2013.
4. *Making Cents*, "Fort Knox, America's Gold Vault" by Dr. Sol Taylor, 4/19/2008.
5. Leonard Augsburger, *Treasure in the Cellar* (Baltimore: Maryland Historical Society, 2008), p.28.
6. Ibid.

Notes

4. THE VOYAGES OF CAPTAIN JOHN

1. *Rare Coin Review* #150, *"The 1934 Baltimore Gold Hoard"* by Leonard Augsburger, November/December 2002, p.38.
2. Ibid.
3. All information regarding the French seizure of the American vessel *The Eliza Davidson* has been derived from the 1885 volume of *Reports of Cases Argued and Adjudged in the Court of Appeals in Maryland* published by M. Curlander of Baltimore. The specific case referenced is *The Charleston Insurance and Trust Company vs. Jas. J. Corner and Thomas Corner*, December, 1844 on pp. 276-289.
4. Ibid.
5. All information regarding the activities of the American vessel *The Eliza Davidson* in both Cuba and Sierra Leone has been derived from a report from the Mixed Court of British and Spanish Justice recorded in the *Correspondence with the British Commissioners at Sierra Leone Regarding the Slave Trade* (From May 11th to December 31st, 1840, inclusive). See the specific case summary "Report of the Case of the Brig 'Eliza Davidson,' Alexander B. Hanna, Master. Sierra Leone, April 24th, 1840."
6. United States. Congress. House. Committee on Commerce, George Washington Toland, Nicholas Philip Trist – 1840. *Report 707.*
7. All information regarding the activities of the American vessel *The Eliza Davidson* in both Cuba and Sierra Leone has been derived from a report from the Mixed Court of British and Spanish Justice recorded in the *"Correspondence with the British Commissioners at Sierra Leone Regarding the Slave Trade* (From May 11th to December 31st, 1840, inclusive)." See the specific case summary *"Report of the Case of the Brig 'Eliza Davidson,' Alexander B. Hanna, Master. Sierra Leone, April 24th, 1840."*

8. Anonymous, *The Authentic Exposition of the K.G.C., Knights of the Golden Circle, or a History of Secession from 1834 to 1861* (C.O. Perrine, 1861), p.6.
9. *The Baltimore Sun*, *"A Bitter Inner Harbor Legacy: The Slave Trade,"* by Ralph Clayton, 7/12/2000.
10. www.msa.maryland.gov. *"Baltimore City, Maryland – Historical Chronology."*
11. www.mdhs.org. *"Maryland State Colonization Society Papers, 1827-1871, MS 571."*
12. Ibid.
13. Thomas A. Horrocks, Harold Holzer, and Frank J. Williams, editors, *The Living Lincoln* (Southern Illinois University, 2011), p.192.
14. David C. Keehn, *Knights of the Golden Circle: Secret Empire, Southern Secession, Civil War* (Louisiana State University Press, 2013), p.73.
15. www.immigrantships.net. *Immigrant Ships Transcriber Guild.* The Bark "Ann Eliza" Rio de Janeiro, Brazil to Baltimore, Maryland, March 3, 1841.

5. LET THE CIRCUS BEGIN

1. Leonard Augsburger, *Treasure in the Cellar* (Baltimore: Maryland Historical Society, 2008), p.11.
2. Ibid., p.19.
3. *Baltimore News*, 9/3/1934, p.3.
4. *Baltimore American*, 9/2/1934, p.3
5. *Baltimore Evening Sun*, 9/1/1934, p.13.
6. Ibid., 9/6/1934, p.38.
7. Leonard Augsburger, *Treasure in the Cellar* (Baltimore: Maryland Historical Society, 2008), pp.34-35.
8. *Baltimore Evening Sun*, 9/1/1934, p.13.
9. Leonard Augsburger, *Treasure in the Cellar* (Baltimore: Maryland Historical Society, 2008), p.35.
10. Ibid., p.30.
11. *Baltimore Sun*, 4/23/1936, p.26.
12. *Baltimore Evening Sun*, 9/11/1934, p.34.

Notes

13. *Baltimore Sun*, 9/15/1934, p.20.
14. Leonard Augsburger, *Treasure in the Cellar* (Baltimore: Maryland Historical Society, 2008), pp.50-51.
15. *Rare Coin Review* #150, *"The 1934 Baltimore Gold Hoard"* by Leonard Augsburger, November/December 2002, p.36.
16. Leonard Augsburger, *Treasure in the Cellar* (Baltimore: Maryland Historical Society), p.29.
17. Ibid., p.49.
18. Ibid., pp.11-12.
19. Testimony of Theodore Jones, BCCC#2, docket A-579, 1934.
20. Leonard Augsburger, *Treasure in the Cellar* (Baltimore: Maryland Historical Society, 2008), p.48.
21. *Rare Coin Review* #150, *"The 1934 Baltimore Gold Hoard"* by Leonard Augsburger, November/December 2002, p.38.
22. Ibid.
23. Ibid., p.37.
24. Leonard Augsburger, *Treasure in the Cellar* (Baltimore: Maryland Historical Society, 2008), p.7.
25. Ibid.
26. Ibid., p.8.
27. Ibid., p.9.
28. Ibid.
29. Ibid., p.11.
30. Ibid., p.10.
31. Ibid.
32. Testimony of Theodore Jones, BCCC#2, docket A-579, 1934.
33. Leonard Augsburger, *Treasure in the Cellar* (Baltimore: Maryland Historical Society, 2008), p.68.
34. *Rare Coin Review* #150, *"The 1934 Baltimore Gold Hoard"* by Leonard Augsburger, November/December 2002, p.39.
35. Leonard Augsburger, *Treasure in the Cellar* (Baltimore: Maryland Historical Society, 2008), p.41.
36. Ibid., p.52.
37. Ibid., p.51.

6. BIRTH OF THE KGC

1. www.ushistory.org. *"13a.The Declaration of Independence and Its Legacy."*
2. www.wikipedia.org. *"Slavery in the United States."*
3. Ibid. *"Act Prohibiting Importation of Slaves."*
4. James A. Morone, *Hellfire Nation: The Politics of Sin in American History* (Yale University press, 2004), p.154.
5. www.pbs.org. *"Africans in America, Part 3 – Nat Turner's Rebellion."*
6. Anonymous, *An Authentic Exposition of the "K.G.C." Knights of the Golden Circle, or, a History of the Secession from 1834 to 1861* (Charles Perrine, Publisher, Indianapolis, IN, 1861), p.6.
7. David C. Keehn, *Knights of the Golden Circle: Secret Empire, Southern Secession, Civil War* (Louisiana State University Press, 2013), p.41.
8. *1841 Maryland Colonization Society Journal (Vol. 1, No.1)*, p.11. James Corner is listed as a member of the Baltimore City delegation.
9. Anonymous, *An Authentic Exposition of the "K.G.C." Knights of the Golden Circle, or, a History of the Secession from 1834 to 1861* (Charles Perrine, Publisher, Indianapolis, IN, 1861), p.6.
10. Ibid.
11. www.wikipedia.org. *"John C. Calhoun."*
12. Thomas G. West, *Vindicating the Founders: Race, Sex, Class, and Justice in the Origins of America* (Rowman & Littlefield, 1997), p.33.
13. Irving H. Bartlet, *John C. Calhoun, A Biography* (W. W. Norton & Company, 1994), p.228.
14. Warren Getler and Bob Brewer, *Rebel Gold: One Man's Quest to Crack the Code Behind the Secret Treasure of the Confederacy* (Simon & Schuster, 2003), p.46.
15. *"Why Non-Slaveholding Southerners Fought,"* Address to the Charleston Library Society given by Gordon Rhea, January 25, 2011.

Notes

16. www.wikipedia.com "*John A. Quitman.*"
17. John D. Winters, The Civil War in Louisiana (Louisiana State University Press, 1963), p.64.
18. Warren Getler and Bob Brewer, *Rebel Gold: One Man's Quest to Crack the Code Behind the Secret Treasure of the Confederacy* (Simon & Schuster, 2003), pp.48-52.
19. Tom Chaffin, *Fatal Glory: Narciso Lopez and the First Clandestine U.S. War Against Cuba* (The University Press of Virginia, 1996), pp.80-81.
20. David C. Keehn, *Knights of the Golden Circle: Secret Empire, Southern Secession, Civil War* (Louisiana State University Press, 2013), p.11.
21. www.wikipedia.org. "*Crabb Massacre.*"
22. www.wikipedia.org. "William Walker (filibuster)."
23. www.wikipedia.org "Franklin Pierce."
24. Robert E. May, *Manifest Destiny's Underworld: Filibustering in Antebellum America* (University of North Carolina Press, 2002), pp.257-258.
25. Ibid., p.84.
26. David C. Keehn, *Knights of the Golden Circle: Secret Empire, Southern Secession, Civil War* (Louisiana State University Press, 2013), pp.13-14.
27. BreAnn Rumsch, *Franklin Pierce: 14th President of the United States* (ABDO Publishing, Minnesota, 2009), p.12.
28. Robert E. May, *John A. Quitman: Old South Crusader* (Louisiana State University Press, 1984), p.294.
29. Robert E. May, *Manifest Destiny's Underworld: Filibustering in Antebellum America* (University of North Carolina Press, 2002), p.35.
30. Randolph P. Campbell, "Knights of the Golden Circle" from the Handbook of Texas Online.
31. www.wikipedia.org. "*George W.L. Bickley.*"
32. Warren Getler and Bob Brewer, *Rebel Gold: One Man's Quest to Crack the Code Behind the Secret Treasure of the Confederacy* (Simon & Schuster, 2003), pp.16-17.
33. David C. Keehn, *Knights of the Golden Circle: Secret Empire, Southern Secession, Civil War* (Louisiana State University Press, 2013), p.6.

34. Ibid., p.7.
35. Leslie Stephen (editor), *Dictionary of National Biography 17* (Smith, Elder & Co., London, England, 1889) p. 264-266.
36. David C. Keehn, *Knights of the Golden Circle: Secret Empire, Southern Secession, Civil War* (Louisiana State University Press, 2013), p.7.
37. Ibid., p.8.
38. Frank L. Klement, *Dark Lanterns: Secret Political Societies, Conspiracies, and Treason Trials in the Civil War* (Louisiana State University Press, 1989), pp.7-8.
39. Mark C. Carnes, *Secret Ritual and Manhood in Victorian America* (Yale University, 1989) pp.7-8.
40. Frank L. Klement, *Dark Lanterns: Secret Political Societies, Conspiracies, and Treason Trials in the Civil War* (Louisiana State University Press, 1989), p.8.
41. David C. Keehn, *Knights of the Golden Circle: Secret Empire, Southern Secession, Civil War* (Louisiana State University Press, 2013), p.10.
42. Ibid.
43. George W.L. Bickley, "The American Colonization and Steamship Company of '1'" in *Rules, Regulations, and Principals of the K.G.C.* found in the Bickley Papers at the National Archives.
44. www.battlehymn.com. *Straight Talk – "All Wars Are Debt-Financed"* by Dane Phillips, May 10, 2013.
45. Robert E. May, *John A. Quitman: Old South Crusader* (Louisiana State University Press, 1984), pp.291-295.
46. Frank L. Klement, *Dark Lanterns: Secret Political Societies, Conspiracies, and Treason Trials in the Civil War* (Louisiana State University Press, 1989), p.8.
47. Robert E. May, *John A. Quitman: Old South Crusader* (Louisiana State University Press, 1984), p.251.
48. Warren Getler and Bob Brewer, *Rebel Gold: One Man's Quest to Crack the Code Behind the Secret Treasure of the Confederacy* (Simon & Schuster, 2003), pp.61-65.
49. www.wikipedia.org. "National Hotel disease."

50. Robert E. May, *John A. Quitman: Old South Crusader* (Louisiana State University Press, 1984), p.328.
51. Warren Getler and Bob Brewer, *Rebel Gold: One Man's Quest to Crack the Code Behind the Secret Treasure of the Confederacy* (Simon & Schuster, 2003), p.55.
52. Ibid., p.56.
53. Anonymous, *Edmund Wright: His Adventures With and Escape from the Knights of the Golden Circle*, (J.R. Hawley, Cincinnati, 1864), p.54.
54. www.knightsofthegoldencircle.webs.com. "Home."
55. *Continental Monthly*, May 1862, p.576.
56. *Southern Broad-Axe, West Point, MS, July 20, 1859, p.2., c.5.*
57. *Old-Line Democrat, Little Rock, AR, August 16, 1860, p.2., c.2.*

7. BALTIMORE AND THE SLAVE TRADE

1. L. Diane Barnes, Brian Schoen, and Frank Towers, *The Old South's Modern Worlds: Slavery, Region, and the Nation in the Age of Progress* (Oxford University Press, 2011), p.278.
2. Peter Kolchin, *American Slavery: 1619-1877* (New York: Hill and Wang, 1993), pp. 81-82.
3. www.pathways.thinkport.org. *"Pathways to Freedom: Maryland and the Underground Railroad."*
4. *Baltimore Sun, "Slave or Free, Blacks Made an Impact on City,"* by Jacques Kelly, August 23, 1994.
5. John Mack Faragher (editor), *The Encyclopedia of Colonial and Revolutionary America* (New York: Facts on File, 1990), p.257.
6. Matthew Page Andrews, History of Maryland (Doubleday, New York 1929), p. 146.
7. *Baltimore Sun, "The Secret History of City Slave Trade,"* by Scott Shane, June 20, 1999.
8. *Baltimore Sun, "A Bitter Inner Harbor Legacy: The Slave Trade,"* by Ralph Clayton, July 12, 2000.
9. www.civilwartalk.com. *"Slave Pens."*

10. *Baltimore Sun, "The Secret History of City Slave Trade,"* by Scott Shane, June 20, 1999.
11. Ibid.
12. *Baltimore Sun, "A Bitter Inner Harbor Legacy: The Slave Trade,"* by Ralph Clayton, July 12, 2000.
13. *Baltimore Sun, "The Secret History of City Slave Trade,"* by Scott Shane, June 20, 1999.
14. James Monroe Gregory, *Frederick Douglass the Orator* (Wiley & Co., Springfield, MA 1893), pp.103-104.
15. *Baltimore Sun, "The Secret History of City Slave Trade,"* by Scott Shane, June 20, 1999.
16. www.wikipedia.com. *"History of Slavery in Maryland."*
17. *The Baltimore Chronicle, "Baltimore Should Have a Memorial to Victims of its Slave Market,"* by Ralph Clayton, October 24, 2005.
18. Charles MacKay, *Life and Liberty in America: Sketches of a Tour in the United States and Canada* (Harper & Brothers, New York, 1859) p.270.
19. www.mdhs.org. *"Key Items Tell Maryland Emancipation Story."*
20. Bryan Prince, *A Shadow on the Household: One Enslaved Family's Incredible Struggle for Freedom* (McClelland & Stewart, 2009), p.11.
21. *Ordinances of the Corporation of the City of Baltimore from 1823-1827 Inclusive* (reprinted by John Cox, Baltimore, 1876).
22. *Various city directories and advertisements in 19th-century Baltimore periodicals list James Armstrong & Co. as being located on Concord Street near the Pratt Street Bridge.*
23. John Thomas Scharf, *History of Baltimore City and County, Maryland* (Louis H. Everts, Philadelphia, 1881), p.184.
24. As derived from publicly available shipping and port records from the 1830s, 1840s, and 1850s. The majority of Captain Mattison's travels seem to have taken him to New Orleans, Havana, Rio di Janeiro, Mexico, Latin America in general, California, and also Hawaii.

25. *The Baltimore Underwriter*, May 1868, Vol. III, No. 11., in a listing of the officers of the American Fire Insurance Company of Baltimore.
26. Leonard Augsburger, *Treasure in the Cellar* (Baltimore: Maryland Historical Society, 2008), p.47.
27. *Rare Coin Review* #150, *"The 1934 Baltimore Gold Hoard"* by Leonard Augsburger, November/December 2002, p.38.
28. Baltimore City directories of the 1860s show Captain John J. Mattison residing at 88 Broadway Avenue, just a few blocks east of S. Eden St.
29. Testimony of Margaret Saulsbury Short and Elizabeth Saulsbury Audoun, BCCC#2, docket A-579, 1934.
30. Maryland Court of Appeals, Records and Briefs, April 1935, cases 35-36, Saulsbury brief, p.20.
31. *Baltimore Sun, "The Secret History of City Slave Trade,"* by Scott Shane, June 20, 1999.
32. Ibid.

8. SWORN TESTIMONY

1. Testimony of Theodore Jones, BCCC#2, docket A-579, 1934.
2. Ibid.
3. Leonard Augsburger, *Treasure in the Cellar* (Baltimore: Maryland Historical Society, 2008), p.56.
4. Ibid.
5. Testimony of Henry Grob, BCCC#2, docket A-579, 1934.
6. Leonard Augsburger, *Treasure in the Cellar* (Baltimore: Maryland Historical Society, 2008), p.56.
7. Ibid., p.57.
8. Ibid., p.12.
9. Ibid., pp.59-60.
10. Ibid., pp.60-61.
11. *The Daily Record*, Baltimore, 2/16/1935, p.3.
12. *Baltimore Sun*, 1/27/1935, p.6.

13. Leonard Augsburger, *Treasure in the Cellar* (Baltimore: Maryland Historical Society, 2008), pp.63-64.
14. BCCC#2, docket A-579, 1934, p.234.
15. Testimony of Margaret Saulsbury Short and Elizabeth Saulsbury Audoun, BCCC#2, docket A-579, 1934.
16. *Rare Coin Review* #150, *"The 1934 Baltimore Gold Hoard"* by Leonard Augsburger, November/December 2002, pp.37-38.
17. Ibid., p.38.
18. Testimony of Margaret Saulsbury Short, BCCC#2, docket A-579, 1934.
19. *The Daily Record*, Baltimore, 2/11/1935, p.3.
20. Leonard Augsburger, *Treasure in the Cellar* (Baltimore: Maryland Historical Society, 2008), p.75.
21. Ibid.
22. Ibid., p.77.
23. Testimony of tenant Harry Fleischer, BCCC#2, docket A-579, 1934.
24. French Exhibit A, Maryland Court of Appeals records and briefs, April 1935, docket #35.

9. A BAND OF BROTHERS

1. John Thomas Scharf, *History of Baltimore City and County, Maryland* (Louis H. Everts, Philadelphia, 1881), p.184.
2. Ibid.
3. Testimony of Margaret Saulsbury Short and Elizabeth Saulsbury Audoun, BCCC#2, docket A-579, 1934.
4. Ibid.
5. Maryland Court of Appeals, Records and Briefs, April 1935, cases 35-36, Saulsbury brief, p.20.
6. John Thomas Scharf, *History of Baltimore City and County, Maryland* (Louis H. Everts, Philadelphia, 1881), p.184.
7. Genealogical research and notes on the Sauslbury family provided by Leonard Augsburger.

8. Edward T. Schultz, *History of Freemasonry in Maryland* (Medairy & Co., Baltimore, 1888), p.33.
9. John Thomas Scharf, *History of Baltimore City and County, Maryland* (Louis H. Everts, Philadelphia, 1881), p.184.
10. Ibid., pp.183-184.
11. www.msa.maryland.gov. Archives of Maryland, Historical List, Baltimore City Council, Second Branch, 1846-1900.
12. *Journal of the Proceedings of the Second Branch City Council of Baltimore, Sessions 1868-1869* (E.G. Armiger, Baltimore City Printer, 1869).
13. *The Baltimore Underwriter and Internal Revenue Record* (May 1868, Volume III, No. II), p.166. See the Board of Directors listed for the American Fire Insurance Company of Baltimore.
14. *Miscellaneous Documents of the House of Representatives (printed during the First Session of the thirty-Sixth Congress, 1859-1860).* See the section on Maryland's Contested Election and the list of voters surveyed, p.150.

10. THE CAPTAIN COMES HOME

1. Derived from various 1850s commercial shipping records made available by port cities across the Western hemisphere.
2. www.odysseymarine.com. Web site of Odyssey Marine Exploration, a publicly traded company in the United States.
3. www.wikipedia.org. Albert W. Hicks.
4. *The Life, Trial, Confession, and Execution of Albert W. Hicks, the Pirate and Mutineer* (Dewitt Publishing House, New York, 1860). All of the accounts of the crimes committed by Hicks, as well as his voyage with Captain John J. Mattison on his vessel *Maria*, were taken from Hicks' transcribed confession.
5. Ibid., p.52.
6. Ibid., p.50.

7. www.wikipedia.com. *"Liberty Island."*
8. Leonard Augsburger, *Treasure in the Cellar* (Baltimore: Maryland Historical Society, 2008), p.7.
9. *The Baltimore Underwriter and Internal Revenue Record* (May 1868, Volume III, No. II), p.166. See the Board of Directors listed for the American Fire Insurance Company of Baltimore.
10. Edward T. Schultz, *History of Freemasonry in Maryland* (Medairy & Co., Baltimore, 1888), p.414.
11. Leonard Augsburger, *Treasure in the Cellar* (Baltimore: Maryland Historical Society, 2008), p.71.
12. *Rare Coin Review* #150, *"The 1934 Baltimore Gold Hoard"* by Leonard Augsburger, November/December 2002, pp.37-38.
13. From the 1870 federal census taken door-to-door in Baltimore, MD, Third Ward.
14. Baltimore City directories of the 1860s show Captain John J. Mattison residing at 88 Broadway Avenue, just a few blocks east of S. Eden St.
15. Post-Civil War city directories show Captain John E. Stevens residing on East Baltimore Avenue, just a few blocks north of S. Eden St.
16. Leonard Augsburger, *Treasure in the Cellar* (Baltimore: Maryland Historical Society, 2008), pp.71-72.
17. David C. Keehn, *Knights of the Golden Circle: Secret Empire, Southern Secession, Civil War* (Louisiana State University Press, 2013), pp.10 & 28.
18. Leonard Augsburger, *Treasure in the Cellar* (Baltimore: Maryland Historical Society, 2008), p.46.
19. *Rare Coin Review* #150, *"The 1934 Baltimore Gold Hoard"* by Leonard Augsburger, November/December 2002, p.38.
20. Charles R. Schultz, *Forty-niners 'round the Horn* (University of South Carolina Press, 1999) pp.316 & 338.
21. Warren Getler and Bob Brewer, *Rebel Gold: One Man's Quest to Crack the Code Behind the Secret Treasure of the Confederacy* (Simon & Schuster, 2003), p.18.

22. David C. Keehn, *Knights of the Golden Circle: Secret Empire, Southern Secession, Civil War* (Louisiana State University Press, 2013), p.20.
23. Testimony of Margaret Saulsbury Short, BCCC#2, docket A-579, 1934.
24. Leonard Augsburger, *Treasure in the Cellar* (Baltimore: Maryland Historical Society, 2008), p.72.
25. Anonymous, *The Great Conspiracy* (Philadelphia, Barclay & Co., 1866), p.26.
26. Testimony of Margaret Saulsbury Short, BCCC#2, docket A-579, 1934.
27. David C. Keehn, *Knights of the Golden Circle: Secret Empire, Southern Secession, Civil War* (Louisiana State University Press, 2013), p.17.
28. Ibid., p.2.
29. www.knightsofthegoldencircle.webs.com.
30. Leonard Augsburger, *Treasure in the Cellar* (Baltimore: Maryland Historical Society, 2008), p.70.
31. Ibid.
32. Warren Getler and Bob Brewer, *Rebel Gold: One Man's Quest to Crack the Code Behind the Secret Treasure of the Confederacy* (Simon & Schuster, 2003), p.149.
33. www.pbs.org *"The Proclamation of Amnesty and Reconstruction."*
34. Leonard Augsburger, *Treasure in the Cellar* (Baltimore: Maryland Historical Society, 2008), p.72.
35. Ibid., p.47.
36. *The Baltimore Underwriter and Internal Revenue Record* (May 1868, Volume III, No. II), p.166. See the Board of Directors listed for the American Fire Insurance Company of Baltimore.
37. From the 1870 federal census taken in Baltimore, MD, Third Ward.
38. Leonard Augsburger, *Treasure in the Cellar* (Baltimore: Maryland Historical Society, 2008), p.22.

11. HERE COMES THE JUDGE

1. Testimony of Theodore Jones and Henry Grob, BCCC#2, docket A-579, 1934.
2. Testimony of property manager Benjamin Kalis, BCCC#2, docket A-579, 1934.
3. Testimony of tenant Harry Fleischer, BCCC#2, docket A-579, 1934.
4. Leonard Augsburger, *Treasure in the Cellar* (Baltimore: Maryland Historical Society, 2008), p.77 and also the testimony of Bessie Jones, BCCC#2, docket A-579, 1934.
5. Leonard Augsburger, *Treasure in the Cellar* (Baltimore: Maryland Historical Society, 2008), p.7.
6. *Rare Coin Review* #150, *"The 1934 Baltimore Gold Hoard"* by Leonard Augsburger, November/December 2002, p.39.
7. *The Pacific Reporter* (contains decisions of the Supreme Courts for the Western states), Volume 74, 1904, West Publishing Company, St. Paul, "Danielson vs. Roberts" pp. 913-915.
8. *Rare Coin Review* #150, *"The 1934 Baltimore Gold Hoard"* by Leonard Augsburger, November/December 2002, p.39.

12. MOBTOWN USA

1. Carl Leon Bankston, *Encyclopedia of American Immigration* (Salem Press, 2010), pp.476-477.
2. www.wikipedia.org. *"Baltimore (Demographics)."*
3. *The Magazine for the National Endowment for the Humanities*, "Gangs of Baltimore" by Martin Ford, May/June 2008, Vol. 29, No. 3.
4. *Baltimore Sun, "The Gangs of Baltimore,"* by Martin Ford, June 29, 2003.
5. Susan F. Martin, *A Nation of Immigrants* (Cambridge University Press, 2011), p.138.

Notes

6. Bruce Levine, *Conservatism, Nativism, and Slavery: Thomas R. Whitney and the Origins of the Know-Nothing Party* (Journal of American History, 2001), pp. 455-488.
7. www.wikipedia.org. *"Know Nothing."*
8. Allen Jayne, *Lincoln: And the American Manifesto* (Prometheus Book, New York, 2007), p.178.
9. www.wikipedia.org. *"United States presidential election, 1856."*
10. John Wilkes Booth (edited by John Rhodehamel and Louise Taper), *Right or Wrong, God Judge Me: The Writings of John Wilkes Booth* (The Board of Trustees of the University of Illinois, 2007), p.44.
11. *Baltimore Sun, "Think Baltimore's a rough place now? Try the 1850s,"* by Carl Schoettler, January 15, 2006.
12. Matthew Page Andrews, *History of Maryland* (Doubleday, Doran & Co., New York, 1929), pp. 476-477.
13. Joseph Humphrey Desmond, *The Know-Nothing Party: A Sketch* (The New Century Press, 1905), p.129.
14. Frank B. Marcotte, *Six Days in April: Lincoln and the Union in Peril* (Algora Publishing, 2005), p.26.
15. *Baltimore Sun, "Book Recalls Bad Old Days of 19th-century Baltimore"* by Jacques Kelly, August 1, 2006.
16. Robert J. Brugger, *Maryland, A Middle Temperament: 1634-1980* (The Johns Hopkins University Press, 1988), p.260.
17. *The Magazine for the National Endowment for the Humanities, "Gangs of Baltimore"* by Martin Ford, May/June 2008, Vol. 29, No. 3.
18. *Smithsonian Magazine, "The (Still) Mysterious Death of Edgar Allan Poe"* by Natasha Geiling, October 7, 2014.
19. The Wire, "The Mysterious 'Poe Toaster' Did Not Surface for Edgar Allan Poe's 205th Birthday," by Adam Chandler, January 19, 2014.
20. *Miscellaneous Documents of the House of Representatives (printed during the First Session of the thirty-Sixth Congress, 1859-1860).* See the

section on Maryland's Contested Election and the list of voters surveyed, p.150.

21. John Thomas Scharf, *History of Baltimore City and County, Maryland* (Louis H. Everts, Philadelphia, 1881), p.184.

22. *Baltimore Sun, "Violence is an Old Story in 'Mobtown'"* by Scott Shane, November 1, 1992.

13. HARPERS FERRY

1. Scott J. Hammond, Kevin R. Hardwick, and Howard L. Lubert, *Classics of American Political and Constitutional Thought* (Hackett Publishing Company, Indianapolis, 2007), p.304.

2. Jack R. Censer and Lynn Hunt, *Liberty, Equality, and Fraternity: Exploring the French Revolution* (Pennsylvania State University Press, 2001), pp.123-124.

3. www.wikipedia.org. *"Constitution of Haiti."*

4. Ned Sublette, *The World That Made New Orleans: From Spanish Silver to Congo Square* (Lawrence Hill Books, Chicago, 2008), p.261.

5. www.wikipedia.org. *"Nat Turner."*

6. www.civilwar.org/education/history/biographies. *"Harriet Tubman – Underground Railroad 'Conductor', Nurse, Spy."*

7. James D. Horan, *The Pinkertons: The Detective Dynasty That Made History* (Crown Publishers, New York, 1969), p.19.

8. www.wikipedia.org. *"Kansas-Nebraska Act."*

9. www.wikipedia.org. *"Border Ruffian."*

10. Conrad Swackhamer and Spencer Wallace Cone (editors), *The United States Democratic Review, Volume VI* (Lloyd & Co., New York, 1856), p.402.

11. www.wikipedia.org. *"Lawrence Massacre."*

12. www.senate.gov/artandhistory/history/minute. *"May 22, 1856: The Caning of Senator Charles Sumner."*

13. www.ushistory.org/us/31d. *"The Pottawatomie Creek Massacre."*

Notes

14. Richard Reece, *Bleeding Kansas* (ABDO Publishing Co., Minneapolis, 2012), p.87.
15. David S. Reynolds, *John Brown, Abolitionist: The Man Who Killed Slavery, Sparked the Civil War, and Seeded Civil Rights* (Vintage Books, New York, 2005), pp.201-202.
16. www.wikipedia.org. *"John Brown (abolitionist)."*
17. www.wikipedia.org. *"William Quantrill."*
18. www.wikipedia.org. *"Lawrence Massacre."*
19. www.eyewitnesstohistory.com/quantrill.htm. *"William Quantrill Raids, Lawrence, Kansas, 1863."*
20. www.pbs.org. *"American Experience – John Brown's Holy War."* Margaret Washington, historian.
21. Oswald Garrison Villard, *John Brown: 1800-1859* (Houghton Mifflin Company, 1910), p.376.
22. www.pbs.org. *"American Experience – John Brown's Holy War."* The Missouri Raid.
23. Ibid.
24. Otto Scott, *The Secret Six: John Brown and the Abolitionist Movement* (Uncommon Books, 1993).
25. www.kshs.org. *"Kansapedia – Kansas Historical Society."* Cool Things – John Brown Pike.
26. Marian Taylor, *Harriet Tubman: Antislavery Activist* (Chelsea House Publishers, 2004), pp.68-69.
27. www.wsj.com. *"John Brown: The Man Who Started the Civil War?"* by Tony Horwitz, October 26, 2011.
28. www.wikipedia.org. *"John Brown's raid on Harpers Ferry."*
29. James Oliver Horton and Lois E. Horton, Slavery and the Making of America (Oxford University Press, 2006), p.162.
30. www.wikipedia.org. *"John Brown's raid on Harpers Ferry."*
31. Horace Greeley, *The American Conflict: A History* (Part One, 1864), p.292.
32. www.pbs.org. *"American Experience – John Brown's Holy War."* John Brown's Fort.
33. www.wikipedia.org. *"John Brown's raid on Harpers Ferry."*
34. Ibid.

35. James M. McPherson, *Battle Cry of Freedom: The Civil War Era* (Oxford University Press, 2003), p.205.
36. David S. Reynolds, *John Brown Abolitionist: The Man Who Killed Slavery, Sparked the Civil War, and Seeded Civil Rights* (Vintage Books, New York, 2006), pp.339-340.
37. Mario M. Cuomo and Harold Holzer, *Lincoln on Democracy* (Fordham University Press, 2004), p.169.
38. Larry J. Reynolds, *Righteous Violence: Revolution, Slavery, and the American Renaissance* (University of Georgia Press, 2011), p.29.
39. Daniel Stashower, *The Hour of Peril: The Secret Plot to Murder Lincoln before the Civil War* (St. Martin's Press, New York, 2013), p.63.
40. www.investigatinghistory.ashp.curry.edu. *"John Brown's 1859 Harpers Ferry Raid,"* by Bill Friedheim, Borough of Manhattan Community College, CUNY.
41. Franklin Benjamin Sanborn, *The Life and Letters of John Brown: Liberator of Kansas, and Martyr of Virginia* (Robers Brothers, Boston, 1891), p.585.
42. William Edward Burghardt DuBois, John Brown (George W. Jacobs & Company, Philadelphia, 1909), p. 350.
43. www.pbs.org. *"American Experience – John Brown's Holy War."* John Brown's Last Prophecy.
44. Julia Ward Howe, *Reminiscences: 1819–1899* (Houghton, Mifflin: New York, 1899), p.275.
45. Andrew Taylor and Eldrid Herrington (editors), *The Afterlife of John Brown* (Palgrave Macmillan, 2005), pp. 41-42.
46. www.wikiquote.org. *"John Brown (abolitionist)."*
47. Arthur F. Loux, *John Wilkes Booth: Day by Day* (McFarland & Company, Inc. Publishers, North Carolina, 2014), pp.35-36.
48. Nora Titone, *My Thoughts Be Bloody: The Bitter Rivalry Between Edwin and John Wilkes Booth* (Free Press, New York, 2010), p.213.
49. David S. Reynolds, *John Brown Abolitionist: The Man Who Killed Slavery, Sparked the Civil War, and Seeded Civil Rights* (Vintage Books, New York, 2006), p.478.

50. James Cross Giblin, *Good Brother, Bad Brother: The Story of Edwin Booth and John Wilkes Booth* (Clarion Books, New York, 2005), p.57.
51. Nora Titone, *My Thoughts Be Bloody: The Bitter Rivalry Between Edwin and John Wilkes Booth* (Free Press, New York, 2010), pp.215-216.

14. GRAND MASTERS OF THE 33rd DEGREE

1. Edward T. Schultz, *History of Freemasonry in Maryland* (Medairy & Co., Baltimore, 1888), p.713.
2. Ibid.
3. Ibid.
4. Ibid.
5. Ibid.
6. John Thomas Scharf, *History of Baltimore City and County, Maryland* (Louis H. Everts, Philadelphia, 1881), p.184.
7. Ibid., p.183.
8. Quentin R. Skraebic, *The 100 Most Significant Events in American Business: an Encyclopedia* (ABC-CLIO, LLC, California, 2012), pp.31-32.
9. Ibid., p.33.
10. Bruce J. Schulman, *Student's Guide to the Presidency* (CQ Press, Washington, D.C., 2009), p.333.
11. Ruth Clifford Engs, *Clean Living Movements: American Cycles of Health Reform* (Greenwood Publishing Group, Connecticut, 2001), p.85.
12. www.wikipedia.org *"Know Nothing."*
13. Ibid.
14. Ibid.
15. www.wikipedia.org. *"Southern Democrats."*
16. John Thomas Scharf, *History of Baltimore City and County, Maryland* (Louis H. Everts, Philadelphia, 1881), p.184.
17. Henry Eliot Shepherd, *History of Baltimore Maryland from Its Founding as a Town to Its Current Year* (S.B. Nelson, Publisher, 1898), p.112.

18. Edward T. Schultz, *History of Freemasonry in Maryland* (Medairy & Co., Baltimore, 1888), p.289.
19. Ibid.
20. Ibid., pp. 414 and 579.
21. Ibid., p.579.
22. www.gospeltruth.net. Rev. C.G. Finney, *The Character, Claims and Practical Workings of Freemasonry – Chapter VII, Royal Arch Degree* (1869).
23. Edward T. Schultz, *History of Freemasonry in Maryland* (Medairy & Co., Baltimore, 1888), pp.414 and 579.
24. www.wikipedia.org. *"Albert Pike."*
25. Warren Getler and Bob Brewer, *Rebel Gold: One Man's Quest to Crack the Code Behind the Secret Treasure of the Confederacy* (Simon & Schuster, 2003), pp.53-54.
26. Ibid., p.59.
27. Ibid., p.59.
28. Ibid., p.56.
29. www.wikipedia.org. *"United States presidential election, 1860."*
30. Annie Heloise Abel, *The Slaveholding Indians, Vol. II* (Arthur H. Clark Co., Cleveland, 1919), p.172.
31. www.civilwar.org. Battlefields – *"The Battle of Pea Ridge."*
32. www.civilwar.org. Battlefields – *"Cherokees at Pea Ridge."*
33. Albert Pike, *Morals and Dogma* of the Scottish Rite of Freemasonry (Martino Fine Books, 2013).
34. www.freemasonry.bcy.ca. Anti-Masonry – *"Albert Pike Did Not Found the Ku Klux Klan."*
35. Donald G. Lett, Jr., *Phoenix Rising: The Rise and Fall of the American Republic* (Phoenix Rising, 2008), p.67.
36. Warren Getler and Bob Brewer, *Rebel Gold: One Man's Quest to Crack the Code Behind the Secret Treasure of the Confederacy* (Simon & Schuster, 2003), pp.60-61.
37. Ibid., p.89.
38. Ibid., p.89.

15. TRIUMPH OF THE RINKY DINKY DOOS

1. Leonard Augsburger, *Treasure in the Cellar* (Baltimore: Maryland Historical Society, 2008), p.69.
2. *The Baltimore Sun, "Gold Comes Out of the Cellar and Into the Loret"* by Frederick N. Rasmussen, 9/28/2008.
3. Leonard Augsburger, *Treasure in the Cellar* (Baltimore: Maryland Historical Society, 2008), p.86.
4. *Baltimore Evening Sun*, 2/16/1935, p.1.
5. *Rare Coin Review* #150, *"The 1934 Baltimore Gold Hoard"* by Leonard Augsburger, November/December 2002, p.39.
6. Leonard Augsburger, *Treasure in the Cellar* (Baltimore: Maryland Historical Society, 2008), pp. 19-20.
7. *Rare Coin Review* #150, *"The 1934 Baltimore Gold Hoard"* by Leonard Augsburger, November/December 2002, p.39.
8. *Baltimore Evening Sun*, 3/7/1935, p.13.
9. Ibid.
10. *Baltimore Evening Sun*, 4/18/1935, p.8.
11. *Baltimore Evening Sun*, 2/21/1935, p.10.

16. BICKLEY AT THE BORDER

1. www.battlehymn.com. *Straight Talk – "All Wars Are Debt-Financed"* by Dane Phillips, May 10, 2013.
2. David C. Keehn, *Knights of the Golden Circle: Secret Empire, Southern Secession, Civil War* (Louisiana State University Press, 2013), p.14.
3. Anonymous, *The Authentic Exposition of the K.G.C., Knights of the Golden Circle, or a History of Secession from 1834 to 1861* (C.O. Perrine, 1861), p.57.
4. Warren Getler and Bob Brewer, *Rebel Gold: One Man's Quest to Crack the Code Behind the Secret*

Treasure of the Confederacy (Simon & Schuster, 2003), pp.16-18.

5. www.tshaonline.org. Texas State Historical Association, *"Knights of the Golden Circle."*

6. David C. Keehn, *Knights of the Golden Circle: Secret Empire, Southern Secession, Civil War* (Louisiana State University Press, 2013), p.11.

7. Anonymous, *The Authentic Exposition of the K.G.C., Knights of the Golden Circle, or a History of Secession from 1834 to 1861* (C.O. Perrine, 1861), pp.27-28.

8. David C. Keehn, *Knights of the Golden Circle: Secret Empire, Southern Secession, Civil War* (Louisiana State University Press, 2013), p.12.

9. www.tshaonline.org. Texas State Historical Association, *"Knights of the Golden Circle."*

10. David C. Keehn, *Knights of the Golden Circle: Secret Empire, Southern Secession, Civil War* (Louisiana State University Press, 2013), p.25.

11. Anonymous, *The Authentic Exposition of the K.G.C., Knights of the Golden Circle, or a History of Secession from 1834 to 1861* (C.O. Perrine, 1861), p.8.

12. Warren Getler and Bob Brewer, *Rebel Gold: One Man's Quest to Crack the Code Behind the Secret Treasure of the Confederacy* (Simon & Schuster, 2003), pp.18.

13. David C. Keehn, *Knights of the Golden Circle: Secret Empire, Southern Secession, Civil War* (Louisiana State University Press, 2013), p.27.

14. Anonymous, *The Authentic Exposition of the K.G.C., Knights of the Golden Circle, or a History of Secession from 1834 to 1861* (C.O. Perrine, 1861), p.9.

15. David C. Keehn, *Knights of the Golden Circle: Secret Empire, Southern Secession, Civil War* (Louisiana State University Press, 2013), p.27.

16. Ibid.

17. Ibid., p.18.

18. www.allempires.com. *"The Mexican American War."*

Notes

19. www.historynet.com. *"Home Grown Terrorists,"* by Beth Rowland, July 8, 2015.
20. David C. Keehn, *Knights of the Golden Circle: Secret Empire, Southern Secession, Civil War* (Louisiana State University Press, 2013), p.20.
21. Jon E. Lewis, *The Mammoth Book of Conspiracies* (Constable Robinson, 2012).
22. David C. Keehn, *Knights of the Golden Circle: Secret Empire, Southern Secession, Civil War* (Louisiana State University Press, 2013), pp.15-16.
23. Ibid., p.28.
24. *Arkansas True Democrat, "The K.G.C. in Action,"* September 7, 1859.
25. www.wikipedia.org. *"Sam Houston."*
26. David C. Keehn, *Knights of the Golden Circle: Secret Empire, Southern Secession, Civil War* (Louisiana State University Press, 2013), pp.35-36.
27. www.wacoheartoftexas.com. *"Grand Lodge of Texas."*
28. James L. Haley, *Sam Houston* (University of Oklahoma Press, 2002), p.397.
29. Ibid., p.392.
30. *New York Times, "Position of Gov. Houston,"* March 30, 1861.
31. David C. Keehn, *Knights of the Golden Circle: Secret Empire, Southern Secession, Civil War* (Louisiana State University Press, 2013), p.32.
32. Josefina Zoraida Vazquez and Lorenzo Meyer, *The United States and Mexico* (The University of Chicago Press, 1995), p.65.
33. David C. Keehn, *Knights of the Golden Circle: Secret Empire, Southern Secession, Civil War* (Louisiana State University Press, 2013), p.33.
34. Ibid., p.21.
35. Thomas G. Dyer, *Secret Yankees: The Union Circle in Confederate Atlanta* (Johns Hopkins University Press, 1999), p.34.
36. Ibid.
37. David C. Keehn, *Knights of the Golden Circle: Secret Empire, Southern Secession, Civil War* (Louisiana State University Press, 2013), p.40.

38. www.tshaonline.org. Texas State Historical Association, *"Knights of the Golden Circle."*
39. Mark A. Lause, *A Secret Society History of the Civil War* (The University of Illinois, 2011), pp. 92 and 98.
40. David C. Keehn, *Knights of the Golden Circle: Secret Empire, Southern Secession, Civil War* (Louisiana State University Press, 2013), p.42.
41. www.knights-of-the-golden-circle.blogspot.com. *"The Knights of the Golden Circle."*
42. David C. Keehn, *Knights of the Golden Circle: Secret Empire, Southern Secession, Civil War* (Louisiana State University Press, 2013), p.42.
43. Michael L. Collins, *Texas Devils: Rangers and Regulars on the Lower Rio Grande, 1846-1861* (University of Oklahoma Press, 2008), pp.224-227.
44. David C. Keehn, *Knights of the Golden Circle: Secret Empire, Southern Secession, Civil War* (Louisiana State University Press, 2013), p.44.
45. Letter from George Bickley's nephew, Charles, to the Raleigh Press, defending his uncle, published in the *Norfolk Southern Argus*, May 15, 1861.
46. David C. Keehn, *Knights of the Golden Circle: Secret Empire, Southern Secession, Civil War* (Louisiana State University Press, 2013), pp.51-52.
47. Ibid.
48. *The Weekly Telegraph of Houston*, November 27, 1860.
49. Anonymous, *The Authentic Exposition of the K.G.C., Knights of the Golden Circle, or a History of Secession from 1834 to 1861* (C.O. Perrine, 1861), pp.35-36.
50. Ibid., p.75.
51. David C. Keehn, *Knights of the Golden Circle: Secret Empire, Southern Secession, Civil War* (Louisiana State University Press, 2013), p.89.
52. William Curtis Nunn, *Ten More Texans in Gray* (Hill Jr. College Press, 1980), p.73.
53. Justin Farrell, *The Battle for Yellowstone: Morality and the Sacred Roots of Environmental Conflict* (Princeton University Press, 2015), p.70.

54. Horace Greeley, *The American Conflict: A History of the Great Rebellion* (O.D. Case & Company, 1866), p.350.
55. Frank L. Klement, *Dark Lanterns: Secret Political Societies, Conspiracies, and Treason Trials in the Civil War* (Louisiana State University Press, 1989), p.8.
56. Ibid., p.33 and the *Baltimore Sun*, August 17, 1867.
57. James Hagy, *"George Washington Lafayette Bickley: The Early Years,"* Historical Sketches of Southwest Virginia (Publication 6, 1972).
58. Benn Pitman, *The Trials for Treason at Indianapolis, Disclosing the Plans for Establishing a North-Western Confederacy* (Moore, Wilstach & Baldwin, Cincinnati, OH, 1865), p.24.
59. Curtis A. Early and Gloria J. Early, *Ohio Confederate Connection: Facts You may Not Know about the Civil War* (iUniverse, 2010), p.205.
60. www.bbc.com. BBC News, *"Victorian Strangeness: The Lawyer Who Shot Himself Proving His Case,"* August 16, 2014.
61. Anonymous, *The Authentic Exposition of the K.G.C., Knights of the Golden Circle, or a History of Secession from 1834 to 1861* (C.O. Perrine, 1861), p.21.
62. www.wikipedia.org. *"Caleb Cushing."*
63. *The Philadelphia Inquirer, "The Great Northwest Conspiracy,"* July 29, 1864.

17. THE 1861 BALTIMORE PLOT TO KILL LINCOLN

1. Charles T. McClenachan, *The Book of the Ancient and Accepted Scottish Rite of Freemasonry* (Masonic Publishing and Manufacturing Co., New York, 1868), p.606.
2. Eric H. Walther, *The Fire-Eaters* (Louisiana State University Press, 1992), p.75.

3. Anonymous, *The Authentic Exposition of the K.G.C., Knights of the Golden Circle, or a History of Secession from 1834 to 1861* (C.O. Perrine, 1861), p.16.
4. Michael J. Kline, *The Baltimore Plot: The First Conspiracy to Assassinate Abraham Lincoln* (Westholme Publishing, PA, 2013), p.355.
5. Edited by Harold Holzer, Craig L. Symonds, and Frank J. Williams, *Exploring Lincoln: Great Historians Reappraise Our Greatest President* (Fordham University press, 2015), p.201.
6. www.wikipedia.org. *"Baltimore Plot."*
7. Edward Steers, *Blood on the Moon: The Assassination of Abraham Lincoln* (The University Press of Kentucky, 2005), p.19.
8. Daniel Mark Epstein, *Lincoln's Men: The President and His Private Secretaries* (Harper Collins, New York, 2009), p.17.
9. Daniel Stashower, *The Hour of Peril: The Secret Plot to Murder Lincoln before the Civil War* (St. Martin's Press, 2013), p.266.
10. Ibid., p.95.
11. William A. Tidwell, *Come Retribution: The Confederate Secret Service and the Assassination of Lincoln* (University Press of Mississippi, 1988), p.229.
12. *The Baltimore Underwriter and Internal Revenue Record* (May 1868, Volume III, No. II), p.166.
13. https://en.wikipedia.org/wiki. *"Kate Warne."*
14. Corey Recko, *A Spy for the Union: the Life and Execution of Timothy Webster* (McFarland & Company, Inc. Publishers, 2013).
15. https://en.wikipedia.org/wiki. *"Kate Warne."*
16. John Mason Potter, *Thirteen Desperate Days* (The University of Michigan, 1964), p.118.
17. Harry Ezratty, *Baltimore in the Civil War: The Pratt Street Riot and a City Occupied* (The History Press, Charleston, SC, 2010), p.49.
18. Dorothy Sterling, *We Are Your Sisters: Black Women in the Nineteenth Century* (W.W. Norton & Company, 1984), p.149.

19. Al Benson, Jr. and Walter Donald Kennedy, *Lincoln's Marxists* (Pelican Publishing Company, 2011), p.164.

20. Arnie Bernstein, *The Hoofs and Guns of the Storm: Chicago's Civil War Connections* (Lake Claremont Press, Chicago, 2003), pp.148-149.

21. Anonymous, *An Authentic Exposition of the "K.G.C." Knights of the Golden Circle, or, a History of the Secession from 1834 to 1861* (Charles Perrine, Publisher, Indianapolis, IN, 1861), pp.34-35.

22. David C. Keehn, *Knights of the Golden Circle: Secret Empire, Southern Secession, Civil War* (Louisiana State University Press, 2013), p.104.

23. Ibid.

24. Walter Stahr, *Seward: Lincoln's Indispensable Man* (Simon & Schuster, New York, 2012), p.280.

25. Harry Ezratty, *Baltimore in the Civil War: The Pratt Street Riot and a City Occupied* (The History Press, Charleston, SC, 2010), p.49.

26. Michael J. Kline, *The Baltimore Plot: The First Conspiracy to Assassinate Abraham Lincoln* (Westholme Publishing, PA, 2013), pp.94-97.

27. Harry Ezratty, *Baltimore in the Civil War: The Pratt Street Riot and a City Occupied* (The History Press, Charleston, SC, 2010), p.50.

28. Ibid.

29. William A. Tidwell, *Come Retribution: The Confederate Secret Service and the Assassination of Lincoln* (University Press of Mississippi, 1988), p.228.

30. Norma Barret Cuthbert, *Lincoln and the Baltimore Plot*, from the Davies Report (Huntington Library, 1949), p.92.

31. Michael J. Kline, *The Baltimore Plot: The First Conspiracy to Assassinate Abraham Lincoln* (Westholme Publishing, PA, 2013), p.425.

32. Harry Ezratty, *Baltimore in the Civil War: The Pratt Street Riot and a City Occupied* (The History Press, Charleston, SC, 2010), p.49.

33. Michael J. Kline, *The Baltimore Plot: The First Conspiracy to Assassinate Abraham Lincoln* (Westholme Publishing, PA, 2013), pp.76-77.

34. *Miscellaneous Documents of the House of Representatives (printed during the First Session of the thirty-Sixth Congress, 1859-1860)*. See the section on Maryland's Contested Election and the list of voters surveyed, p.150.
35. Testimony of Margaret Saulsbury Short, BCCC#2, docket A-579, 1934.
36. Daniel Stashower, *The Hour of Peril: The Secret Plot to Murder Lincoln before the Civil War* (St. Martin's Press, 2013), p.216.
37. Michael J. Kline, *The Baltimore Plot: The First Conspiracy to Assassinate Abraham Lincoln* (Westholme Publishing, PA, 2013), p.89.
38. William A. Tidwell, *Come Retribution: The Confederate Secret Service and the Assassination of Lincoln* (University Press of Mississippi, 1988), pp.328-330
39. Michael J. Kline, *The Baltimore Plot: The First Conspiracy to Assassinate Abraham Lincoln* (Westholme Publishing, PA, 2013), pp.86-87.
40. Ibid., pp.313-314.
41. Ibid., pp.296-297.
42. Edited by Harold Holzer, Craig L. Symonds, and Frank J. Williams, *Exploring Lincoln: Great Historians Reappraise Our Greatest President* (Fordham University press, 2015), p.31.
43. Norma Barret Cuthbert, *Lincoln and the Baltimore Plot*, from the Davies Report (Huntington Library, 1949), p.92.
44. Michael J. Kline, *The Baltimore Plot: The First Conspiracy to Assassinate Abraham Lincoln* (Westholme Publishing, PA, 2013), pp.291-293.
45. Norma Barret Cuthbert, *Lincoln and the Baltimore Plot*, from the Allan Pinkerton Report, February 15, 1861 (Huntington Library, 1949), pp.32-34.
46. Michael J. Kline, *The Baltimore Plot: The First Conspiracy to Assassinate Abraham Lincoln* (Westholme Publishing, PA, 2013), p.183.
47. Ibid., p.128.
48. Ibid., pp.124-128.

Notes

49. Lucius Eugene Chittenden, *Recollections of President Lincoln and His Administration* (Harper & Brothers, New York, 1891), pp.61-62.
50. William A Tidwell, *April '65, Confederate Covert Action in the American Civil War* (Kent State University Press, 1995), p.126.
51. "Norwegian Sailors in American Waters" published by the Norwegian-American Historical Association (NAHA) in 1933. See Chapter 6, Norwegian-American Yachting Sailors where in 1851, Captain John E. Stevens, president of the New York Yacht Club, sailed the yacht "America" in an international yacht race.
52. Wikipedians (editors), *Abraham Lincoln* (from Pedia Press), p.219.
53. Corey Recko, *A Spy for the Union: the Life and Execution of Timothy Webster* (McFarland & Company, Inc. Publishers, 2013), p.53.
54. Daniel Stashower, *The Hour of Peril: The Secret Plot to Murder Lincoln before the Civil War* (St. Martin's Press, 2013), p.115.
55. David Chambers Mearns (editor), *The Lincoln Papers: The Story of the Collection, with Selections to July 4, 1861*, Volume 2 (MacMillan, 1950), p.431.
56. Michael J. Kline, *The Baltimore Plot: The First Conspiracy to Assassinate Abraham Lincoln* (Westholme Publishing, PA, 2013), pp.56-57.
57. Corey Recko, *A Spy for the Union: the Life and Execution of Timothy Webster* (McFarland & Company, Inc. Publishers, 2013), p.55.
58. Daniel Stashower, *The Hour of Peril: The Secret Plot to Murder Lincoln before the Civil War* (St. Martin's Press, 2013), p.228.
59. Norma Barret Cuthbert, *Lincoln and the Baltimore Plot*, from the Allan Pinkerton Report, February 21, 1861 (Huntington Library, 1949), pp.64.
60. Daniel Stashower, *The Hour of Peril: The Secret Plot to Murder Lincoln before the Civil War* (St. Martin's Press, 2013), p.214.

61. Henry Clay Whitney, *Lincoln the Citizen, February 12, 1809 to March 4, 1861* (The Current Literature Publishing Co., New York, 1907), p.301.
62. Allan Pinkerton, *History and Evidence of the Passage of Abraham Lincoln from Harrisburg, PA , to Washington, D. C., on the 22nd and 23rd of February 1861* (Biblio Bazaar Reprint, 2010).
63. John C. Waugh, *One Man Great Enough: Abraham Lincoln's Road to Civil War* (Harcourt Books, 2007), pp.393-394.
64. Edward Steers, *Blood on the Moon: The Assassination of Abraham Lincoln* (The University Press of Kentucky, 2005), pp.19-20.
65. Ibid., p.20.
66. Wayne Whipple, *The Story-Life of Lincoln* (The John C. Winston Co., Philadelphia,1908), pp.379-380.
67. Arnie Bernstein, *The Hoofs and Guns of the Storm: Chicago's Civil War Connections* (Lake Claremont Press, Chicago, 2003), p.150.
68. Norma Barret Cuthbert, *Lincoln and the Baltimore Plot*, from William Herndon's notes on an 1866 interview with Norman Judd (Huntington Library, 1949), pp.112.
69. Norma Barret Cuthbert, *Lincoln and the Baltimore Plot*, from the Allan Pinkerton Report, February 22, 1861 (Huntington Library, 1949), p.79.
70. Lamon, Ward Hill, *The Life of Abraham Lincoln: His Birth to His Inauguration as President (*James R. Osgood and Company, Boston, 1872), p.513.
71. Henry Clay Whitney, *Lincoln the Citizen, February 12, 1809 to March 4, 1861* (The Current Literature Publishing Co., New York, 1907), p.303.
72. Jane Singer and John Stewart, *Lincoln's Secret Spy: The Civil War Case That Changed the Future of Espionage* (Rowman & Littlefield, 2015), p. 63.
73. Norma Barret Cuthbert, *Lincoln and the Baltimore Plot*, from the Allan Pinkerton Report, February 22, 1861 (Huntington Library, 1949), p.72.
74. Festus Paul Summers, *The Baltimore and Ohio in the Civil War* (G.P. Putnam's Sons, 1939), p.46.

Notes

75. Jay Bonansinga, *Pinkerton's War: The Civil War's Greatest Spy and the Birth of the U.S. Secret Service* (Lyons Press, CT, 2012), pp.109-112.
76. Daniel Stashower, *The Hour of Peril: The Secret Plot to Murder Lincoln before the Civil War* (St. Martin's Press, 2013), pp.281-286.
77. Norma Barret Cuthbert, *Lincoln and the Baltimore Plot*, from the Allan Pinkerton Report, February 22, 1861 (Huntington Library, 1949), p.79.
78. www.wikipedia.org. *"Kate Warne."*
79. Jane Singer and John Stewart, *Lincoln's Secret Spy: The Civil War Case That Changed the Future of Espionage* (Rowman & Littlefield, 2015), p.64.
80. Lucius Eugene Chittenden, *Recollections of President Lincoln and His Administration* (Harper & Brothers, New York, 1891), p.66.
81. Edited by Harold Holzer, Craig L. Symonds, and Frank J. Williams, *Exploring Lincoln: Great Historians Reappraise Our Greatest President* (Fordham University press, 2015), p.31.
82. *The Philadelphia Inquirer, "The Story About Baltimore"* 2/25/1861.
83. Daniel Stashower, *The Hour of Peril: The Secret Plot to Murder Lincoln before the Civil War* (St. Martin's Press, 2013), p.266.
84. Herbert Mitgang, *Abraham Lincoln: A Press Portrait* (Fordham University Press, 2000), p.231.

18. BALTIMORE AT WAR

1. Anonymous, *Edmund Wright: His Adventures With and Escape from the Knights of the Golden Circle*, (J.R. Hawley, Cincinnati, 1864), p.56.
2. www.nps.gov/fomc/learn/historyculture/the-pratt-street-riot.htm. Fort McHenry – *"The Pratt Street Riot."*
3. www.en.wikipedia.org/wiki/. *"President Lincoln's 75,000 Volunteers."*

4. David C. Hinze and Karen Farnham, *The Battle of Carthage: Border War in Southwest Missouri July 5, 1861* (Savas Publishing Company, 1997), p. 21.
5. E. Polk Johnson, *History of Kentucky and Kentuckians, Vol. 1* (The Lewis Publishing Company, 1912), p.305.
6. William Curtis Nunn, *Ten More Texans in Gray* (Hill Jr. College Press, 1980), p.73.
7. Frederick W. Seward, *Seward at Washington: 1846-1861* (Derby and Miller, New York, 1891), p.502.
8. John P. Mains and Louis Philippe McCarty, *The Annual Statistician and Economist* (L.P. McCarty, San Francisco and New York, 1888), p.50.
9. www.en.wikipedia.org/wiki. *"Baltimore Riot of 1861."*
10. John Lockwood and Charles Lockwood, *The Siege of Washington: The Untold Story of the Twelve Days That Shook the Union* (Oxford University Press, 2011), p.92.
11. Editors Robert Underwood Johnson and Clarence Clough Buel, *Battles and Leaders of the Civil War* (The Century Company, New York, 1884-1887), p.150.
12. Benson J. Lossing, *Pictorial History of the Civil War in the United States* (Applewood Books, Massachusetts, 1866), p.412.
13. Harry Ezratty, *Baltimore in the Civil War: The Pratt Street Riot and a City Occupied* (The History Press, Charleston, SC, 2010), p.55.
14. George William Brown, *Baltimore and the 19th of April, 1861* (John Hopkins University, Baltimore, 1887), p.50.
15. www.civilwarguide.info/battles/. *"Baltimore Riot of 1861."*
16. George William Brown, *Baltimore and the 19th of April, 1861* (John Hopkins University, Baltimore, 1887).
17. Ibid., pp.48-51.
18. Michael J. Kline, *The Baltimore Plot: The First Conspiracy to Assassinate Abraham Lincoln* (Westholme Publishing, PA, 2013), p 350.
19. www.welcometobaltimorehon.com/. *"Pratt Street Riots, April 19, 1861."*

Notes

20. Harry Ezratty, *Baltimore in the Civil War: The Pratt Street Riot and a City Occupied* (The History Press, Charleston, SC, 2010), pp.65-69 and www.en.wikipedia.org/wiki. *"Baltimore Riot of 1861."*
21. James F. Simon, *Lincoln and Chief Justice Taney: Slavery, Secession, and the President's War Powers* (Simon and Schuster, 2006), p.185.
22. Frank B. Marcotte, *Six Days in April: Lincoln and the Union in Peril* (Algora Publishing, 2005), p.56.
23. Harry Ezratty, *Baltimore in the Civil War: The Pratt Street Riot and a City Occupied* (The History Press, Charleston, SC, 2010), p.64.
24. George William Brown, *Baltimore and the 19th of April, 1861* (John Hopkins University, Baltimore, 1887), p.63.
25. William Blair Lord and Henry M. Parkhurst, *The Debates of the Constitutional Convention of the State of Maryland: Assembled at the City of Annapolis, Wednesday, April 27, 1864* (Printed by Richard P. Bayly, Annapolis, 1864), p.411.
26. William Lee Miller, *President Lincoln: The Duty of a Statesman* (Vintage Books, a division of Random House, 2009), p.115.
27. George L.P. Radcliffe, *Governor Thomas H. Hicks of Maryland and the Civil War* (The Johns Hopkins Press, Baltimore, 1901), p.54.
28. Edward T. Schultz, *History of Freemasonry in Maryland* (Medairy & Co., Baltimore, 1888), p.414.
29. George L.P. Radcliffe, *Governor Thomas H. Hicks of Maryland and the Civil War* (The Johns Hopkins Press, Baltimore, 1901), p.57.
30. Michael J. Kline, *The Baltimore Plot: The First Conspiracy to Assassinate Abraham Lincoln* (Westholme Publishing, PA, 2013), pp.357-358.
31. Ibid., p.358.
32. Ibid., p.359.
33. George William Brown, *Baltimore and the 19th of April, 1861* (John Hopkins University, Baltimore, 1887), p.58.

34. Michael J. Kline, *The Baltimore Plot: The First Conspiracy to Assassinate Abraham Lincoln* (Westholme Publishing, PA, 2013), p.358.
35. Ibid., p.357.
36. John Thomas Scharf, *History of Baltimore City and County, Maryland* (Louis H. Everts, Philadelphia, 1881), p.130.
37. Michael J. Kline, *The Baltimore Plot: The First Conspiracy to Assassinate Abraham Lincoln* (Westholme Publishing, PA, 2013), p.358.
38. *Boston Commonwealth*, April 22, 1865.
39. *The Abraham Lincoln Papers at the Library of Congress, Series 1. General Correspondence. 1833-1916. Helen M. Linscott to Abraham Lincoln, Monday, November 14, 1864.*
40. John Lockwood and Charles Lockwood, *The Siege of Washington: The Untold Story of the Twelve Days That Shook the Union* (Oxford University Press, 2011), p.185.
41. www.msa.maryland.gov/msa/. Maryland State Archives, *"The General Assembly Moves to Frederick, 1861."*
42. Michael J. Kline, *The Baltimore Plot: The First Conspiracy to Assassinate Abraham Lincoln* (Westholme Publishing, PA, 2013), p.14.
43. www.welcometobaltimorehon.com/. *"Pratt Street Riots, April 19, 1861."*
44. Harry Ezratty, *Baltimore in the Civil War: The Pratt Street Riot and a City Occupied* (The History Press, Charleston, SC, 2010), p.99.
45. Benson J. Lossing, *Pictorial History of the Civil War in the United States* (Applewood Books, Massachusetts, 1866), pp.449-450.

19. AUCTION DAY

1. *Baltimore Evening Sun*, 2/21/1935, p.14.
2. *Rare Coin Review* #150, *"The 1934 Baltimore Gold Hoard"* by Leonard Augsburger, November/December 2002, p.39.
3. Ibid., p.43.
4. Leonard Augsburger, *Treasure in the Cellar* (Baltimore: Maryland Historical Society, 2008), p.95.
5. *Baltimore Sun*, 4/30/1935, p.5.
6. *Baltimore Evening Sun*, 5/2/1935, p.40.
7. Leonard Augsburger, *Treasure in the Cellar* (Baltimore: Maryland Historical Society, 2008), p.87.
8. Ibid., pp.90-91.
9. Ibid., p.91.
10. Ibid., p.92.
11. Ibid., pp.90-91.
12. Ibid., p.93.
13. Ibid., p.92.
14. *Baltimore Evening Sun*, 5/3/1935, p.15, and *Baltimore News*, 9/3/1935, p.2.
15. *Baltimore Sun,* 4/23/1936, p. 26.
16. Baltimore City Circuit Court #2, case 20020, 1935.
17. *Baltimore Sun,* 4/23/1936, p. 26.
18. *Findlay vs. Jones*, BCCC #, file 21483A.
19. Leonard Augsburger, *Treasure in the Cellar* (Baltimore: Maryland Historical Society, 2008), p.101.
20. Ibid., p.83.
21. Testimony given regarding the "second" gold discovery, BCCC #2, 9/20/1935 and also Leonard Augsburger, *Treasure in the Cellar* (Baltimore: Maryland Historical Society, 2008), p.97.
22. Leonard Augsburger, *Treasure in the Cellar* (Baltimore: Maryland Historical Society, 2008), p.110.

20. 2,000 GOLD COINS IN "THE FOUNTAIN"

1. Matthew Page Andrews, *The Fountain Inn Diary* (Richard R. Smith, New York, 1948), p.27.
2. Ibid., pp.63-64.
3. www.nps.gov/parkhistory. *Fort McHenry – "Star Spangled Banner."*
4. Matthew Page Andrews, *The Fountain Inn Diary* (Richard R. Smith, New York, 1948).
5. Michael J. Kline, *The Baltimore Plot: The First Conspiracy to Assassinate Abraham Lincoln* (Westholme Publishing, PA, 2013), p 425.
6. *Miscellaneous Documents of the House of Representatives (printed during the First Session of the thirty-Sixth Congress, 1859-1860).* See the section on Maryland's Contested Election and the list of voters surveyed, p.150.
7. John Thomas Scharf, *History of Baltimore City and County, Maryland* (Louis H. Everts, Philadelphia, 1881), p.499 and Matthew Page Andrews, *The Fountain Inn Diary* (Richard R. Smith, New York, 1948), p.85.
8. Charles Lewis Francis, *Narrative of a Private Soldier in the Volunteer Army of the United States, During a Portion of the Period Covered by the Great War of the Rebellion of 1861* (War College Series, 2015), p.10 and Frank B. Marcotte, *Six Days in April: Lincoln and the Union in Peril* (Algora Publishing, 2005), p.29.
9. Daniel Stashower, *The Hour of Peril: The Secret Plot to Murder Lincoln before the Civil War* (St. Martin's Press, 2013), p.216.
10. *The New York Times, The Great Fever Plot; Examination of the Notorious Dr. Blackburn at Toronto* (May 26, 1865).
11. www.wikipedia.org. *"Dr. Luke P. Blackburn."*
12. Edward Steers, Jr. (editor), *The Trial: The Assassination of President Lincoln and theTrial of the Conspirators* (The University Press of Kentucky, 2003), pp.55-56.

13. Jane Singer, *The Confederate Dirty War: Arson, Bombings, Assassination and Plots for Chemical and Germ Attacks on the Union* (McFarland & Co., 2005), p 78.
14. *Halifax Morning Call*, May 29, 1865.
15. Ibid.
16. Ibid.
17. Ibid.
18. *The New York Times, The Great Fever Plot; Examination of the Notorious Dr. Blackburn at Toronto* (May 26, 1865).
19. *Halifax Morning Call*, May 29, 1865.
20. www.wikipedia.org. *"Dr. Luke P. Blackburn."*
21. Nancy Disher Baird, *Luke Pryor Blackburn: Physician, Governor, Reformer* (The University of Kentucky Press, 1979), p.35.
22. Edward Steers, Jr. (editor), *The Trial: The Assassination of President Lincoln and the Trial of the Conspirators* (The University Press of Kentucky, 2003), pp.38.
23. *Halifax Morning Call*, May 29, 1865.
24. www.archive.org. *"The Papers of Randolph Abbott Shotwell. Vol. II."* A publication by the North Carolina Historical Commission.
25. Matthew Page Andrews, *The Fountain Inn Diary* (Richard R. Smith, New York, 1948), p.85.
26. *New York Times*, September 7, 1870.
27. Matthew Page Andrews, *The Fountain Inn Diary* (Richard R. Smith, New York, 1948), p.91.
28. *Miscellaneous Documents of the House of Representatives (printed during the First Session of the thirty-Sixth Congress, 1859-1860).* See the section on Maryland's Contested Election and the list of voters surveyed, p.150.
29. Ibid., p.162.
30. Genealogical research and notes on the Sauslbury family provided by Leonard Augsburger.
31. Daniel Stashower, *The Hour of Peril: The Secret Plot to Murder Lincoln before the Civil War* (St. Martin's Press, 2013), p.216.

32. Leonard Augsburger, *Treasure in the Cellar* (Baltimore: Maryland Historical Society, 2008), p.46.
33. www.coinauctionhelp.com. *"Indian Princess, Gold Dollar."* Published list of dates, mint marks, and mintage for the U.S. gold dollars.
34. *Miscellaneous Documents of the House of Representatives (printed during the First Session of the thirty-Sixth Congress, 1859-1860).* See the section on Maryland's Contested Election and the list of voters surveyed.

21. CONFEDERATE *007*

1. *New York Times,* "Important News from Maryland; Arrest of Marshal Kane," June 28, 1861.
2. www.politico.com. *"Union Troops Arrest John Merryman for Treason, May 25, 1861,"* by Andrew Glass, May 25, 2012.
3. *Boston Commonwealth,* April 22, 1861, p.2.
4. www.msa.maryland.gov/msa. Maryland State Archives, *"Ex Parte Merryman."*
5. Michael J. Kline, *The Baltimore Plot: The First Conspiracy to Assassinate Abraham Lincoln* (Westholme Publishing, PA, 2013), p 374.
6. Orville J. Victor, *The History, Civil, Political, and Military of the Southern Rebellion* (James D. Torry, Publisher, New York 1861), p.146.
7. deFrancis Folsom, *Our Police: A History of the Baltimore Police Force From the First Watchman to the Latest Appointee* (J.D. Ehlers & Co., 1888), p.57.
8. Harry Ezratty, *Baltimore in the Civil War: The Pratt Street Riot and a City Occupied* (The History Press, Charleston, SC, 2010), p.19.
9. Frank Key Howard, *Fourteen Months in American Bastilles* (Kelly, Hedian & Piet, 1863), p.54. and Matthew Kent, University of Maryland Francis King Carey School of Law, paper titled "Displaced by a force to which they yielded but could not resist – *A Historical and Legal Analysis of Mayor and City*

Council of Baltimore v. Charles Howard et.al." from 2011.

10. Charles W. Mitchell, Maryland Voices of the Civil War (Johns Hopkins University Press, Baltimore, 2007), p.273.

11. Robert Nicholson Scott, The War of the Rebellion: A Compilation of the Official Records of the Union and Confederate Armies (Washington: Government Printing Office, 1894), p.657.

12. Charles W. Mitchell, Maryland Voices of the Civil War (Johns Hopkins University Press, Baltimore, 2007), p.291.

13. Gordon Samples, Lust for Fame – The Stage Career of John Wilkes Booth (McFarland & Co, Inc., North Carolina, 1982), p.170.

14. John Y. Simon, Harold Holzer, and Dawn Vogel, Lincoln Revisited: new Insights from the Lincoln Forum (Fordham University Press, New York 2007), pp.320-321.

15. William A. Tidwell, Come Retribution: The Confederate Secret Service and the Assassination of Lincoln (University Press of Mississippi, 1988), p.331.

16. Ibid., p.166.

17. Report of the Judge Advocate General on the "Order of American Knights," or "Sons of Liberty" – a Western Conspiracy in Aid of the Southern Rebellion (Government Printing Office, Washington, DC, 1864).

18. Jennifer L. Weber, Copperheads: The Rise and Fall of Lincoln's Opponents in the North (Oxford University Press, 2006), p.118.

19. Adam Mayers, Dixie and the Dominion: Canada, the Confederacy, and the War for the Union (Dundurn press, Toronto 2003), p.159 and William A. Tidwell, Come Retribution: The Confederate Secret Service and the Assassination of Lincoln (University Press of Mississippi, 1988), p.330.

20. Michael J. Kline, The Baltimore Plot: The First Conspiracy to Assassinate Abraham Lincoln (Westholme Publishing, PA, 2013), pp.377-378.

21. Captain Robert D. Minor, CSN, to Admiral Franklin Buchanan, CSN, in the Official Records of the Union

and *Confederate Navies* (U.S. Government Printing Office, Washington, D.C., 1880-1881, Series 1, Vol. 2), pp.822-828.

22. William A. Tidwell, *Come Retribution: The Confederate Secret Service and the Assassination of Lincoln* (University Press of Mississippi, 1988), pp.179-180.

23. Michael J. Kline, *The Baltimore Plot: The First Conspiracy to Assassinate Abraham Lincoln* (Westholme Publishing, PA, 2013), p.378.

24. Warren Getler and Bob Brewer, *Rebel Gold: One Man's Quest to Crack the Code Behind the Secret Treasure of the Confederacy* (Simon & Schuster, 2003), p.19.

25. William A. Tidwell, *Come Retribution: The Confederate Secret Service and the Assassination of Lincoln* (University Press of Mississippi, 1988), p.187.

26. *Charleston Mercury*, July 20, 1864.

27. www.cia.gov. *"Intelligence in the Civil War"* (publication of the CIA, Public Affairs of the Central Intelligence Agency, Washington, D.C.), see the section "Conspiracy in Canada" pp.42-46.

28. Ibid., p.45.

29. Nancy Disher Baird, Luke Pryor Blackburn: Physician, Governor, Reformer (The University Press of Kentucky, 1979), p.26.

30. John W. Headley, *Confederate Operations in Canada and New York* (Neale Publishing Co., 1906), p.264.

31. www.cia.gov. *"Intelligence in the Civil War"* (publication of the CIA, Public Affairs of the Central Intelligence Agency, Washington, D.C.), see the section "Conspiracy in Canada" p.45.

32. *The McGill Daily, "John Booth Lived Here: How Montreal Fell for the Confederacy,"* by Matt Herzfeld, January 26, 2012.

33. www.stalbansraid.com. The St. Alban's Raid. *"The Northernmost Land Action of the Civil War."*

34. James David Horan, *Confederate Agent: A Discovery in History* (New York: Crown Publishers, Inc, 1954), p.170 and Russ A. Pritchard Jr, *Raiders of the Civil*

War: Untold Stories of Actions Behind the Lines (The Lyons Press, 2005), p.96.

35. www.stalbansraid.com. The St. Alban's Raid. *"The Northernmost Land Action of the Civil War."*
36. Robin W. Winks, *The Civil War Years: Canada and the United States* (McGill-Queens University Press, 1998), p.334.
37. Edward Steers, Jr. (editor), *The Trial: The Assassination of President Lincoln and the Trial of the Conspirators* (The University Press of Kentucky, 2003), p.39.
38. Ibid., p.53.
39. Warren Getler and Bob Brewer, *Rebel Gold: One Man's Quest to Crack the Code Behind the Secret Treasure of the Confederacy* (Simon & Schuster, 2003), p.70.
40. John D. Lawson, *American State Trials – section on "The Lincoln Conspirators"* (F.H. Thomas Law Book Co., St. Louis, 1917), pp.558-559.
41. James D. Horan, *Confederate Agent: A Discovery in History* (Crown, New York, 1954), p.13.
42. Terry Alford, *Fortune's Fool: The Life of John Wilkes Booth (Oxford University press, 2015)*, p.186.
43. Ibid.
44. William A. Tidwell, *Come Retribution: The Confederate Secret Service and the Assassination of Lincoln* (University Press of Mississippi, 1988), pp.329 and 333.
45. Edward Steers, *Blood on the Moon: The Assassination of Abraham Lincoln* (The University Press of Kentucky, 2005), pp.73-74.
46. Arthur F. Loux, *John Wilkes Booth: Day by Day* (McFarland & Company, Inc. Publishers, North Carolina, 2014), p.178.
47. Edward Steers, Jr. (editor), *The Trial: The Assassination of President Lincoln and the Trial of the Conspirators* (The University Press of Kentucky, 2003), p.39.
48. Adam Mayers, *Dixie and the Dominion: Canada, the Confederacy, and the War for the Union* (Dundurn press, Toronto 2003), p.160.

49. William A Tidwell, *April '65, Confederate Covert Action in the American Civil War* (Kent State University Press, 1995), p.146.
50. *New York Times*, April 28, 1865.
51. Ronald J. Pastore and John O'Melveney Woods, *Jesse James' Secret* (Createspace Independent Publishing, 2014), p.119.
52. Izola Forrester, *This One Mad Act* (Hale, Cushman, and Flint, Boston MA, 1937), in the preface.
53. David C. Keehn, *Knights of the Golden Circle: Secret Empire, Southern Secession, Civil War* (Louisiana State University Press, 2013), p.180.
54. Ibid., p.187.

22. THE CANDLE MERCHANT OF EDEN STREET

1. Maryland State Archives, Chancery Papers Index, 1849, MSA S 1432, April 11, 1849, *William Pinkney Whyte vs. Andrew Saulsbury and William Hamilton.* BA. Insolvent estate of Saulsbury – grocery store in BC.
2. John Thomas Scharf, *History of Baltimore City and County, Maryland* (Louis H. Everts, Philadelphia, 1881), p.184.
3. Ibid.
4. Genealogical research and notes on the Sauslbury family provided by Leonard Augsburger.
5. John Thomas Scharf, *History of Baltimore City and County, Maryland* (Louis H. Everts, Philadelphia, 1881), p.184.
6. Ibid.
7. Leonard Augsburger, *Treasure in the Cellar* (Baltimore: Maryland Historical Society, 2008), pp.71-72.
8. Anonymous, *The Great Conspiracy* (Philadelphia, Barclay & Co., 1866), p.26.
9. www.knightsofthegoldencircle.webs.com. "Home."

Notes

10. Leonard Augsburger, *Treasure in the Cellar* (Baltimore: Maryland Historical Society, 2008), p.61.
11. From the 1870 federal census taken door-to-door in Baltimore, MD, Third Ward, as well as genealogical research and notes on the Sauslbury family provided by Leonard Augsburger.
12. Testimony of Margaret Saulsbury Short and Elizabeth Saulsbury Audoun, BCCC#2, docket A-579, 1934.
13. Ibid.
14. *Rare Coin Review* #150, *"The 1934 Baltimore Gold Hoard"* by Leonard Augsburger, November/December 2002, p.38.
15. Ibid., p.37.
16. Leonard Augsburger, *Treasure in the Cellar* (Baltimore: Maryland Historical Society, 2008), pp.46-47.
17. Ibid., p.47.
18. Ibid.
19. Ibid., p.71.
20. Report from the Mixed Court of British and Spanish Justice recorded in the *Correspondence with the British Commissioners at Sierra Leone Regarding the Slave Trade* (From May 11th to December 31st, 1840, inclusive). See the specific case summary "Report of the Case of the Brig 'Eliza Davidson,' Alexander B. Hanna, Master. Sierra Leone, April 24th, 1840."
21. John Thomas Scharf, *History of Baltimore City and County, Maryland* (Louis H. Everts, Philadelphia, 1881), p.184.
22. *The Baltimore Underwriter and Internal Revenue Record* (May 1868, Volume III, No. II), p.166. See the Board of Directors listed for the American Fire Insurance Company of Baltimore.
23. *New York Times*, September 7, 1870.
24. Testimony of Elizabeth Saulsbury Audoun, BCCC#2, docket A-579, 1934.
25. *Journal of the Proceedings of the Second Branch City Council of Baltimore, at the Sessions 1867-1868* (John Cox, Baltimore City Printer, 1868) *Journal of the Proceedings of the Second Branch City Council of*

Baltimore, Sessions 1868-1869 (E.G. Armiger, Baltimore City Printer, 1869).
26. Ibid., and also Leonard Augsburger, Treasure in the Cellar (Baltimore: Maryland Historical Society, 2008), p.62.
27. Leonard Augsburger, Treasure in the Cellar (Baltimore: Maryland Historical Society, 2008), p.62.
28. Ibid.

23. A THIEF IN THE NIGHT

1. Testimony given regarding the "second" gold discovery, BCCC #2, 9/20/1935 and also Leonard Augsburger, *Treasure in the Cellar* (Baltimore: Maryland Historical Society, 2008), p.110.
2. Leonard Augsburger, *Treasure in the Cellar* (Baltimore: Maryland Historical Society, 2008), p.83.
3. Ibid. p.102.
4. *Rare Coin Review* #150, *"The 1934 Baltimore Gold Hoard"* by Leonard Augsburger, November/December 2002, p.39.
5. *Baltimore Evening Sun*, 9/3/1935, p.40.
6. *Baltimore Evening Sun*, 9/11/1934, p.34.
7. Leonard Augsburger, *Treasure in the Cellar* (Baltimore: Maryland Historical Society, 2008), pp.101-103.
8. *Washington Post*, 10/3/1935, p.11.
9. Testimony of Henry Grob, BCCC #2, 9/20/1935
10. *Baltimore News*, 9/3/1935, p.2.
11. Leonard Augsburger, *Treasure in the Cellar* (Baltimore: Maryland Historical Society, 2008), pp.103-104.
12. *Rare Coin Review* #150, *"The 1934 Baltimore Gold Hoard"* by Leonard Augsburger, November/December 2002, p.39.
13. *Baltimore Evening Sun*, 9/3/1935, p.8.
14. Leonard Augsburger, *Treasure in the Cellar* (Baltimore: Maryland Historical Society, 2008), p.105.
15. *Baltimore Evening Sun*, 9/17/1935, p.11.

16. Testimony of Theodore Jones and Henry Grob, BCCC #2, 9/20/1935
17. Leonard Augsburger, *Treasure in the Cellar* (Baltimore: Maryland Historical Society, 2008), pp.110-111.
18. Ibid., p.116.
19. Testimony of Philip Rummel, BCCC #2, 9/20/1935.
20. *Rare Coin Review* #150, *"The 1934 Baltimore Gold Hoard"* by Leonard Augsburger, November/December 2002, pp.39-40.
21. Leonard Augsburger, *Treasure in the Cellar* (Baltimore: Maryland Historical Society, 2008), p.109.
22. *Baltimore Sun*, 9/21/1935, p.4.
23. *Daily Record*, Baltimore, 10/5/1935, p.3.
24. Inventory of coins purchased by the Merrills, BCCC #2, 9/20/1935.
25. Ruth Grob's bank deposits introduced as evidence, BCCC #2, 9/20/1935.
26. Leonard Augsburger, *Treasure in the Cellar* (Baltimore: Maryland Historical Society, 2008), pp.114.
27. Ibid., p.118.
28. Ibid., p.119.
29. Ibid., p.120.
30. *"French vs. Jones* Case Chronology," File 21483A, BCCC #2, 10/8/1935.

24. THE NIGHT THEY DROVE OLD DIXIE DOWN

1. "The Night They Drove Old Dixie Down," released in 1969 by The Band. Writer Robbie Robertson, label Capitol Records. The most successful English-language cover of the song was a version by Joan Baez released in 1971, which peaked at number three on the *Billboard* Hot 100 chart in the US in October of that year.
2. Frederick Hatch, *Protecting President Lincoln: The Security Effort, the Thwarted Plots and the Disaster at*

Ford's Theater (McFarland & Co., North Carolina, 2011), p.66.

3. Michael J. Kline, *The Baltimore Plot: The First Conspiracy to Assassinate Abraham Lincoln* (Westholme Publishing, PA, 2013), pp. 376-378.
4. Mark A. Lause, *A Secret Society History of the Civil War* (The University of Illinois, 2011), p. 142.
5. www.wikipedia.org. *"John H. Winder."*
6. William A. Tidwell, *Come Retribution: The Confederate Secret Service and the Assassination of Lincoln* (University Press of Mississippi, 1988), pp.61 and 146, and also www.wikipedia.org. *"George Proctor Kane."*
7. Ibid., p 146.
8. Jack E. Schairer, *Lee's Bold Plan for Point Lookout: The Rescue of Confederate Prisoners That Never Happened* (McFarland & Co., North Carolina, 2008), p.130.
9. *Hallowed Ground Magazine*, *"Stalking John Wilkes Booth,"* by Bob Allen, Summer 2015 issue.
10. Terry Alford, Fortune's Fool: *The Life of John Wilkes Booth (Oxford University Press, 2015),* p.185.
11. www.wikipedia.org. *"Dahlgren Affair."*
12. John C. Fazio, *Decapitating the Union: Jefferson Davis, Judah Benjamin and the Plot to Assassinate Lincoln* (McFarland & Co., North Carolina, 2015), p.21.
13. www.wikipedia.org. *"Dahlgren Affair."*
14. www.historynet.com/jefferson-davis. *"The Dahlgren Papers Revisited."*
15. Michael J. Kline, *The Baltimore Plot: The First Conspiracy to Assassinate Abraham Lincoln* (Westholme Publishing, PA, 2013), pp. 376-378.
16. Ulysses Simpson Grant (edited by John F. Marszalek), *The Best Writings of Ulysses S. Grant* (Southern Illinois University Press, 2015), pp. 62-63.
17. Arthur F. Loux, *John Wilkes Booth: Day by Day* (McFarland & Company, Inc. Publishers, North Carolina, 2014), p.184.

Notes

18. Adam Mayers, *Dixie and the Dominion: Canada, the Confederacy, and the War for the Union* (Dundurn press, Toronto 2003), pp.157-158.
19. Edward Steers, *Blood on the Moon: The Assassination of Abraham Lincoln* (The University Press of Kentucky, 2005), p.61.
20. Adam Mayers, *Dixie and the Dominion: Canada, the Confederacy, and the War for the Union* (Dundurn press, Toronto 2003), pp.157-158.
21. Kate Clifford Larson, *The Assassin's Accomplice: Mary Surratt and the Plot to Kill Abraham Lincoln* (Basic Books, New York, 2008), pp.64-65.
22. Frederick Hatch, *Protecting President Lincoln: The Security Effort, the Thwarted Plots and the Disaster at Ford's Theater* (McFarland & Co., North Carolina, 2011), p.81.
23. John C. Fazio, *Decapitating the Union: Jefferson Davis, Judah Benjamin and the Plot to Assassinate Lincoln* (McFarland & Co., North Carolina, 2015), p.107.
24. William A. Tidwell, *Come Retribution: The Confederate Secret Service and the Assassination of Lincoln* (University Press of Mississippi, 1988), p 339.
25. James L. Swanson and Daniel R. Weinberg, *Lincoln's Assassins: Their Trial and Execution* (HarperCollins, 2006), p.51.
26. Edward Steers, *Blood on the Moon: The Assassination of Abraham Lincoln* (The University Press of Kentucky, 2005), p.73.
27. Clara E. Laughlin, *The Death of Lincoln* (Doubleday, Page & Company, New York, 1909), p. 216.
28. Edward Steers, Jr. (editor), *The Trial: The Assassination of President Lincoln and the Trial of the Conspirators* (The University Press of Kentucky, 2003), p.45.
29. Kate Clifford Larson, *The Assassin's Accomplice: Mary Surratt and the Plot to Kill Abraham Lincoln* (Basic Books, New York, 2008), pp.65-66.
30. Gene Smith, *Lee and Grant: A Dual Biography* (Promontory Press, 1989), p.246.

31. Edward L. Ayers, Lewis L. Gould, David M. Oshinsky, and Jean R. Souderlund, *American Passages: A History of the United States* (Wadsworth, Cengage Learning), p. 426.
32. Donald Vaughan, *The Everything Civil War Book* (Adams Media Corp., Massachusetts, 2000), p.70.
33. John Wilkes Booth (edited by John Rhodehamel and Louise Taper), *Right or Wrong, God Judge Me: The Writings of John Wilkes Booth* (The Board of Trustees of the University of Illinois, 1997), p.15.
34. Edward Steers, *Blood on the Moon: The Assassination of Abraham Lincoln* (The University Press of Kentucky, 2005), p.162.
35. Paul Simpson, *That's the Way They Want You to Think: Conspiracies Real, Possible, and Paranoid* (Zenith Press, 2012), p.10.
36. Edward Steers, Jr. (editor), *The Trial: The Assassination of President Lincoln and the Trial of the Conspirators* (The University Press of Kentucky, 2003), pp.144-145.
37. John C. Fazio, *Decapitating the Union: Jefferson Davis, Judah Benjamin and the Plot to Assassinate Lincoln* (McFarland & Co., North Carolina, 2015), pp.84-85.
38. William A. Tidwell, *Come Retribution: The Confederate Secret Service and the Assassination of Lincoln* (University Press of Mississippi, 1988), p 61.
39. *New York Daily Graphic*, March 22, 1876.
40. Michael J. Kline, *The Baltimore Plot: The First Conspiracy to Assassinate Abraham Lincoln* (Westholme Publishing, PA, 2013), p. 386.
41. Frank B. Marcotte, *Six Days in April: Lincoln and the Union in Peril* (Algora Publishing, 2005), p.30.
42. *Boston Commonwealth*, April 22, 1861, p.2.
43. Gordon Samples, *Lust for Fame – The Stage Career of John Wilkes Booth* (McFarland & Co, Inc., North Carolina, 1982), p.170.
44. Terry Alford, *Fortune's Fool: The Life of John Wilkes Booth* (Oxford University press, 2015), p.185 and the *New York Daily Graphic*, March 22, 1876.

45. William A. Tidwell, *Come Retribution: The Confederate Secret Service and the Assassination of Lincoln* (University Press of Mississippi, 1988), p xii.
46. William Marvel, *Mr. Lincoln Goes to War* (Houghton Mifflin Company, 2006), p.297.
47. Charles W. Mitchell, *Maryland Voices of the Civil War* (Johns Hopkins University Press, Baltimore, 2007), p.291.
48. Leonard F. Guttridge and Ray A. Neff, Dark Union: *The Secret Web of Profiteers, Politicians, and Booth Conspirators That Led to Lincoln's Death* (Wiley, 2003), p. 31 and *Izola Louise Forrester, This One Mad Act* (Hale, Cushman, and Flint, 1937), p.198.
49. W.C. Jameson, *Return of Assassin John Wilkes Booth* (Republic of Texas Press, 1998), p.146.
50. *The McGill Daily, "John Booth Lived Here: How Montreal Fell for the Confederacy,"* by Matt Herzfeld, January 26, 2012.
51. *Izola Louise Forrester, This One Mad Act* (Hale, Cushman, and Flint, 1937), p.181.
52. W.C. Jameson, *John Wilkes Booth Beyond the Grave* (Taylor Trade Publishing, MD, 2013), p.170.
53. John W. Headley, *Confederate Operations in Canada and New York* (Neale Publishing Co., 1906), p.243.
54. Paul Taylor, *Old Slow Town: Detroit During the Civil War* (Wayne State University Press, 2013), p.173.
55. William Gilmore Beymer, *Scouts and Spies of the Civil War* (University of Nebraska Press, 2003), p.199.
56. *New York Daily Graphic*, March 22, 1876.
57. Adam Mayers, *Dixie and the Dominion: Canada, the Confederacy, and the War for the Union* (Dundurn press, Toronto 2003), p.159.
58. *New York Daily Graphic*, March 22, 1876.
59. Ibid.
60. Ibid.
61. Marshall P. Waters, PhD, *"Confederate Treasury – the Final Disposition,"* (paper written in 2007).
62. Jefferson Davis (edited by Lynda L. Crist), *The Papers of Jefferson Davis: Vol. II, September 1864 to May, 1865* (Louisiana State University Press, 2003), p.525.

63. John C. Inscoe (editor), *The Civil War in Georgia: A New Georgia Encyclopedia Companion* (The University of Georgia Press, 2011), p.104.
64. Frank L. Klement, *Dark Lanterns: Secret Political Societies, Conspiracies, and Treason Trials in the Civil War* (Louisiana State University Press, 1989), p.218.
65. David J. Phillips, *On This Day, Vol. 1* (iUniverse, New York, 2007), p.102.
66. *"The* Missing Confederate Gold: Raid at Chennault, *Georgia, May 24, 1865"* by Marshall P. Waters III. Published in the *Surratt Courier Newsletter* (affiliate of the Surratt House museum), December 2009, Volume XXXIV No. 12, pp 3-9.
67. Larry Gordon, *The Last Confederate General: John C. Vaughn and His East Tennessee Cavalry* (Zenith Press, Minneapolis, 2009), p. 160.
68. Bill Yenne, *Lost Treasure: A Guide to Buried Riches* (Berkley Books, New York, 1999), p.117.
69. Ibid., p.118.
70. *"The* Missing Confederate Gold: Raid at Chennault, *Georgia, May 24, 1865"* by Marshall P. Waters III. Published in the *Surratt Courier Newsletter* (affiliate of the Surratt House museum), December 2009, Volume XXXIV No. 12, pp 3-9.
71. Ray Chandler, *The Last Days of the Confederacy in Northeast Georgia* (The History Press, South Carolina, 2015), p.83.
72. Brad Meltzer with Keith Ferrell, *History Decoded: The 10 Greatest Conspiracies of All Time* (A&E Television networks, LLC, 2013), p.18.
73. *"Lost Confederate Gold"* episode of the History Channel show "Decoded" with Brad Meltzer in December 30, 2010.
74. Brad Meltzer with Keith Ferrell, *History Decoded: The 10 Greatest Conspiracies of All Time* (A&E Television networks, LLC, 2013), pp.17-18.
75. *"Lost Confederate Gold"* episode of the History Channel show "Decoded" with Brad Meltzer in December 30, 2010. Interview portion with Dr. Marshall P. Waters.

Notes

76. Ibid. Portion with Bob Brewer at the Danville Cemetery.
77. www.historynewsnetwork.org. *"Mystery of Lost Confederate Gold"* by Wesley Millett and Gerald White, May 19, 2008.
78. Ibid.
79. Ibid.
80. Ibid.
81. *"The* Missing Confederate Gold: Raid at Chennault, *Georgia, May 24, 1865"* by Marshall P. Waters III. Published in the *Surratt Courier Newsletter* (affiliate of the Surratt House museum), December 2009, Volume XXXIV No. 12, pp 3-9.
82. Jefferson Davis (edited by Lynda L. Crist), *The Papers of Jefferson Davis: Vol. II, September 1864 to May, 1865* (Louisiana State University Press, 2003), p.525.
83. www.wikipedia.org. "George Proctor Kane" and Frank B. Marcotte, *Six Days in April: Lincoln and the Union in Peril* (Algora Publishing, 2005), p.163.
84. Robert Alonzo Brock and Virgil Anson Lewis, *Virginia and Virginians* (H.H. Hardesty, Richmond, 1888), p.790.
85. John Thomas Scharf, *History of Baltimore City and County, Maryland* (Louis H. Everts, Philadelphia, 1881), p.210.
86. Ibid.
87. Ibid.
88. Ibid.
89. Frank B. Marcotte, *Six Days in April: Lincoln and the Union in Peril* (Algora Publishing, 2005), p.163.
90. www.wikipedia.org. "George Proctor Kane."
91. Edward T. Schultz, *History of Freemasonry in Maryland* (Medairy & Co., Baltimore, 1888), p.414.
92. John Thomas Scharf, *History of Baltimore City and County, Maryland* (Louis H. Everts, Philadelphia, 1881), p.184.
93. *The New York Times, "Death of Baltimore's Mayor; The Life of a Prominent Ex-Rebel and Member of Lee's Staff,"* June 24, 1878, special dispatch to the *New York Times.*

25. THE CANDLE GOES OUT

1. Leonard Augsburger, *Treasure in the Cellar* (Baltimore: Maryland Historical Society, 2008), p.162 and BCCC #2, docket A-579, 1934.
2. Maryland State Archives, Chancery Papers Index, 1849, MSA S 1432, April 11, 1849, *William Pinkney Whyte vs. Andrew Saulsbury and William Hamilton. BA.* Insolvent estate of Saulsbury - grocery store in BC.
3. Testimony of Margaret Saulsbury Short and Elizabeth Saulsbury Audoun, BCCC#2, docket A-579, 1934.
4. Ibid.
5. The collected obituaries of Andrew Saulsbury are given into evidence in BCCC #2, docket A-579, 1934.
6. Leonard Augsburger, *Treasure in the Cellar* (Baltimore: Maryland Historical Society, 2008), pp.47-48.
7. Ibid., p.62 and the collected obituaries of Andrew Saulsbury are given into evidence in BCCC #2, docket A-579, 1934.
8. www.wikipedia.org. *"Michael O'Laughlen."*
9. Leonard Augsburger, *Treasure in the Cellar* (Baltimore: Maryland Historical Society, 2008), pp.47-48.
10. Ibid., p.185.
11. Baltimore City Register of Wills (Inventories), 1874, JHB 99, 365-378.
12. Leonard Augsburger, *Treasure in the Cellar* (Baltimore: Maryland Historical Society, 2008), p.61.
13. John Thomas Scharf, *History of Baltimore City and County, Maryland* (Louis H. Everts, Philadelphia, 1881), p.184.
14. Ibid.
15. Gordon Samples, *Lust for Fame: The Stage Career of John Wilkes Booth* (McFarland & Company, North Carolina 1998), p.170.
16. www.wikipedia.org. *"George Proctor Kane."*

17. Edward T. Schultz, *History of Freemasonry in Maryland* (Medairy & Co., Baltimore, 1888), pp.713-717.
18. Ibid. p.579.
19. John Edward Semmes, *John H.B. Latrobe and His Times* (The Norman, Remington Co, Baltimore, MD, 1917), p.417.
20. *Proceedings of the Grand Lodge of Maryland, A.F. and A.M.* as put out by the Grand Lodge of Maryland (Griffin, Curley, & Co., 1887), p.50.
21. *Proceedings of the Grand Lodge of Colorado, A.F. and A.M.* as put out by the Grand Lodge of Colorado (W.F. Robinson & Co., 1892), p.103/Appendix.
22. www.wikipedia.org. *"Albert Pike."*
23. *The National Bankruptcy News,* April 15, 1899, p. Maryland, p.245. Action brought against the company by Martha C. Pough of Massachusetts, an investor in Jas. Armstrong & Co. headed by Thomas Armstrong.

26. HENRY AND THEODORE'S LONG WAIT

1. Leonard Augsburger, *Treasure in the Cellar* (Baltimore: Maryland Historical Society, 2008), p.107.
2. BCCC #2, equity docket 43A, folio 720, 1937.
3. Leonard Augsburger, *Treasure in the Cellar* (Baltimore: Maryland Historical Society, 2008), pp.108-113.
4. *Baltimore Evening Sun,* 8/25/1937, p.32.
5. Testimony recorded in BCCC #2, 9/20/1935.
6. *Baltimore Evening Sun,* 1/31/1936, p.42.
7. Ibid.
8. Leonard Augsburger, *Treasure in the Cellar* (Baltimore: Maryland Historical Society, 2008), pp.130-131.
9. *Baltimore Evening News,* 9/3/1935, p.40.
10. Leonard Augsburger, *Treasure in the Cellar* (Baltimore: Maryland Historical Society, 2008), p.131.
11. Ibid.

12. *Rare Coin Review* #150, *"The 1934 Baltimore Gold Hoard"* by Leonard Augsburger, November/December 2002, p.41.
13. Ibid., p.42.
14. *Baltimore Sun*, 4/23/1936, p.26.
15. Leonard Augsburger, *Treasure in the Cellar* (Baltimore: Maryland Historical Society, 2008), p.132.
16. *Baltimore Sun*, 10/9/1936, p.37.
17. Leonard Augsburger, *Treasure in the Cellar* (Baltimore: Maryland Historical Society, 2008), p.134.
18. *Baltimore Sun*, 4/251936, p.1.

27. MYSTERY OF THE CODED DUE-BILL

1. Henry Bartlet Maglathlin, New Practical Arithmetic (Robert S. Davis $ Co., Boston, 1875), pp.76-77.
2. Leonard Augsburger, *Treasure in the Cellar* (Baltimore: Maryland Historical Society, 2008), p.47.
3. Private correspondence with Leonard Augsburger, author of *Treasure in the Cellar* (Baltimore: Maryland Historical Society, 2008).
4. Leonard Augsburger, *Treasure in the Cellar* (Baltimore: Maryland Historical Society, 2008), p.61.
5. Ibid.
6. www.wikipedia.org. *"The Art of War."*
7. www.outlawtreasure.worldbreak.com. *"The Knights of the Golden Circle."*
8. Warren Getler and Bob Brewer, *Rebel Gold: One Man's Quest to Crack the Code Behind the Secret Treasure of the Confederacy* (Simon & Schuster, 2003), p.22.
9. Ibid., p.19.
10. Testimony of Margaret Saulsbury Short and Elizabeth Saulsbury Audoun, BCCC#2, docket A-579, 1934.
11. www.allkindsofhistory.worldpress.com. *"The Last Secret of the Hunley."* May 10, 2014.
12. Brian Hicks and Schulyer Krope, *Raising the Hunley: The Remarkable History and Recovery of the Lost*

Confederate Submarine (The Ballantine Publishing Group, 2002), p.26.
13. www.wikipedia.org. *"Pioneer (submarine)."*
14. www.wikipedia.org. *"American Diver."*
15. www.hunley.org. *"Friends of the Hunley."*
16. Ibid.
17. www.wikipedia.org. *"The Hunley."*
18. www.wikipedia.org. *"H.L Hunley (submarine)."*
19. David C. Keehn, *Knights of the Golden Circle: Secret Empire, Southern Secession, Civil War* (Louisiana State University Press, 2013), p.91.
20. www.hunley.org. *"Friends of the Hunley – Lt. George Dixon and the Third Crew."*
21. www.wikipedia.org. *"George E. Dixon."*
22. www.wikipedia.org. *"USS Housatonic (1861)."*
23. www.hunley.org. *"Friends of the Hunley – Finding the Hunley."*
24. www.wikipedia.org. *"H.L. Hunley (submarine) – Recovery of Wreckage."*
25. www.wikipedia.org. *"H.L. Hunley (submarine) – Crew."*
26. Ibid.
27. www.smithsonian.com. *"The Amazing (If True) Story of the Submarine Mechanic Who Blew Himself Up Then Resurfaced as a Secret Agent for Queen Victoria,"* by Mike Dash, June 30, 2014.
28. Ibid.

28. THE SISTERS FINALLY CASH IN

1. Leonard Augsburger, *Treasure in the Cellar* (Baltimore: Maryland Historical Society, 2008), p.120.
2. C. Arthur Eby & Emory H. Niles brief that a re-argument should be granted, 170 Md., 318, 13.
3. Leonard Augsburger, *Treasure in the Cellar* (Baltimore: Maryland Historical Society, 2008), p.132.
4. Ibid., p.128.
5. Ibid., p.132.
6. Ibid.

7. *Rare Coin Review* #150, *"The 1934 Baltimore Gold Hoard"* by Leonard Augsburger, November/December 2002, p.41.
8. Ibid.
9. Leonard Augsburger, *Treasure in the Cellar* (Baltimore: Maryland Historical Society, 2008), p.133.
10. *Baltimore Sun*, 10/2/1936, p.4.
11. Leonard Augsburger, *Treasure in the Cellar* (Baltimore: Maryland Historical Society, 2008), p.134.
12. Ibid.
13. Ibid., p.137.
14. Ibid., p.148.
15. Ibid., p.138.
16. Opinion of Judge Samuel K. Dennis, BCCC #2, 12/28/1937.
17. Leonard Augsburger, *Treasure in the Cellar* (Baltimore: Maryland Historical Society, 2008), p.139.

29. JESSE JAMES IS GONE WITH THE WIND

1. Ted P. Yeatman, *Frank and Jesse James: The Story Behind the Legend* (Cumberland House, TN, 2000), p.27.
2. T.J. Stiles, *Jesse James: Last Rebel of the Civil War* (A.A. Knopf, 2002), p.25.
3. Ron Pastore and John O'Melveny Woods, *Jesse James' Secret* (Intellect Publishing, 2011), p. 43 and Phyllis Appel, *The Missouri Connection: Profiles and the Famous and Infamous* (Smashwords Edition, 2012), p.112.
4. Thomas Goodrich, *War to the Knife: Bleeding Kansas, 1854-1861* (University of Nebraska Press, 1988), pp.136-137.
5. Ted P. Yeatman, *Frank and Jesse James: The Story Behind the Legend* (Cumberland House, TN, 2000), p.30.
6. Barbara Saffer, *Jesse James – Famous Figures of the American Frontier* (Chelsea House Publishers, Philadelphia, 2002), p.58.

Notes

7. Warren Getler and Bob Brewer, *Rebel Gold: One Man's Quest to Crack the Code Behind the Secret Treasure of the Confederacy* (Simon & Schuster, 2003), p.105.
8. Richard N. Piland and Marietta Wislon Boenker, *Independence* (Arcadia Publishing, 2008), p.8.
9. Phillip W. Steele and George Warfel, *The Many Faces of Jesse James* (Pelican Publishing Company, 1998), p.23.
10. Del Schrader, *Jesse James Was One of His Names: The Greatest Cover-up in History by the Famous Outlaw Who Lived 73 Incredible Lives* (Santa Anita Press, 1975), p.57.
11. Jim Feazell, "Jesse" A Supernatural Thriller (iUnivers, Bloomington, 2011), pp.31-32.
12. William A. Settle, *Jesse James Was His Name: Or, Fact and Fiction Concerning the Careers of the Notorious James Brothers of Missouri* (University of Missouri Press, 1966), pp.25-27.
13. Carl R. Green and William R. Sandford, *Jesse James: Wanted Dead or Alive* (Enslow Publishers, NJ, 2009), p.14.
14. www.wikipedia.org. *"Centralia Massacre (Missouri)."*
15. www.tjstiles.net/bio.htm.
16. Troy Taylor, *The Big Book of Missouri Ghost Stories* (Stackpole Books, 2013), p. 241.
17. Nate Hendley, *American Gangsters, Then and Now: An Encyclopedia* (Greenwood Publishing, CA, 2010), p. 105.
18. Ted P. Yeatman, *Frank and Jesse James: The Story Behind the Legend* (Cumberland House, TN, 2000), pp.75-76.
19. Ron Pastore and John O'Melveny Woods, *Jesse James' Secret* (Intellect Publishing, 2011), p. 43 and Phyllis Appel, *The Missouri Connection: Profiles and the Famous and Infamous* (Smashwords Edition, 2012), pp.58-59.
20. Phillip W. Steele, *Outlaws and Gunfighters of the Old West* (Pelican Publishing Company, 1998), p.18.
21. www.wikipedia.org. *"Archie Clement."*

22. Larry C. Bradley, *Jesse James: The Making of a Legend* (Larren Publishers, 1980), p.25.
23. Fred Rosen, *The Historical Atlas of American Crime* (Facts on File, New York, 2005), p.145.
24. The New York Times, *"Iowa Boy Finds $50,000; Gold and Paper Money in a Box Buried in Clinton, Iowa,"* October 30, 1897.
25. Ron Pastore and John O'Melveny Woods, *Jesse James' Secret* (Intellect Publishing, 2011), pp.255-257.
26. Robertus Love, *The Rise and Fall of Jesse James* (University of Nebraska Press, 1990), pp.54-58.
27. Carl R. Green and William R. Sandford, *Jesse James: Wanted Dead or Alive* (Enslow Publishers, NJ, 2009), p.6.
28. Henry J. Walker, *Jesse James "The Outlaw"* (Wallace-Homestead, Des Moines, 1961), p.133.
29. Robert L. Dyer, *Jesse James and the Civil War in Missouri* (University of Missouri Press, 1994), p.58.
30. T.J. Stiles, *Jesse James: Last Rebel of the Civil War* (A.A. Knopf, 2002), pp.224-226.
31. Ibid., p.102.
32. The History Channel, *Jesse James' Hidden Treasure*, 2009 television special.
33. Joseph Cummins, *Heists: Gripping Exposes of the World's Most Notorious Robberies* (Murdoch Books PTY Limited, Australia and the UK, 2011), p.63.
34. T.J. Stiles, *Jesse James: Last Rebel of the Civil War* (A.A. Knopf, 2002), pp.211-226.
35. Robert Barr Smith, *The Last Hurrah of the James-Younger Gang* (University of Oklahoma Press, 2001), p.77.
36. Richard Worth, *Great Robberies* (Chelsea House Publishers, Philadelphia, 2001), pp.42-43.
37. Robert L. Dyer, *Jesse James and the Civil War in Missouri* (University of Missouri Press, 1994), p.59.
38. Donald L. Gilmore, *Riding Vengeance with the James Gang* (Pelican Publishing, Louisiana, 2009), p.204.
39. Robert Barr Smith, *The Last Hurrah of the James-Younger Gang* (University of Oklahoma Press, 2001), pp.186-187.

Notes

40. Ted P. Yeatman, *Frank and Jesse James: The Story Behind the Legend* (Cumberland House, TN, 2000), pp.174-177.
41. Sean McLachlan, *The Last Ride of the James-Younger Gang: Jesse James and the Northfield Raid 1876* (Osprey Publishing 2012), pp.73-74.
42. R.G. Tidwell, *The Frank and Jesse James Saga – The Beginning of the End for the James Gang* (Bluewater Publications, Alabama, 2011), p.210.
43. Aaron Frisch, *Jesse James* (Creative Education, Minnesota, 2006), p.33.
44. William A. Settle, *Jesse James Was His Name: Or, Fact and Fiction Concerning the Careers of the Notorious James Brothers of Missouri* (University of Missouri Press, 1966), pp.117-120.
45. Barbara Saffer, *Jesse James – Famous Figures of the American Frontier* (Chelsea House Publishers, Philadelphia, 2002), p.55.
46. Nate Hendley, *American Gangsters, Then and Now: An Encyclopedia* (Greenwood Publishing, CA, 2010), p. 116.
47. Larry Wood, *Murder and Mayhem in Missouri* (History Press, Charleston, 2013), p.46.
48. Carl W. Breihan, *The Man Who Shot Jesse James* (A.S. Barnes, 1979), p.46.
49. Marley Brant, *The Outlaw Youngers: A Confederate Brotherhood* (Madison Books, Lanham, MD, 1992), p.224.
50. Carl W. Breihan, *The Man Who Shot Jesse James* (A.S. Barnes, 1979), p.62.
51. Ronald J. Pastore and John O'Melveney Woods, *Jesse James' Secret* (Createspace Independent Publishing, 2014).
52. Ibid., p.229.
53. *Liberty Tribune*, April 14, 1882 as quoted in Del Schrader's *Jesse James Was One of His Names: The Greatest Cover-up in History by the Famous Outlaw Who Lived 73 Incredible Lives* (Santa Anita Press, 1975).
54. Carl W. Breihan, *The Man Who Shot Jesse James* (A.S. Barnes, 1979), p.46.

55. Eugene Campbell Barker and Herbert Eugene Bolton, *The Southwestern Historical Quarterly, Vol.44* (Texas State Historical Association, Austin, 1941), p. 301 and David C. Keehn, *Knights of the Golden Circle: Secret Empire, Southern Secession, Civil War* (Louisiana State University Press, 2013), p.121.
56. James R. Knight, *The Battle of Pea Ridge: The Civil War Fight for the Ozarks* (The History Press, Charleston, SC, 2012), p.18.
57. Clara Sue Kidwell, *The Choctaws in Oklahoma: From Tribe to Nation, 1855-1970* (University of Oklahoma Press, 2007), p. 63.
58. Robert Scott, *Blood at Sand Creek: The Massacre Revisted* (Caxton Printers, Idaho, 1994), p.188.
59. Albert Pike, *Morals and Dogma* of the Scottish Rite of Freemasonry (Martino Fine Books, 2013).
60. www.wikipedia.org. *"Joseph O. Shelby."*
61. Ted P. Yeatman, *Frank and Jesse James: The Story Behind the Legend* (Cumberland House, TN, 2000), p.104.
62. Deryl P. Spellmeyer, *Jo Shelby's Iron Brigade* (Pelican Publishing, Louisiana, 2007), p.292.
63. www.wikipedia.org. *"James Timberlake."*
64. Bill Yenne, *Lost Treasure: A Guide to Buried Riches* (Berkley Books, New York, 1999), pp.152-158.
65. www.wikipedia.org. *"Frank James."*
66. Robertus Love, *The Rise and Fall of Jesse James* (University of Nebraska Press, 1990), p.398.
67. William A. Settle, *Jesse James Was His Name: Or, Fact and Fiction Concerning the Careers of the Notorious James Brothers of Missouri* (University of Missouri Press, 1966), pp.142-143.
68. Carl W. Breihan, *The Man Who Shot Jesse James* (A.S. Barnes, 1979), p.54.
69. *History of Clay and Platte Counties,* St. Louis, MO: National Historical Company, 1885. pp. 368-9.
70. Daniel O'Flaherty, *General Jo Shelby: Undefeated Rebel* (University of North Carolina Press, 1954), pp. 383-385.
71. Ron Pastore and John O'Melveny Woods, *Jesse James' Secret* (Intellect Publishing, 2011), p.90.

72. Ibid., p.265.
73. Ibid., pp. 175, 177, 180, and 267.
74. Ibid., pp.124-128.
75. Ibid., pp.264-265.
76. Ibid., pp.233-235
77. Ted P. Yeatman, *Frank and Jesse James: The Story Behind the Legend* (Cumberland House, TN, 2000), p.276.
78. Ron Pastore and John O'Melveny Woods, *Jesse James' Secret* (Intellect Publishing, 2011), pp.266-267.
79. *The Los Angles Times*, April 4, 1882.
80. The History Channel, *Jesse James' Hidden Treasure*, 2009 television special.
81. *The New York Times*, *"Iowa Boy Finds $50,000; Gold and Paper Money Buried in a Box in Clinton, Iowa"* October 30, 1897.

30. GOLDEN DREAMS

1. Leonard Augsburger, *Treasure in the Cellar* (Baltimore: Maryland Historical Society, 2008), p.34.
2. Ibid., p.107.
3. *Baltimore News*, 8/25/1937, p.15.
4. *Rare Coin Review* #150, *"The 1934 Baltimore Gold Hoard"* by Leonard Augsburger, November/December 2002, p.42.
5. Opinion of Judge Samuel K. Dennis, BCCC #2, 12/28/1937.
6. Leonard Augsburger, *Treasure in the Cellar* (Baltimore: Maryland Historical Society, 2008), p.135.
7. Ibid.
8. *Baltimore Evening Sun*, 9/26/1937, p.36.
9. *Baltimore Sun*, 8/25/1937, p.4.
10. Leonard Augsburger, *Treasure in the Cellar* (Baltimore: Maryland Historical Society, 2008), p.163.
11. Ibid.

12. *Rare Coin Review* #150, *"The 1934 Baltimore Gold Hoard"* by Leonard Augsburger, November/December 2002, p.42.
13. Leonard Augsburger, *Treasure in the Cellar* (Baltimore: Maryland Historical Society, 2008), p.149.
14. BCCC #2, equity docket 43A, folio 803, 5/19/1939.
15. Leonard Augsburger, *Treasure in the Cellar* (Baltimore: Maryland Historical Society, 2008), pp.149-150.
16. *Baltimore Sun*, 12/27/1940, p.9.
17. Leonard Augsburger, *Treasure in the Cellar* (Baltimore: Maryland Historical Society, 2008), pp.146-147.

31. THE SOUTH SHALL RISE AGAIN

1. Warren Getler and Bob Brewer, *Rebel Gold: One Man's Quest to Crack the Code Behind the Secret Treasure of the Confederacy* (Simon & Schuster, 2003), originally published in hardcover under the title *Shadow of the Sentinel: One Man's Quest to Crack the Code Behind the Secret Treasure of the Confederacy.*
2. Warren Getler and Bob Brewer, *Rebel Gold: One Man's Quest to Crack the Code Behind the Secret Treasure of the Confederacy* (Simon & Schuster, 2003), p.9.
3. Ibid., p.11.
4. Ibid., p.11.
5. Ibid., p.12.
6. The narrative regarding Mr. Brewer's treasure hunting activities in Arkansas is all derived and condensed from his book, *Rebel Gold*, co-authored with Warren Getler.
7. *Mena Star*, *"When the James Boys, Famed Bandits, Visited Arkansas: Following the Robbery in 1874 of Stage Coach Running Between Malvern and Hot Springs, Band Said to Have Escaped by Way of Old Cove,"* by Bob Berry, May 21, 1931.

Notes

8. Albert Pike, *Morals and Dogma* of the Scottish Rite of Freemasonry (Martino Fine Books, 2013).
9. Edward T. Schultz, *History of Freemasonry in Maryland* (Medairy & Co., Baltimore, 1888), pp.414 and 579.
10. www.en.wikipedia.org. *"Dixie (song)."*
11. Warren Getler and Bob Brewer, *Rebel Gold: One Man's Quest to Crack the Code Behind the Secret Treasure of the Confederacy* (Simon & Schuster, 2003), p.56.
12. Thomas P. Kettel, *History of the Great Rebellion* (L. Stebbins, Hartford, CT 1875), p.31.
13. Warren Getler and Bob Brewer, *Rebel Gold: One Man's Quest to Crack the Code Behind the Secret Treasure of the Confederacy* (Simon & Schuster, 2003), p.79.
14. Ibid., p.252.
15. The History Channel, *Jesse James' Hidden Treasure*, 2009 television special.
16. Warren Getler and Bob Brewer, *Rebel Gold: One Man's Quest to Crack the Code Behind the Secret Treasure of the Confederacy* (Simon & Schuster, 2003), pp.88-90.
17. *Old West Magazine*, *"One Black Pot With a Yellow Fortune,"* by J. Mark Bond (Fall, 1970), pp. 18-19 and 54-55.
18. Warren Getler and Bob Brewer, *Rebel Gold: One Man's Quest to Crack the Code Behind the Secret Treasure of the Confederacy* (Simon & Schuster, 2003), p.90.
19. Del Schrader, *Jesse James Was One of His Names: The Greatest Cover-up in History by the Famous Outlaw Who Lived 73 Incredible Lives* (Santa Anita Press, 1975).
20. Ibid., p.187.
21. Ibid., p.250.
22. Ibid., p.208.
23. Ibid., pp 1 and 9-35.
24. Ronald J. Pastore and John O'Melveney Woods, *Jesse James' Secret* (Createspace Independent Publishing, 2014).

25. Del Schrader, *Jesse James Was One of His Names: The Greatest Cover-up in History by the Famous Outlaw Who Lived 73 Incredible Lives* (Santa Anita Press, 1975), pp. 2, 50, 51, 189, and 274.
26. Ibid., p.275.
27. Ibid., pp.188-198.
28. John Bell, *Rebels on the Great Lakes: Confederate Naval Commando Operations Launched From Canada 1863-1864* (Dundurn, Toronto, 2011), p.156.
29. Warren Getler and Bob Brewer, *Rebel Gold: One Man's Quest to Crack the Code Behind the Secret Treasure of the Confederacy* (Simon & Schuster, 2003), p.112.
30. Henry J. Walker, Jesse James "The Outlaw" (Wallace-Homestead Company, Des Moines, 1961).
31. Ibid., p. 155.
32. Ibdi., p.70.
33. Ibid., p.155.
34. Ibid., p.18.
35. Warren Getler and Bob Brewer, *Rebel Gold: One Man's Quest to Crack the Code Behind the Secret Treasure of the Confederacy* (Simon & Schuster, 2003), p.97.
36. Del Schrader, *Jesse James Was One of His Names: The Greatest Cover-up in History by the Famous Outlaw Who Lived 73 Incredible Lives* (Santa Anita Press, 1975), pp. 133-142.
37. Warren Getler and Bob Brewer, *Rebel Gold: One Man's Quest to Crack the Code Behind the Secret Treasure of the Confederacy* (Simon & Schuster, 2003), p.102.
38. Ibid., pp.121-122.
39. Ibid., pp.130-131.
40. *Treasure Hunter Confidential Newsletter*, April 1990, "Knights of the Golden Circle."
41. Warren Getler and Bob Brewer, *Rebel Gold: One Man's Quest to Crack the Code Behind the Secret Treasure of the Confederacy* (Simon & Schuster, 2003), p.260.
42. Ibid., pp.260-262.
43. Ibid., p.262.

Notes

44. Ibid., p.258.
45. Ibid., p.262.
46. Brad Meltzer with Keith Ferrell, *History Decoded: The 10 Greatest Conspiracies of All Time* (A&E Television networks, LLC, 2013), pp.22-25.

32. VICTORIO PEAK AND BEYOND

1. www.mcguiresplace.net. *"The Treasure of Victorio Peak"* by Bonnie Wayne McGuire.
2. www.coloradomagazineonline.com. *"Mystery of the Lost Gold of Victorio Peak,"* edited by Mel Fenson (from information obtained from web sources), copyright 2010-2011.
3. www.victoriopeak.com. 1977 video interview with Ova "Babe" Noss, property of the Ova Noss Family Partnership.
4. Ibid.
5. Ibid.
6. Barbara Mariott, *Myths and Mysteries of New Mexico* (Morris Book Publishing LLC, 2011), p.82.
7. David Leon Chandler, *100 Tons of Gold* (Doubleday & Co., Inc., New York, 1978), p.110.
8. Affidavit submitted by Milton "Doc" Noss associate B.D. Lampros to the U.S. Secretary of Defense in October, 1952.
9. www.desertusa.com. Desert USA Forums. Victorio Peak Story, "The Gold House" Book 1 Review, excerpt from video interview with Tony Jolley, an associate of Milton "Doc" Noss.
10. Bill Yenne, *Lost Treasure: A Guide to Buried Riches* (Berkley Books, New York, 1999), pp.232-233.
11. David Leon Chandler, *100 Tons of Gold* (Doubleday & Co., Inc., New York, 1978), see photos of artifacts between pages 32 and 33.
12. www.nytimes.com. *"Following 1937 Story of Buried Gold, Family Searches New Mexico's Sands,"* by Dirk Johnson, July 29, 1992.

13. David Leon Chandler, *100 Tons of Gold* (Doubleday & Co., Inc., New York, 1978), pp.121-122.

14. *Alamogordo Daily News*, "Operation Paperclip brought possible criminals to U.S.," by Karl Anderson, July 29, 2007.

15. Barbara Mariott, *Myths and Mysteries of New Mexico* (Morris Book Publishing LLC, 2011), p.84.

16. David Leon Chandler, *100 Tons of Gold* (Doubleday & Co., Inc., New York, 1978), p.134.

17. www.legendsofamerica.com. New Mexico Legends, *"Victorio Peak Treasure"* by Kathy Weiser, updated December, 2012, p.3.

18. www.dailyoddsandends.worldpress.com. *"Victorio Peak Treasure . . . Milton 'Doc' Noss . . . Biggest Con of the 20th Century?"* posted March 29, 2014.

19. Freedom Magazine, *"Gold! The Mystery of the $30 Billion Treasure,"* by Thomas G. Whittle, June 1986.

20. *60 Minutes* television show, episode in 1977 "Gold Fever" with Dan Rather reporting.

21. David Leon Chandler, *100 Tons of Gold* (Doubleday & Co., Inc., New York, 1978), p.143.

22. W.C. Jameson, *Lost Treasures of American History* (Taylor Trade Publishing, Lanham, MD, 2006), p.45.

23. *Lawrence Journal-World*, *"The Secret of Victorio Peak: Golden Treasure or Giant Hoax?"* by Scott McCartney, Associated Press Writer, May 18, 1987.

24. David Leon Chandler, *100 Tons of Gold* (Doubleday & Co., Inc., New York, 1978), pp.148-149 and p.189, and Bill Yenne, *Lost Treasure: A Guide to Buried Riches* (Berkley Books, new York, 1999), p.235.

25. David Leon Chandler, *100 Tons of Gold* (Doubleday & Co., Inc., New York, 1978), p.3. This was an August 10, 1961 communication of the Secret Service.

26. www.legendsofamerica.com. New Mexico Legends, *"Victorio Peak Treasure"* by Kathy Weiser, updated December, 2012, p.4.

27. David Leon Chandler, *100 Tons of Gold* (Doubleday & Co., Inc., New York, 1978), p.151. This report was filed with the commanding general at White Sands Missile Range.

Notes

28. www.nytimes.com. *"Following 1937 Story of Buried Gold, Family Searches New Mexico's Sands,"* by Dirk Johnson, July 29, 1992.
29. David Leon Chandler, *100 Tons of Gold* (Doubleday & Co., Inc., New York, 1978), p.68. Testimony of John Dean III on June 25, 1973 before the Senate subcommittee investigating President Nixon's involvement in the "Watergate" burglary and cover-up.
30. David Leon Chandler, *100 Tons of Gold* (Doubleday & Co., Inc., New York, 1978), p.179.
31. Ibid., p.180.
32. Ibid., pp.164-167 and p.180.
33. Ibid., p.178.
34. Ibid., p.178.
35. Ibid., p.181. This is from a July 26, 1974 Department of the Army memo from K.C. Emerson, aide to Norman Augustine, Assistant Secretary of the Army, to his boss, stating that a group was allowed to enter the White Sands Missile Range for 48 hours and did return with a gold bar.
36. *The Washington Post, "Buried Treasure Sought in Operation Goldfinder,"* by Bill Richards, March 19, 1977.
37. David Leon Chandler, *100 Tons of Gold* (Doubleday & Co., Inc., New York, 1978), p.193.
38. *60 Minutes* television show, episode in 1977 "Gold Fever" with Dan Rather reporting.
39. L.T. Dolphin, W.B. Beatty, and J.D. Tanzi, *"Radar Probing of Victorio Peak, New Mexico."* (Stanford Research Institute, Menlo Park, CA, 1977).
40. *Clovis News Journal* at www.cnjonline.com. *"The Mystery of Buried Treasure,"* by Don McAlavy, May 7, 2003.
41. *Rolling Stone Magazine, "A Hundred Tons of Gold,"* December 18, 1975 which shows photographs obtained from the U.S. Army at Victorio Peak.
42. *PEOPLE Magazine* at www.people.com. *"In Search of a Legend"* by Guy Garcia, Vol. 38, No.11. September 14, 1992.

43. www.legendsofamerica.com. New Mexico Legends, *"Victorio Peak Treasure"* by Kathy Weiser, updated December, 2012, p.4.

44. *Amarillo Globe-News* at www.amarillo.com. *"Army: Gold Hunters Owe $701,091 for Search,"* by the Associated Press, July 18, 1999. Also, Bill Yenne, *Lost Treasure: A Guide to Buried Riches* (Berkley Books, New York, 1999), p.242.

45. Bill Yenne, *Lost Treasure: A Guide to Buried Riches* (Berkley Books, New York, 1999), pp.227-229.

46. www.legendsofamerica.com. New Mexico Legends, *"Victorio Peak Treasure"* by Kathy Weiser, updated December, 2012, p.2.

47. David Leon Chandler, *100 Tons of Gold* (Doubleday & Co., Inc., New York, 1978), p.114.

48. *Lost Treasure*, Time-Life Books, 1991, p.120.

49. Bill Yenne, *Lost Treasure: A Guide to Buried Riches* (Berkley Books, new York, 1999), pp.155-158.

50. Ibid., pp.159-160.

51. David Leon Chandler, *100 Tons of Gold* (Doubleday & Co., Inc., New York, 1978), pp.71-74.

52. W.C. Jameson, *Unsolved Mysteries of the Old West* (Taylor Trade Publishing, Lanham, MD, 2006), p.44.

53. *60 Minutes* television show, episode in 1977 "Gold Fever" with Dan Rather reporting.

54. Ibid.

55. Warren Getler and Bob Brewer, *Rebel Gold: One Man's Quest to Crack the Code Behind the Secret Treasure of the Confederacy* (Simon & Schuster, 2003), pp.109-111.

56. *American Ecclesiastical Review: A Monthly Publication for the Clergy.* Vol. XXII., New York, 1900, p.130.

33. BALTIMORE 2016

1. Testimony of Margaret Saulsbury Short, BCCC #2, docket A-579, 1934.

Notes

2. Leonard Augsburger, *Treasure in the Cellar* (Baltimore: Maryland Historical Society, 2008), p.3.
3. David Harry Bennett, *The Party of Fear: From Nativist Movements to the new Right in American History* (University of North Carolina Press, 1988), p.147.
4. www.wikipedia.org. *"Baltimore (Demographics)"*
5. Ibid.
6. Ray Suarez, *The Old Neighborhood: What We Lost in the Great Suburban Migration, 1966-1999* (The Free Press, Division of Simon & Schuster, 1999), p.132.
7. Robert Moore, *"A Brief Economic History of Modern Baltimore"* (article appeared in the 2004 study "Putting Baltimore's People First: Keys to Responsible Economic Development of our City" by the AFL-CIO).
8. David Simons and Edward Burns, *The Corner: A Year in the Life of an Inner-City Neighborhood* (Broadway Books, 1998).
9. www.wikipedia.org. *"The Wire."*
10. *Bloomberg Business, "The Best TV Show Ever?"* by Thane Peterson, August 25, 2003.
11. *Baltimore Sun, "Young city black men: 56% in trouble – Study of Baltimore says problem is racial bias in U.S. war on drugs"* by Norris P. West, September 1, 1992.
12. Ibid.
13. Ibid.
14. *"A Global Study on the Influence of Neighborhood Contextual Factors on Adolescent Health"* by Kristin Mmari (*Journal of Adolescent Health*, December 2014), Vol. 55, Issue 6.
15. Ibid.
16. www.vocative.com. *"Baltimore Youths Have it Worse Than Those in Nigeria,"* by Elizabeth Kulze, December 1, 2014.
17. Elijah Anderson, *Code of the Street: Decency, Violence, and the Moral Life of the Inner City* (W.W. Norton & Company, 2000).
18. *The Atlantic, "The Code of the Streets,"* by Elijah Anderson, May, 1994.
19. www.wikipedia.org. *"Washington Hill, Baltimore."*

20. *The Daily Mail*, from the Associated Press and reporter Kiri Blakeley, August 10, 2015.

CONCLUSION

1. Matthew Kent, University of Maryland Francis King Carey School of Law, paper titled "Displaced by a force to which they yielded but could not resist – *A Historical and Legal Analysis of Mayor and City Council of Baltimore v. Charles Howard et.al.*" from 2011, pp.4-5.
2. Ibid., p.6.
3. Ibid.
4. David Detzer, *The Turbulent Days Between Fort Sumter and Bull Run* (Harvest Books, 2007).
5. Daniel Stashower, *The Hour of Peril: The Secret Plot to Murder Lincoln before the Civil War* (St. Martin's Press, New York, 2013), p.319.
6. Anonymous, *The Great Conspiracy* (Philadelphia, Barclay & Co., 1866), p.26.
7. www.knightsofthegoldencircle.webs.com.
8. *Civil War Times Illustrated, Volume 40, Issues 1-4* (Historical Times, Inc., 2001), p.34.
9. Ross M. Kimmel, *"Maryland Private Henry Hollyday's Faded Confederate Uniform Holds Many Tales for the Attentive Observer"*, *"America's Civil War"* magazine, January 2001, Volume 13, Issue 6.
10. *New York Times*, April 28, 1865.
11. Jefferson Davis (edited by Lynda L. Crist), *The Papers of Jefferson Davis: Vol. II, September 1864 to May, 1865* (Louisiana State University Press, 2003), p.525.
12. Robert Alonzo Brock and Virgil Anson Lewis, *Virginia and Virginians* (H.H. Hardesty, Richmond, 1888), p.790.
13. Ibid.
14. Walter Lee Brown, *A Life of Albert Pike* (The University of Arkansas Press, 1997), pp.439-440.
15. James Mackay, *Allan Pinkerton: The First Private Eye* (John Wiley & Sons, 1997), p.211.

Notes

16. Ron Pastore and John O'Melveny Woods, *Jesse James' Secret* (Intellect Publishing, 2011), pp.255-257.

17. *Mena Star*, *"When the James Boys, Famed Bandits, Visited Arkansas: Following the Robbery in 1874 of Stage Coach Running Between Malvern and Hot Springs, Band Said to Have Escaped by Way of Old Cove,"* by Bob Berry, May 21, 1931.

18. Warren Getler and Bob Brewer, *Rebel Gold: One Man's Quest to Crack the Code Behind the Secret Treasure of the Confederacy* (Simon & Schuster, 2003), pp.1-2 and 214-218.

19. Ron Pastore and John O'Melveny Woods, *Jesse James' Secret* (Intellect Publishing, 2011), pp.88-91.

20. Ibid., pp.124-128.

21. Carl W. Breihan, *The Man Who Shot Jesse James* (A.S. Barnes, 1979), p.54.

22. Paul Iselin Wellman, *A Dynasty of Western Outlaws* (University of Nebraska Press, 1961), p.127.

23. Ibid., p.126.

24. Terry Rowan, *The American Western Complete Film Guide* (Lulu.com, 2013), p.211.

25. Ron Pastore and John O'Melveny Woods, *Jesse James' Secret* (Intellect Publishing, 2011), p.92-94.

26. Ibid., pp.175-177.

27. *Rolling Stone Magazine*, *"A Hundred Tons of Gold,"* December 18, 1975 which shows photographs obtained from the U.S. Army at Victorio Peak.

28. *60 Minutes* television show, episode in 1977 "Gold Fever" with Dan Rather reporting.

29. Ibid.

30. *America Unearthed* cable television show on with Scott Wolter, March 9, 2014, the episode "Lincoln's Secret Assassins" from the Arts & Entertainment (A&E) Network's H2 channel.

31. Warren Getler and Bob Brewer, *Rebel Gold: One Man's Quest to Crack the Code Behind the Secret Treasure of the Confederacy* (Simon & Schuster, 2003), pp.254-265.

32. Ibid., p.109.

Made in the USA
Middletown, DE
19 September 2017